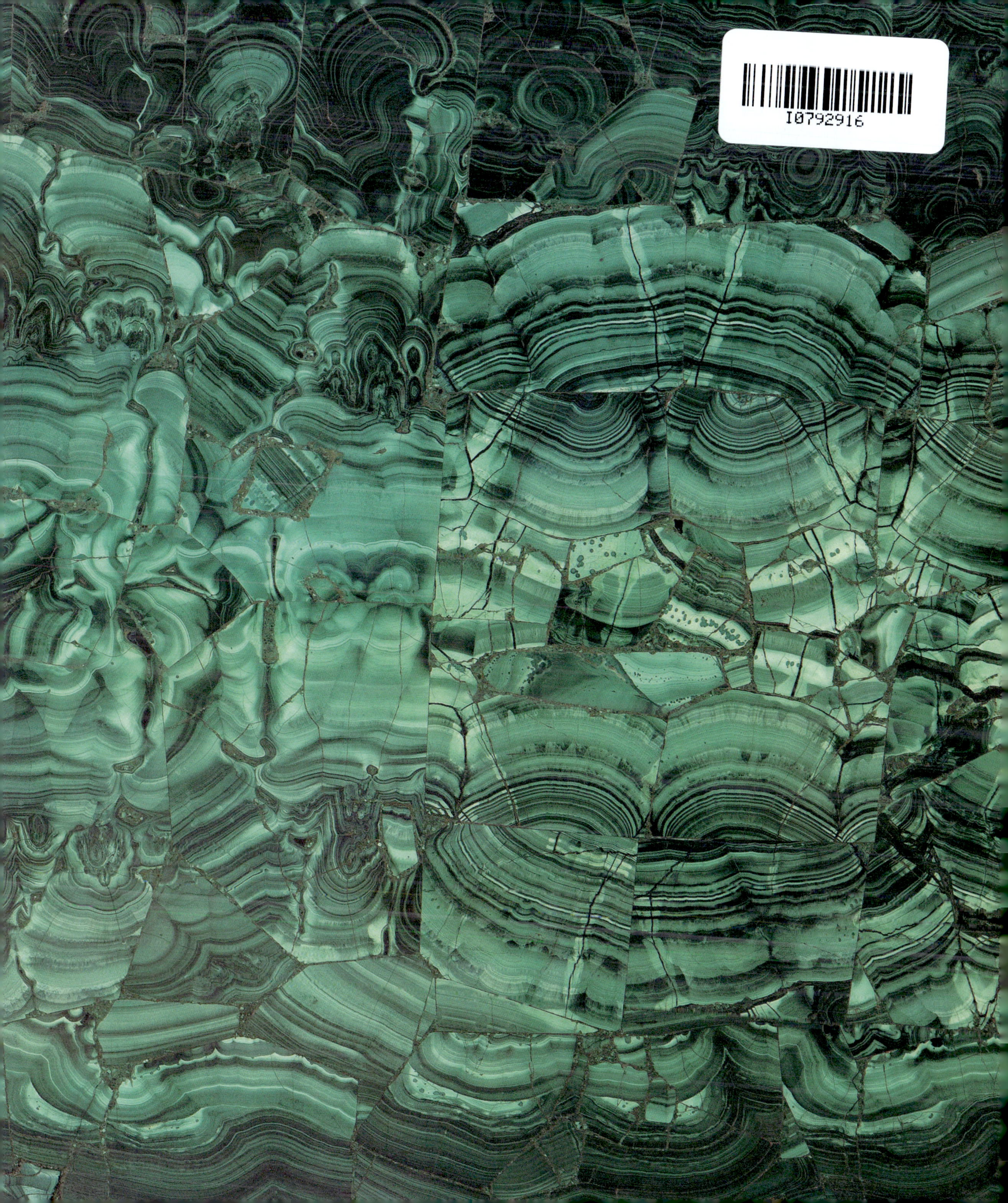

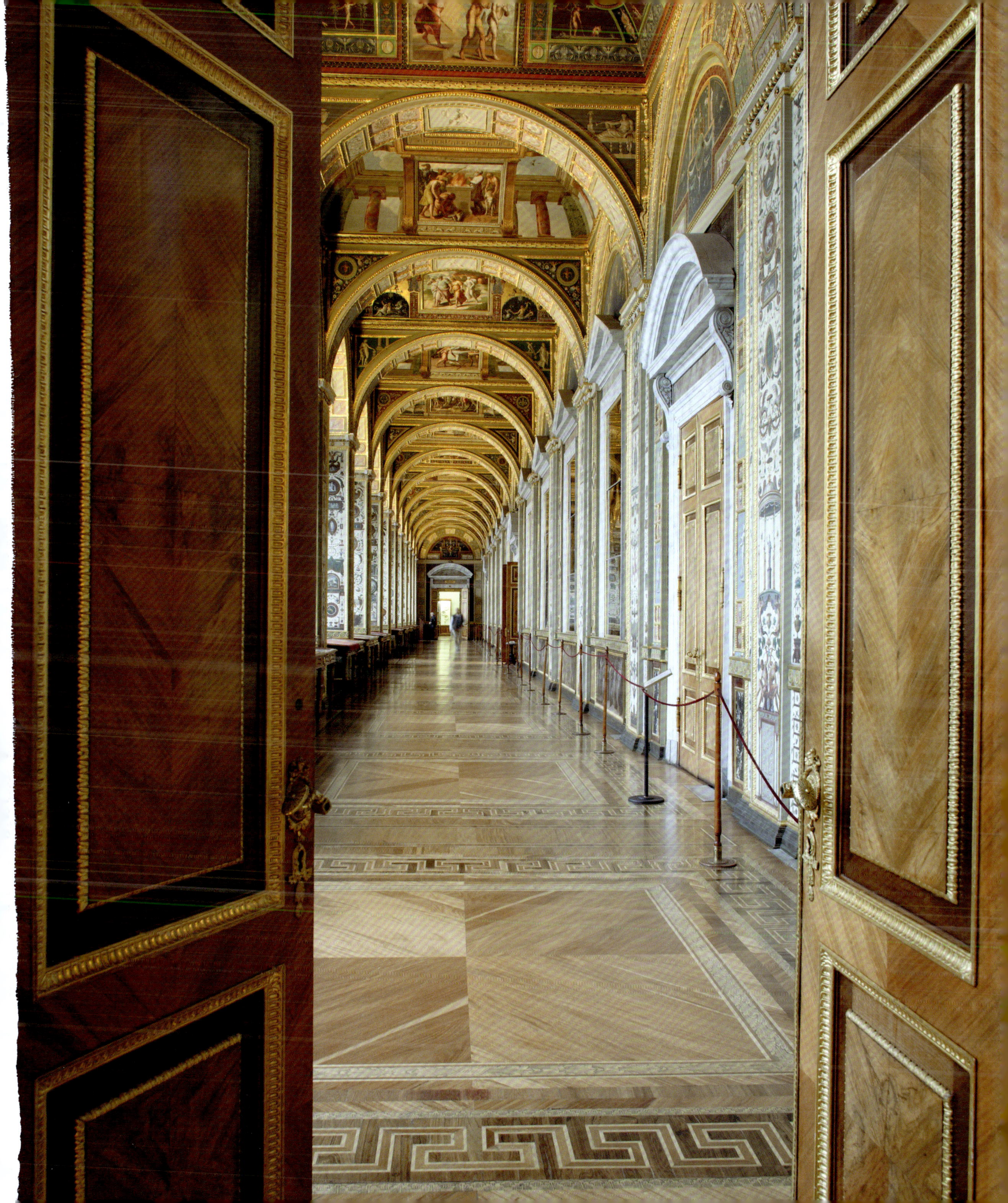

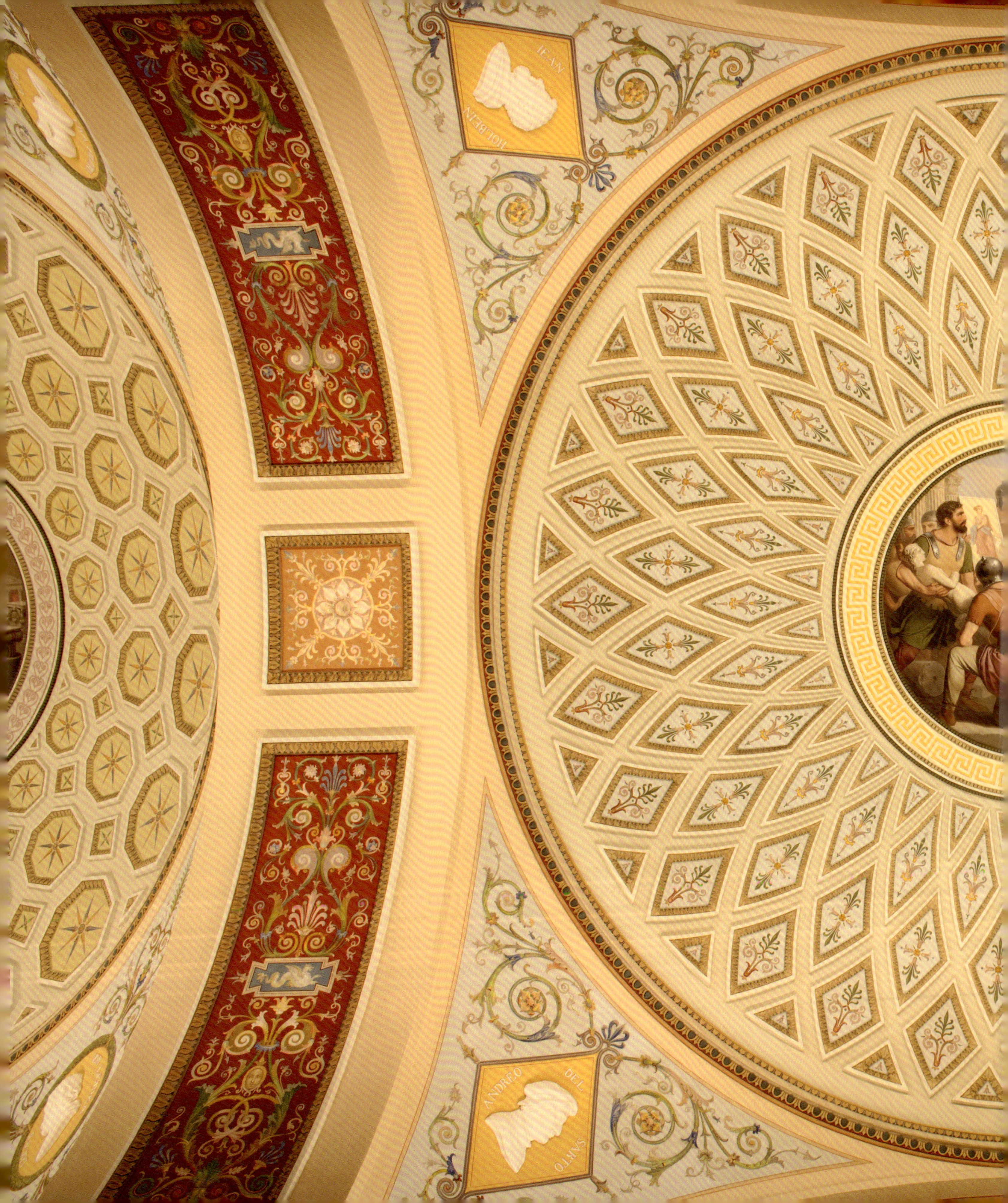
IEAN
HOLBEIN
ANDREO DEL SARTO

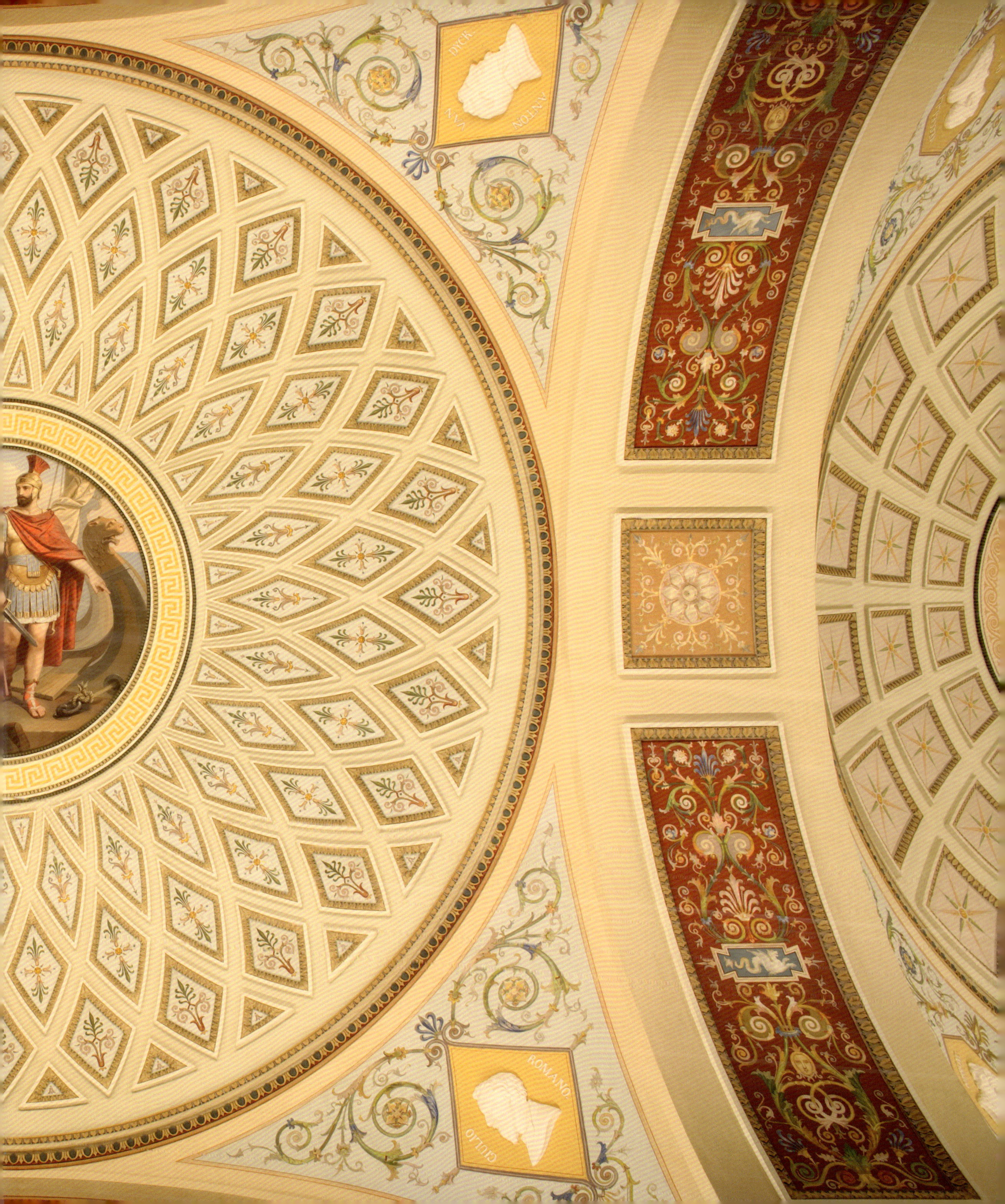
ANTON VAN DICK
GIULIO ROMANO

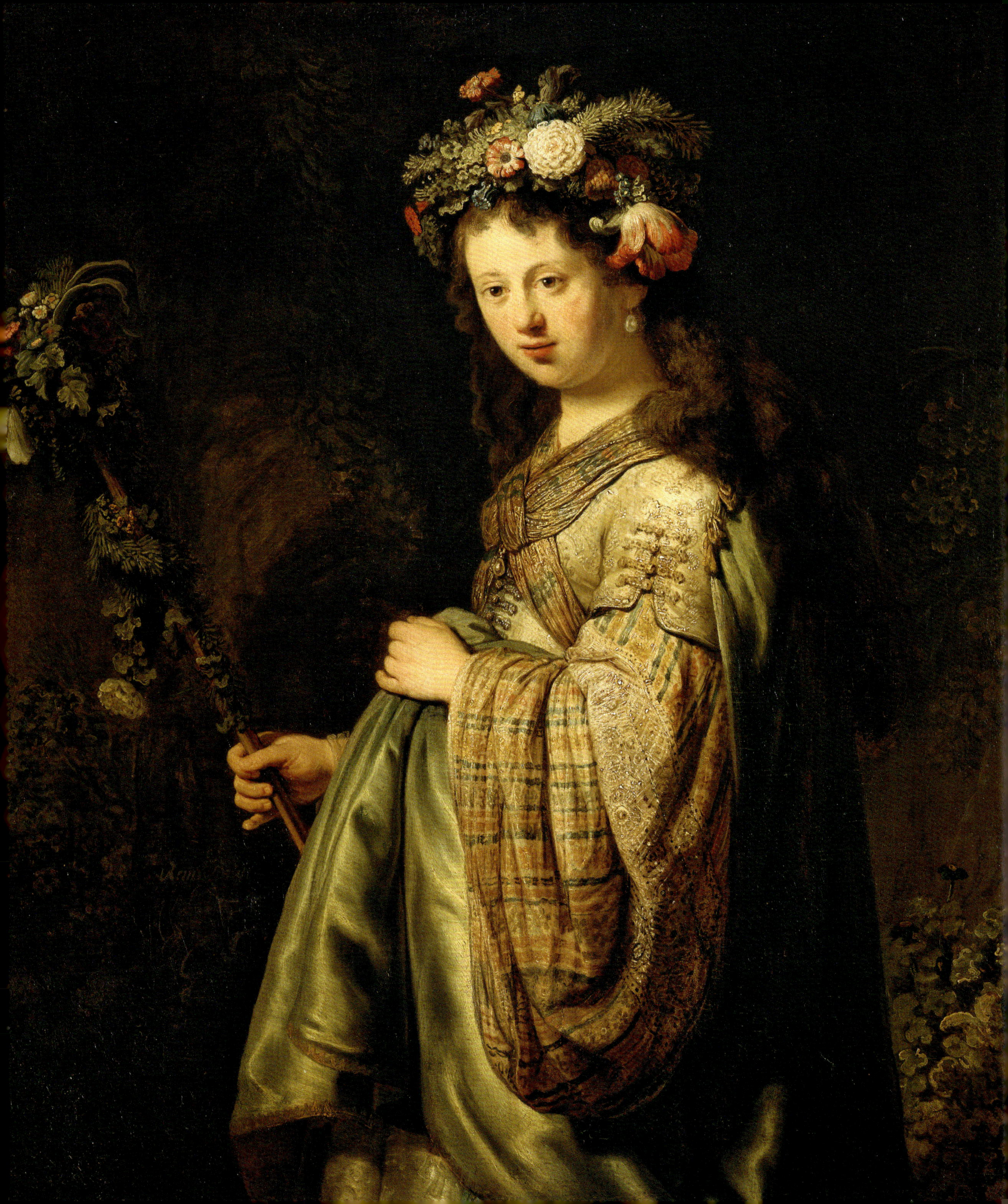

THE HERMITAGE

250 MASTERWORKS

Foreword by

MIKHAIL PIOTROVSKY

In association with the

HERMITAGE MUSEUM

RIZZOLI Electa

arca publishers

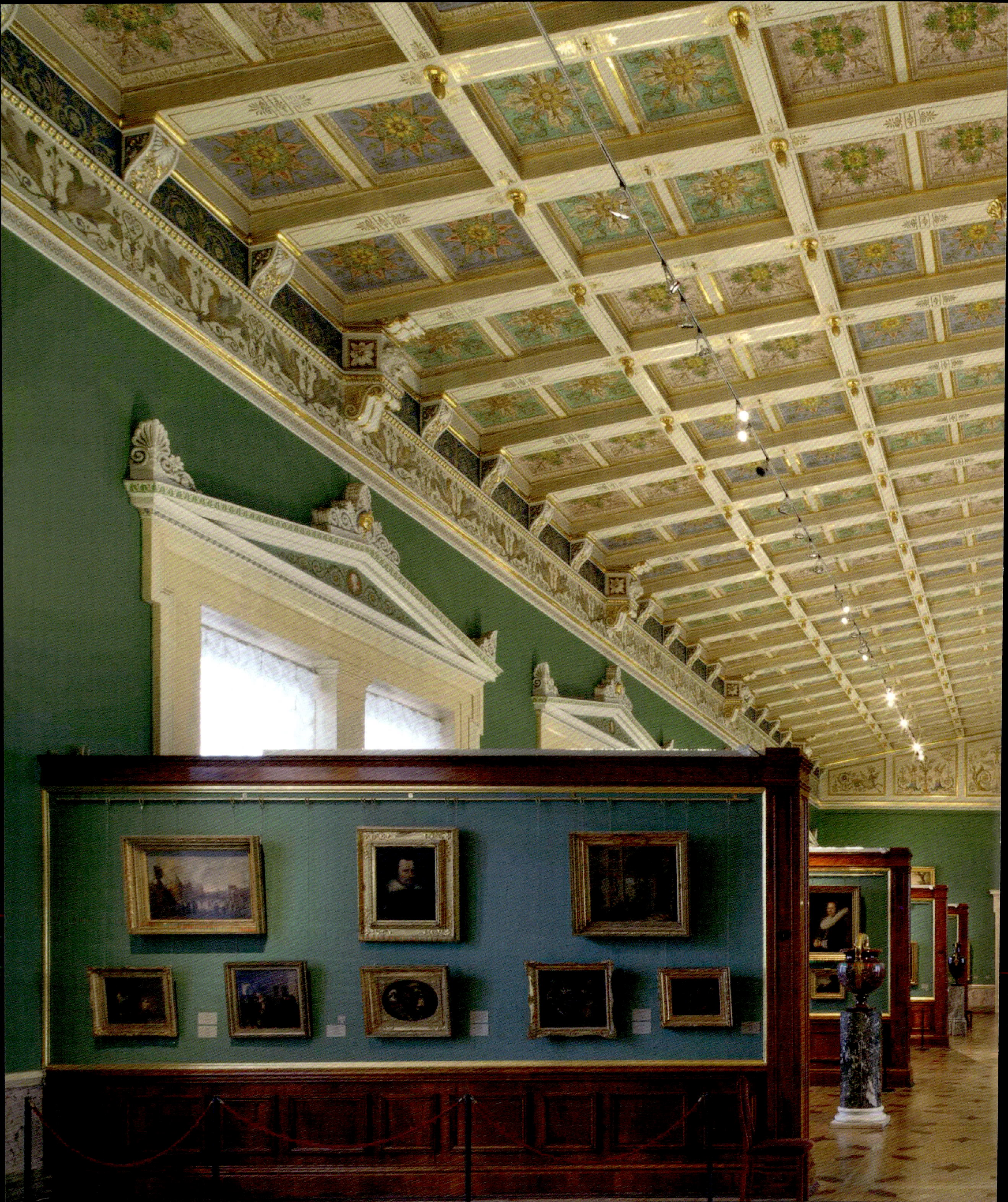

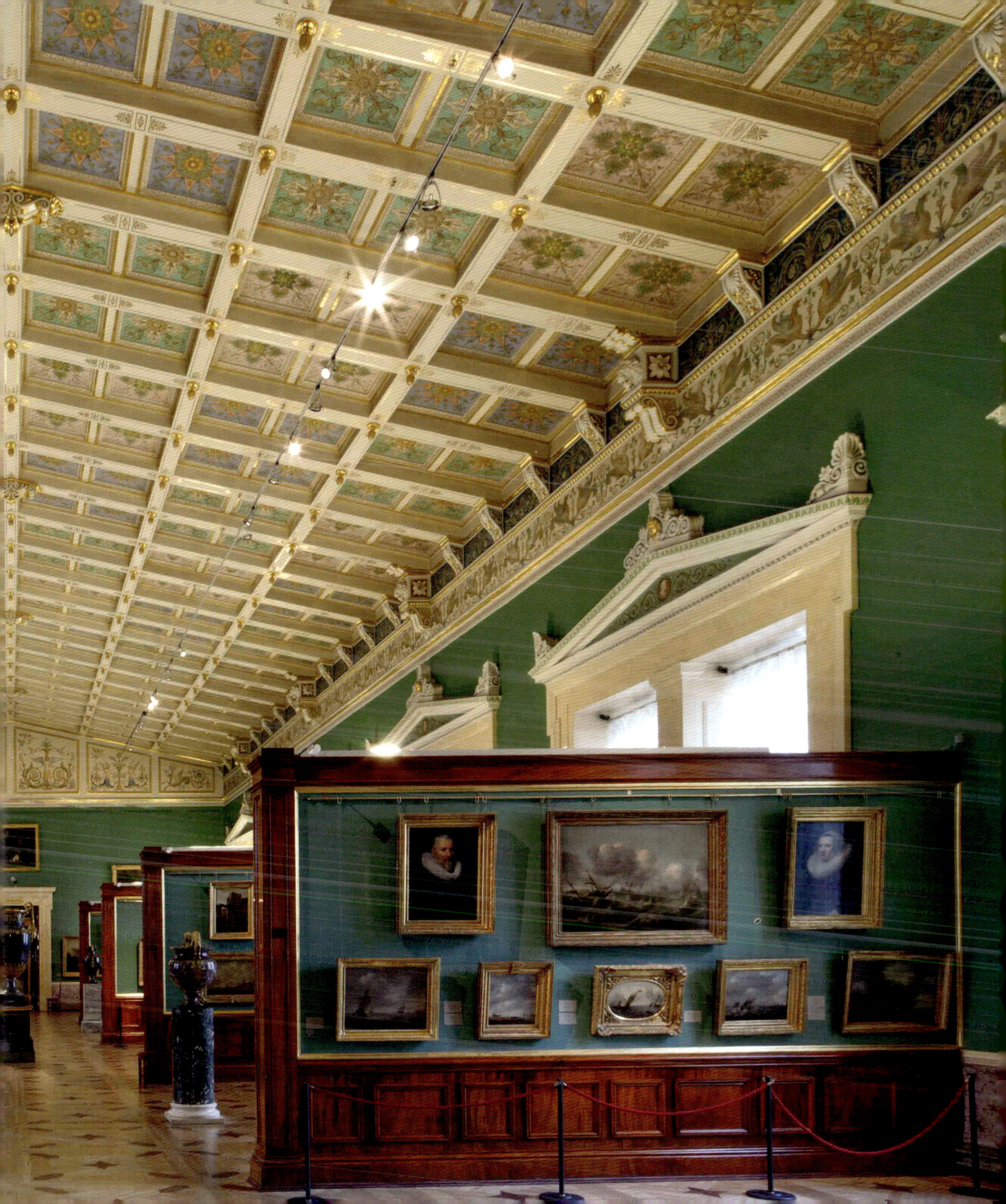

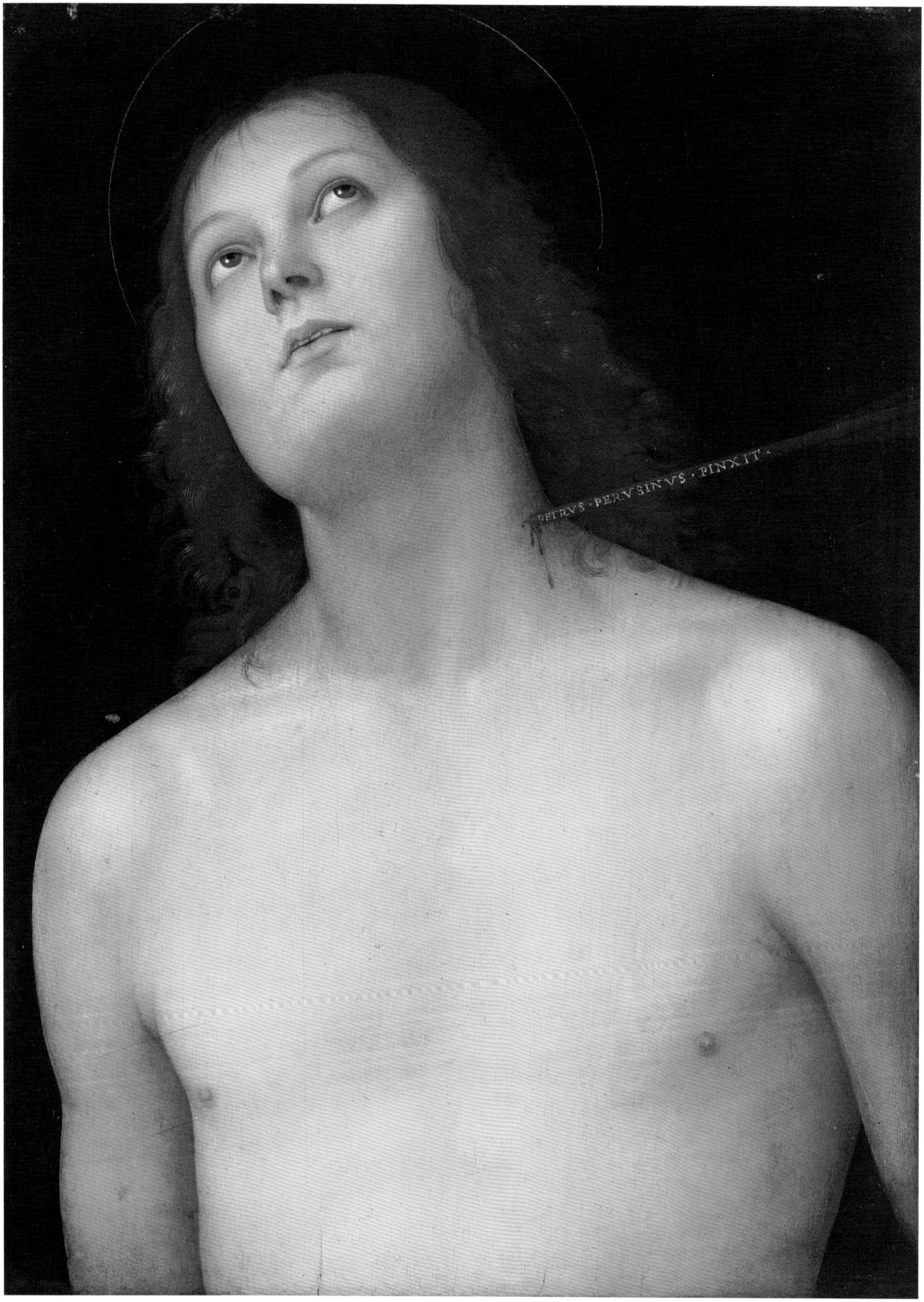
PETRVS · PERVSINVS · PINXIT ·

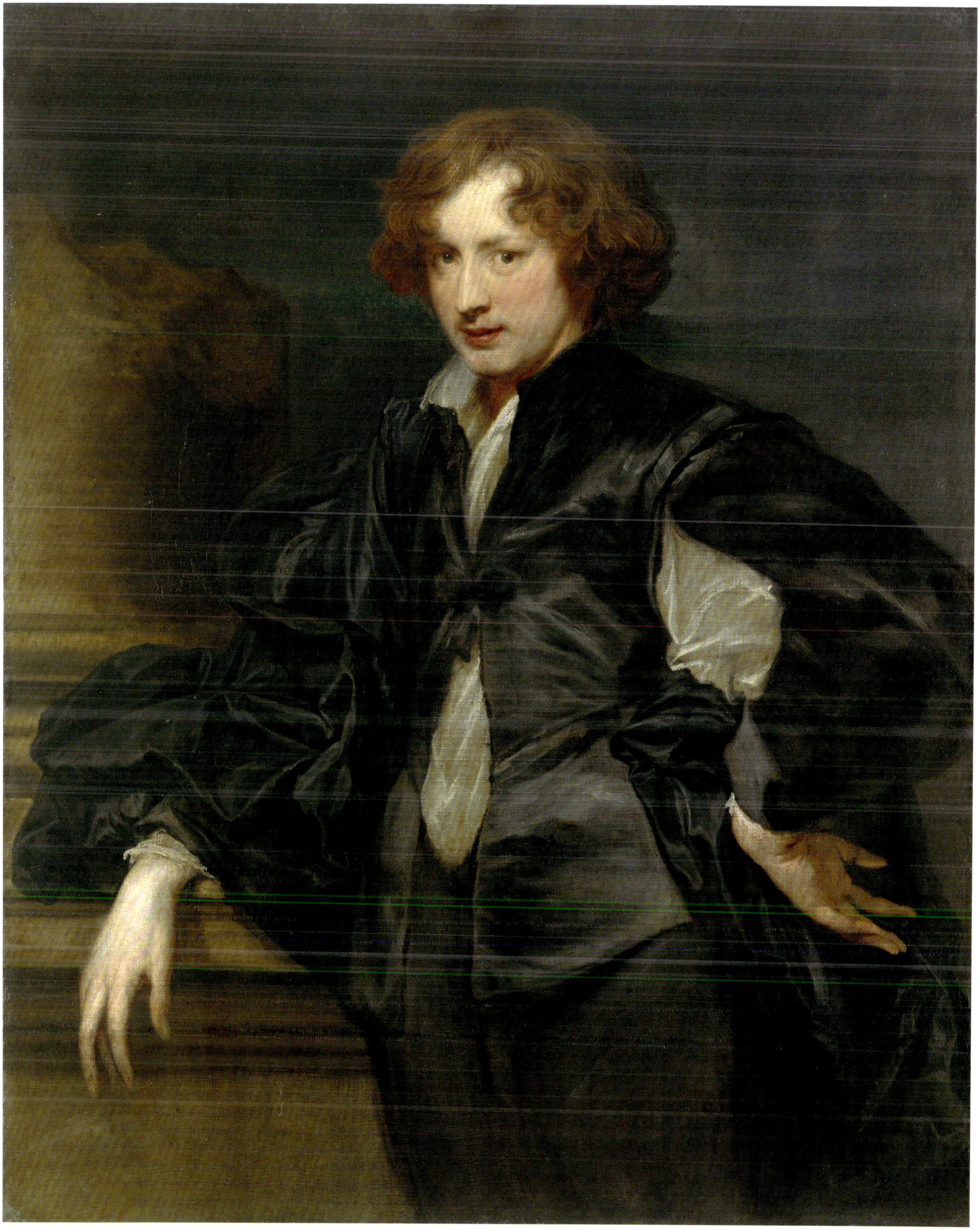

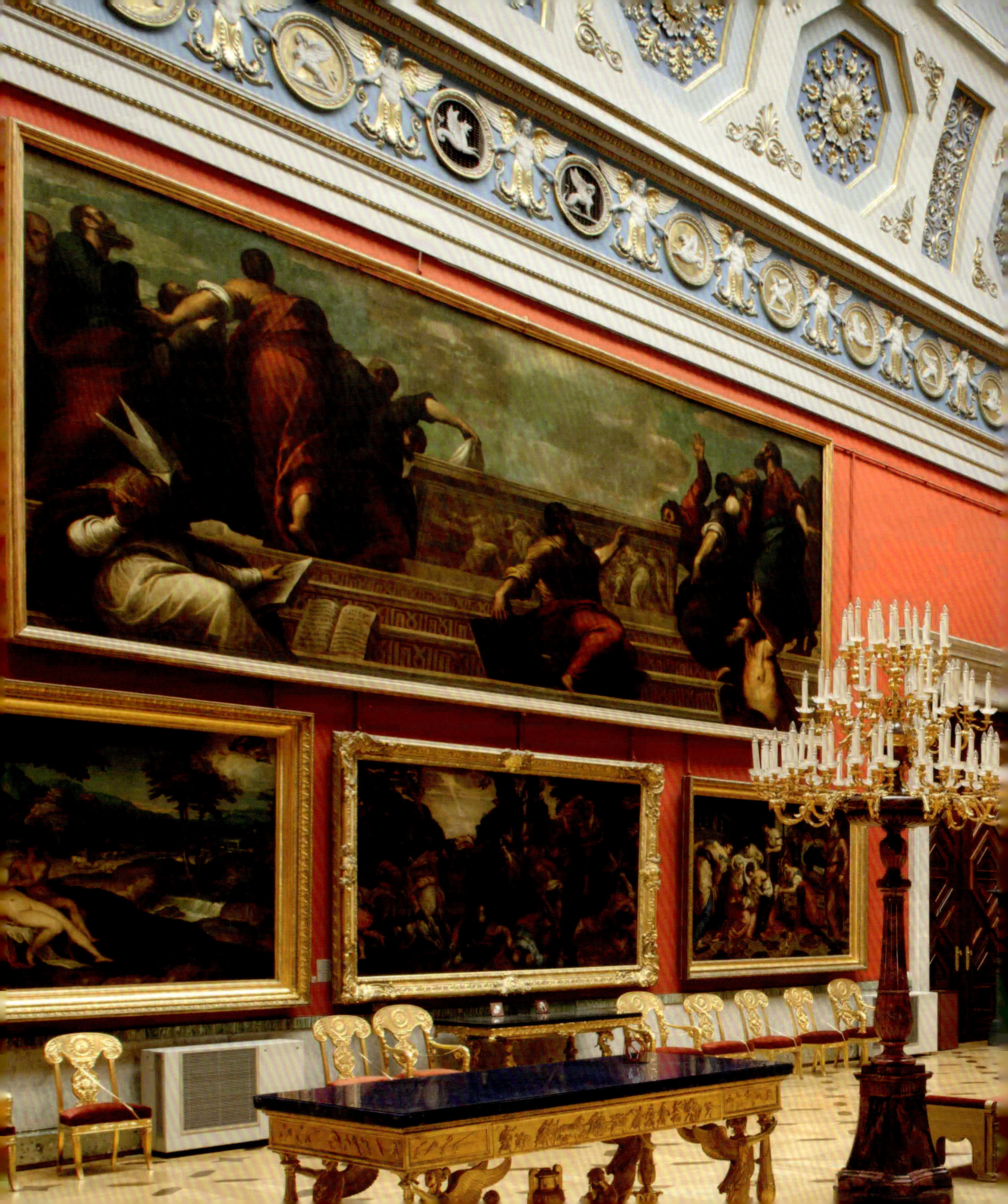

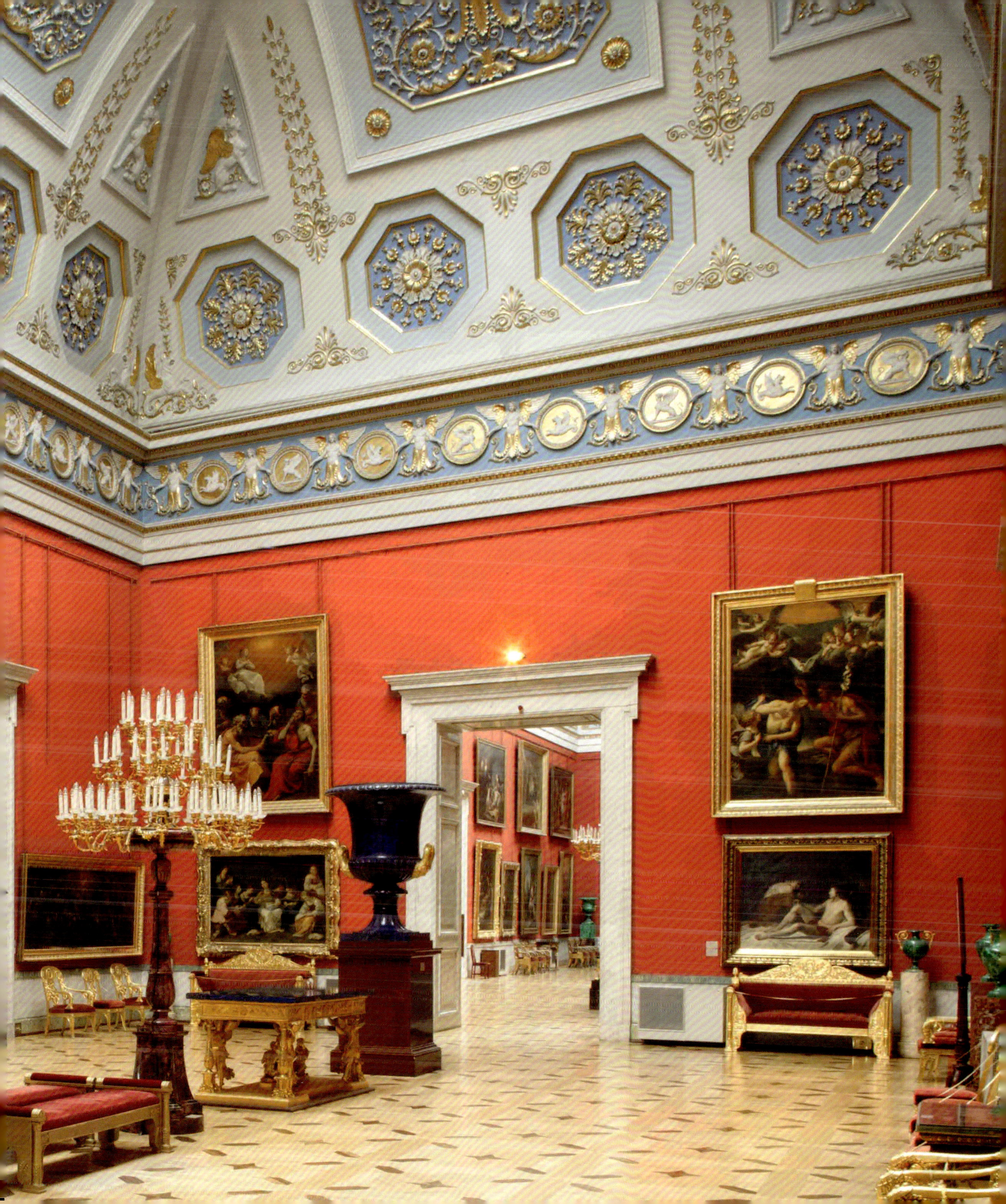

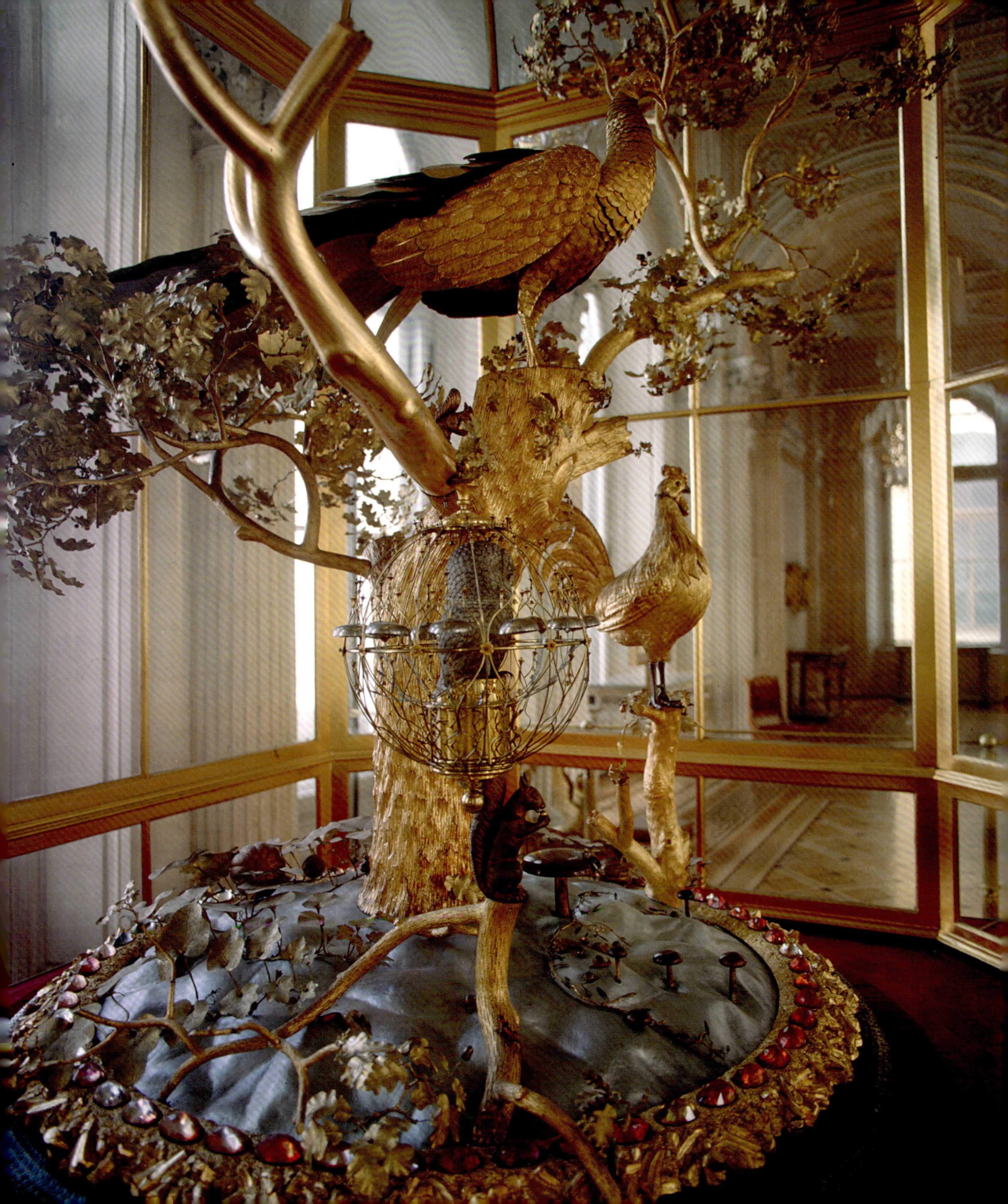

Contents

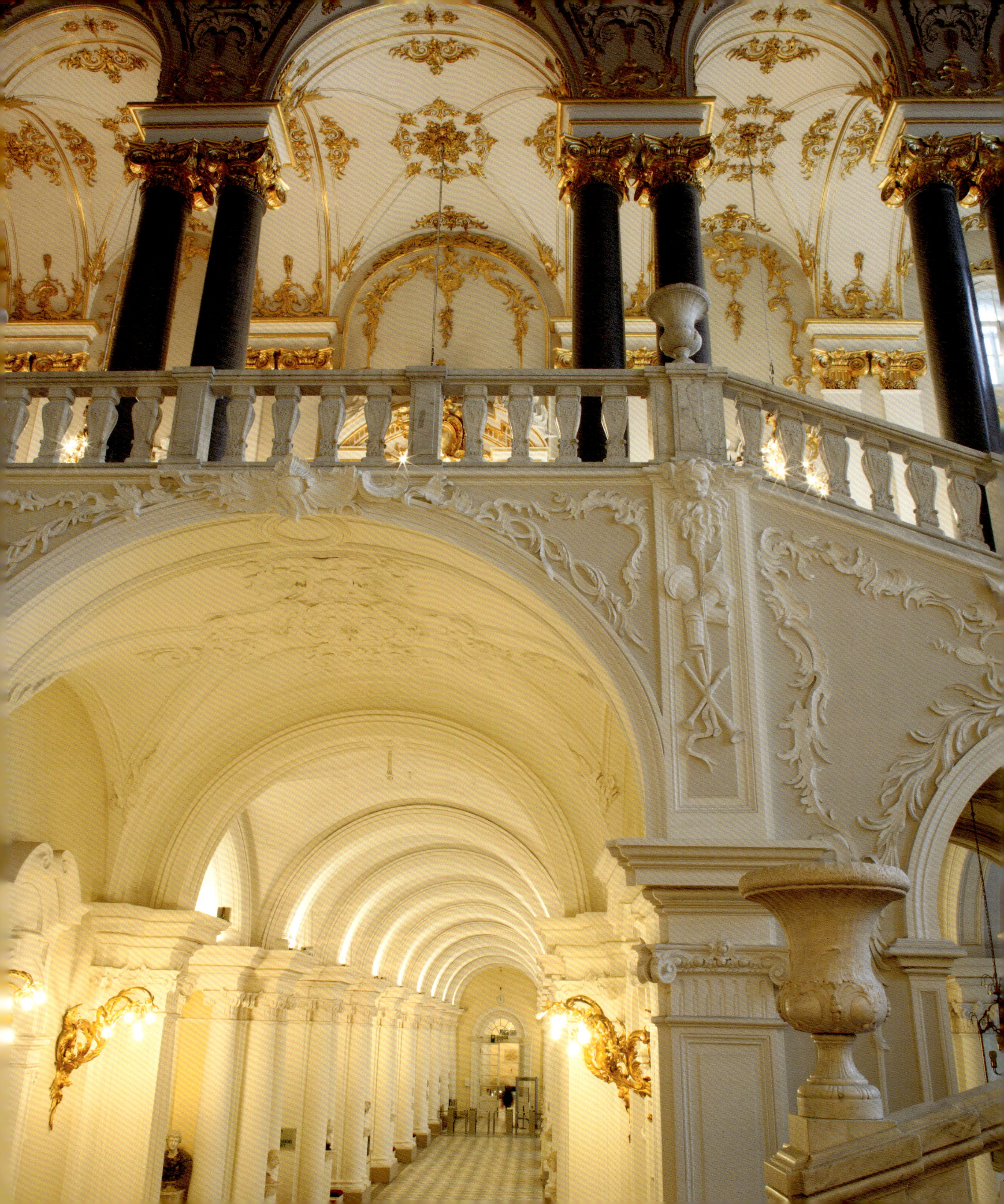

A Long Two Hundred and Fifty Years

In 1764 the Russian empress Catherine II, known today as Catherine the Great, bought several hundred select paintings for her palace. They had been prepared for King Frederick the Great of Prussia, but he was not able to purchase the collection because he had been bankrupt by the war with Russia. Thus, from the very beginning the royal art collection was a symbol of Russia's strength and power. The empress hung the paintings delivered to St. Petersburg in the Hermitage, the pavilion intended for "secluded" meetings and unofficial receptions for friends and guests. The Hermitage became the name for the royal museum, which grew, with purchases of the best collections in Europe and the new buildings and galleries built to house them.

Although Catherine was pure German, there were few rulers of Russia who cared so zealously about the prestige and Russian character of the country. She embodied the dreams of Peter the Great by making Russia a great power. She understood that the concept of *great* encompassed not only economy and army but also art collections. She willed this understanding to her descendants who ruled Russia. The Hermitage became not simply a museum but also a barometer of the country's condition. By offering European art within its walls, the museum made it part of Russian culture—the Russian culture open to the entire world, of which Dostoyevsky spoke so eloquently in his speech about Pushkin.

Alexander I, the conqueror of Napoleon, followed his grandmother Catherine in adding new collections to the Hermitage. His younger brother, Nicholas I, built the New Hermitage, a special building that even today is considered a masterpiece of museum architecture, and

opposite: *The Main (Jordan) Staircase in the Winter Palace.*

Nicholas I made the Hermitage a public museum (1851). The Hermitage walls and collections tell the story of world art and of Russian collectors, of the Russian love of fine arts, of Russian politics, of the three evacuations of the collections during fateful wars, and of the three revolutions they withstood. The Hermitage lived through eras of expansion and of destruction after the Russian Revolution. Its paintings remember and can recount the time of Bloody Sunday and the storm of the Winter Palace, and the horrible Nazi blockade of Leningrad. The museum survived in difficult times, of which there have been many in Russian history, and helped the Russian people and their culture survive.

Gradually the Hermitage turned into an encyclopedic museum, presenting an uninterrupted discourse of the most varied cultures of the West and the East within the context of Russian culture. The Hermitage may be an encyclopedia of world culture, but it is written in Russian. Rembrandt and Rubens, Raphael and Leonardo, Velázquez and Friedrich, Matisse and Picasso, Kandinsky, Malevich, Kabakov, the Taurida Venus, the Scythian deer, and Buddhist and Byzantine icons lead a special life in the buildings of the Winter Palace; the Old, New, and Small Hermitages; the Hermitage Theater; and the building of the General Staff. They blend into Russian architecture and Russian history and yet they do not, thereby accentuating them.

Today the Hermitage is a global museum whose exhibitions and satellites make it present throughout the world and over the Internet. It is the pride and the symbol of Russia. One of the most accessible museums in the world, its collections and interiors give pleasure to and feed the minds of the most varied categories of visitors, from those who know nothing about art to those who seek its most sophisticated manifestations, from the amateur to the connoisseur. It welcomes vacationing tourists and demanding St. Petersburgers alike. It recounts, it teaches, it lectures. In the new Russia, the Hermitage, as one of the main museums of the world, remains a source of knowledge and pleasure while remaining a sensitive barometer of the mood and condition of the country and the world.

In these days of the virtual and illusory, the museum successfully shows people that real art has the power and energy to change a person's life. It was ever thus. This book presents 250 masterpieces including *The Sacrifice of Isaac* by Rembrandt, *Portrait of a Lady-in-Waiting to the Infanta Isabella* by Rubens, *St. Sebastian* by Titian, *The Lute Player* by Caravaggio, *Boy with a Dog* by Picasso, and *The Dance* and *Music* by Matisse. In fact, there are many more. Art is boundless in principle. Today the Hermitage is doing everything to ensure that this boundlessness brings joy to everyone. This book is one of the ways to do it.

—Mikhail Piotrovsky

opposite: *The Gallery of the History of Ancient Painting in the New Hermitage.*

following spread: *The Pavilion Hall in the Small Hermitage.*

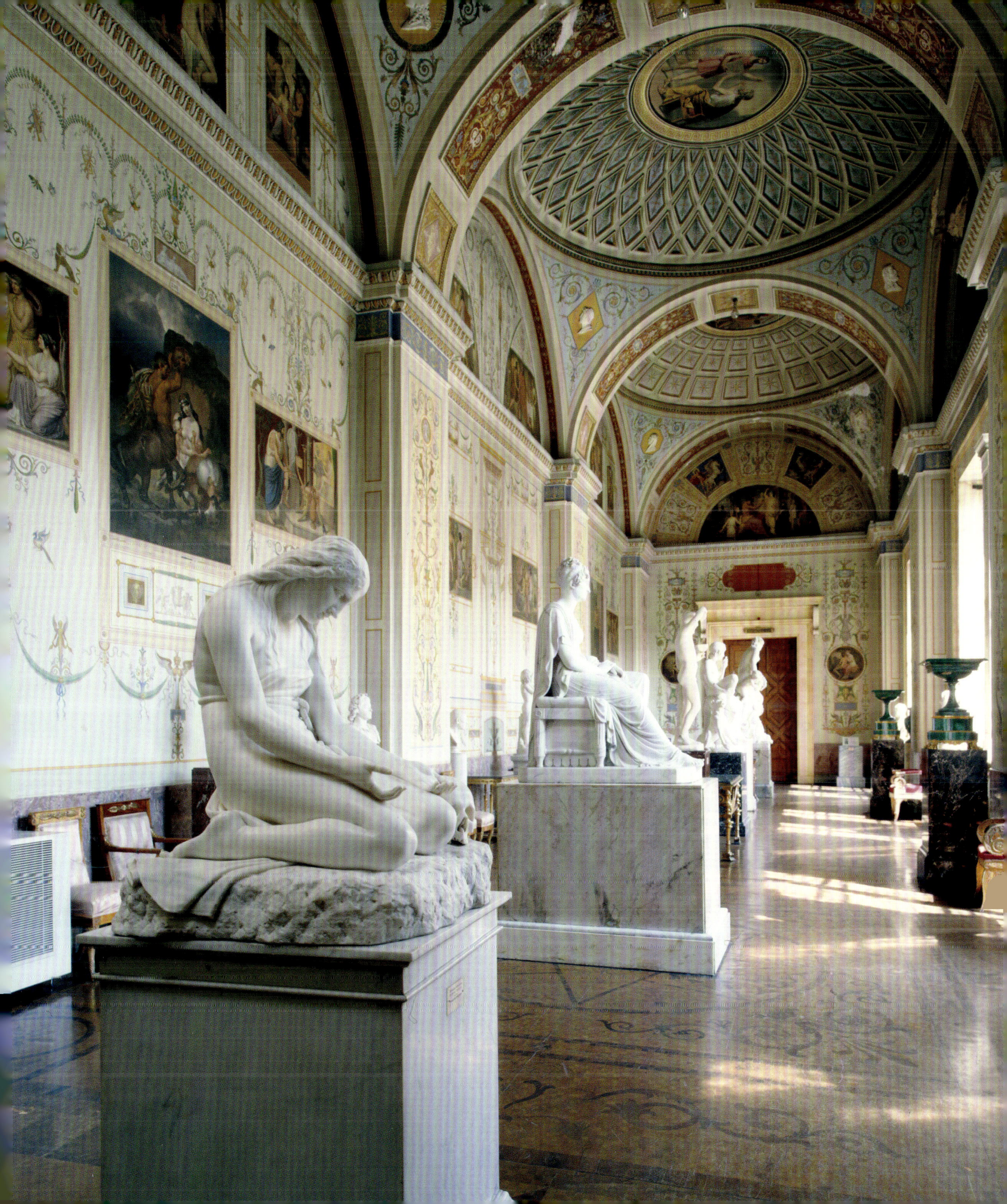

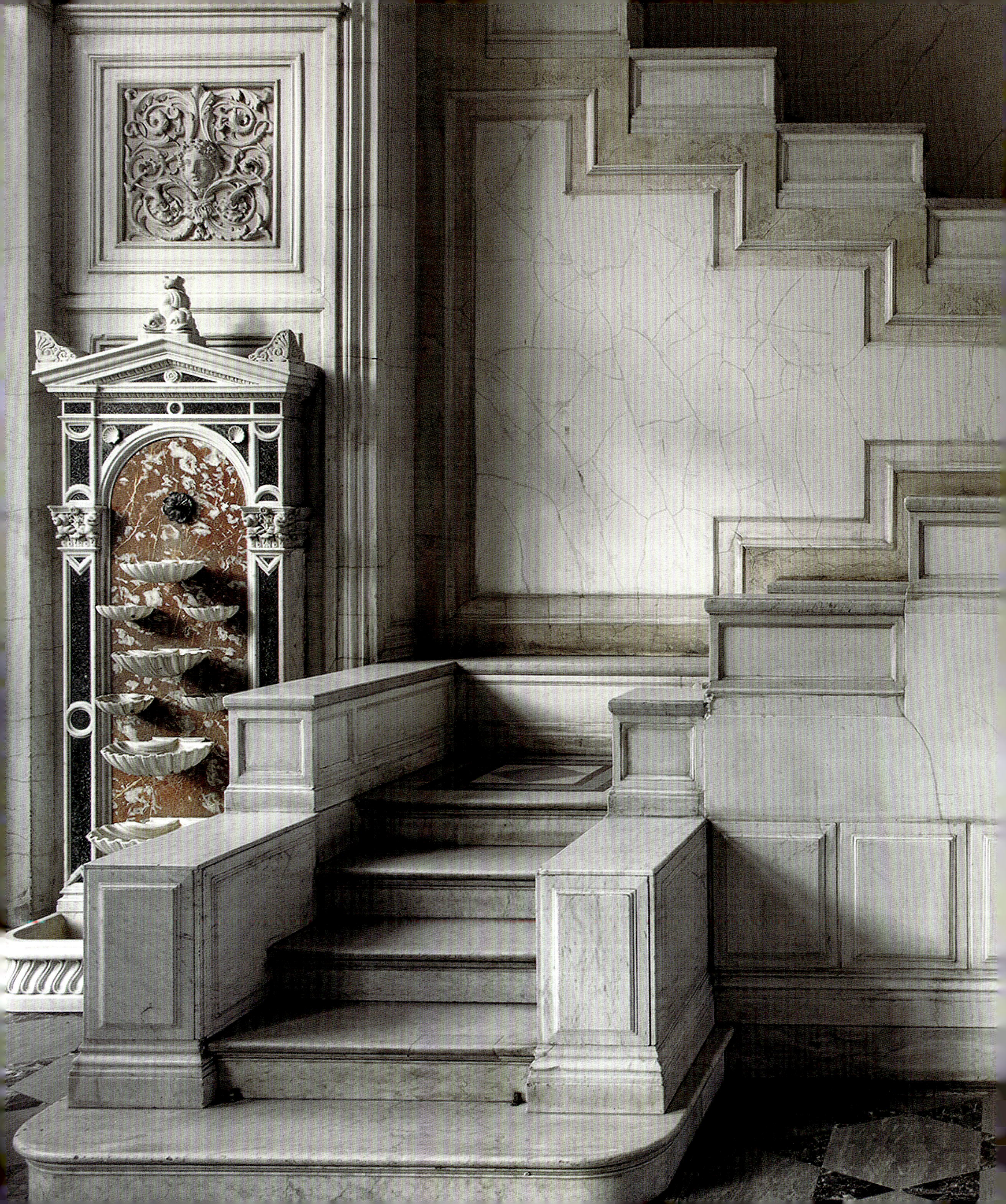

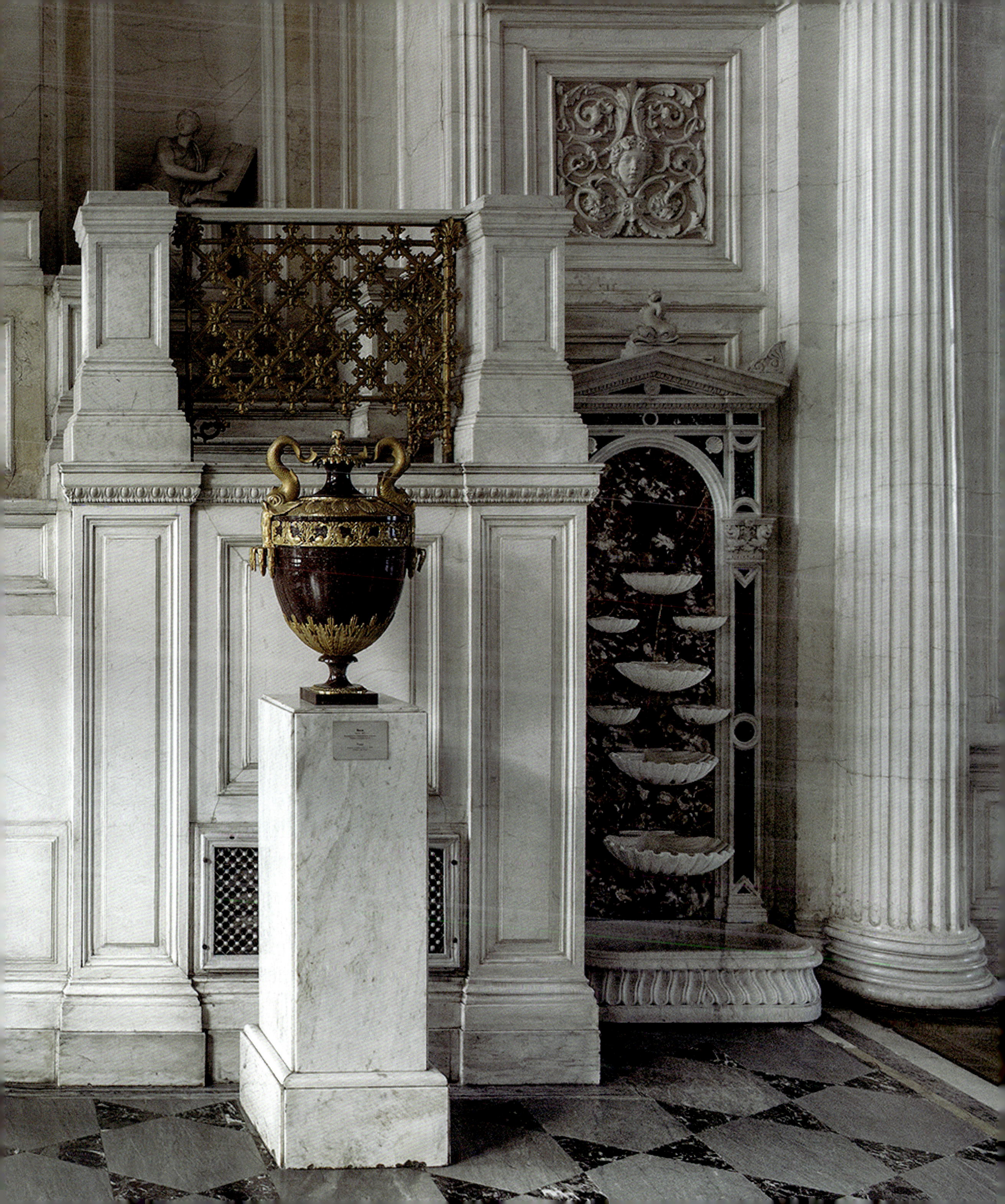

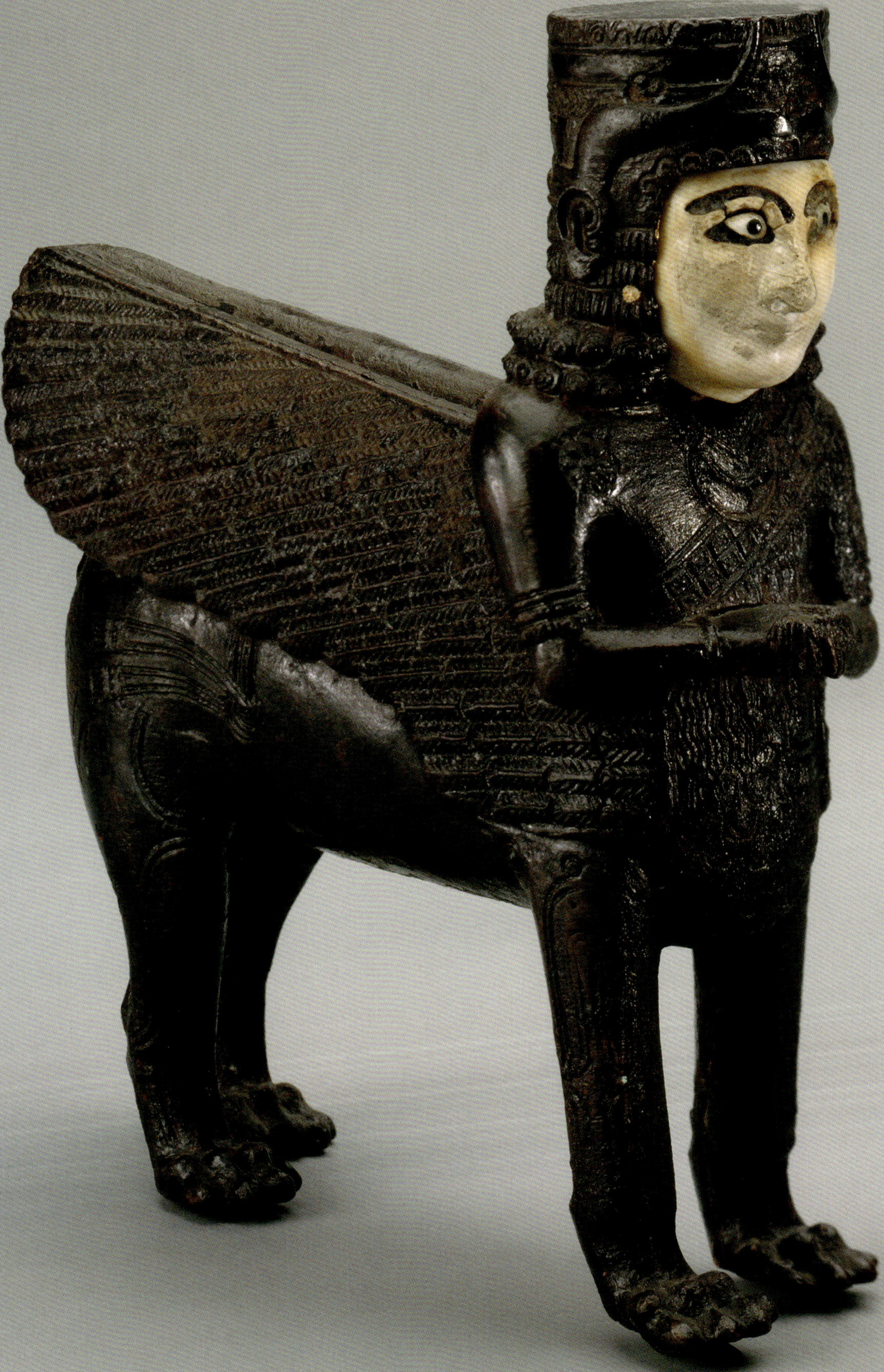

Ancient Egyptian, Near Eastern, and Asian Art

Throne Ornament in the Form of a Sphinx. URARTU. 7TH CENTURY B.C. BRONZE WITH TRACES OF GILDING, INLAID WHITE STONE. $6\frac{1}{4}$ IN. (16 CM) HIGH.

The hollow figurine of a winged lion with a human torso and head crowned with a tiara once adorned a throne in a palace or temple. It is unique, made using an expensive and laborious technique that allowed only a single cast from a wax model. It was originally covered with extremely thin gold foil, and the grooves on the wings were filled with a red paste.

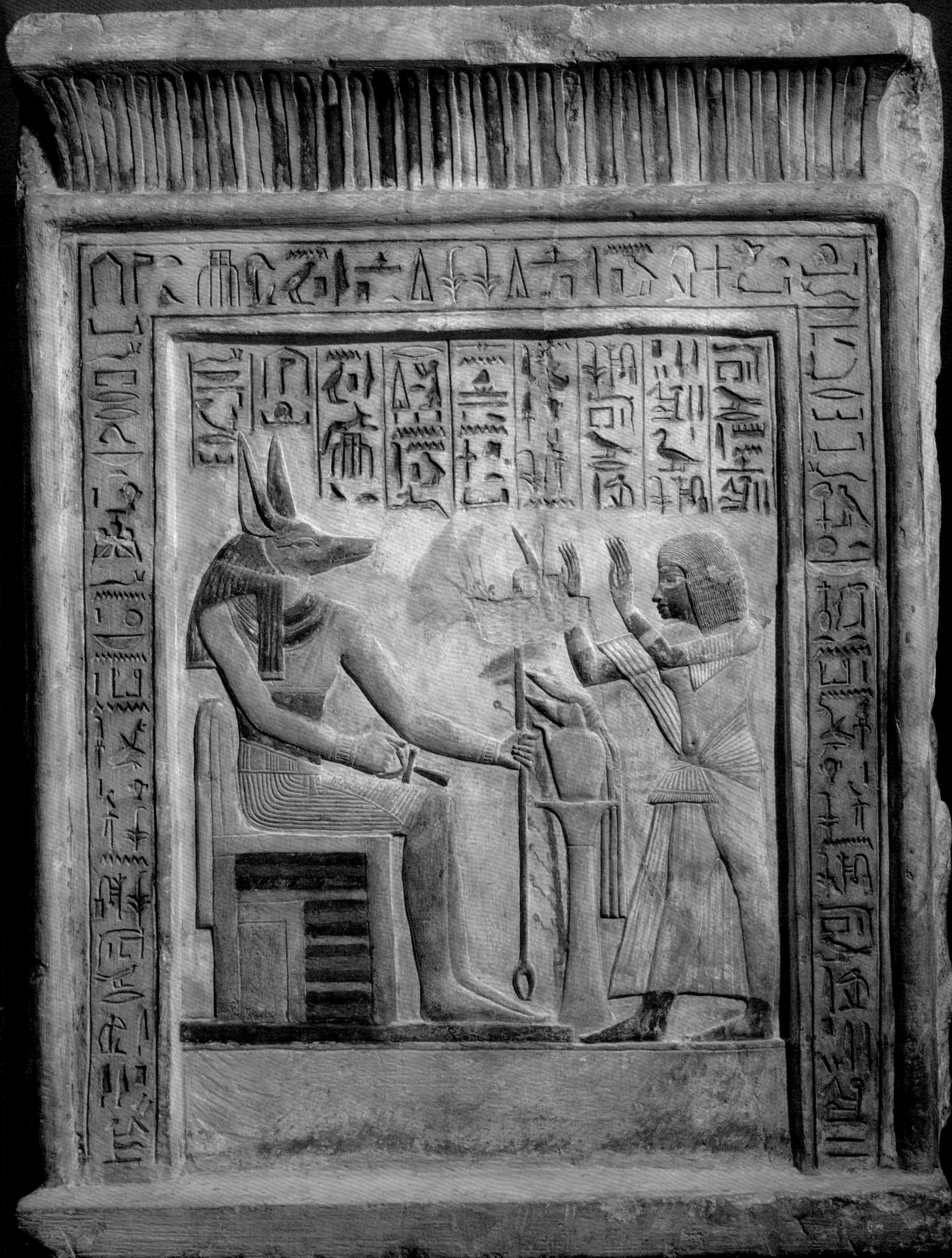

opposite: *The Stela of Ipi.*
NEW KINGDOM, ANCIENT EGYPT. SECOND HALF OF THE 14TH CENTURY B.C. (18TH DYNASTY). LIMESTONE. 37⅜ × 28 IN. (95 × 71 CM).

Ipi was a high-ranking official, the royal scribe and fan-bearer to Tutankhamun. That pharaoh's reign was marked by a reaction to the religious reforms of his predecessor, Amenhotep IV (Akhenaton), and the resumption of worship of the ancient gods. Depictions of these begin to appear again on objects in the tombs of private individuals. This stela, showing Ipi praying before the god Anubis, is among the earliest artifacts of that type.

right: *Statue of Amenemhat III.*
MIDDLE KINGDOM, ANCIENT EGYPT. LATE 19TH–EARLY 18TH CENTURY B.C. BLACK GRANITE (DIORITE). 35 IN. (86.5 CM) HIGH.

The reign of the pharaoh Amenemhat III was marked by military successes and economic prosperity, accompanied by large-scale construction. This statue is a superb example of the realistic royal portrait common in ancient Egypt. Amenemhat is dressed in a pleated skirt and wears a *nemes*, the royal headcloth. The indentations at the temple were made to attach a false beard, another attribute of supreme power.

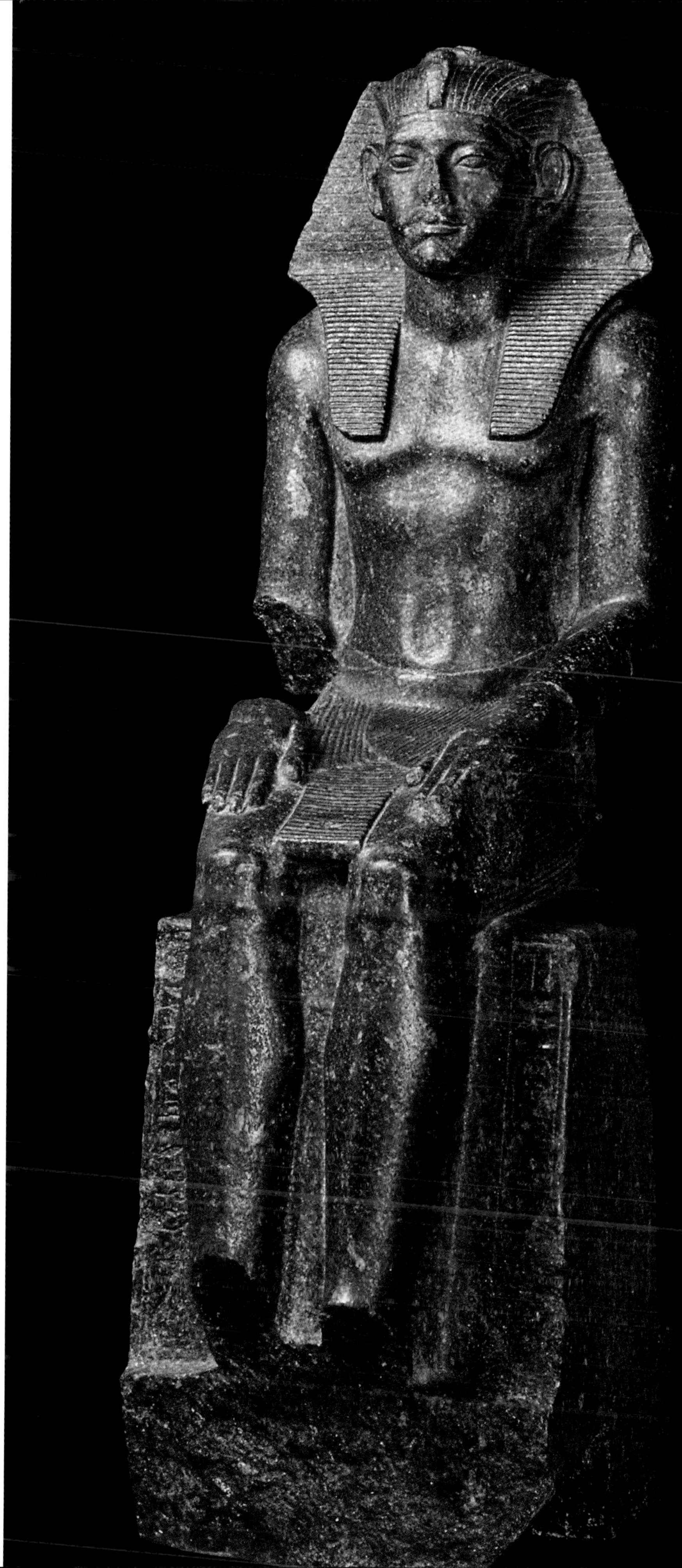

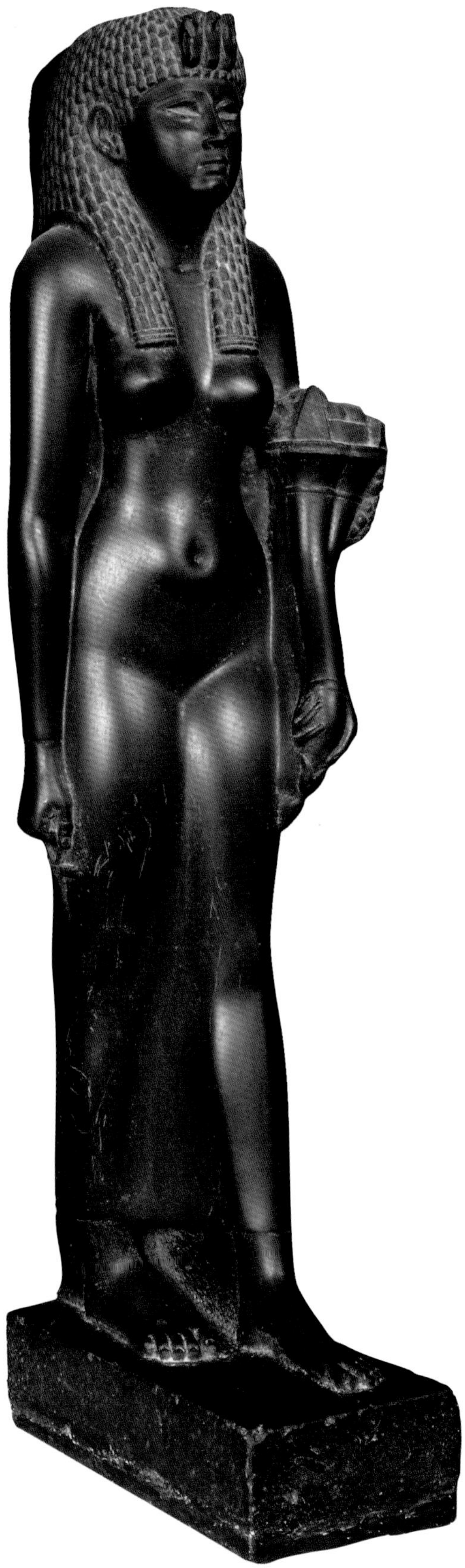

left: *Statue of Queen Cleopatra VII.* 51–33 B.C. BLACK BASALT. 41¾ IN. (105 CM) HIGH.

One of the best sculptural depictions of a ruler of Ptolemaic Egypt, in terms of workmanship and state of preservation, this statue conforms to the traditional Egyptian canon. In the figure's right hand is an ankh, an Egyptian symbol of life, and in her left, a horn of plenty, an attribute adopted from Greece. The three uraei (sacred asps) in the wig are specific to depictions of Cleopatra VII, while the cornucopia also occurs in statues of earlier rulers.

opposite: *Portrait of a Young Woman.* FAYUM, EGYPT. FIRST HALF OF THE 2ND CENTURY. ENCAUSTIC PAINT ON PANEL. 12⅝ × 5⅜ IN. (32.2 × 13.5 CM).

The practice of making burial portraits such as this one, to be placed over the face of a mummy and within the wrappings, arose in Egypt in Roman times, in the first century A.D., uniting features of ancient Egyptian and Greco-Roman traditions. In accordance with the canon, the woman's face, though painted in fine detail, represents an ideal type and lacks strong individuality.

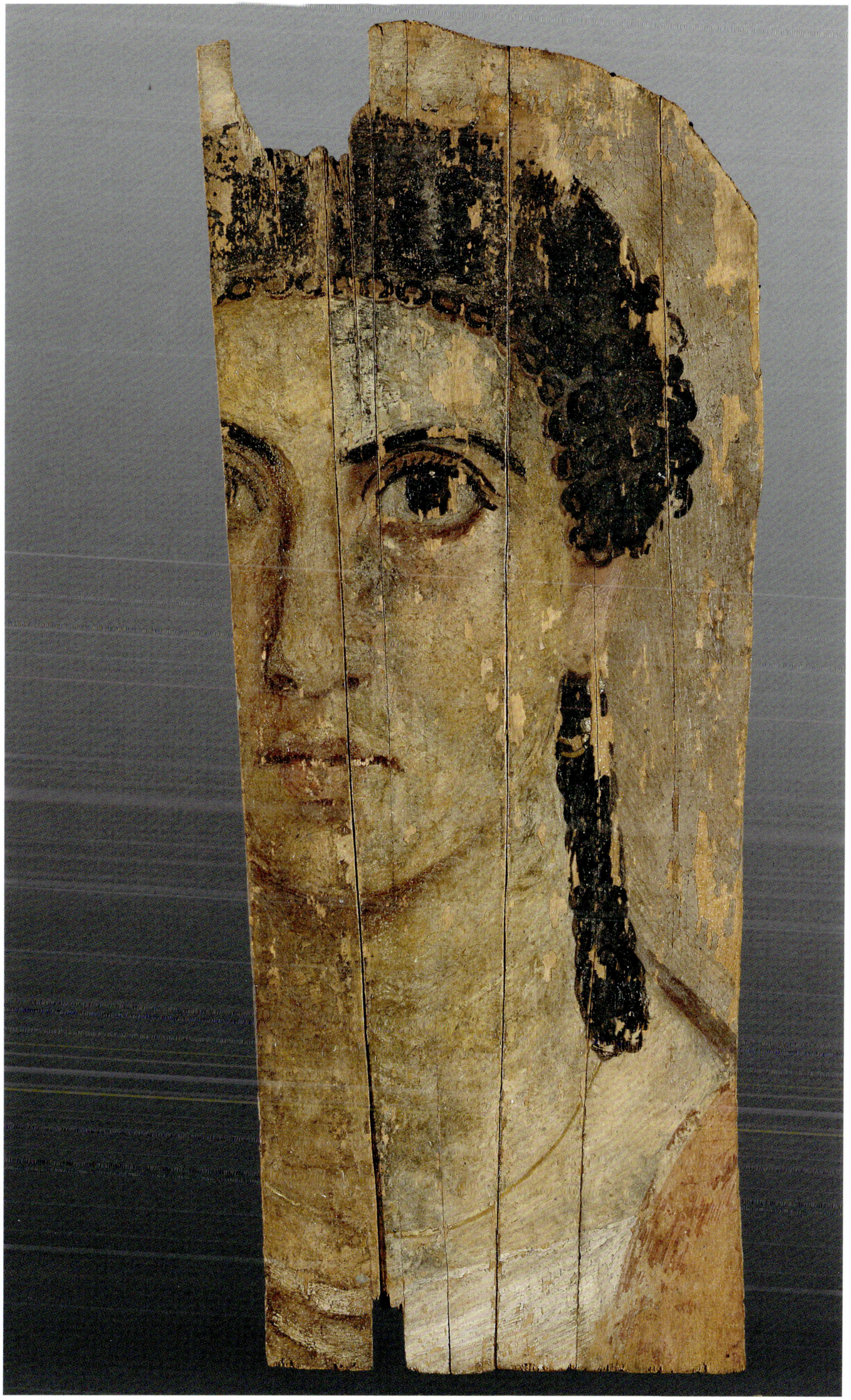

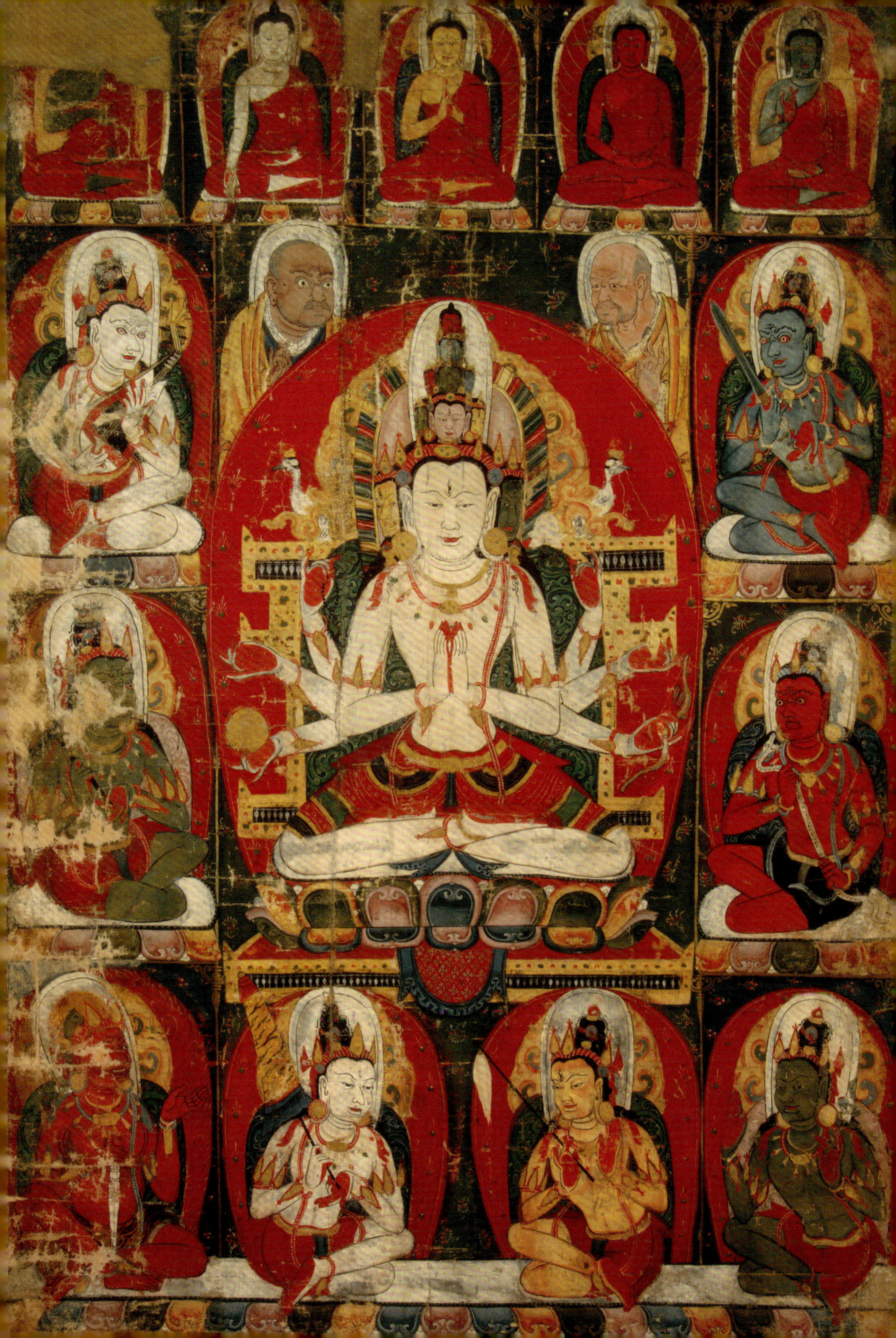

right: *Portrait of an Official.* 12TH CENTURY. KHARA-KHOTO, HSI HSIA (A TANGUT STATE IN PRESENT-DAY NORTHWESTERN CHINA). DISTEMPER PAINTS AND INDIA INK ON PAPER. 17¾ × 12½ IN. (45 × 31.8 CM).

A prominent place in the Hermitage is reserved for the artworks of the Tangut, the people who created the state of Hsi Hsia, which perished in the Mongol invasion of 1227. Tangut culture became known through the discoveries made in 1908–9 by Piotr Kozlov's expedition to the lost fortress of Khara-Khoto. This portrait of an elderly official, who cannot be identified due to the lack of any text, follows the portraiture canon of the Chinese Sung era.

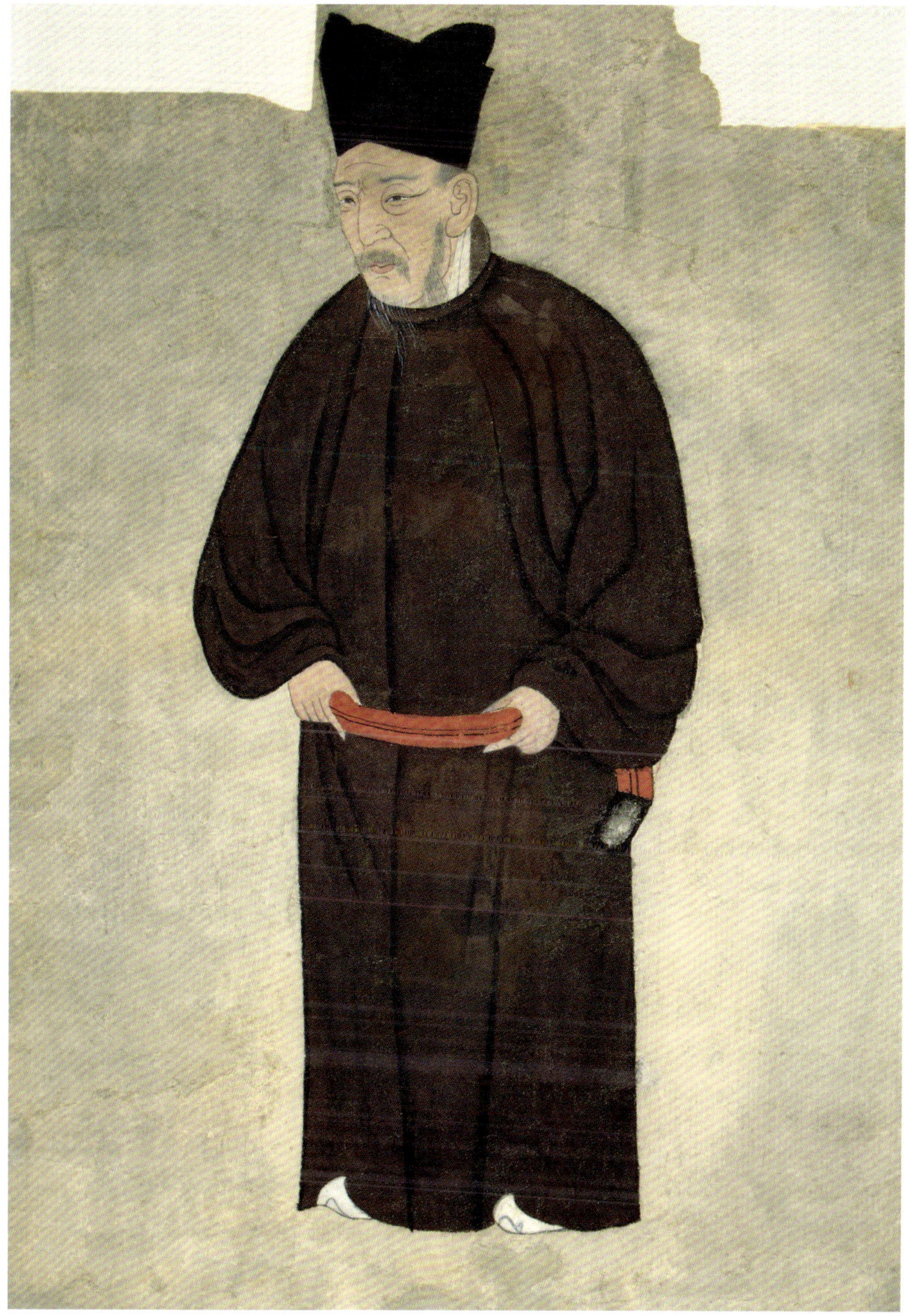

opposite: *The Eleven-Faced Bodhisattva Avalokitesvara.* 12TH CENTURY. KHARA-KHOTO, HSI HSIA (A TANGUT STATE IN PRESENT-DAY NORTHWESTERN CHINA). DISTEMPER PAINTS ON CANVAS. 52 × 37 IN. (132 × 94 CM).

Buddhism was an important influence in the formation of Tangut culture. The Hermitage *tangka* (religious painting) depicts the bodhisattva of mercy and compassion Avalokitesvara on a lotus throne. The two main arms, placed together in the *anjami mudra* gesture, hold the wish-fulfilling jewel. The central figure is symmetrically surrounded by other deities of Buddhist mythology. Behind the *mandorla* (radiance) in which the Avalokitesvara is depicted, two monks are shown, one young with a grotesque face, the other old and pleasant looking.

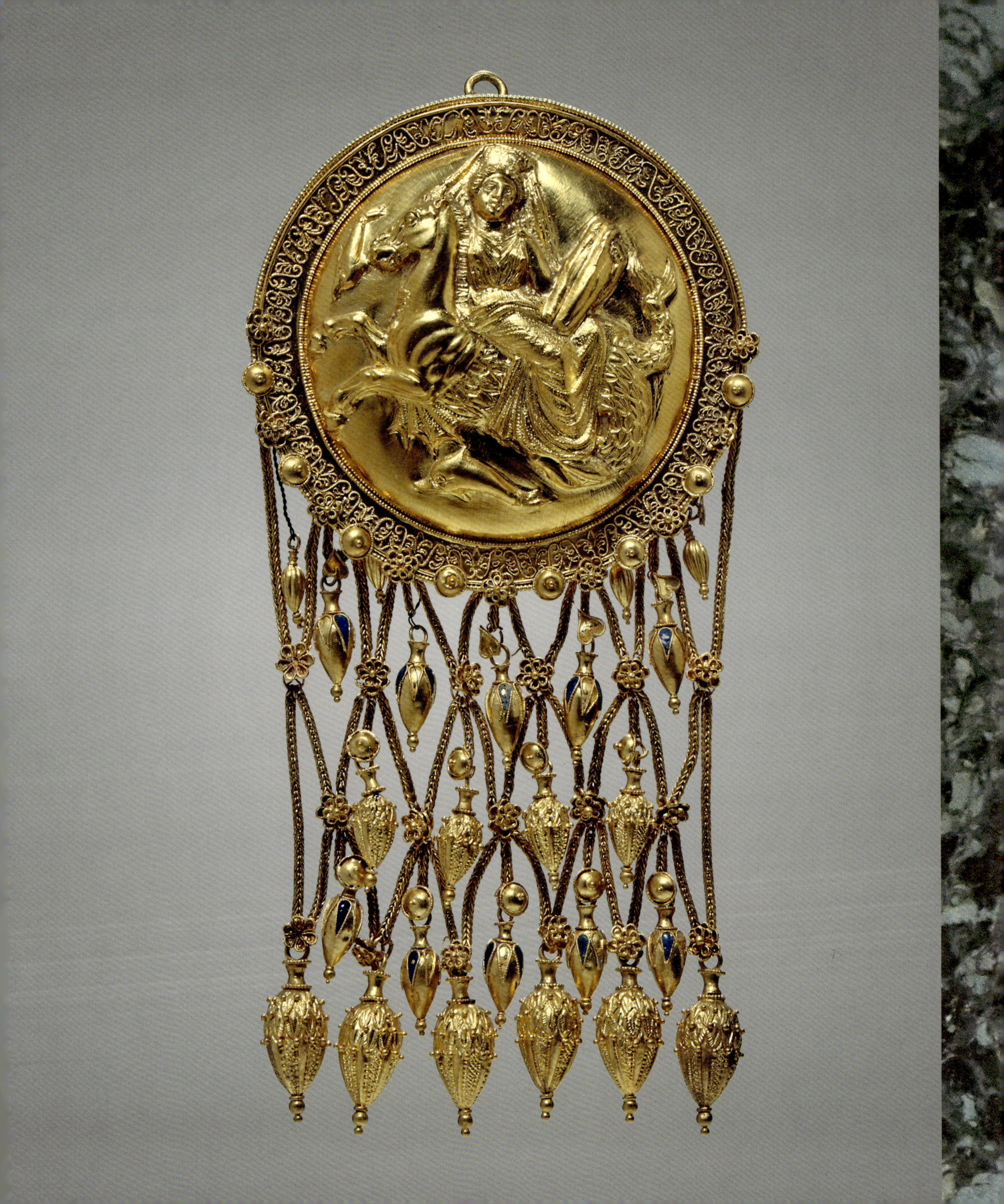

Scythian and Bosporan Antiquities

Temporal Pendant with a Depiction of a Nereid on a Hippocampus in a Medallion. 330–300 B.C. BIG TWIN BURIAL MOUND, BOSPORAN KINGDOM, TAMAN PENINSULA, RUSSIA. GOLD AND ENAMEL. 6⅛ IN. (15.5 CM) HIGH.

This pendant is one of a pair attached to the sides of a *kalathos* to dangle at the wearer's temples. The relief ornament on the medallion shows a sea nymph, or nereid, riding a hippocampus, a fantastic mix of horse and fish. This may be Thetis, the mother of the ancient Greek hero Achilles, or one of her companions. The subject derives from an episode in the *Iliad* in which Achilles is brought armor made by Hephaestus, the god of metalworking.

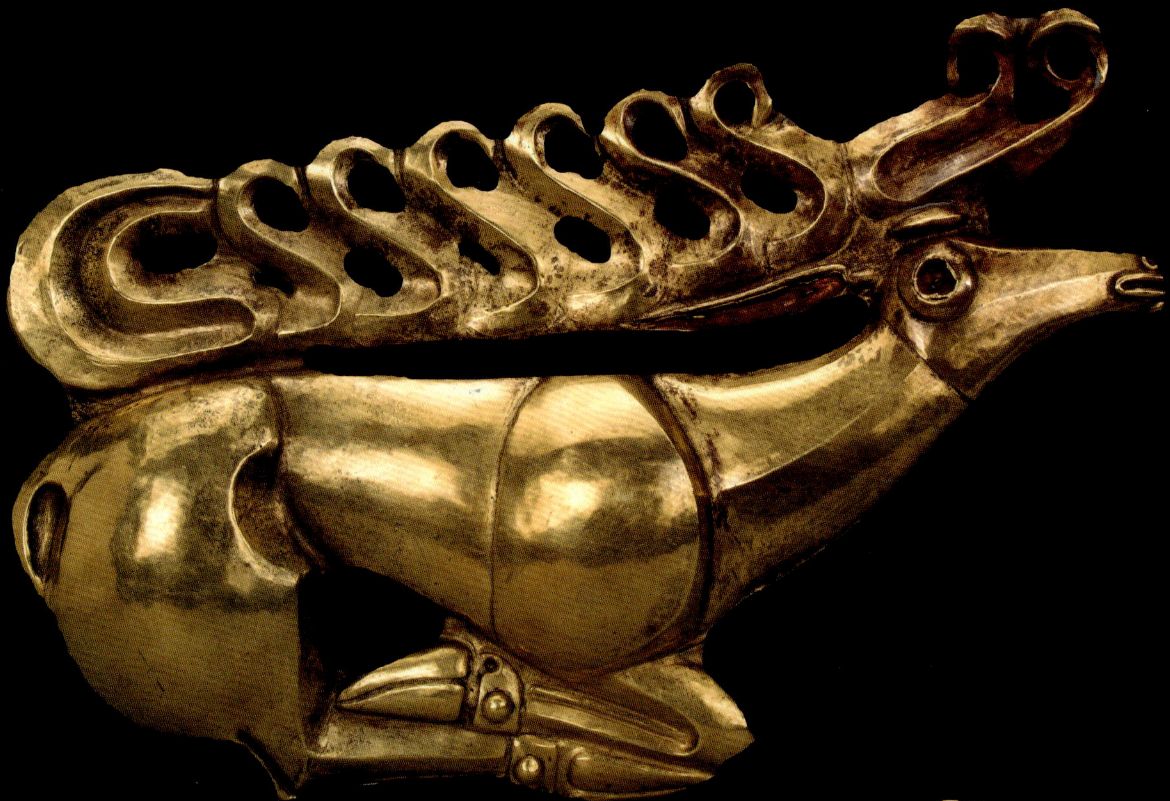
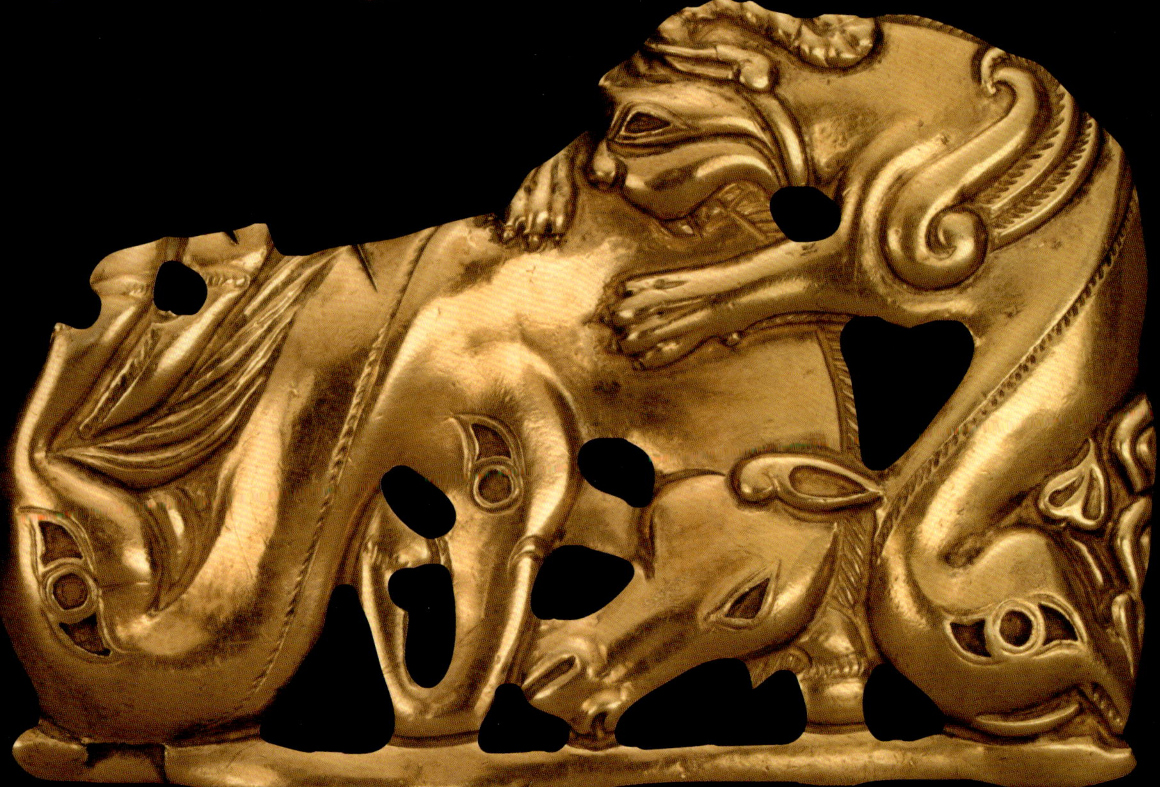

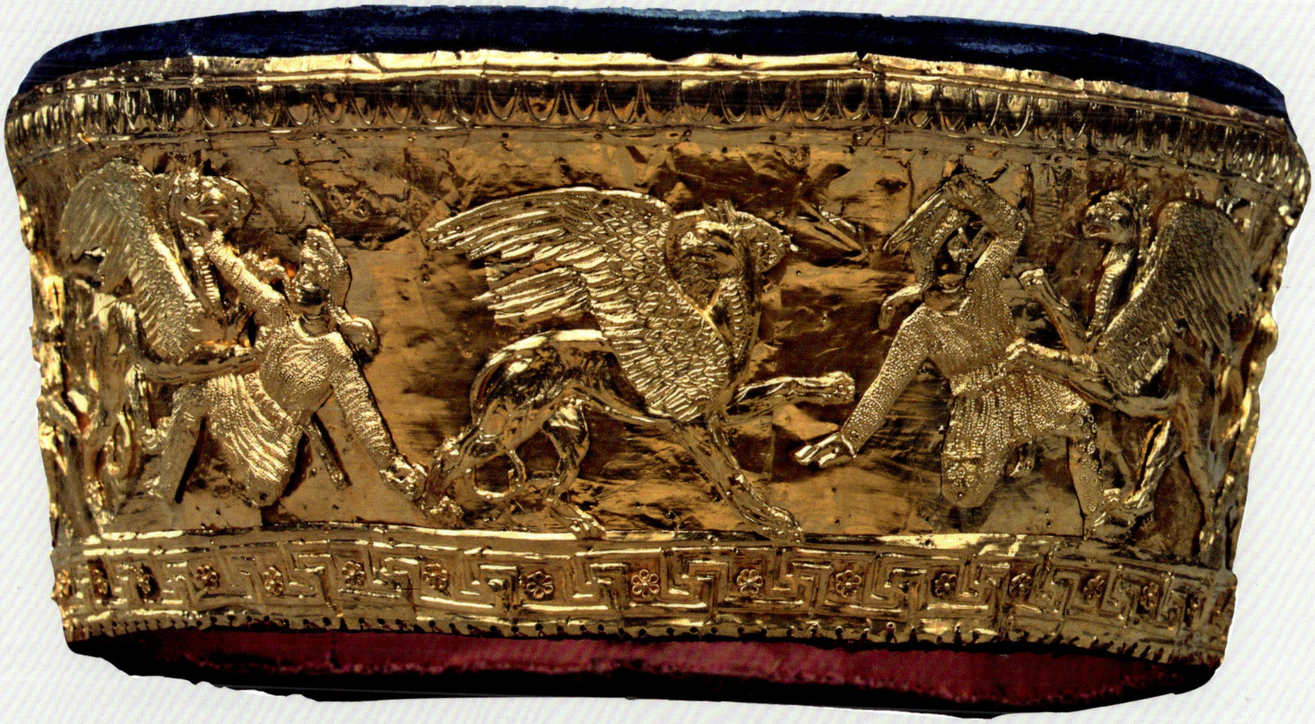

opposite, top: *Plaque in the Form of a Deer.* BURIAL MOUND NEAR THE COSSACK VILLAGE OF KOSTROMSKAYA, KUBAN RIVER BASIN, KRASNODAR TERRITORY, RUSSIA. LATE 7TH CENTURY B.C. GOLD. 12½ IN. (31.7 CM) LONG, 7½ IN. (19 CM) HIGH.

This plaque once embellished a shield or bow case that may have belonged to a member of the clan's tribal aristocracy. The relief is a masterpiece of Scythian metalworking and a copybook example of the mature Animal Style. An accurate depiction of the deer is combined with a decorative yet concise treatment of the details; it is shown as if prepared for a ritual sacrifice. Sockets in the eye and ear were originally filled with an inlay, now lost.

opposite, bottom: *Attacking a Horse.* 4TH–3RD CENTURY B.C. GOLD. 7⅝ IN. (19.3 CM) LONG.

The relief on this openwork plate, from Peter the Great's Siberian collection, depicts a horse being attacked by a gryphon, a subject typical of the Scythians' Animal Style, which evidently related to their religious conceptions. The dynamism of the figures of the monster and its struggling prey combines with fanciful stylization: the bodies twisted into an S shape and the ornamental treatment of the details. The shoulders, haunches, and eyes of the animals have sockets for colored insets now lost.

above: *Headdress in the Form of a Kalathos Bearing a Depiction of a Battle between the Arimapsi and Gryphons.* BIG TWIN BURIAL MOUND, BOSPORAN KINGDOM, TAMAN PENINSULA, RUSSIA. 330–300 B.C. GOLD. 4 IN. (10 CM) HIGH, 10¼ IN. (26 CM) DIAMETER.

This ritual headdress in the form of a *kalathos* (flared basket), is among the priestly attributes associated with the cults of several fertility deities. This richly decorated example consists of thirty interconnected plates. The figurative scene shows a battle between men in barbarian (oriental) clothing and fantastic monsters, one of a group of myths that probably formed in the northern Black Sea area as a result of a symbiosis between the beliefs of the ancient Greek colonists and local legends.

below, left: *Comb Bearing a Depiction of a Battle Scene.* SOLOKHA BURIAL MOUND, DNIEPER RIVER BASIN, ZAPOROZHYE REGION, UKRAINE. LAST THIRD OF THE 5TH–EARLY 4TH CENTURY B.C. GOLD. 5 IN. (12.6 CM) HIGH, 4 IN. (10.2 CM) WIDE.

The scene on the back of this gold comb probably illustrates a Scythian legend or myth or perhaps a glorified historical episode: the culmination of the dynastic conflict between the sons of the Scythian king Ariapithes. The shape repeats those made of a combination of metal and bone or wood often found in the burials of the Scythian aristocracy. It is a masterpiece of Greek metalworking made for a Scythian client.

below, right: *Belt Plate Showing a Tree, Horses, and Two Personages over the Body of a Hero.* 5TH–4TH CENTURY B.C. GOLD. 4¾ IN. (12.1 CM) HIGH, 6 IN. (15.2 CM) WIDE.

This openwork cast and chased plate takes the form of a relief that apparently depicts a scene from a heroic epic of the ancient Altai nomads: the revival of a hero by his wife and brother beneath a poplar tree. The figures' dress, the weapons, and the horses' harnesses look identical to authentic objects found by the Soviet archaeologists who excavated the frozen Pazyryk and Tuektin burial mounds, in the Altai Mountains.

opposite: *Male Mask.* FROM A 3RD-CENTURY BURIAL IN THE NECROPOLIS OF PANTICAPEUM; KERCH, UKRAINE. GOLD. 10 IN. (25.5 CM) HIGH.

A dish from the same burial in which this mask was found bears an inscription that includes the name of King Rescuporides. On this basis, the grave was determined to be royal and the mask considered a funerary depiction of the monarch. But no consensus has been reached on his identity—eight rulers of the Bosporan kingdom were named Rescuporides. The plot thickens with the dating of the mask, which appears to be older than any other object in the complex.

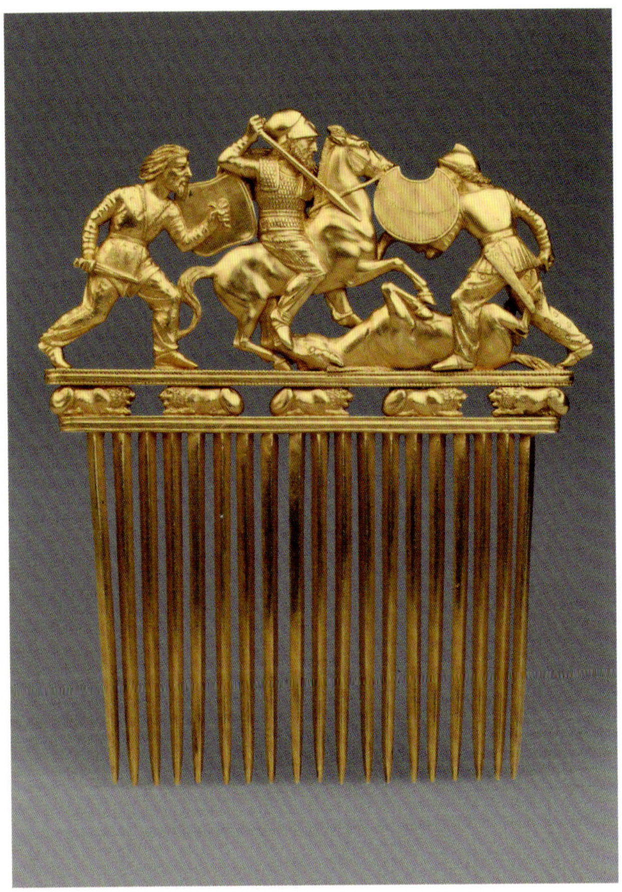

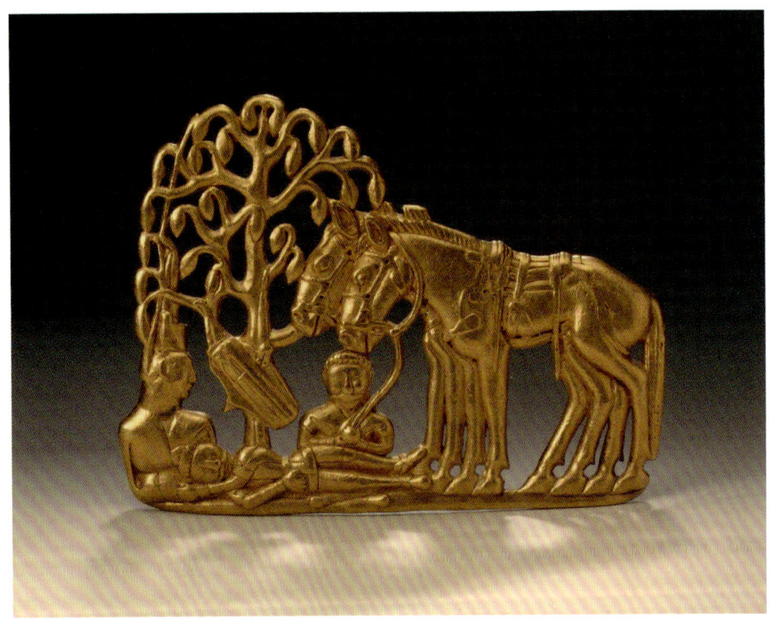

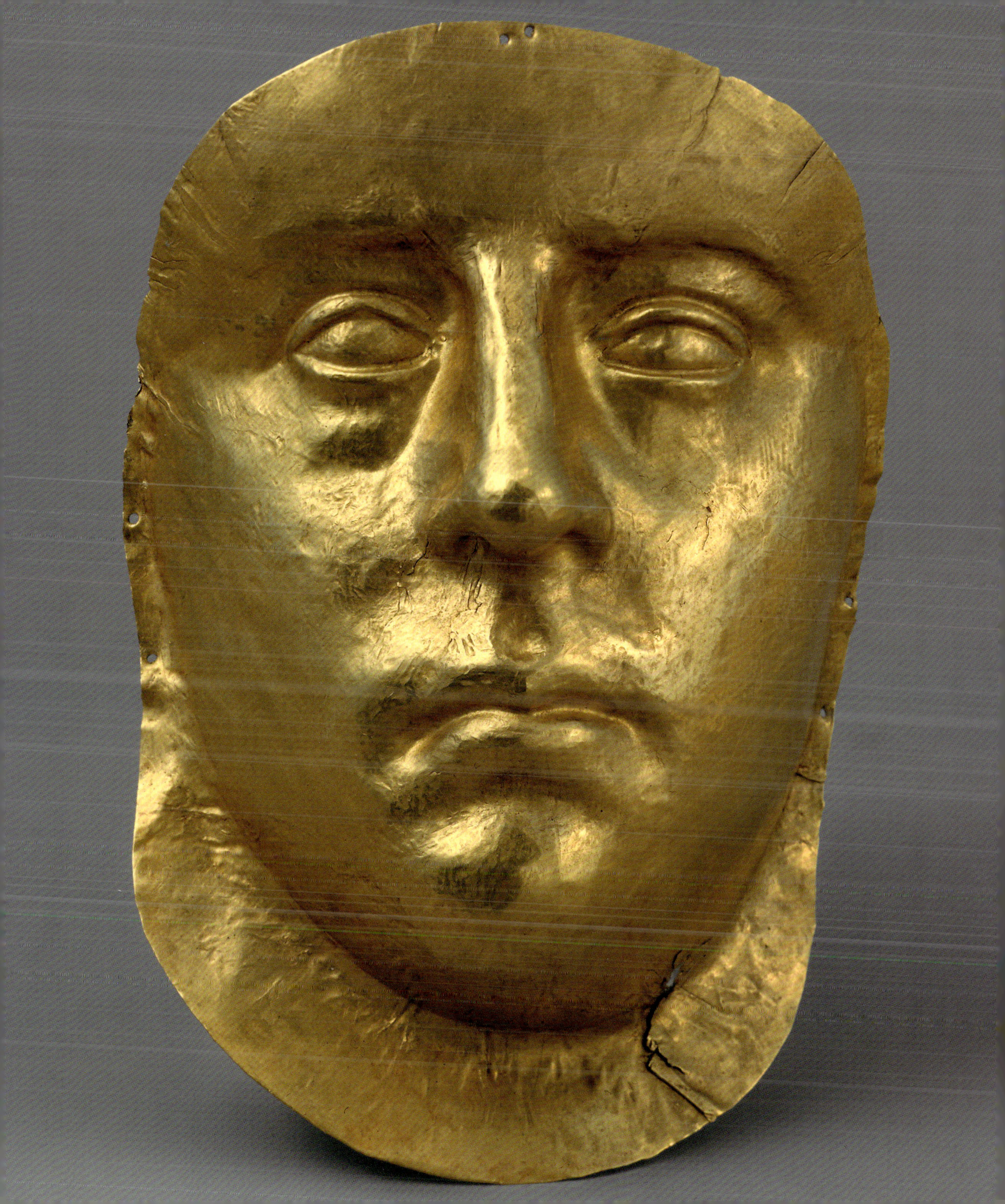

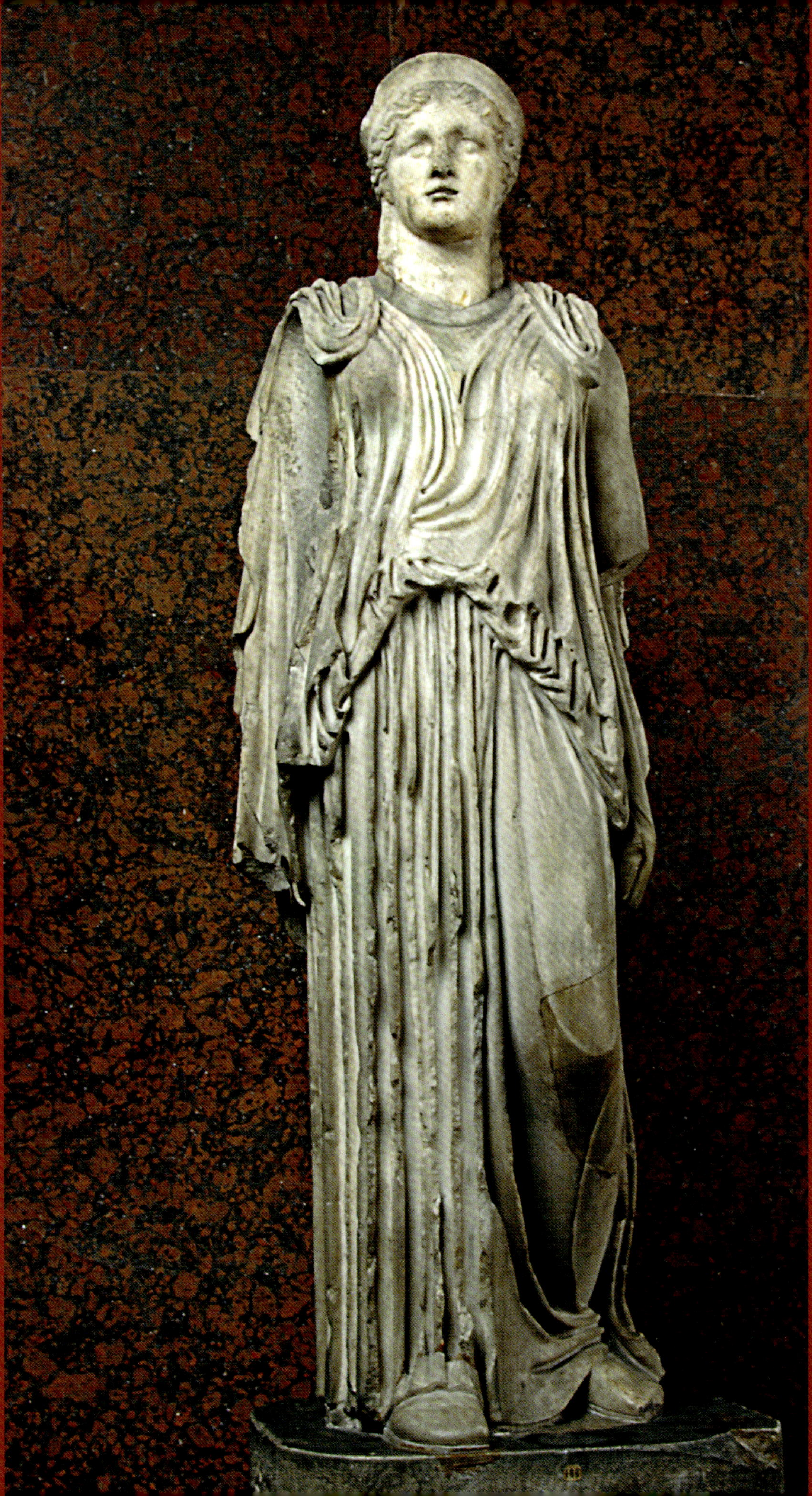

Greek and Roman Antiquities

Statue of Demeter. ROMAN WORK BASED ON A 5TH-CENTURY-B.C. GREEK ORIGINAL; 2ND CENTURY A.D. (?). MARBLE. 52 3/8 IN. (133 CM) HIGH.

Judging by the small size and decorative details, this statue likely served as an architectural element, possibly a caryatid, rather than as a cult object. The goddess wears a *peplos*, or loose female garment. The head, a later addition but also ancient, is believed to be based on a lost monumental statue of Demeter.

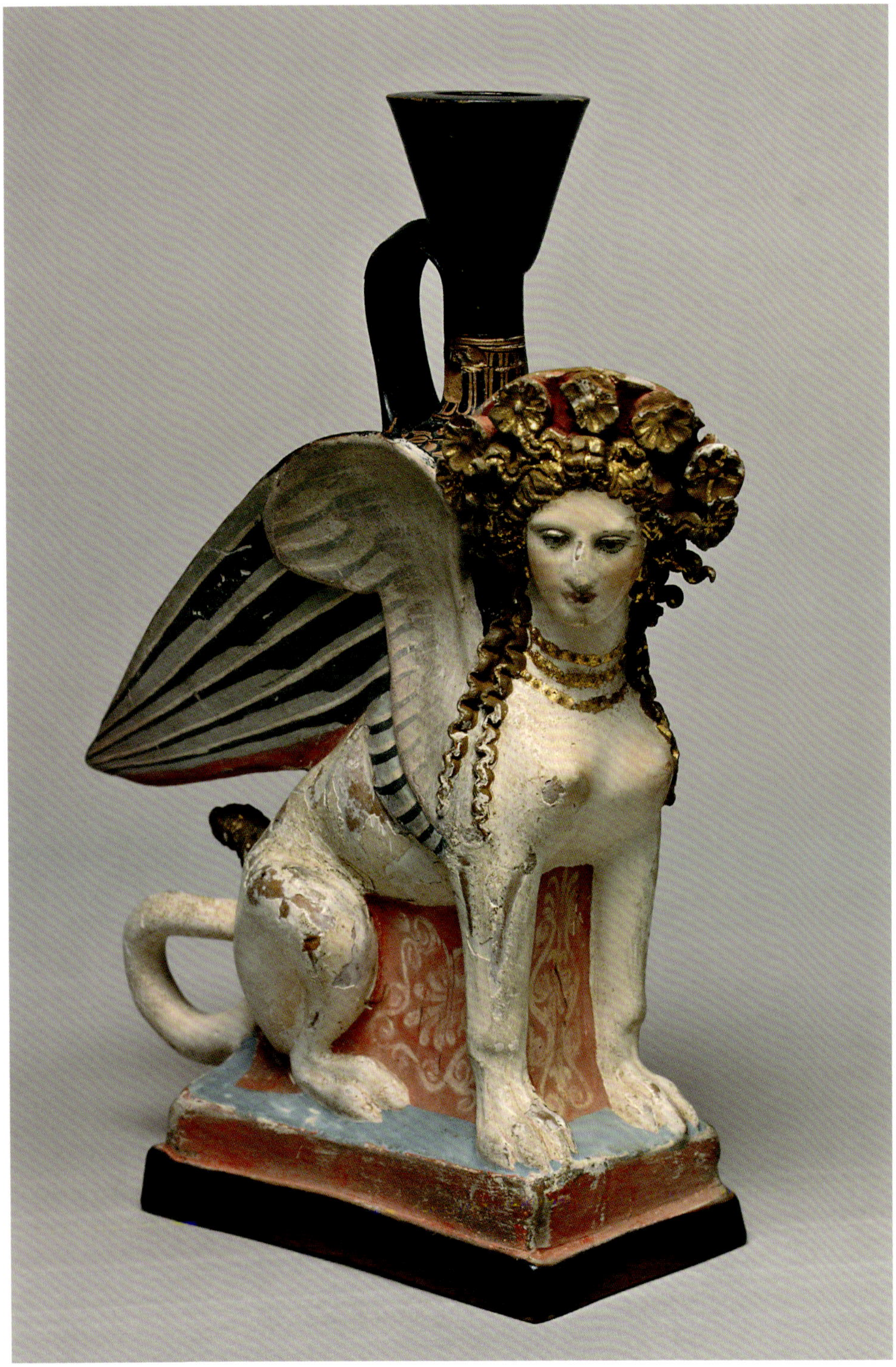

left: *Figured Lekythos in the Form of a Sphinx.* ATTICA. LATE 5TH–FIRST QUARTER OF THE 4TH CENTURY B.C. EARTHENWARE. 8 1/4 IN. (21 CM) HIGH.

This sphinx-shaped lekythos—a vessel used to store aromatic oils—was discovered in 1869 during the excavation of a female burial site in the necropolis of the ancient city of Phanagoria. It is a rare example of the combination of red-figure decoration with polychrome painting applied after firing. The original paints have survived with minimal losses, providing an idea of the range of colors used to embellish classical sculpture.

opposite: *Aphrodite and Eros.* BOEOTIA (TANAGRA). FIRST QUARTER OF THE 3RD CENTURY B.C. TERRACOTTA. 7 1/4 IN. (18.5 CM) HIGH.

In contrast to most Tanagra statuettes, which were produced in small series, this example is unique. The complex composition required several molds, with the parts attached with slip before firing. Unlike most cult statues of Aphrodite, the goddess is shown seated on a klismos chair with her son in her lap. The rattle was added by a 19th-century restorer. If not for the wings on Eros's back, it would be hard to recognize the Olympian deities in this idyllic composition.

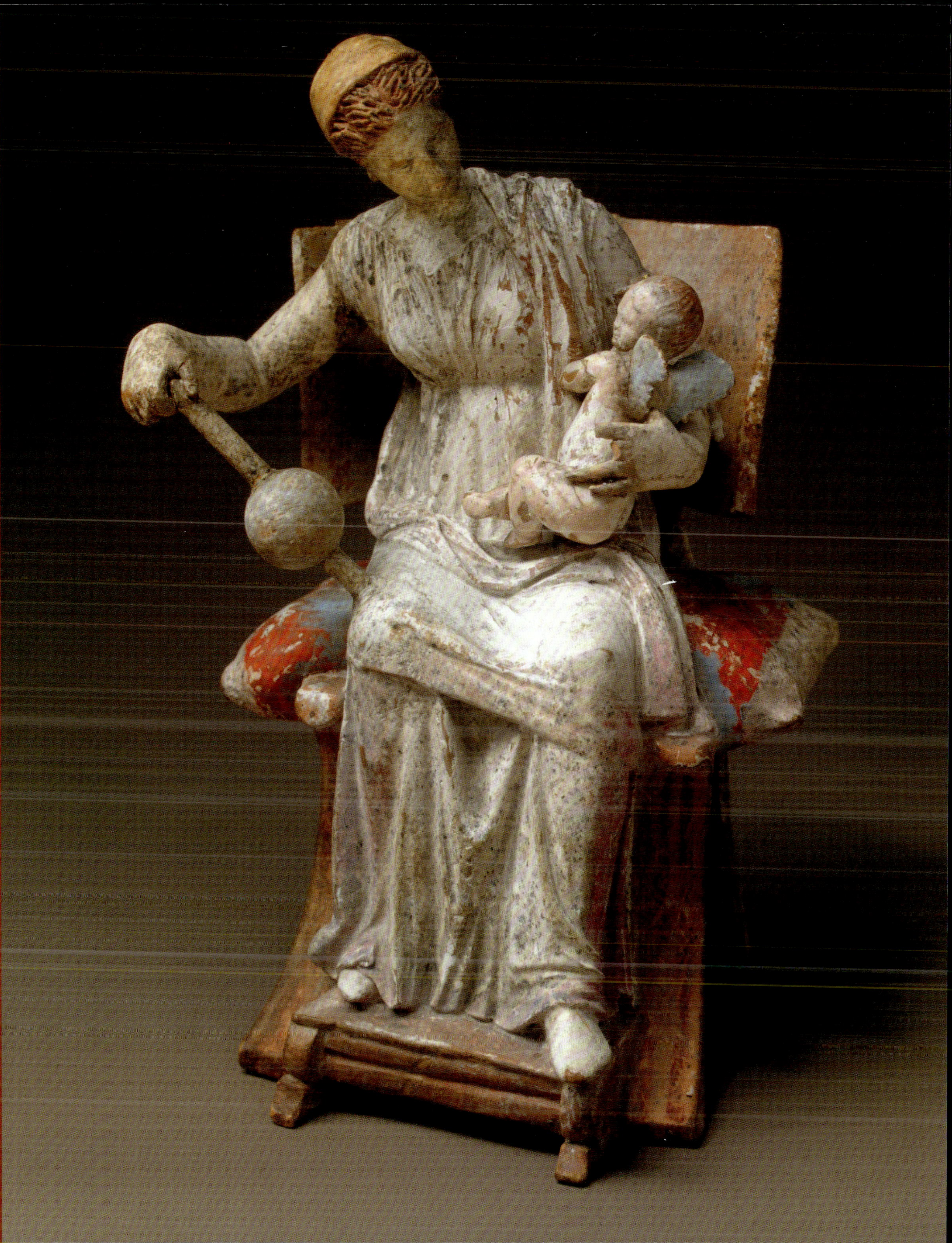

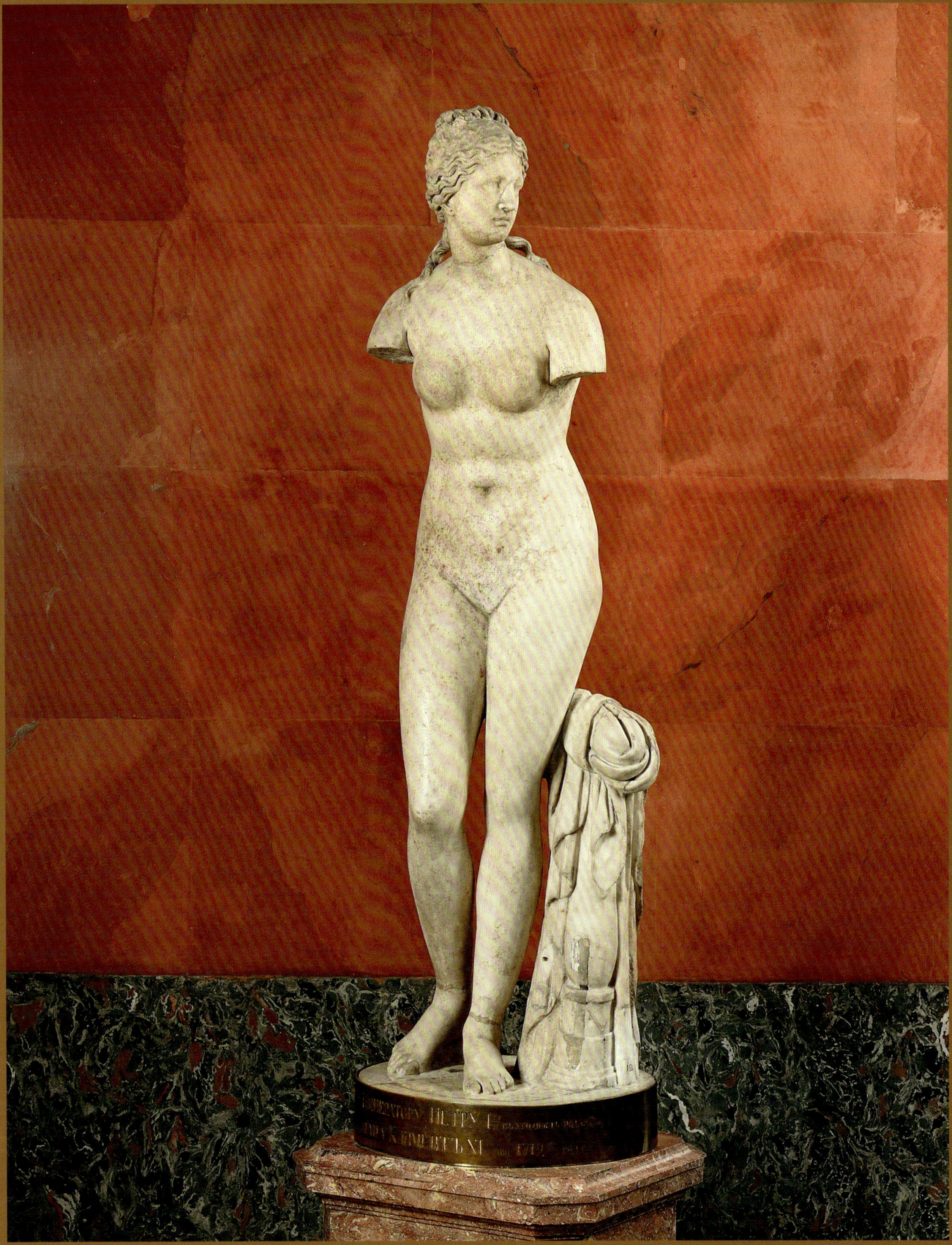

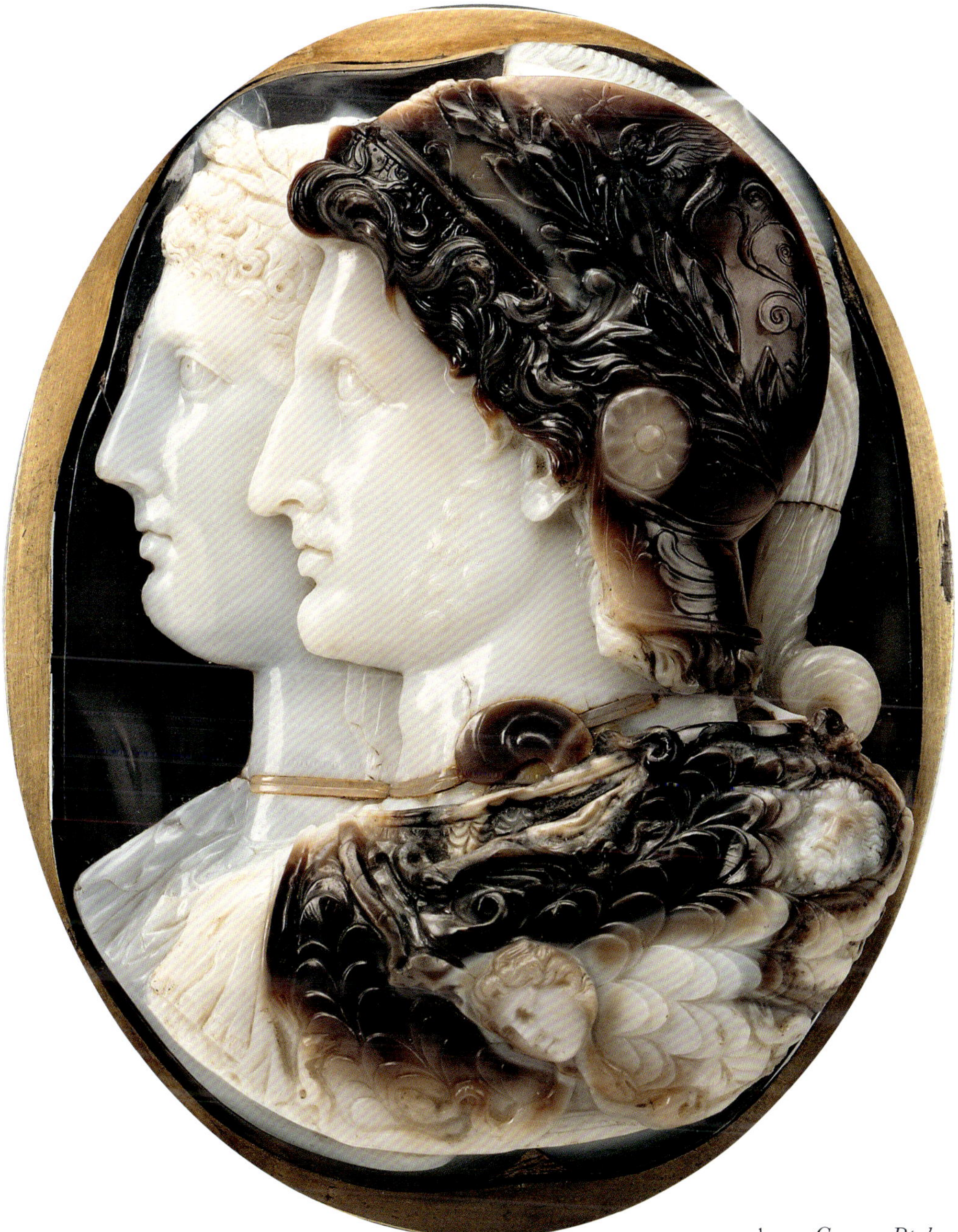

above: *Cameo, Ptolemy II and Arsinoe II (Gonzaga Cameo).* ALEXANDRIA. 3RD CENTURY B.C. AGATE. $6^{1}/_{8} \times 4^{5}/_{8}$ IN (15.7 × 11.8 CM).

This masterpiece of official art depicts Ptolemy II Philadelphus ("sister-loving") and Arsinoe II Philadelpha ("brother-loving"), rulers of Hellenistic Egypt, as Olympian gods. The queen's head shawl symbolizes the new deities' sacred marriage. Marriage between close relatives and deification of living monarchs were customary in ancient Egypt, and so were also used to establish the continuity and legitimacy of nonnative dynasties.

opposite: *The Taurida Venus.* ROMAN REPLICA OF A HELLENISTIC STATUE(?). MARBLE. $66^{1}/_{2}$ IN. (169 CM) HIGH.

This statue was one of the first ancient sculptures to enter the Hermitage. Acquired in 1721, during the reign of Peter the Great, it adorned the Summer Garden before being moved to the Taurida Palace, for which it is named. The statue is considered to be a Roman copy of a Hellenistic original, but recently it was suggested that it is an authentic Greek cult statue of the 2nd century B.C.

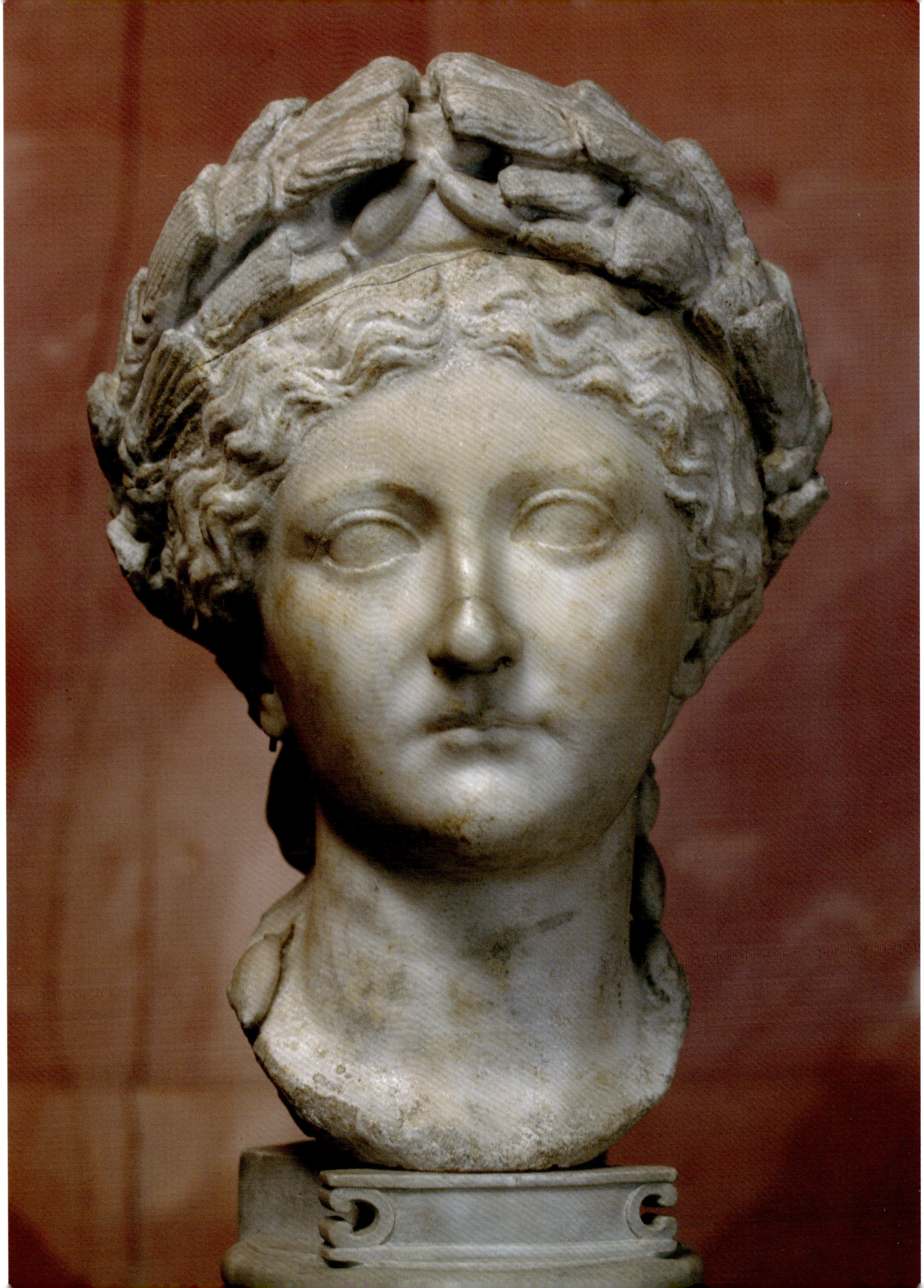

right: *Statue of Augustus in the Guise of Jupiter.* FIRST HALF OF THE 1ST CENTURY. MARBLE. 72⅞ IN. (185 CM).

The Italian Neoclassical sculptor Filippo Gnaccarini, who restored this badly damaged statue found during excavations at Cumae, added to it the attributes of Jupiter (a scepter and figure of Victory on an orb). Augustus was indeed depicted in this way in the reigns of his successors, beginning with Tiberius (r. A.D. 14–A.D. 37), who established the official cult of the deified late emperor.

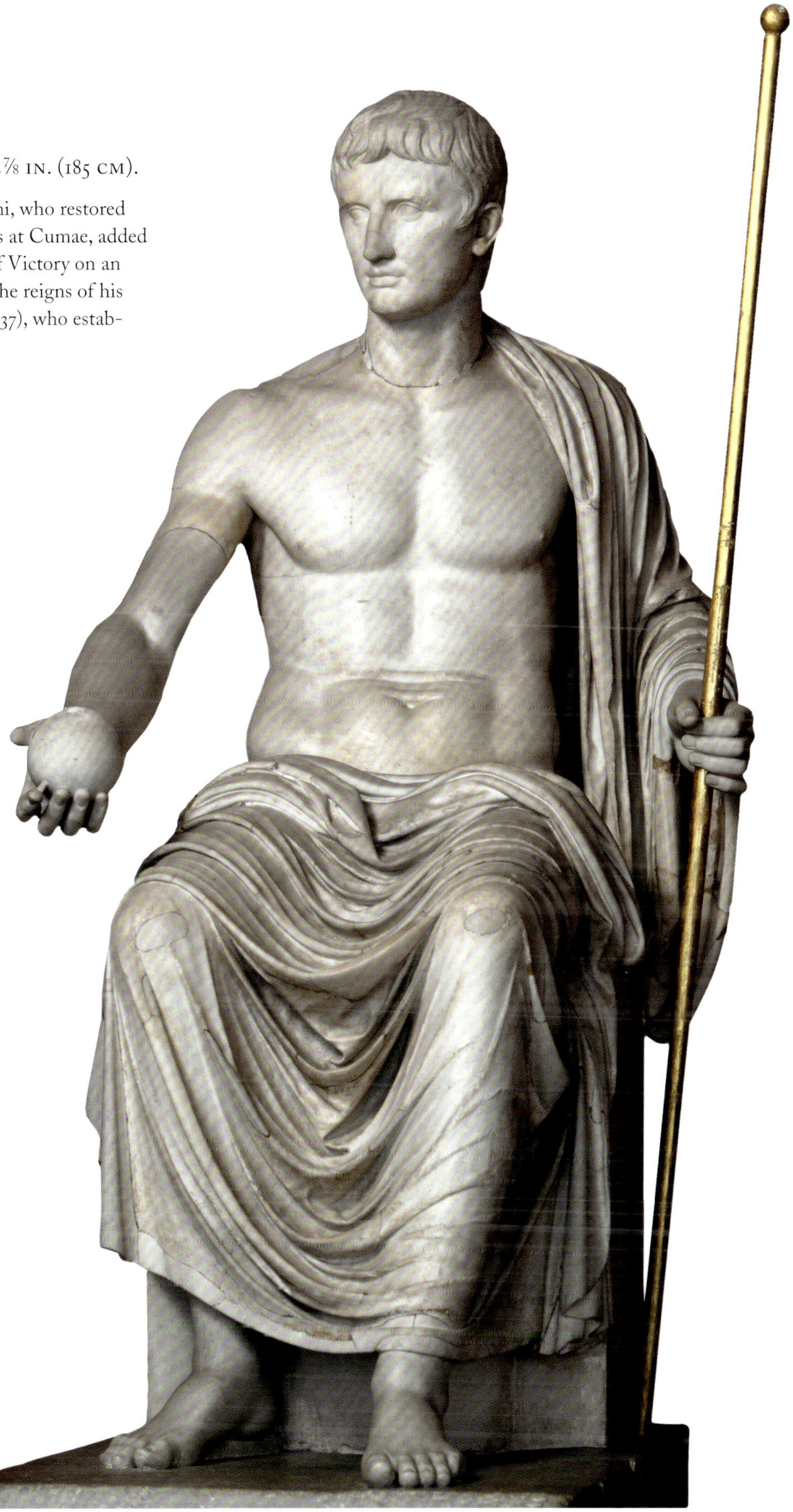

opposite: *Portrait of Livia.* 1ST CENTURY A.D. MARBLE. 13⅜ IN. (34 CM) HIGH

Livia Drusilla (58 B.C.–A.D 29) was the first Roman woman in whose honor altars were constructed and statues erected. At age twenty, she married the emperor Augustus and, after his death, enjoyed nearly unlimited power. The portrait head (part of a larger statue) presents her in the guise of Ceres-Augusta, high priestess of the cult of Divine Augustus.

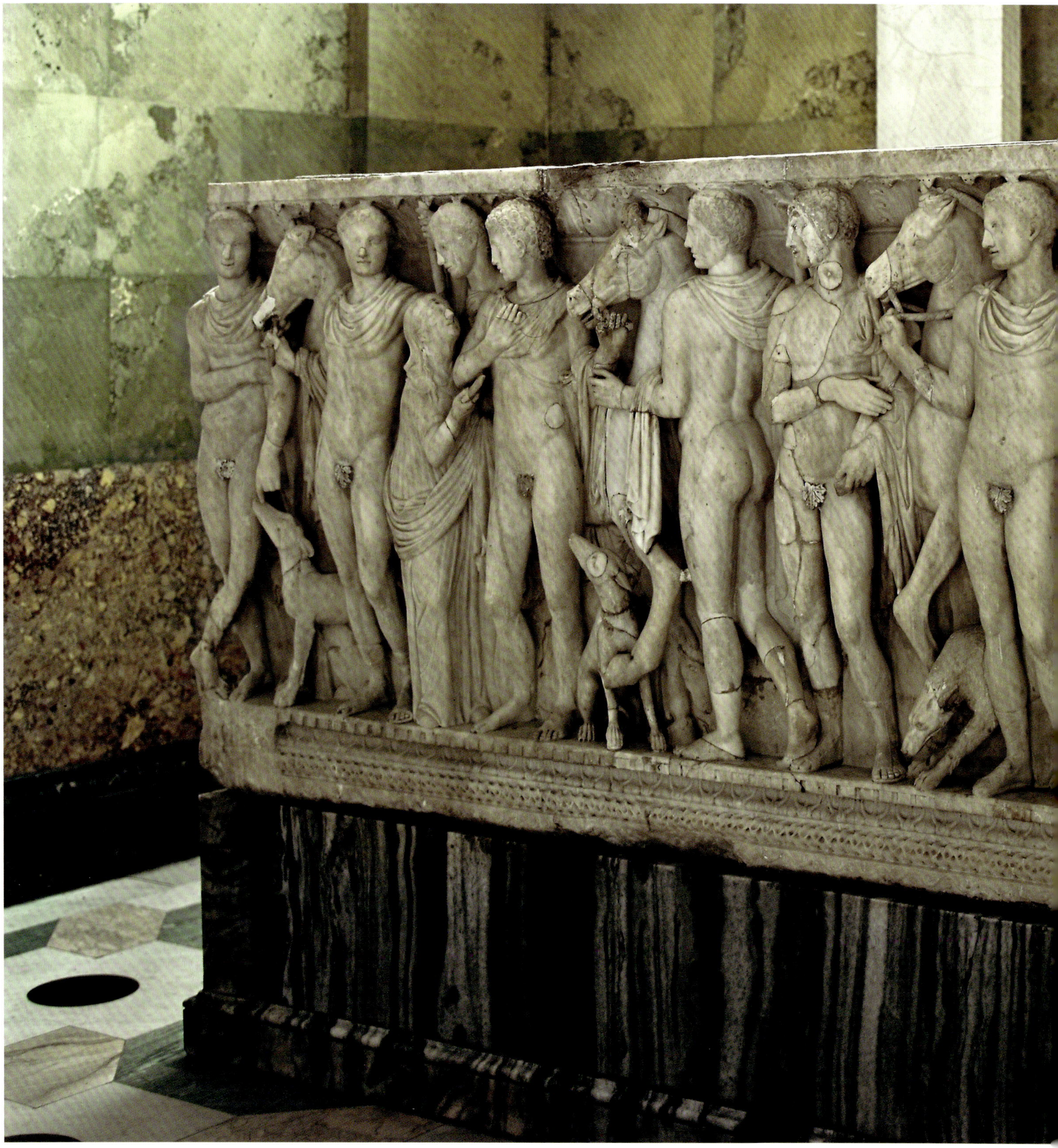

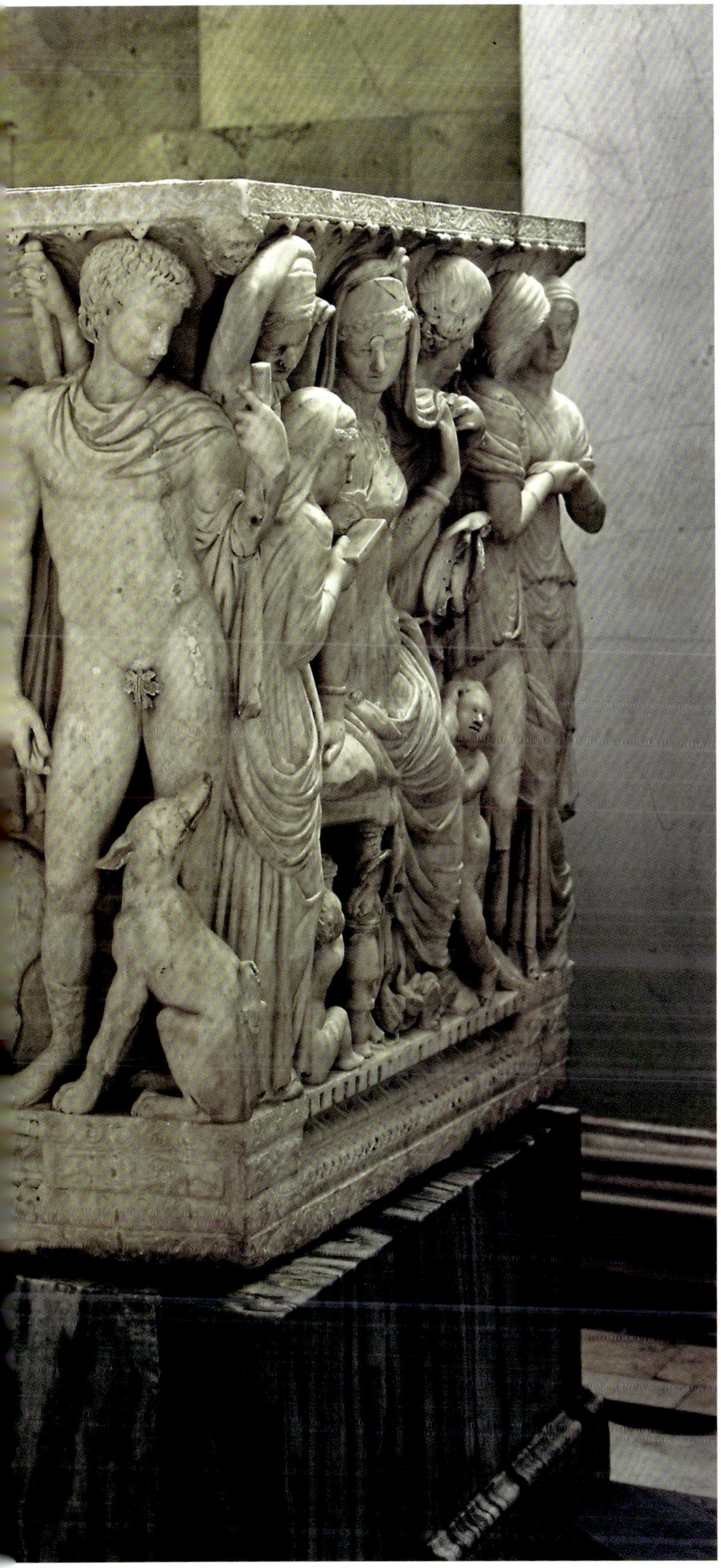

Sarcophagus, Hippolytus and Phaedra. ATTICA. MID-3RD CENTURY. MARBLE. $49\frac{1}{4}$ IN. (125 CM) HIGH.

According to Greek myth, the passionate hunter Hippolytus angered Aphrodite by his preference for Artemis. Aphrodite exacted revenge by making Phaedra, his father's young wife, fall in love with him. The sarcophagus shows the moment when Hippolytus rejects Phaedra's advances, setting off a chain of tragic events that ended in Phaedra's suicide and Hippolytus's death.

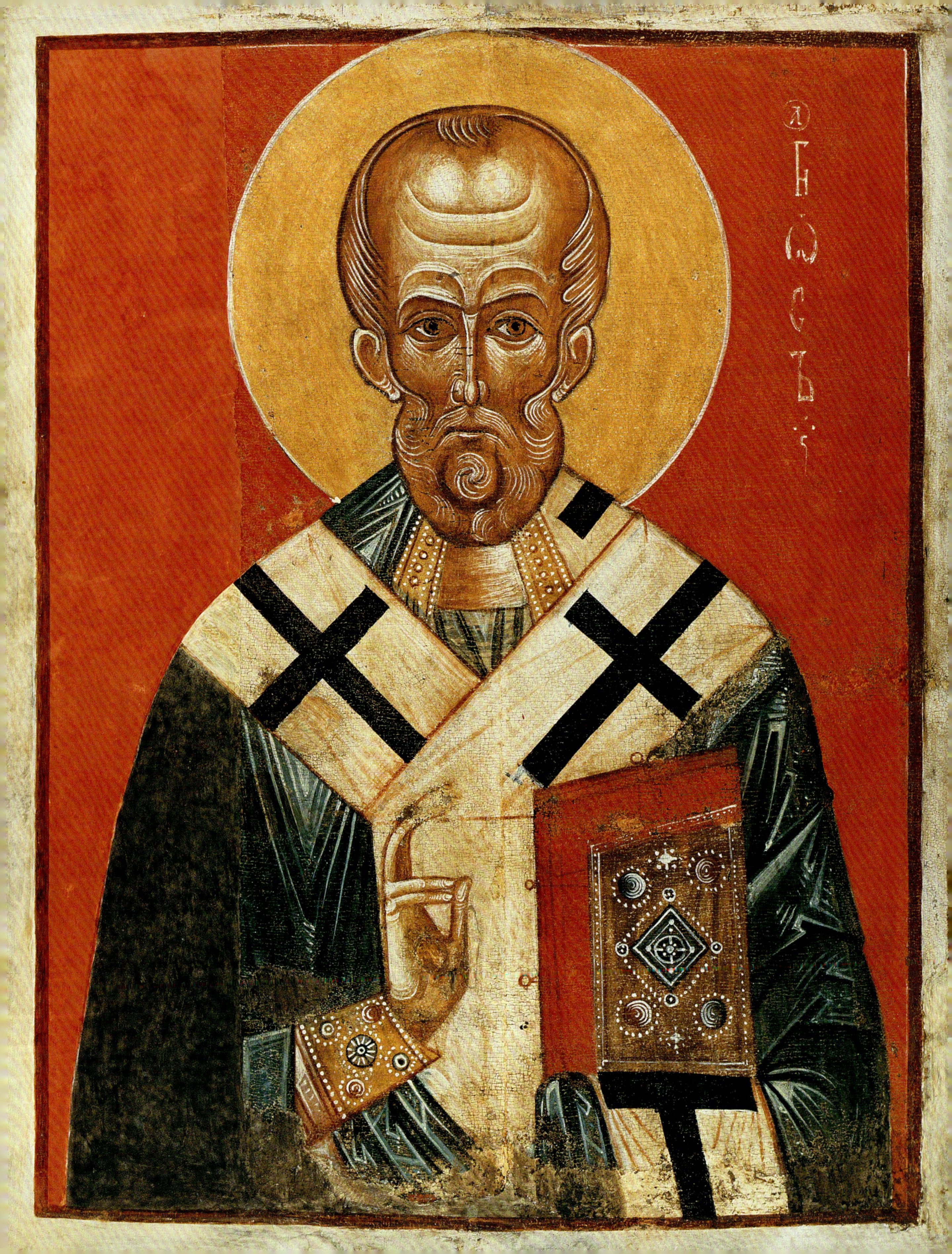

Byzantine and Ancient Russian Art

St. Nicholas the Wonder-Worker. NOVGOROD. LATE 13TH–EARLY 14TH CENTURY. EGG TEMPERA ON GESSOED PANEL. 42 3/8 × 31 1/4 IN. (107.7 × 79.5 CM).

Nicholas, the most highly venerated saint in Early Rus', is depicted half-length in this Novgorodian icon, giving a blessing with his right hand and holding the Gospel in his left, which is covered by the end of his omophorion (a liturgical stole worn by Orthodox bishops). This iconography of the saint is traditional for 13th-century Novgorod. The red background is a characteristic feature of the Novgorodian school of icon-painting.

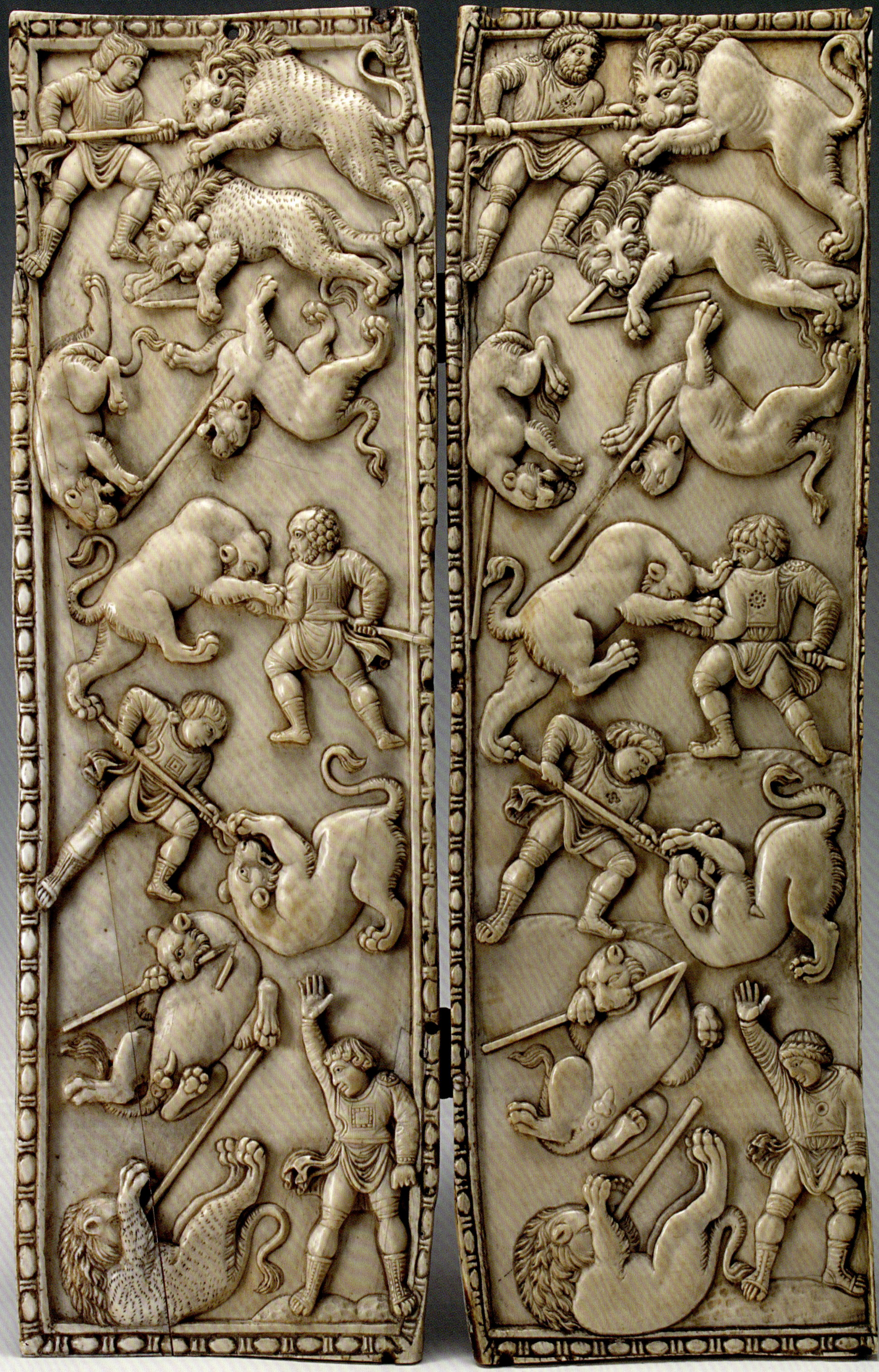

opposite: *Diptych with Church Scenes.*
CONSTANTINOPLE (?)/ALEXANDRIA (?). 5TH CENTURY.
CARVED IVORY. EACH PANEL 13 × 4 1/8 IN. (33 × 10.5 CM).

In contrast to the majority of early Byzantine ivory diptychs, this example does not depict a consul embarking on the office to which there were annual elections in Constantinople. It probably served as an invitation to the games held in the capital's hippodrome each year on January 1, on the occasion of the consular elections.

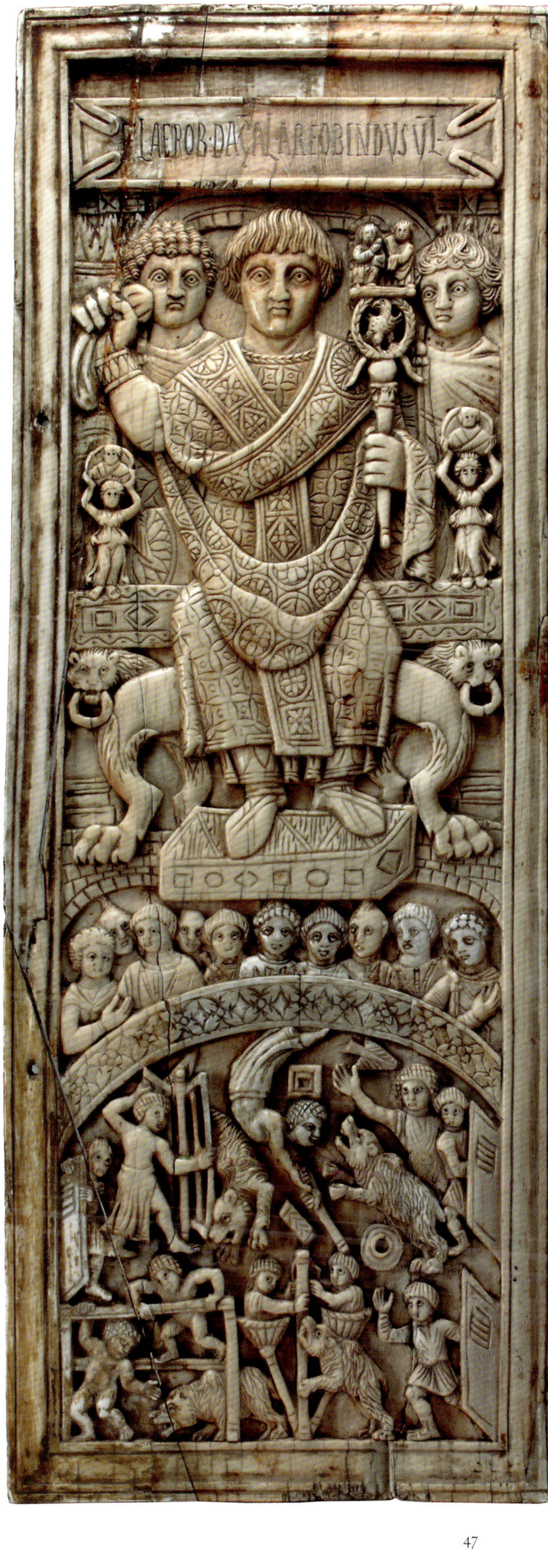

right: *Leaf of a Diptych of Consul Areobindus.*
CONSTANTINOPLE. 506. CARVED IVORY. 14 7/8 × 5 1/2 IN. (37.6 × 14 CM).

Flavius Areobindus Dagalaiphus, shown in an armchair at the opening of the circus games, signals for the spectacle to begin. "A man of nobility," as the inscription above proclaims, he was a Goth who married a granddaughter of Emperor Valentinian III (r. 425–55). He held the office of consul in the Byzantine capital in 506, under Emperor Anastasius I (r. 491–518). Atop his scepter is a depiction of the emperor presenting him with a scroll listing his rights.

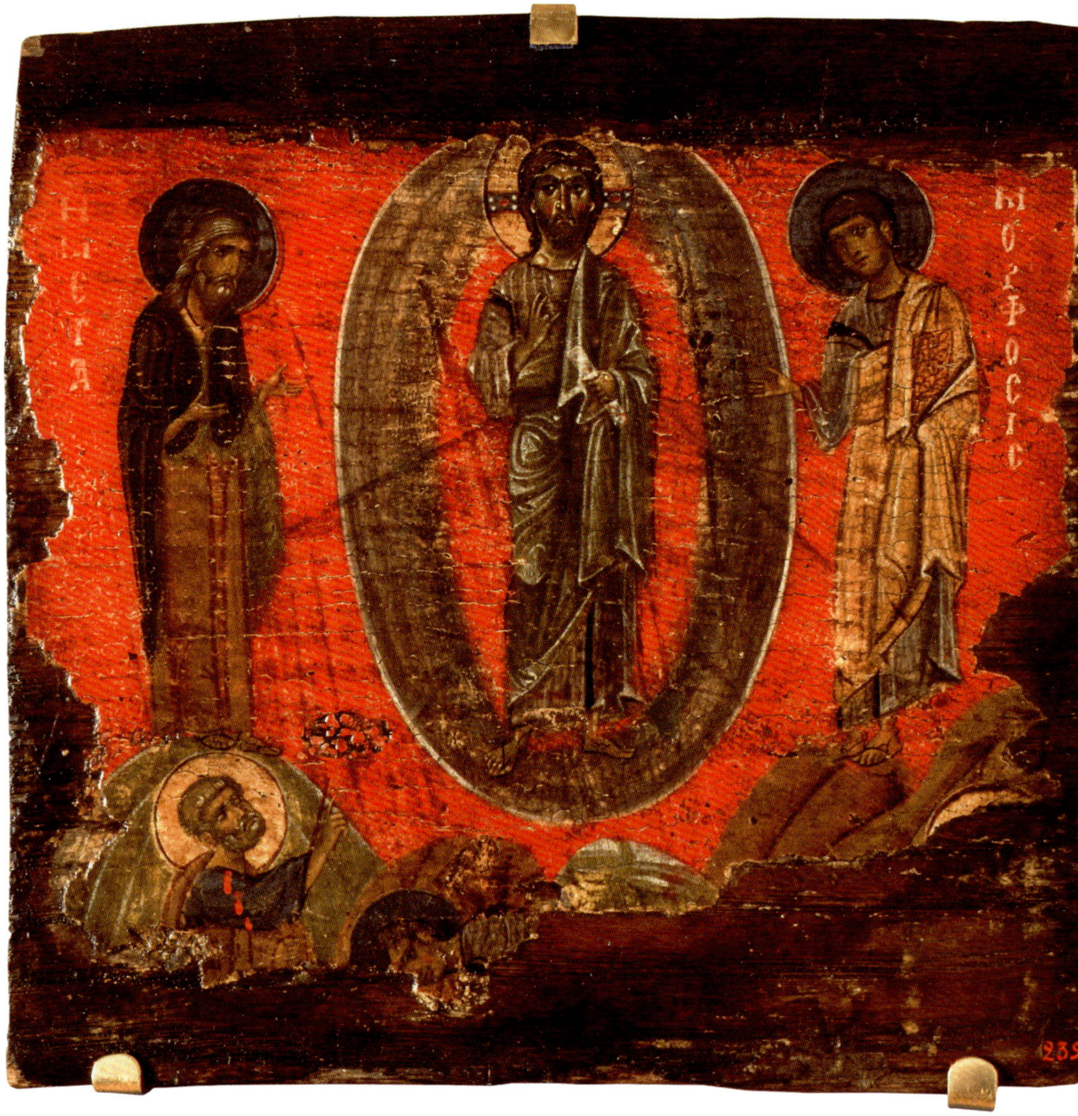

above: *The Transfiguration.* BYZANTIUM. 12TH CENTURY. EGG TEMPERA ON PANEL. 9⅛ × 9⅜ IN. (23.2 × 23.7 CM).

This icon was part of the *epithelium*, a horizontal board that came above the local tier in an iconostasis, that depicts the great Christian feasts. The archaeologist Piotr Sevastyanov brought this icon to Russia from Mount Athos in 1860. Although the red ground is not typical for Byzantine icons, it is not unknown in the medieval period. Red had great symbolic meaning in Byzantine iconography: it represented not only fire and purification but also the blood of Christ.

opposite: *Christ Pantocrator.* NORTHERN PAINTING. SECOND HALF OF THE 13TH CENTURY. EGG TEMPERA ON PANEL WITH A FINE LAYER OF GESSO. 25⅜ × 16⅜ IN. (64.5 × 41.5 CM).

This icon is among the four earliest works in the Hermitage belonging to the circle known as Northern Painting. Christ is depicted on a black background, giving the blessing with his right hand and holding an open Gospel in his left. Stylistic and iconographic features that include a certain simplification of the image and attention to the ornamentation of the clothing indicate that the icon was created in one of the centers of northern European Russia.

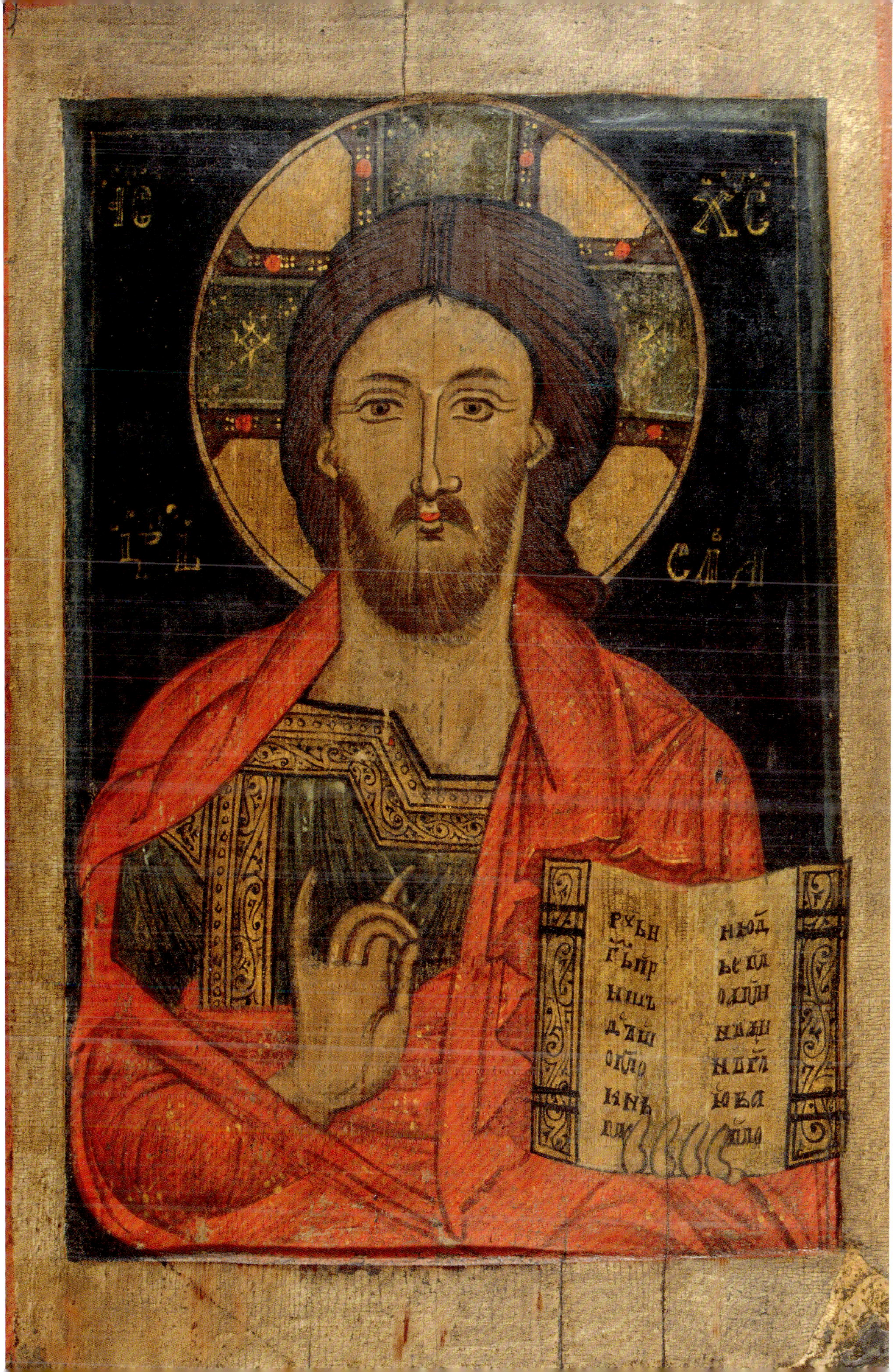

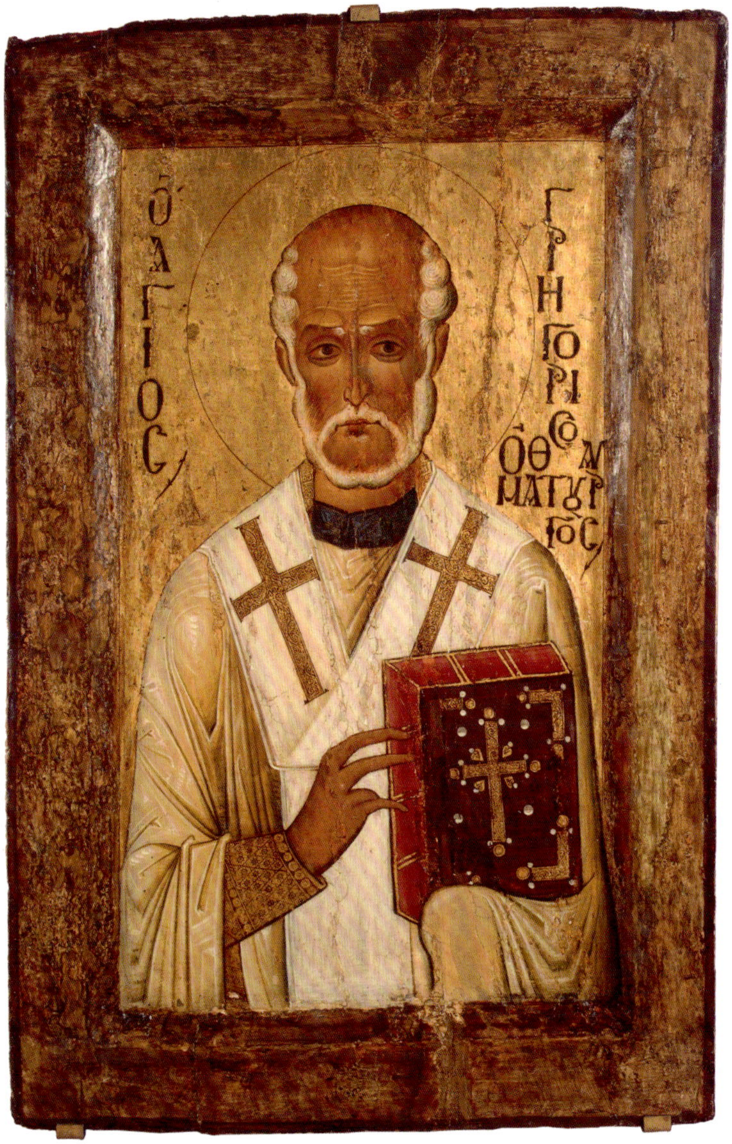

left: *St. Gregory Thaumaturge.* CONSTANTINOPLE. FIRST HALF OF THE 12TH CENTURY. TEMPERA ON WALNUT PANEL. 31⅞ × 20⅞ IN. (81 × 53 CM).

This icon depicts Gregory, sainted Bishop of Neocaesarea (ca. 213–270/275). A missionary and theologian, Gregory was a pupil of Origen of Alexandria, one of the foremost Fathers of the Church, and himself among those who formulated the doctrine of the Trinity. The Hermitage work is a masterpiece of Byzantine icon-painting. The artist produced an individualized, almost portrait image. Proper appreciation of the work is somewhat marred by the loss of the precious metal mount that originally covered the icon.

opposite: *St. Nicholas, with Scenes from His Life (Nicholas of Zaraisk).* NOVGOROD. FIRST HALF OF THE 16TH CENTURY. EGG TEMPERA ON GESSOED PANEL WITH GILDING. 65 × 45¼ IN. (165 × 115 CM).

One traditional type of Russian icon depicted a saint in the center surrounded by scenes of his life. Here, these include the birth of St. Nicholas, his consecration as deacon and bishop, and his miracles. The saint is shown in his bishop's robes, his right hand raised in blessing, his left holding the Gospel. Legend has it that the Byzantine prototype for this version was brought to the town of Zaraisk in the 13th century.

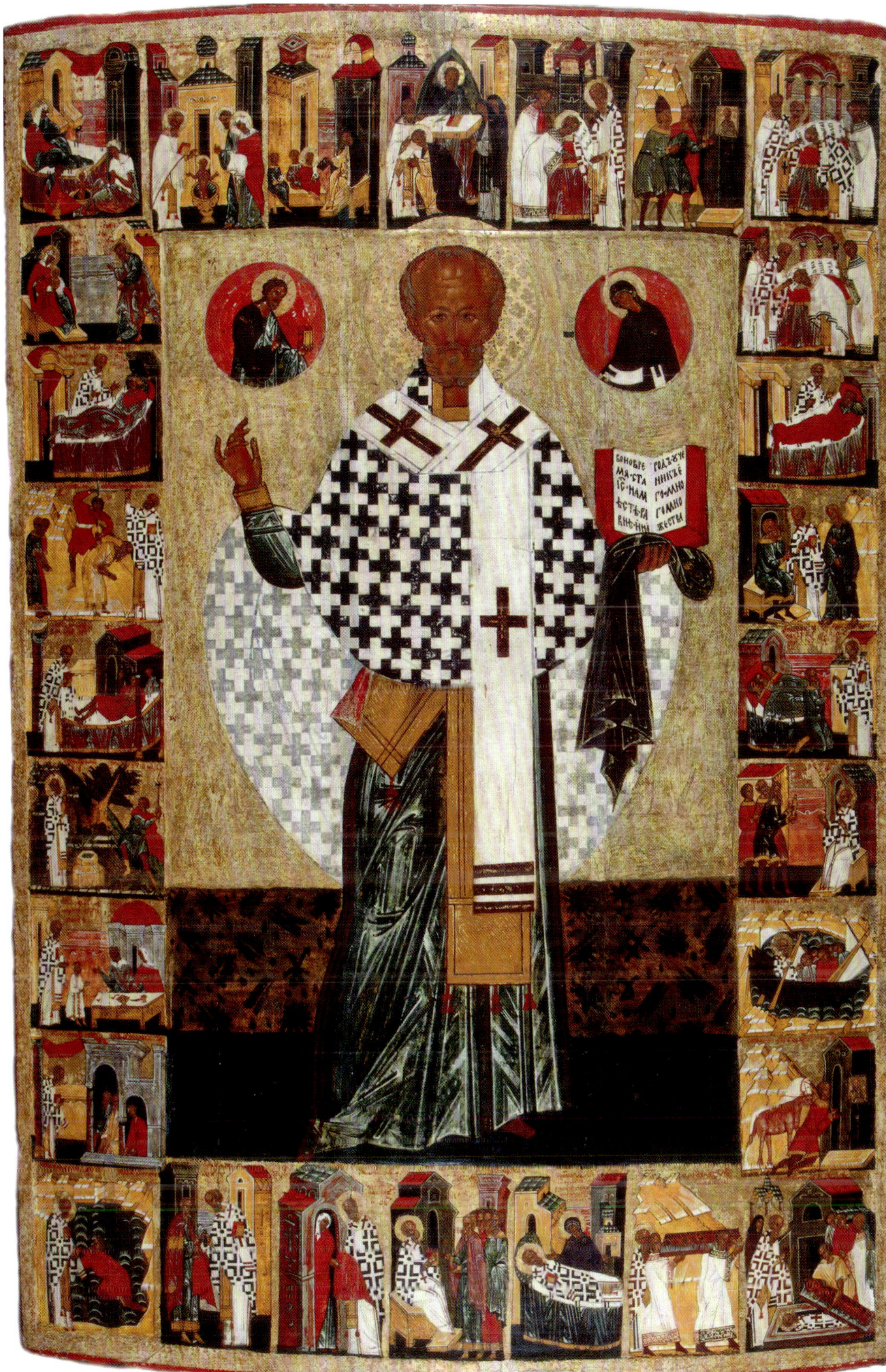

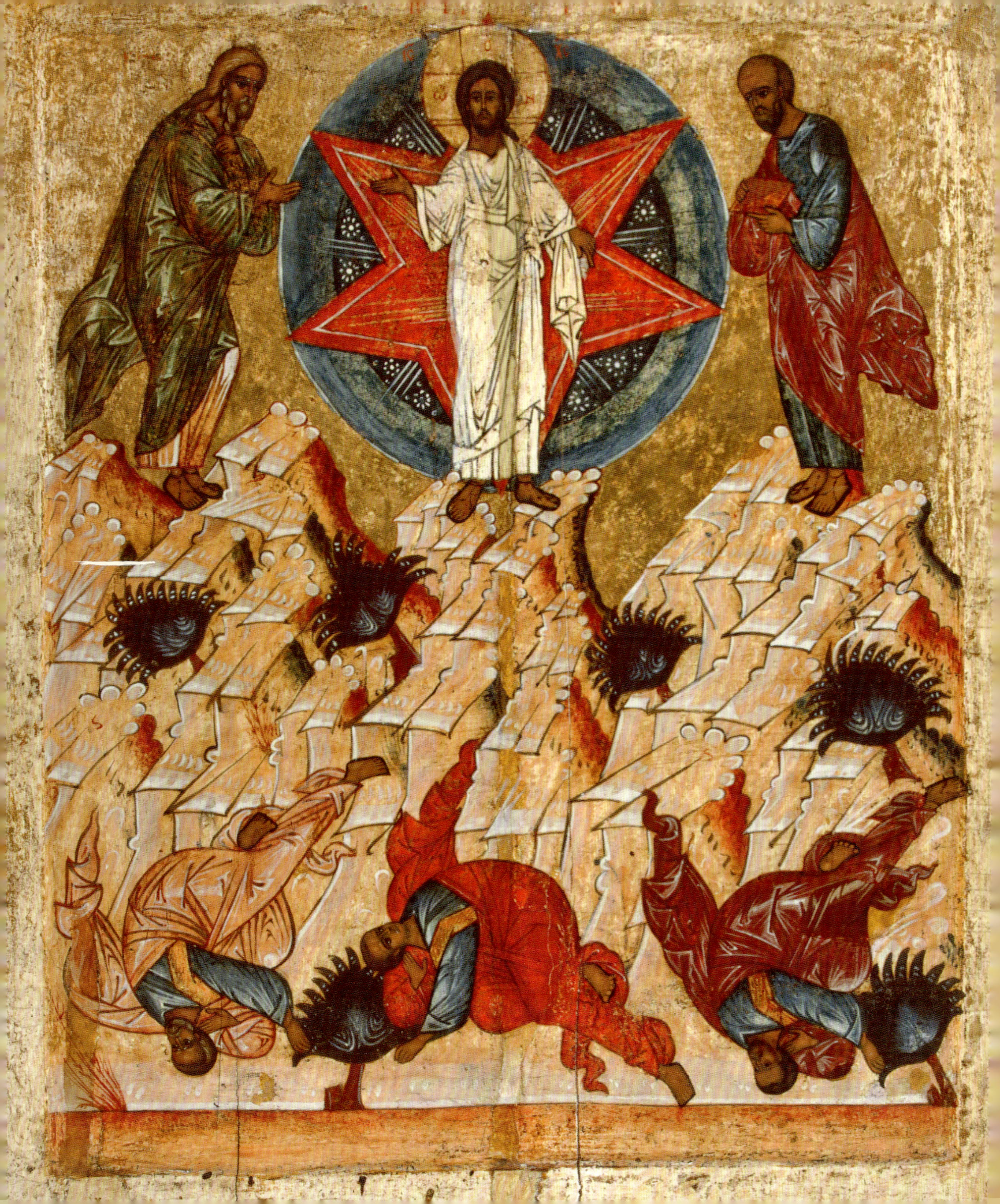

opposite: *The Transfiguration.* NOVGOROD. 16TH CENTURY. EGG TEMPERA ON GESSOED PANEL WITH GILDING. 30¾ × 24 IN. (78 × 61 CM).

The Gospel account of Christ in Glory on the summit of Mount Tabor is presented here in brief and with certain peculiarities. Christ's right hand, for example, is open and not closed in a gesture of blessing. The whiteness of his clothing is stressed by the dark background in the form of a red six-pointed star with gold rays, inscribed in a circle instead of the traditional almond-shaped *mandorla*.

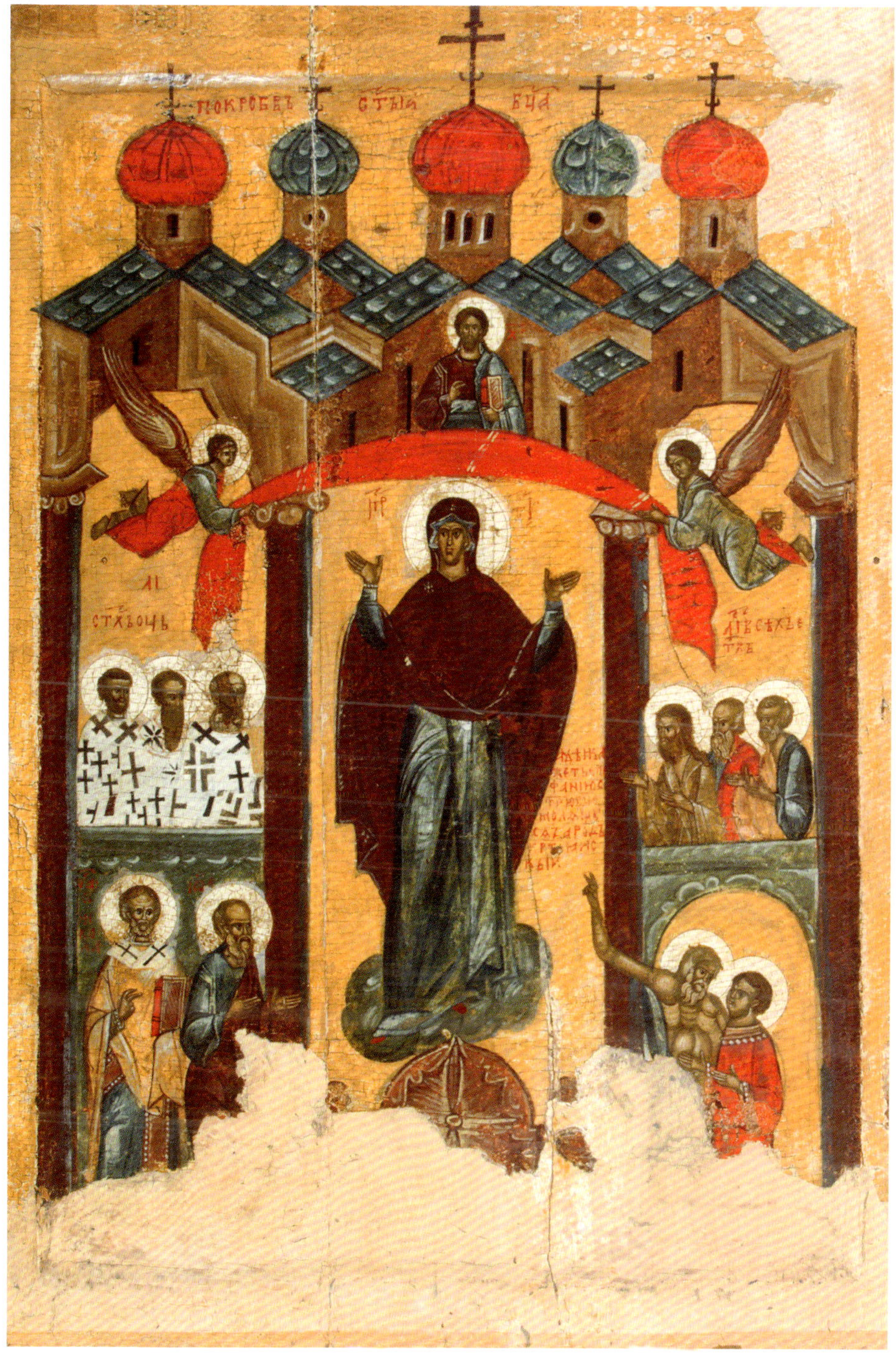

above. *The Intercession of the Virgin.* 15TH CENTURY. EGG TEMPERA ON GESSOED PANEL. 29⅛ × 20 × 1 IN. (74 × 51 × 2.5 CM).

The intercession of the Virgin on behalf of humankind is symbolized by a veil that she spread over worshippers in a vision, witnessed by the holy fool Andrew, that took place in a Constantinople church in 910, when Byzantium was under threat from the Saracens. Andrew and his young companion Epiphanius are among the saints depicted in the icon. The Feast of the Intercession, established by the Eastern Church in memory of this event, is particularly celebrated in Russia.

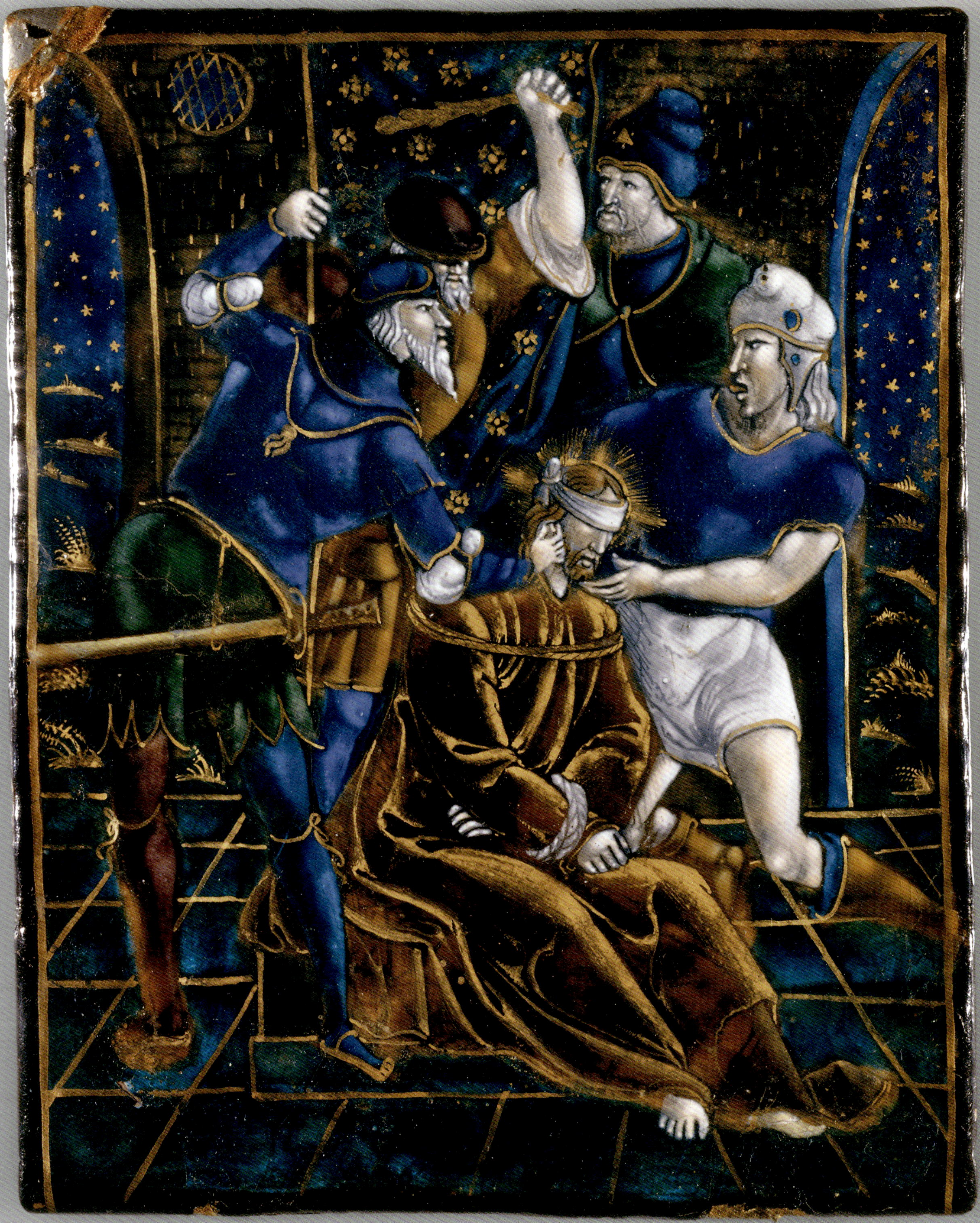

Medieval European Decorative Arts

CIRCLE OF COLIN NOUALIER. *The Mocking of Christ.* LIMOGES. SECOND QUARTER OF THE 16TH CENTURY. COPPER, ENAMEL, POLYCHROME PAINTING, AND CLEAR COUNTER-ENAMELLING. 8⅛ × 6⅜ IN. (20.6 × 16.3 CM).

Painted enamel plaques assembled into miniature altarpieces were popular in the 16th century. The series of twelve plaques depicting the Passion to which this example belongs was based on engravings by Lucas van Leyden. Graphic prototypes were typical for the "new school" of Limoges enamel that emerged in the 1530s.

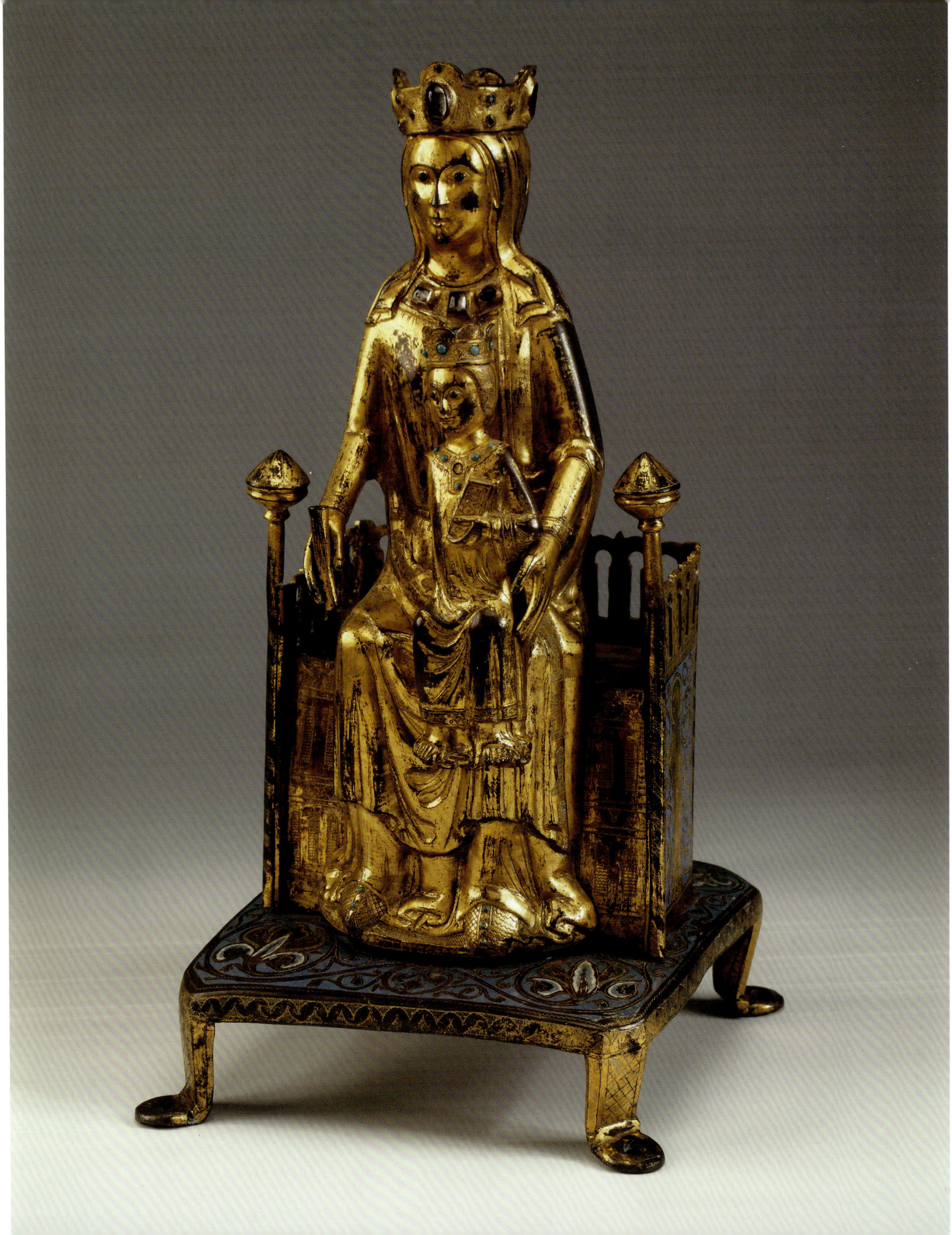

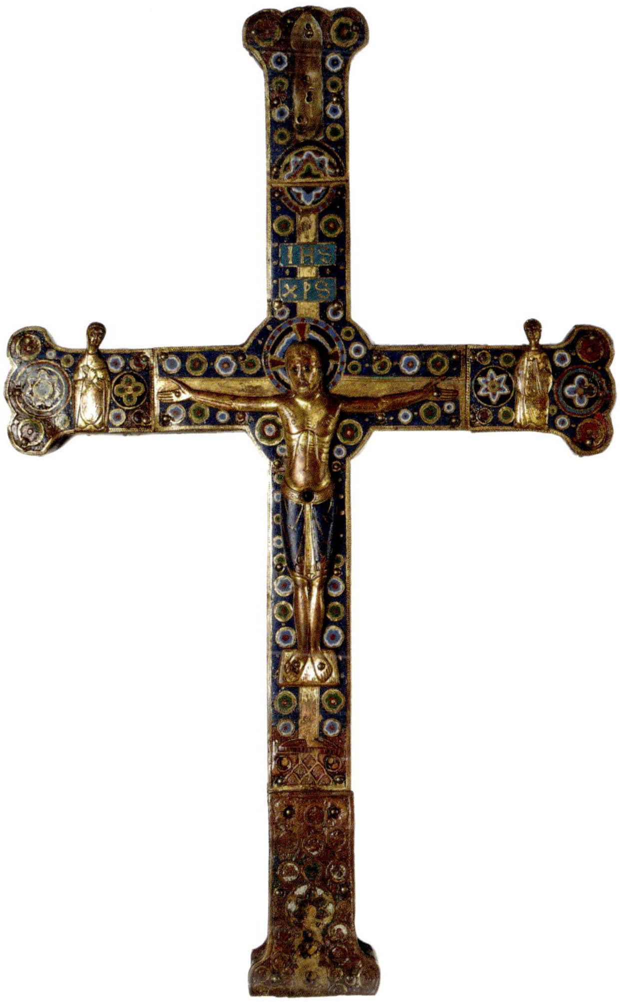

opposite: *Pyx Depicting the Virgin and Child.* LIMOGES. MID-13TH CENTURY. OPAQUE ENAMEL ON COPPER (CHAMPLEVÉ TECHNIQUE) WITH GLASS. 15½ IN. (39 CM) HIGH.

This reliquary takes the form of the Virgin Mary and the Christ Child seated on a cubic throne; the pierced balustrade is identical to the characteristic decoration on the crests of Limoges caskets. The throne's side walls show an Annunciation scene, while at the back is a little door that, researchers suggest, indicates this sculptural group was used to store the consecrated Host.

above: *Processional Cross.* LIMOGES. FIRST QUARTER OF THE 13TH CENTURY. WOOD, COPPER, BRASS, OPAQUE ENAMEL (CHAMPLEVÉ TECHNIQUE), GLASS, GILDING. 23 × 14½ IN. (58.7 × 37 CM).

On feast days associated with the Holy Cross, crosses such as this were carried on poles in procession or placed on a stand on the altar. Some contained particles of the "True Cross," discovered in Jerusalem around 320. This example, made from wood covered with brass sheets, is decorated with enamel insets and applied figures of Christ, Mary, and St. John. The back features Christ in a *mandorla*, with the symbols of the Evangelists at the ends of the arms.

below: *Reliquary of St. Elizabeth of Hungary.* FRANCE. MID-13TH CENTURY. WOOD, SILVER, PRECIOUS AND SEMIPRECIOUS STONES, GLASS. 22⅞ IN. (58 CM) HIGH.

This reliquary, which frames a figure of Saint Elizabeth, was made by Parisian jewelers. Elizabeth's name is given in an inscription on the base. The daughter of a Hungarian king, Elizabeth was married at an early age to a duke of Thuringia, who died, soon after, on his way to the Crusades. The widowed duchess devoted herself to the sick and impoverished, becoming a symbol of Christian charity. She was canonized within five years of her death.

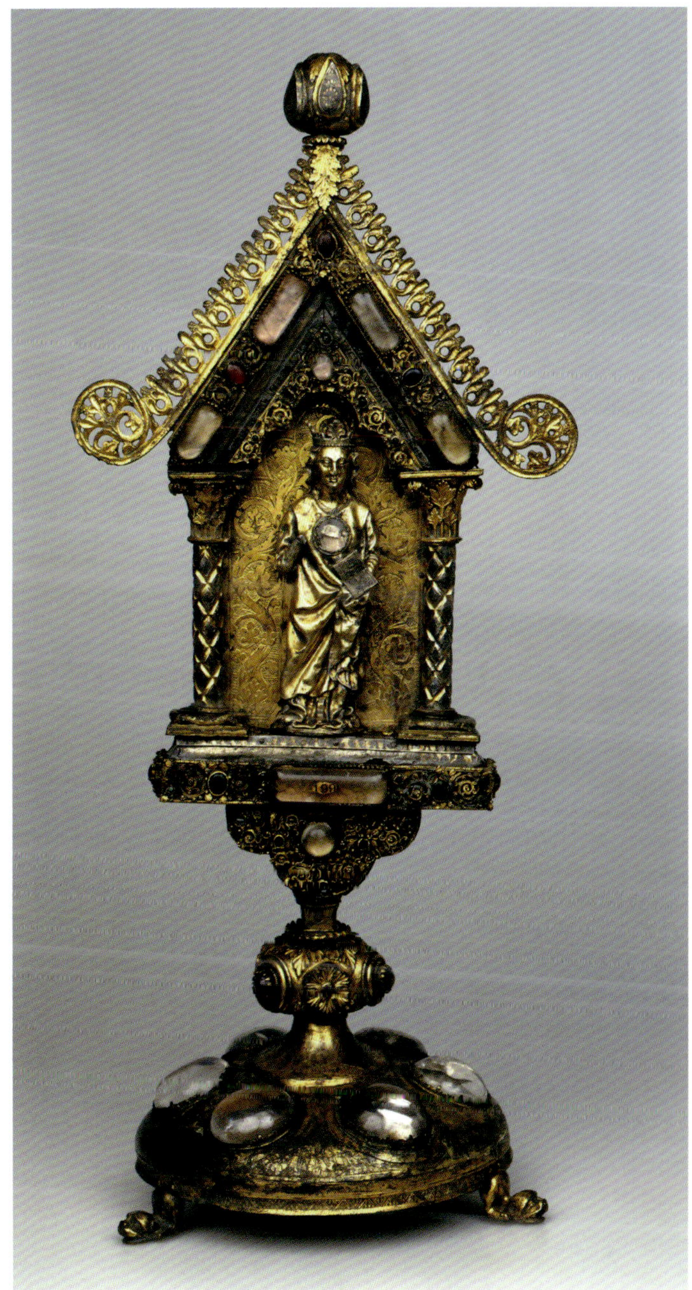

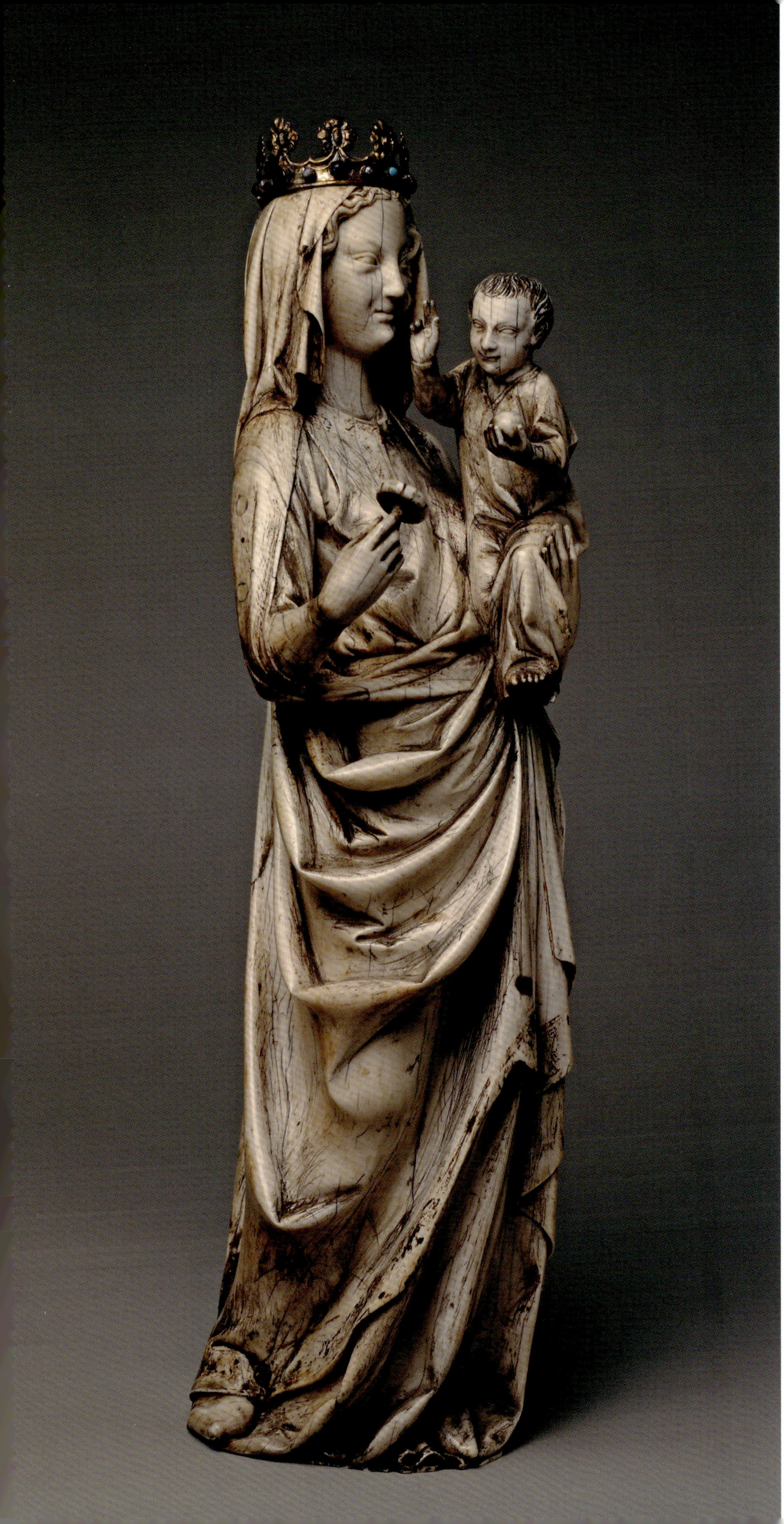

The Virgin and Child. FRANCE. FIRST HALF OF THE 14TH CENTURY. IVORY WITH TRACES OF PAINT, METAL, PRECIOUS STONES, FILIGREE WORK. 17¾ IN. (45 CM) HIGH.

Figures such as this one, reproducing a type that had formed in large-scale Gothic statuary, were intended for the domestic chapels of wealthy families. In them Mary has lost the static, stern expressiveness of Romanesque works and acquired features of a courtly lady. The natural curve of her figure is emphasized by the folds of the cloak, which the craftsman delineated with great skill.

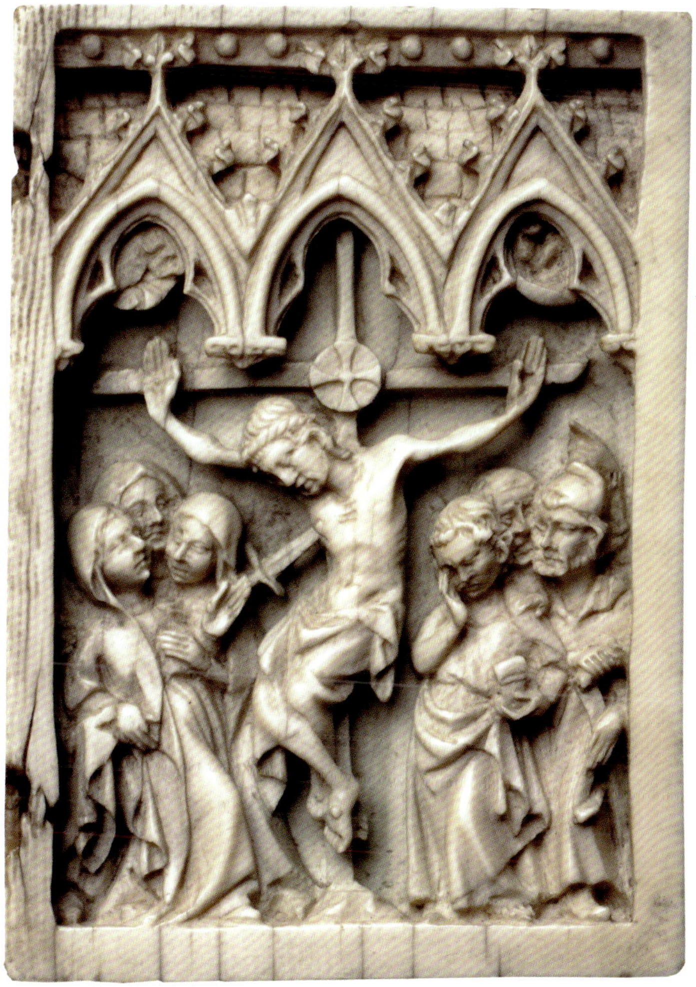

left: *Panel of a Diptych with a Depiction of the Crucifixion.* GERMANY. LATE 14TH CENTURY. CARVED IVORY, WITH TRACES OF GREEN PAINT. 6 × 3⅜ IN. (15 × 8.5 CM).

Such diptychs, reproducing in miniature the large altar compositions that adorned medieval cathedrals, served as an aid to prayer in domestic chapels or on journeys. When depicting Gospel events, irrespective of where they occurred, Gothic ivory-carvers always placed them in an architectural setting. Besides providing compositional completeness and decorative effect, this approach enabled artisans to give their miniature devotional pieces greater similarity to church interiors.

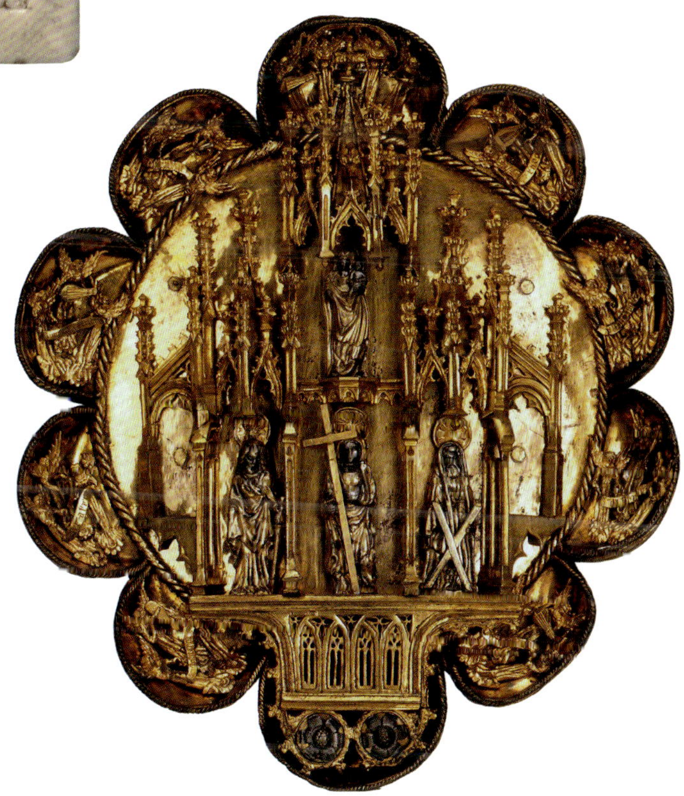

right: *Agraffe with a Depiction of the Virgin and Saints.* 15TH CENTURY. LOWER SAXONY. COPPER AND SILVER WITH GILDING. 8½ IN. (21.5 CM) HIGH.

This massive clasp for a bishop's vestments was acquired by Alexander Bazilevsky in 1874 and came into the Hermitage as part of his collection. It bears relief images of the Virgin and Saints Helen, Andrew, and James with little figures of angels making music. A German inscription reads: "I, Derick the jeweler, undertook to make the clasp entirely from copper apart from the four silver depictions." Latin inscriptions on banderoles give the names of the nine orders of angels.

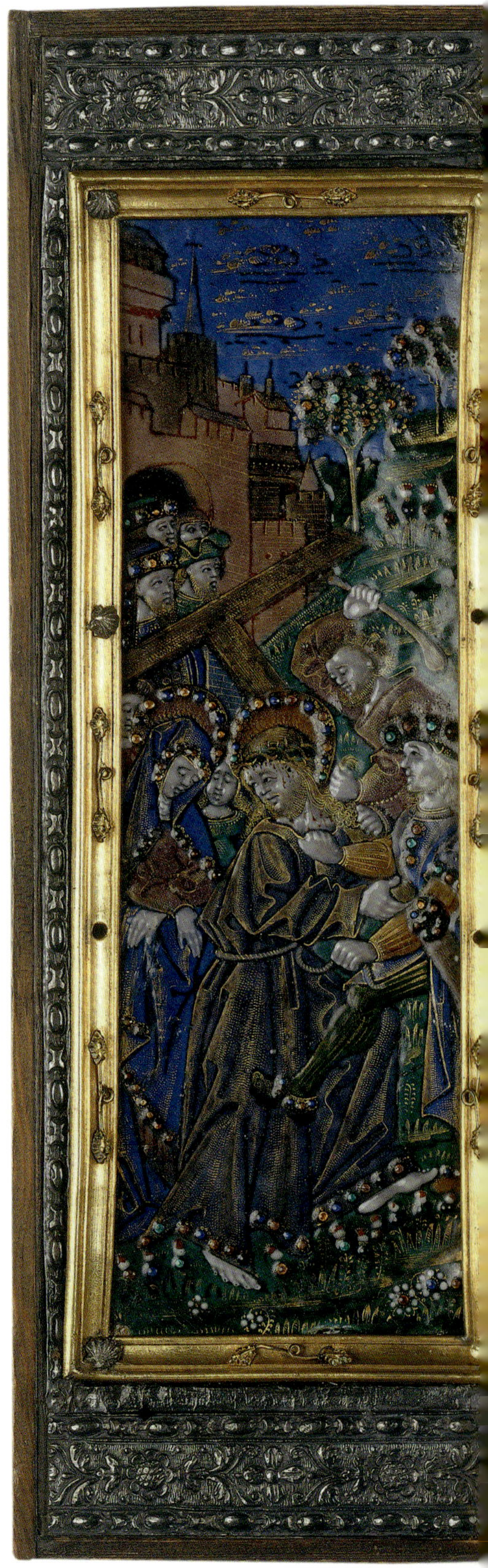

WORKSHOP OF THE MASTER OF THE ORLEANS.
Triptych: Carrying the Cross; Crucifixion; Lamentation.
FRANCE. LATE 15TH–EARLY 16TH CENTURY. COPPER, ENAMEL, WOOD, SILVER MOUNTS, WITH POLYCHROME PAINTING AND GILDING. 11⅞ × 15 IN. (30 ×38 CM).

The abundant use of enamel cabochons—drop-shaped convex projections with foil beneath—was characteristic of "old school" Limoges enamelers, including this workshop. Another distinctive feature is the virtuoso way the clothing folds have been painted in gold. The central Crucifixion scene features angels collecting blood flowing from Christ's hands. The soul of Dismas, the penitent thief to Christ's right, is shown as an infant being carried away by an angel, while the unrepentant Gestas's soul is taken by a devil.

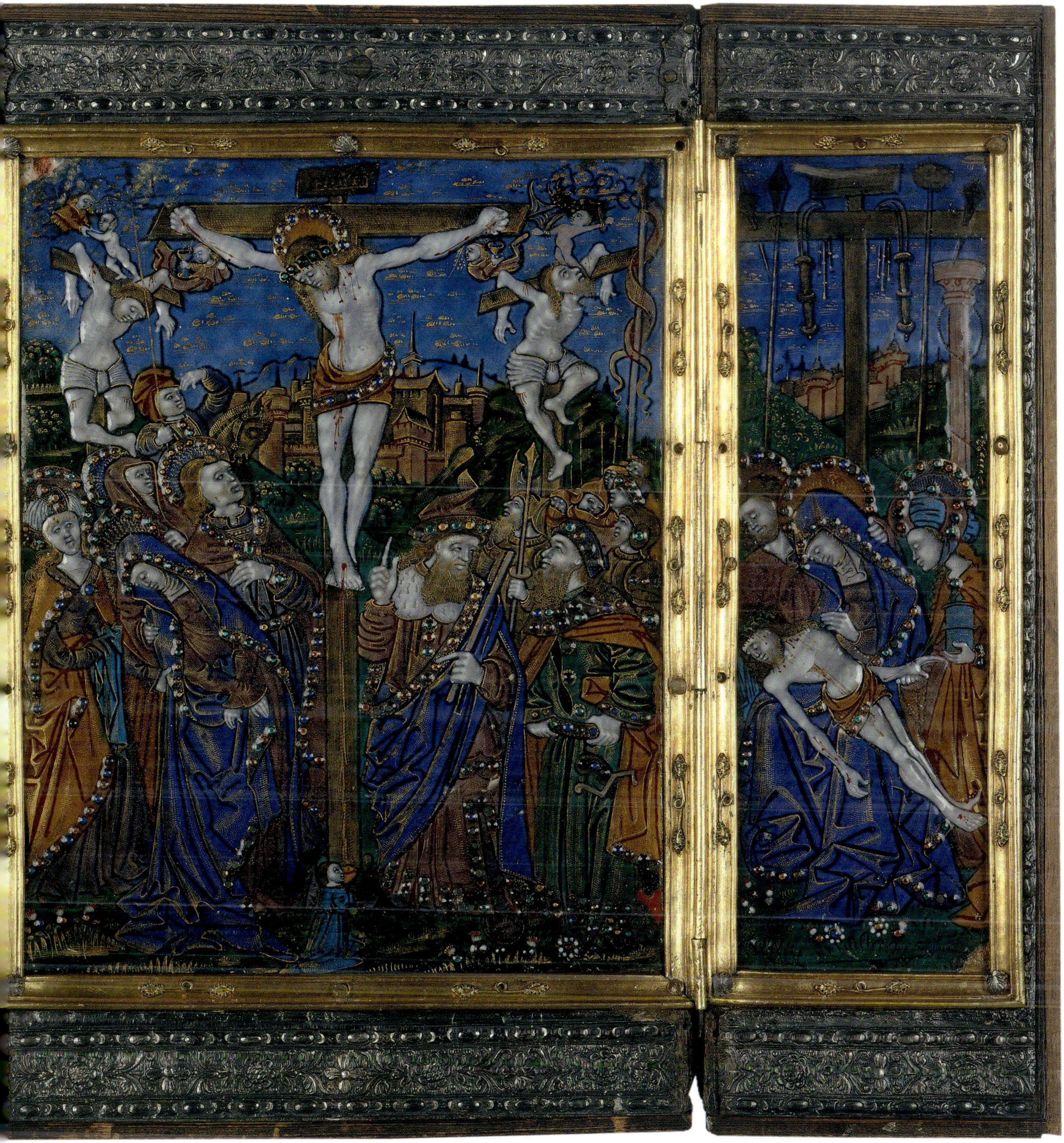

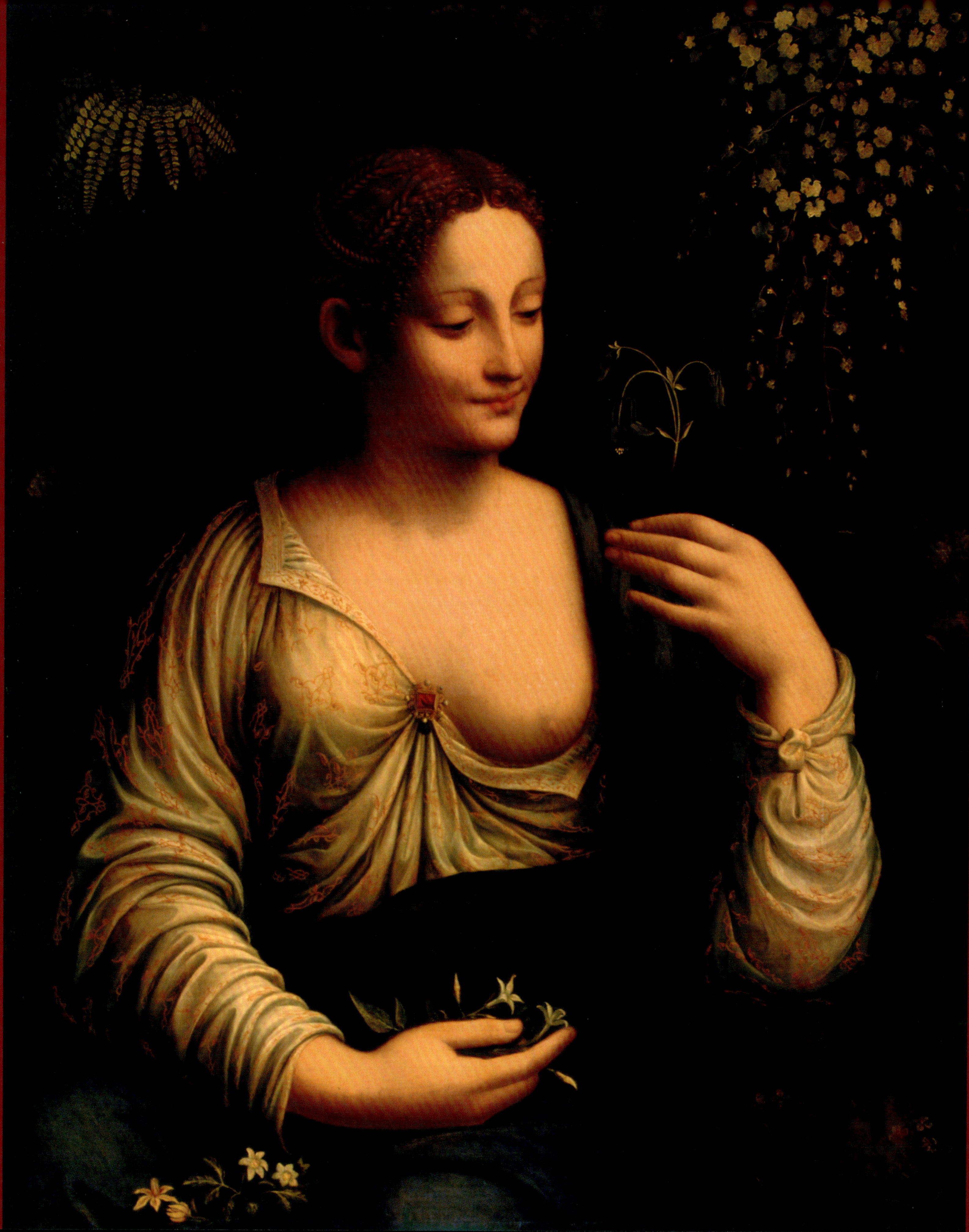

Western European Painting, 13th–Early 18th Century

FRANCESCO MELZI. *Flora.* BETWEEN 1510 AND 1515. OIL ON CANVAS
30 × 24⅞ IN. (76 × 63 CM).

Melzi, Leonardo da Vinci's favorite pupil, followed the master to France and remained with him to the end of his life. He used a number of his teacher's devices—soft sfumato, restrained colors, and the unknown sitter's elegant pose and mysterious half-smile—which is why this painting was long attributed to Leonardo. Some scholars have believed it to be a portrait of a noble lady at the court of François I; others suggest it is Mona Lisa.

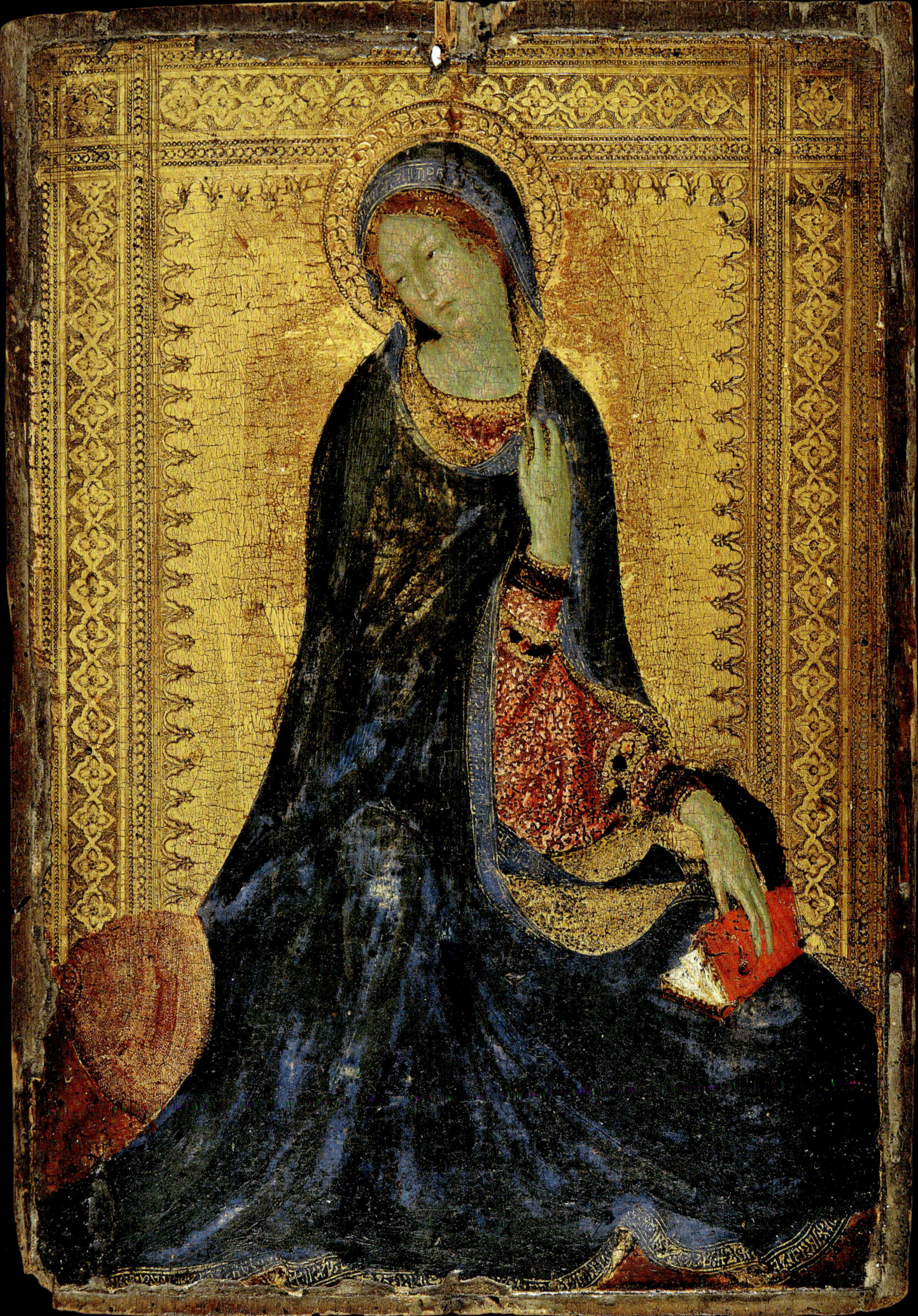

opposite: SIMONE MARTINI.
The Virgin from an Annunciation.
1339–42. TEMPERA ON PANEL.
12 × 8½ IN. (30.5 × 21.5 CM).

Simone Martini, a pupil of Duccio, brought fame to his native Siena. His refined, exquisite style impressed aristocratic customers. Petrarch called him "the master of our time," and according to Vasari, the epitaph above the artist's tomb read: "To the most celebrated of all painters." Here, Martini's archangel is holding not a lily, a symbol of purity traditional for this subject, but an olive branch. The choice may have stemmed from the lily's association with Siena's rival city, Florence.

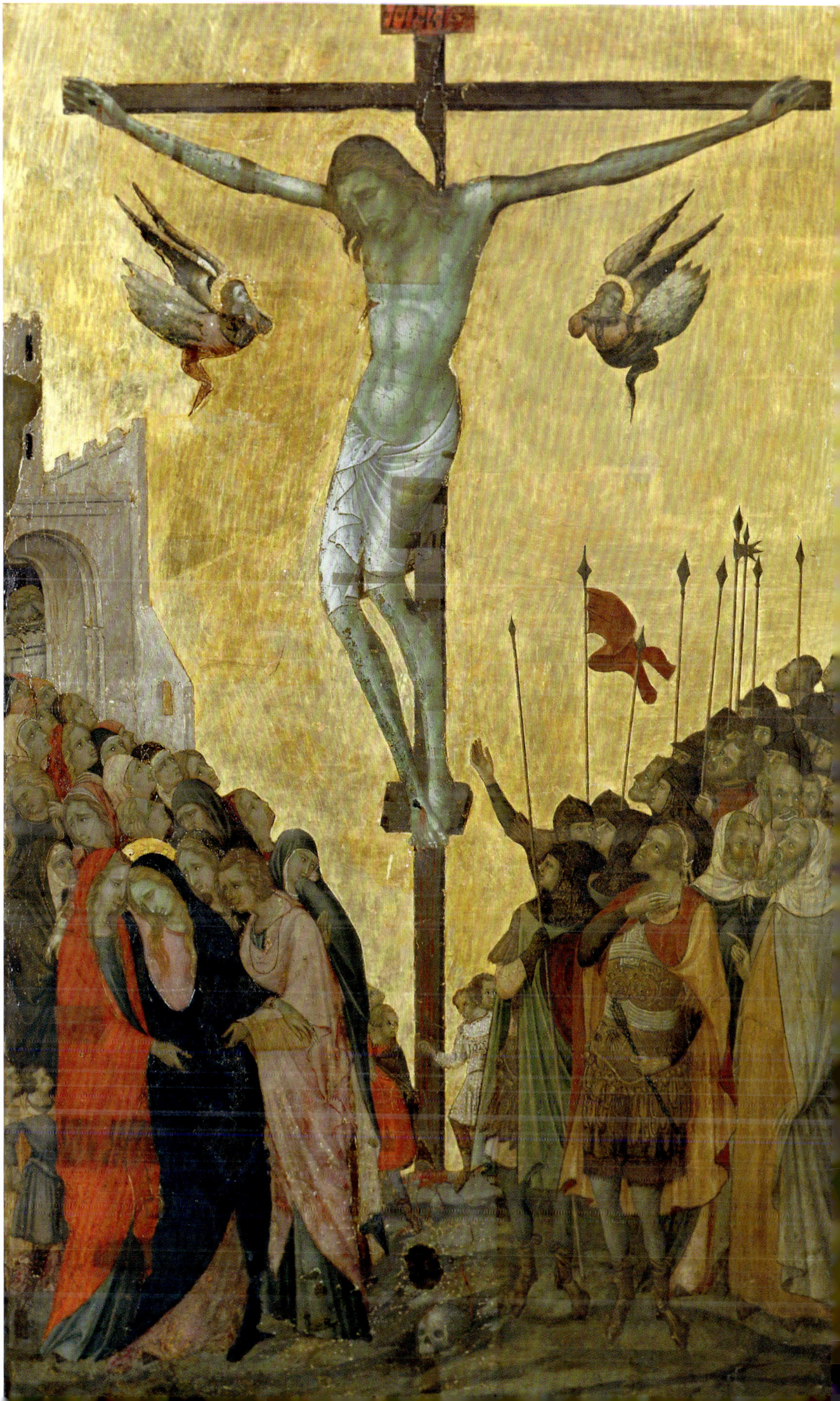

right: UGOLINO LORENZETTI. *Calvary.*
CA. 1350. TEMPERA ON PANEL.
36 × 21⅞ IN. (91.5 × 55.5 CM).

This altarpiece is probably among the early works of a Sienese artist active between 1320 and 1360. It displays features that derive from the Byzantine artistic tradition: the depiction of figures on different scales, the placement of the groups, and architecture shown from several viewpoints simultaneously. Ugolino Lorenzetti's later paintings are closer to Gothic art, demonstrating the artist's familiarity with the work of Simone Martini and Pietro Lorenzetti.

ANTONIO DI FIRENZE. *Madonna and Child with a Sainted Bishop, John the Baptist, and Angels.* FIRST HALF OF THE 15TH CENTURY. TEMPERA ON PANEL. 59½ × 33½ IN. (151 × 85 CM).

This double-sided work would have been carried in religious processions. Because he is shown holding a tower, the saint on the left may be Liberius of Ravenna or Zenobius of Florence. The Crucifixion scene on the reverse repeats the composition by Fra Angelico in the Montecarlo monastery church. The depiction at the foot of the Cross—of monks holding scourges and wearing hoods with only slits for the eyes—suggests that this work was commissioned by the Capuchin order.

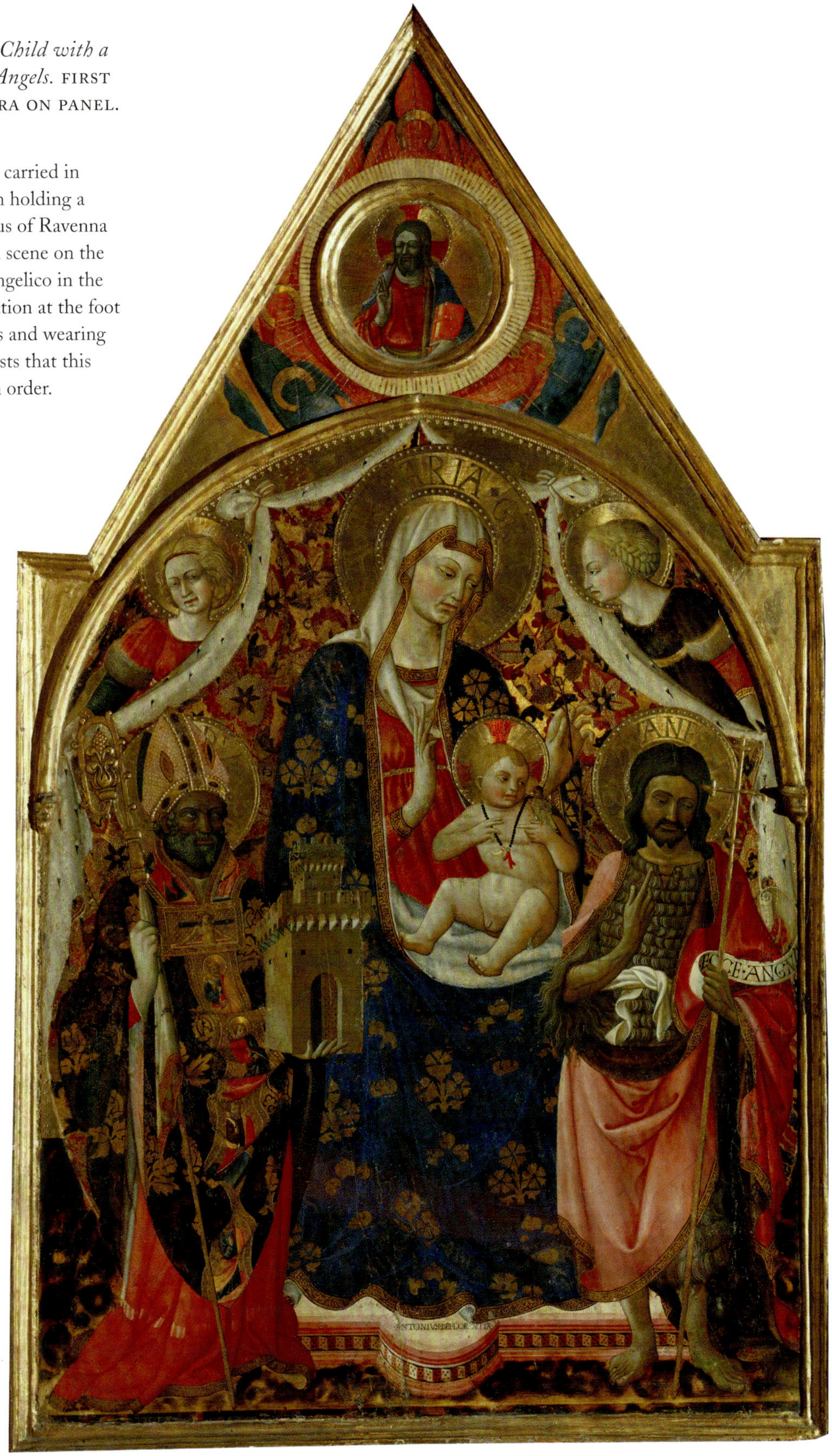

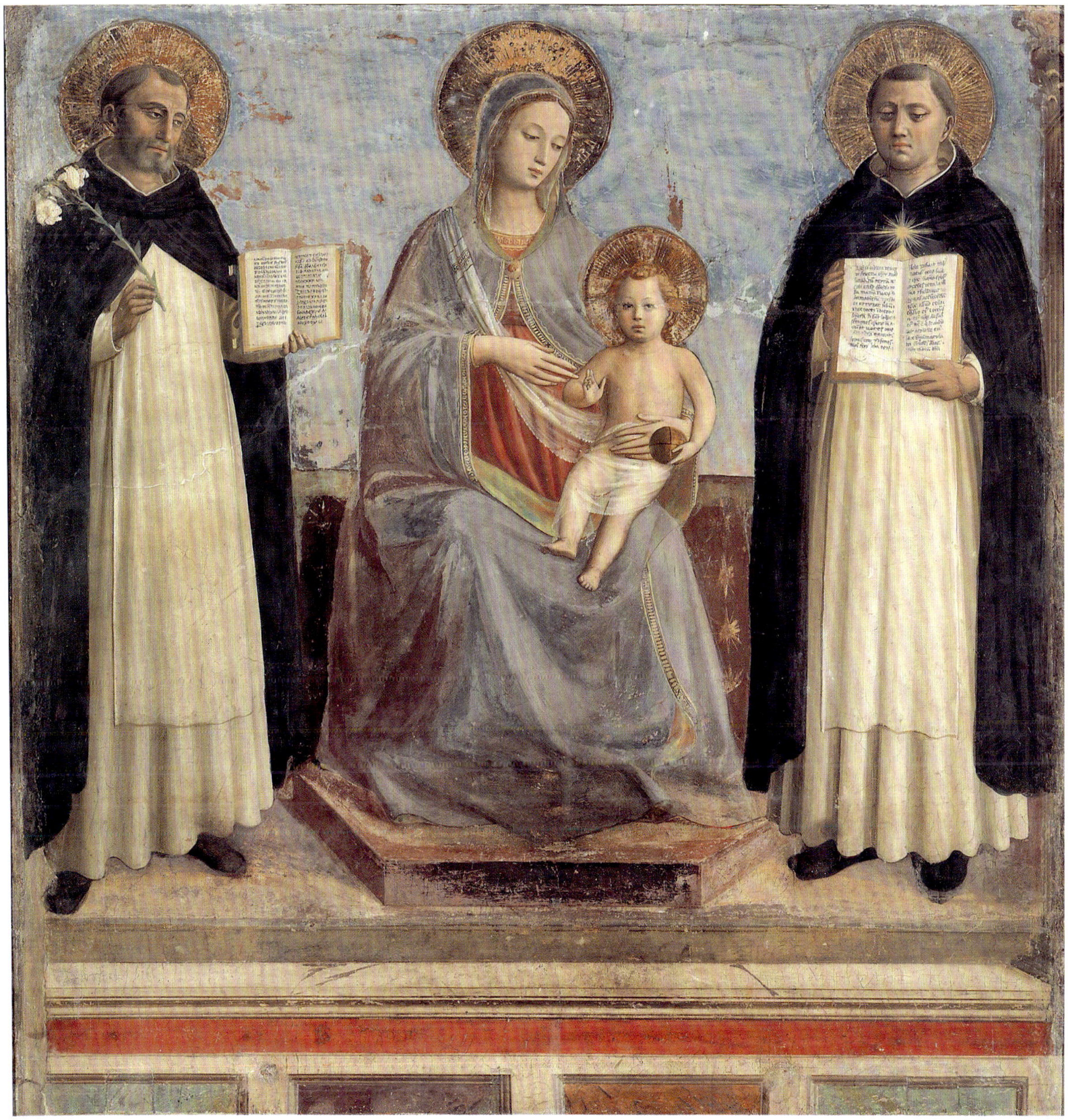

FRA ANGELICO (GUIDO DI PIETRO). *The Virgin and the Child with Saints Dominic and Thomas Aquinas.* BETWEEN 1424 AND 1430. FRESCO. 77 1/8 × 73 5/8 IN. (196 × 187 CM).

This work is part of a fresco cycle that Angelico created in the San Domenico monastery in Fiesole, where he was prior. The artist's devotion to his religious calling did not prevent him from becoming an innovator in painting. Without pursuing the dynamic action and spatial depth sought by most of his contemporaries, he achieves a sculpture-like monumentality that—like the airy translucence of his paints, especially those in the murals—links him with Piero della Francesca.

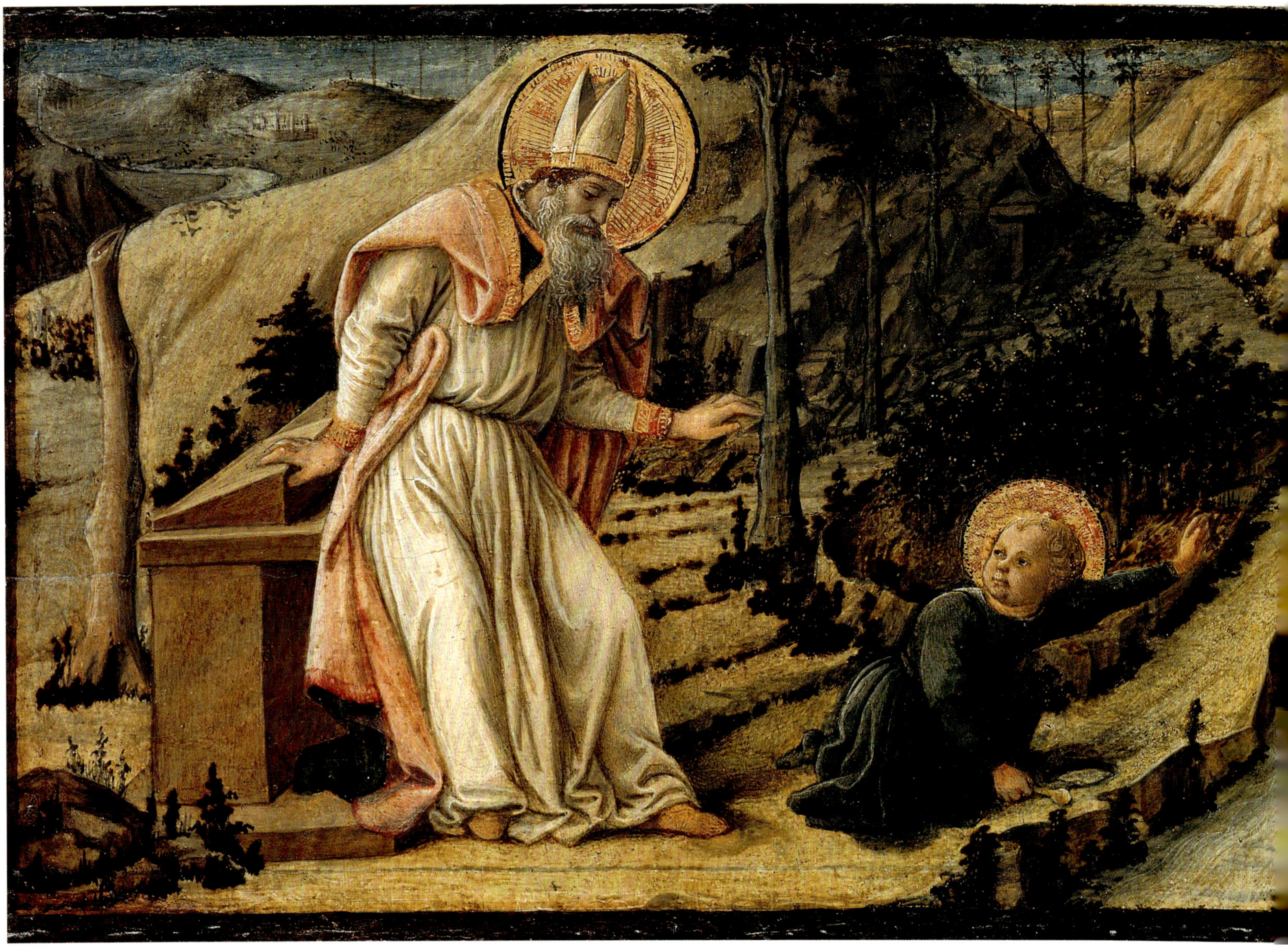

FRA FILIPPO LIPPI. *The Vision of St. Augustine.* LATE 1450S–EARLY 1460S. TEMPERA AND OIL ON PANEL. 11 × 20¼ IN. (28 × 51.5 CM).

The subject here is from the life of St. Augustine of Hippo (354–430). According to legend, while pondering the mystery of the Trinity, the bishop had a vision of a child using a spoon to transfer water from the sea into a puddle. When Augustine questioned him, the child explained that his pursuit was no less futile than the bishop's attempts to understand the Trinity. Here, the sea is represented by a stream, and the Trinity by a disk containing three profiles.

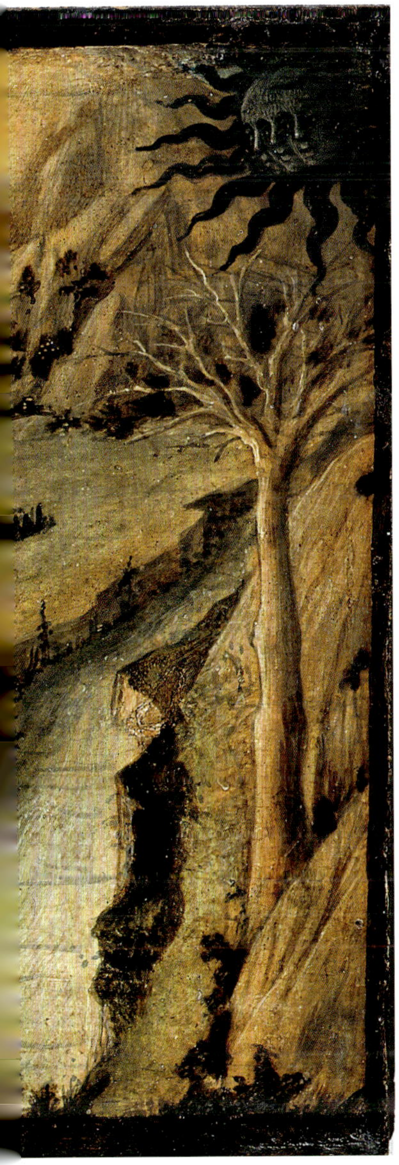

FILIPPINO LIPPI. *Adoration of the Christ Child.* MID-1480S.
OIL ON COPPER. 20⅞ IN. (53 CM) DIAMETER.

Filippino Lippi, the son of the artist Fra Filippo Lippi, was a pupil of the famous Sandro Botticelli. Like his teacher, Filippino Lippi gave preference to elongated proportions and exquisite forms. Against the background of a Tuscan landscape, Mary and the angels worship the newborn Christ. This Adoration is one of the first paintings in Italian art in which the landscape is in keeping with the mood and appearance of the personages.

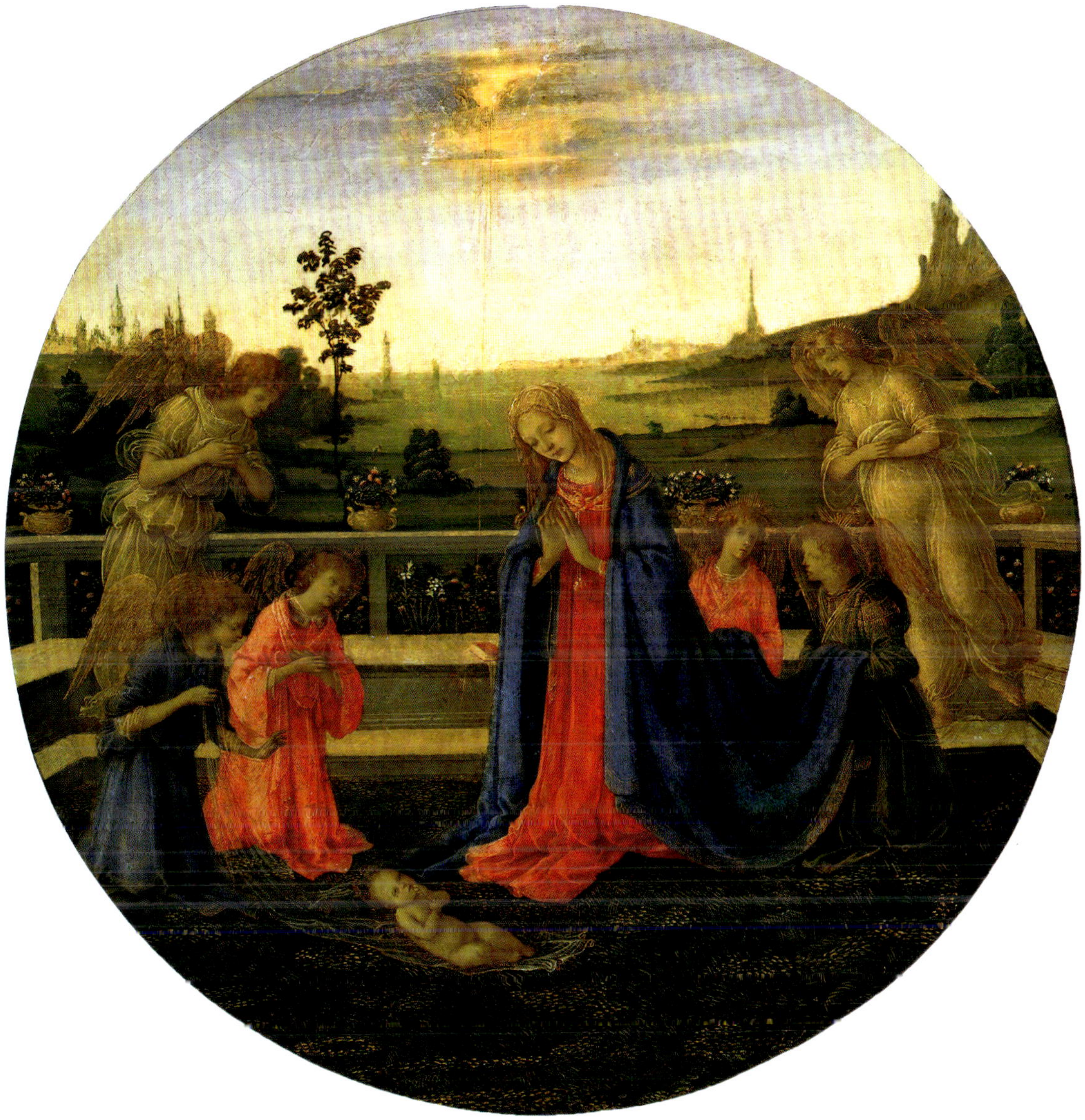

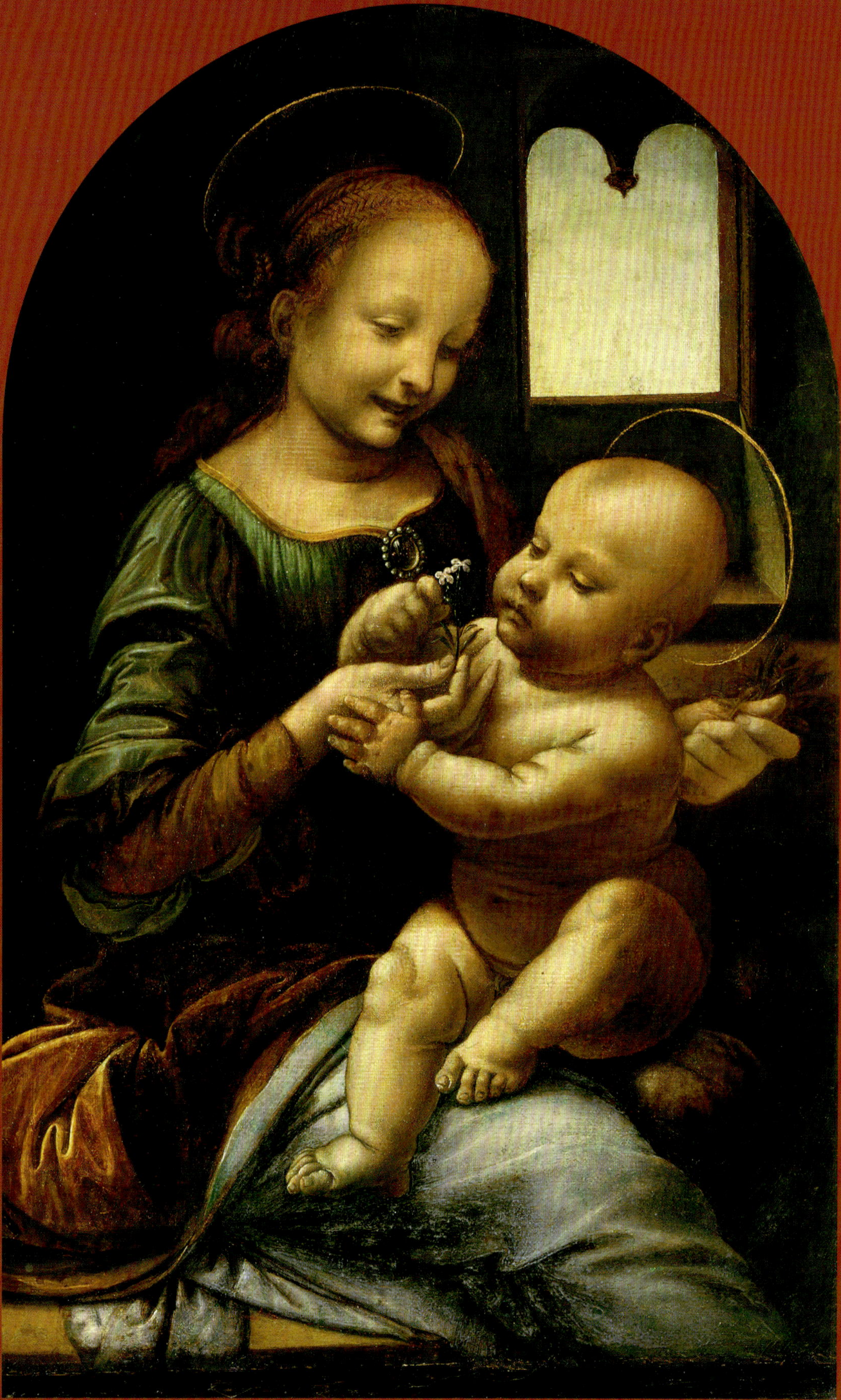

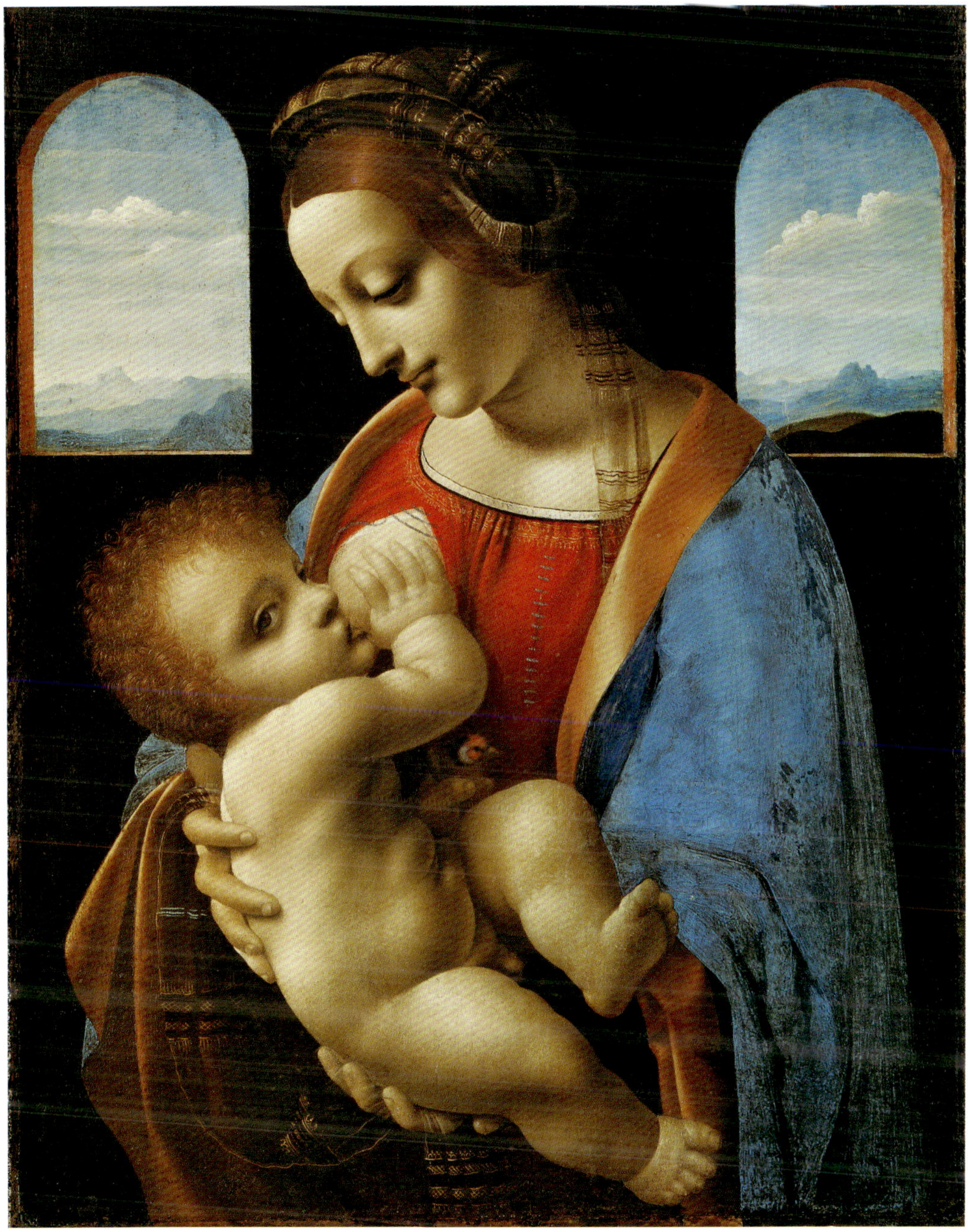

left: LEONARDO DA VINCI. *Madonna with the Child (Litta Madonna).* 1490–91. TEMPERA ON CANVAS (TRANSFERRED FROM PANEL). 16½ × 13 IN. (42 × 33 CM).

Leonardo is among those geniuses for whom perfection does not exclude simplicity. In tempera, already superseded by oils, which permitted finer chiaroscuro modeling, he presents the traditional image of the Virgin of Humility through the contrast of tender flesh tones, the scarlet of her blouse, and the blue of her cape, which is echoed in the azure landscape beyond. Enclosed by masterly drawing in a sculptural form, these resonant colors form an absolute balance of earthly and heavenly.

opposite: LEONARDO DA VINCI. *Madonna with a Flower (Benois Madonna).* 1478–80. OIL ON CANVAS (TRANSFERRED FROM PANEL). 19½ × 12½ IN. (49.5 × 31.5 CM).

According to one theory, this painting is a political allegory that refers to the events of the Pazzi conspiracy of 1478, a plot in which Giuliano dei' Medici was killed and that nearly cost the life of his brother Lorenzo. The Christ Child's gaze is fixed not on the flower in the Virgin's hand but rather on the rounded patches of light reflected in the brooch on her breast, possibly an allusion to the *palle*, or balls, in the arms of the Medici family.

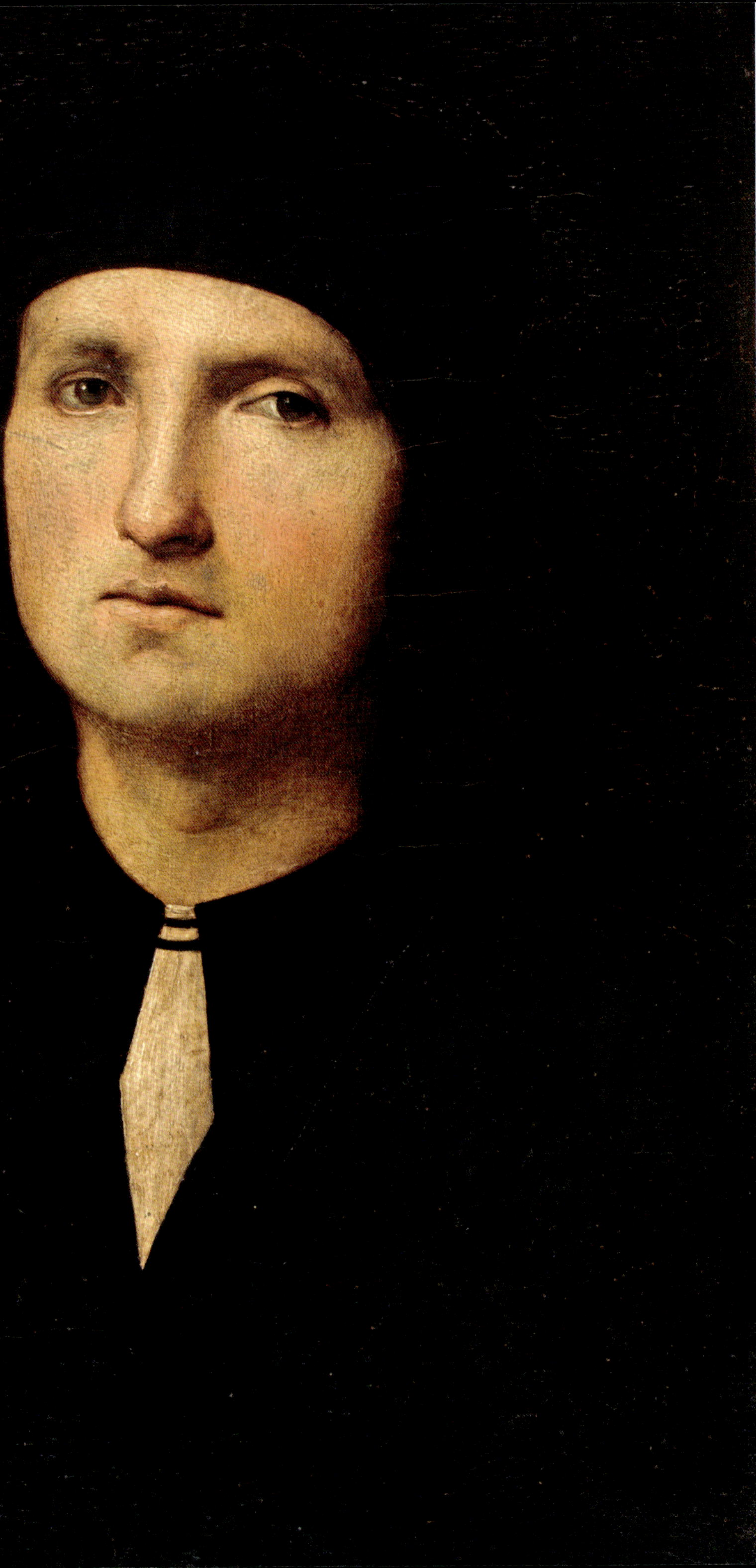

opposite: PIETRO PERUGINO (PIETRO VANNUCCI). *Portrait of a Young Man.* CA. 1500. OIL ON CANVAS (TRANSFERRED FROM PANEL). 17¾ × 10 IN. (45 × 25.5 CM).

The "dove-like gaze"—as contemporaries described the dreamily pious visual appeal to heaven that typifies Perugino's personages—is also seen in this secular painting. Identification of the model is complicated by the artist's evident indifference to the depiction of individual characteristics and achievements. But it is the very impersonality that is remarkable in the portraits of an artist who was more concerned with the compositional arrangement of figures and spatial rhythm.

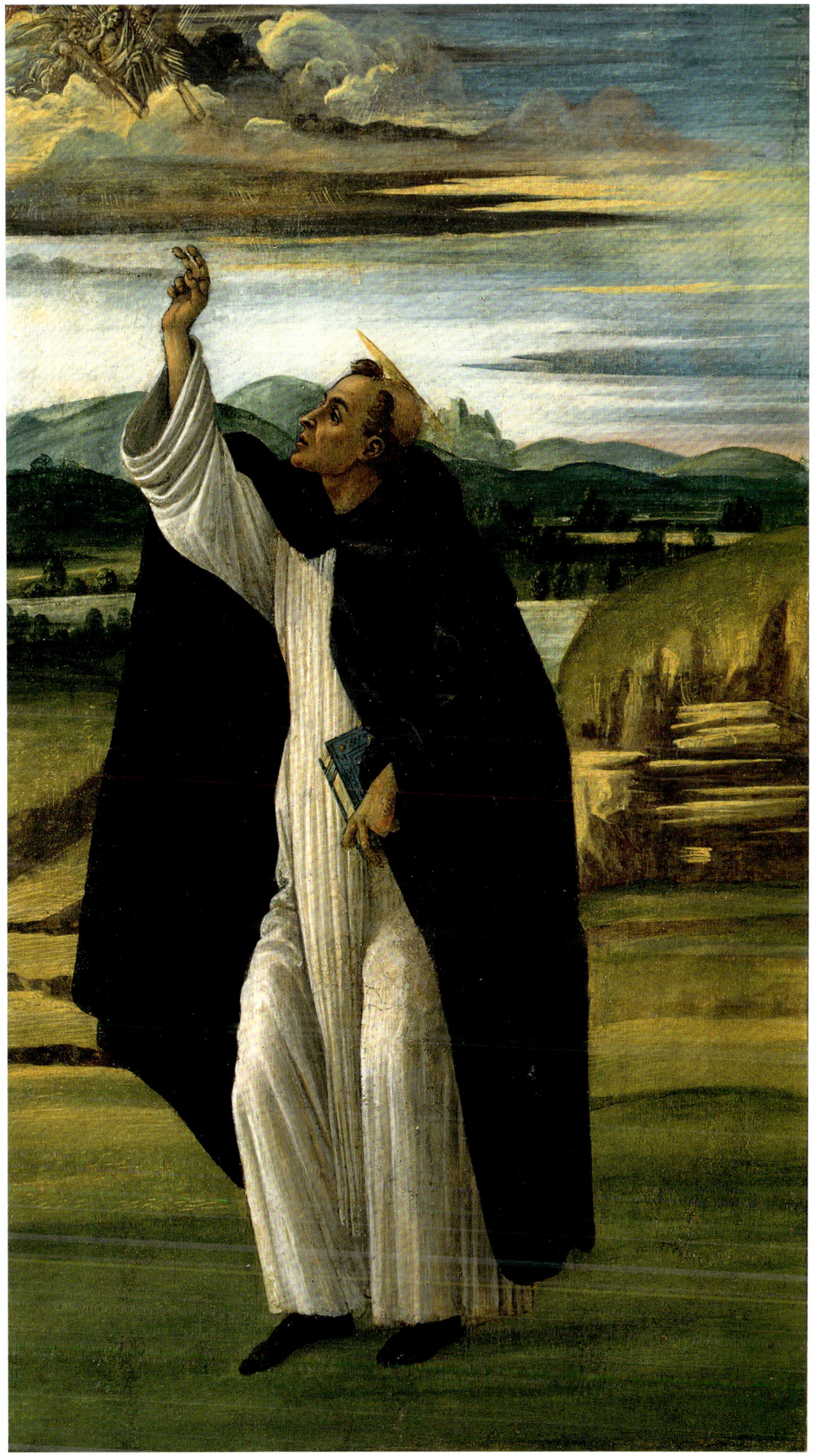

right: SANDRO BOTTICELLI (ALESSANDRO DI MARIANO DEI FILIPEPI). *St. Dominic.* 1490S. TEMPERA AND OIL ON CANVAS (TRANSFERRED FROM PANEL). 17½ × 10¼ IN. (44.5 × 26 CM).

A pupil of Fra Filippo Lippi, Botticelli was among the most gifted painters working at the court of Lorenzo the Magnificent. Here, the founder of the Dominican order of monks is presented in an iconographic manner that is rarely seen: above the saint, whose hand is raised in a gesture of blessing, is a half-figure of Christ surrounded by angels heralding the Last Judgment.

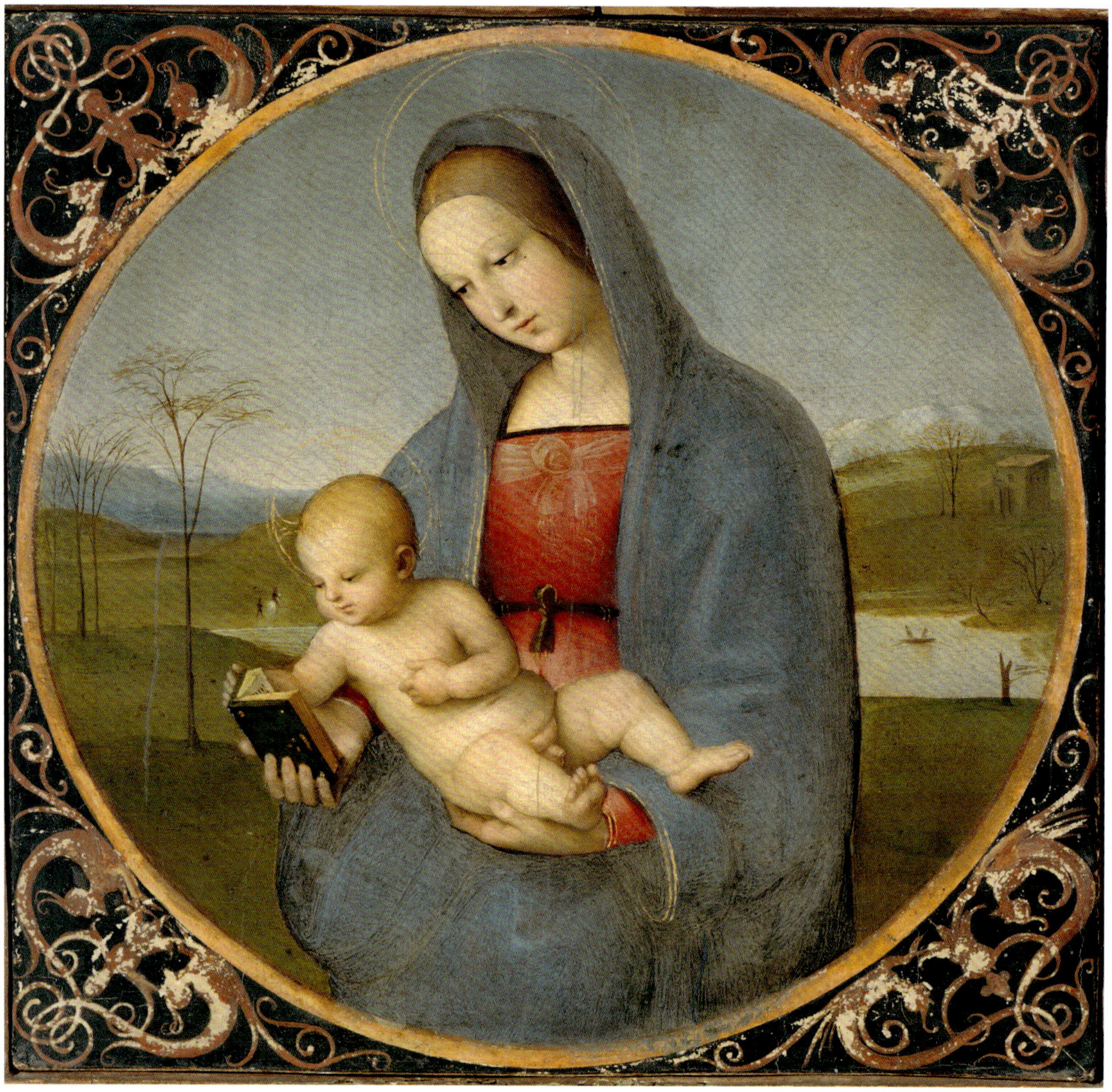

above: RAPHAEL (RAFFAELLO SANTI). *The Conestabile Madonna.* 1502–3. TEMPERA ON CANVAS (TRANSFERRED FROM PANEL). 6 7/8 × 7 IN. (17.5 × 18 CM).

Restoration of this tondo revealed that Raphael originally showed the Virgin holding a pomegranate and not a book. This painting forms a cohesive whole with the frame, which was made to the artist's design. He likely painted the work, perhaps as a commission from the Perugian noble Alfani Diamante, before moving to Florence in 1504. In the 18th century the Alfanis became related to the Conestabile family, from whom Alexander II bought the painting in 1871.

opposite: RAPHAEL (RAFFAELLO SANTI). *The Holy Family (Madonna with the Beardless Joseph).* 1506. OIL AND TEMPERA ON CANVAS (TRANSFERRED FROM PANEL). 28 1/2 × 22 1/2 IN. (72.5 × 57 CM).

In this traditional depiction of Mary, the Infant Jesus, and Joseph, a sense of spiritual unity is achieved through the organization of space, the skillful alternation of colors, and the figures' outlines, which form a compositional oval. Raphael invested his subjects with realistic features: the Virgin's dress and hairstyle reflect Florentine fashion of the day, while Joseph, in defiance of tradition, is depicted without a beard—the reason this painting is sometimes called the Madonna with the Beardless Joseph.

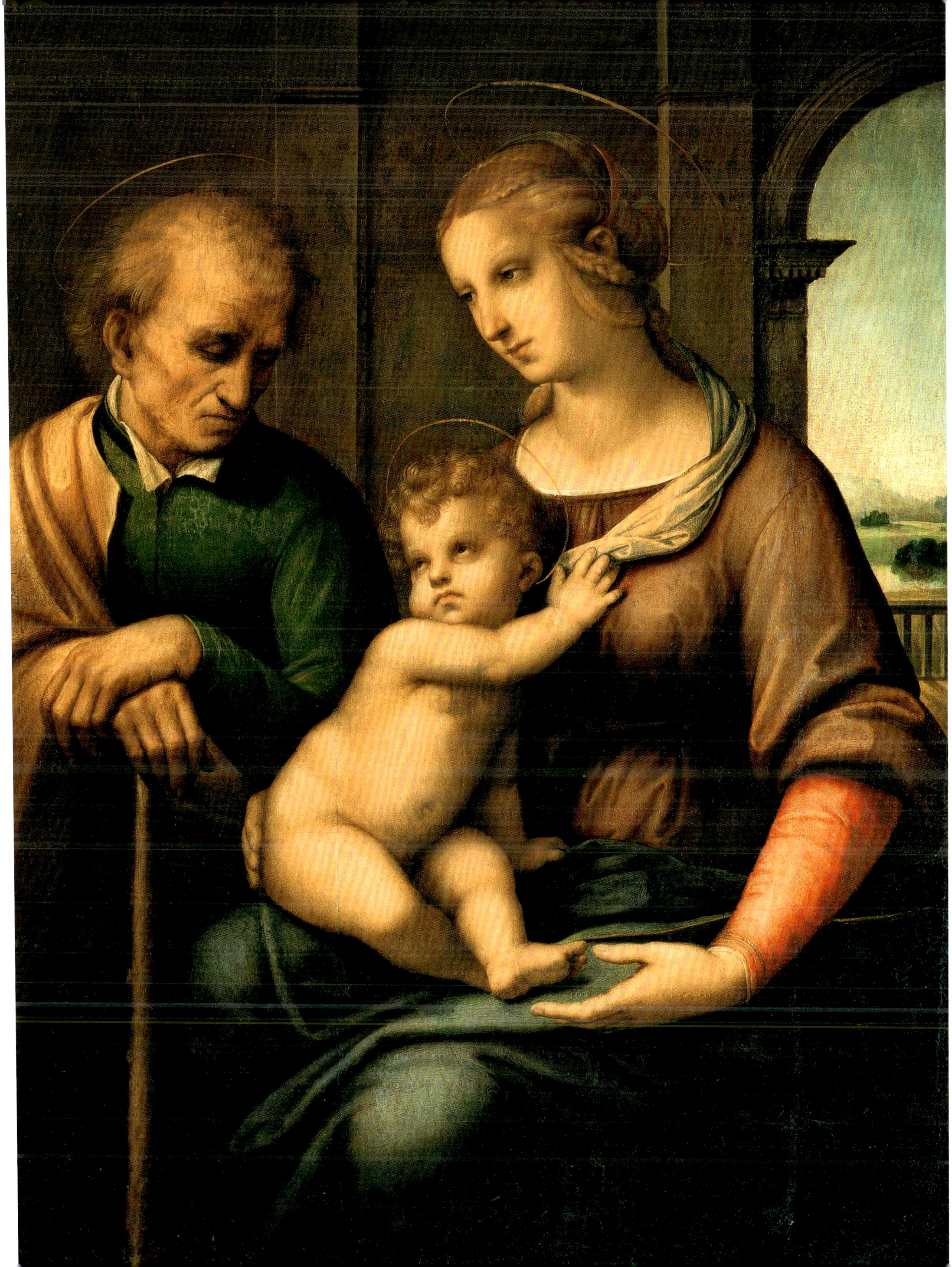

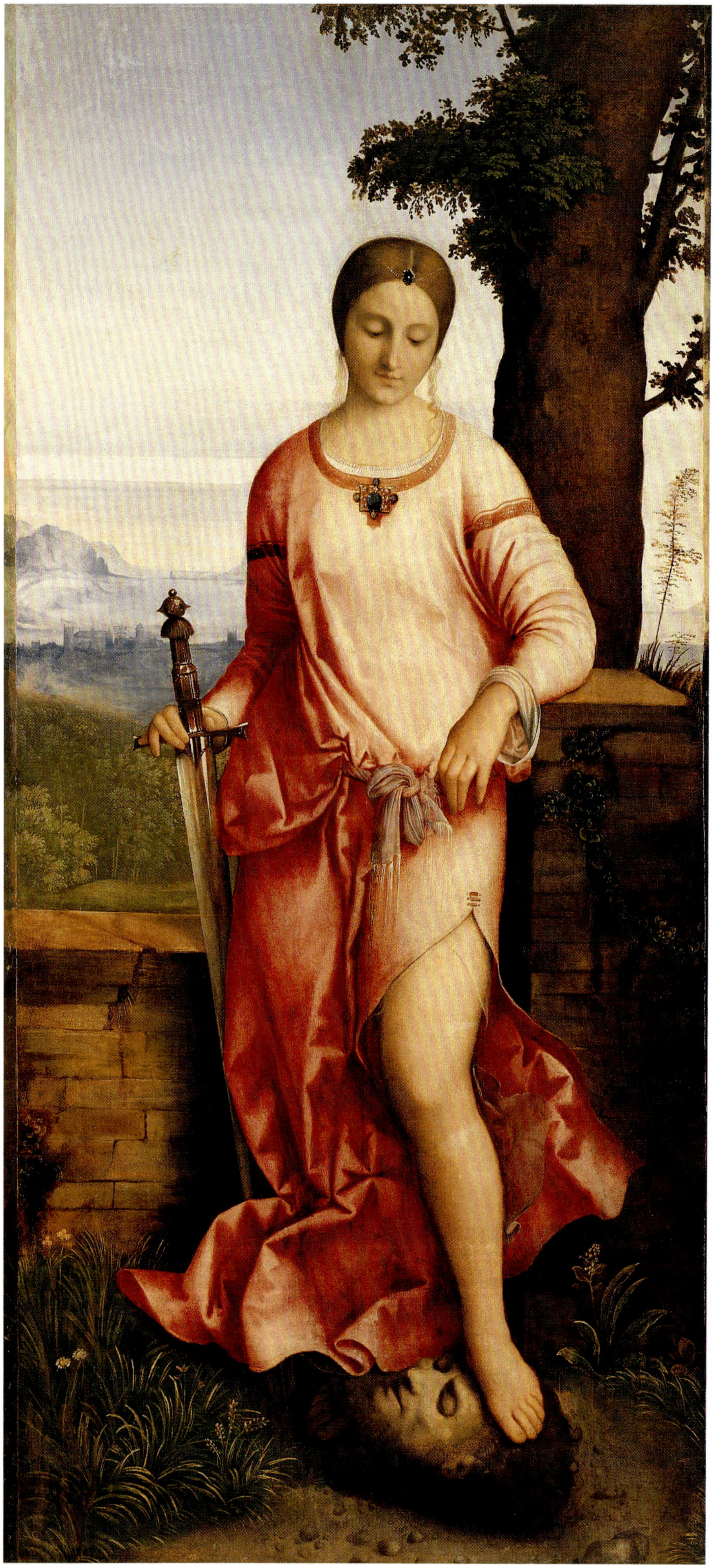

left: GIORGIONE (GIORGIO BARBARELLI DA CASTELFRANCO). *Judith.* CA. 1504. OIL ON CANVAS (TRANSFERRED FROM PANEL). 56⅝ × 26⅛ IN. (144 × 66.5 CM).

The apocryphal tale of Judith, who saved her native city from an Assyrian invasion, was often illustrated during the Renaissance. Giorgione eschewed the tradition of depicting the moment the heroine cut off the head of the enemy commander Holofernes and, instead, created a lyrical image of his subject reflecting on her deed. The cool of the morning landscape and her enchanting figure convey an idea of the world as a harmonious whole, in which life and death are inextricably linked.

opposite: JACOPO PONTORMO (JACOPO CARRUCCI). *Madonna and Child with St. Joseph and John the Baptist.* 1520S. OIL ON CANVAS. 47¼ × 38½ IN. (120 × 98.5 CM).

Pontormo was an outstanding exponent of early Florentine Mannerism—a Late Renaissance style whose followers rejected the principle of harmony and sought their own artistic language. Pontormo treats the traditional subject in a new way: the composition is deliberately disrupted by intersecting volumes and contrasting patches of color. The red and green seem particularly bright alongside the pale pink face of the Virgin and the body of the Christ Child.

following spread: TITIAN (TIZIANO VECELLIO). *The Flight into Egypt.* 1507. OIL ON CANVAS. 81 × 132¼ IN. (206 × 336 CM).

Titian's early masterpiece was created when he was about nineteen; he had just finished his course at Giovanni Bellini's studio and was working closely with Giorgione. In the works of both artists at this time, the landscape is an important element of the picture. Using his own observations of nature, Titian convincingly depicts the cavalcade of travelers—Joseph, Mary and Child, and James, the brother of the Lord, who leads the donkey—within a horizontal composition marked by the trees.

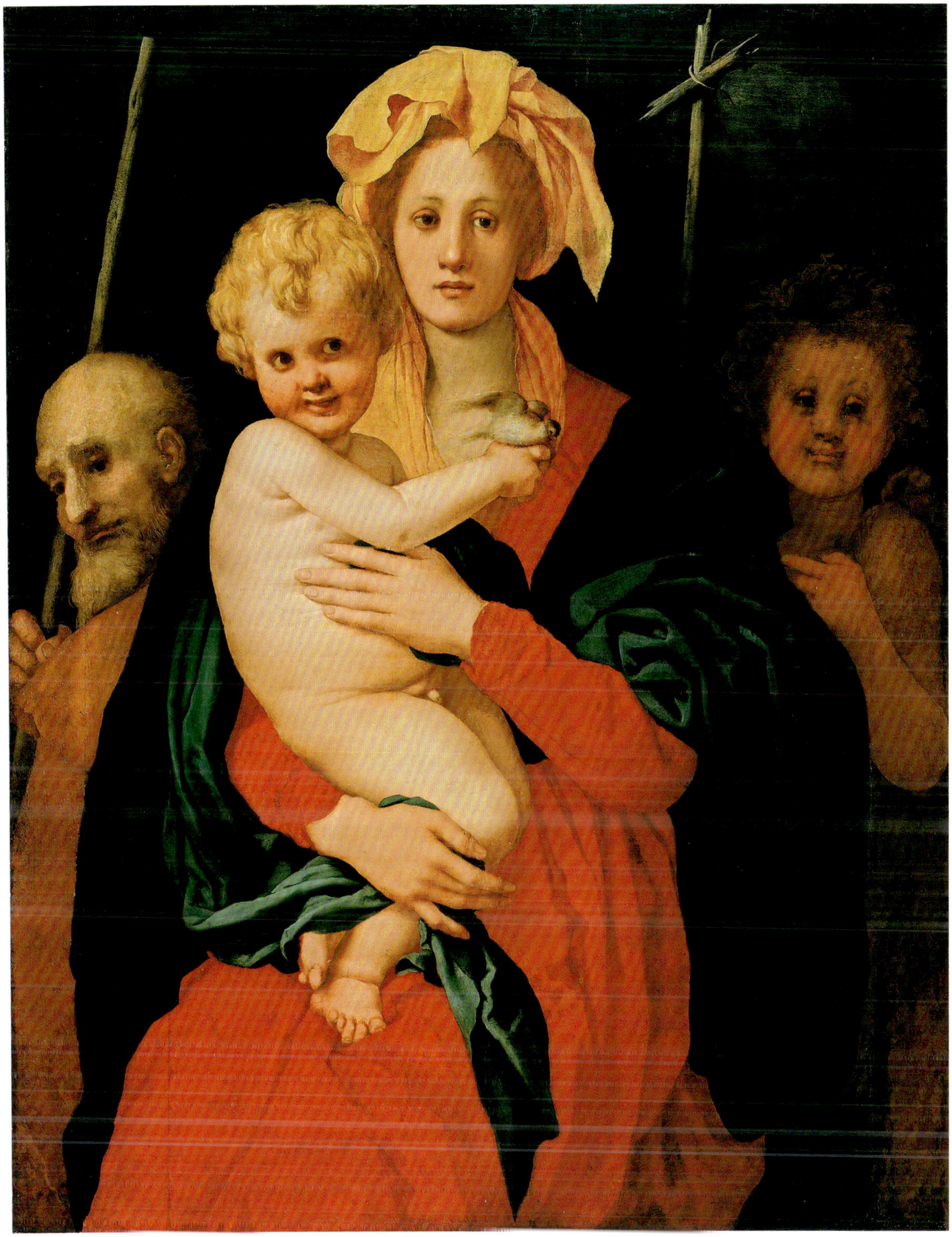

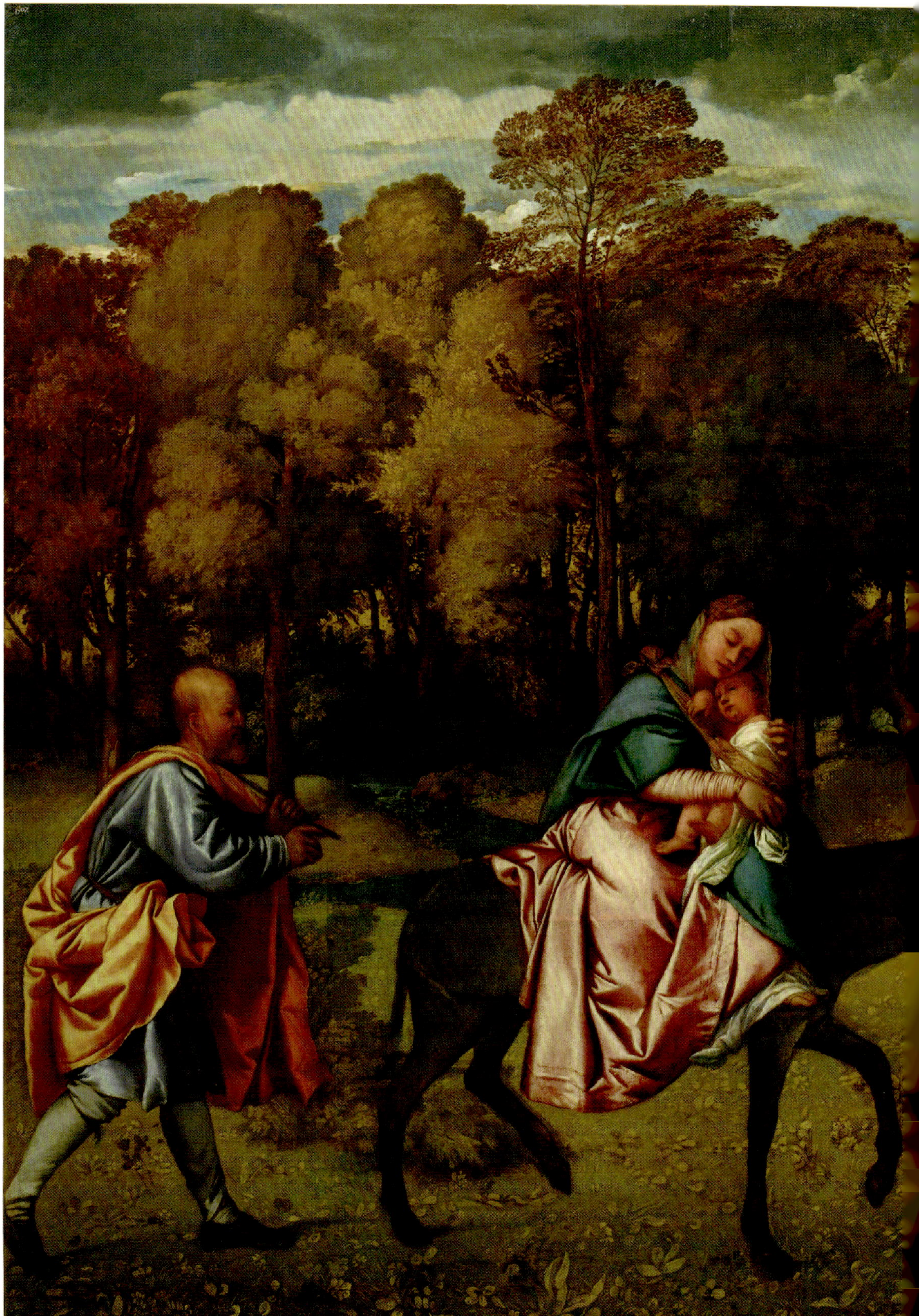

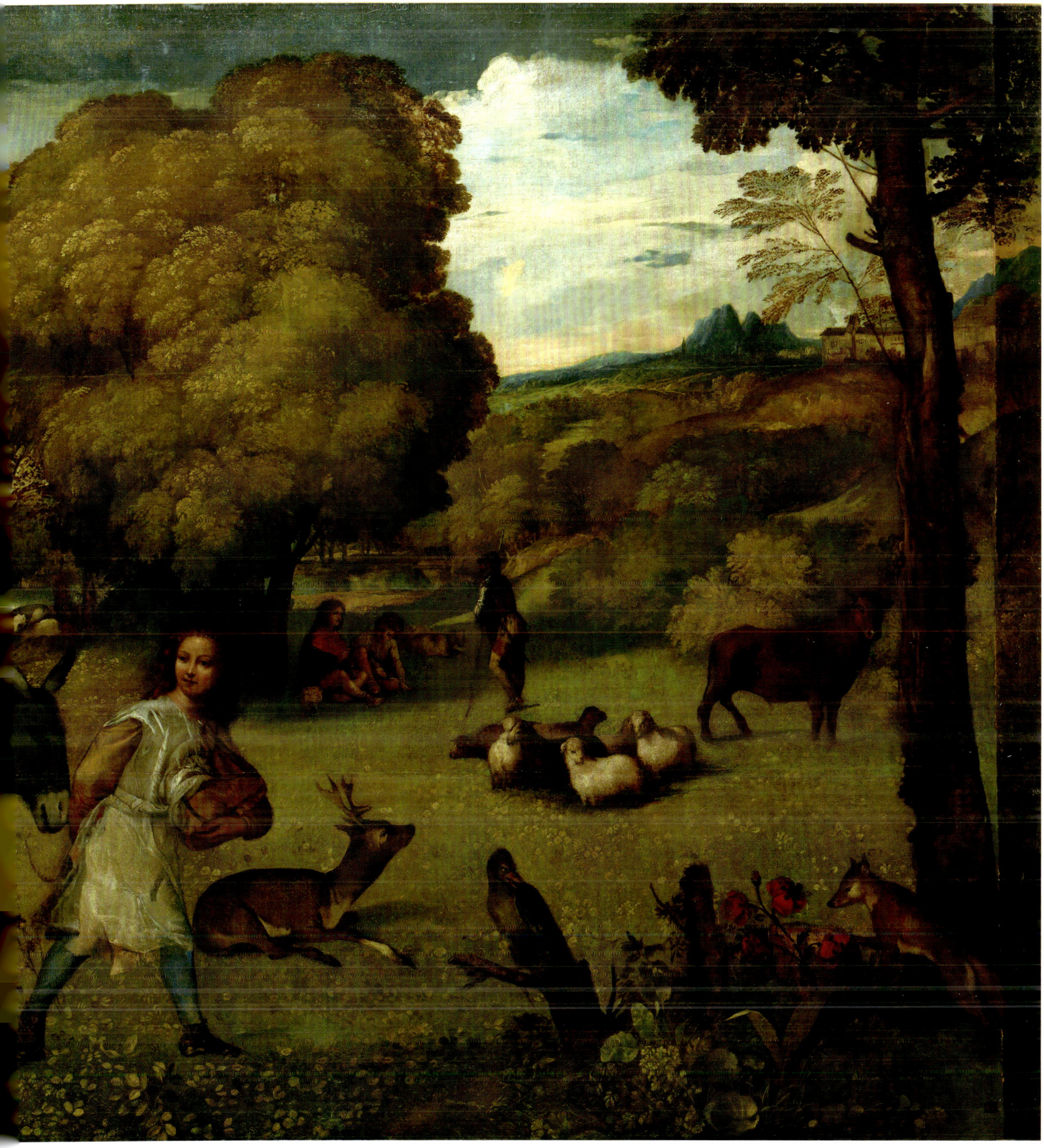

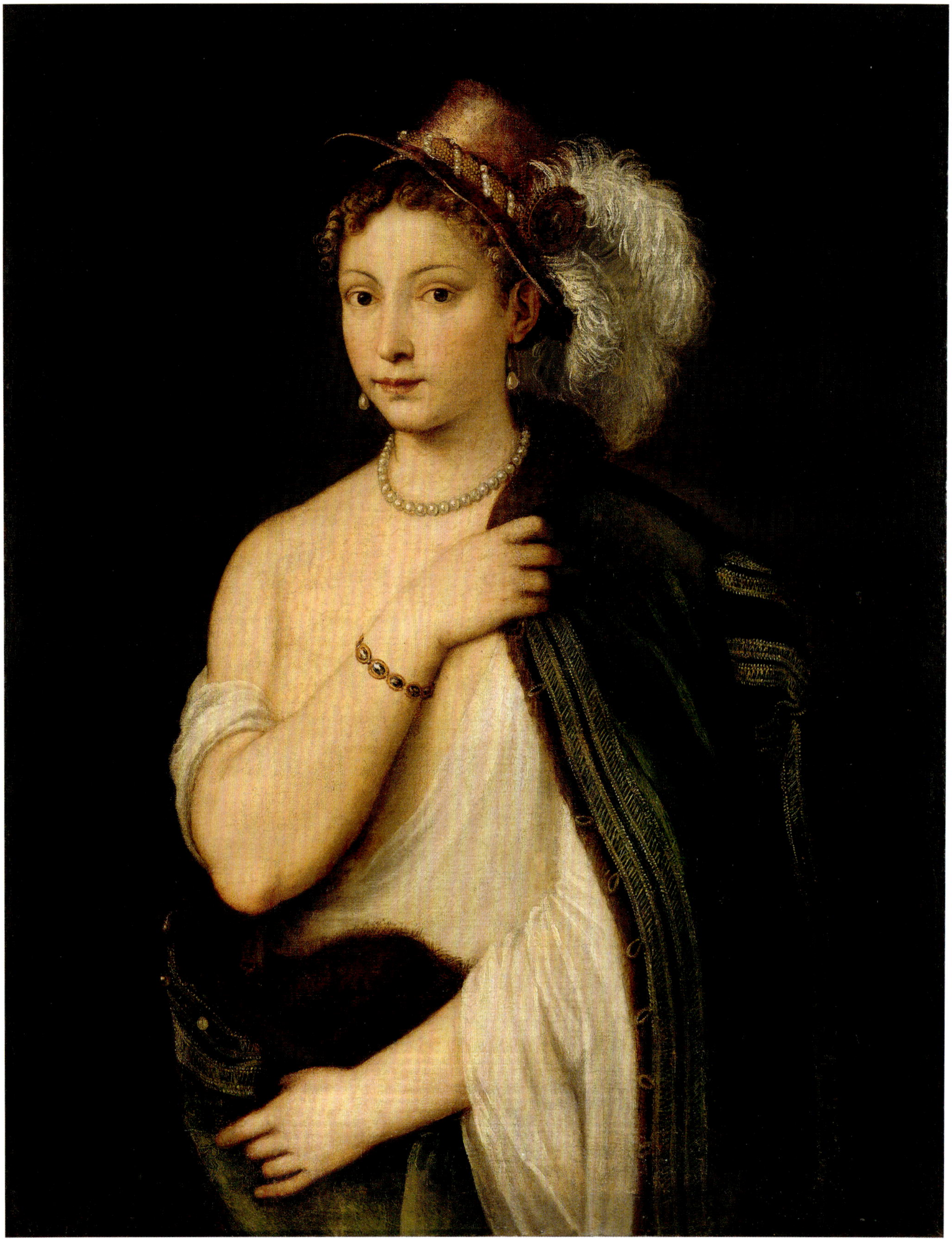

opposite: TITIAN (TIZIANO VECELLIO). *Portrait of a Young Woman.* CA. 1536. OIL ON CANVAS. 37¾ × 29½ IN. (96 × 75 CM).

The crispness and precision of the contours in this portrait, unusual for the mature Titian, have caused specialists to doubt its current attribution. But the refined eroticism is typical of an artist who several times depicted Venuses uninhibitedly demonstrating their nakedness in the setting of a rich Italian house. Here, he does without mythological pretext; the beautiful model has even been perceived as the celebrated patroness of the arts Eleonora Gonzaga, the wife of the Duke of Urbino.

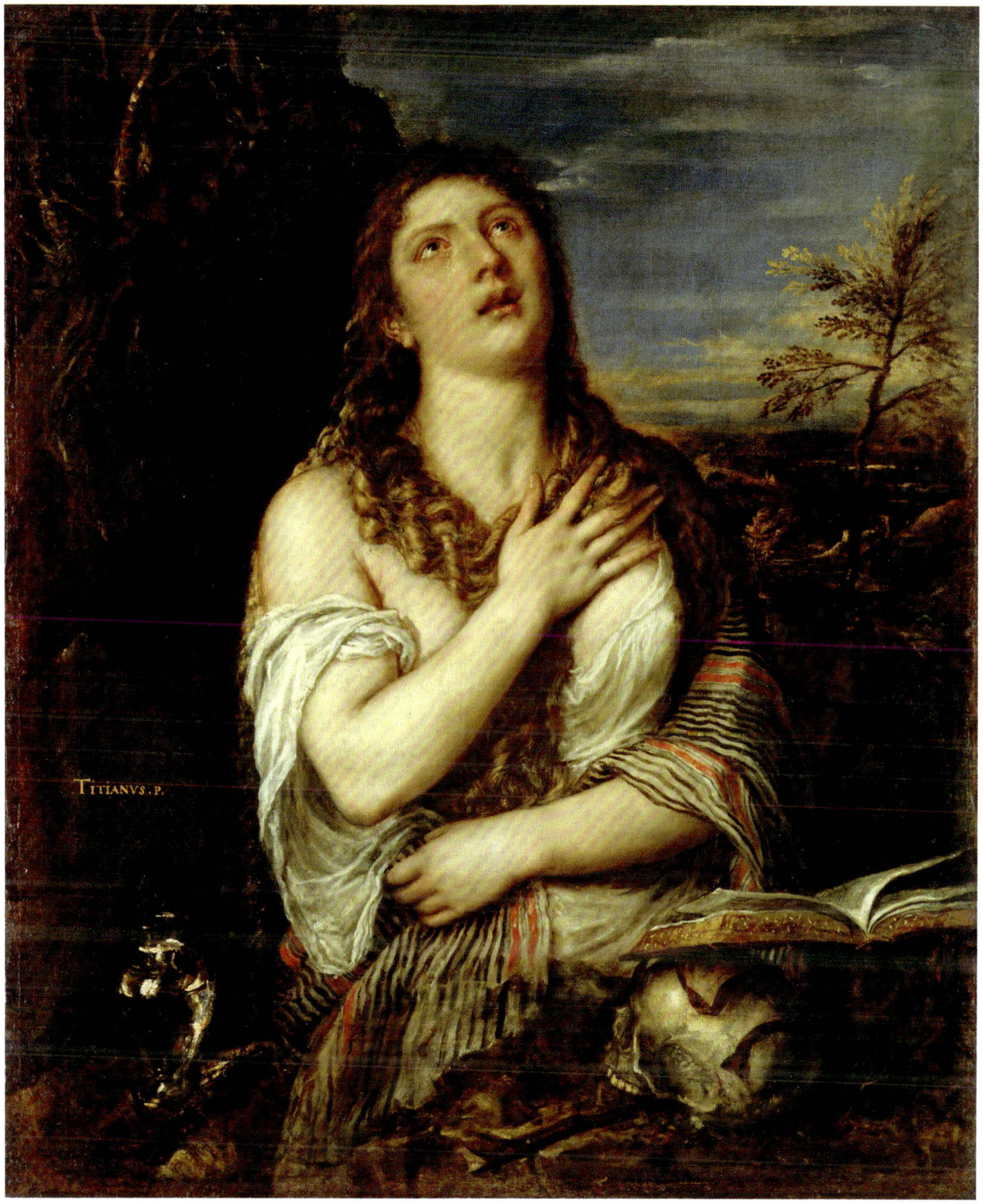

above: TITIAN (TIZIANO VECELLIO). *The Repentant Mary Magdalene.* 1560s. OIL ON CANVAS. 46 ⅞ × 38 ⅛ IN. (119 × 97 CM).

According to legend, after meeting Christ the sinful Mary Magdalene withdrew to the desert where she mourned her previous sins. Titian depicted Mary Magdalene several times but the Hermitage version is justly considered the best—the artist himself did not part with the painting until the end of his days. After the artist's death his son sold his house together with the painting to the patrician Cristoforo Barbarigo. The canvas came into the Hermitage in 1850.

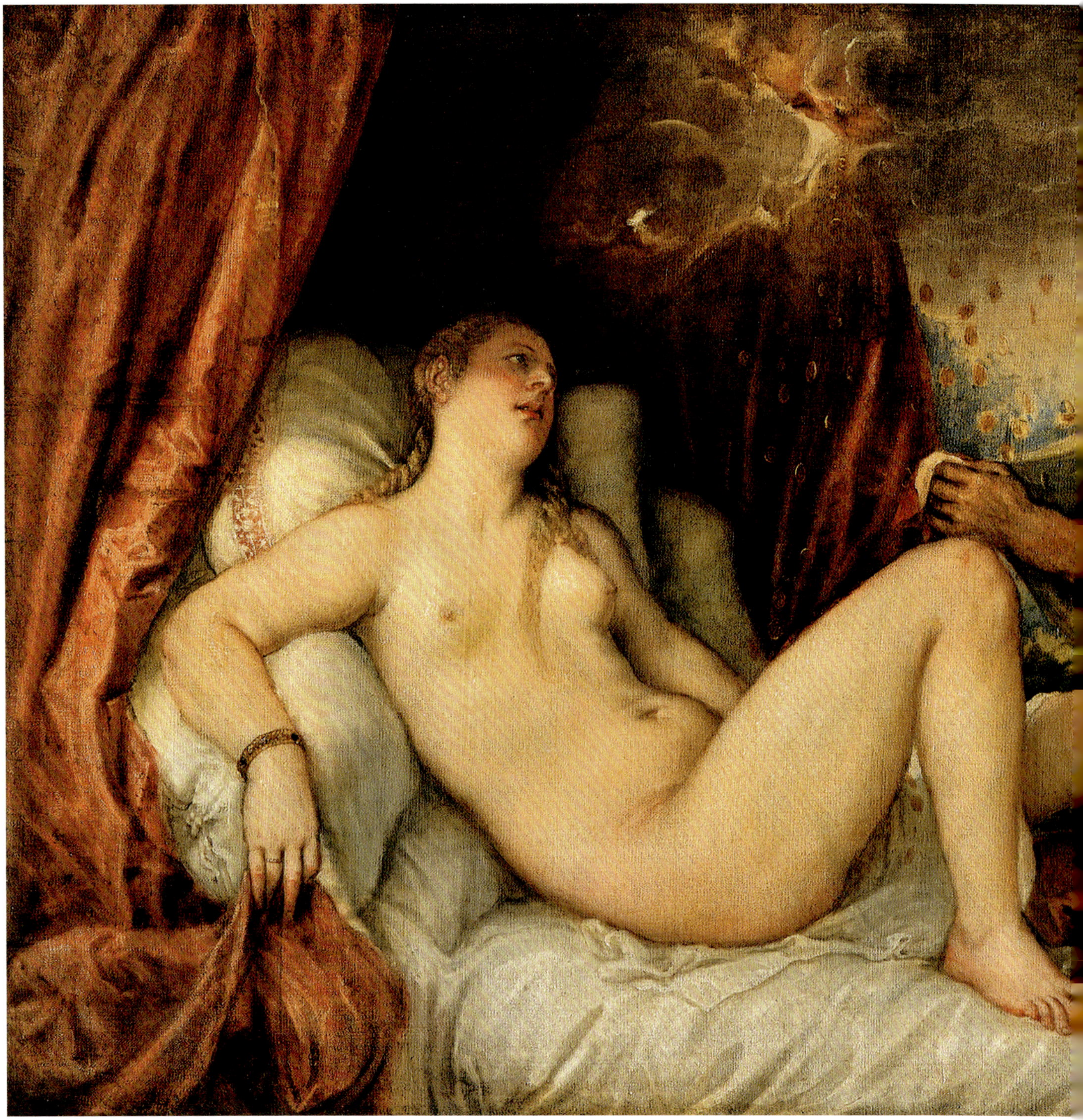

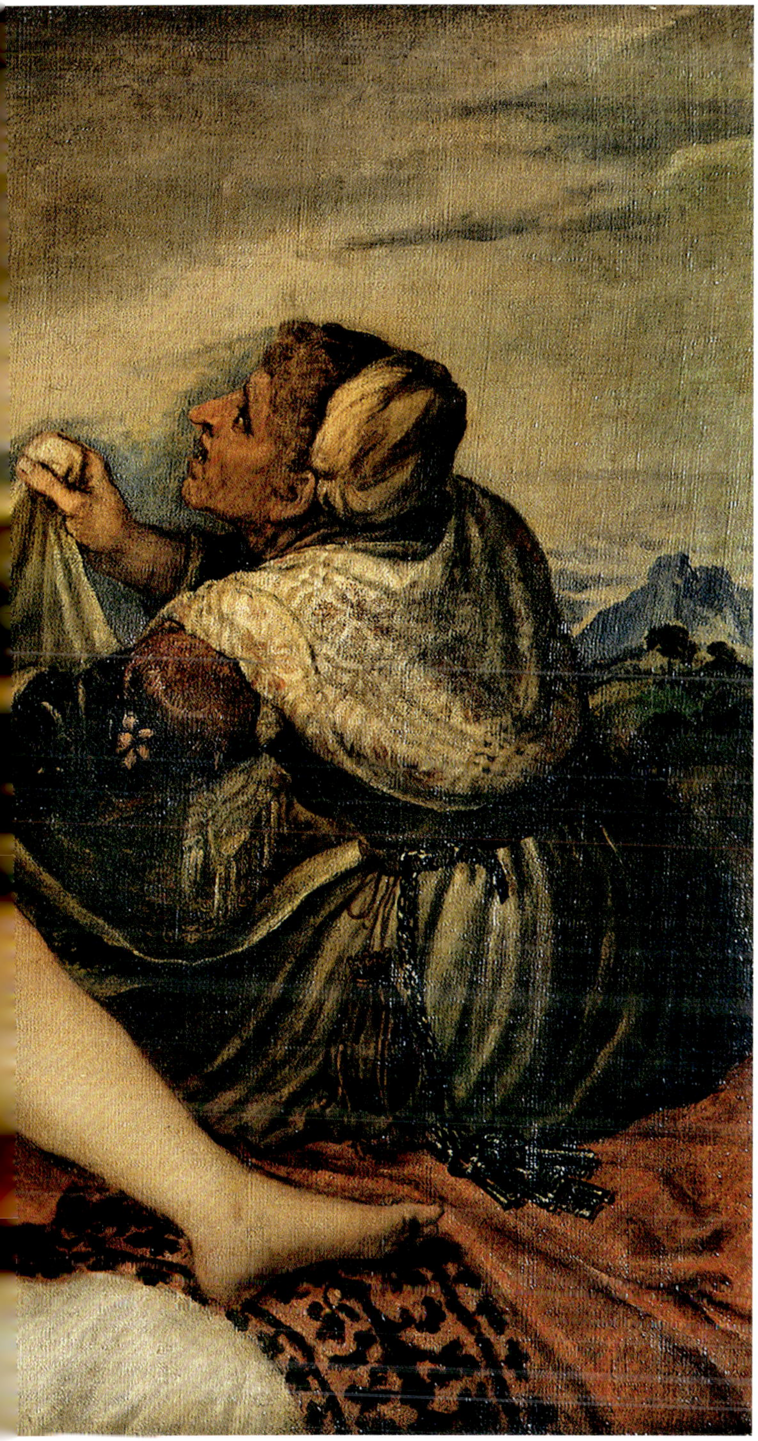

TITIAN (TIZIANO VECELLIO). *Danaë*. CA. 1554. OIL ON CANVAS. $47\frac{1}{4} \times 73\frac{5}{8}$ IN. (120 × 187 CM).

According to *The Amours of Jupiter*, the mythical king Acrisius was scared by an oracle predicting his death at the hands of a son born to his daughter Danaë, and so he locked her in a tower. Jupiter fell in love with the maiden, turning into a golden shower to reach her. Titian conveys the heat of passion by dividing the painting: on the right, the servant catches gold coins in her skirt, while on the left, Danaë's body reigns.

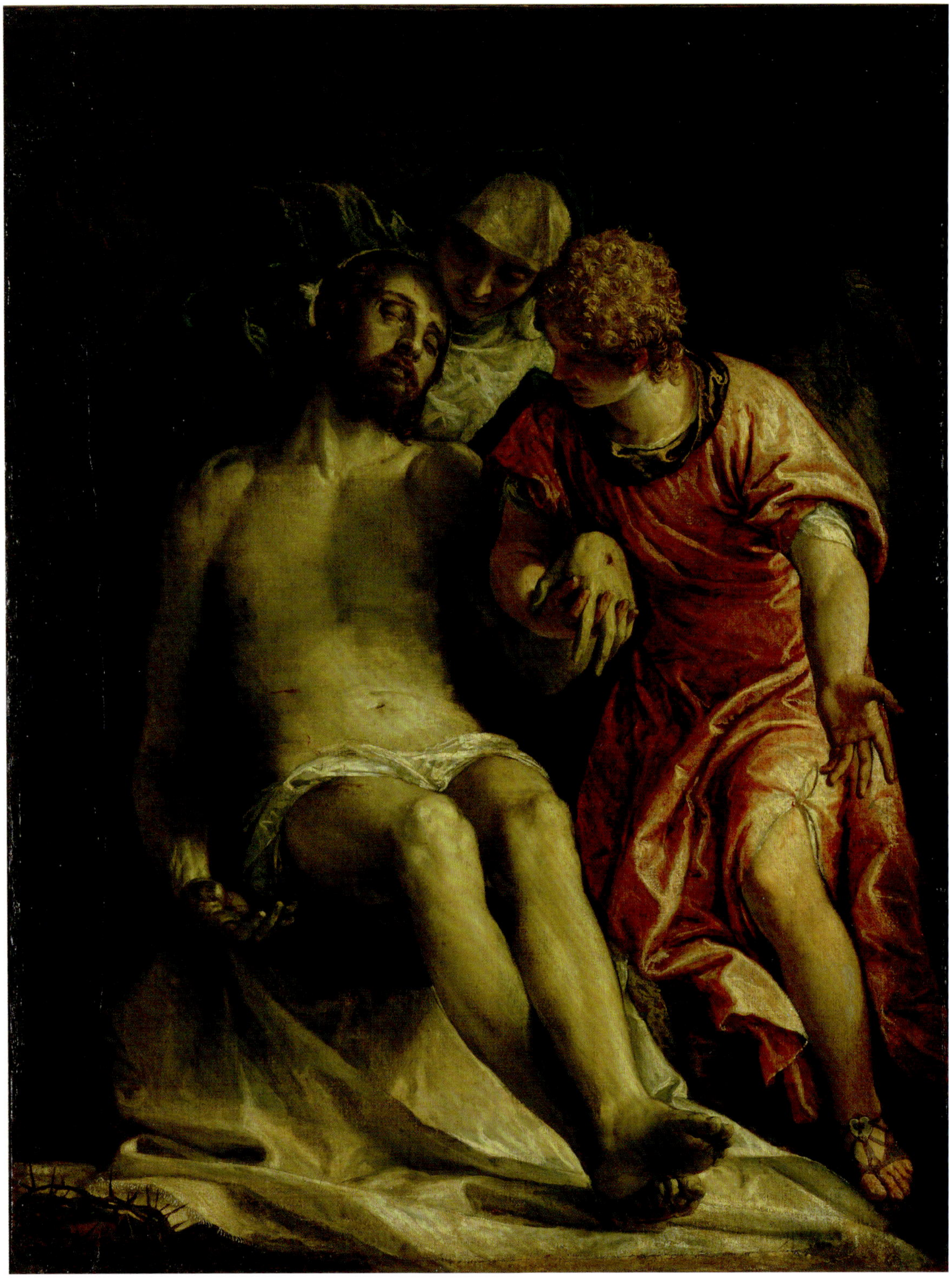

PAOLO VERONESE (PAOLO CAGLIARI). *The Lamentation.* BETWEEN 1576 AND 1582.
OIL ON CANVAS. $57\frac{7}{8} \times 43\frac{7}{8}$ IN. (147 × 111.5 CM).

The Lamentation, one of the best works by Veronese, was created for the Church of Santi Giovanni e Paolo in Venice. The figures depicted are the Virgin Mary and an angel bent over the body of Christ. An X ray of the painting showed that a second angel supported the Savior's body on the left, but was painted out by the artist. The dramatic effect is achieved by the contrast of warm and cold colors.

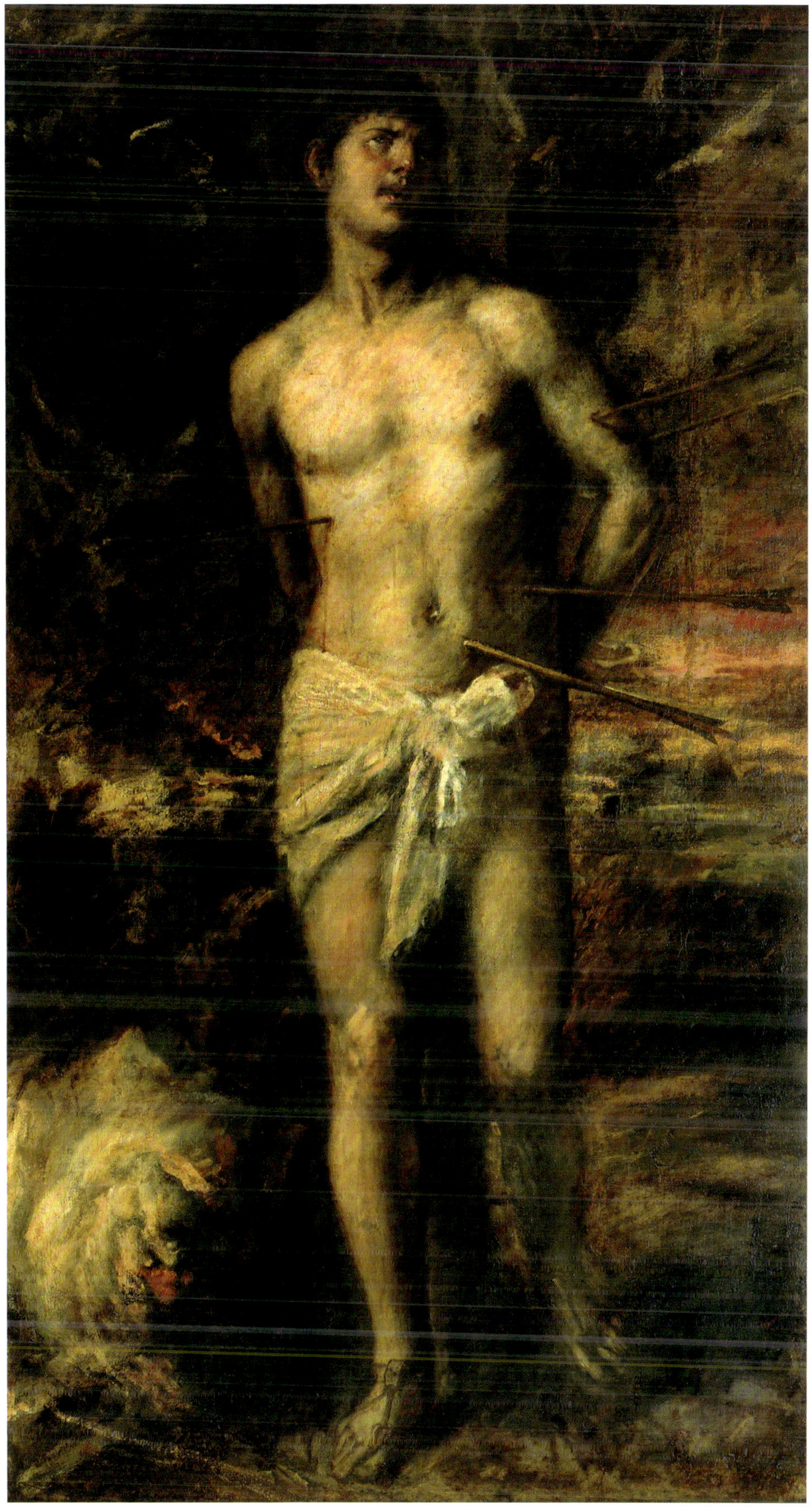

TITIAN (TIZIANO VECELLIO). *St. Sebastian.* CA. 1570. OIL ON CANVAS. $82\frac{5}{8} \times 45\frac{1}{4}$ IN. (210 × 115 CM).

The flesh remained one of the main objects of Titian's reflections even in the last years of his life. Here, it is no longer the regal flesh of Venus or Danaë but rather the suffering flesh of the martyr that, at the same time, rejects suffering. It is filled not with greatness but instead with strength, and that strength is expressed directly, by the flesh of the painting itself. St. Sebastian is undoubtedly beautiful, but it is the beauty of torment.

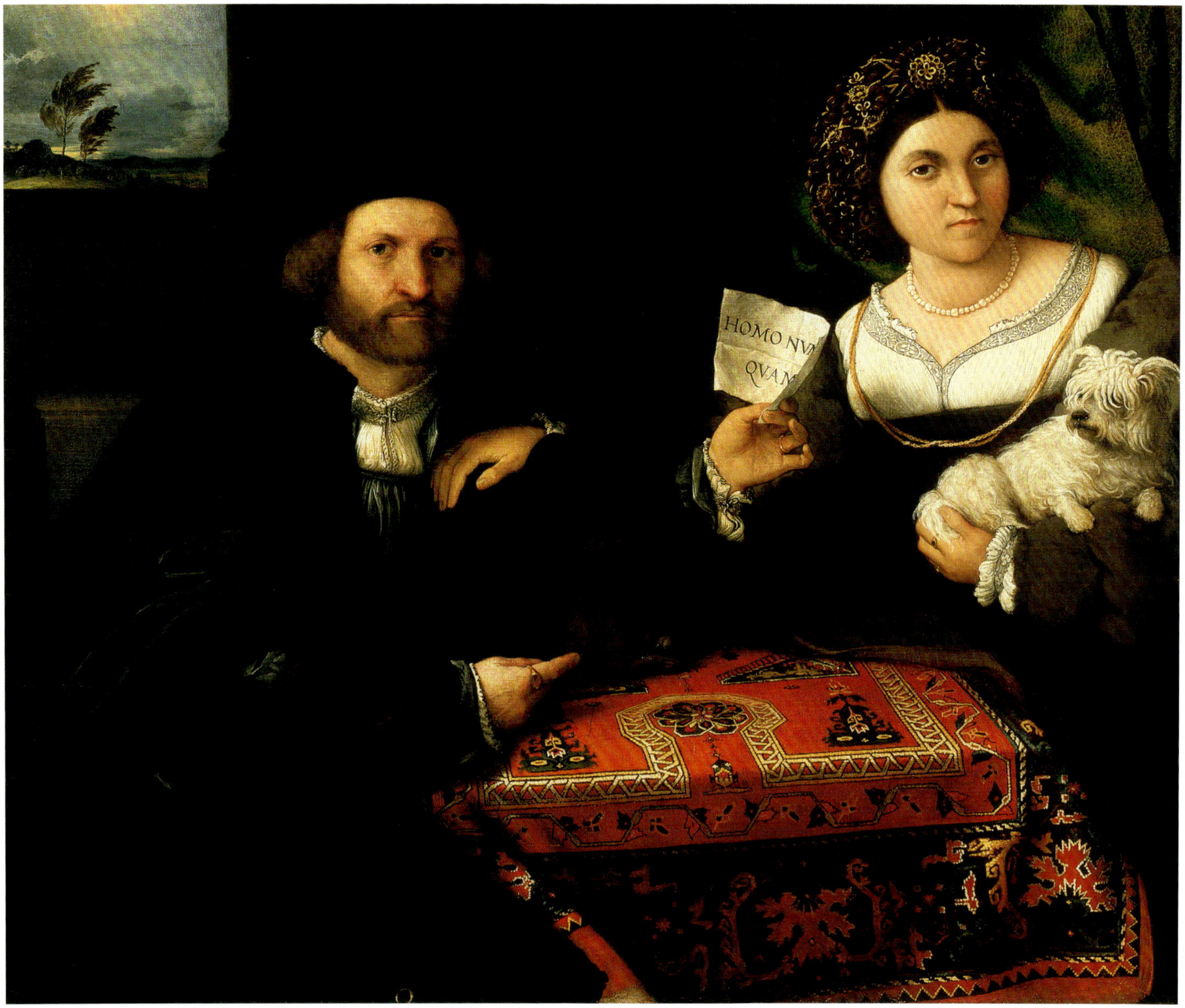

LORENZO LOTTO. *Family Portrait.* 1523–24. OIL ON CANVAS. 37 3/4 × 45 5/8 IN. (96 × 116 CM).

The dog symbolizes faithfulness and constancy, whereas the Latin inscription reads HOMO NUNQUAM, or "A man never." (The probable continuation is "behaves like a male squirrel," an animal, so it was believed in the Middle Ages, that drove the female from the dray in winter to avoid sharing his store of food.) The old-fashioned attributes and overt posing of the couple do not interfere with the portrait's astonishing naturalness, achieved thanks to Lotto's relaxed and ironic eye.

CARAVAGGIO (MICHELANGELO MERISI DA CARAVAGGIO). *The Lute Player.* CA. 1595. OIL ON CANVAS. 37 × 61 3/8 IN. (94 × 119 CM).

The crack in the lute, the damaged pear, the music of a madrigal well-known at the end of the 16th century, and the musician's sad look leave no doubt that this painting is an allegory of unrequited love. At the same time, the strong chiaroscuro and tangible materiality of the still life, so abundant and carefully executed, are clear testimony to the original style and uncompromising character of the twenty-two-year-old Caravaggio.

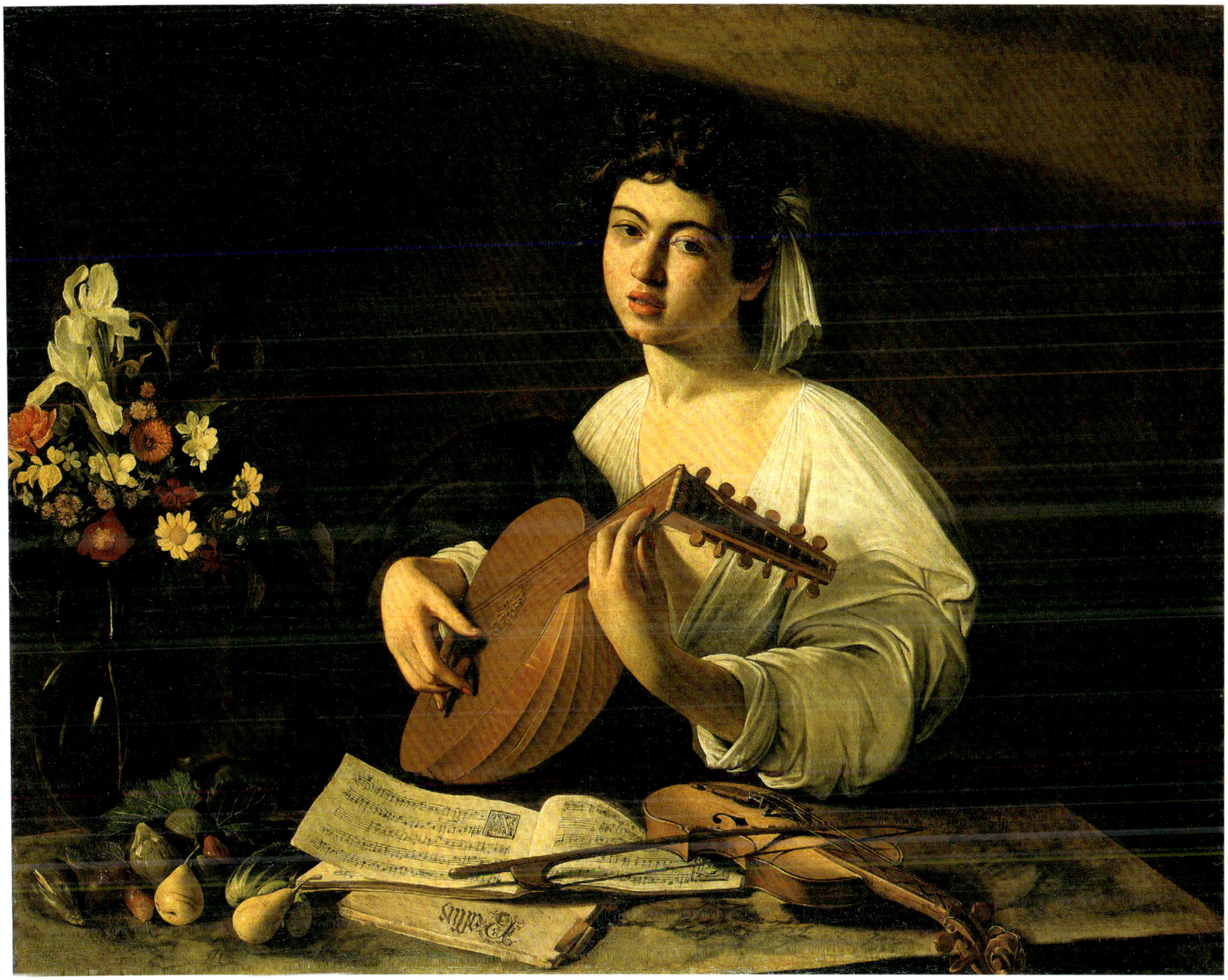

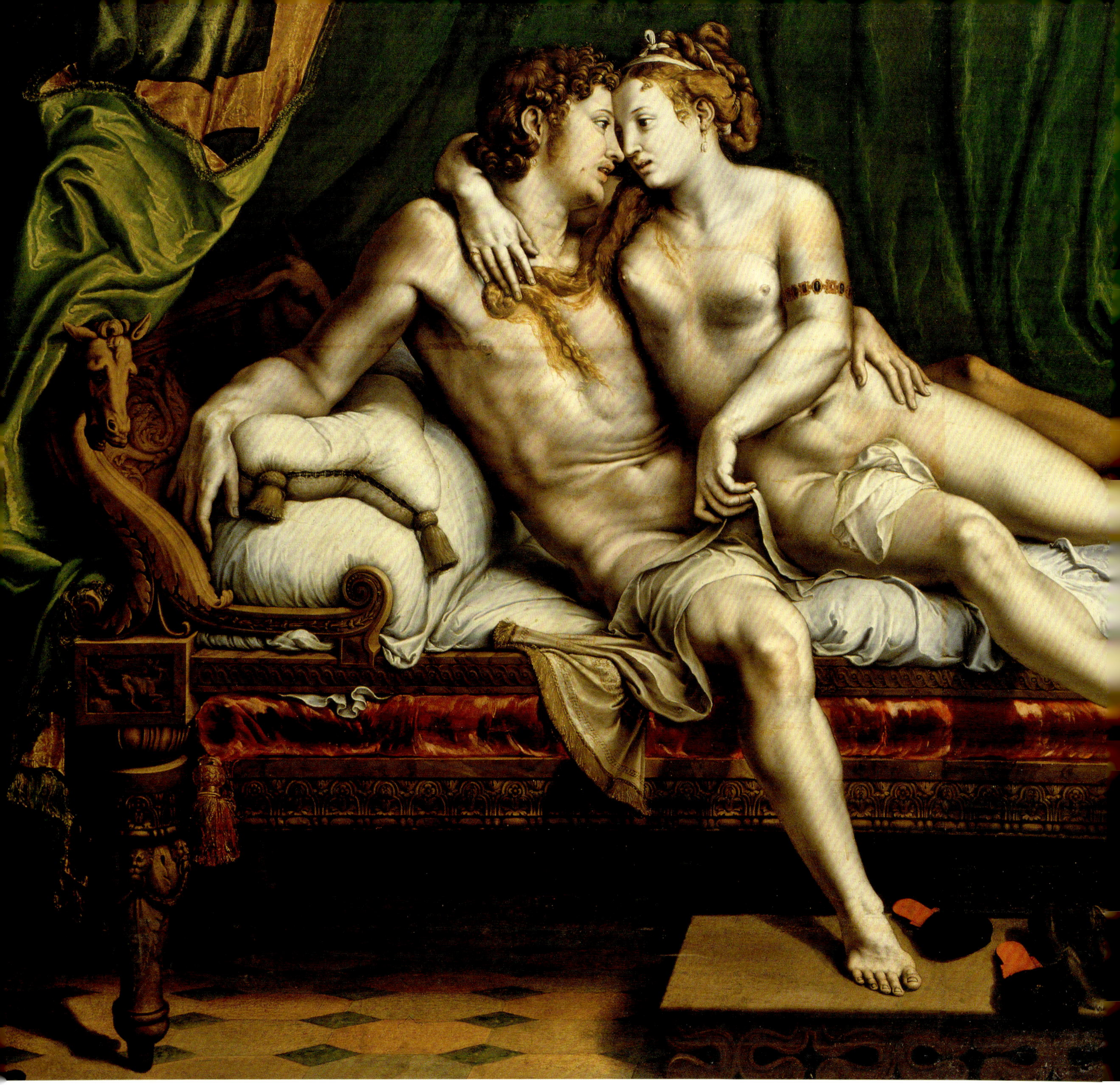

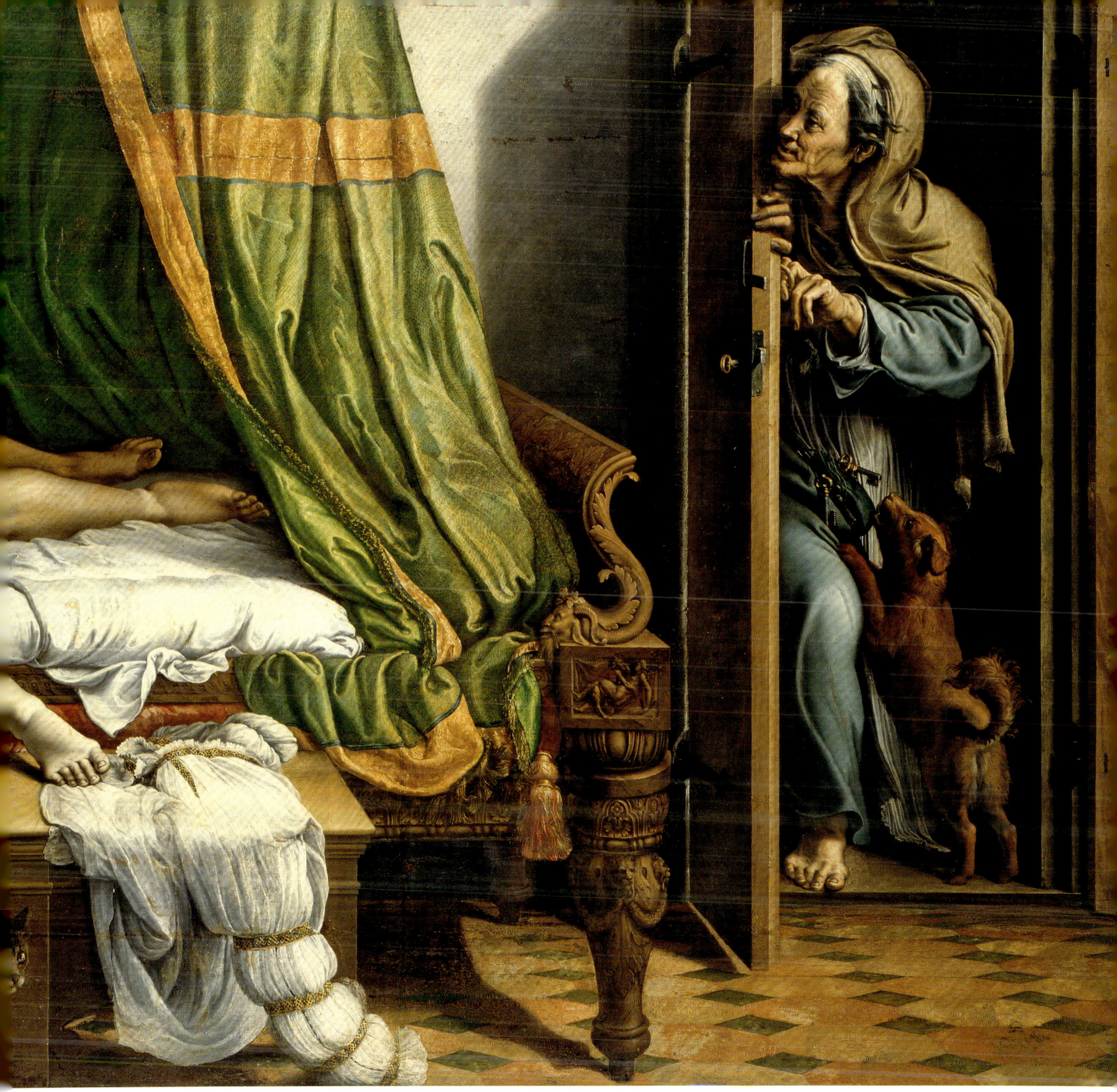

GIULIO ROMANO (GIULIO PIPPI). *Love Scene*. 1524–26. OIL ON CANVAS. 64⅛ × 132⅝ IN. (163 × 337 CM).

Among Raphael's most gifted pupils, Giulio Romano began with monumental murals reminiscent of the works of his teacher. Soon, however, he freed himself of Raphael's influence and Renaissance ideals. His later, independent work reflects the Mannerist search for a new means of expression. According to one interpretation, this painting depicts the romance between Zeus and Alcmene. It has also been suggested that it alludes to the secret marriage of Federigo II Gonzaga and Isabella Boschetti.

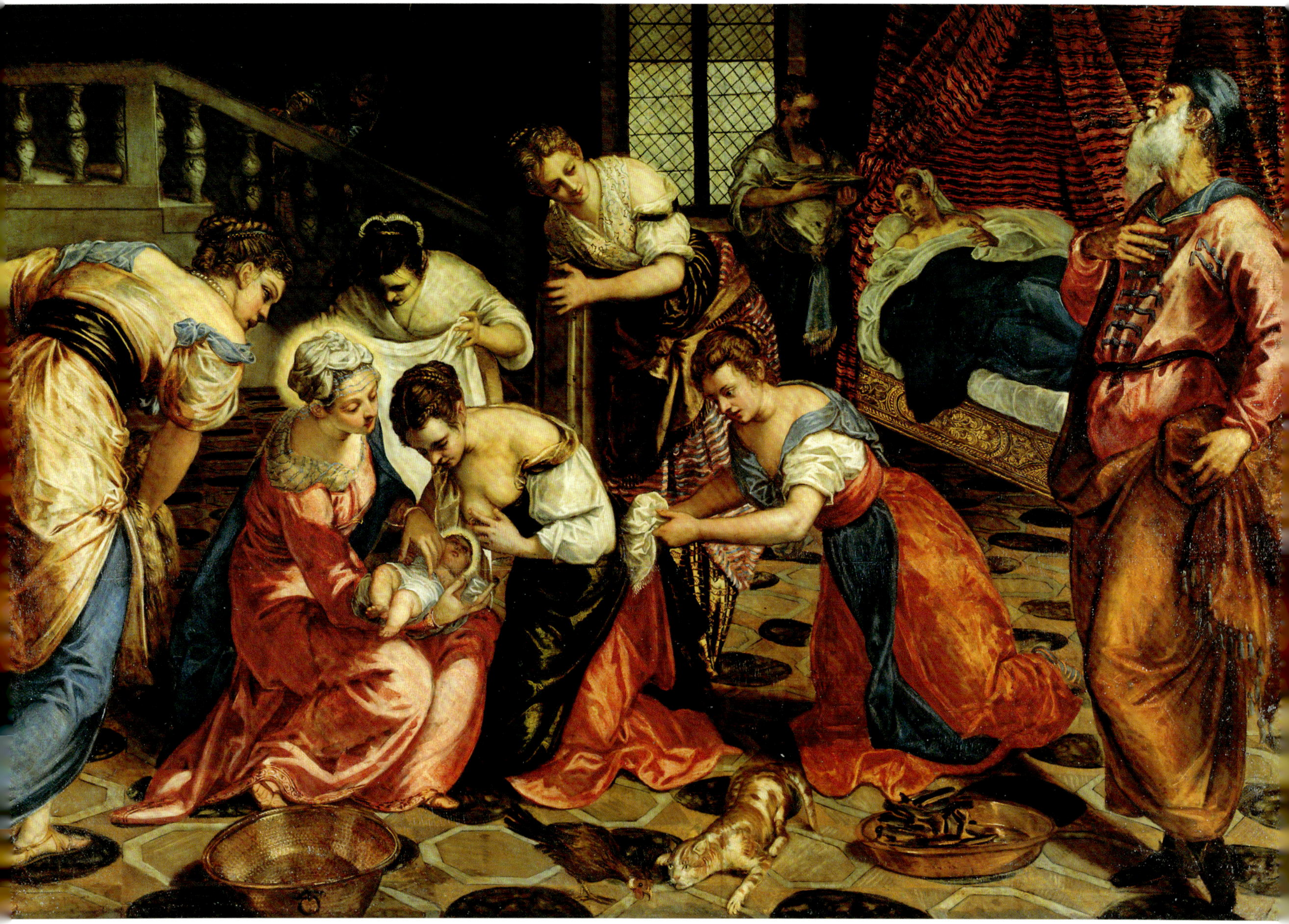

JACOPO TINTORETTO (JACOPO ROBUSTI). *The Nativity of John the Baptist.* CA. 1550. OIL ON CANVAS. 71¼ × 104¾ IN. (181 × 266 CM).

Tintoretto's oeuvre is marked by a keen sense of chaos. In any subject he finds action, and in any action he finds many disconnected actions. This is true of his account of John the Baptist's nativity, which is an eloquent depiction of the turmoil reigning in any home at the birth of a child. The saint's mother, Elizabeth, recuperates on the bed and the Virgin Mary holds the newborn as his father recovers the power of speech, in accordance with the prophecy.

JACOPO TINTORETTO (JACOPO ROBUSTI). *St. George.* 1543–44. OIL ON CANVAS. 48⅛ × 36¼ IN (122 × 92 CM).

The brilliant representative of Venetian Mannerism, Tintoretto received numerous commissions for large-scale works to be hung high up in churches or lay brotherhoods. His famous "downward slope" compositions, in which he placed small figures at the top or in the background, and large ones in the foreground, allowed viewers to see and feel the action represented in the painting. The use of this device is quite obvious in this comparatively small canvas.

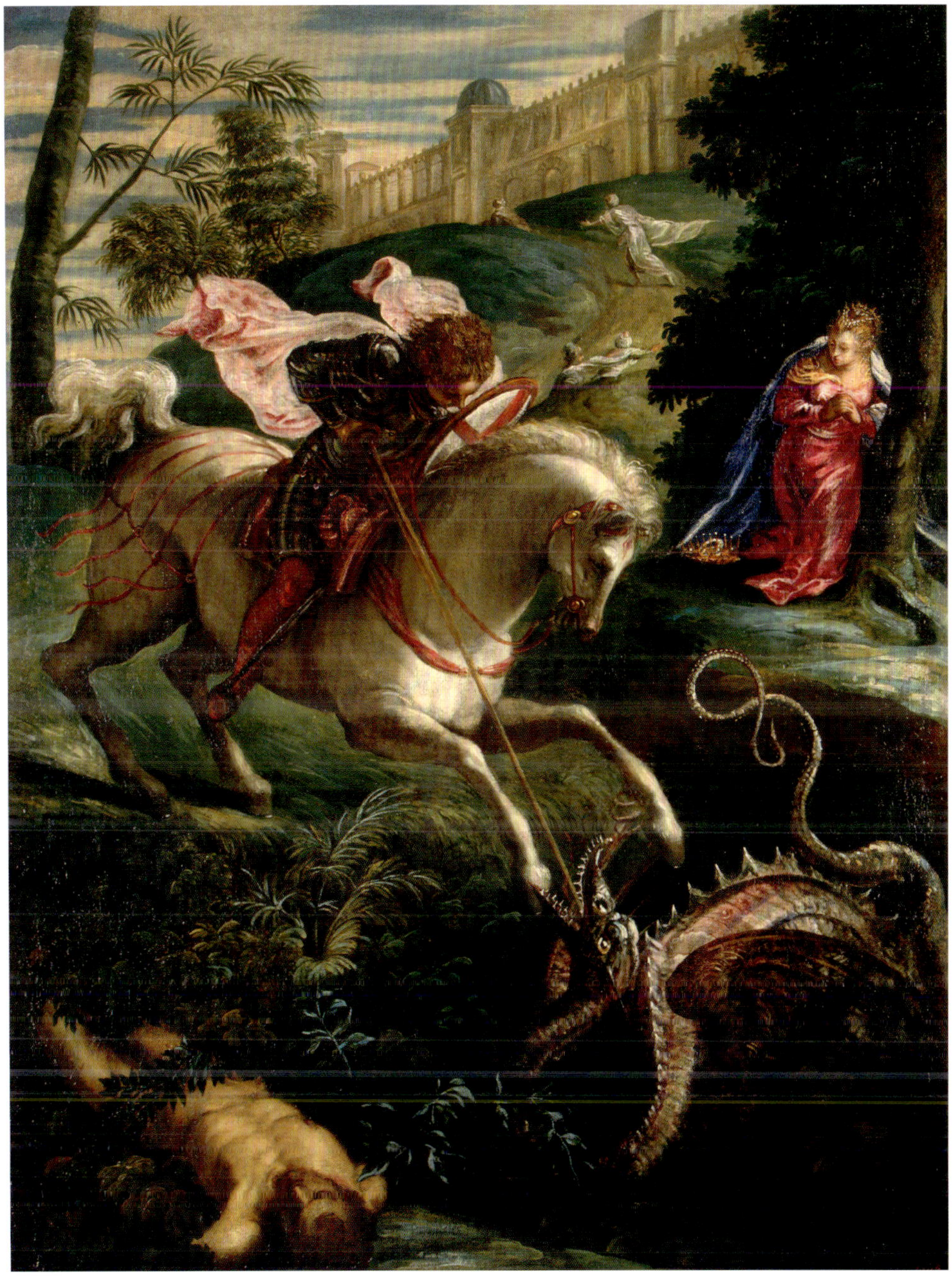

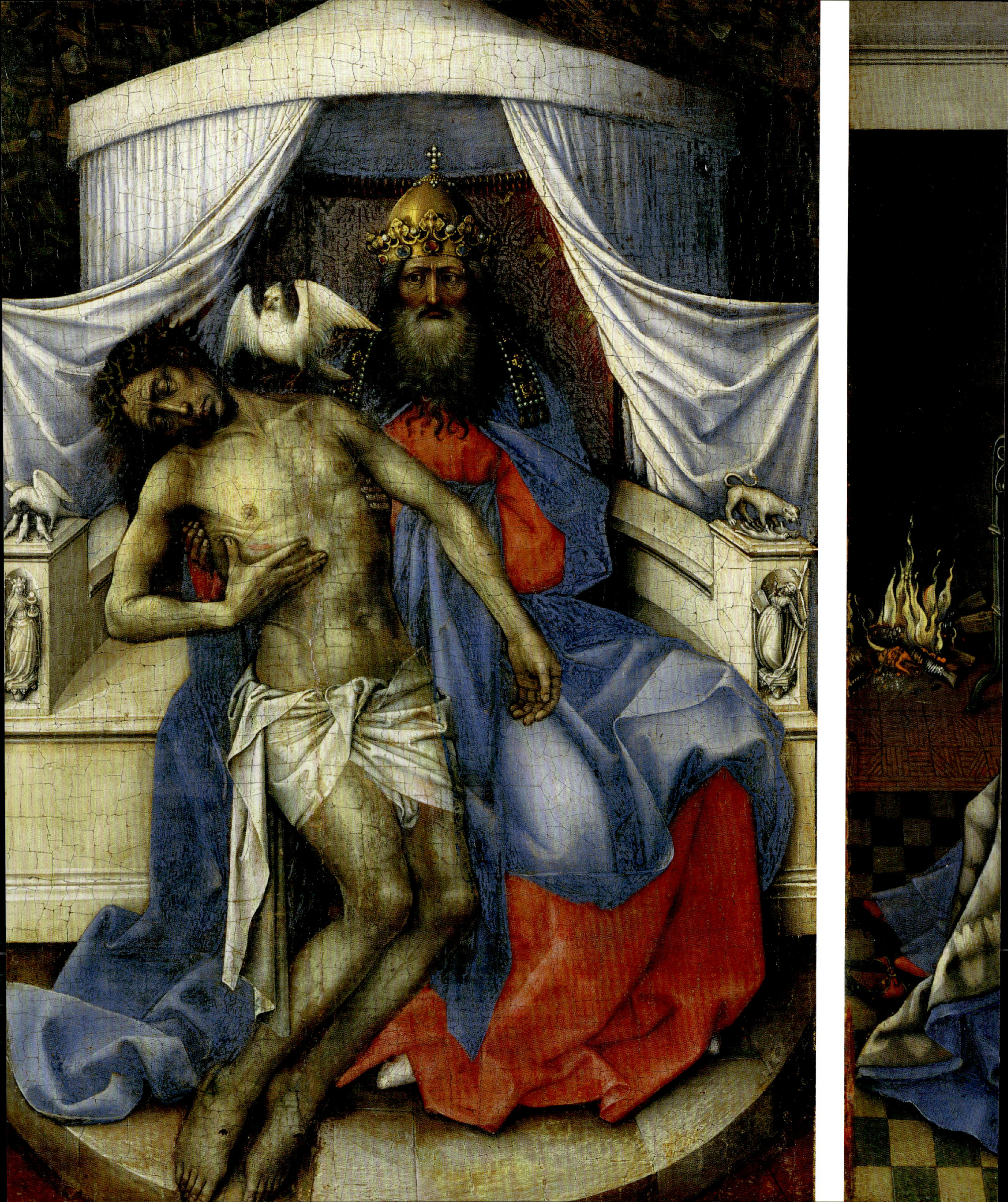

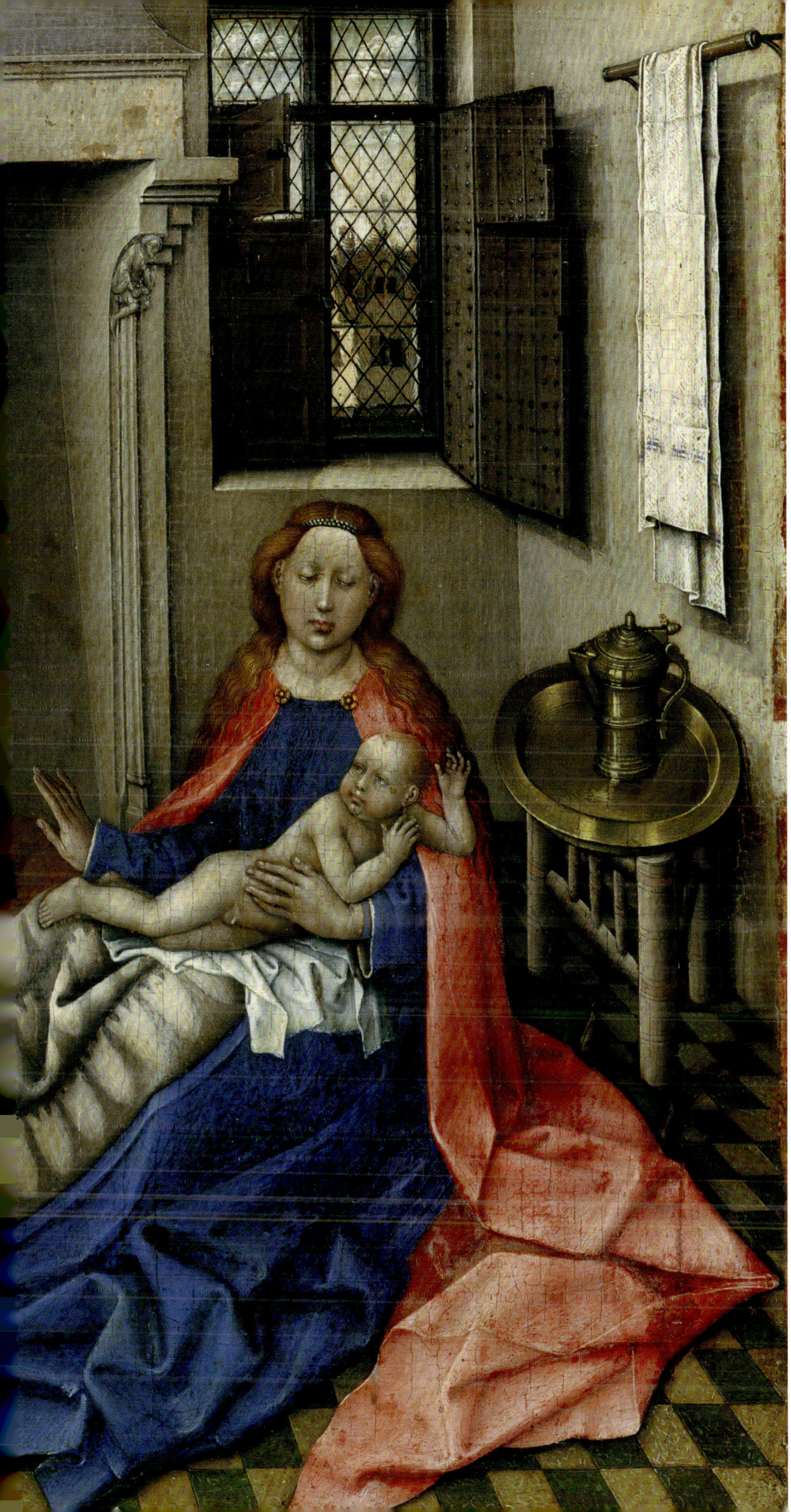

ROBERT CAMPIN. *The Holy Trinity. Virgin and Child by the Fireplace.* DIPTYCH. 1430S. OIL ON PANEL. EACH PANEL 13 1/2 × 9 5/8 IN. (34.3 × 24.5 CM).

Marked by a beautiful palette and glowing paints, this diptych was executed in the technique introduced by Campin's contemporary Jan van Eyck. A traditional approach is evident in the left-hand panel, which is arranged in the style of an icon painting: the body of Christ is in the arms of God the Father, with a dove symbolizing the Holy Spirit perched on his shoulder. The right-hand panel is less conservative: Campin depicted Mary in the guise of a Low Countries townswoman in a contemporary burgher home.

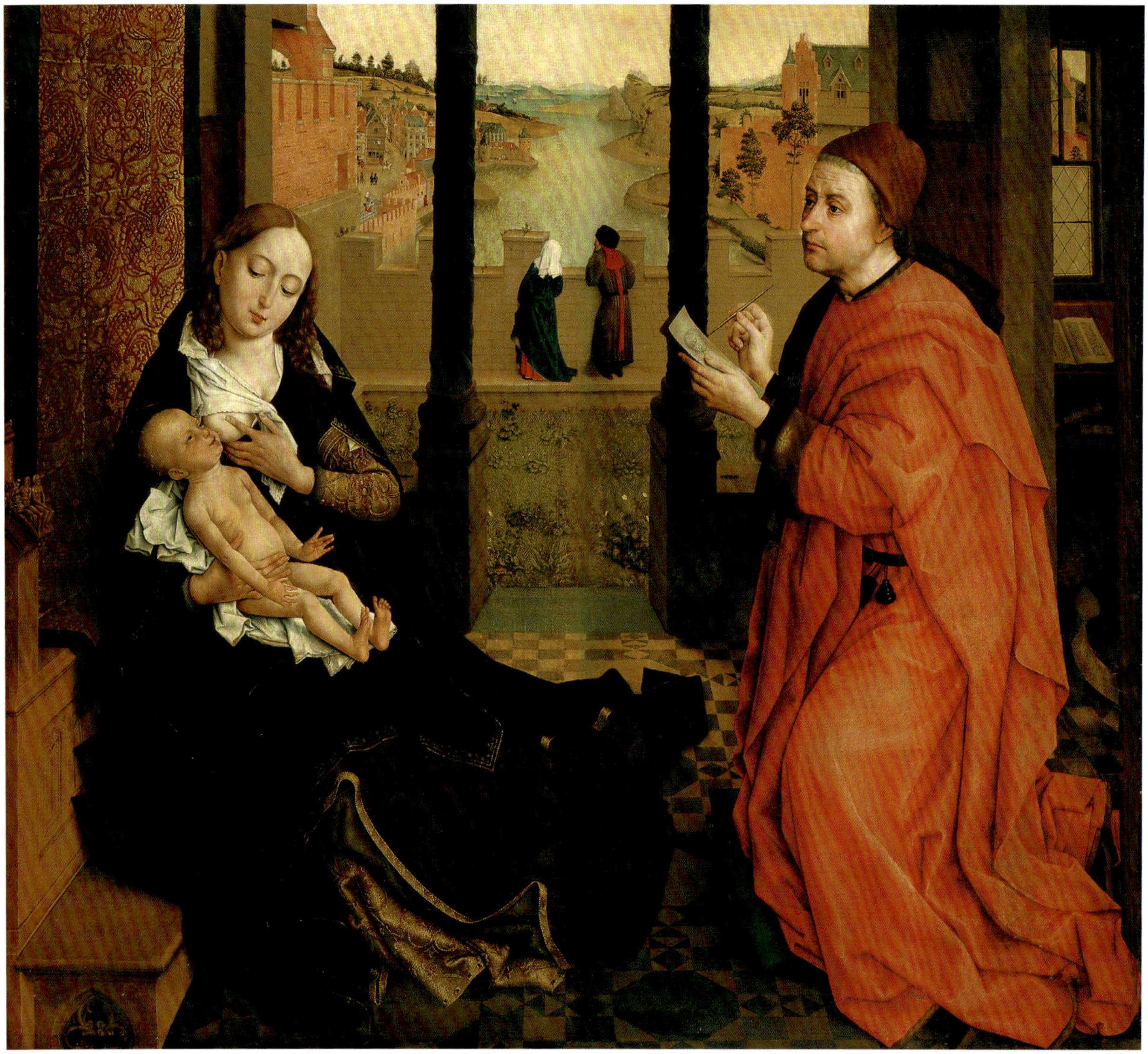

above: ROGIER VAN DER WEYDEN. *St. Luke Drawing the Virgin.* 1430S.
OIL ON CANVAS (TRANSFERRED FROM PANEL). $40\frac{3}{8} \times 42\frac{3}{4}$ IN. (102.5 × 108.5 CM).

According to legend, St. Luke painted the likeness of the Virgin Mary, who appeared to him in a vision, the subject of this work. Mary's parents are depicted in the background. The evangelist, who supposedly practiced medicine, is shown dressed like a Flemish doctor. It has been suggested that this image is a self-portrait as the way in which Luke holds the stylus resembles the technique artists used to avoid smudging drawings with the heel of the hand.

opposite: GEERTGEN TOT SINT JANS (?). *St. Bavo.* LAST THIRD OF THE 15TH CENTURY.
OIL ON CANVAS. $14\frac{3}{8} \times 11\frac{7}{8}$ IN. (36.5 × 30 CM).

Bavo, a knight and landowner who at the end of his life distributed his wealth to the poor and took monastic vows, is the patron saint of several Low Country cities, including Haarlem, where Geertgen tot Sint Jans worked. Geertgen was one of the first artists in the Netherlands to show a particular interest in landscape, and in the depths of this work's simple, unspectacular background we see a church, possibly one of the cathedrals dedicated to the saint.

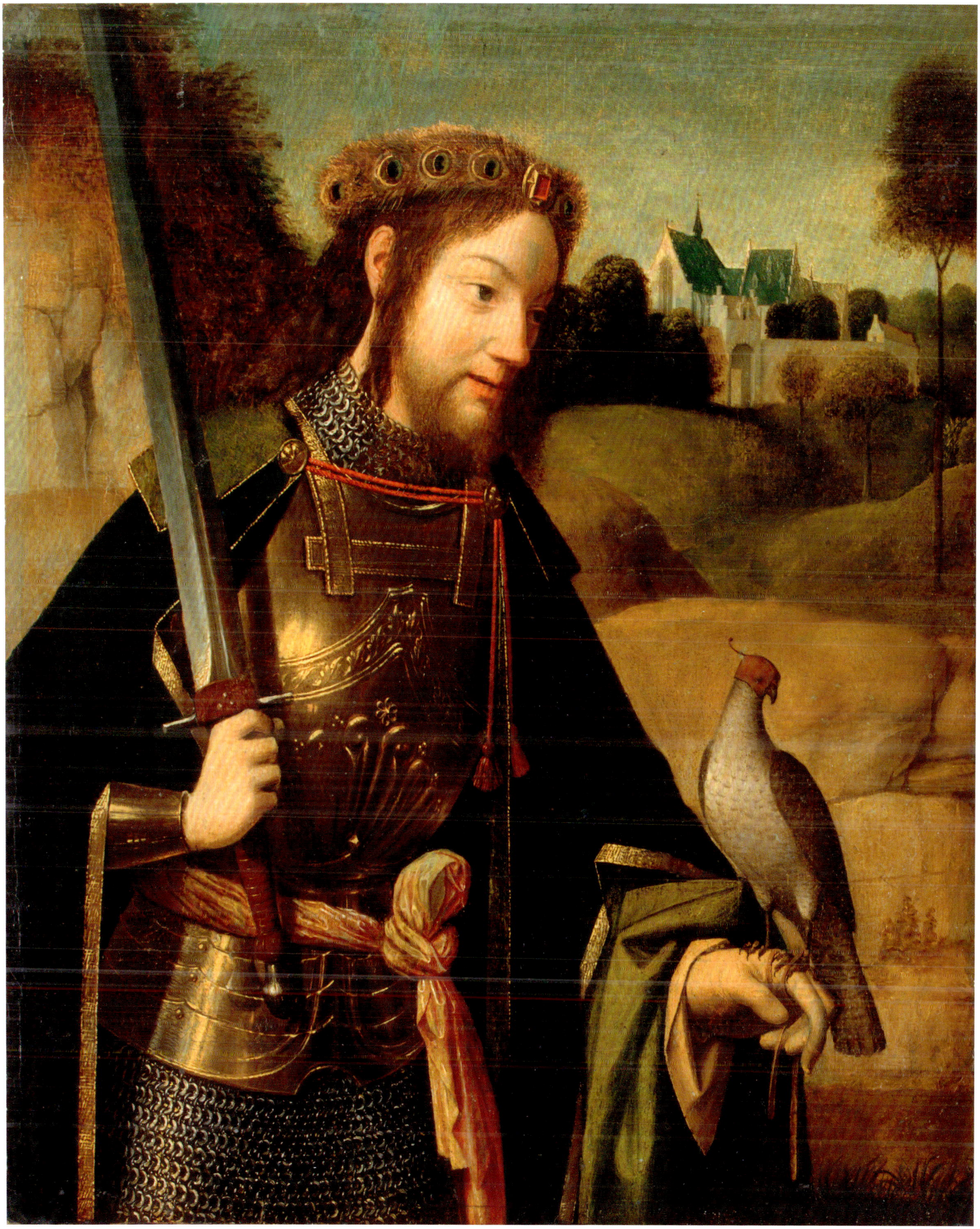

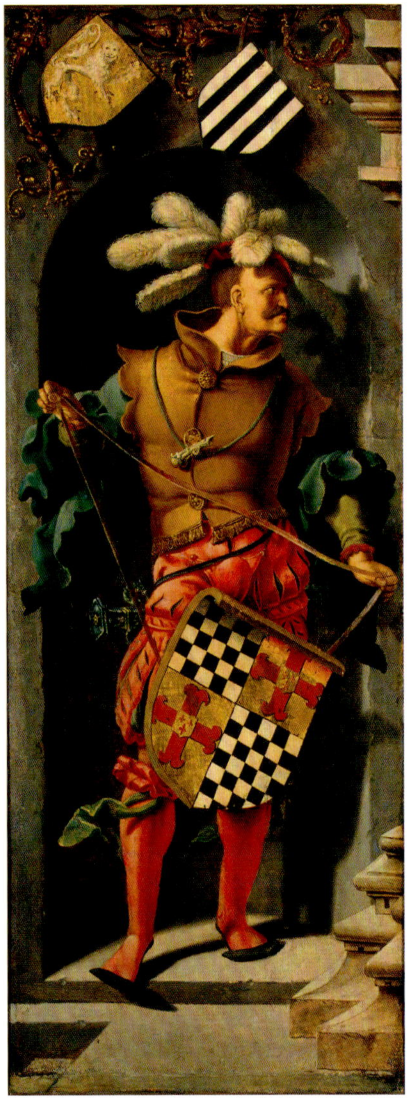

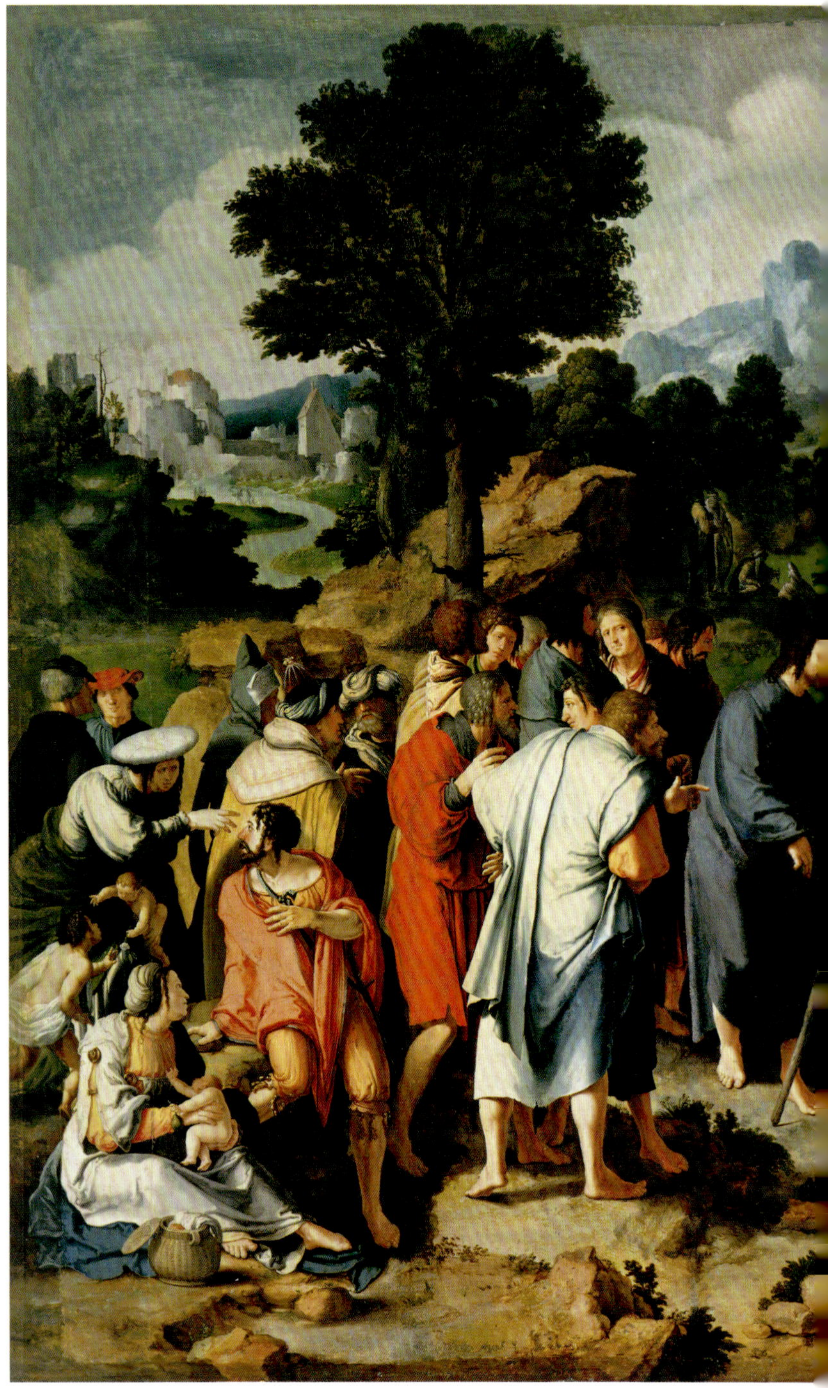

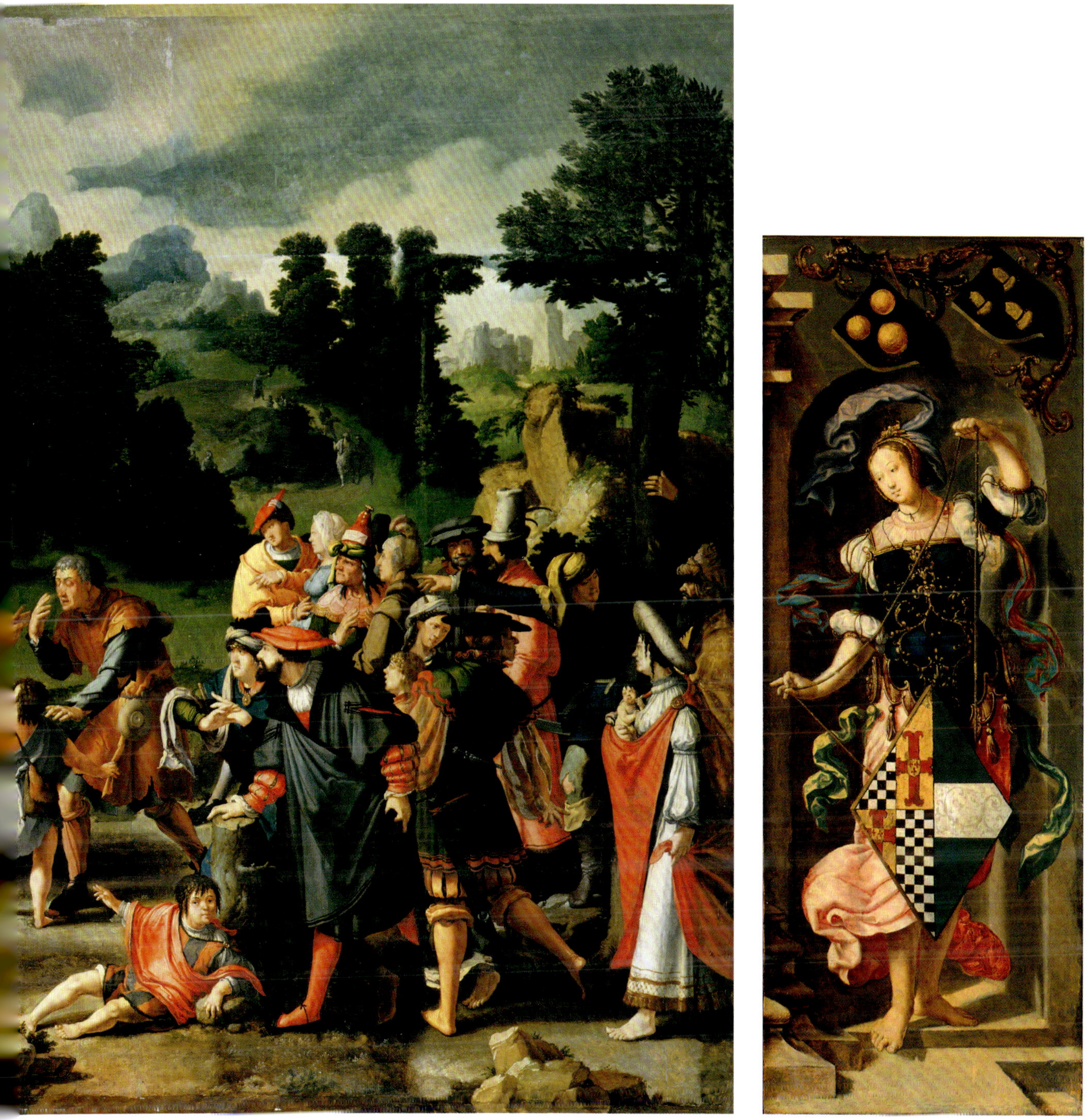

LUCAS VAN LEYDEN. *The Healing of the Blind Man of Jericho.* 1531. OIL ON CANVAS. 15 1/2 × 385 1/2 IN. (CENTRAL PANEL: 115.7 × 217.3 CM; LATERAL PANELS: 89 × 33.5 CM).

This painting was probably commissioned by the Leyden hospital. Originally a triptych that was later converted to canvas, it was opened on important occasions. Heralds demonstrating the donors' coat of arms were depicted on the outer side of the lateral wings, while the inner side, together with the central panel, was given over to the main composition: the story of Christ curing the blind man and a reminder to the sick about the spiritual healing of true believers.

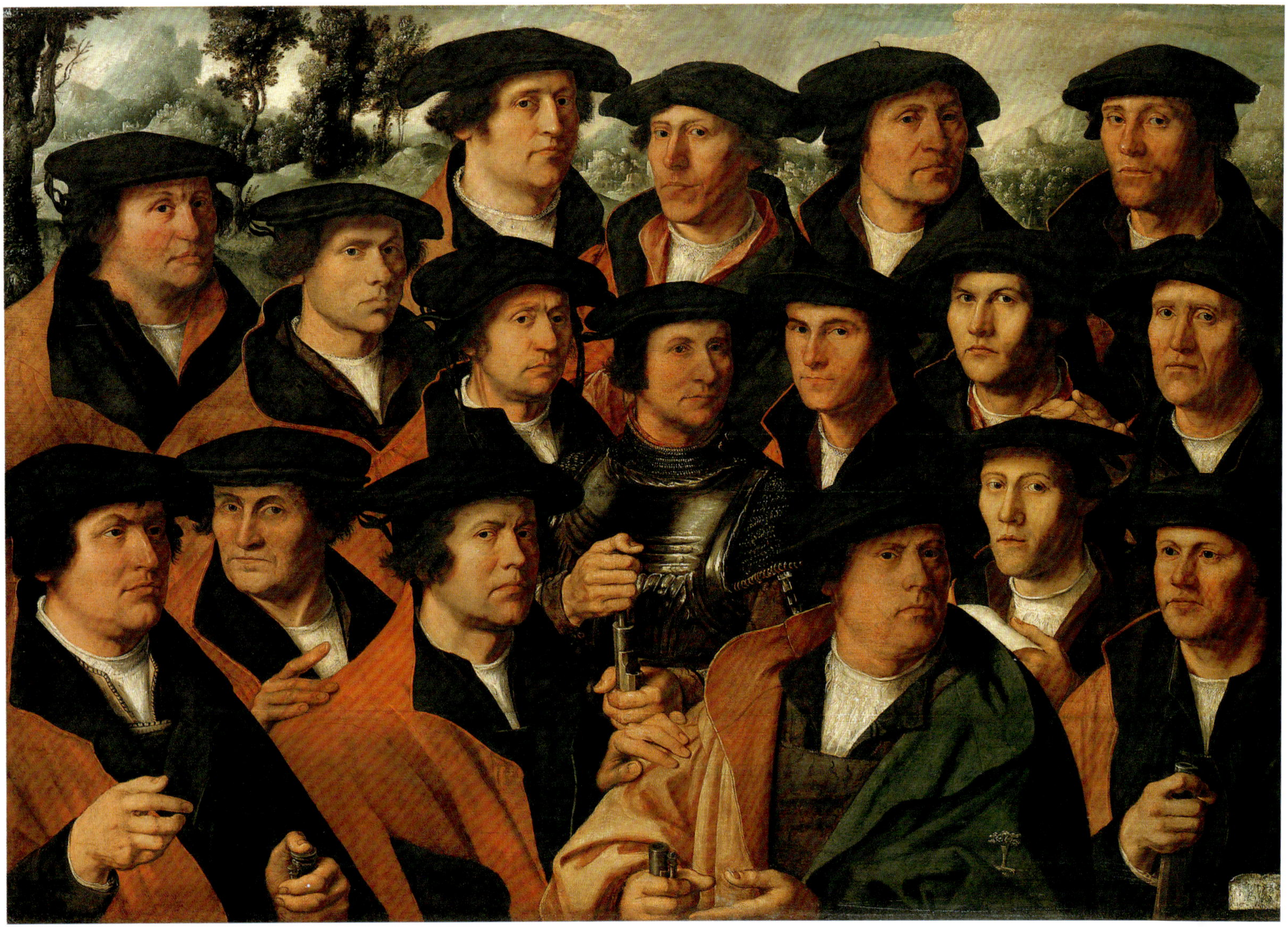

DIRK JACOBSZ. *Group Portrait of the Amsterdam Shooting Corporation.* 1532.
OIL ON CANVAS (TRANSFERRED FROM PANEL). 45 ¼ × 63 IN. (115 × 160 CM).

This painting is among the earliest group portraits created to adorn the interiors of public buildings. The likenesses of seventeen marksmen are arranged mechanically in three rows. Their membership in the corporation—a kind of volunteer militia—is indicated by the red and blue capes. The corporation's badge, an eagle's talon, appears on the cape of one of the front row figures.

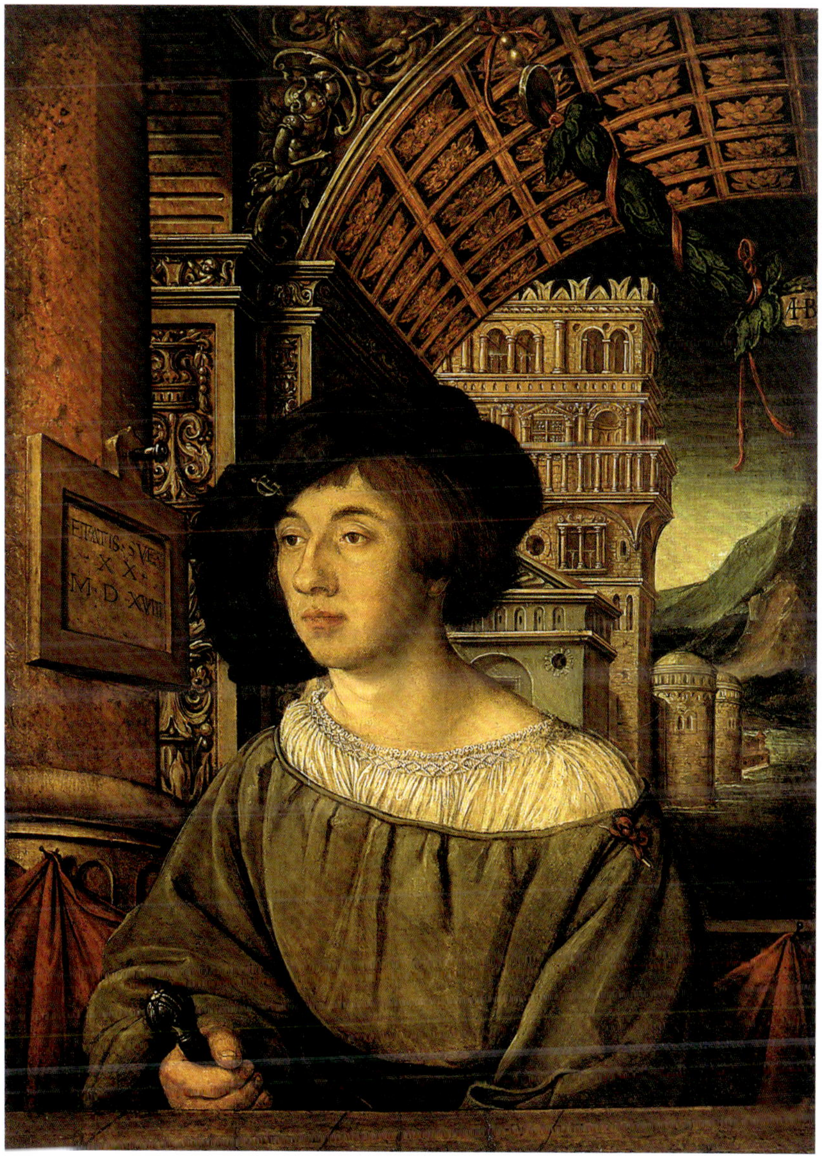

AMBROSIUS HOLBEIN. *Portrait of a Young Man.* 1518. TEMPERA AND OIL ON PANEL. $17\frac{3}{8} \times 12\frac{3}{4}$ IN. (44 × 32.5 CM).

As indicated by the Latin inscription in the cartouche that gives the date of the portrait, the subject was twenty years old. The composition, the turn of the figure, and the asymmetrical cropping of the arch give grounds for suggesting that, originally, this was a double portrait. If customary practice is a guide, the missing part of the painting may have been a depiction of the man's wife or bride to be.

right: MASTER OF THE FEMALE HALF-LENGTHS. *The Virgin and Child.* FIRST HALF OF THE 16TH CENTURY. OIL ON PANEL. 21 × 16 5/8 IN. (53.2 ×42.4 CM).

Though in Northern Europe an interest in the depiction of nature arose and was gradually developed throughout the 15th and 16th centuries, the landscapes painted by local masters were used only as backgrounds for figurative compositions. The Virgin and Christ-Child, who reaches for a platter of grapes and cherries—the symbols of Christ's human essence and the celestial fruit that he brought—do not correlate with nature, the only possible link between them the branchy tree reminiscent of the Tree of Life.

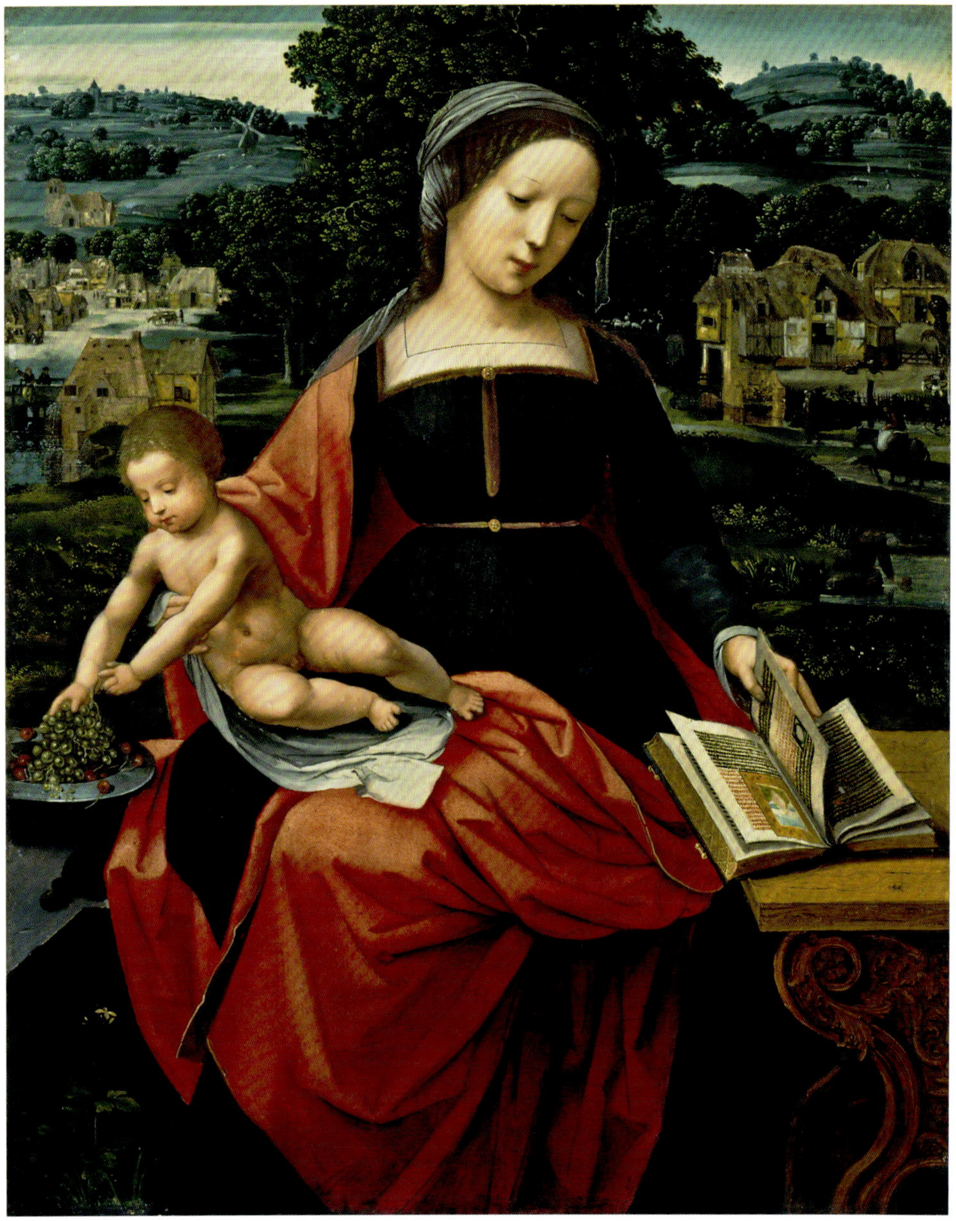

opposite: MASTER OF THE FEMALE HALF-LENGTHS. *Female Musicians.* FIRST HALF OF THE 16TH CENTURY. OIL ON PANEL. 21 ×14 3/4 IN. (53.2 × 37.5 CM).

The author of this painting acquired his "name" due to the existence of a number of similar canvases depicting female "half-lengths." Netherlandish burghers often commissioned paintings of women playing musical instruments as an allegoric representation of love. This idea is supported by the text of the aria shown: "I shall give you joy, my friend, and lead you to the place where your hope aspires; as long as I live, I shall always be with you, and even when I die, my soul will remember you."

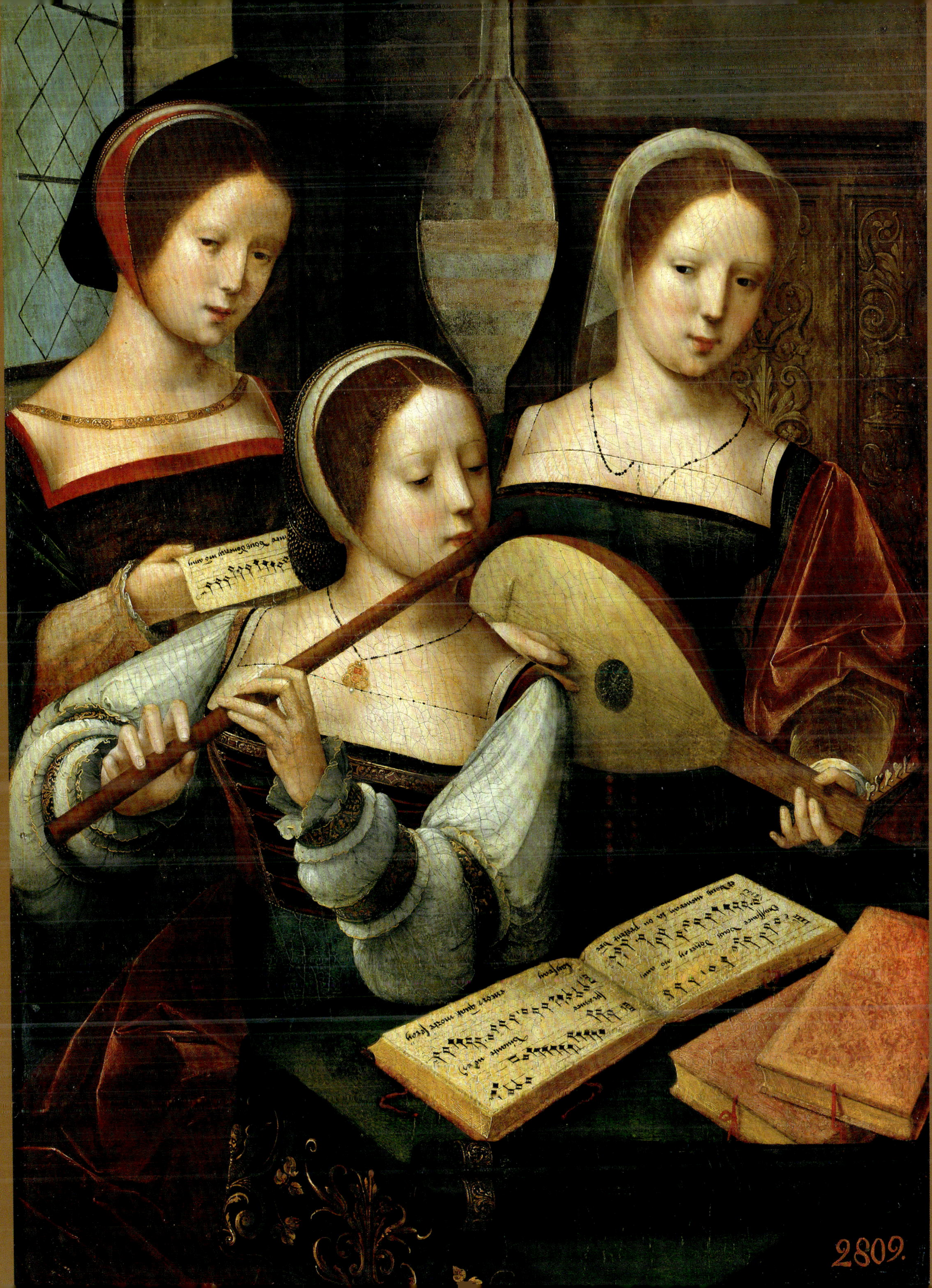
2809.

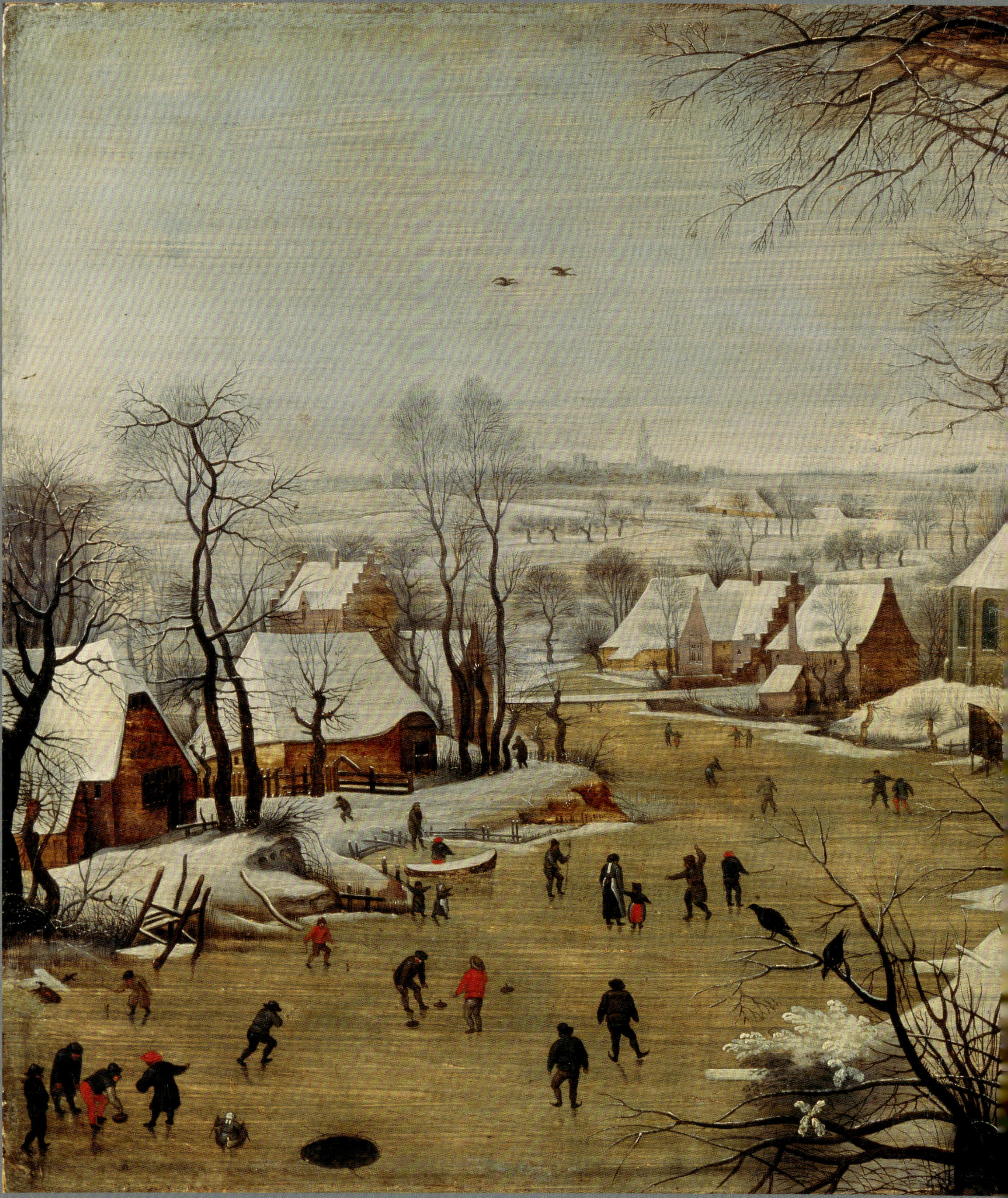

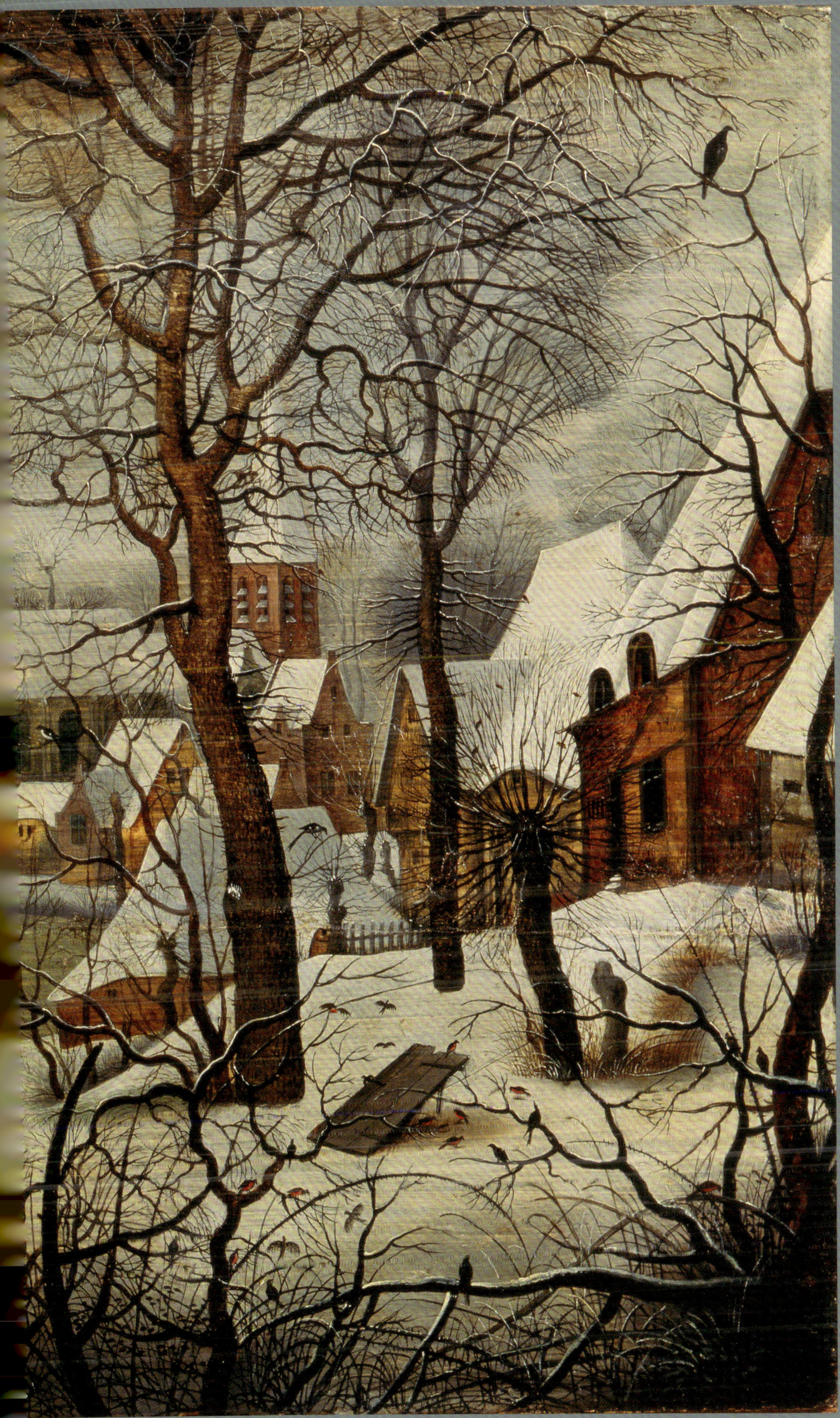

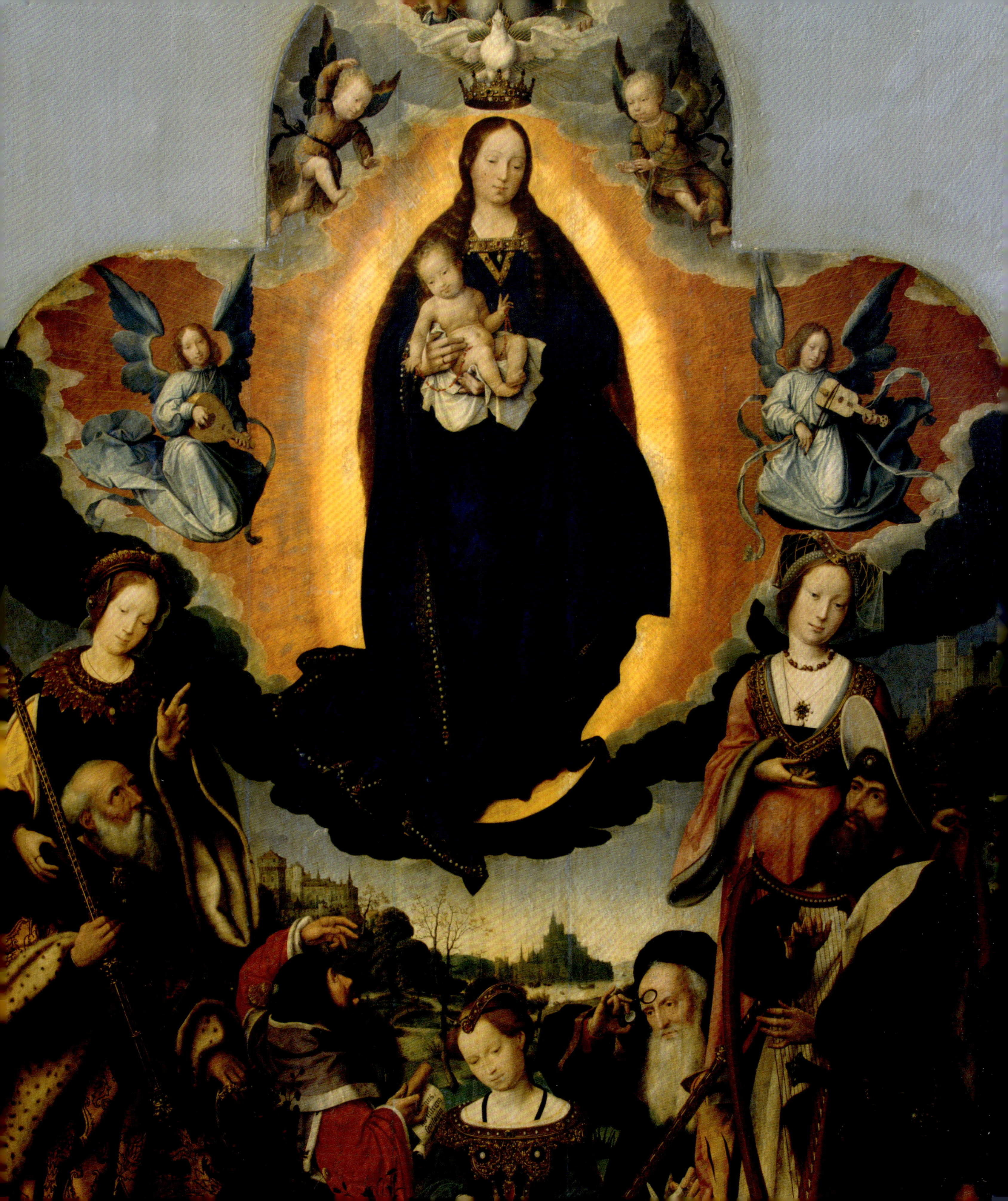

previous spread: PIETER BRUEGHEL THE YOUNGER (?). *Winter Landscape with Skaters and a Bird Snare.* BETWEEN 1615 AND 1620. OIL ON PANEL. 14⅞ × 22 IN. (37.8 × 55.7 CM).

Pieter Brueghel the Elder and his sons Pieter and Jan belong to one of the most renowned dynasties in European painting. The sons made many copies of their famous father's canvases. Though the original of this work, a landscape by Pieter Brueghel the Elder, is among the first secular paintings in the Netherlands, the biblical implications remain: skating, a popular pastime in the Netherlands, serves as a reminder of the thin barrier separating life from death.

opposite: JAN PROVOST. *The Virgin in Glory.* 1524. OIL ON CANVAS (TRANSFERRED FROM PANEL). 80 × 59½ IN. (203 × 151 CM).

This altarpiece is filled with figures and objects that form a network of biblical allusions. Glory is represented by the *mandorla*, the aureola surrounding the Mother of God, who stands on a moon and clouds that separate the earthly and heavenly worlds. Angels praise her with music echoed below by King David, the composer of psalms. Sibyls appear in the center and on the sides. The figures are conventional. Though the earthly landscape is painted in perspective, the heavens remain symbolically flat.

right: LUCAS CRANACH THE ELDER. *Venus and Cupid.* 1509. OIL ON CANVAS (TRANSFERRED FROM PANEL). 83⅞ × 40⅛ IN. (213 × 102 CM).

Among the great masters of the Northern Renaissance, Cranach blended the traditions of the Italian Renaissance and the religious morality of the Reformation. The graceful goddess of love and beauty in this work is both the embodiment of beauty and a symbol of sin. While drawing viewers' attention to the goddess's curves, Cranach warns, with an inscription at the top: "Reject Cupid's lasciviousness with all your might, or else Venus will possess your blinded soul."

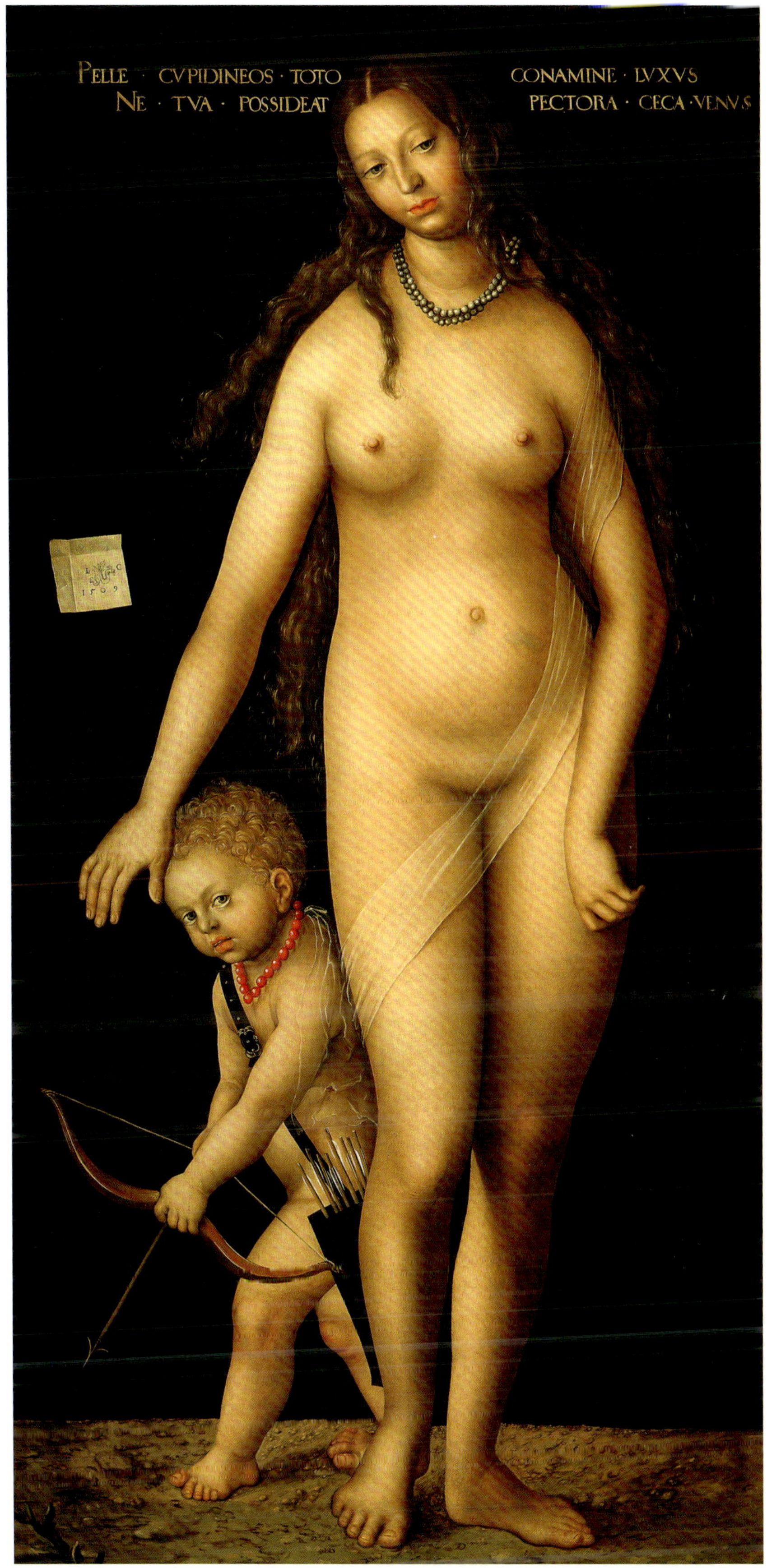

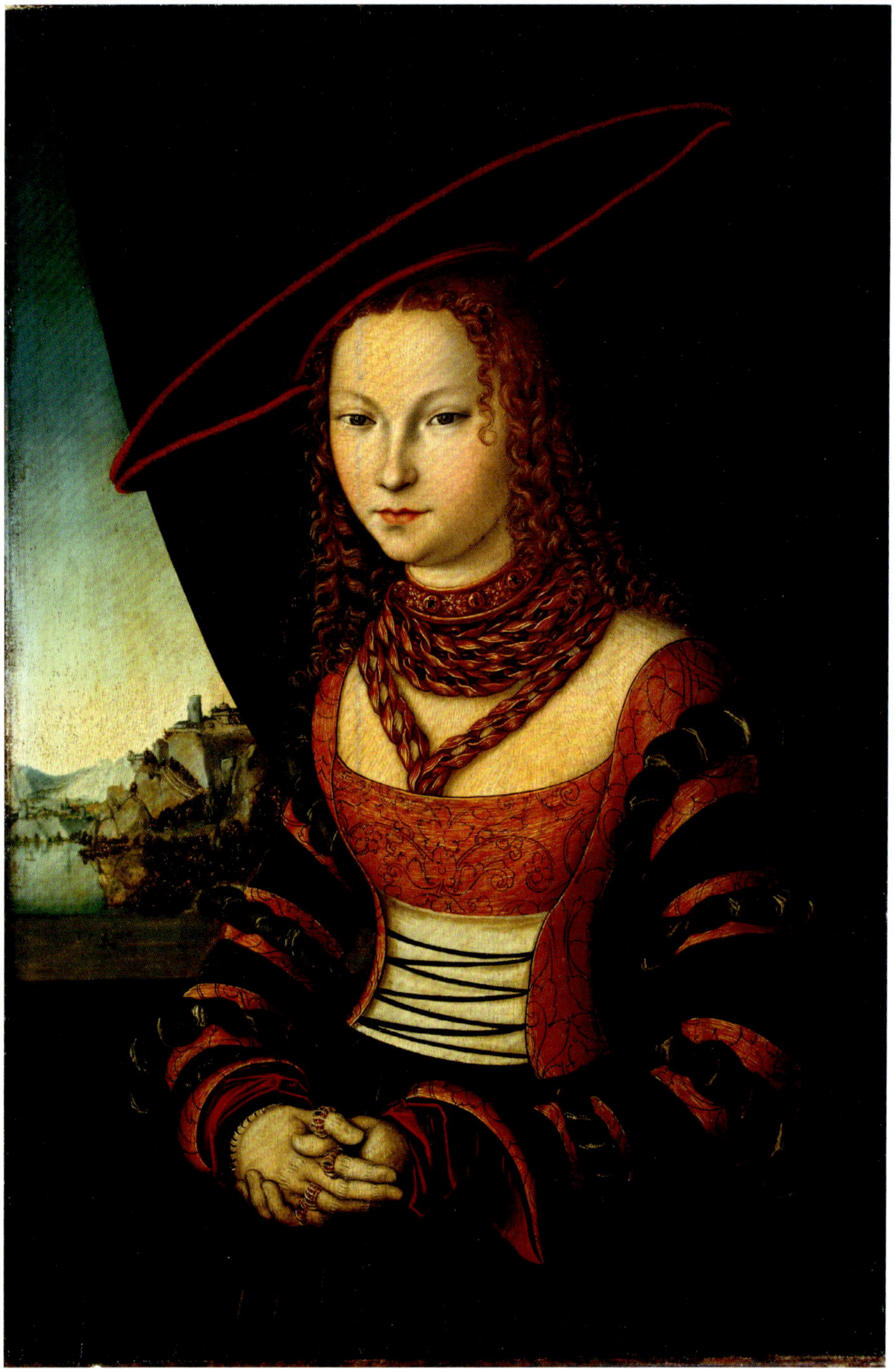

left: LUCAS CRANACH THE ELDER. *Portrait of a Woman.* 1526. OIL ON PANEL. 34⅞ × 23 IN. (88.5 × 58.5 CM).

Cranach's brushwork is devoid of tenderness and more closely resembles the effects of an engraver's burin. His color scheme is founded on simple combinations of local colors, and, although he had mastered Renaissance illusionism, he was in no hurry to abandon stiff Gothic outlines. Yet no small part of his income came from courtly scenes with nude figures and portraits of beauties such as this one, and so his devotion to a painting style that seems alien to eroticism might be regarded as calculation that paid off.

opposite: LUCAS CRANACH THE ELDER. *Virgin and Child under the Apple Tree.* CA. 1530. OIL ON CANVAS (TRANSFERRED FROM PANEL). 34¼ × 23¼ IN. (87 × 59 CM).

The symbolic content of this painting is connected with the Christian dogma of the Fall and Salvation of the human race: the Christ-Child is holding an apple and bread—symbols of original sin and its redemption. Mary is a second Eve, redeeming the sin of the first ancestress. While retaining a link with the devices of Gothic art, the painter produced what is already a Renaissance work. Sitting beneath the apple-tree, Cranach's Virgin is reminiscent of a refined society lady.

following spread: UNKNOWN SPANISH MASTER OF THE 15TH-CENTURY CASTILIAN SCHOOL (CIRCLE OF SANCHO DE ZAMORA?). *The Entombment.* TEMPERA AND OIL ON PANEL. 37 × 76⅜ IN. (94 × 194 CM).

The Gothic conventionality of this painting's composition did not hinder the artist from investing it with a keenness of feelings—religious and broader human ones. The piercingly bright stripe of blood stretching along Christ's pale body repeats and emphasizes the lifeless fracture of its lines. The color is echoed by the clothing of the mourners as well as the flowers, whose expressiveness is far from symbolic. The donor who commissioned the painting for a church is shown by the coffin.

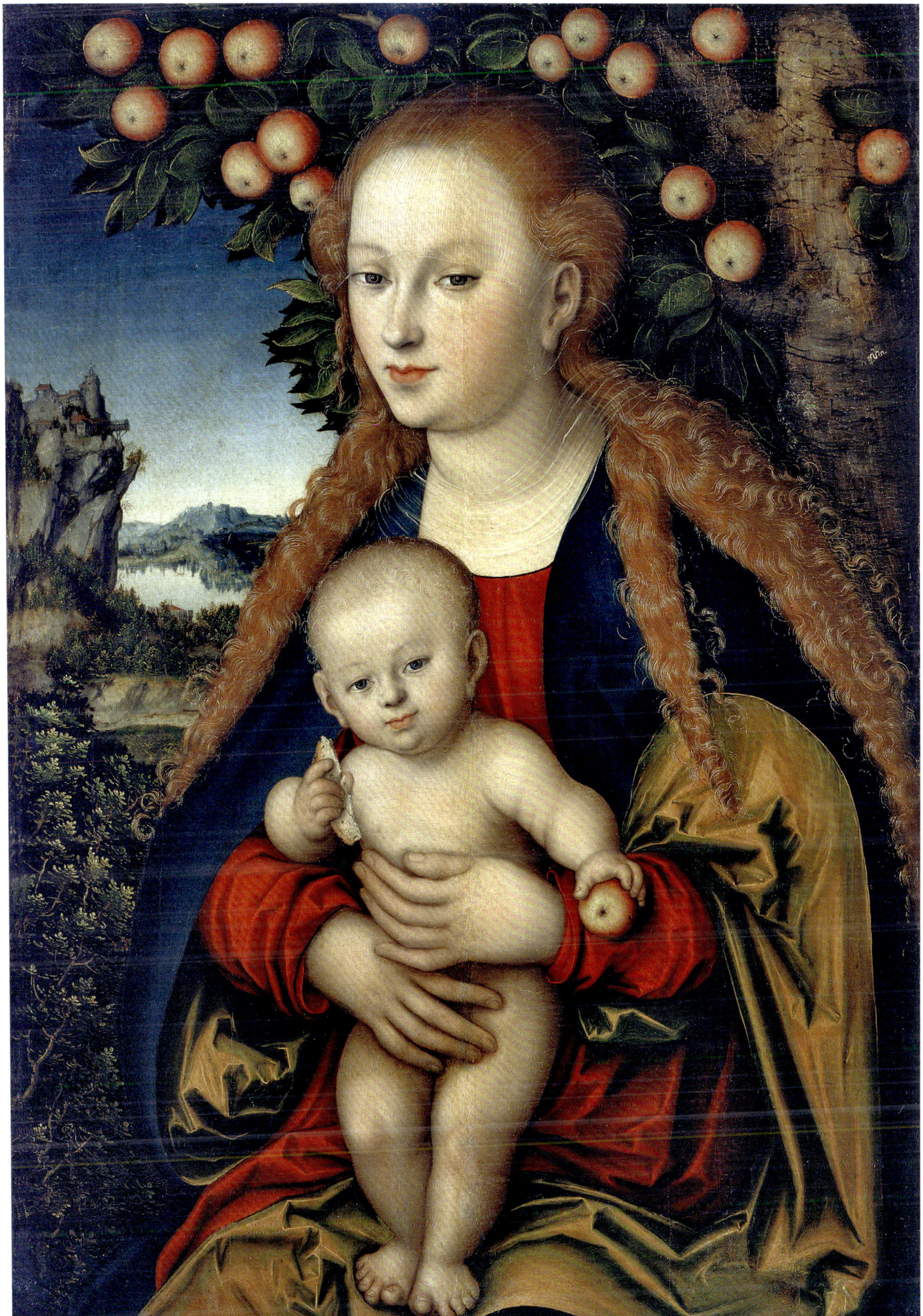

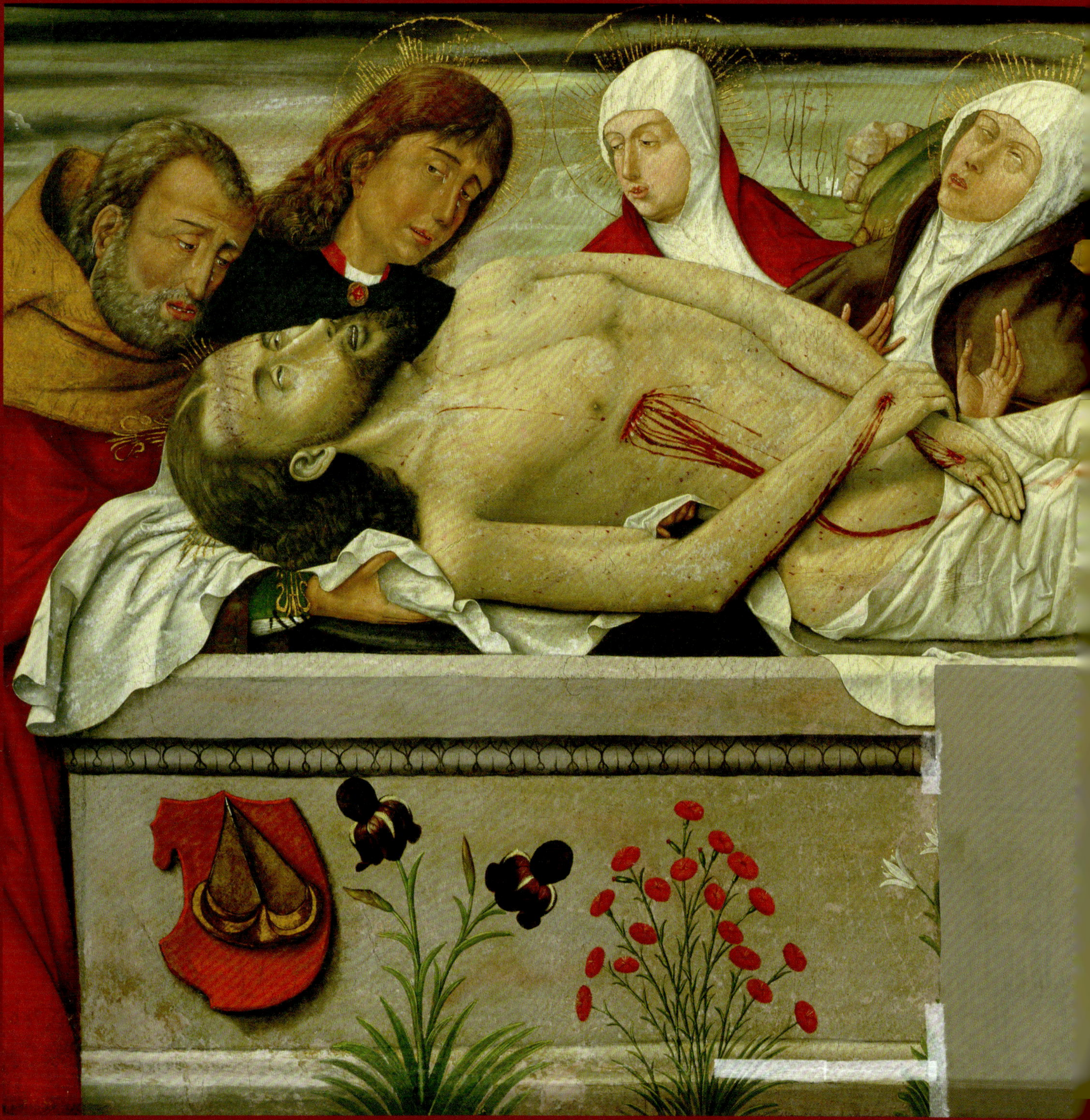

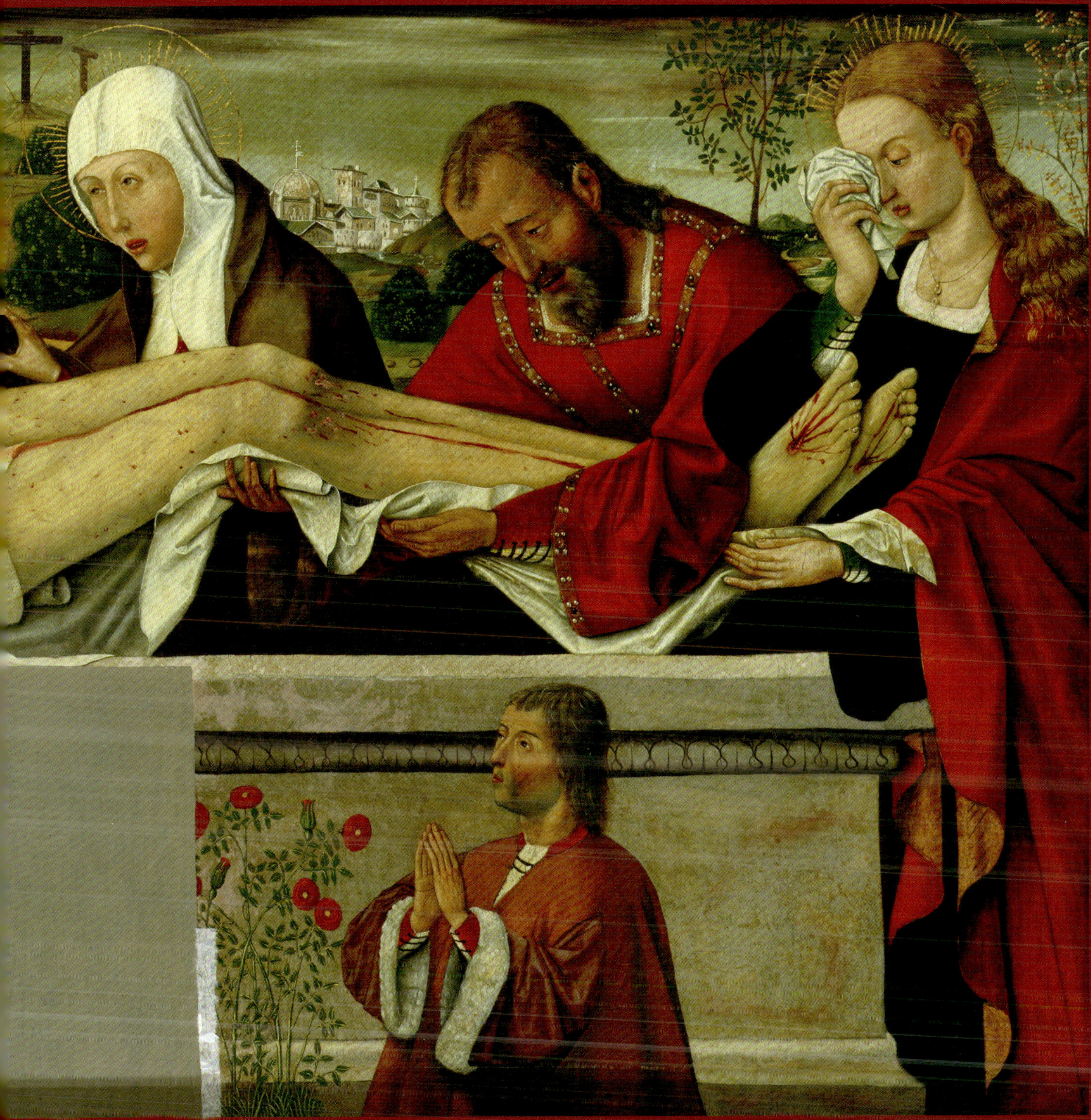

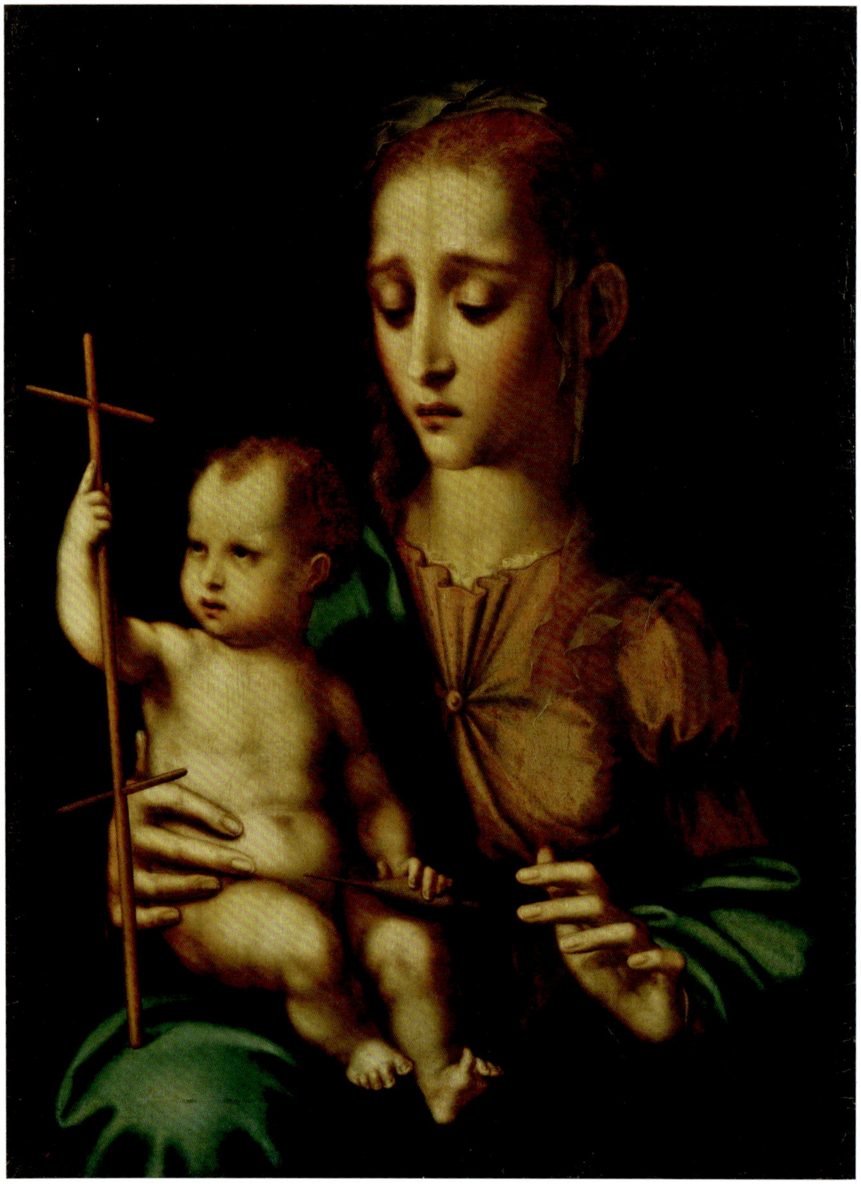

above: LUIS DE MORALES. *The Virgin and Child.* 1570s. OIL ON CANVAS (TRANSFERRED FROM PANEL). 28 1/8 × 20 1/2 IN. (71.5 × 52 CM).

Luis de Morales was nicknamed "El Divino," or "the Divine," and the central themes of his work are suffering and Christian sacrifice. In the treatment of the images, one senses the traditions of the Middle Ages, which endured in Spain. The Virgin in the Hermitage painting is an embodiment of universal sorrow and tragedy. She looks at her son with boundless spiritual pain. The spindle and distaff in the form of a cross symbolize the death that awaits the Christ-Child.

opposite: EL GRECO (DOMENICOS THEOTOCOPOULOS). *The Apostles Peter and Paul.* BETWEEN 1587 AND 1592. OIL ON CANVAS. 47 7/8 × 41 3/8 IN. (121.5 × 105 CM).

Among the first joint depictions in Spanish painting of the apostles Peter and Paul, this work depicts their dispute in Antioch, in which Paul rebuked Peter for lacking the boldness to share a communal meal with former pagans. The key theme of the painting is the clash of contradictory human characters. The contrast of the images is underlined by the composition, the color scheme, and the gestures of the pair: the humble, irresolute Peter (on the left) and the strong-willed, irreconcilable Paul (on the right).

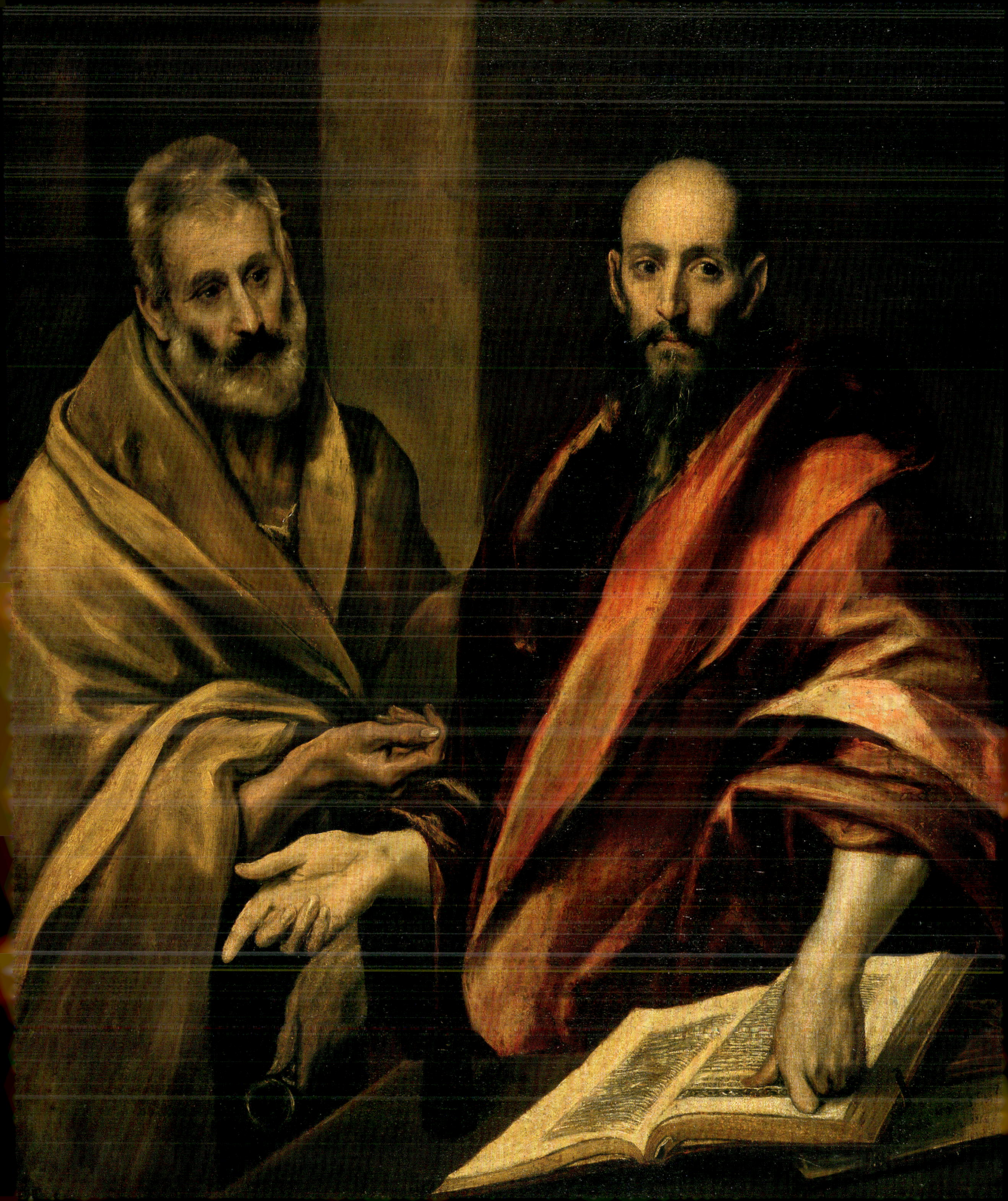

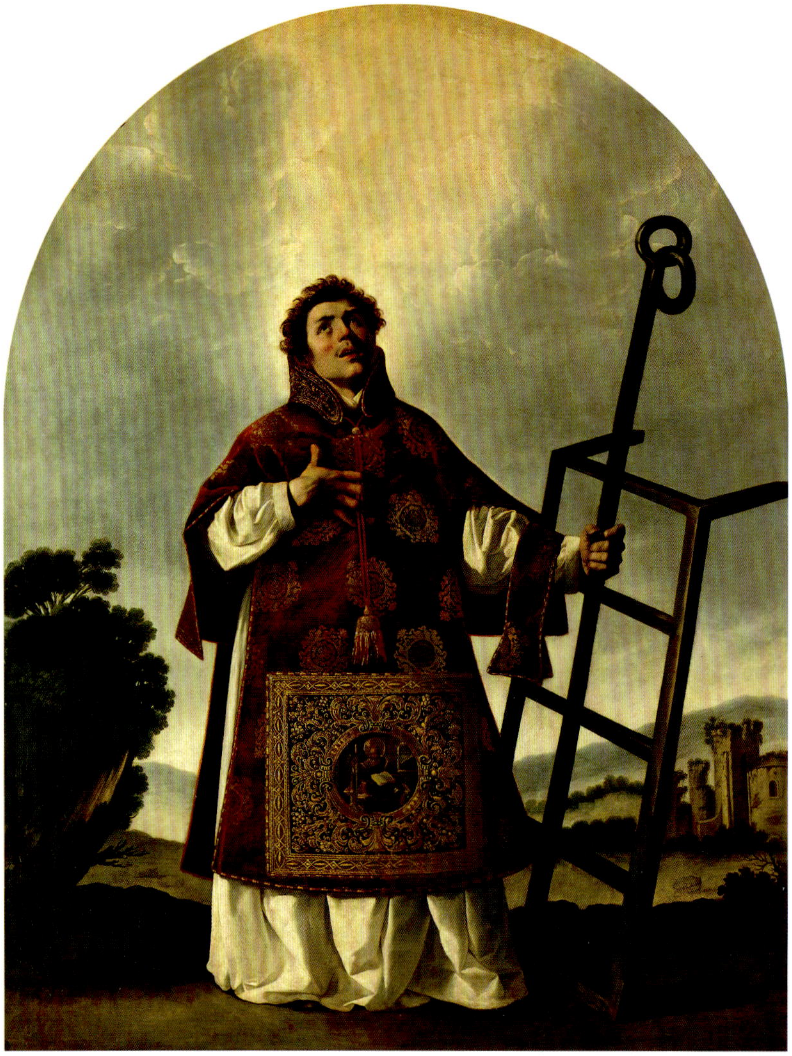

left: FRANCISCO DE ZURBARÁN. *St. Lawrence.* 1636. OIL ON CANVAS. 115 × 88 1/2 IN. (292 × 225 CM).

Unlike other geniuses of the Spanish golden age, Zurbarán appears modest, lacking their boldness of innovation and technical virtuosity. But he was more strongly connected with traditional Spanish piety, with its ardor and tendency to mysticism. Acclaimed by his contemporaries, he executed many commissions for monastery buildings. The Monastery of San José was the source of this portrait of St. Lawrence, shown in deacon's vestments with the instrument of his martyrdom, the gridiron on which he was said to have been roasted alive.

opposite: FRANCISCO DE ZURBARÁN. *The Girlhood of the Virgin.* CA. 1660. OIL ON CANVAS. 29 × 21 IN. (73.5 × 53.5 CM).

Zurbarán's exalted and naïve piety and his close affinity with popular culture expressed themselves in his amazing gift as a colorist. The pure, bright, intensive hues of his paintings, most often dictated by Christian symbolism, seem automatically combined, yet they come together in unexpected poignant harmonies. Here, the red of Mary's dress signifies love and charity; the white of the stitching purity and innocence; and the green, youth and the enclosed garden of paradise, one more symbol of immaculacy.

following spread, left: DIEGO VELÁZQUEZ. *Portrait of Don Gaspar de Guzman y Pimental, Count-Duke of Olivares.* CA. 1638. OIL ON CANVAS. 26 3/8 × 21 1/2 IN. (67 × 54.5 CM).

This prime minister of Philip IV began his career with a dizzying rise and ended it with a no-less-vertiginous fall, spending his last years in exile. When his star was ascending, he introduced the young Velázquez to the king, and the artist painted his powerful patron several times. In this portrait, made shortly before Olivares suffered a series of defeats in both his foreign policy projects and court intrigues, his face clearly betrays fatigue and disillusionment.

following spread, right: JUAN PANTOJA DE LA CRUZ. *Portrait of Diego de Villamayor.* 1605. OIL ON CANVAS. 35 × 28 IN. (89 × 71 CM).

Pantoja de la Cruz worked at the courts of Phillip II and Phillip III, where he produced many formal depictions of Spanish grandees, in which he combined outward splendor with a truthful presentation of the appearance and character of the model. In keeping with early 17th-century tradition, the subject of this work is shown in knightly armor. Though it invests him with significance and grandeur, the youth decked out in iron and lace bears little resemblance to a warrior.

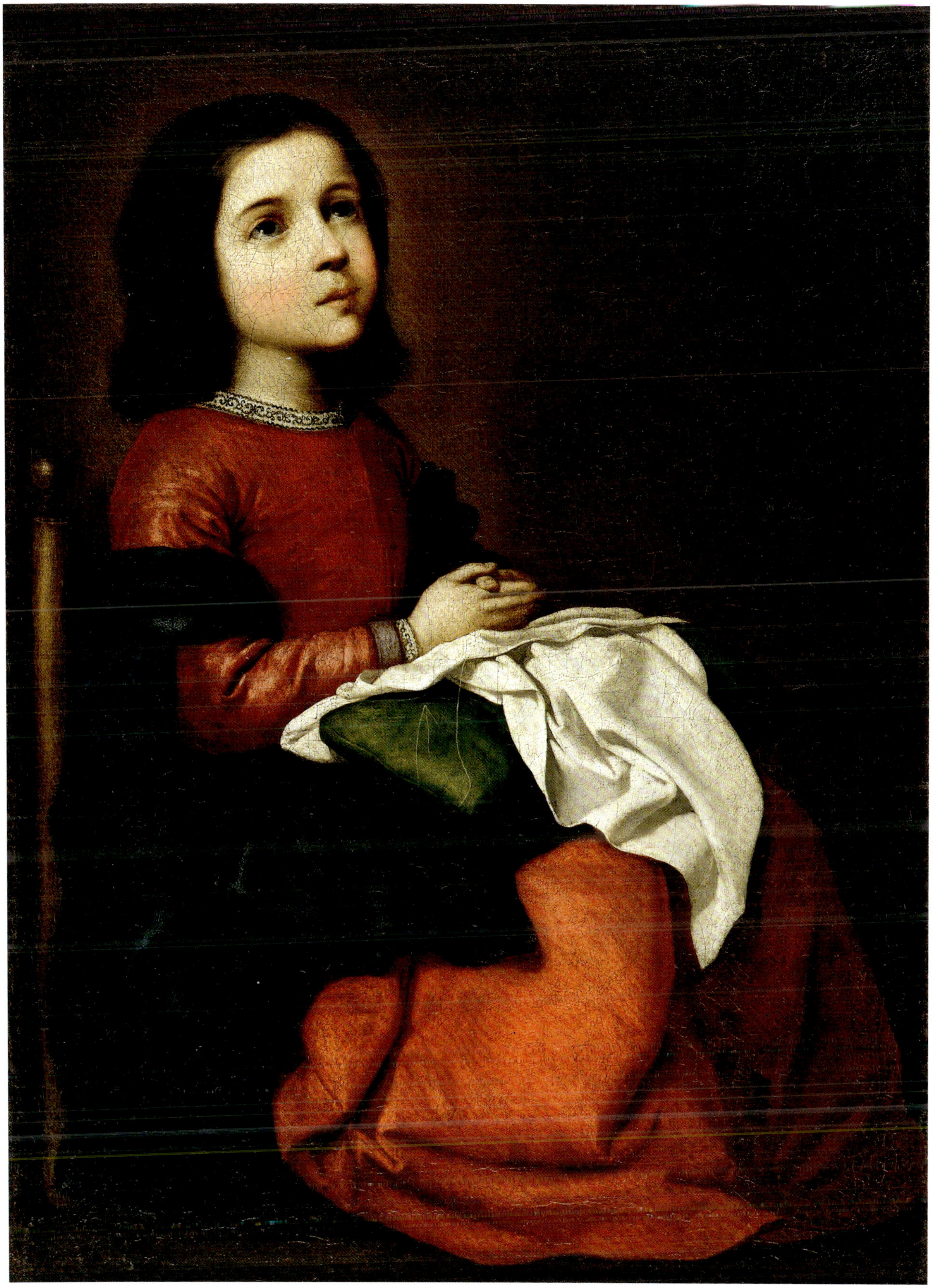

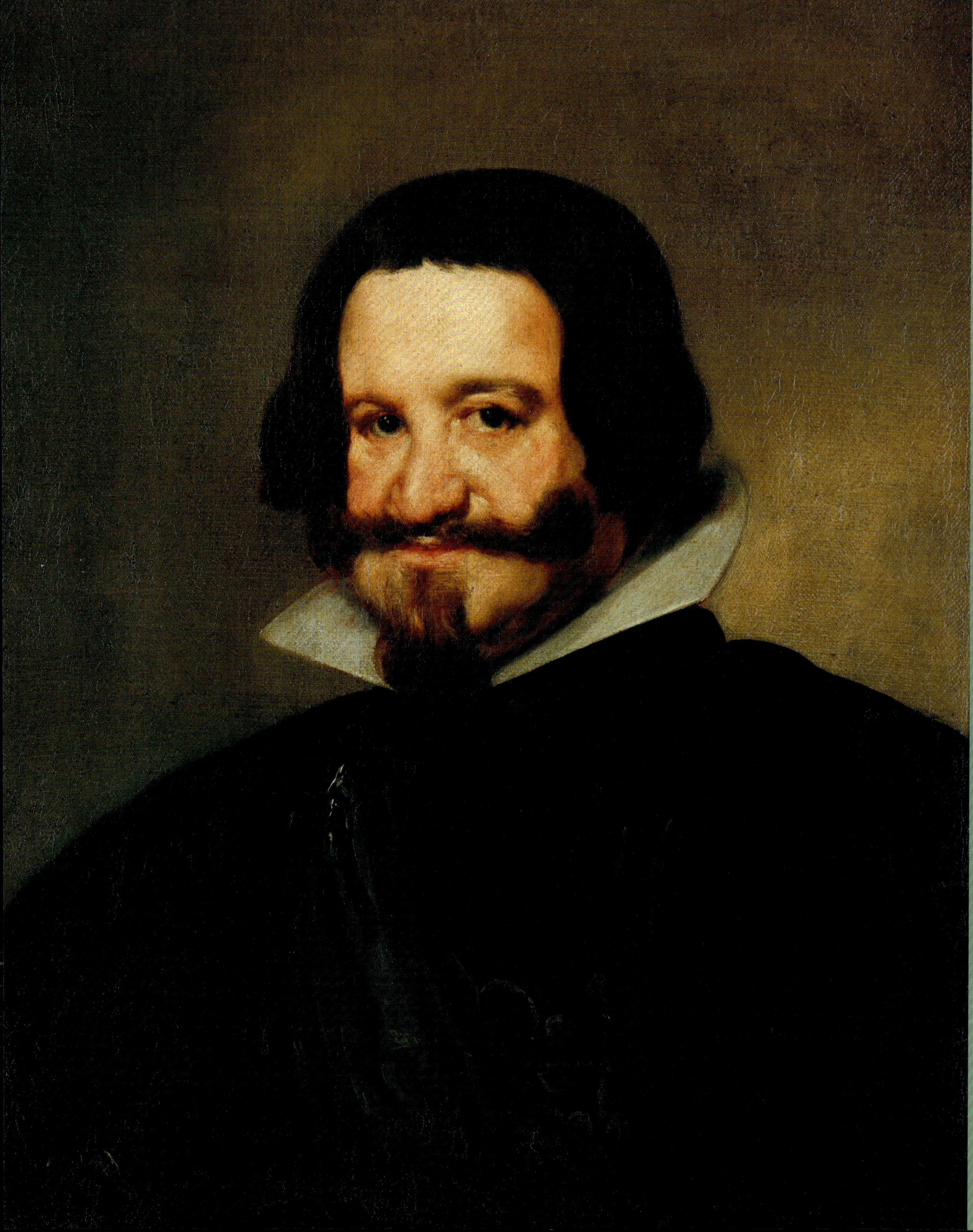

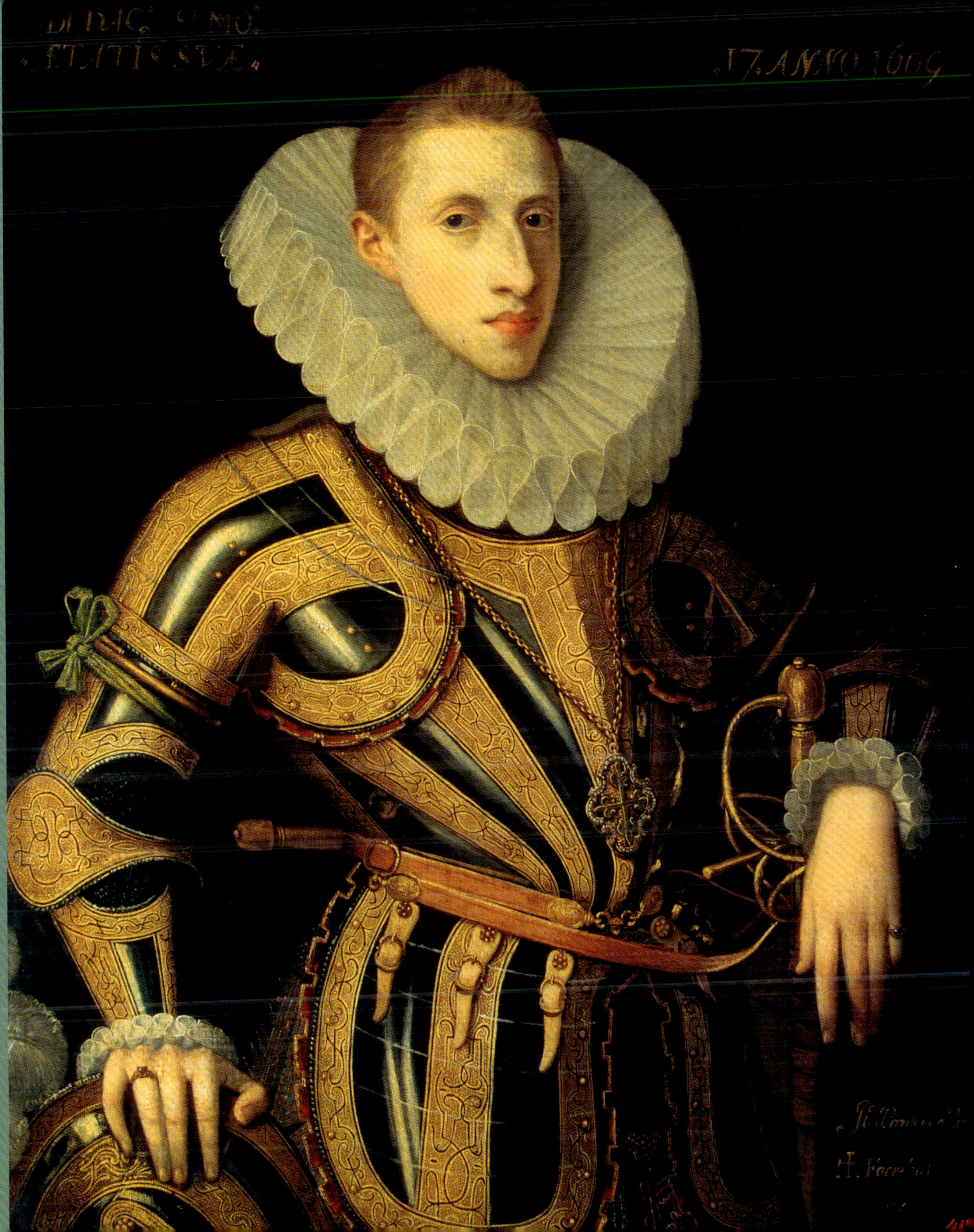
ÆTATIS SVÆ
17 ANNO 1609

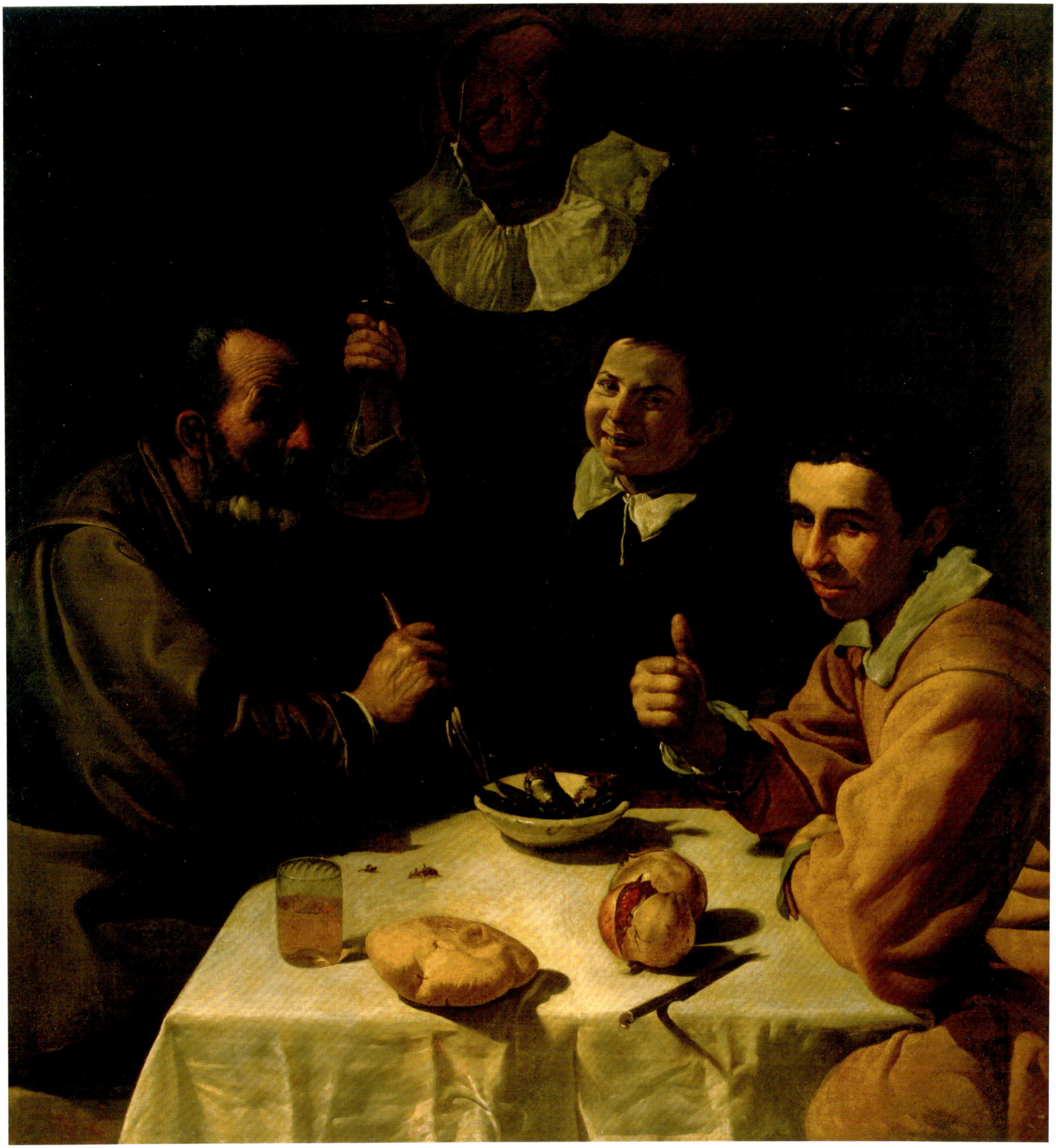

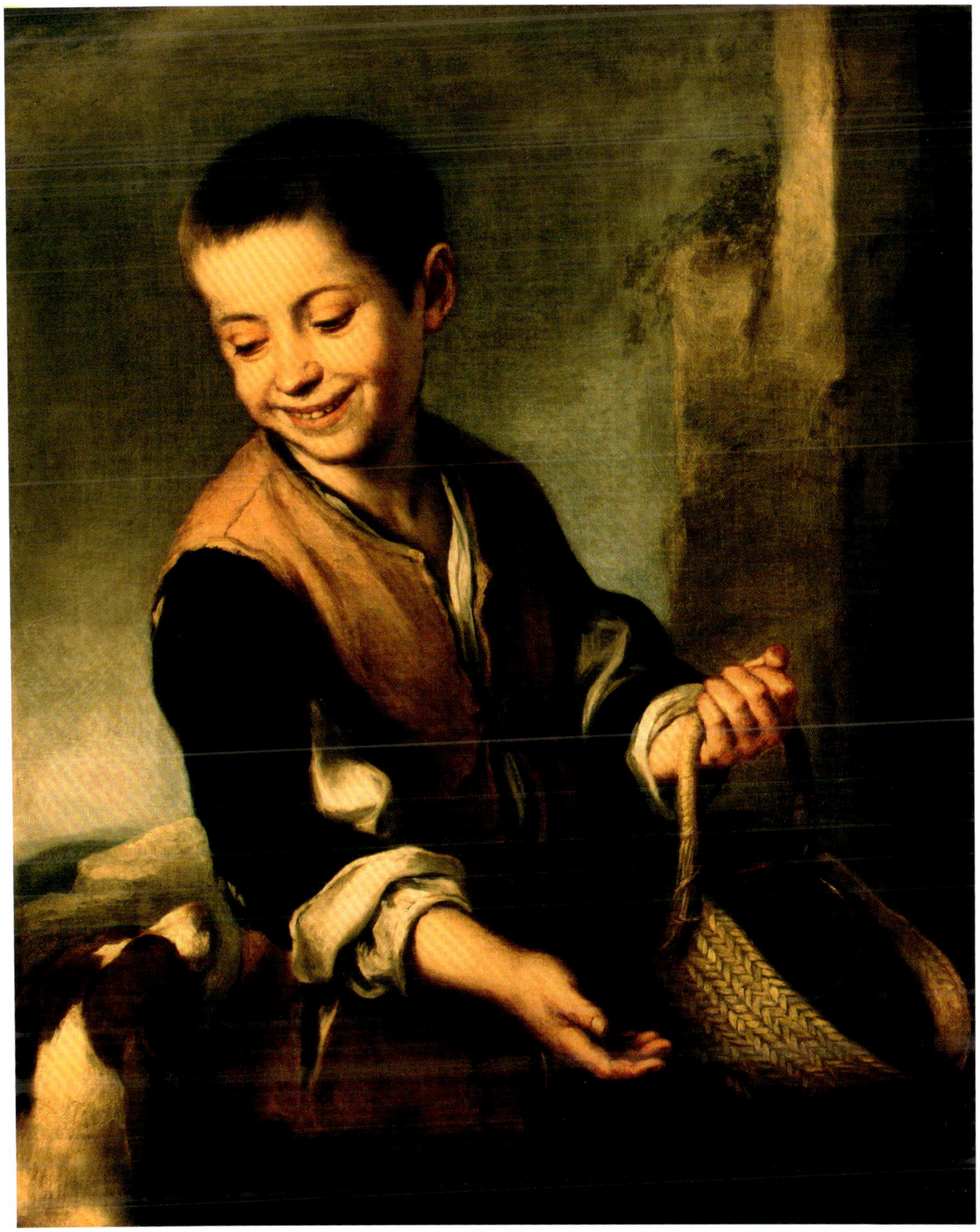

left: BARTOLOMÉ ESTEBAN MURILLO. *Boy with a Dog*. BETWEEN 1655 AND 1660. OIL ON CANVAS. 27½ × 23⅝ IN. (70 × 60 CM).

Bartolomé Esteban Murillo, the last major Spanish painter of the 17th century, enjoyed great fame in his own lifetime. Murillo's paintings were in such demand that the king issued a decree banning their removal from the country. *Boy with a Dog* is one of Murillo's finest genre compositions. The image of a street urchin delighted by a dog is enchanting in its sincerity. The companion piece—*Girl with Fruit*—is on display in the Pushkin Museum of Fine Arts.

opposite: DIEGO VELÁZQUEZ. *Breakfast*. CA. 1617. OIL ON CANVAS. 42¾ × 40⅛ IN. (108.5 × 102 CM).

Fascinated with the depiction of genre scenes, or bodegones, Velázquez produced lively, expressive images of people engaged in their everyday affairs. Seeking as realistic a depiction as possible, the artist employed the device of contrasting lighting, in which the influence of Caravaggio is unarguably present. This painting has an allegorical subtext. Depicted are the three ages, the three aspects of human life. The personages are united by a morning meal consisting of fish, pomegranate, bread, and wine—symbols of Christ.

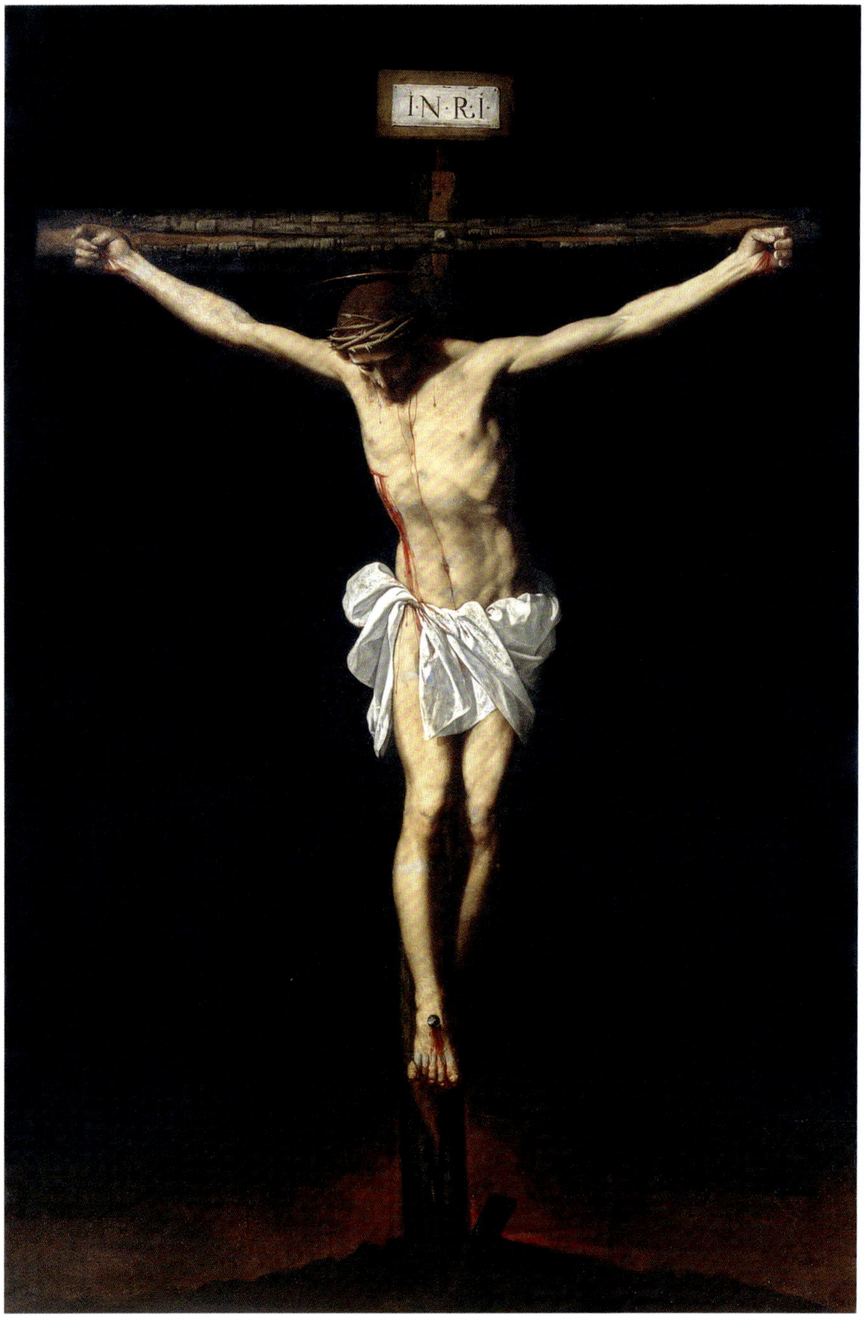

left: ALONSO CANO. *The Crucifixion.* CA. 1636–38, OIL ON CANVAS. 104 3/8 × 68 1/8 IN. (265 ×173 CM).

Especially common in Spain, compositionally pared-down Crucifixion scenes, which differ from the theatrical scenes of the Middle Ages and Renaissance with their abundance of action and detail, were frequently commissioned after the Council of Trent (1545–63), whose resolutions were aimed at strengthening Catholic morality and faith. This large altarpiece, apparently painted for a Dominican monastery, is intended to be viewed from below and to encourage prayerful concentration.

opposite: BARTOLOMÉ ESTEBAN MURILLO. *The ("Walpole") Immaculate Conception.* 1680. OIL ON CANVAS. 76 3/4 × 57 IN. (195 ×145 CM)

The subject of the Immaculate Conception was extremely popular in Spain at the onset of the Reformation and many Spanish artists turned to it in their works, including Murillo, who painted more than a dozen canvases based on the words from the Apocalypse describing it. The name of Walpole preserved in the title of the painting means that the canvas originally had been part of Robert Walpole's collection, which was later bought by Catherine II.

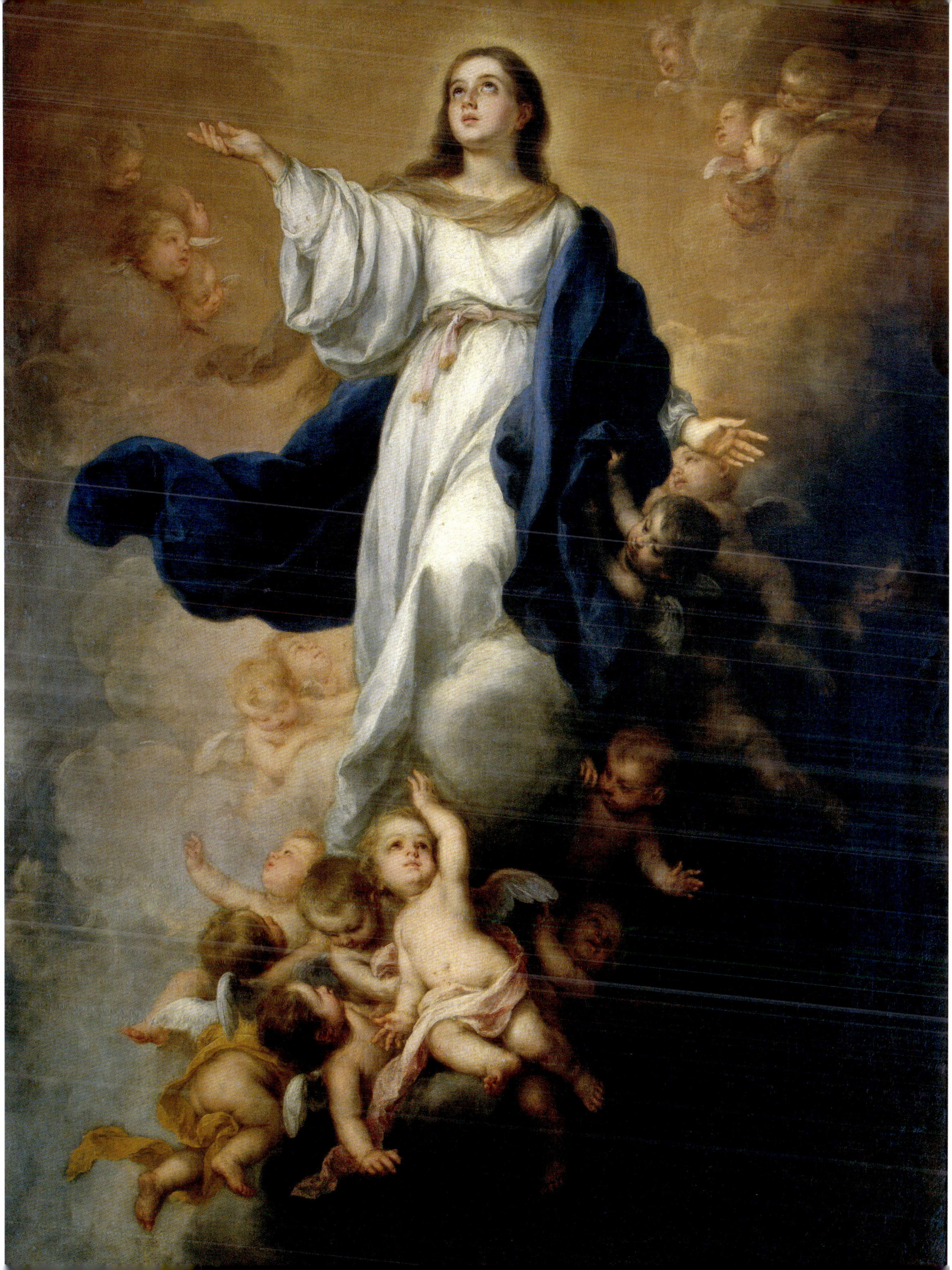

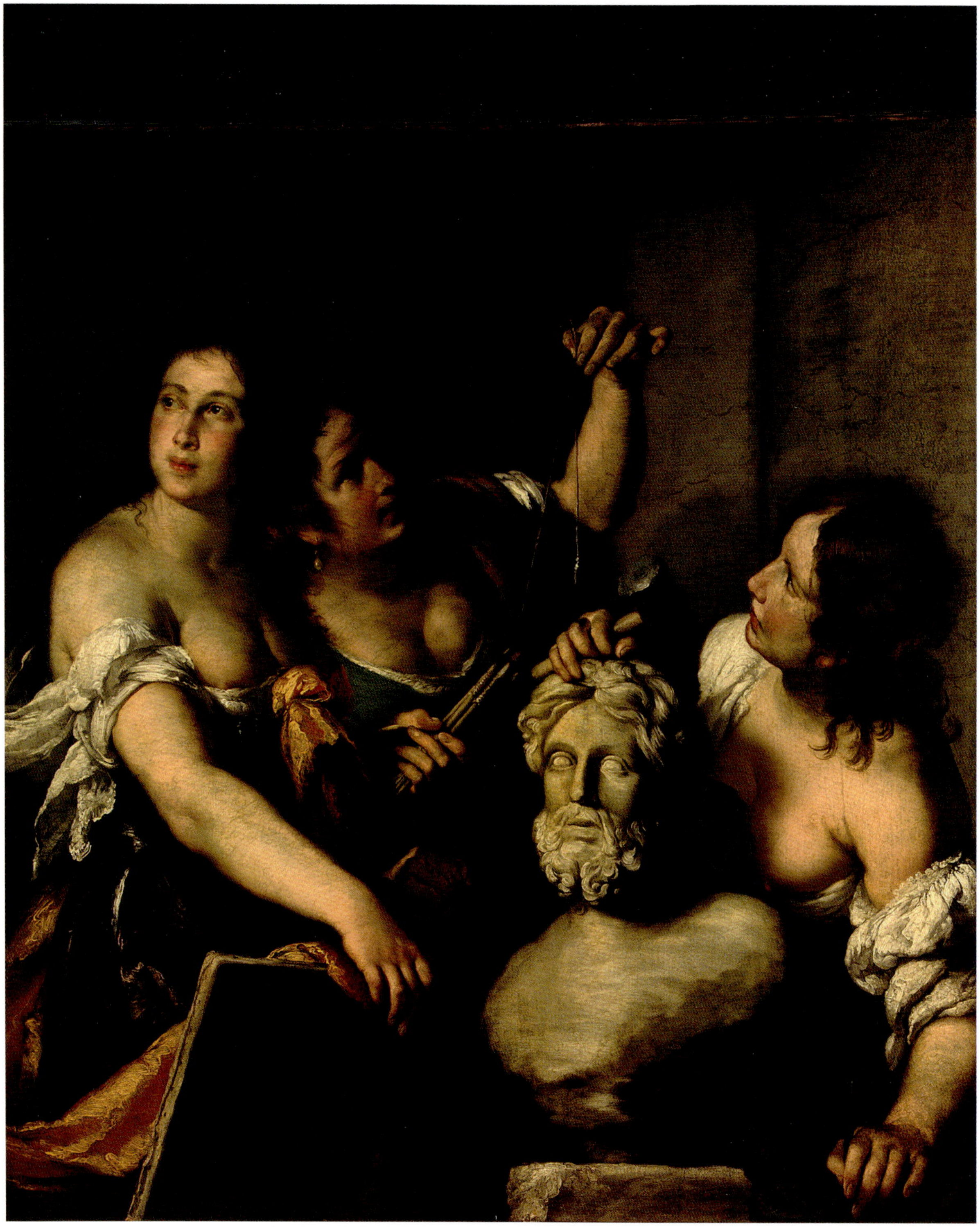

opposite: BERNARDO STROZZI. *Allegory of the Arts.* CA. 1640. OIL ON CANVAS. 60 × 55 IN. (152 × 140 CM).

In his treatise *Ars Poetica*, Roman poet Horace points out the similarity of poetry and painting, asserting the right of poets to let loose their imaginations in the way done by their artist contemporaries. For the painters of Italian Renaissance his words "*ut pictura poesis*" (as is painting so is poetry) became a motto in their struggle for professional prestige. Strozzi, in this allegory, shows Painting, Architecture, and Sculpture, declaring their equal rights by placing the figures around the bust of Homer.

below: BERNARDO STROZZI. *The Healing of Tobit.* CA. 1635. OIL ON CANVAS. 62¼ × 88 IN. (158 × 223.5 CM).

Gathered around Tobit are his wife, Anna; their son Tobias; the dog that accompanied Tobias and the angel on their dangerous journey; and the fish that nearly killed Tobias before he caught it and used its organs to make a medicine to restore his father's eyesight. For Strozzi, color is the main means of expression, so bright and rich compared to his other paintings that it seems an eloquent metaphor for the end to the old man's blindness.

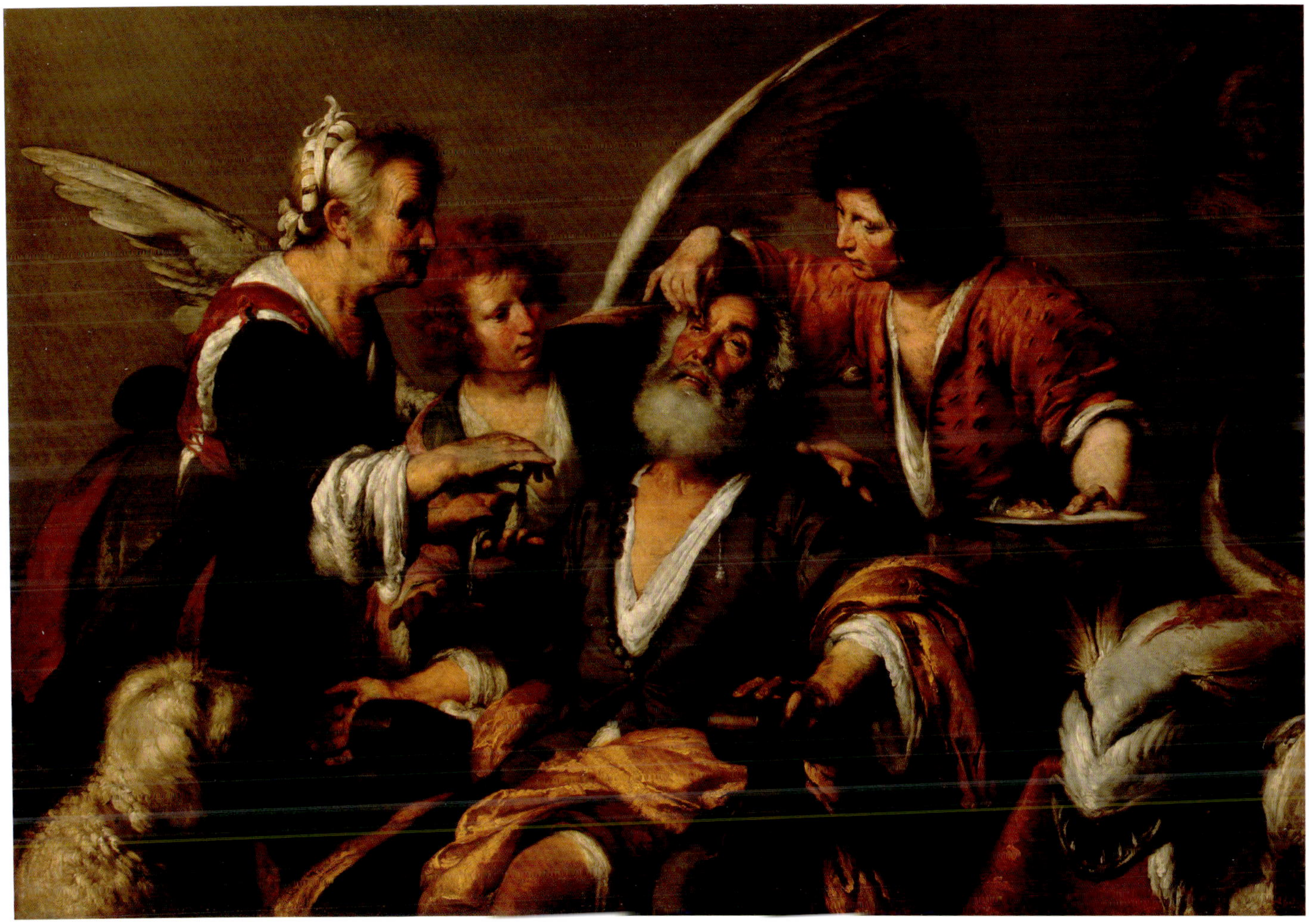

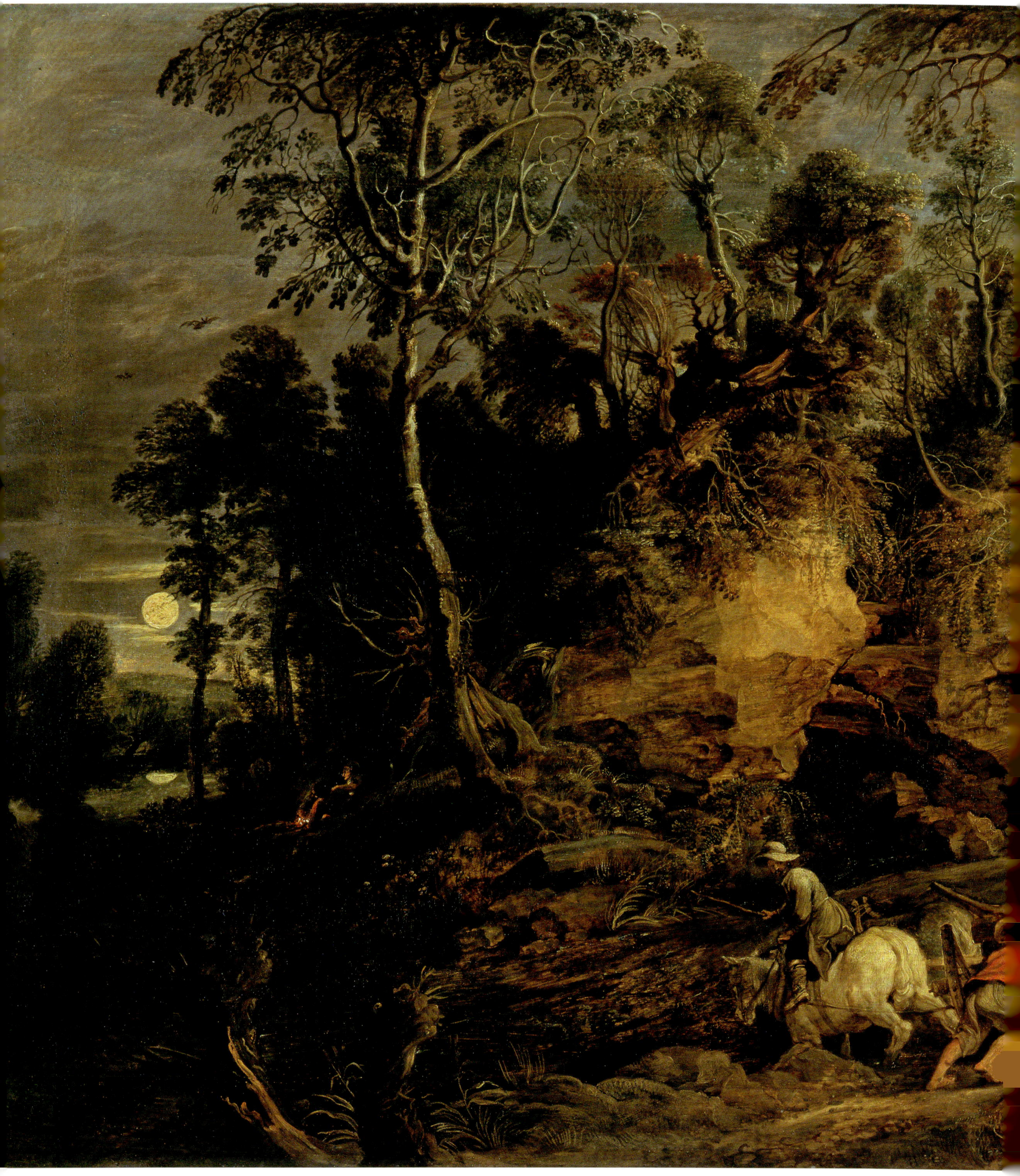

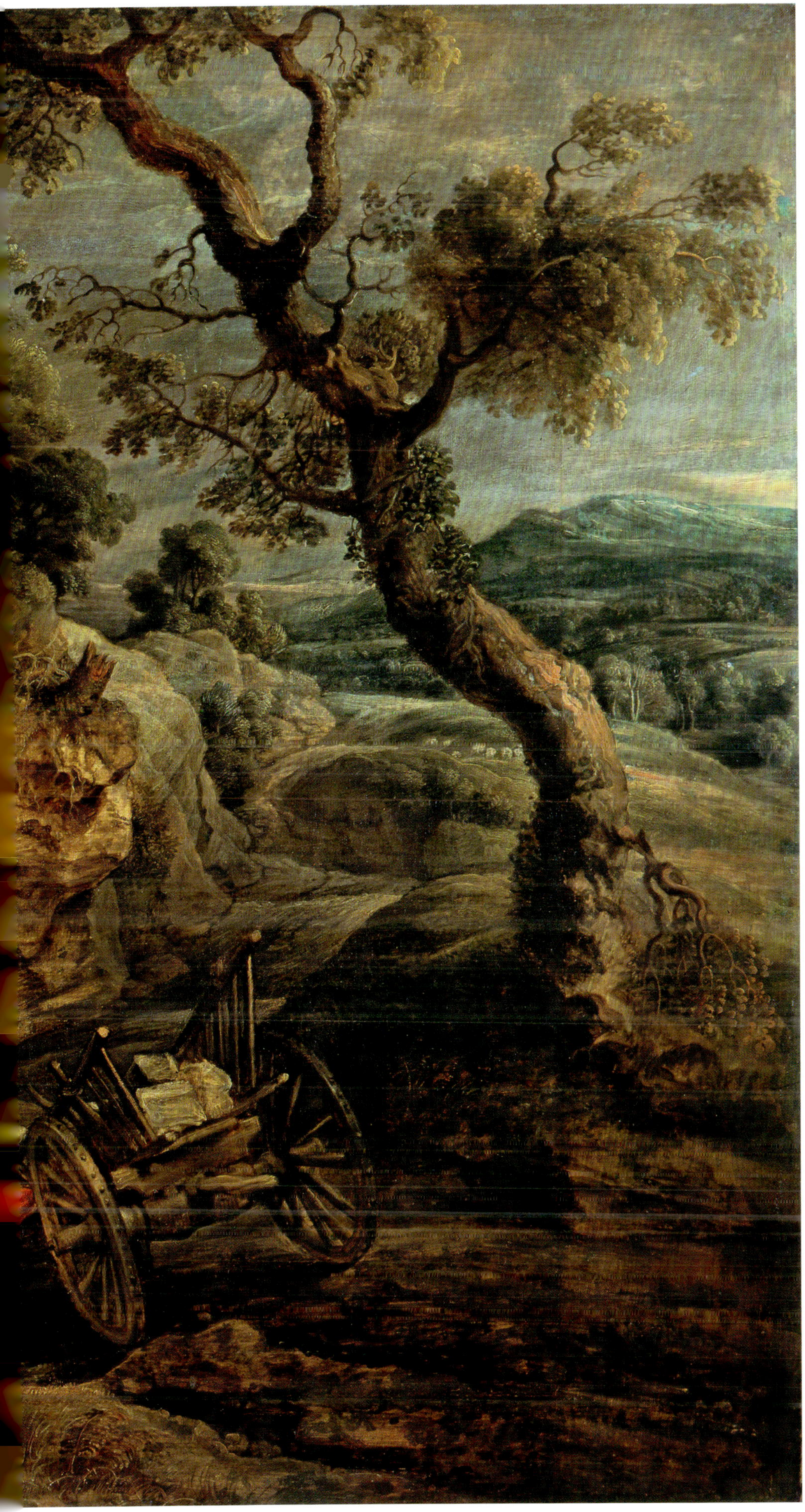

PETER PAUL RUBENS. *The Stone Haulers.* CA. 1620. OIL ON CANVAS (TRANSFERRED FROM PANEL). $33\frac{7}{8} \times 49\frac{7}{8}$ IN. (86 × 126.5 CM).

A magnificent painter and the head of a large studio often commissioned to create grand decorative ensembles for palaces and churches, Rubens was nevertheless attached to a less pompous genre—the landscape. In his youth, Rubens was influenced by a German master of nocturnal landscapes, Adam Elsheimer, and in later years he befriended Jan Brueghel the Younger, whose works he acquired for his private collection. Rubens's own landscapes are full of mighty movements of nature, the play of titanic forces ruling the world and incommensurate with humans. The man's desperate efforts to compete with nature are shown in the figures of stone haulers.

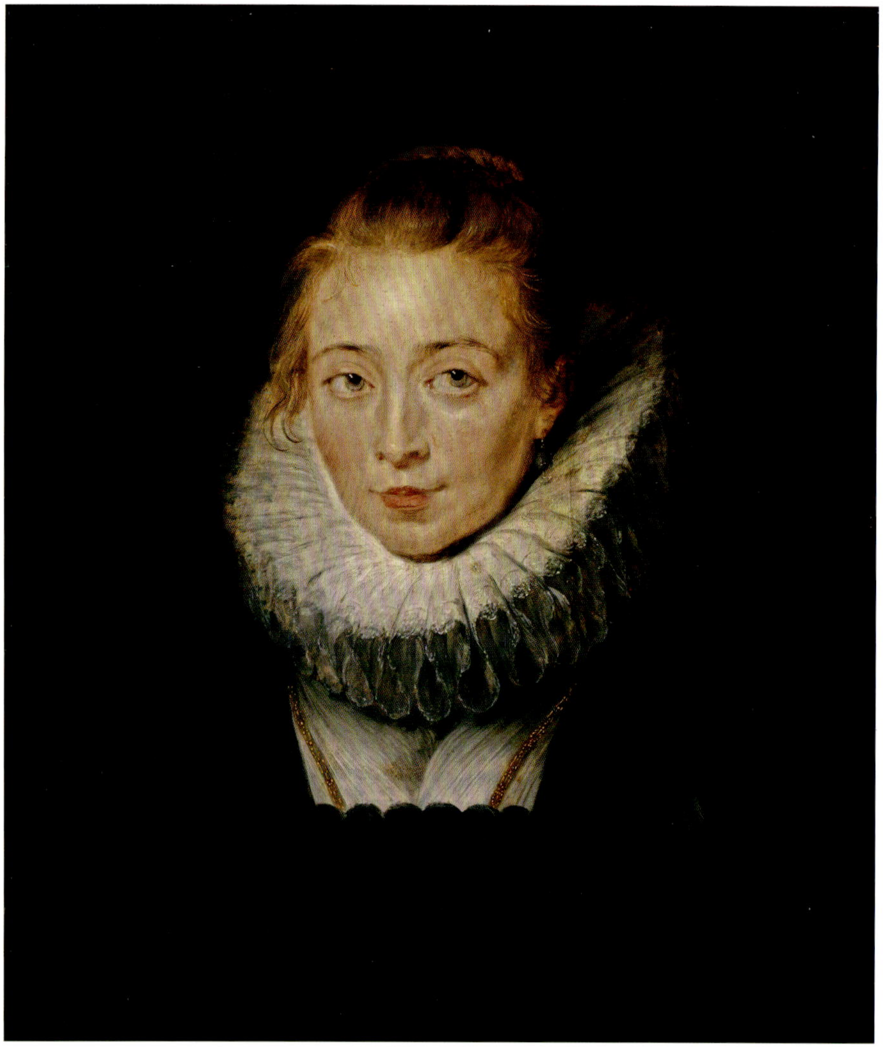

above: PETER PAUL RUBENS. *Portrait of a Lady-in-Waiting to the Infanta Isabella.* MID-1620S. OIL ON PANEL. 25 1/8 × 18 7/8 IN. (64 × 48 CM).

This portrait is considered a posthumous depiction of Rubens's daughter, Clara Serena, who died in 1623 at the age of twelve. In this tender depiction of a young lady, Rubens set down the picture of his daughter already grown-up, which he had in his mind's eye. The title given to the portrait was prompted by the inscription on a preparatory drawing that is in the Albertina collection in Vienna.

opposite: PETER PAUL RUBENS. *The Descent from the Cross.* CA. 1617–18. OIL ON CANVAS. 117 × 78 3/4 IN. (297 × 200 CM).

After the success of the altar triptych on this subject, which Rubens painted for the Antwerp cathedral in 1612, he produced several variants for different churches. In this one, which adorned the Capuchin church in Lierre, the composition has undergone significant changes. The artist reduced the number of figures and increased the scale of Christ, focusing the attention on his body and the kinsfolk and disciples, who do not so much support him as simply touch his body.

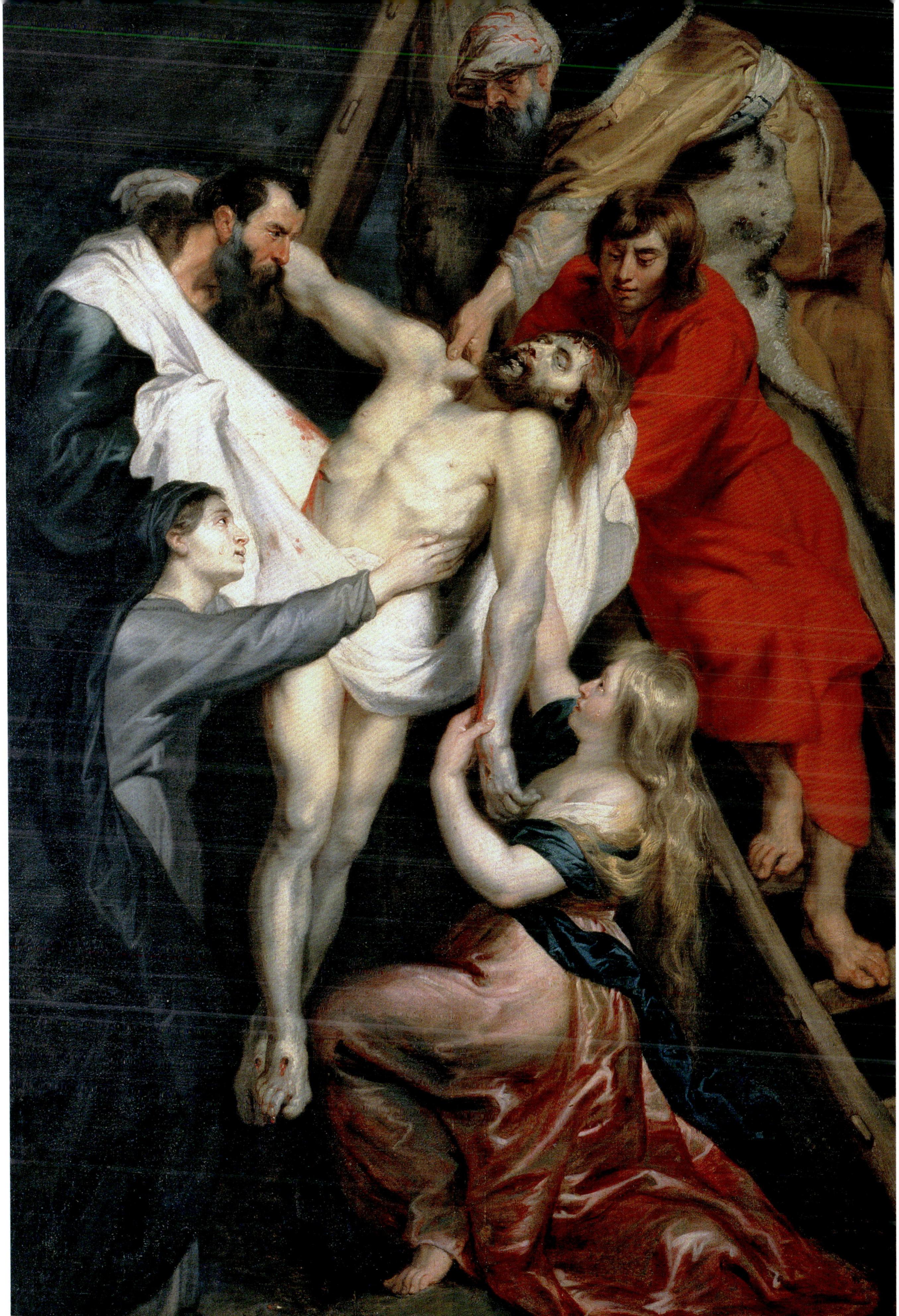

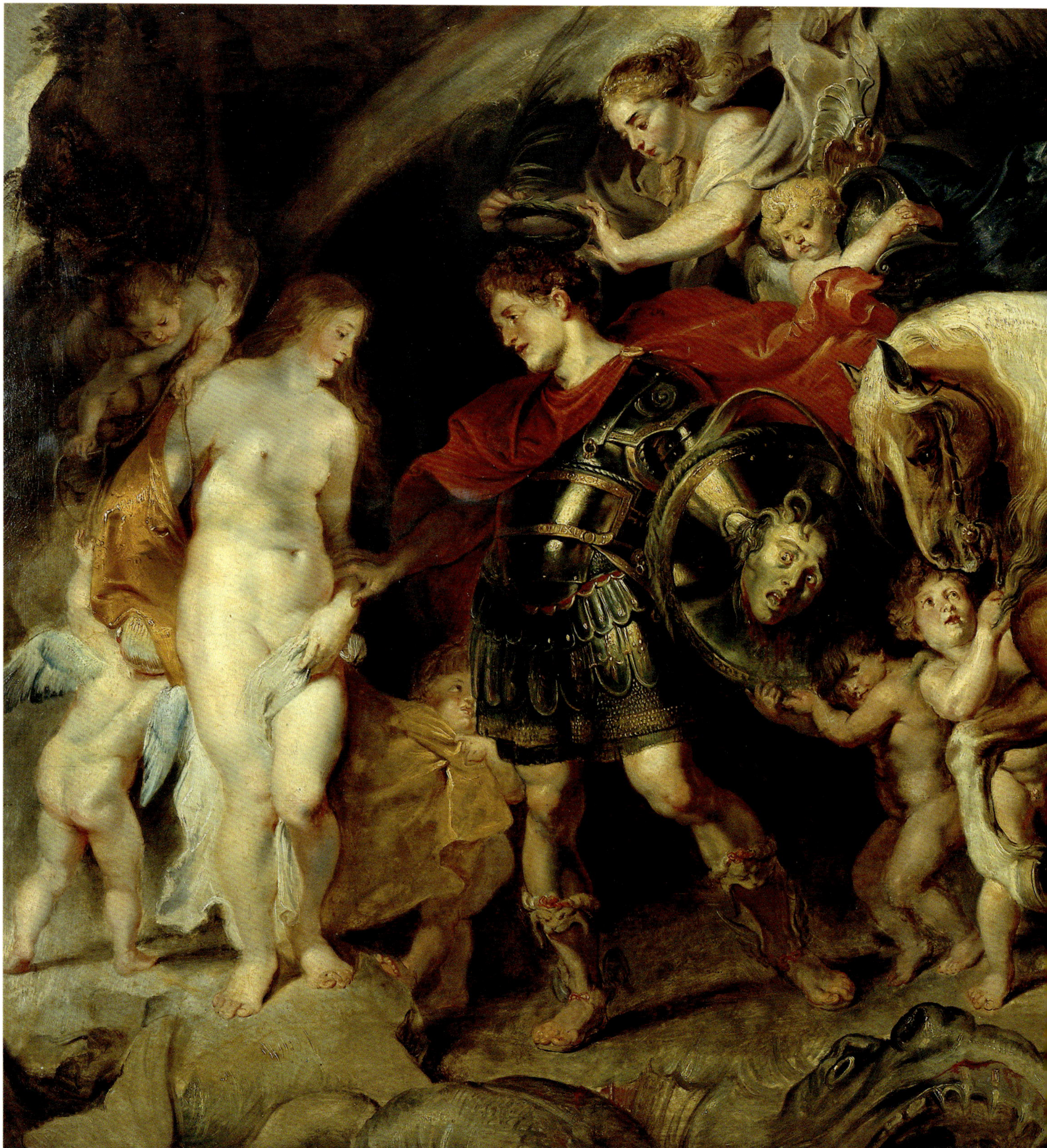

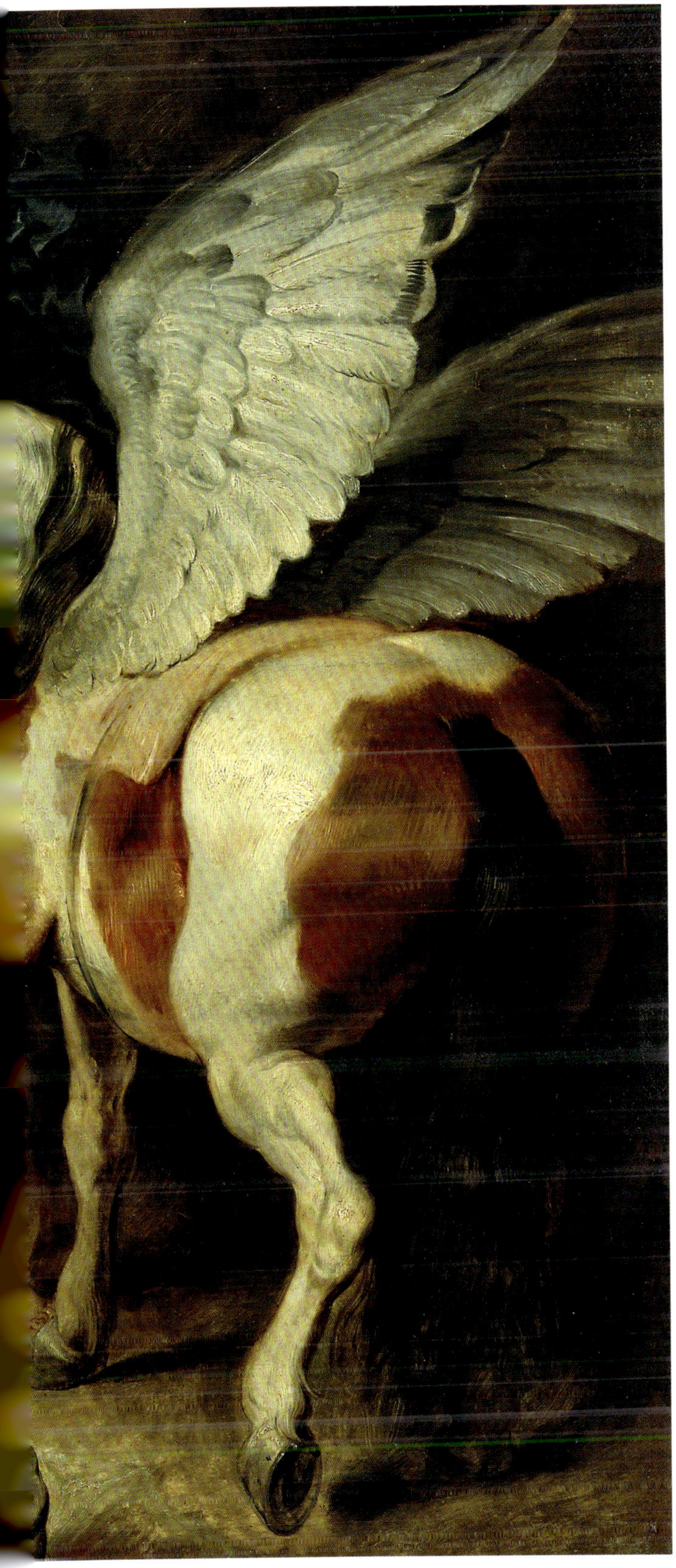

PETER PAUL RUBENS. *Perseus and Andromeda.* CA. 1632. OIL ON CANVAS. $39\frac{1}{8} \times 54\frac{3}{4}$ IN. (99.5 × 139 CM).

This painting is one of the museum's first—as well as one of its best—works by Rubens. Certain elements in the presentation of the mythological subject may seem superfluous: in order to arrive in time to rescue the princess being sacrificed to the terrible monster, either the winged sandals alone or the magical horse Pegasus would have been enough. Still, together the details form a rich yet exceptionally balanced composition extolling the triumph of love.

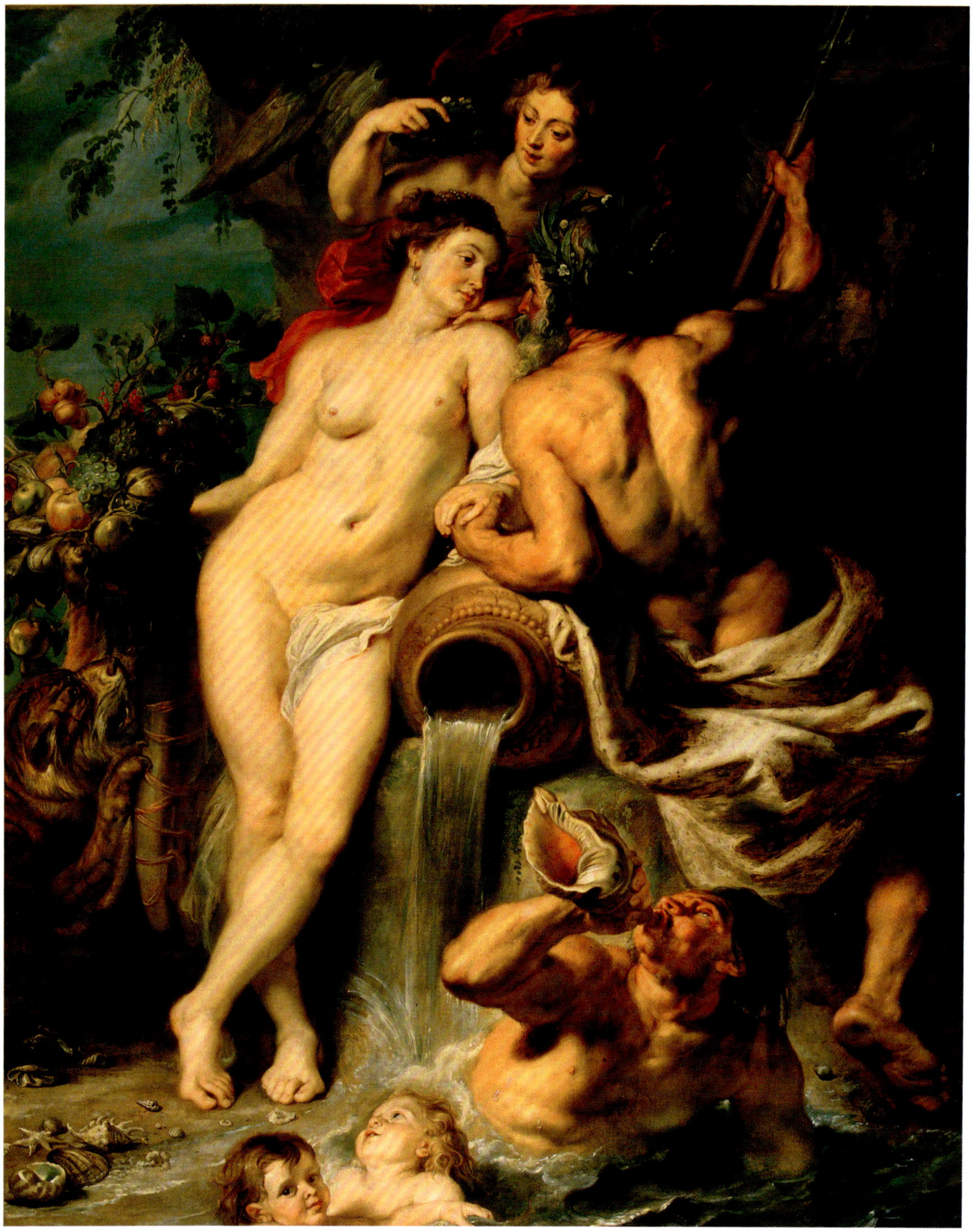

left: PETER PAUL RUBENS. *The Union of Earth and Water.* CA. 1618. OIL ON CANVAS. 87½ × 71 IN. (222.5 × 180.5 CM).

Though based on a mythological subject—the marriage between Cybele, the goddess of the earth, and the sea god Neptune—this painting may also be an expression of Rubens's contemporaries' dream that the Dutch would lift their blockade from the mouth of the River Scheldt, giving Flanders access to the sea. There is justification for a wider interpretation: a glorification of the union of principles—earth and water, male and female, the foundations of earthly life, harmony and perpetual renewal.

opposite: PETER PAUL RUBENS. *Bacchus.* BETWEEN 1638 AND 1640. OIL ON CANVAS. 75⅛ × 63½ IN. (191 ×161.3 CM).

Rubens depicted Bacchus, the ancient god of wine-making, on several occasions. Rubens's subject is far removed from ancient ideals. This feast attended by a satyr, a maenad, and cupids is a hymn to unbridled lack of restraint, the elemental, and the earthly. The canvas was executed in an almost sketchlike, free manner of painting. Painted in the last years of the artist's life, this work was particularly dear to its maker, and he kept it in his studio until death.

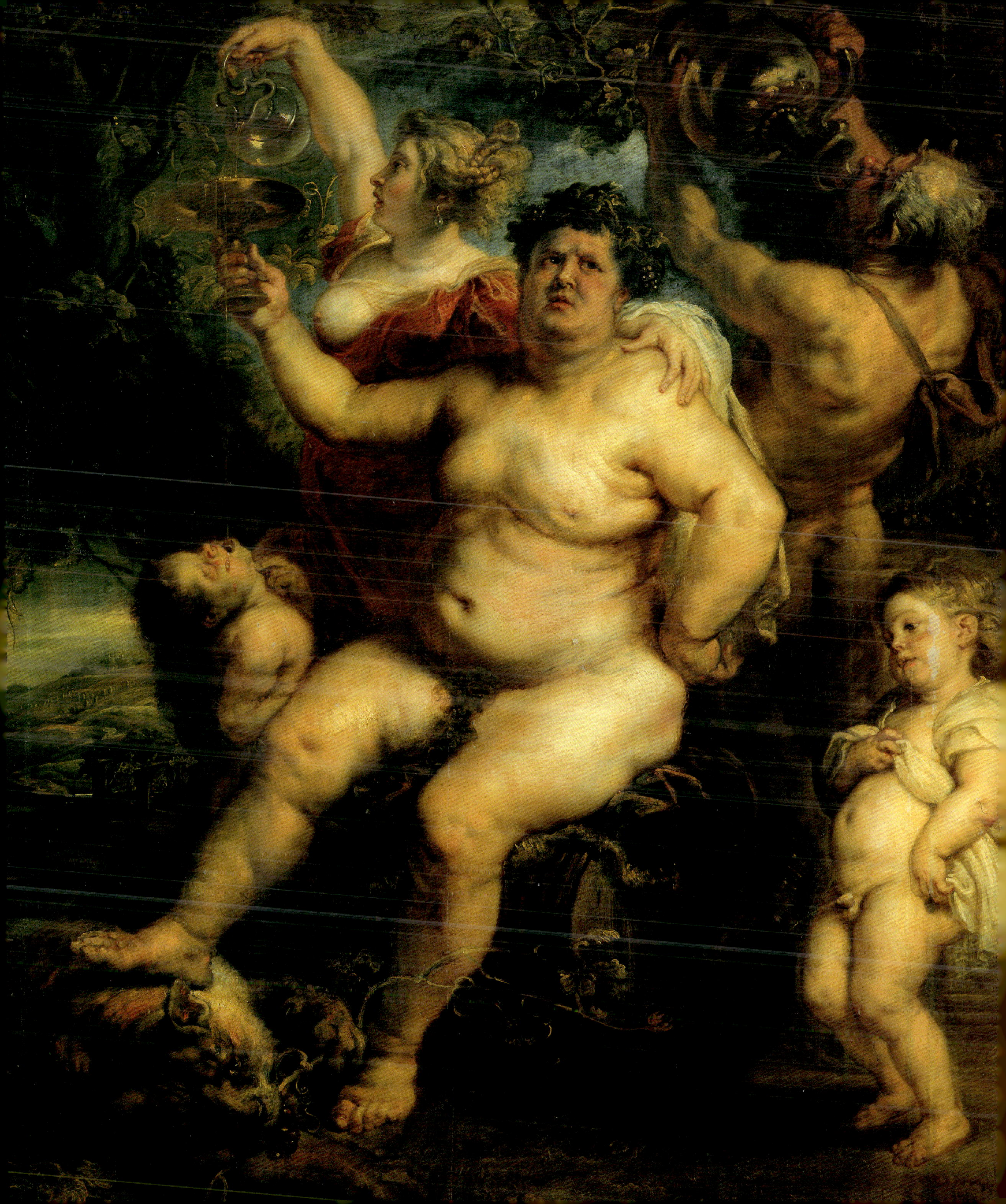

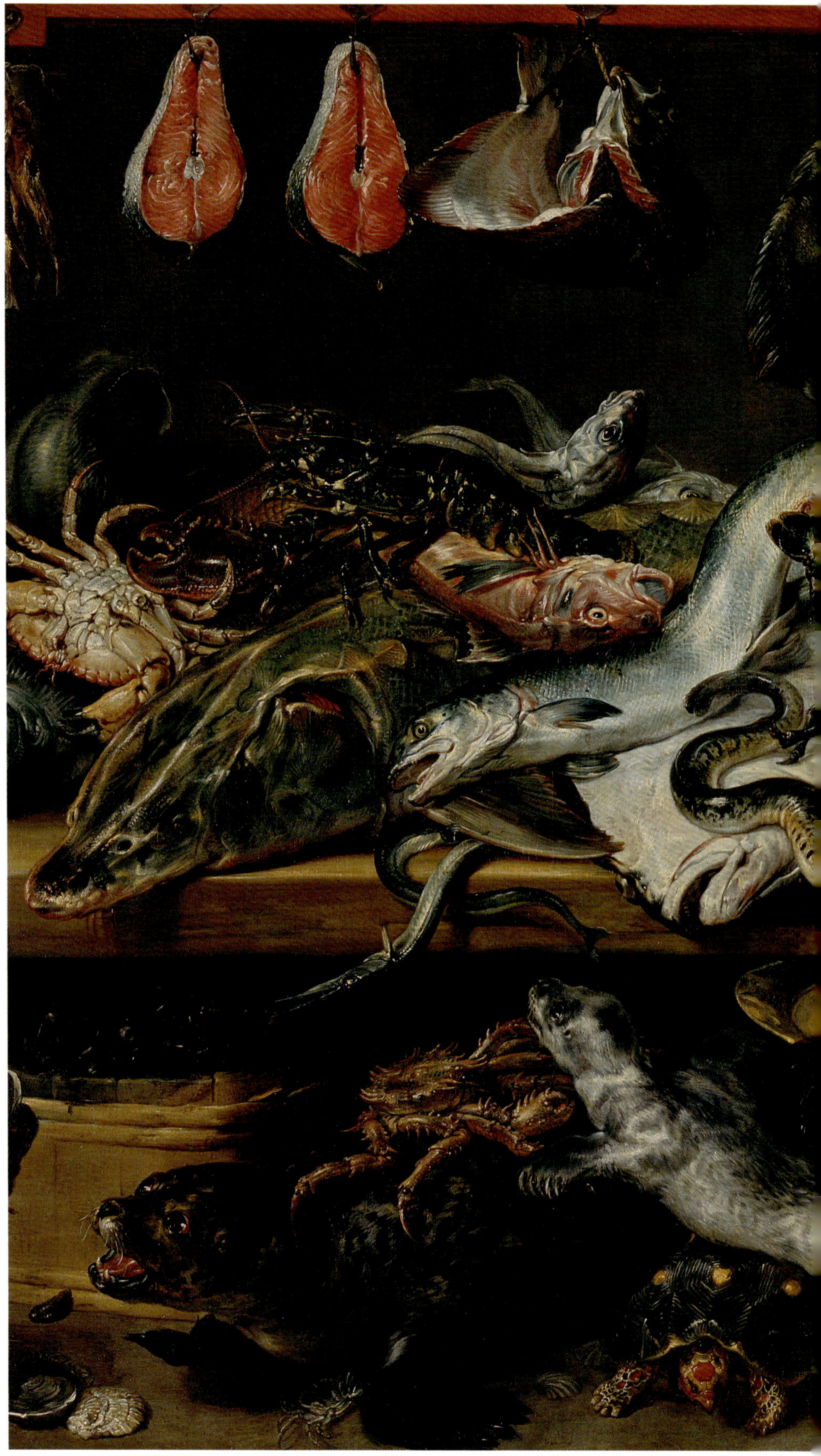

FRANS SNYDERS. *Fish Stall.* BETWEEN 1618 AND 1621. OIL ON CANVAS. 81 1/2 × 134 1/4 IN. (207 × 341 CM).

The sinuous lines of fish, familiar from childhood to an artist whose father owned one of Antwerp's biggest eating-houses, seem made for dynamic Baroque compositions. The precision with which Snyders depicts the denizens of seas and rivers delights zoologists, but the abundance of his many depictions of fish stalls is ruled not by any Linnaean hierarchy: the crustaceans whose shedding of their shells symbolizes the resurrection are superior to the dead fish.

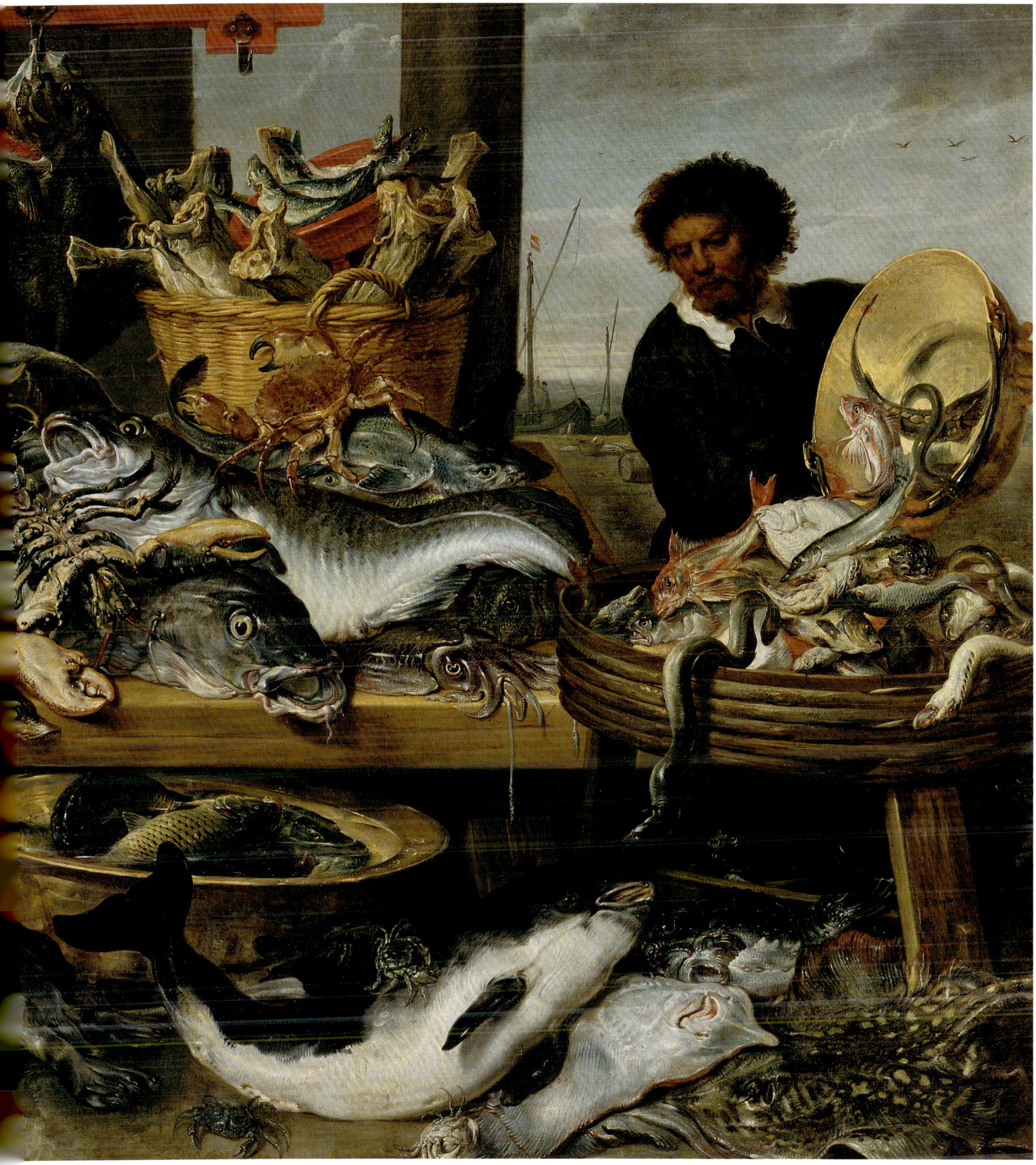

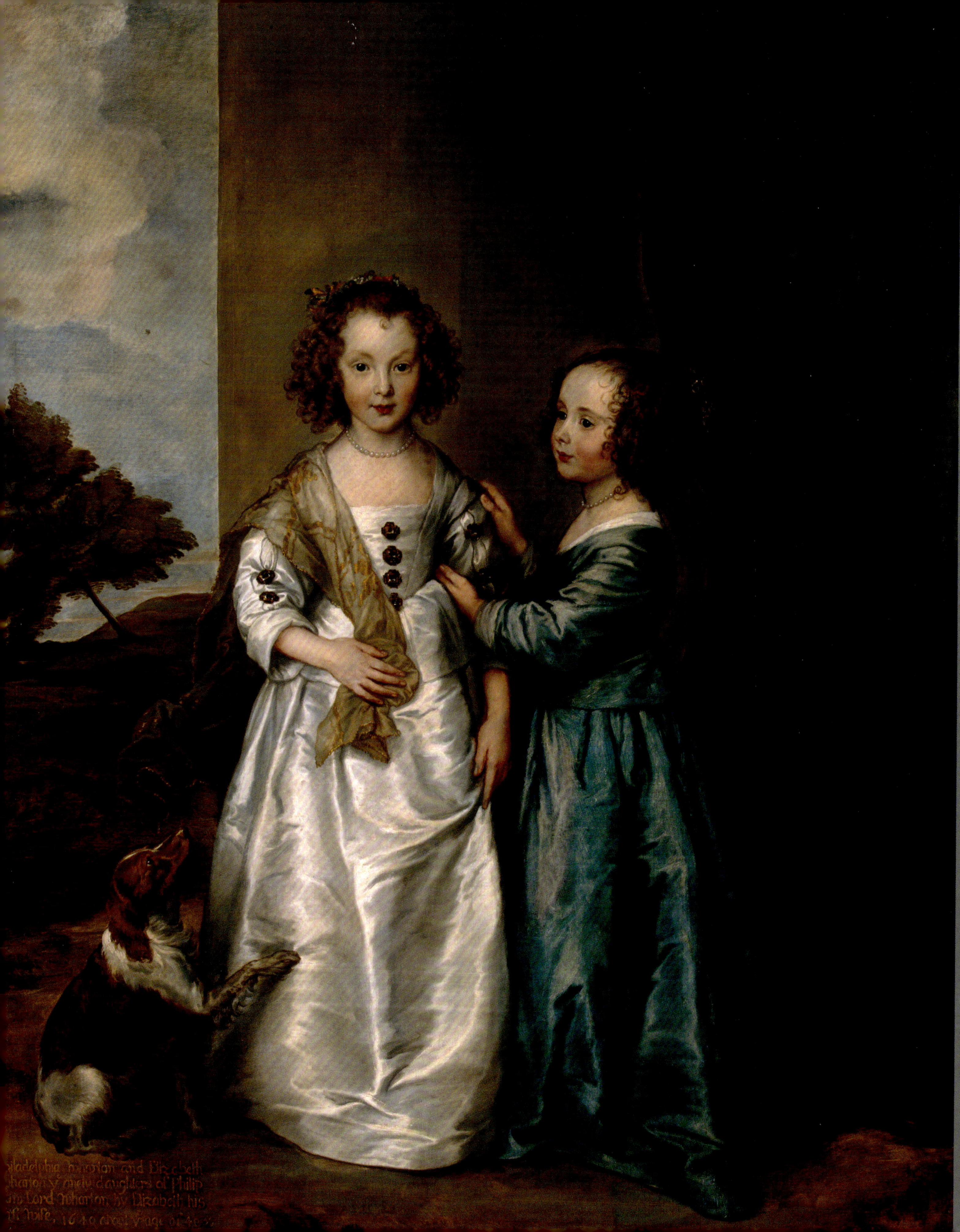

opposite: ANTHONY VAN DYCK. *Portrait of the Sisters Elizabeth and Philadelphia Wharton.* 1640. OIL ON CANVAS. $63^{3}/_{4} \times 51^{1}/_{8}$ IN. (162×130 CM).

In the second half of the 1630s, after his second marriage, Philip, 4th Lord Wharton, an active participant in the Civil War and Cromwell's supporter, commissioned Van Dyck to paint portraits of his family members. The baron's daughters from his first marriage—to Elizabeth Wandesford who died in 1635—are depicted in elegant dresses that create the main color accents in the canvas and display the artist's Flemish feeling of texture. The recent loss in the family is symbolized by the bending tree in the background.

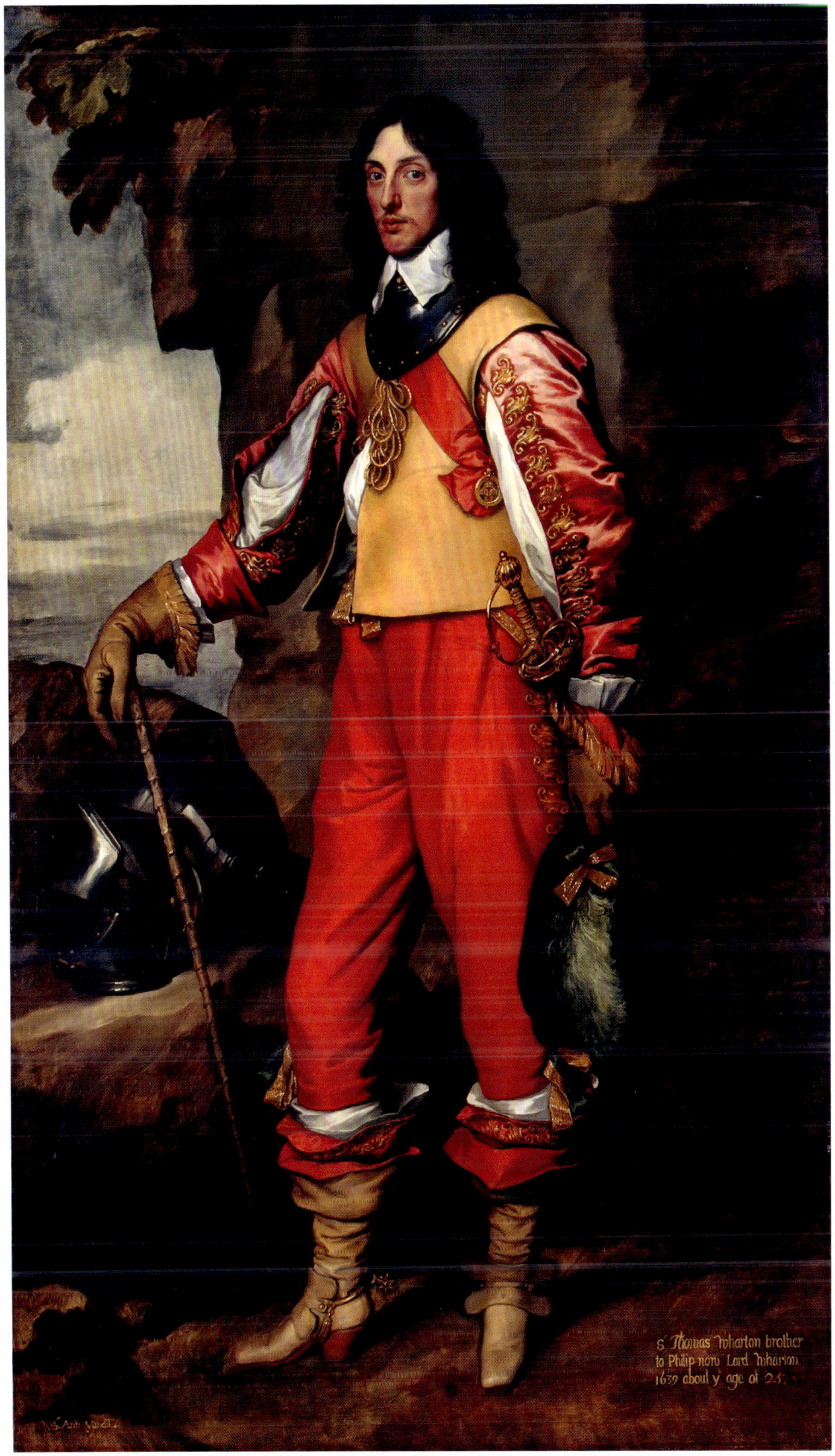

right: ANTHONY VAN DYCK. *Portrait of Sir Thomas Wharton.* SECOND HALF OF THE 1630S. OIL ON CANVAS. $85^{1}/_{2} \times 50^{1}/_{2}$ IN. (217×128.5 CM).

As court painter to Charles I of England between 1632 and 1641, van Dyck fully revealed his talent for formal portraiture. In his depictions of English aristocrats, his subjects' status and strong qualities are conveyed not just by pose and attributes, but also by purely painterly features: resonant color combinations, exquisite texture, and free brushwork. A devotion to a grand style that permitted—and even turned to advantage—an artistically uninhibited manner became, through his example, a distinguishing feature of English painting.

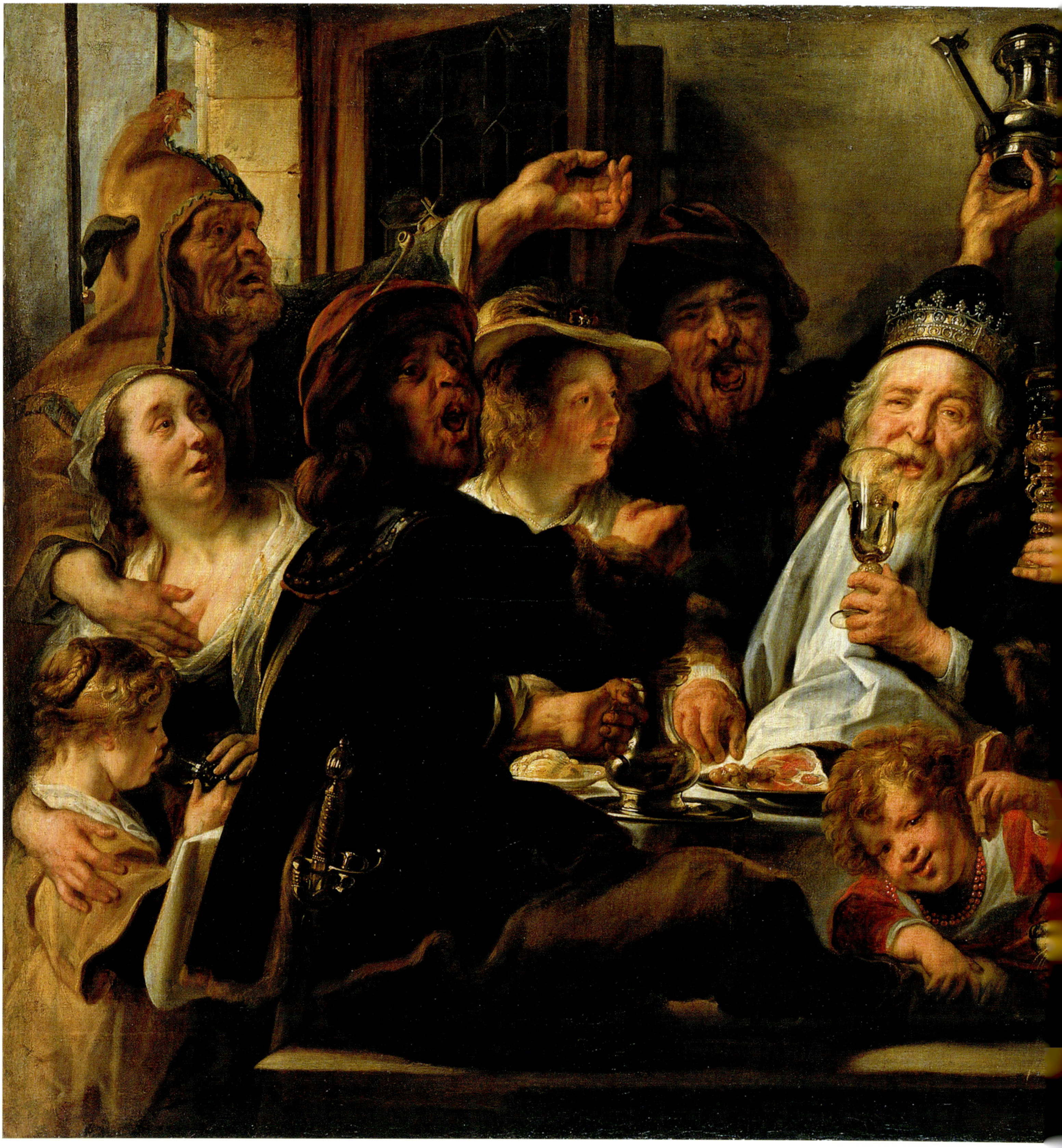

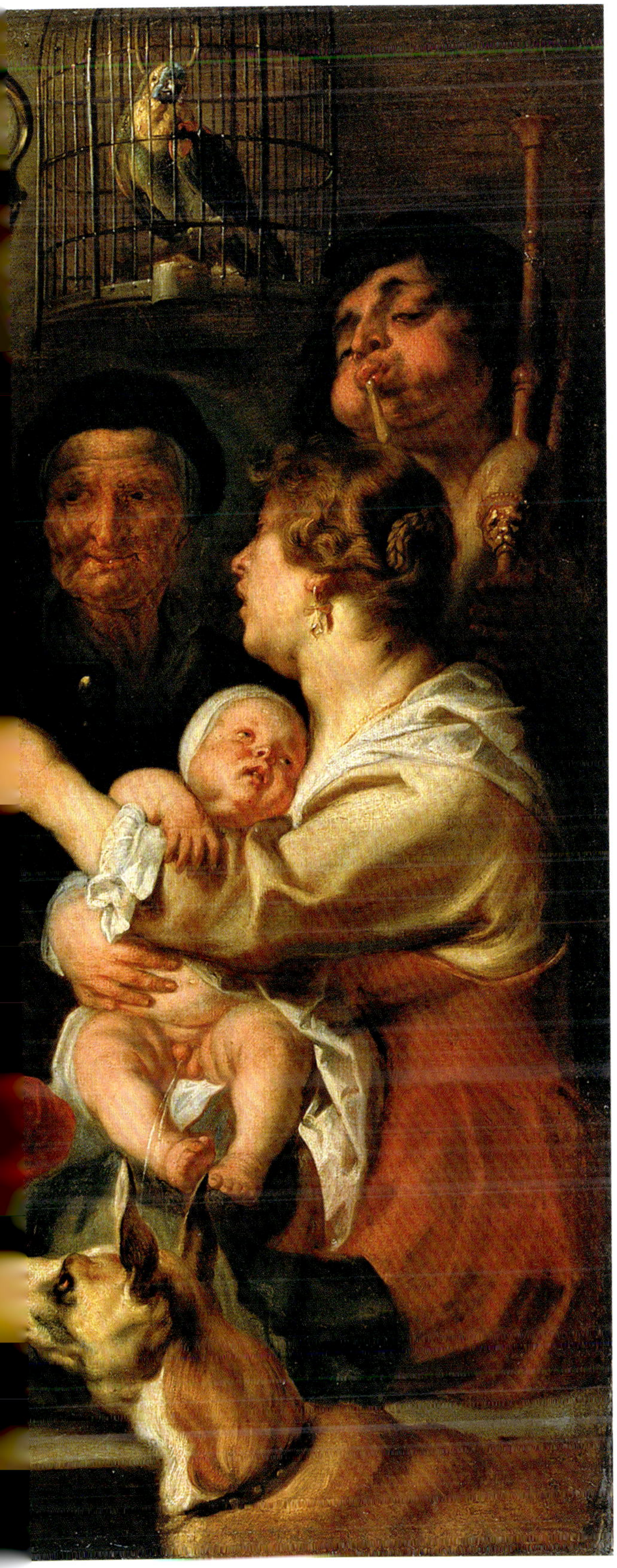

JACOB JORDAENS. *The Bean King.* CA. 1638.
OIL ON CANVAS. 61⅞ × 83 IN. (157 × 211 CM).

The Bean King is among the greatest masterpieces of the Flemish Baroque. The subject is inspired by the festivities held each year in the Low Countries on the Epiphany, when, according to Christian legend, the Magi came to worship the Christ-Child. By tradition, a pie was served with a bean baked into it. Whoever found the bean in his or her slice was declared "monarch" for the evening and directed to choose a consort and appoint courtiers.

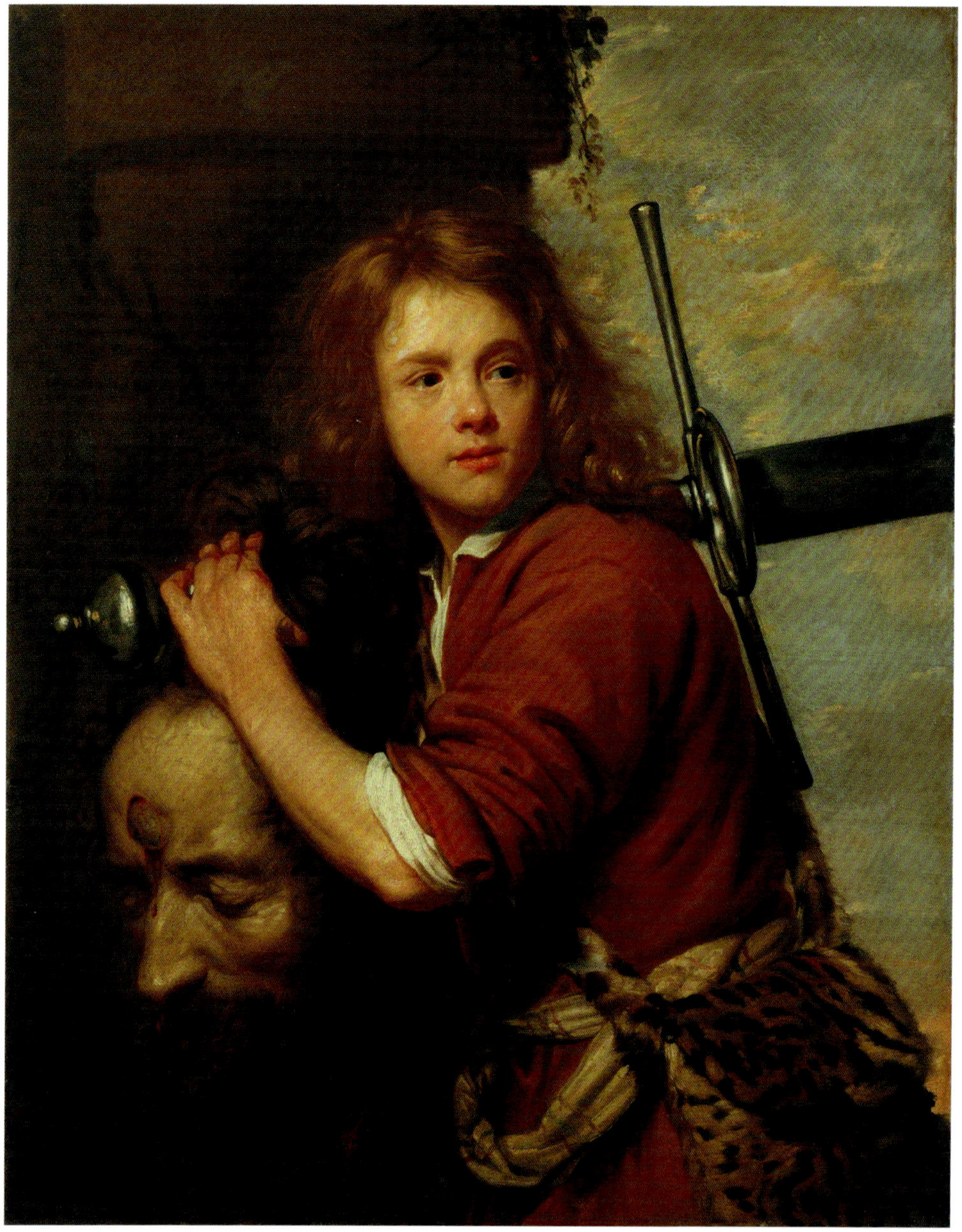

left: JACOB VAN OOST THE ELDER. *David with the Head of Goliath.* 1643. OIL ON CANVAS. 40⅛ × 32 IN. (102 × 81 CM).

When depicting the aftermath of the victory gained by David, the future king of Israel, over the Philistine giant Goliath, the artist was likely inspired by Caravaggio's work on the same subject. Like the great Italian master, he invested the scene with almost shocking naturalism, inspiring worldly reflections about the triumph of youth over age, beauty over ugliness.

opposite: REMBRANDT HARMENSZ. VAN RIJN. *The Sacrifice of Isaac.* 1635. OIL ON CANVAS. 76 ×52 IN. (193 × 132 CM).

The composition's theatrical dynamics, based on eloquent gestures, link this early but already mature painting by Rembrandt with the European aesthetics of the Baroque. Between the movements of Abraham's hands (the left covering his son's face before he kills him; the right stopped at the last moment on God's command) and the angel's exhorting gesture, a whole spectacle unfolds. It lasts only an instant yet encompasses the brutal collision of faith and fatherly love.

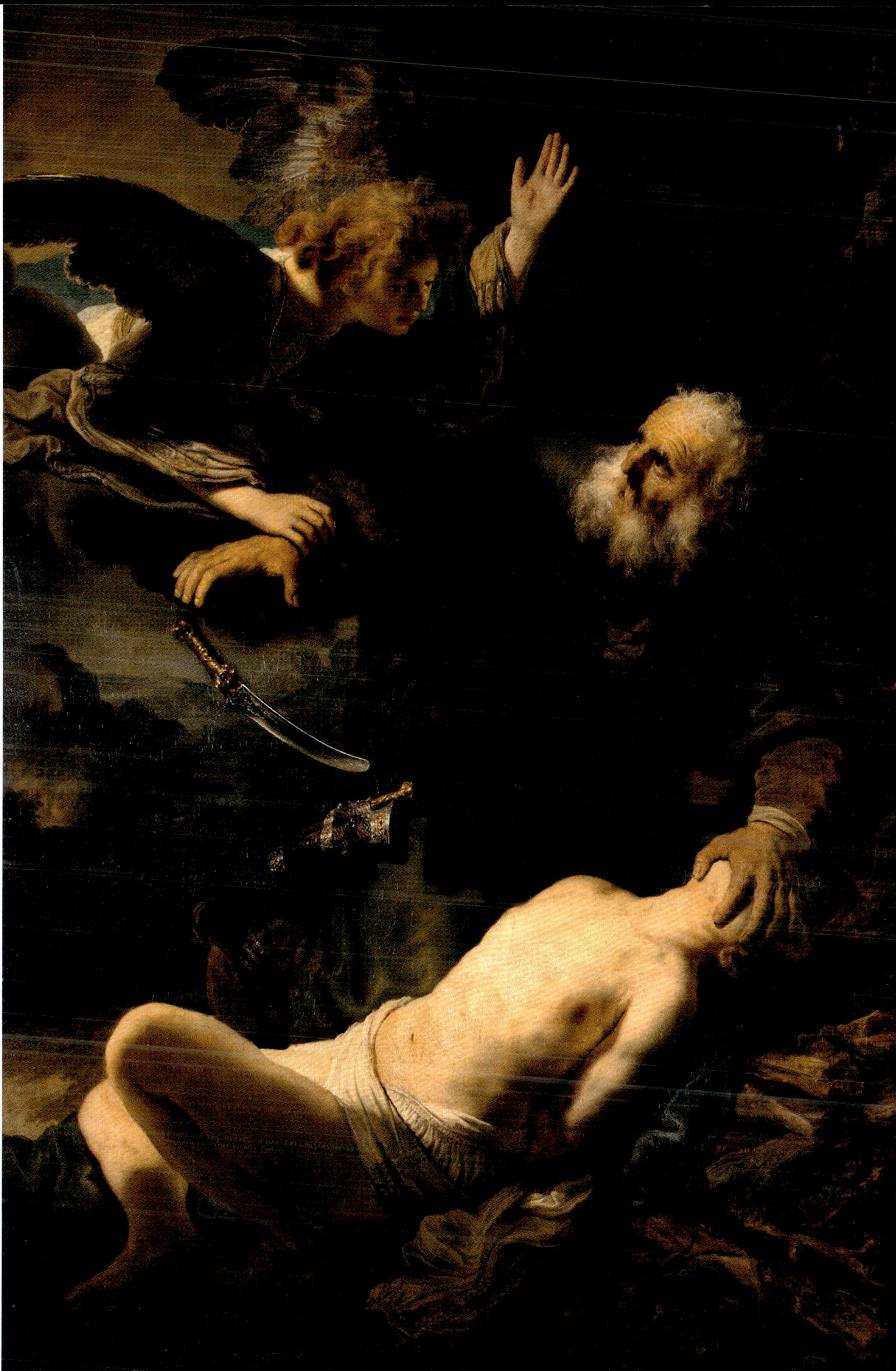

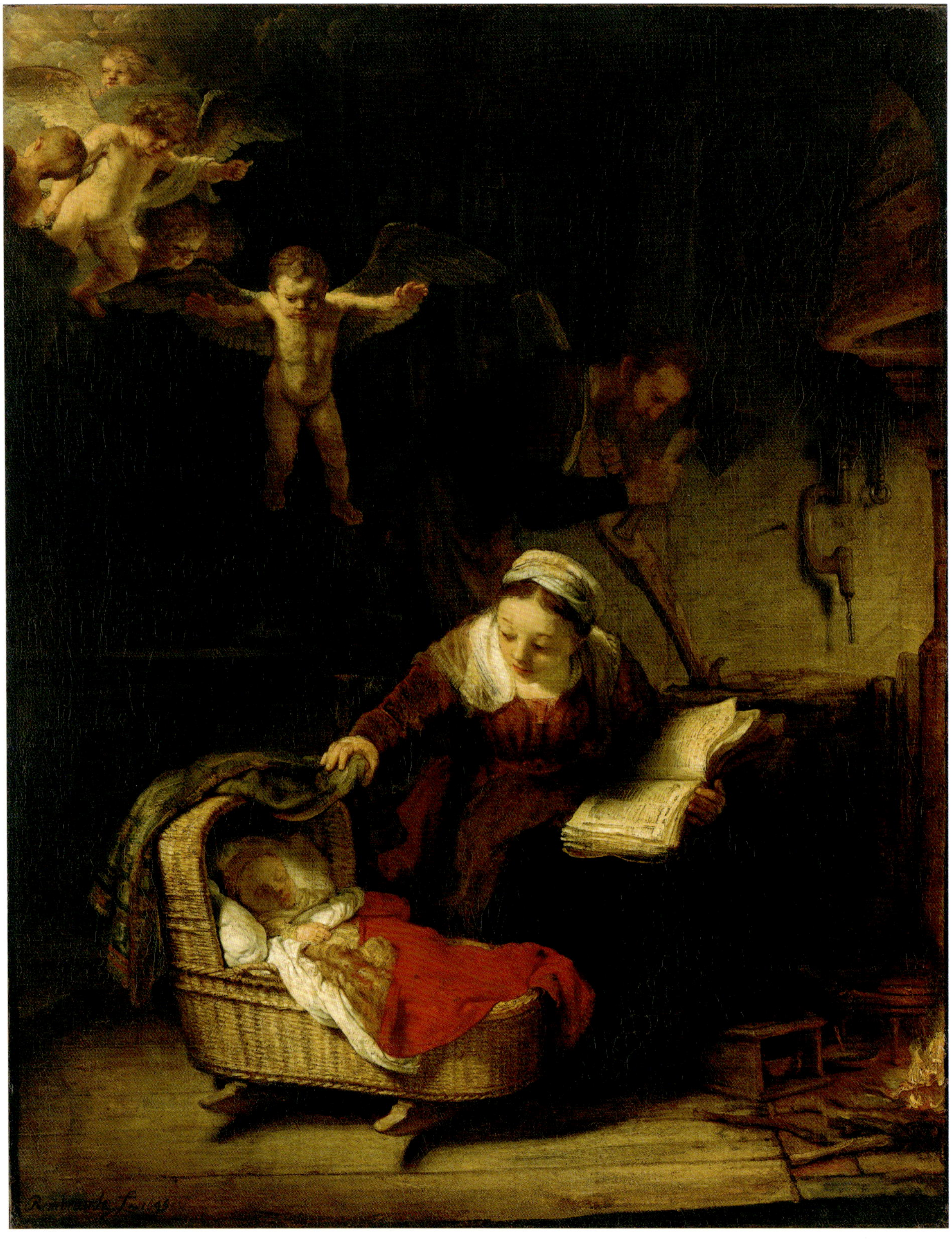

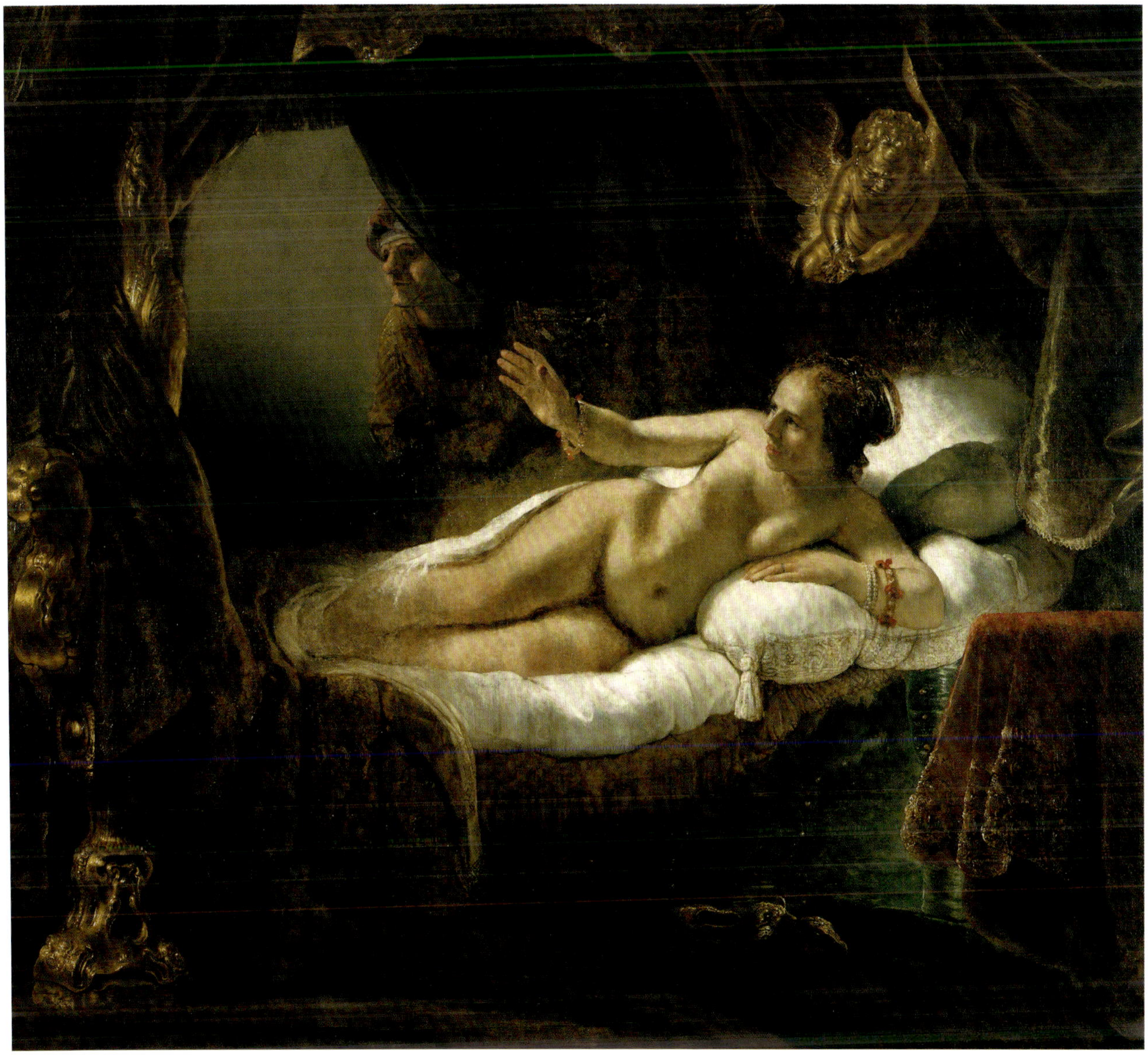

opposite: REMBRANDT HARMENSZ. VAN RIJN. *The Holy Family.* 1645. OIL ON CANVAS. 46 × 35 7/8 IN. (117 × 91 CM).

Rembrandt depicted the Holy Family often in drawings and paintings, seeking the best composition for a subject that almost literally expresses the idea of Christ's dual human and divine nature. Here, the scene takes place in an ordinary Dutch home. The carpenter father is busy at work while the mother watches over her sleeping child. The miracle enters unbeknownst to the personages: descending on waves of light, the angel brings down an invisible veil between two worlds, the earthly and the divine.

above: REMBRANDT HARMENSZ. VAN RIJN. *Danaë.* 1636. OIL ON CANVAS. 72 7/8 × 79 3/4 IN. (185 × 202.5 CM).

The rendering of mythological and religious subjects in more prosaic imagery, a characteristic of 17th-century Dutch and Flemish painting, led Rembrandt not to a delight in the material richness of the world or the poetry of everyday life, but instead to the metaphysics of the sublime. Behind the spicy details of one of Jupiter's love affairs, Rembrandt's Danaë addresses the Christian theme of the spiritualization of the flesh: instead of the usual shower of gold, her body is enveloped in a soft light.

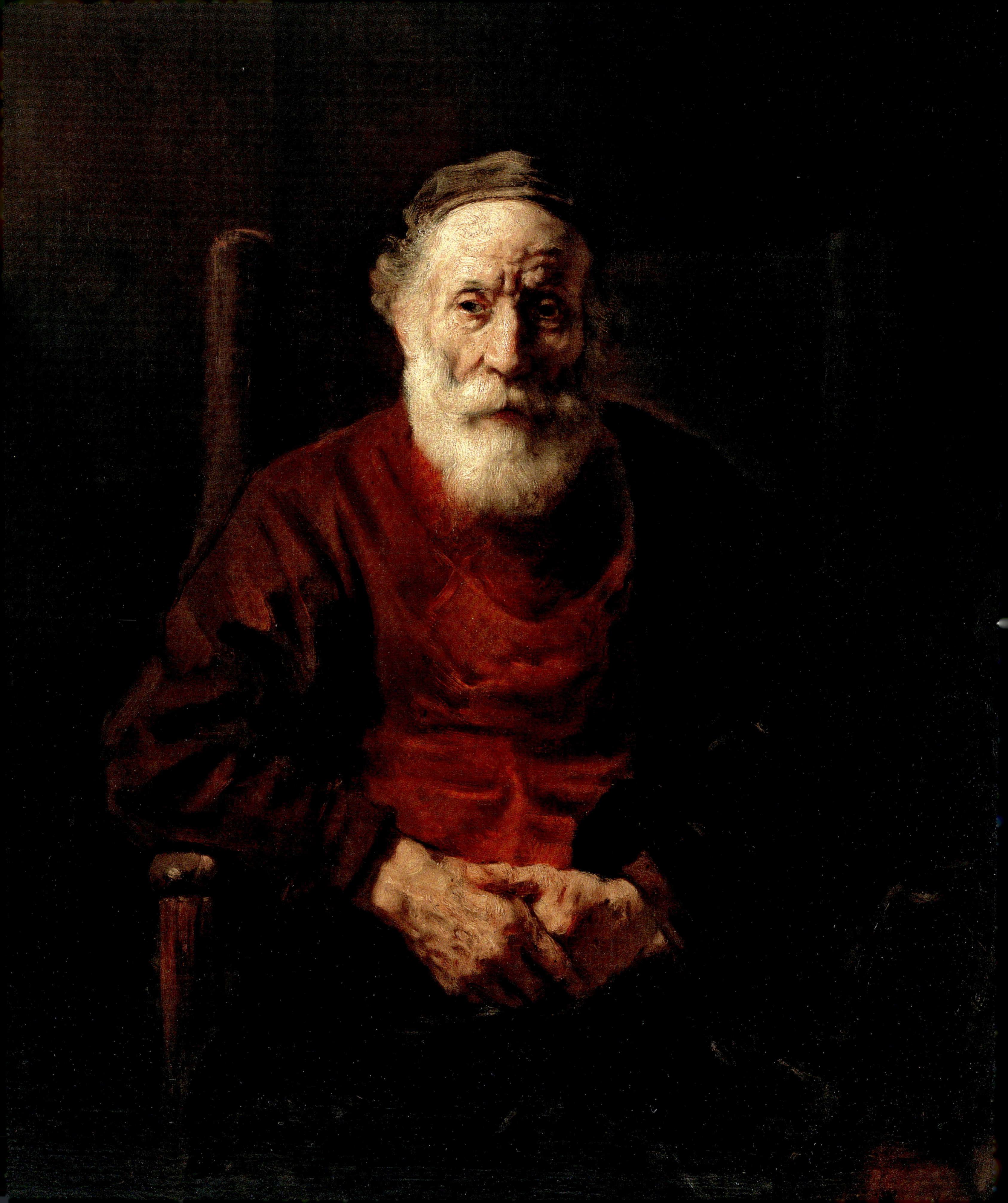

below: REMBRANDT HARMENSZ. VAN RIJN. *Portrait of the Poet Jeremias de Decker.* 1666. OIL ON CANVAS. 28 × 22 IN. (71 ×56 CM).

The Hermitage cannot boast even one painted self-portrait by Rembrandt, but this portrait, created shortly before his death, of a friend who knew the artist well seems part of a silent dialogue. Rembrandt depicts himself in the eyes of the other, so fixed and sharp is the poet's gaze, whose depth is intensified by the shadow of the broad brim of a hat that covers half the face.

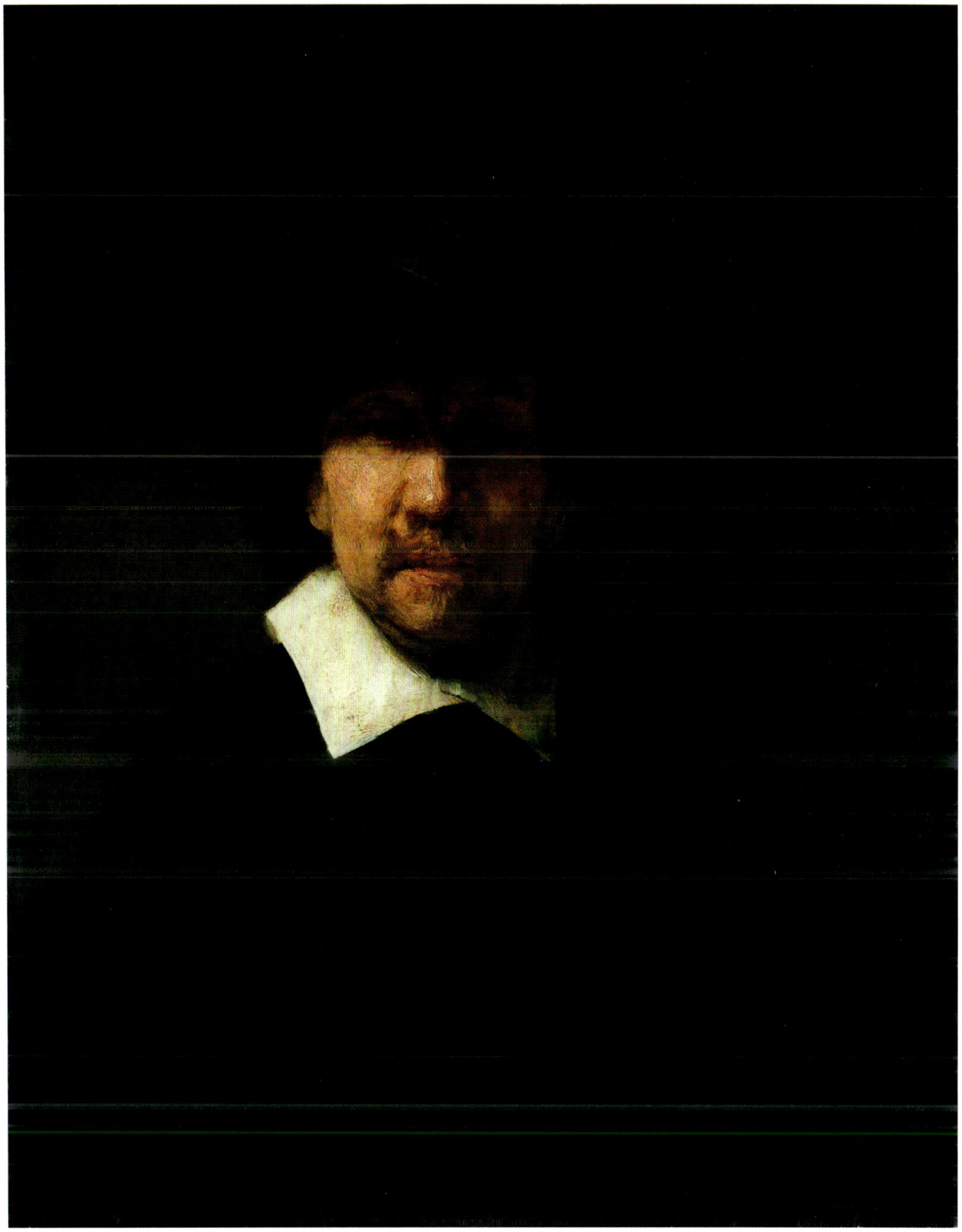

opposite: REMBRANDT HARMENSZ. VAN RIJN. *Portrait of an Old Man in Red.* CA. 1652/54. OIL ON CANVAS. 42½ × 34 IN. (108 ×86 CM).

Although ascetic in the use of color, this portrait is exceptionally varied in the brushstrokes. The complex relief of the old man's face and hands calls to mind these words from the Austrian poet Rainer Maria Rilke: "Do not Rembrandt's secret and greatness lie perhaps in his having seen and painted people as landscapes? . . . He could paint portraits because he looked deeply into faces, as if into lands with a distant horizon and a high, cloudy, shifting sky."

right: REMBRANDT HARMENSZ. VAN RIJN. *The Descent from the Cross.* 1634. OIL ON CANVAS. 62¼ × 46 IN. (158 × 117 CM).

In 1633 and 1634 Rembrandt produced several painted and etched versions of this subject, reflecting a search for the most expressive arrangement and lighting and his gradual movement away from Rubens's composition. This canvas can be regarded as the final stage of that quest: Rembrandt uses light of varying intensity to pick out not only Christ but also Mary on the right and the women on the left, shifting the sense of tragedy from the event to how those close to Jesus experienced it.

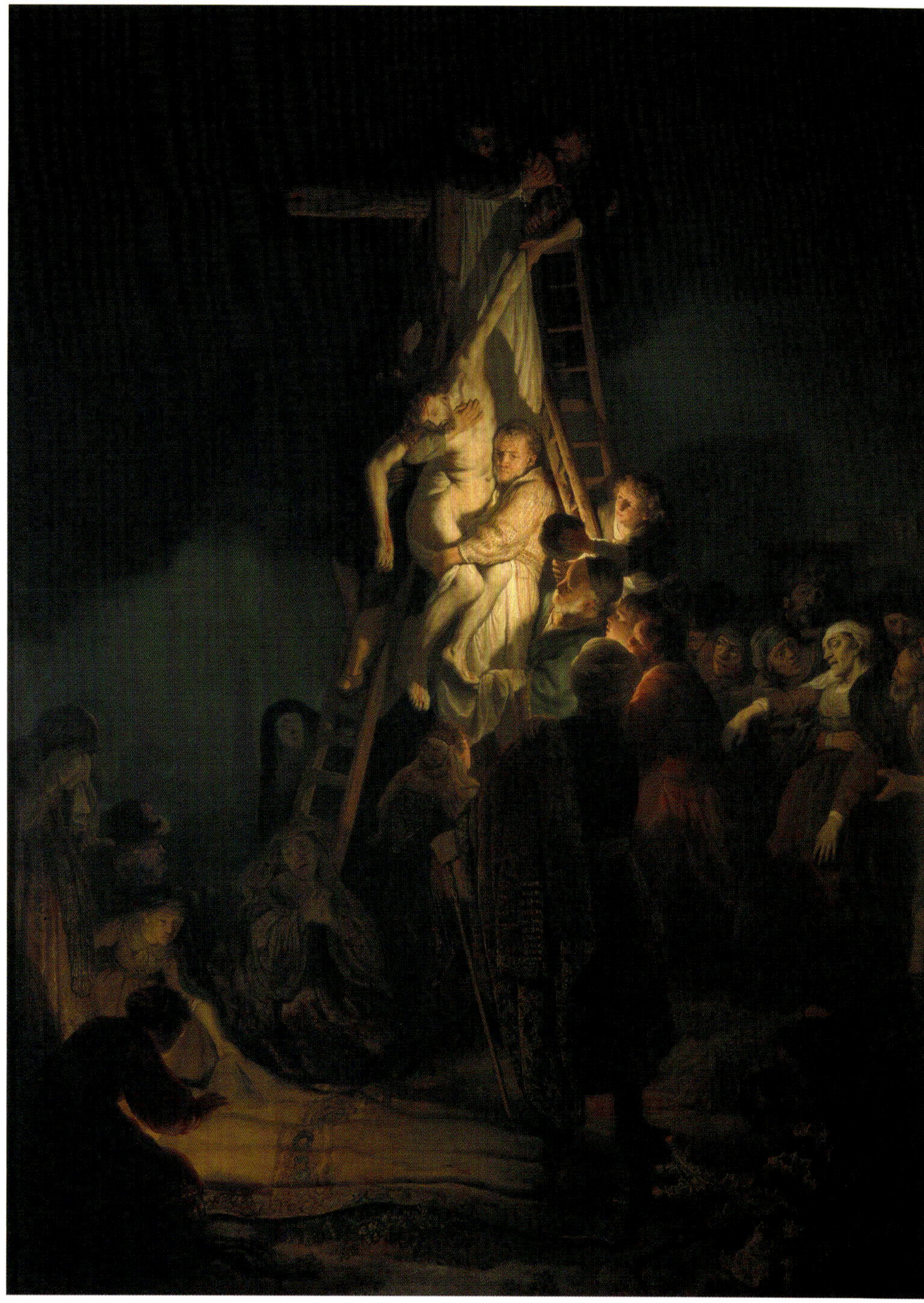

opposite: REMBRANDT HARMENSZ. VAN RIJN. *David and Jonathan.* 1642. OIL ON CANVAS. 28¾ × 24¼ IN. (73 × 61.5 CM).

This painting was purchased in the early 18th century for Peter the Great and adorned the gallery at his Monplaisir palace in Peterhof, Russia's first art collection. It is now believed to reference an early episode in the story of the great and righteous Old Testament king. David bids farewell to his friend, King Saul's son, after Jonathan has warned him of his father's intention to dispose of David as a potential rival.

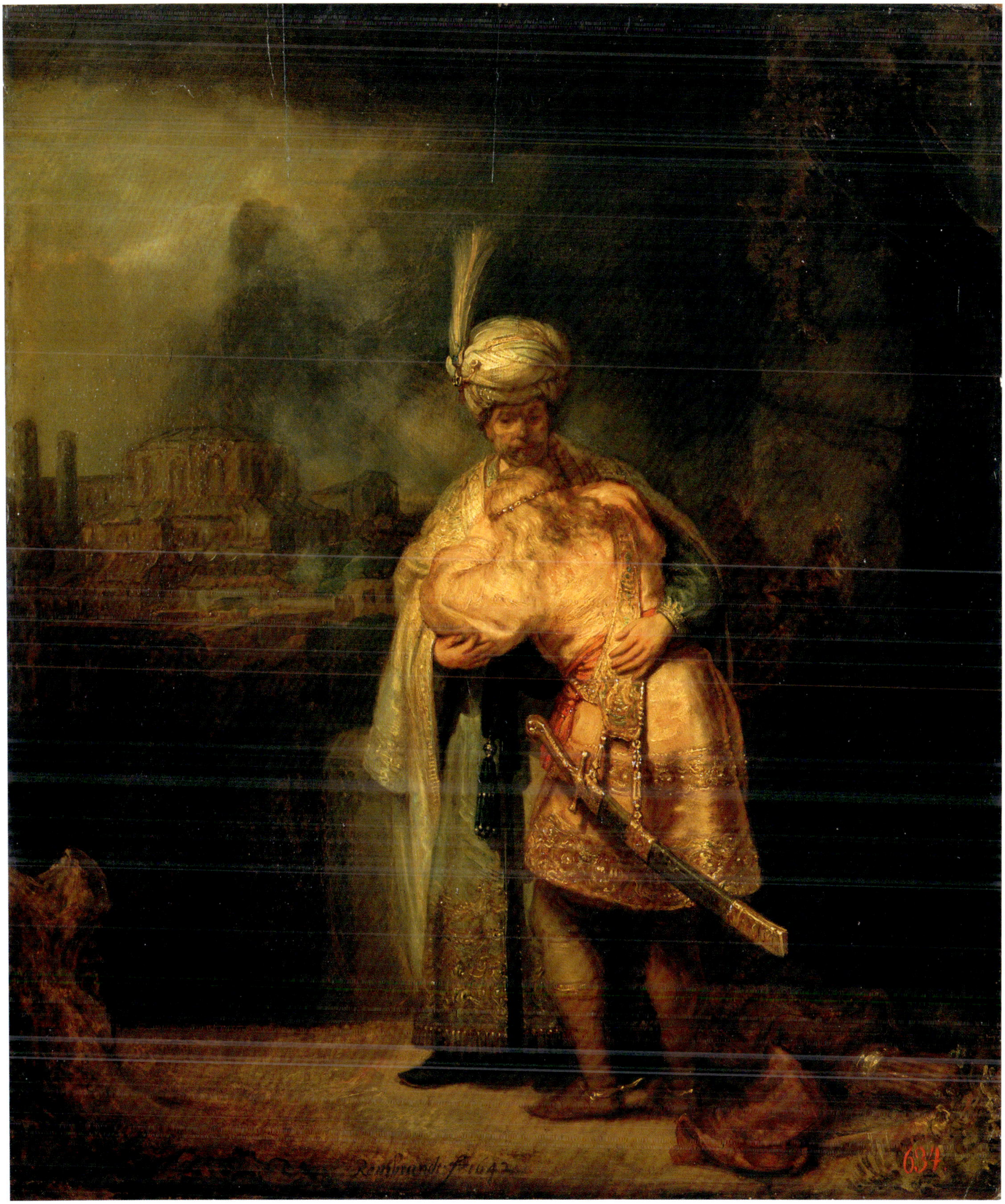

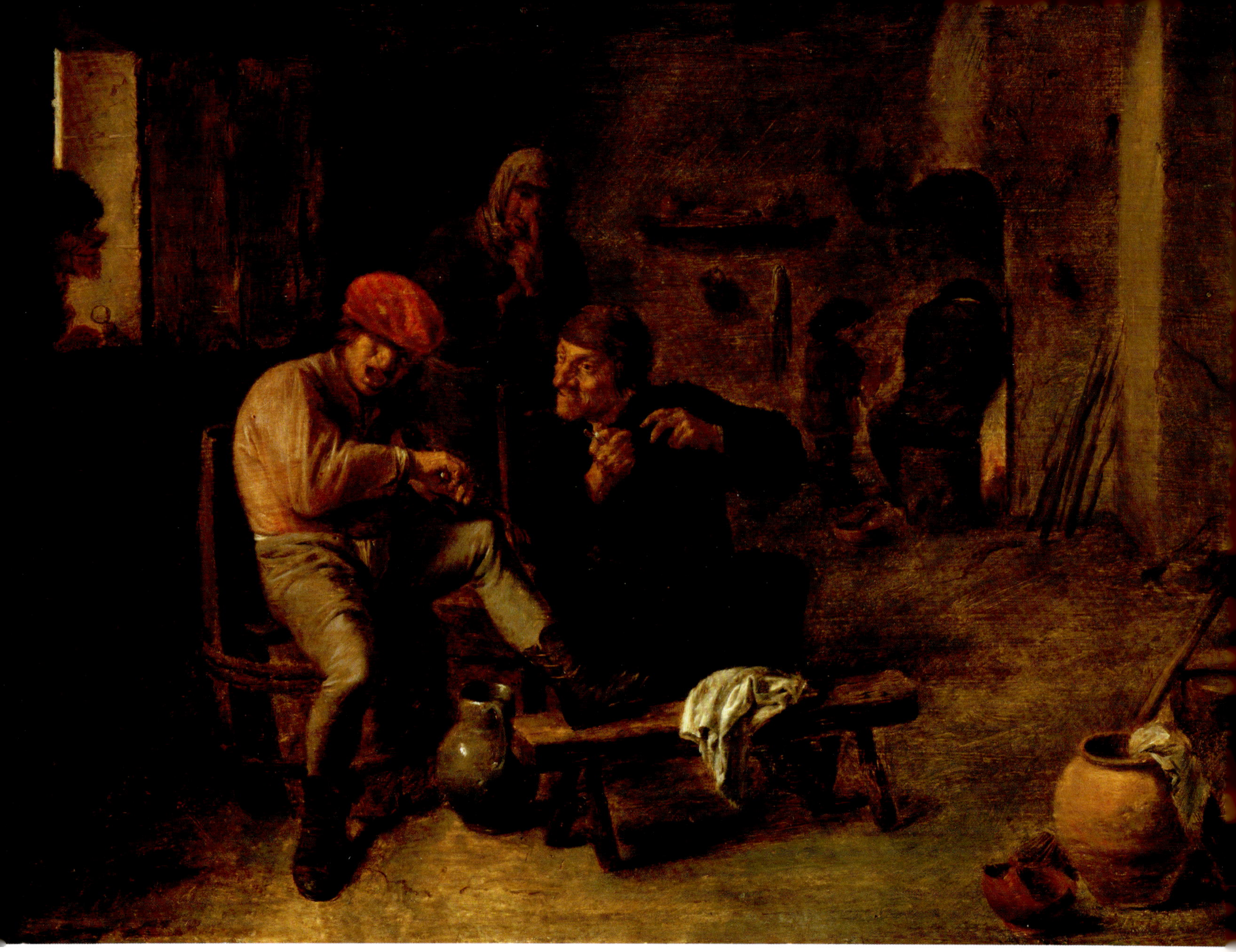

ADRIAEN BROUWER. *Scene in a Tavern (Village Fiddler).* BETWEEN 1634 AND 1638. OIL ON PANEL. 9⅞ × 13⅛ IN. (25 × 33.5 CM).

The peasant genre became prevalent in 17th-century Dutch painting. Among its earliest major exponents was Brouwer, who in 1623–24 moved from Flanders to Haarlem, one of many immigrants drawn by the city's economic growth. He adopted the Netherlandish tradition of depicting scenes from the life of common people, which dates back to Pieter Breughel the Elder and Hieronymus Bosch. Here, it is enlivened by a taste for everyday details and humor, and the personages exhibit the explosive temperament of the Dutch.

ADRIAEN VAN OSTADE. *A Fight.* 1637. OIL ON PANEL. 9⅞ × 13⅛ IN. (25 × 33.5 CM).

Scenes from everyday life had been introduced into European painting by Pieter Brueghel the Elder and became frequent subjects for Dutch painters, including Adriaen van Ostade who used the newly invented technique of tone painting. The characteristic dimness seems quite appropriate for this scene of fighting. Such works were very popular among rich burgers and, later, aristocrats who enjoyed a hearty laugh at the expense of the lowbred. The painting may be also regarded as an allegory of tactile perception.

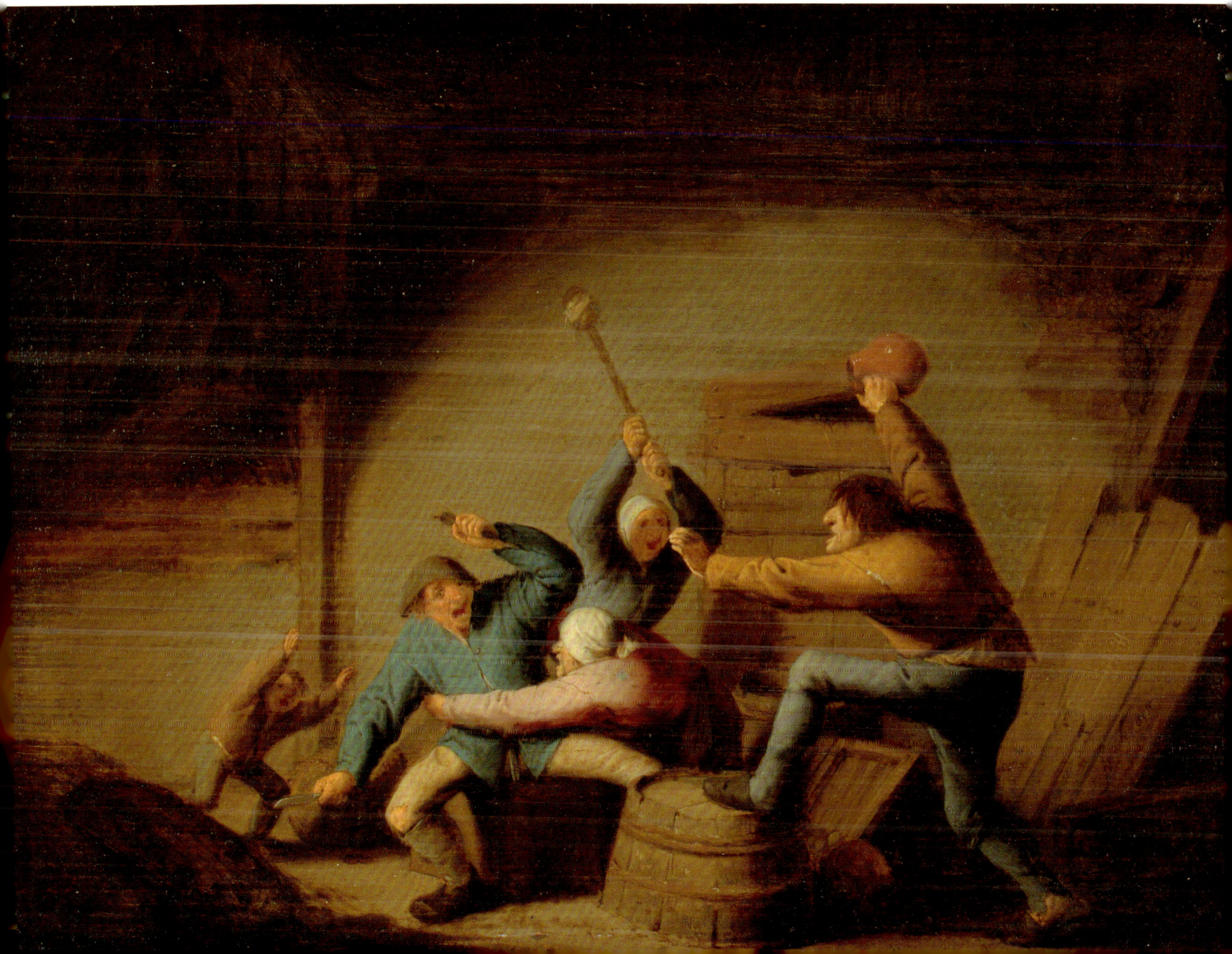

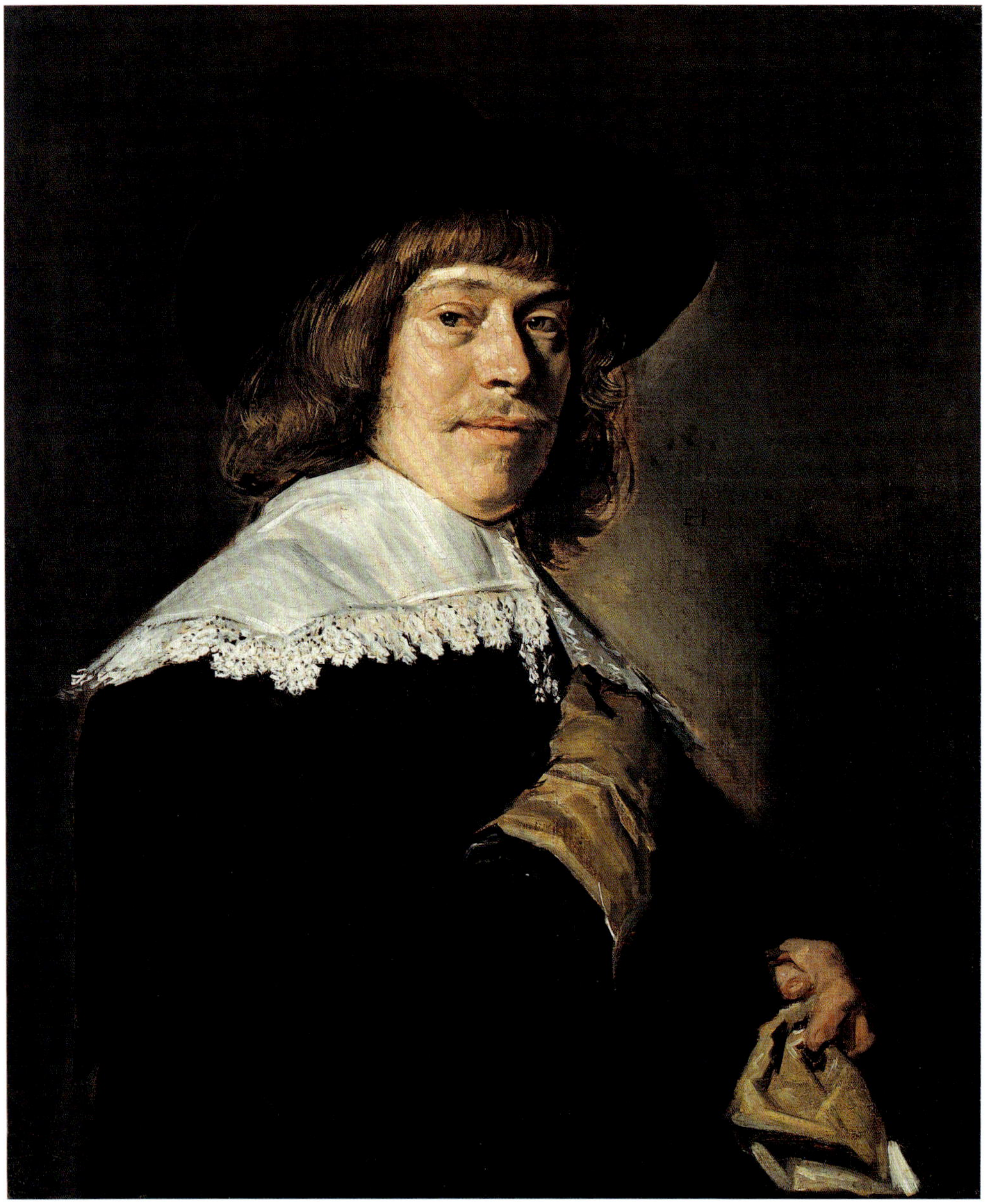

left: FRANS HALS. *Portrait of a Young Man Holding a Glove.* CA. 1650. OIL ON CANVAS. $31\frac{1}{2} \times 26\frac{1}{8}$ IN. (80×66.5 CM).

Now considered one of the finest portraitists in the history of painting, Hals was regarded in his own lifetime as a mere journeyman painter. Here an economic use of paints, in both variety and application, did not prevent him from creating an eloquent, substantial image of a sybarite with full lips and a gourmet's nose, crowned with the thick hair of a ladies' man. The sad gaze and cursorily painted details give the subject the charm of a dandy.

opposite: GERARD TERBORCH. *Portrait of Catarina van Leunink.* AFTER 1654. OIL ON CANVAS. $31\frac{1}{2} \times 23\frac{1}{4}$ IN. (80×59 CM)

In the second half of the 17th century, Terborch began painting smaller size, full-length portraits of Dutch nobility against neutral, often dark, backgrounds, a practice that ensured his success and prosperity. Though priced at a relatively low cost for the time, these works are nevertheless marked by the artist's exceptional mastery in depicting clothes, hands, and faces, while their intimate character made them ideal decoration for the private rooms or study of the buyer's house.

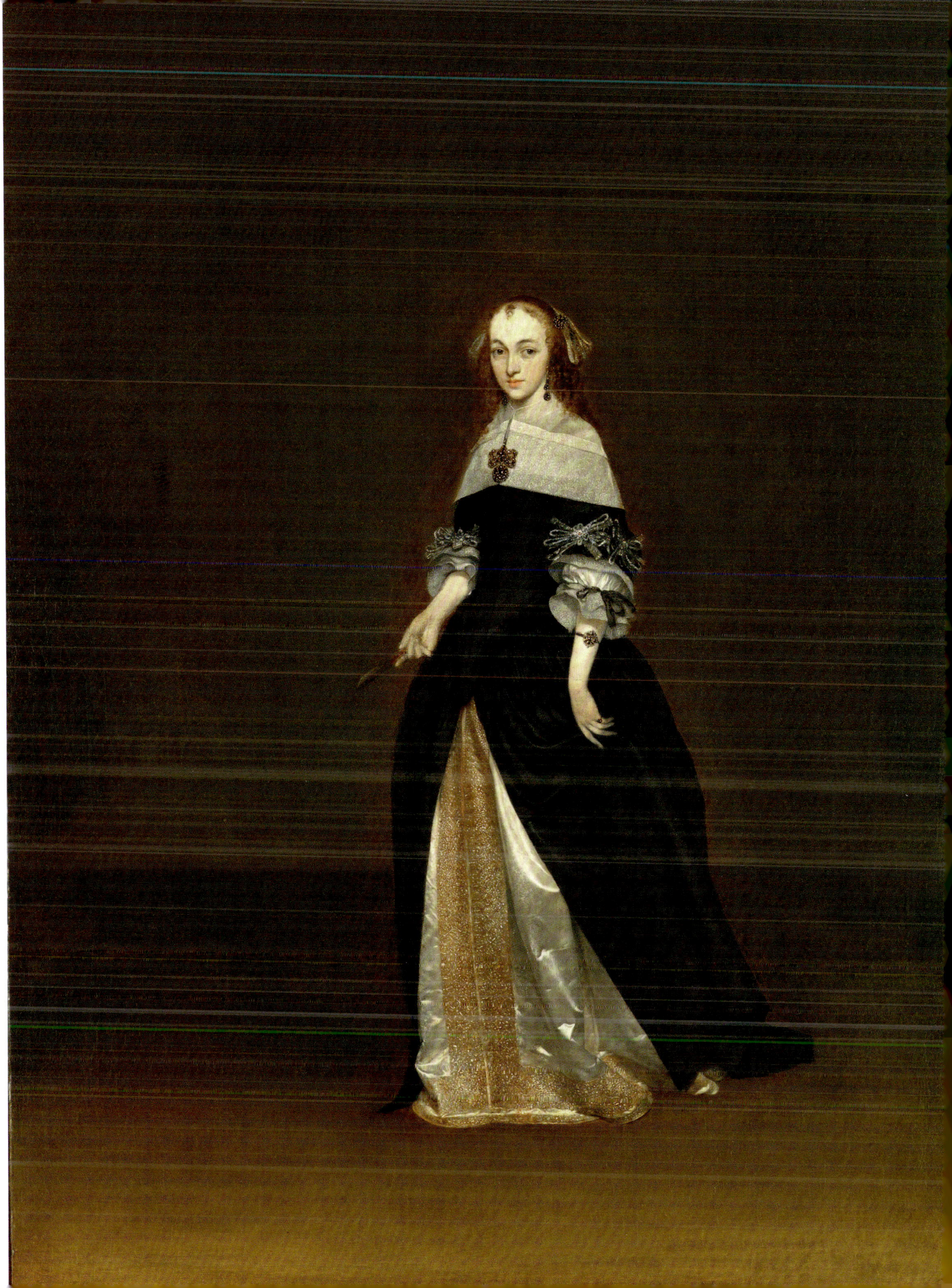

GERARD TERBORCH. *Reading a Letter.* LATE 17TH CENTURY. OIL ON CANVAS. 27 1/2 × 21 1/4 IN. (70 × 54 CM).

Writing, sending, receiving, and reading letters were popular subjects in the genre painting of Holland's golden age. Located on the North Sea coast, Holland, after winning political independence, became the crossroads of the world's sea routes and its citizens started to travel much more than before. A girl or a woman expecting the return of her beloved or her husband is a typical character in such a situation.

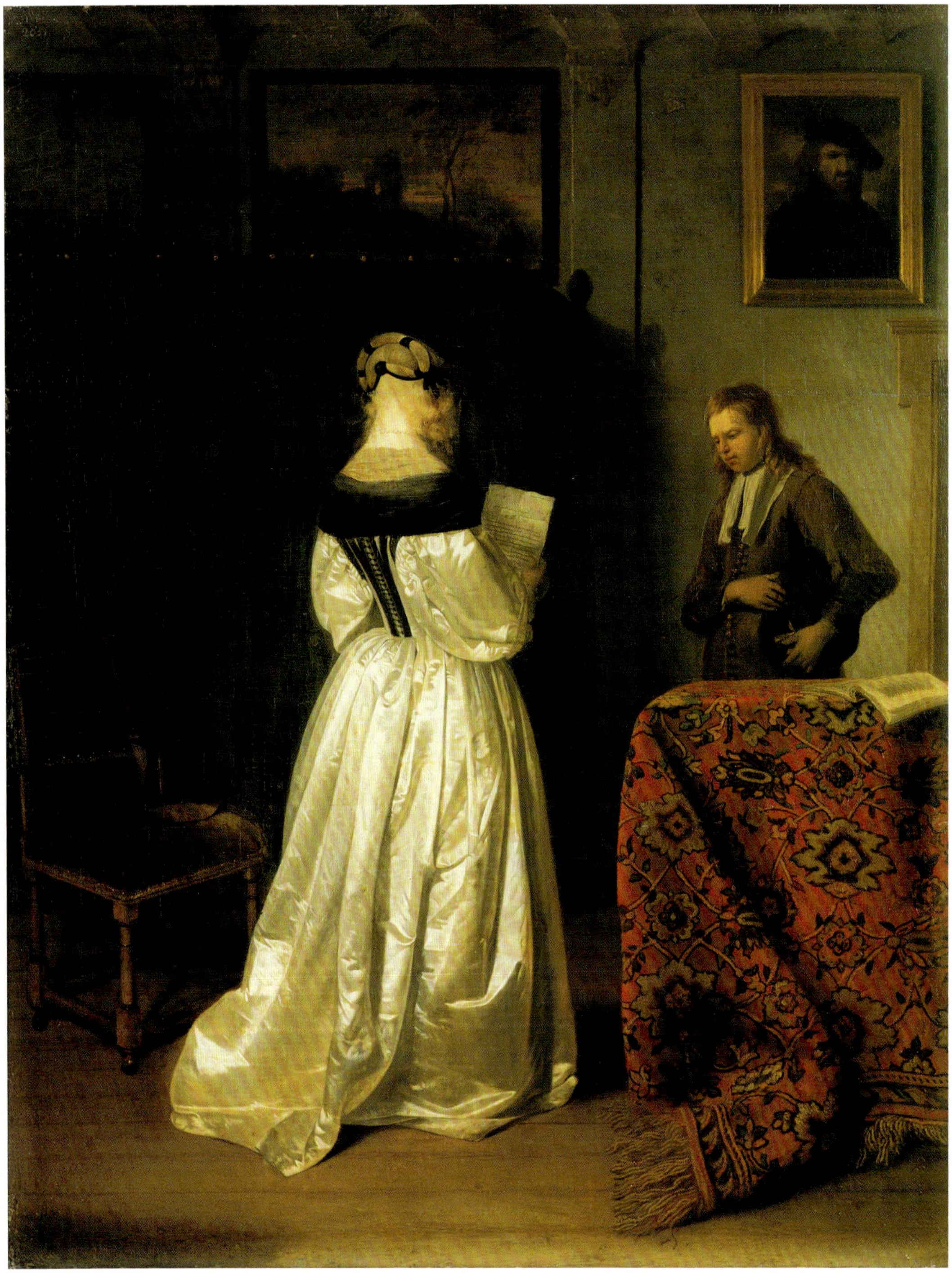

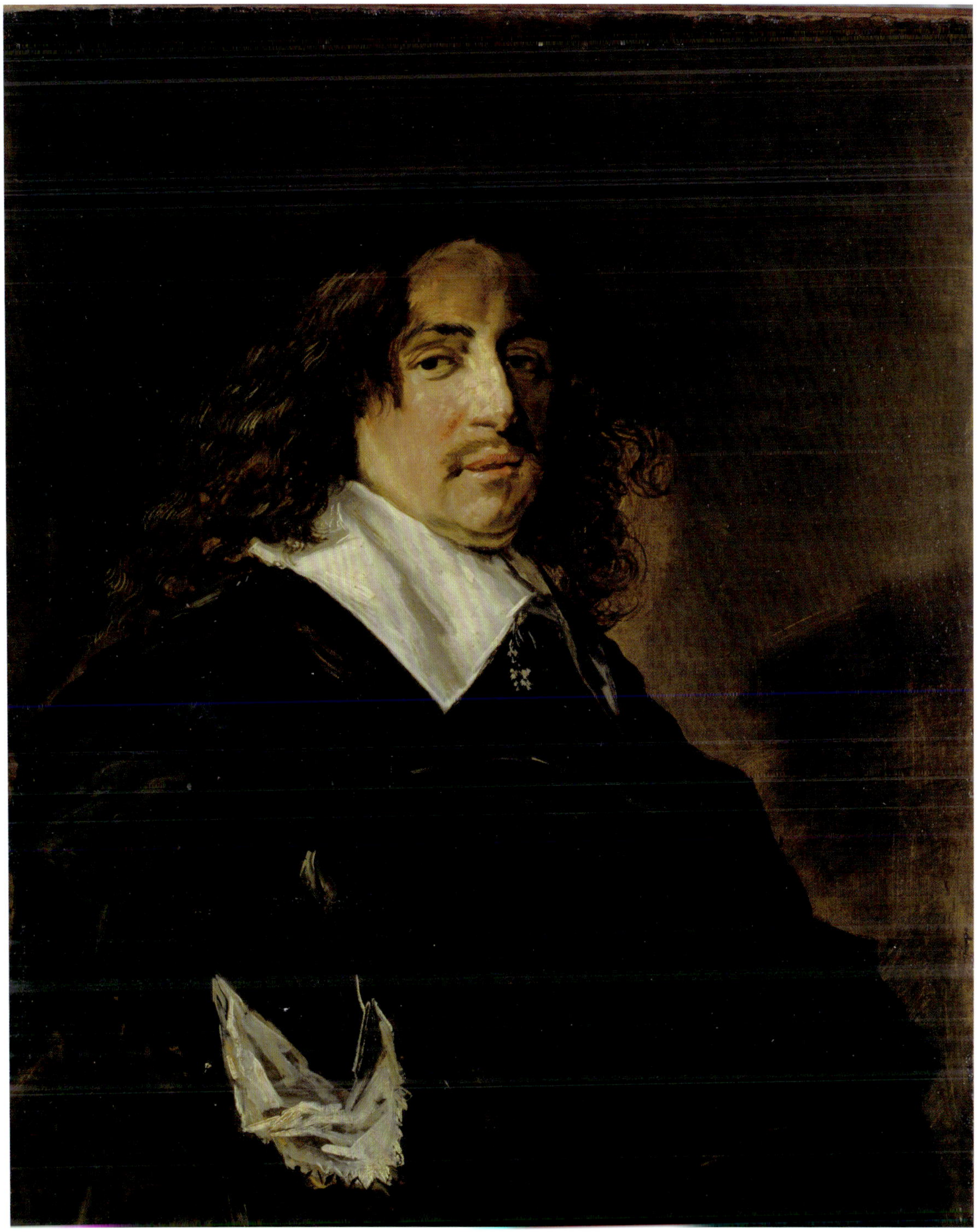

FRANS HALS. *Portrait of a Man.* BEFORE 1660. OIL ON CANVAS.
33¼ × 26⅜ IN. (84.5 × 67 CM).

Only the late Hals knew how to preserve the strict precision of a virtuoso painter without keeping his nervous irritation in check. The almost abstract, chromatic perfection does not impede the impression of truthfulness: the white patch in the foreground, for which it is hard to find an explanation in the subject, emerges from the darkness of the cape with the same sharpness sensed in the model's arrogant gaze and grumpily crumpled chin.

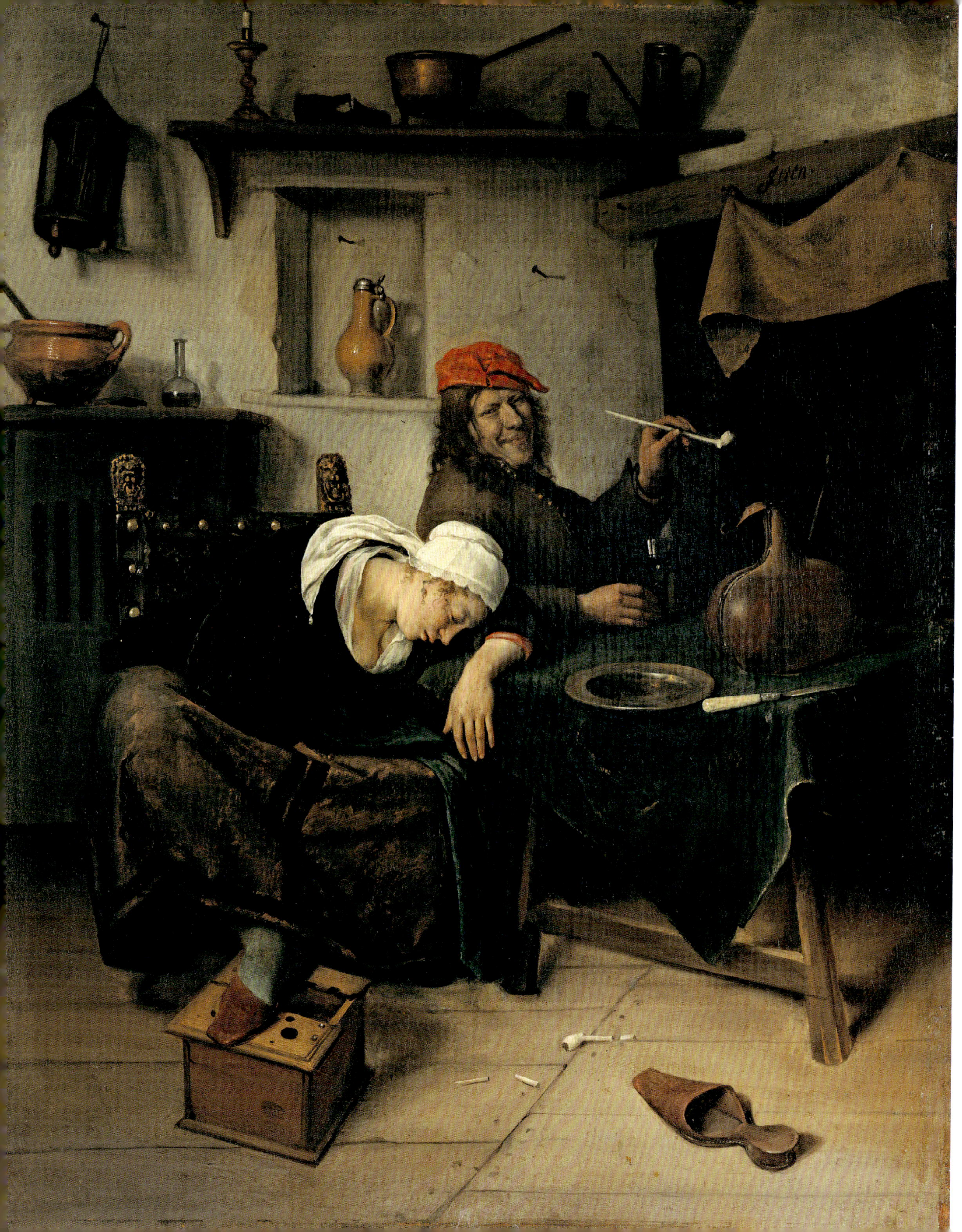

opposite: JAN STEEN. *The Revelers.* CA. 1660. OIL ON PANEL. $15^{3}/_{8}$ × $11^{7}/_{8}$ IN. (39 × 30 CM).

The Dutch Revolution of 1568 flung the country into a war with Spain that lasted off and on for eighty years. It was also the start of a stormy economic boom. In Steen's work, this era of euphoria, of daily changes and dangerous temptations, is reflected in an ambiguity that cannot always be resolved. The drunken couple are Steen and his wife, whose disorderly home points out the distressing moral that vice leads to ruin.

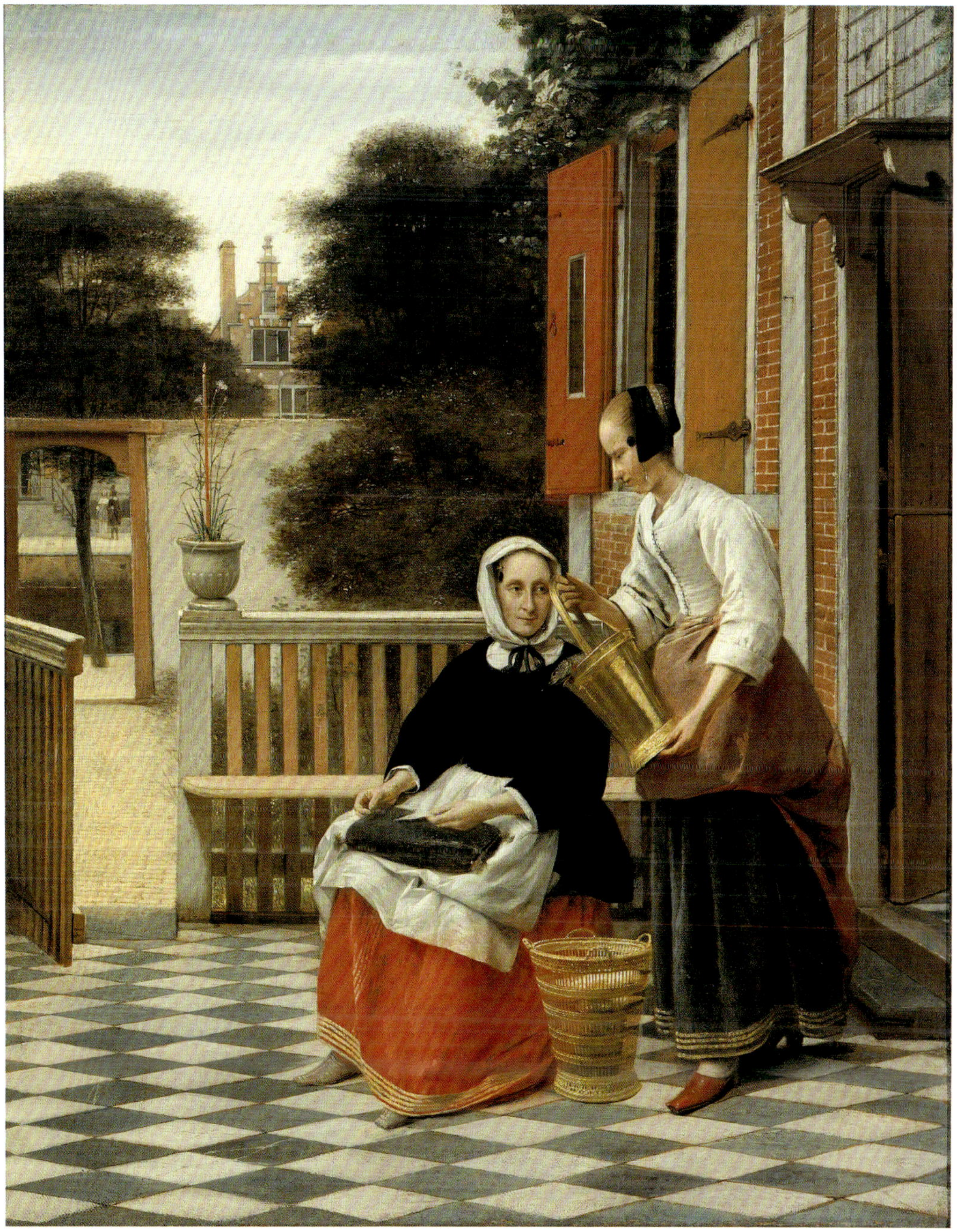

above: PIETER DE HOOCH. *A Woman and Her Maid.* CA. 1660. OIL ON CANVAS. $20^{7}/_{8}$ × $16^{1}/_{2}$ IN. (53 × 42 CM).

Despite not belonging to the genre, de Hooch's paintings fit the description of a still life. Strictly constructed perspective, skillful chiaroscuro, and bright colors create a sense of a frozen moment that encompasses eternity. Among his innovations was the inclusion of adjoining rooms or a street, which enables the viewer to determine the time and place of their creation. Judging by the canal, this airy work was painted in Amsterdam after de Hooch's move there in 1661.

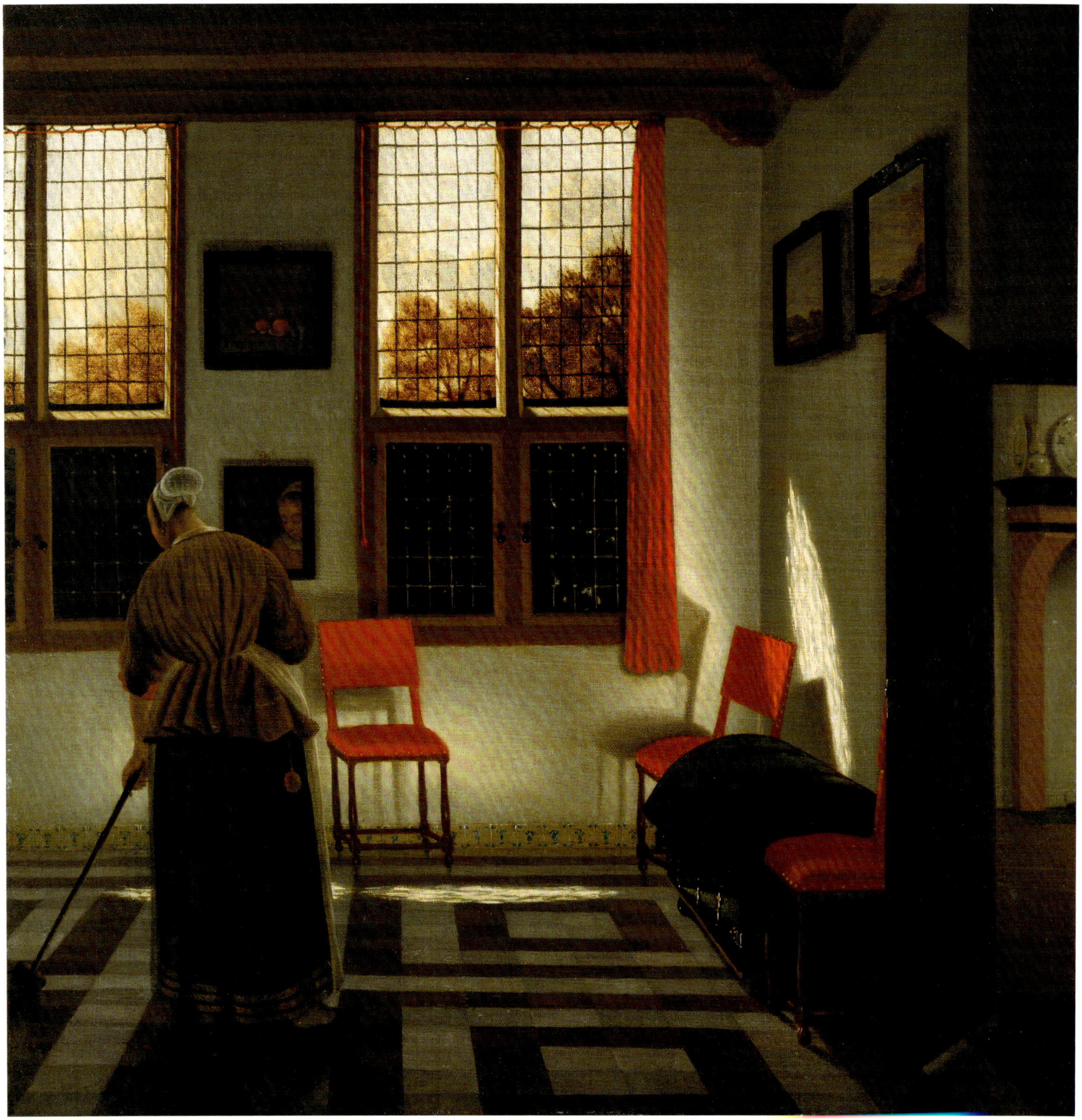

PIETER JANSSENS ELINGA. *Room in a Dutch House.* LATE 1660S–EARLY 1670S. OIL ON CANVAS. 24 1/4 × 23 1/4 IN. (61.5 × 59 CM).

Order in everything was a main virtue in Protestant Holland. That is why many paintings of this period, especially the works of Delft masters, and Pieter Janssens Elinga, in particular, look like a quiet hymn to Order. In this painting, the idea of order is expressed by a sparkling clean, prosperous house with the accurate lines of square floor tiles, rectangular window grates, walls, and pictures. And the bright light on the walls suggests God's blessing.

FRANS JANSZ VAN MIERIS THE ELDER. *Lady at Her Toilette.* CA. 1659–60. OIL ON PANEL. 20¼ × 15½ IN. (51.5 × 39.5 CM).

In the works by Frans Jansz van Mieris the Elder, contemporaries were impressed not only by the mastery of his delicate brushstrokes but also by the captivating story told with numerous details and innuendos. Good-humoredly the painter is shaking a finger at his heroine, while she is playing with her dog. The maid's critical gaze makes it perfectly clear: probably the lady is overcome by a love malady suggested by details such as a letter on the table, a candle near the bed, and pretty green shoes.

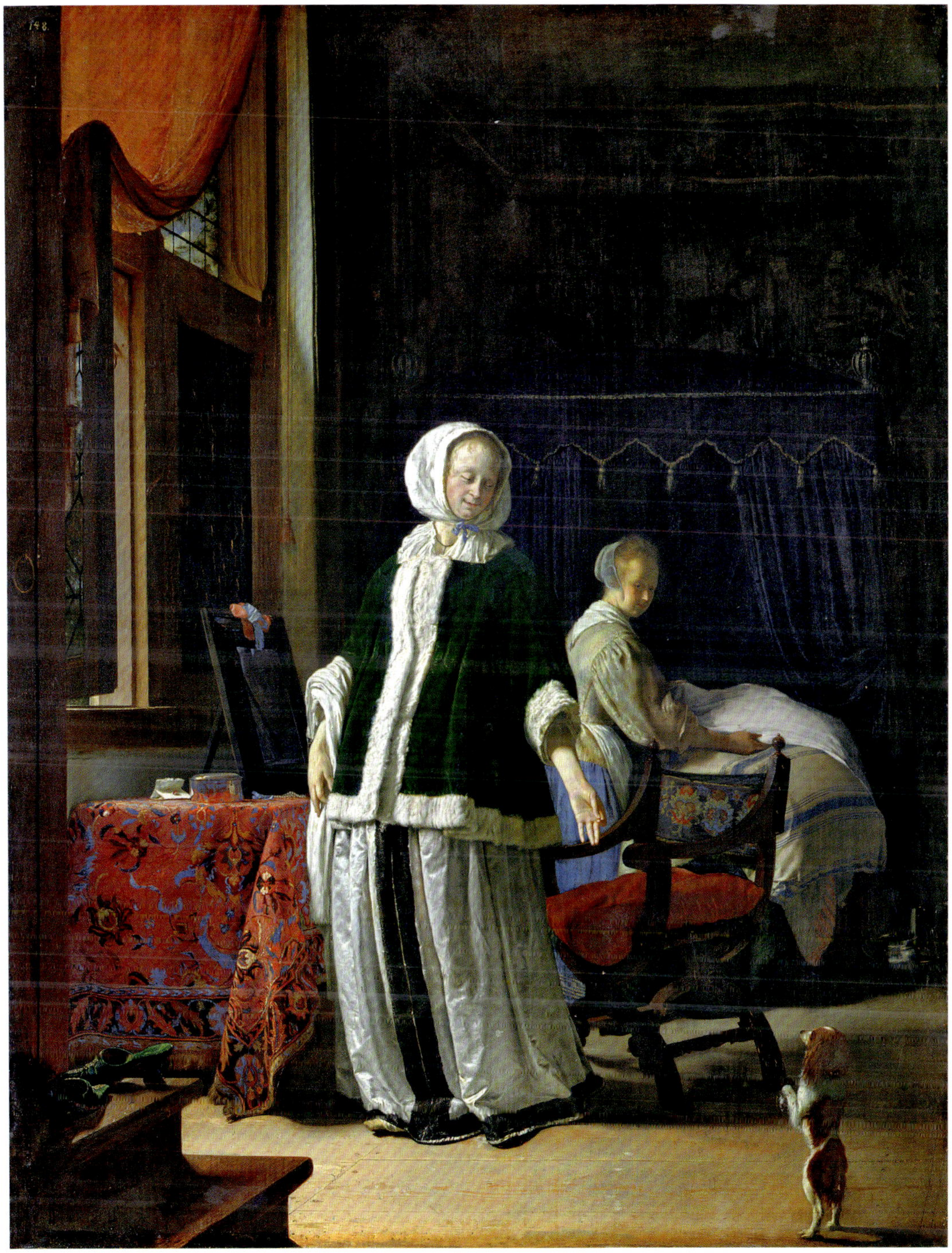

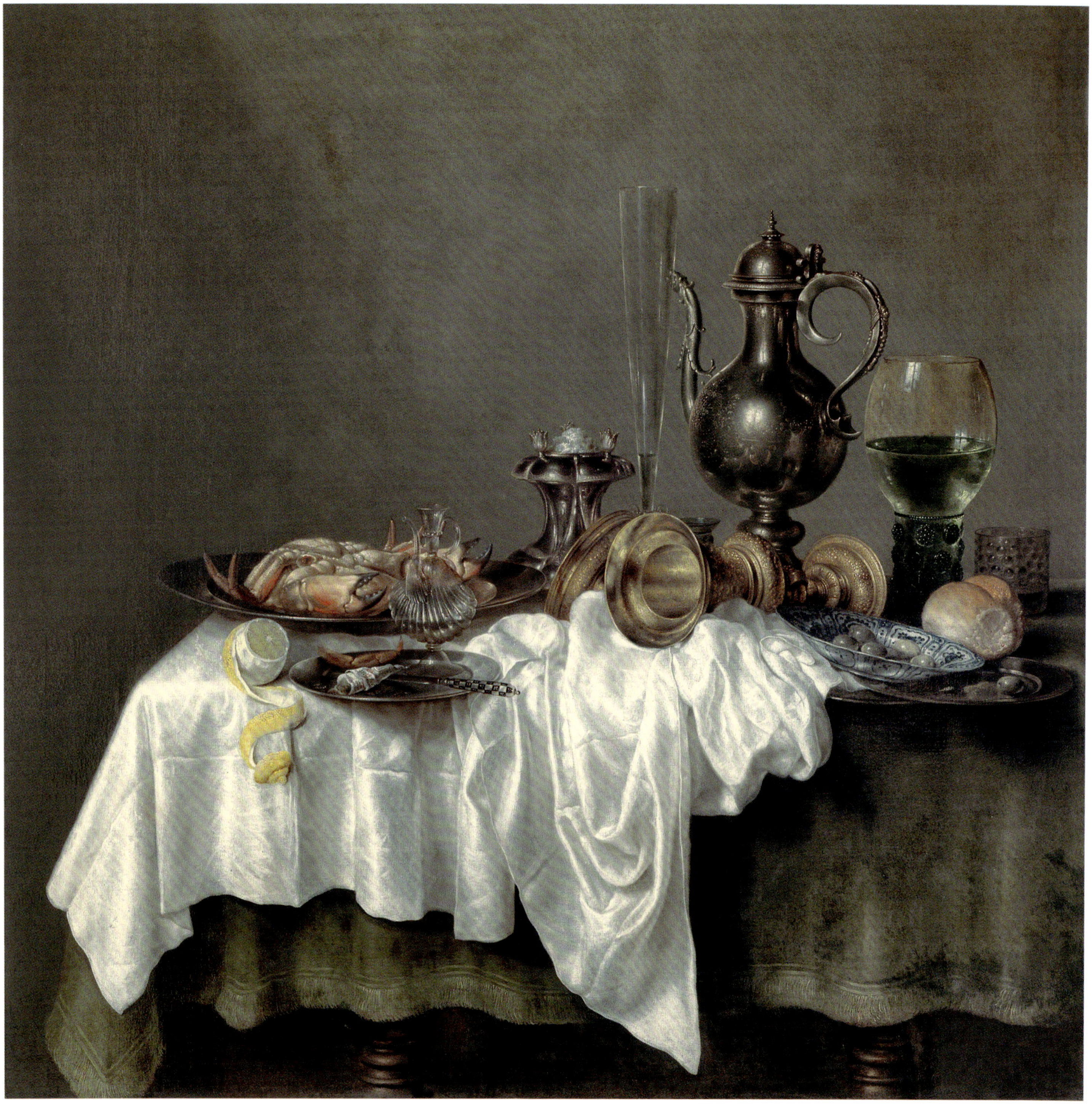

WILLEM CLAESZ HEDA. *Breakfast with a Crab.* 1648. OIL ON CANVAS.
46½ × 46½ IN. (118 × 118 CM).

Looking at *Breakfast* it is easy to understand how the 17th-century Dutch came up with the term *stilleven*, or "still life." The painting is transfused with a sense of domestic warmth and cozy sufficiency. The unfinished glass of wine, the plate moved to the edge of the table, the lemon, the crusty roll, and the huge crab testify to the recent presence of the master of the house, to his tastes and habits.

right: WILLEM KALF. *Dessert.* OIL ON CANVAS. 41 3/8 × 34 1/2 IN. (105 × 87.5 CM).

Gradually the role of decorativeness expanded in the Dutch still life. Kalf, recognized as a great artist by contemporaries (rare for exponents of this genre), owed his fame to the effective combination of a set of elements that appear in different positions and at different angles in painting after painting: bright yellow and orange fruit, an oriental carpet with a deep red-and-black pattern, and exquisitely decorated tableware that gleams against a dense black background.

below: BALTHASAR VAN DER AST. *Still Life with Fruits, Shells and Insects.* 1620S. OIL ON PANEL. 29 1/2 × 41 IN. (75 × 104 CM).

Acute interest in the world in all its manifestations was pervasive in 17th-century Holland. Fascination with the diversity of nature can be easily felt in the works by Balthasar van der Ast, one of the founders of Dutch still-life painting, in which flowers, fruits, shells, insects, and outlandish birds are scrupulously depicted in the minutest detail. At the same time the painter warns us in an allegoric language about the danger of sin, inevitability of punishment, and necessity of repentance.

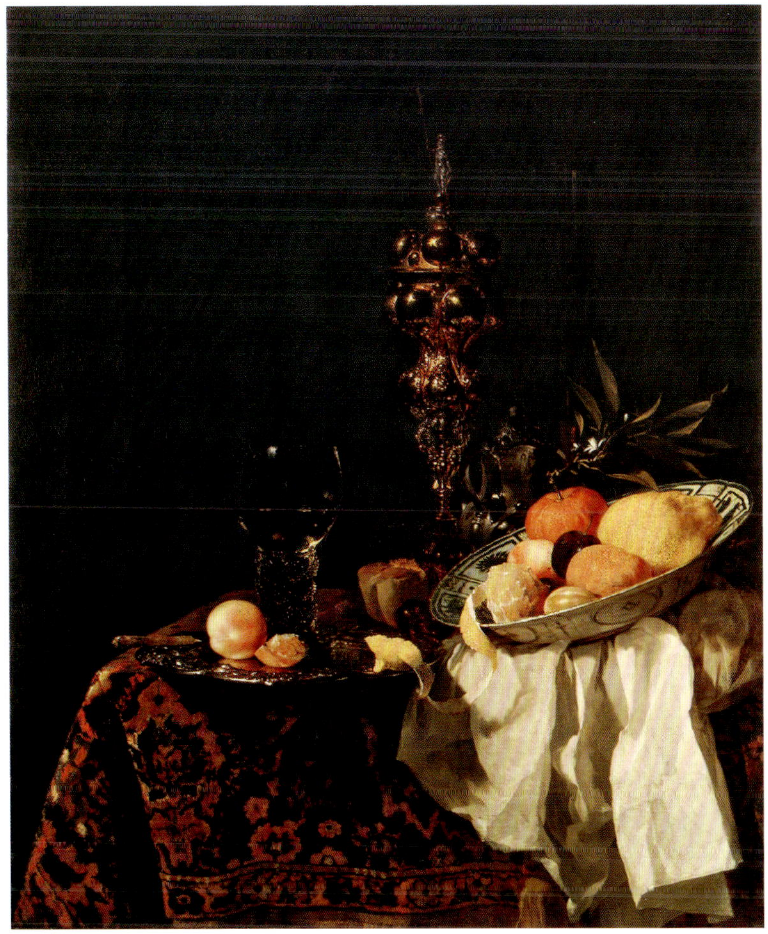

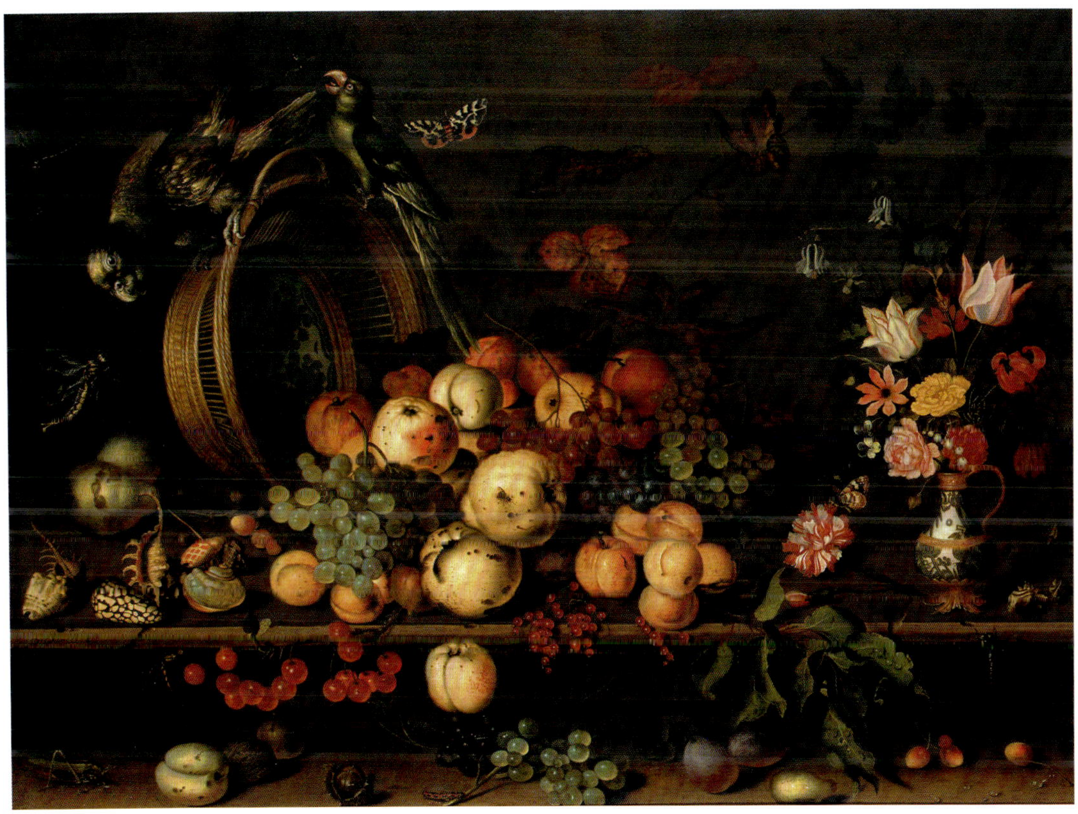

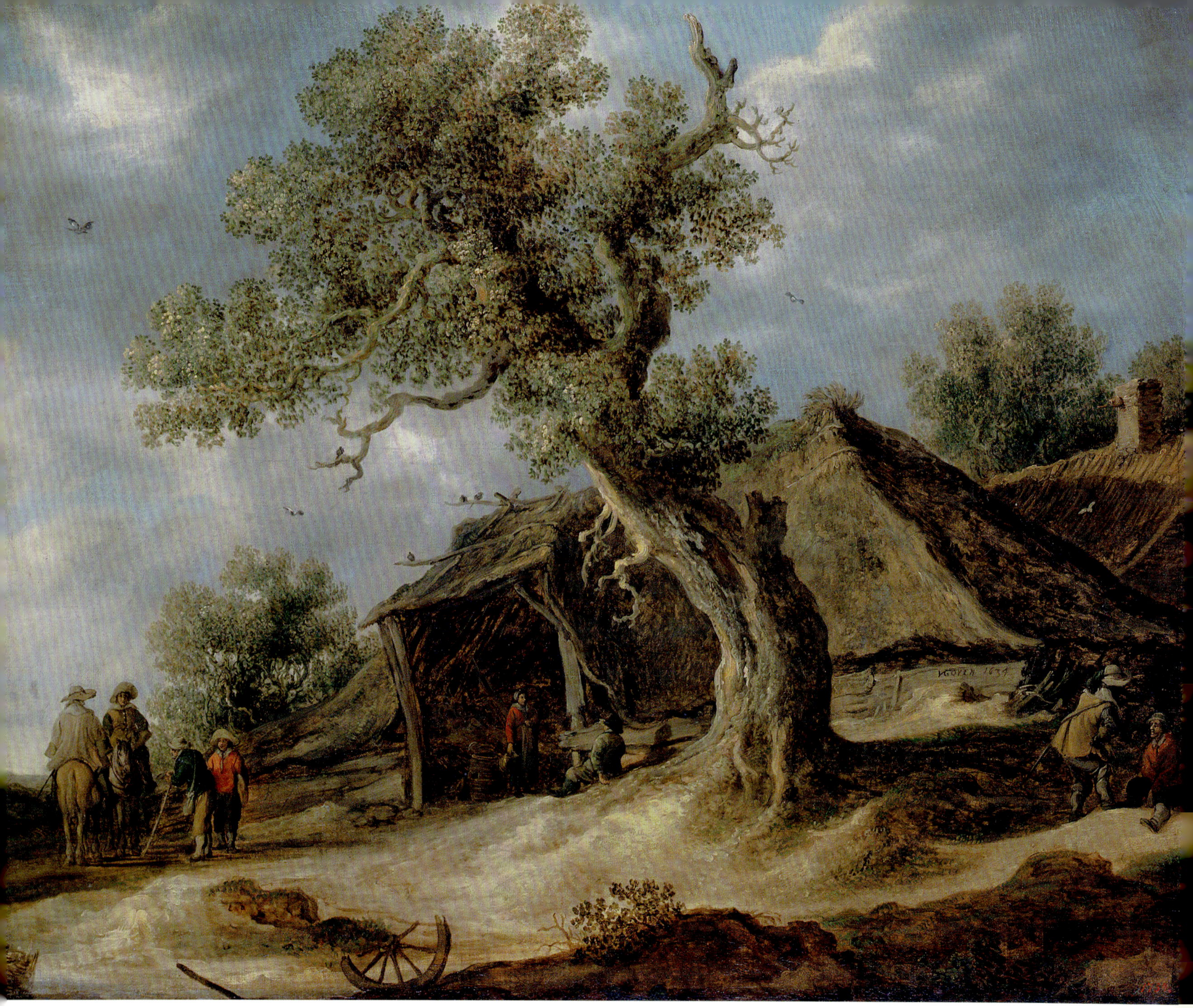

JAN JOZEFSZ VAN GOYEN. *Landscape with an Oak.* 1634.
OIL ON CANVAS. 34 1/4 × 41 3/8 IN. (87 × 105 CM).

With Salomon van Ruysdael, van Goyen was a founder of the Haarlem school of Dutch landscape painting. A tireless draftsman, he left many sketches made from nature; it's possible his paintings were inspired by real-life impressions rather than invented in the studio, and yet they do have metaphysical content. The fresh foliage on the old sturdy tree and the peasants bustling around the lopsided shack prompt thoughts of the continuation of a way of life established over centuries, regardless of daily hardships.

JACOB ISAACKSZ VAN RUISDAEL. *Seashore.* LATE 1660S–EARLY 1670S. OIL ON CANVAS. 20 1/2 × 26 3/4 IN. (52 × 68 CM).

Ruisdael's sea is usually neither spectacularly stormy nor peaceful, as in the works of many of his contemporary seascape painters, who depicted the water as an extension of a Dutch town. In fact, he depicts the determining component of his country's atmosphere: the wind that constantly stirs up waves and agitates clouds in the boundless sky. By eschewing excessively thorough detail, he sometimes manages to convey a fleeting impression, extending a hand to the pioneers of 19th-century French plein air painting.

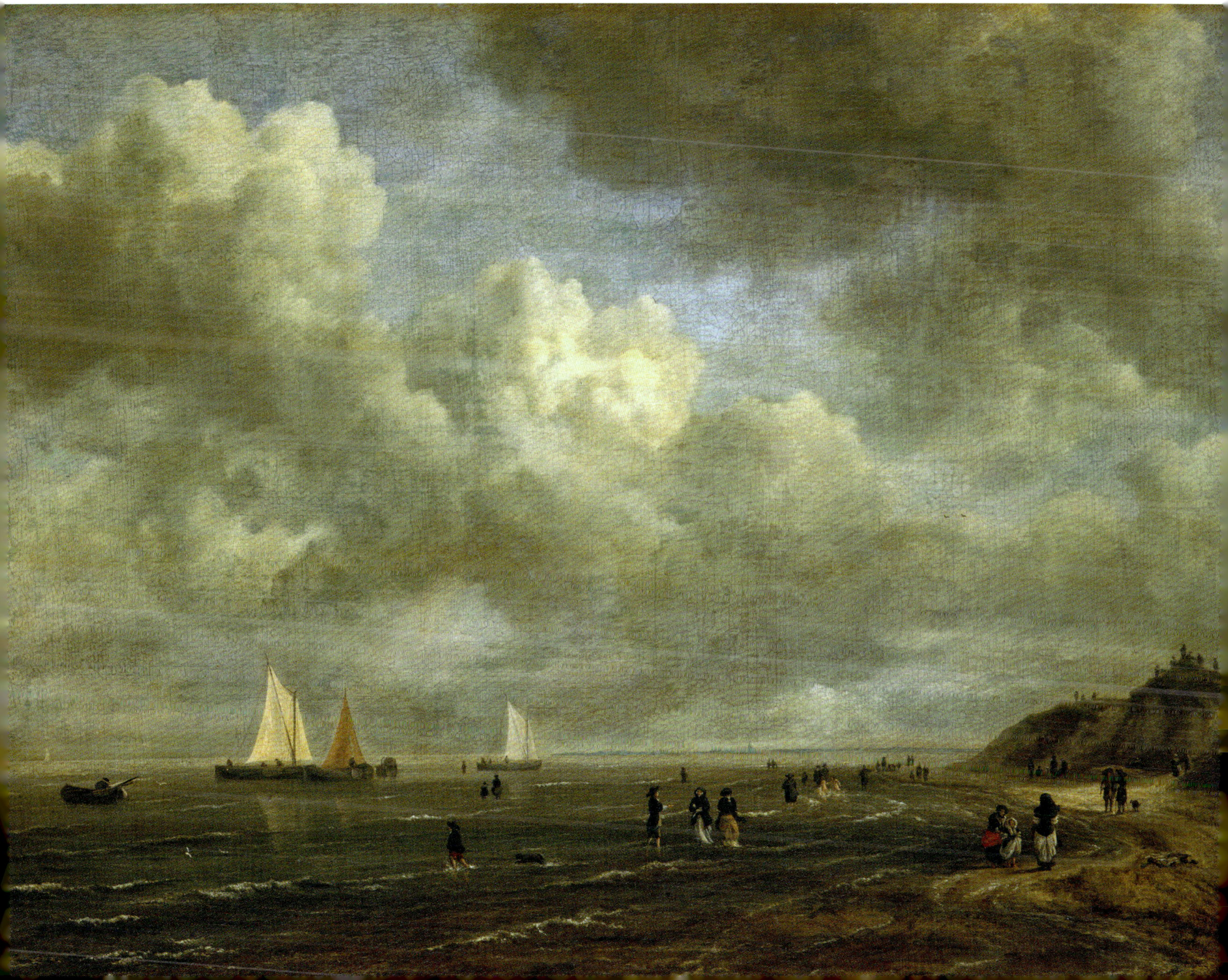

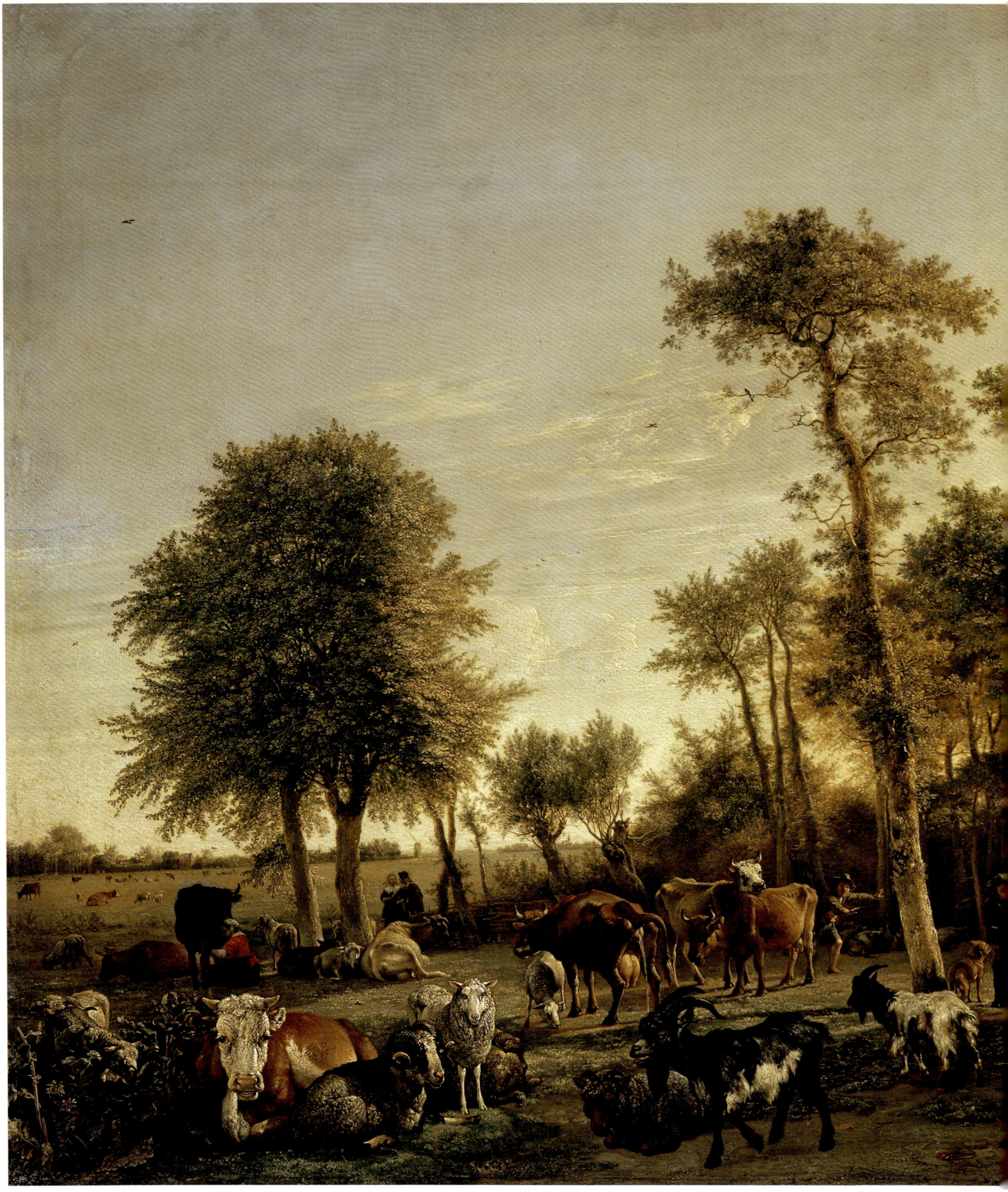

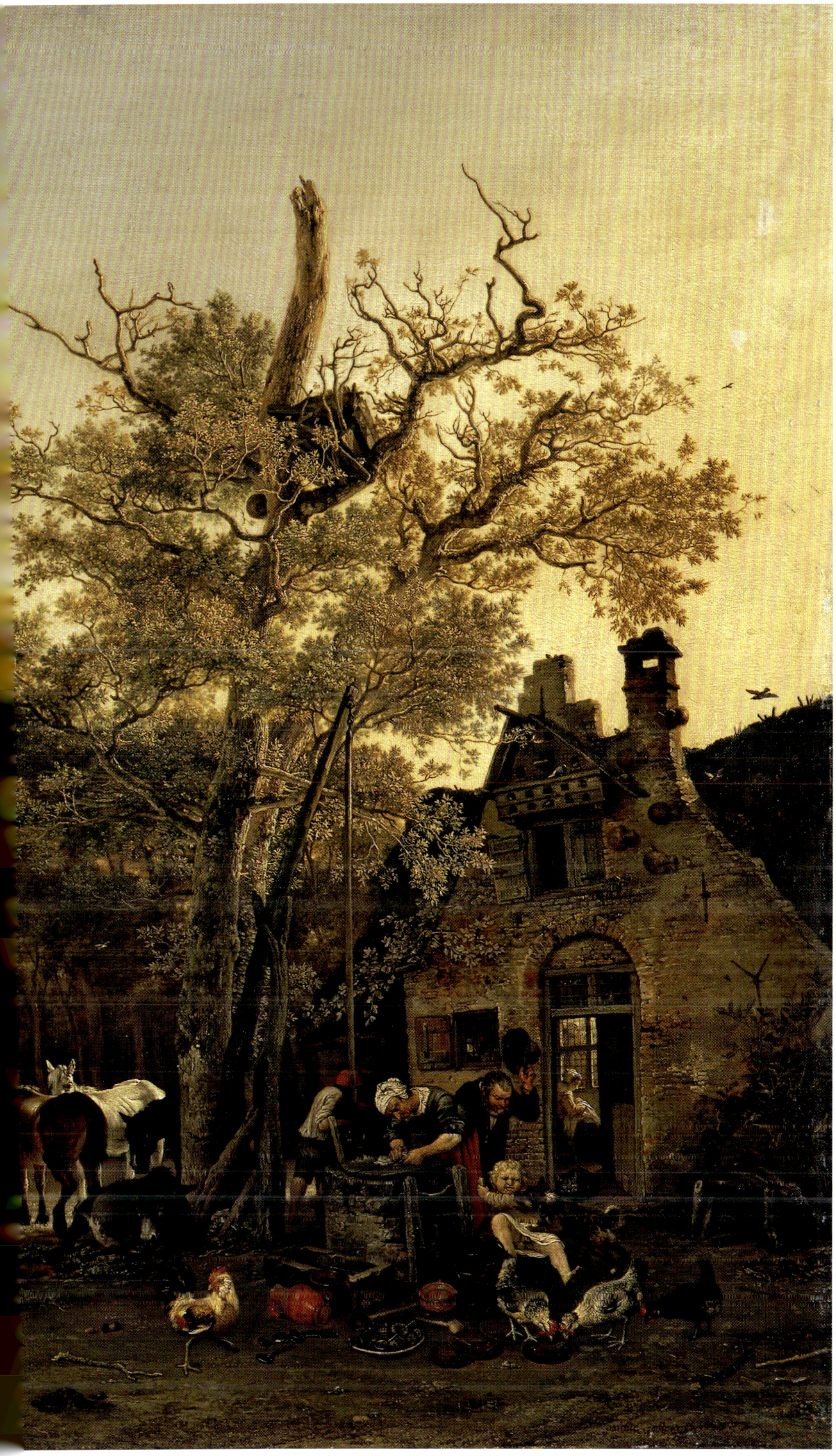

PAULUS POTTER. *The Farm.* 1649. OIL ON CANVAS. $31^{7}/_{8} \times 45^{1}/_{2}$ IN. (81 × 115.5 CM).

The Farm acquired a certain notoriety due to its extremely naturalistic depiction of domestic animals. Nowadays, it is impossible not to notice the overlap between the coarse materiality, which combines strangely with a delicate painting technique in Potter's work, and the famous scene at the agricultural show in Flaubert's novel *Madame Bovary*, in which the banal presentation of awards to the breeders is similarly intercut with the ardent speeches of the seducer.

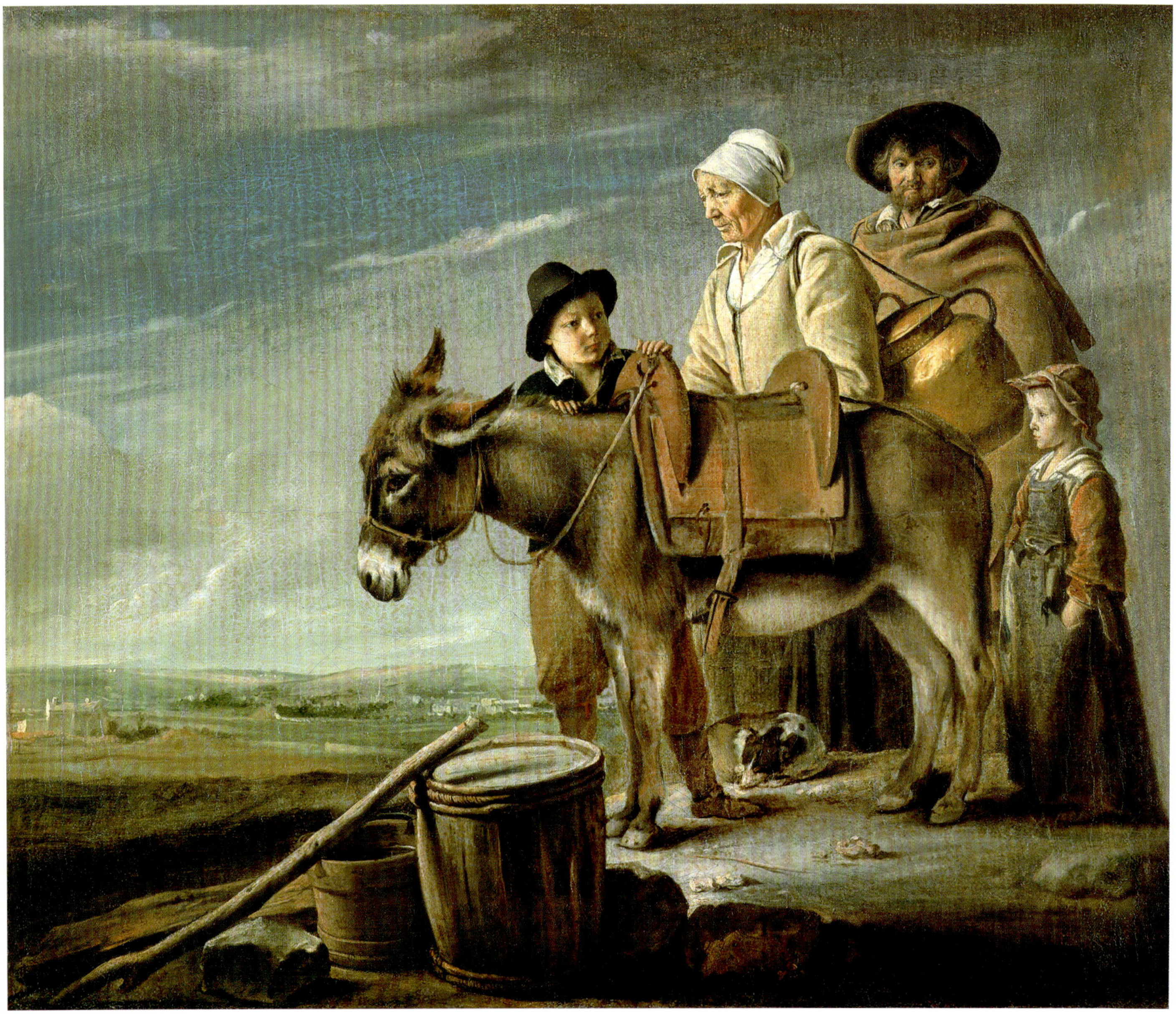

LOUIS LE NAIN. *The Milkmaid's Family.* 1640S. OIL ON CANVAS. 20 × $23^{1}/_{4}$ IN. (51 × 59 CM).

Unlike in contemporary Dutch genre painting, Le Nain's compositions indicate neither peasant labors and leisure nor the common people's hard lot. Indeed, the expensive copper churn and clothing evoke prosperity. This family is more a symbolic expression of the unity between the inhabitants of central France and their native land. The contrived combination of a monumental group standing on a hillock as if on a pedestal, with a majestic panoramic view unfolding behind, has a certain elevated pomp.

LOUIS LE NAIN. *Visit to Grandmother.* CA. 1645–48. OIL ON CANVAS. 22 7/8 × 28 3/4 IN. (58 × 73 CM).

Louis Le Nain was one of three painter brothers who worked together, mainly on commissions from the Parisian aristocracy; in the 1640s they turned their hand to peasant scenes, which had come in to fashion. Devoid of technical luster, their interiors are striking for the interweaving of several melodic threads: approaching and retreating figures, illuminated and shady areas, and the glances the personages seem to give each other just before turning a common, hospitable gaze to the viewer and the world.

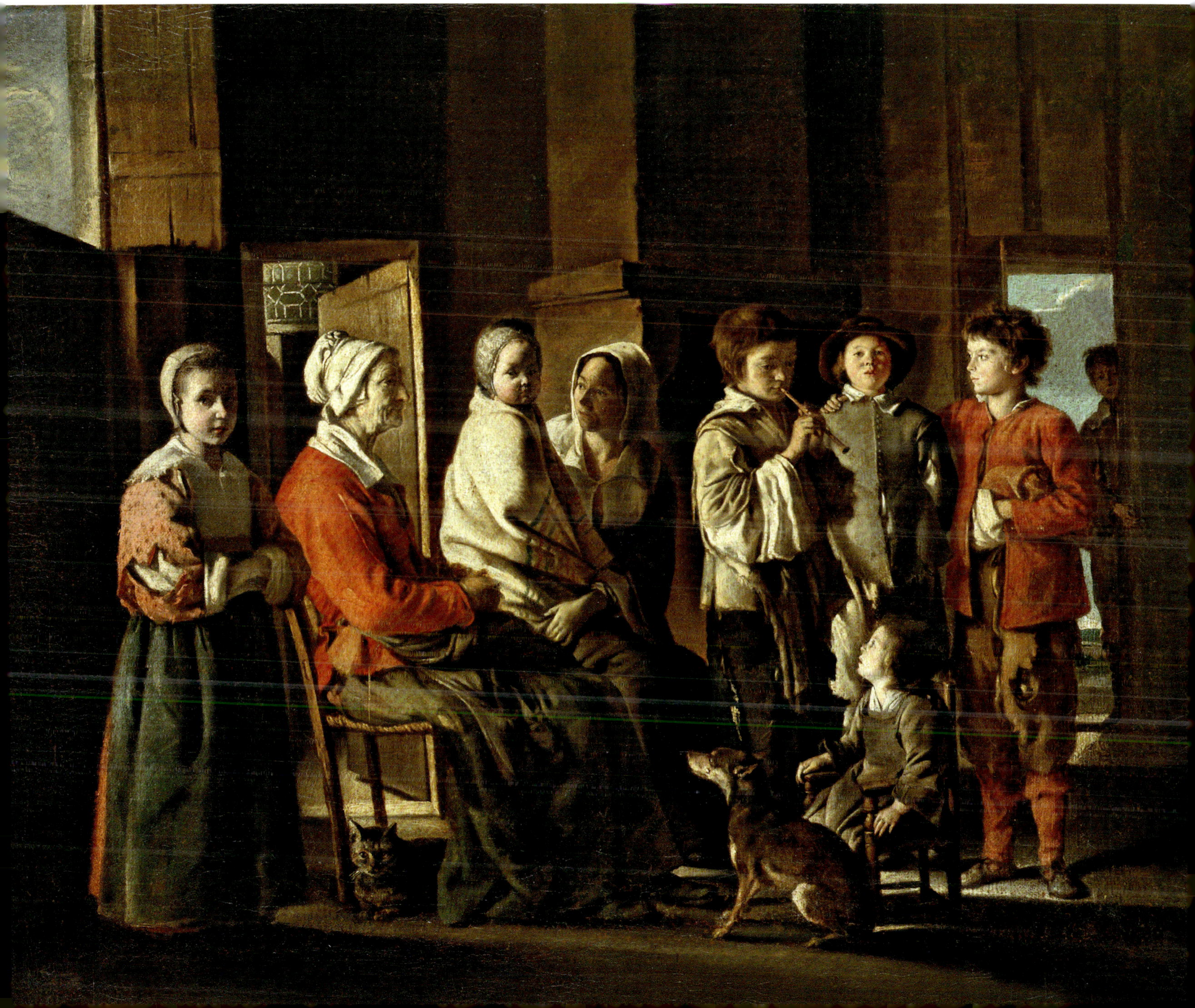

JACQUES BELLANGE. *The Lamentation.* 1615–16. OIL ON CANVAS. $45\frac{1}{4} \times 69$ IN. (115 × 175 CM).

Today Bellange's work is recognized as one of the most enigmatic phenomena in European culture around the turn of the 17th century, and the Hermitage canvas, as a unique masterpiece of French Mannerism. The guttering flame of the candle that fills the painting with an unreal light, the mysterious figures of the mourners whose attire is a strange mixture of historical dress and contemporary 17th-century fashion, and the blue-black color scheme endow the religious scene with the character of a mystic rite.

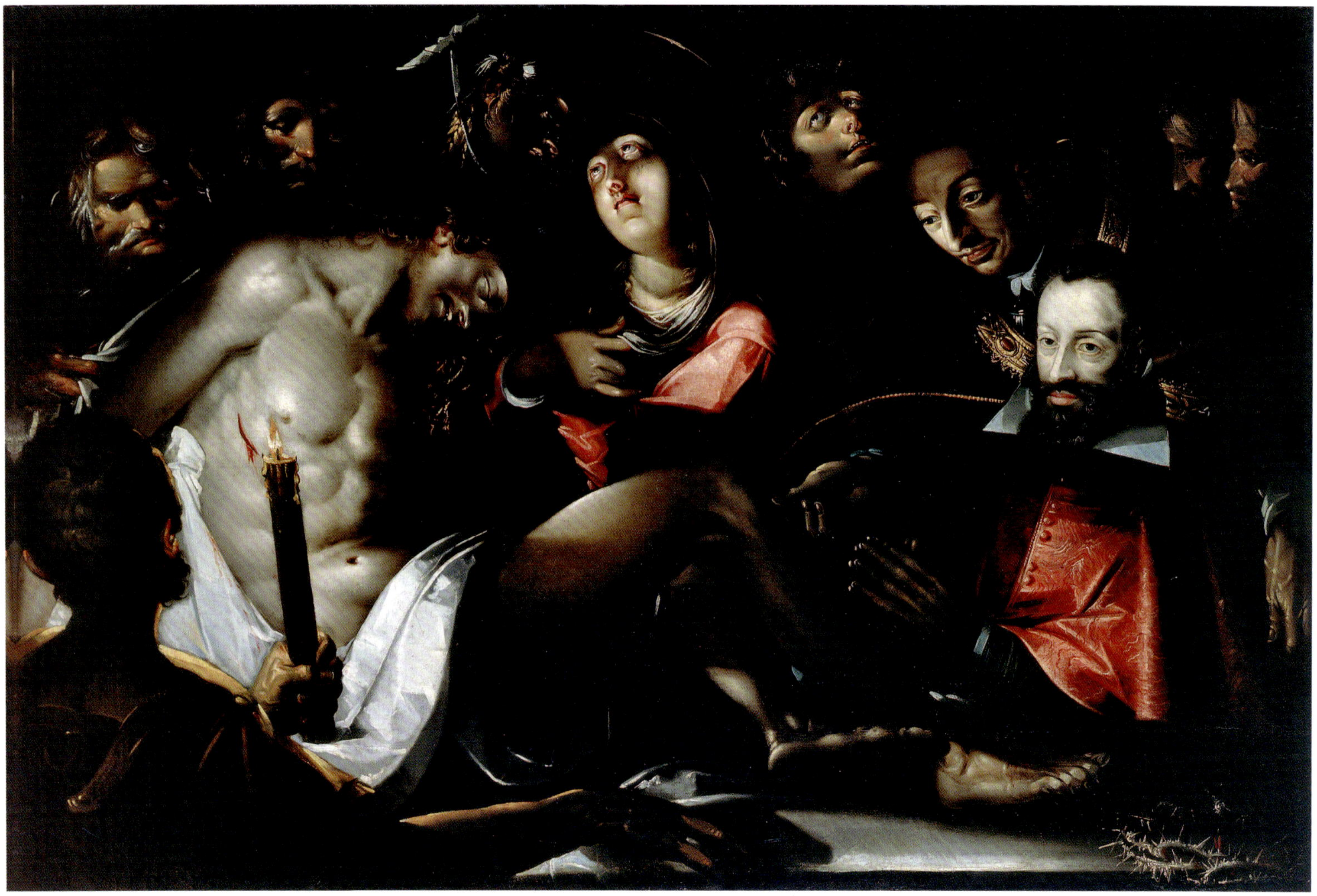

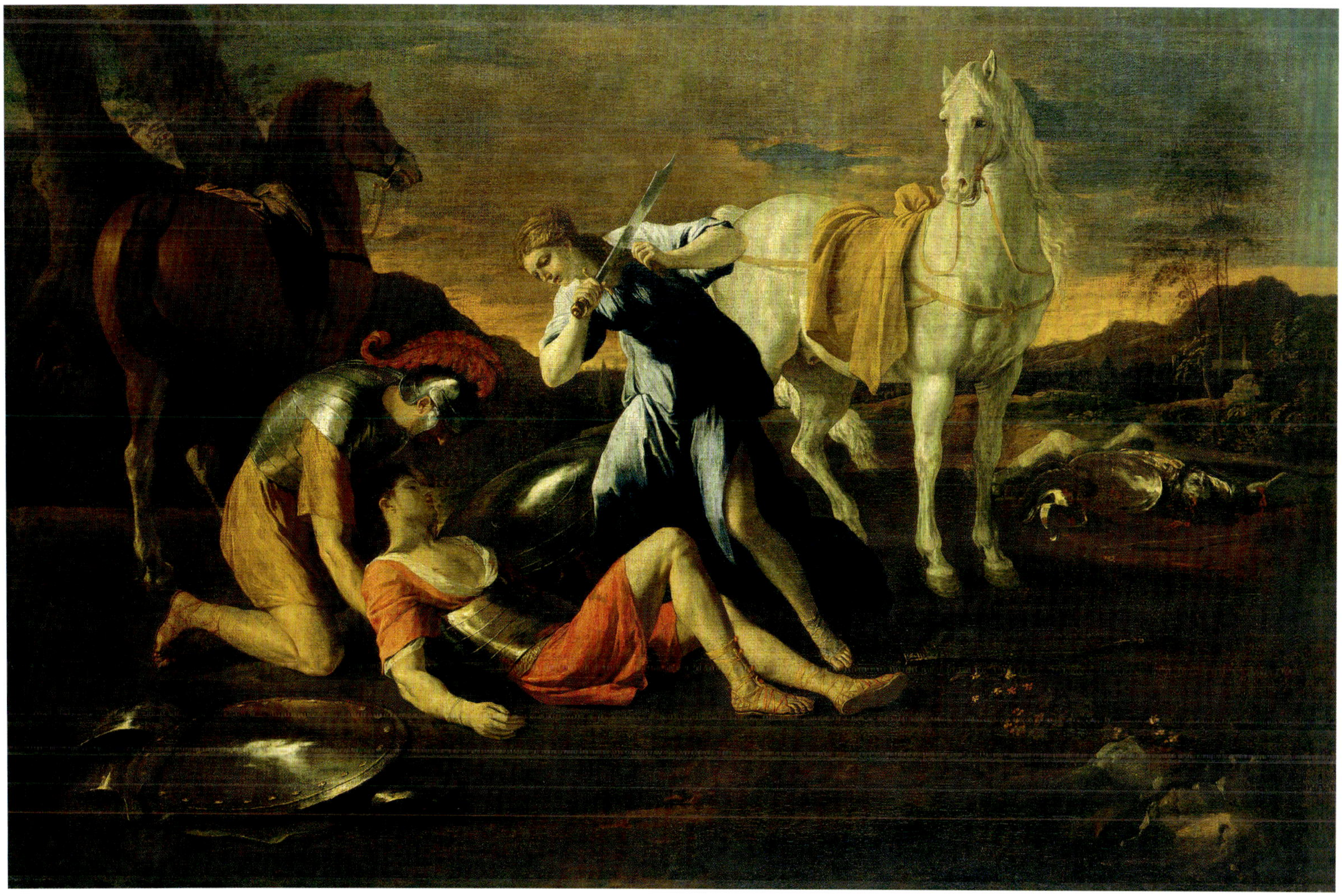

NICOLAS POUSSIN. *Tancred and Erminia.* LATE 1620S–EARLY 1630S. OIL ON CANVAS. 38 1/2 × 57 5/8 IN. (98.5 × 146.5 CM).

This painting illustrates a key moment in Torquato Tasso's poem *Jerusalem Delivered*, when Erminia, the daughter of the king of Antioch, uses the magical power of her hair to save her wounded sweetheart, the crusader Tancred. Poussin demonstrates his ability to moderate passions while presenting an enchanting balance of influences. Neither anatomical precision, nor the eloquence of gestures, nor the power of bright patches of color becomes an end in itself, but together they produce a formula of love and duty that we read without being distracted by superfluous effects.

NICOLAS POUSSIN. *The Battle of the Israelites and Amelikites.* 1624–25.
OIL ON CANVAS. 38 3/8 × 52 3/4 IN. (97.5 × 134 CM).

Poussin's paintings display a highly idiosyncratic French rationalism. Already in this early work, one of the first painted after his arrival in Italy, he places two radically distinct subjects—the "thick of the battle" and Moses praying (which ultimately decides the outcome)—into a tight picture space, distorting proportions but, in exchange, achieving unity and extreme intensity of action.

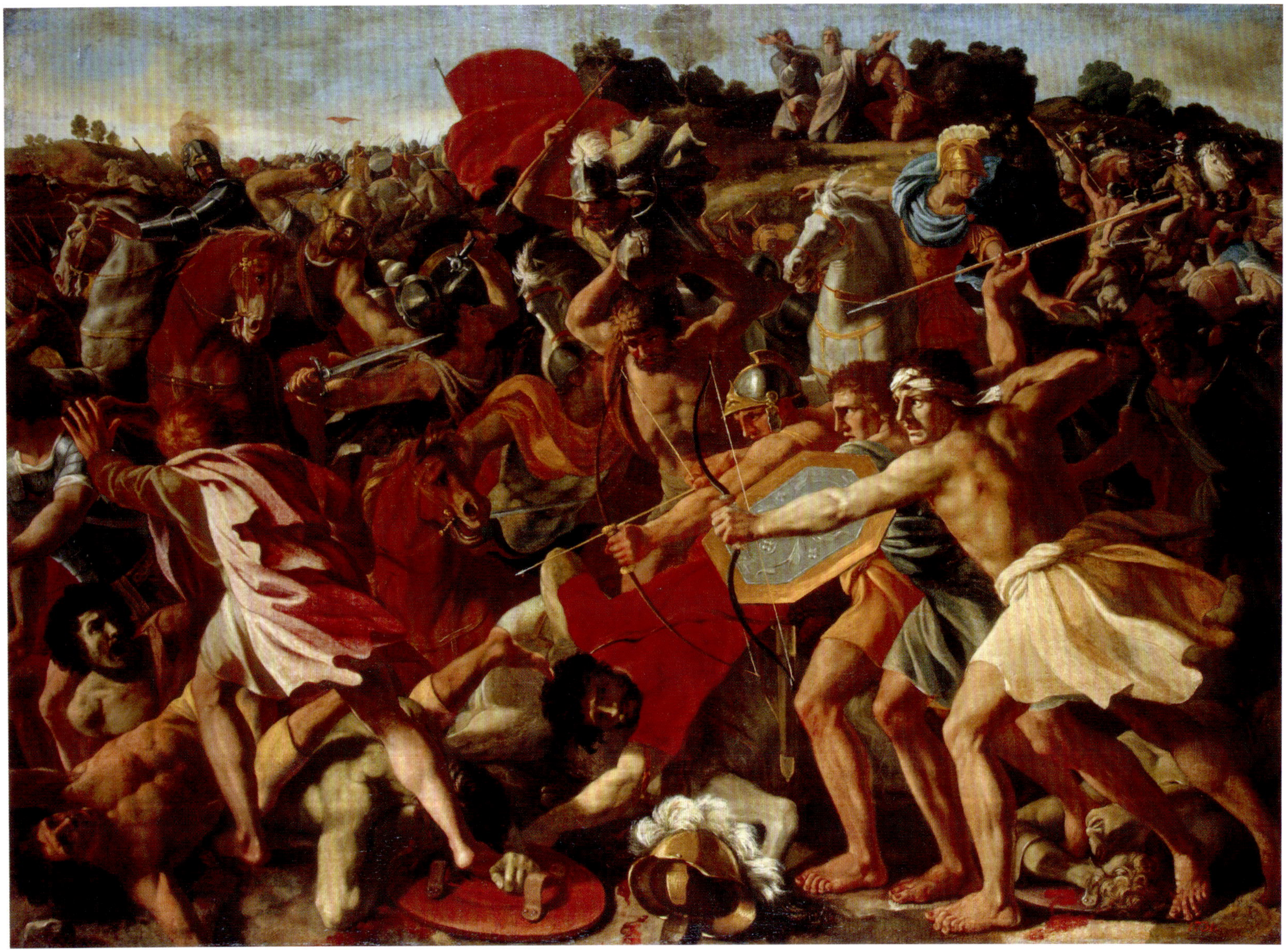

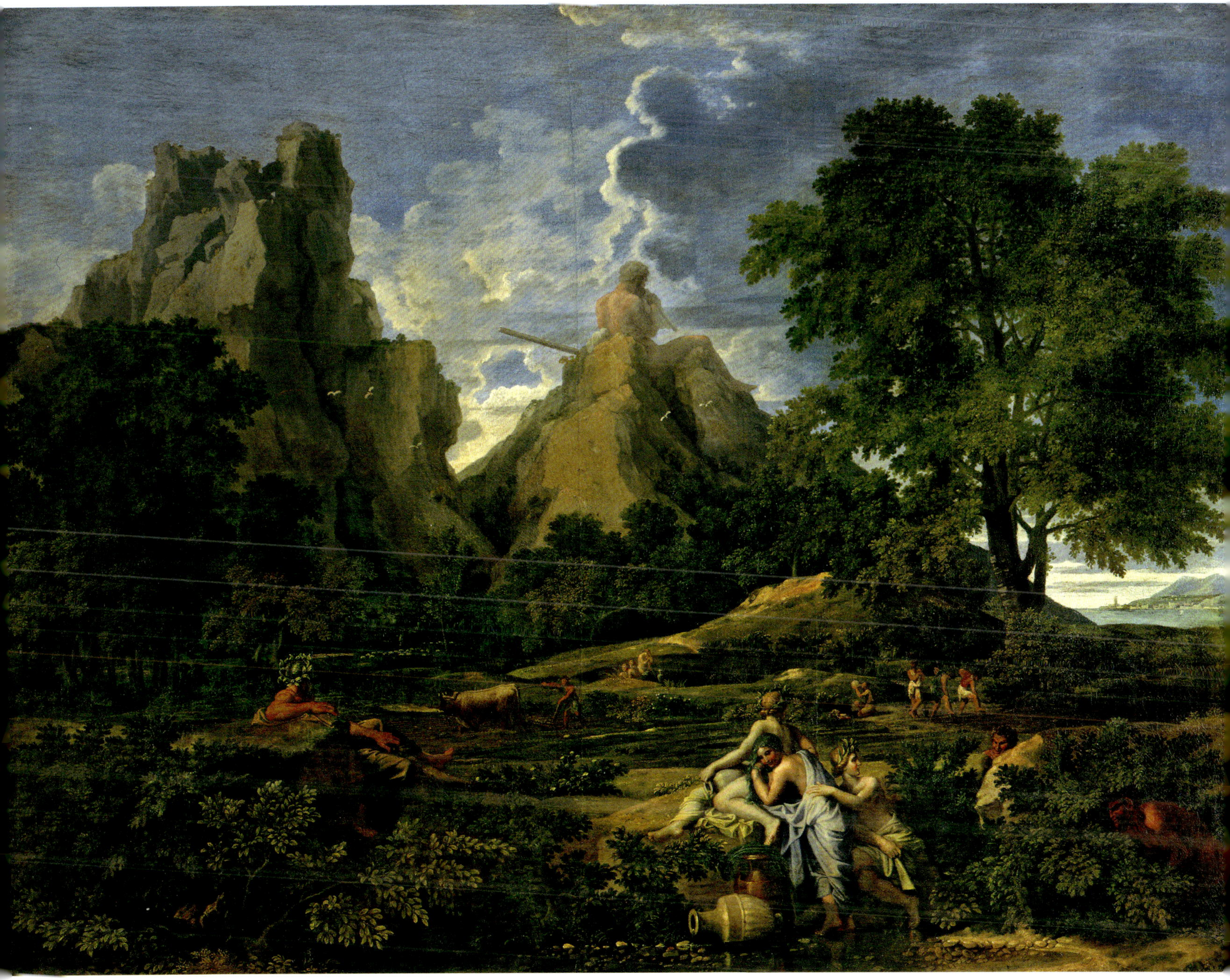

NICOLAS POUSSIN. *Landscape with Polyphemus*. 1649. OIL ON CANVAS. 59 × 78 3/8 IN. (150 × 199 CM).

Poussin's landscapes are striking for his indifference to the illusion of boundless distance, although he mastered the techniques used to produce it. He requires only a small theatrical space to allow our eye to delve into and assess the scale of the valley and the mountains, to notice the Cyclops playing his pipes beneath the sky, and even to enjoy his music, which swells toward the foreground in colors that grow ever more intense, attaining clarity among the deities at the painting's edge.

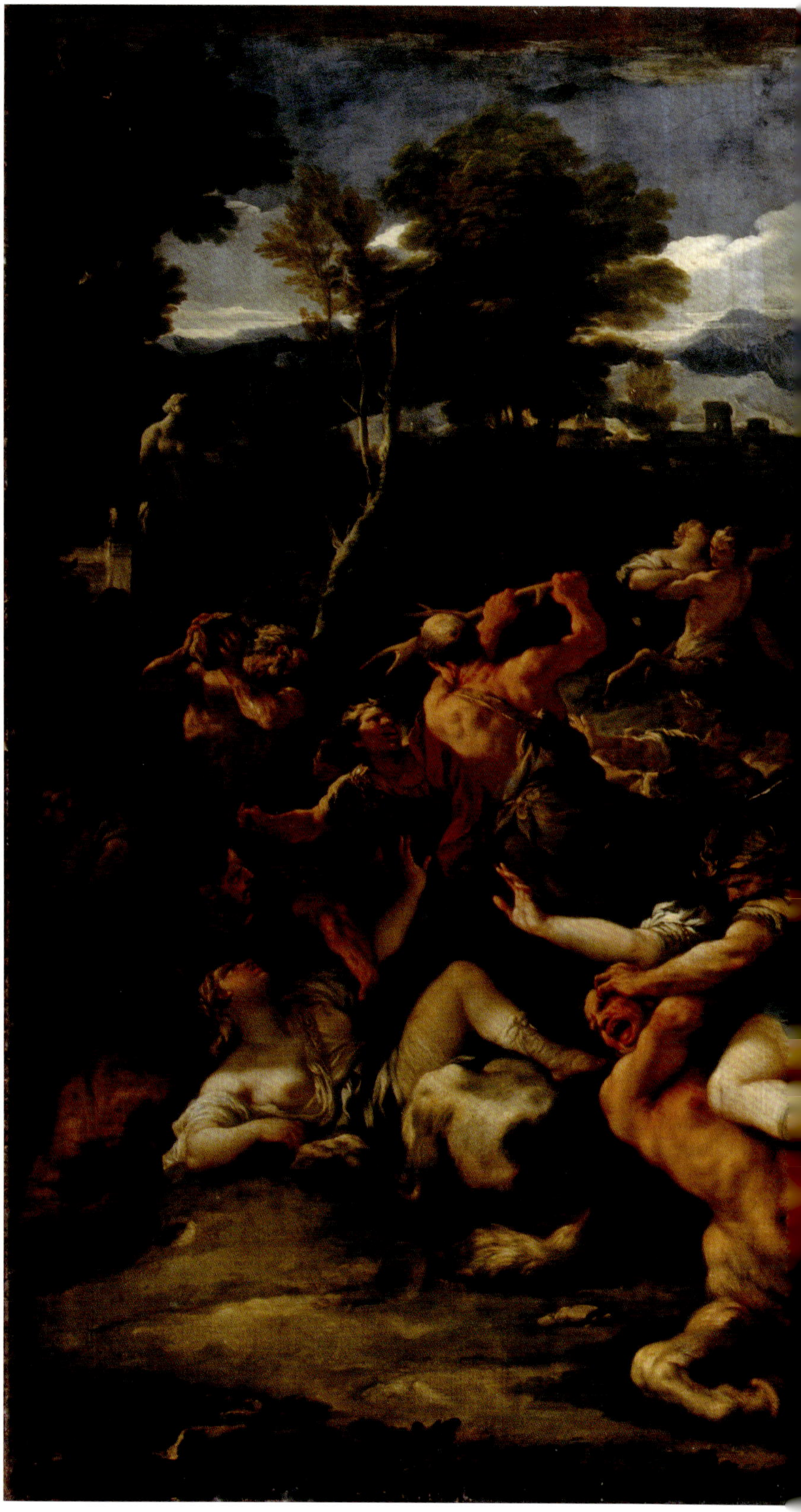

LUCA GIORDANO. *Battle between the Lapiths and the Centaurs.* 1688. OIL ON CANVAS. 100 3/8 × 153 1/2 IN. (255 × 390 CM).

The conflict between the Lapiths, a semi-mythical tribe of giants, and the Centaurs is supposed to have broken out at their king's wedding, when the Centaurs tried to abduct the bride. Giordano persuasively presents the details while demonstrating the breadth of his abilities. In the foreground, passions rage and threaten to spill off the canvas as the delightful natural wealth in the landscape recalls the happy celebration so rudely interrupted.

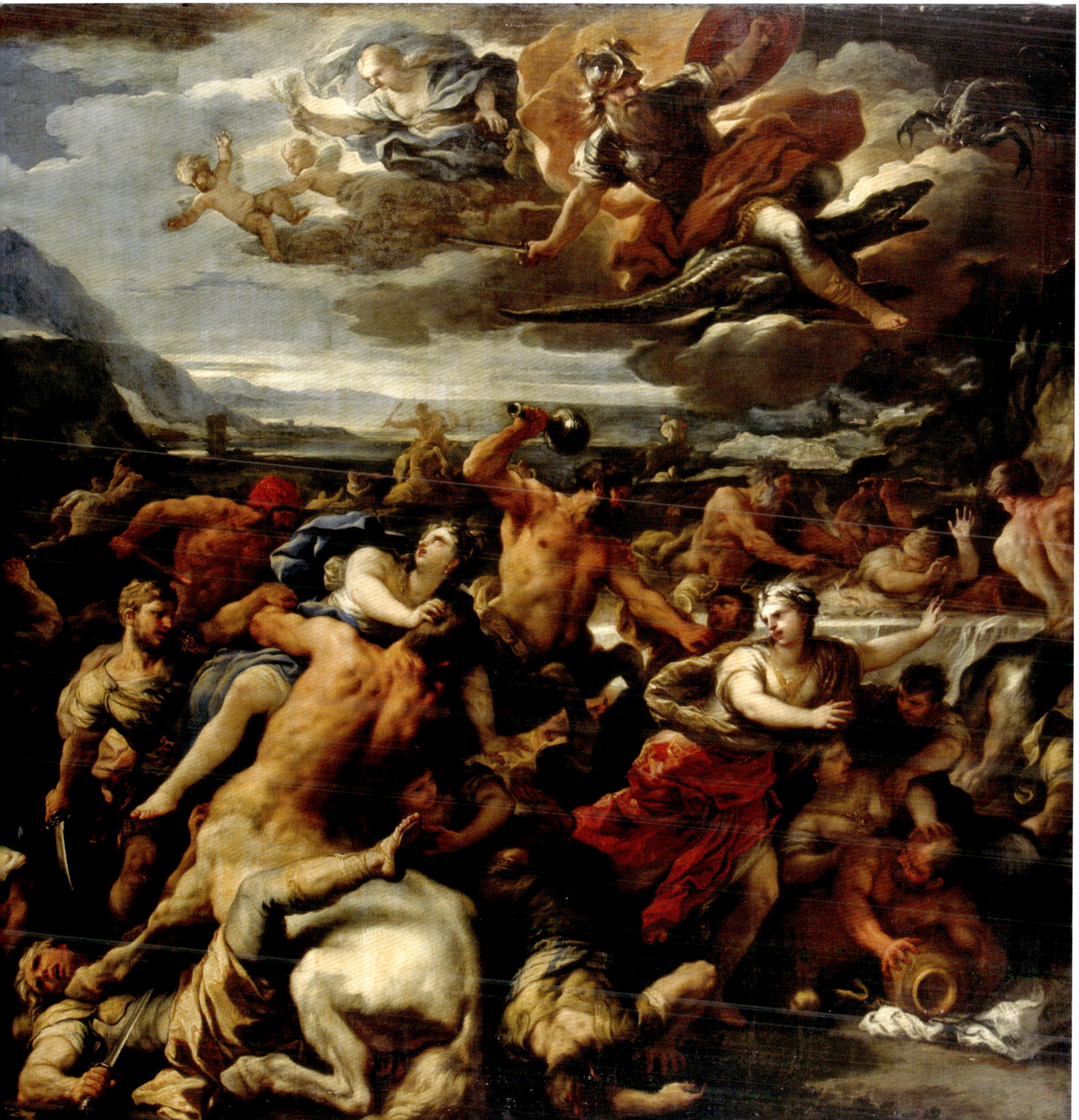

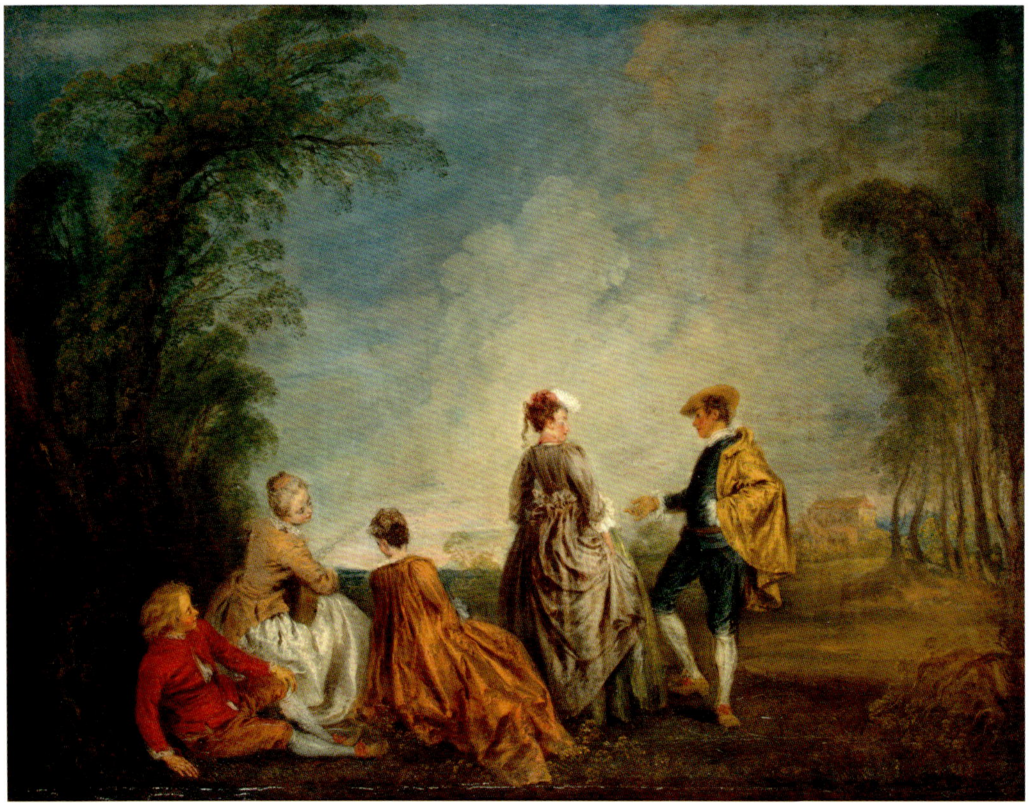

left: ANTOINE WATTEAU. *An Embarrassing Proposal.* CA. 1716. OIL ON CANVAS. 25 1/2 × 33 1/4 IN. (65 × 84.5 CM).

Watteau is celebrated as a master of fêtes galantes, little scenes of the carefree, elegant life of the upper classes. In this scene, exquisite ladies and gentlemen relax in the bosom of nature. They talk, laugh, flirt, and playact—without any regard for the viewer—in the special world of the Rococo era, where fantasy and reality are mixed up. There is neither action nor event, but only the barely detectable nuances of moods and emotions.

right: ANTOINE WATTEAU. *Actors of the Comédie-Française.* CA. 1712. OIL ON PANEL. 7 7/8 × 9 7/8 IN. (20 × 25 CM).

This tiny composition, the earliest of the Hermitage's paintings by Watteau, consists of four virtuoso portraits displaying both character and vivid immediacy. Only the head of the young black boy is a stock image, like the roles he probably performed on stage. The dense painting contains a multitude of shades applied with small, fastidious brushstrokes and is no less rich in color than the artist's gallant scenes set in the open air.

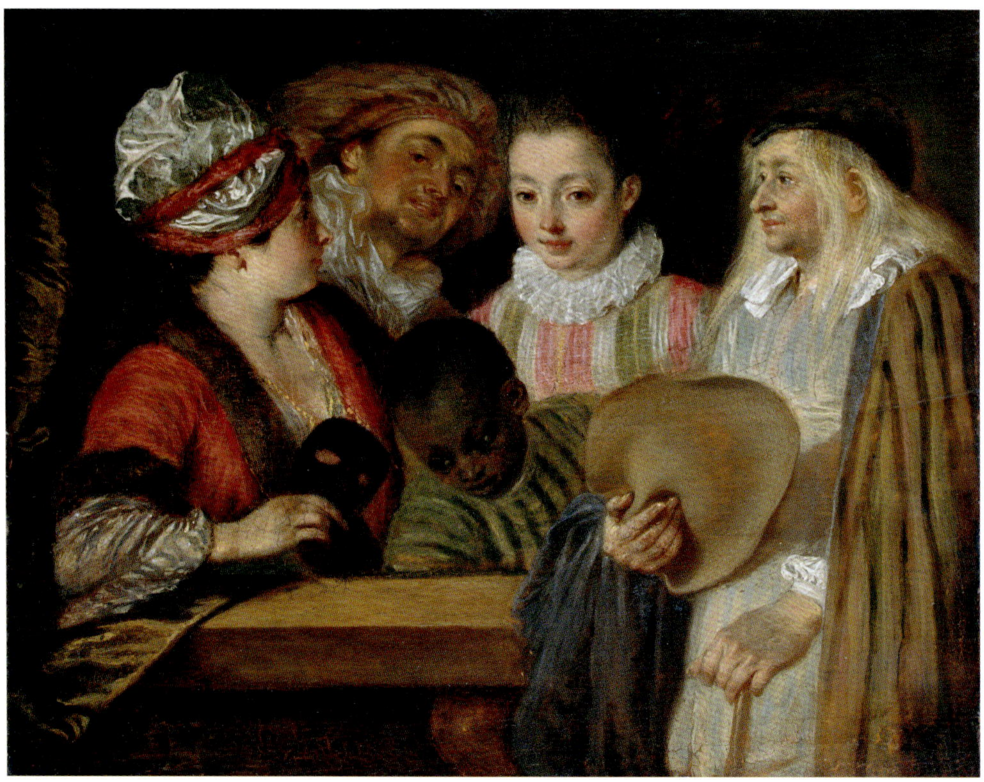

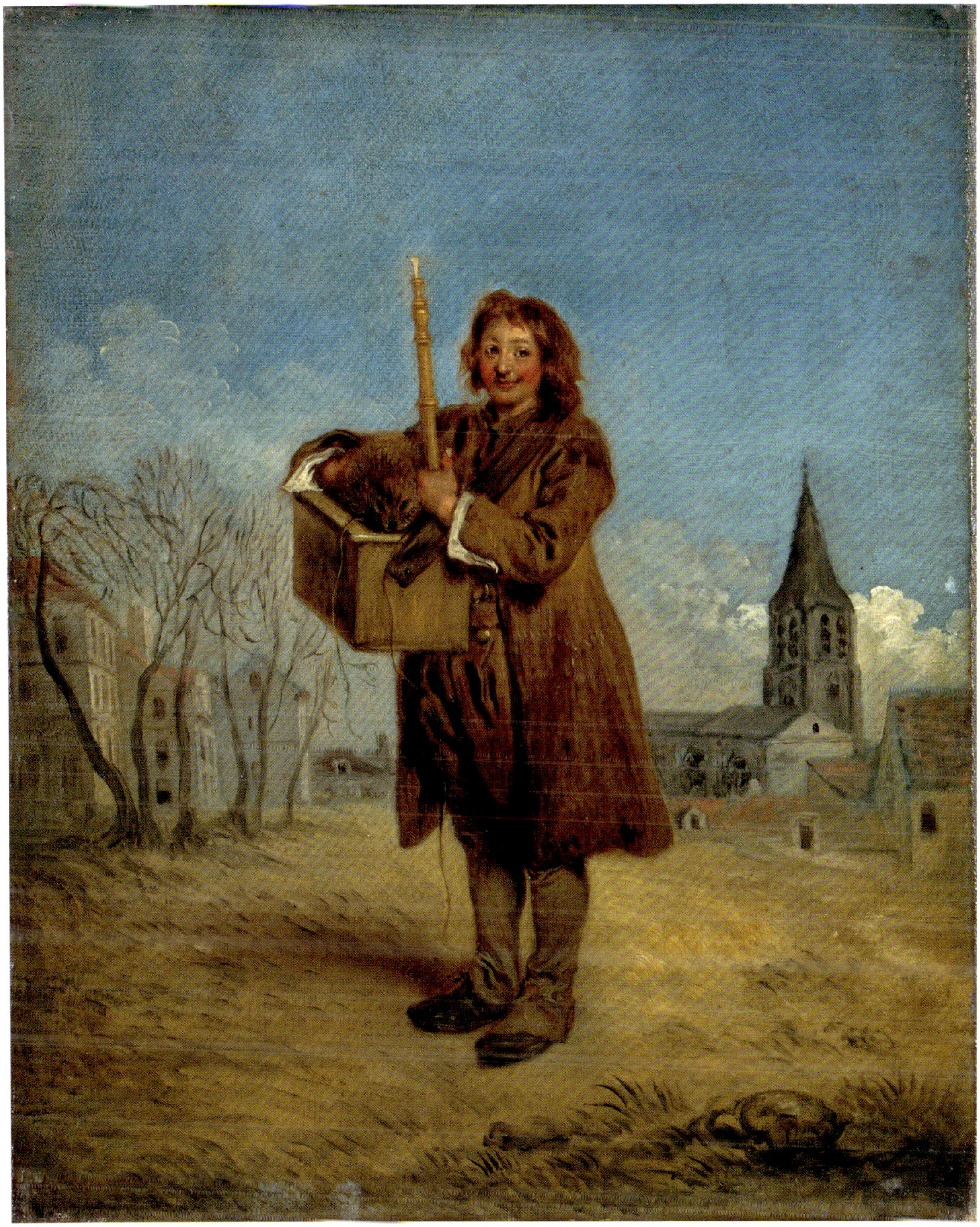

ANTOINE WATTEAU. *Savoyard with a Marmot.* 1716.
OIL ON CANVAS. 16 × 12 3/4 IN. (40.5 × 32.5 CM).

Everything here is archaic: the peasant type posing awkwardly in the center has its origins in 17th-century engravings; the landscape seems completely separate, like a theatrical backdrop. But in Watteau's hands these vestiges of the past become a retrospective view that is not only touching but also intelligent. Even the timidity evident in the molding of the figure works to the benefit of the stylization.

below: ANTOINE WATTEAU. *A Capricious Woman ("La Boudeuse").* CA. 1718. OIL ON CANVAS. 16 1/2 × 13 3/8 IN. (42 × 34 CM).

The closeup view reveals the artificiality of Watteau's world yet enhances its charm. The smooth carpet of the lawn, the trees with twisted trunks, and the leaves each painted separately call to mind "Le Douanier" Rousseau. Yet, the fine painting of the faces and the tangible shifting of the silk, nervously crumpled in the heroine's hand, prompt suspicion that Watteau deliberately used the naïveté of the landscape to echo the childish distress of a girl in a woman's body.

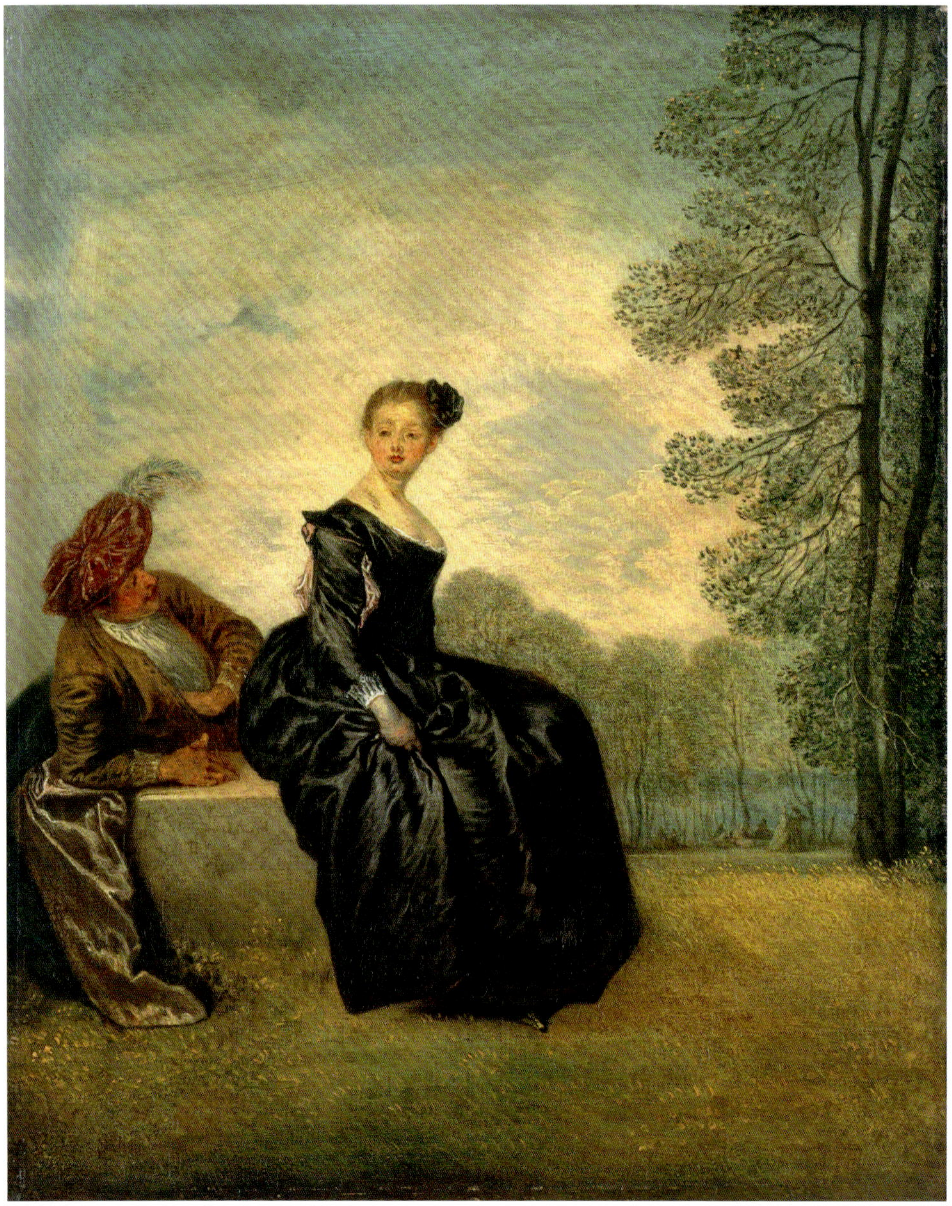

opposite: FRANÇOIS LE MOYNE. *Female Bather.* MID-1720S. OIL ON CANVAS. 54 3/8 × 42 IN. (138 × 106.5 CM).

Le Moyne created this painting during his time in Venice and Rome, and the sculptural molding of the figures and the drapes painted with bright local colors show the Italian influence. Yet the carefree eroticism, which no longer needs the justification of a mythological or biblical subject, and attention to fleeting bodily sensations make this work a typical example of the French Rococo.

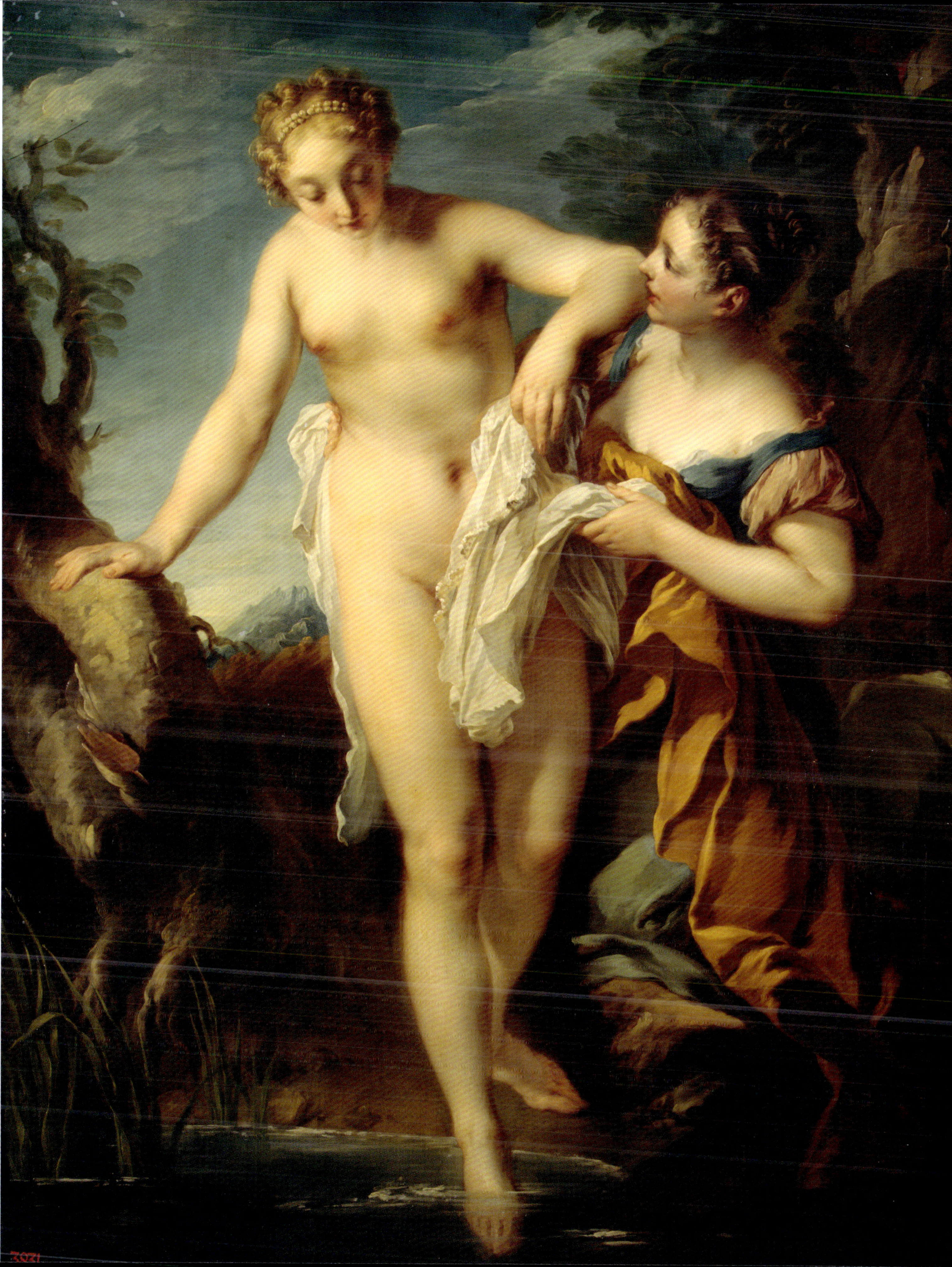

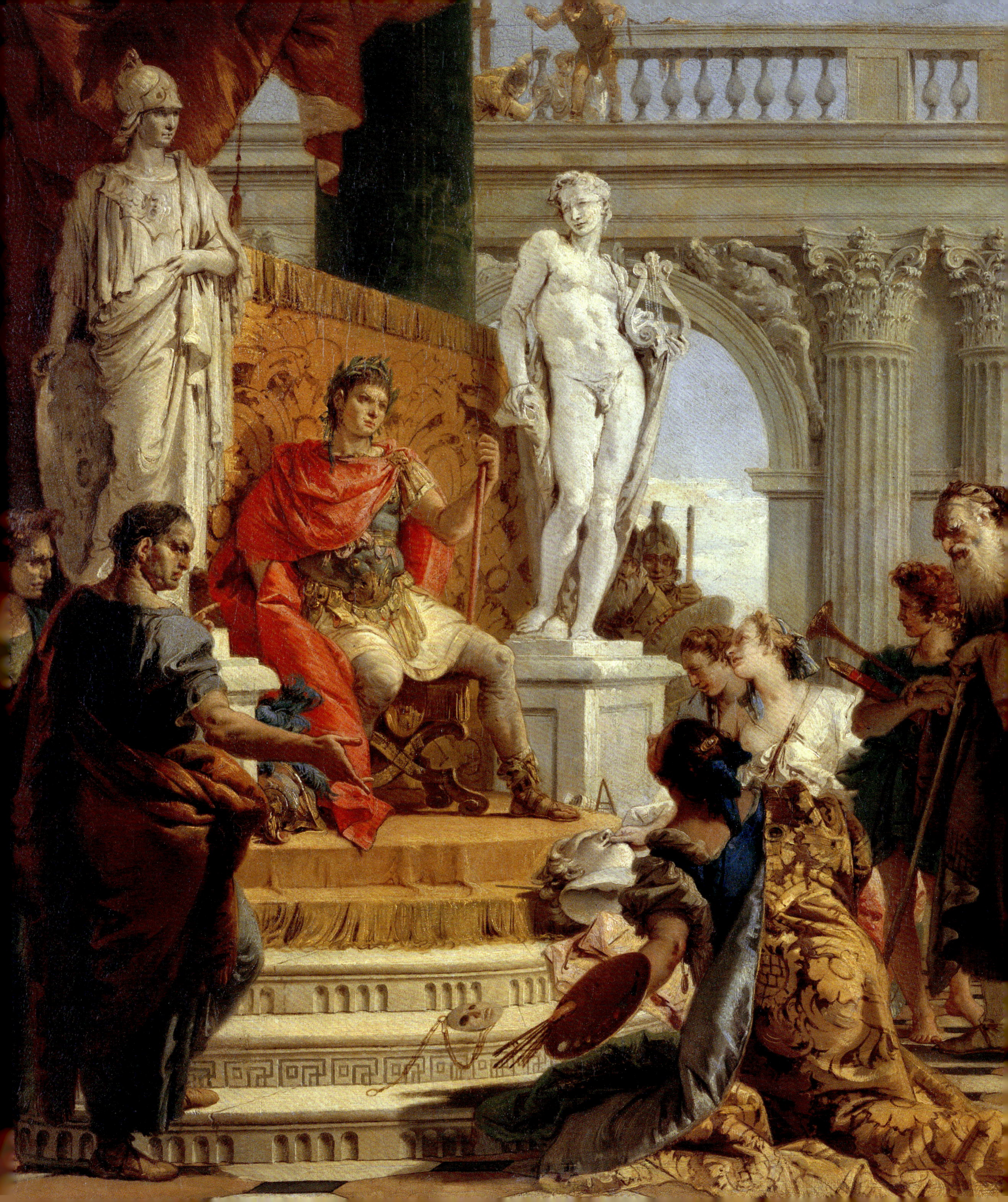

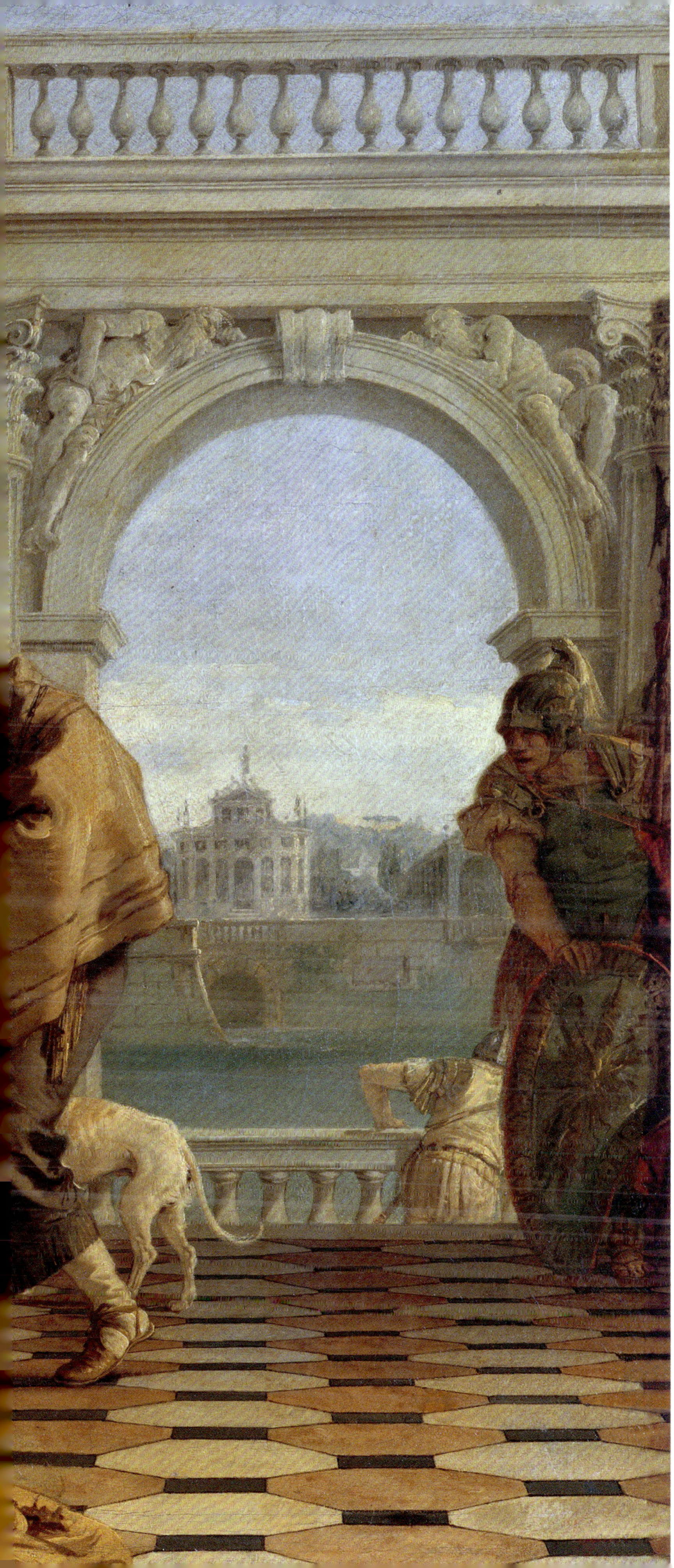

GIOVANNI BATTISTA TIEPOLO. *Maecenas Presenting the Liberal Arts to Augustus.* 1743. OIL ON CANVAS. 27 3/8 × 35 IN. (69.5 × 89 CM).

This painting was originally a gift to the major collector Heinrich Brühl, the powerful prime minister of Elector Frederick Augustus II of Saxony, also King Augustus III of Poland. It came into the Hermitage when Catherine II purchased Brühl's entire collection early in the museum's history. In presenting an ancient example of patronage of the arts, Tiepolo was extolling one of the characteristics of an enlightened monarchy, which the Russian empress was also seeking to establish.

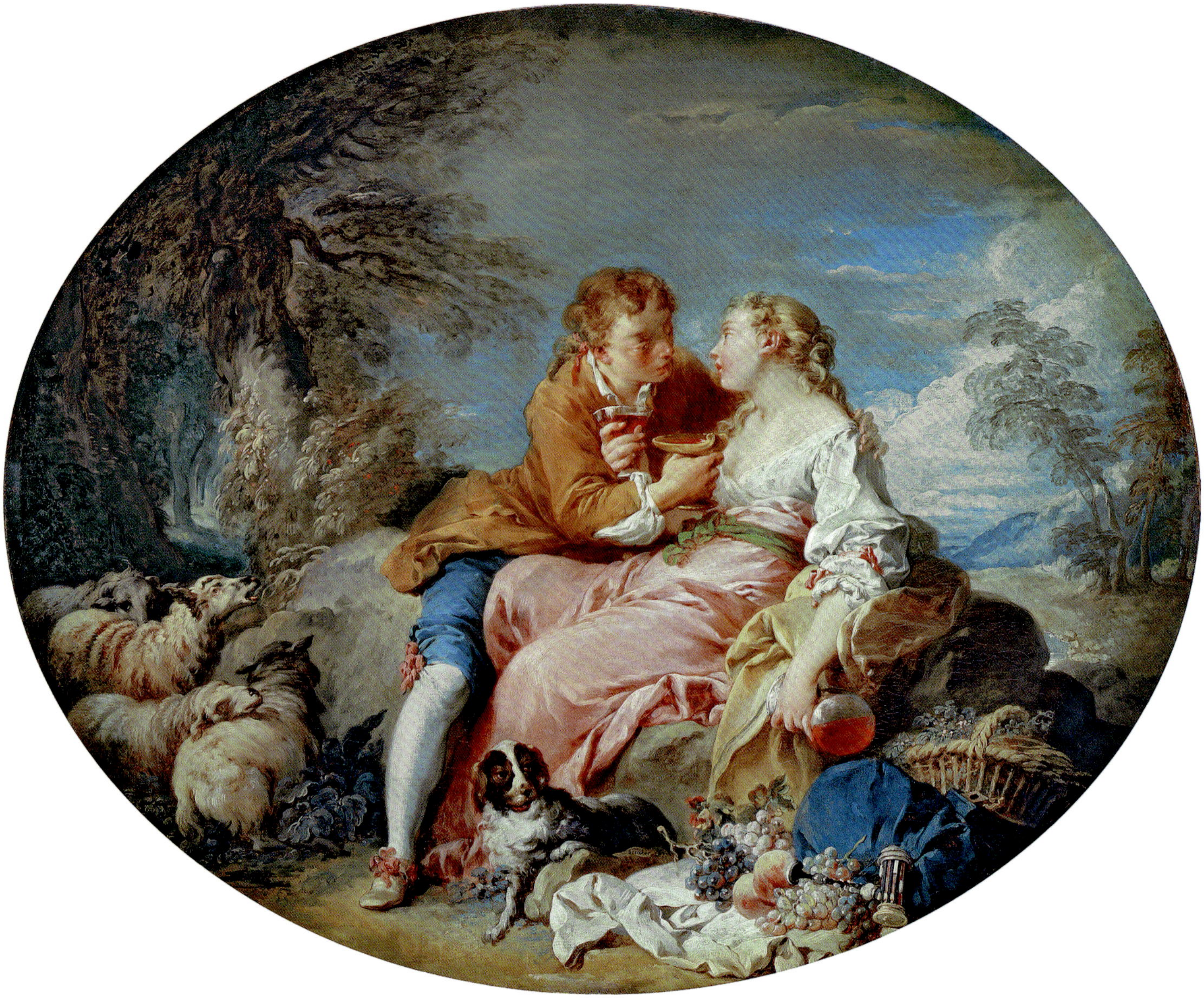

FRANÇOIS BOUCHER. *Pastoral Scene.* 1740S. OIL ON CANVAS. 24 × 29 1/2 IN. (61 × 75 CM) OVAL.

In Boucher's ingenuous pastoral scenes, the desire to please—which in combination with a predilection for captivating subjects and monumental theatrics would lead to the decline of 19th-century academic Neoclassicism—enchants us with its pure aestheticism, just as it did Diderot and his contemporaries.

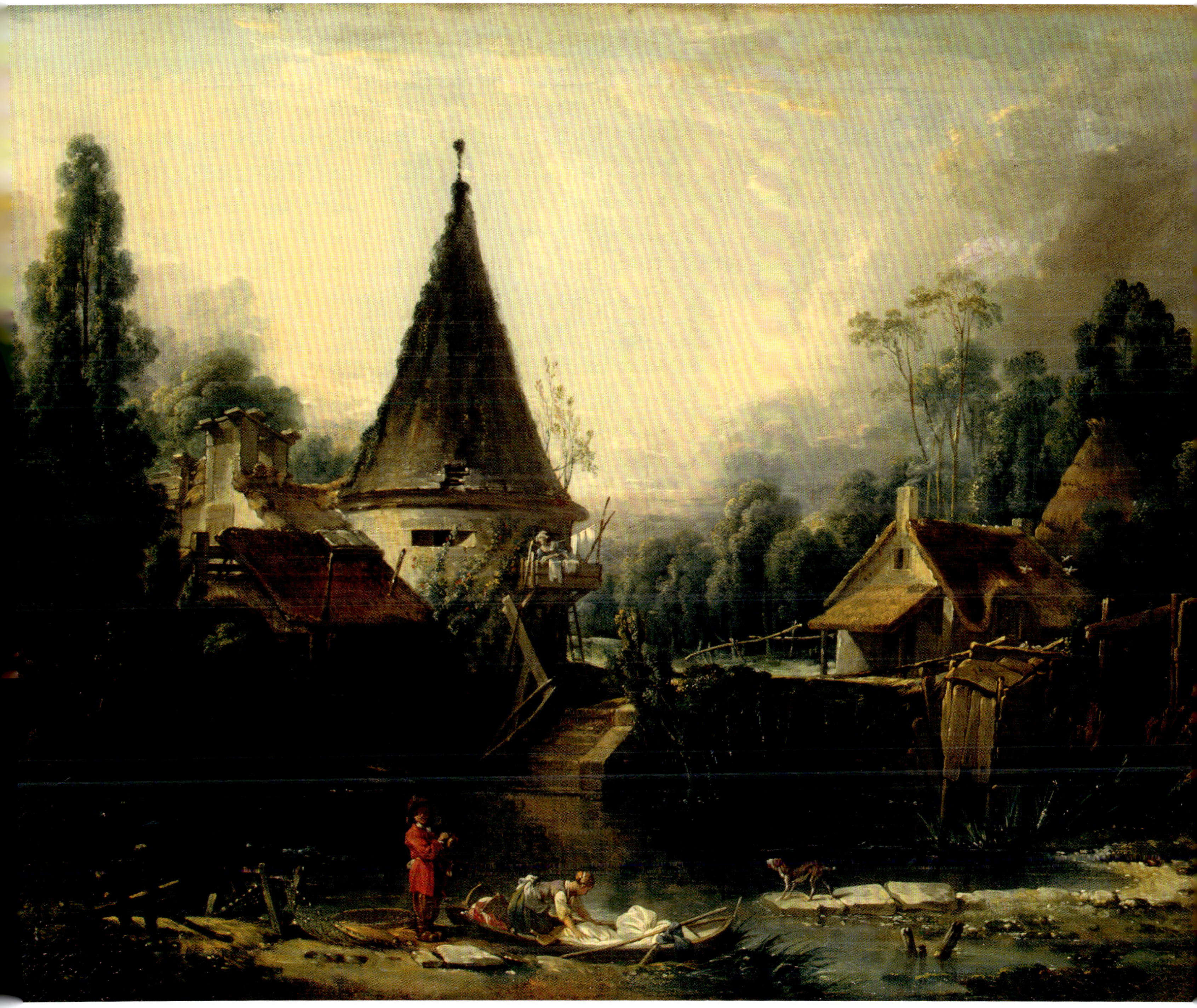

FRANÇOIS BOUCHER. *Landscape near Beauvais.* EARLY 1740S.
OIL ON CANVAS. 19 1/4 × 22 7/8 IN. (49 × 58 CM).

In the same way that nudity was finally emancipated in Rococo art (in Boucher's oeuvre, courtesans are seen basking in bed), landscape rid itself of the last vestiges of narrative. Born of the artist's imagination and deriving conflict-free unity from this, this scene nonetheless consists entirely of details, including the girl calmly doing the laundry, the thoughtful boy next to her, and the doves fluttering above the roof of the cottage.

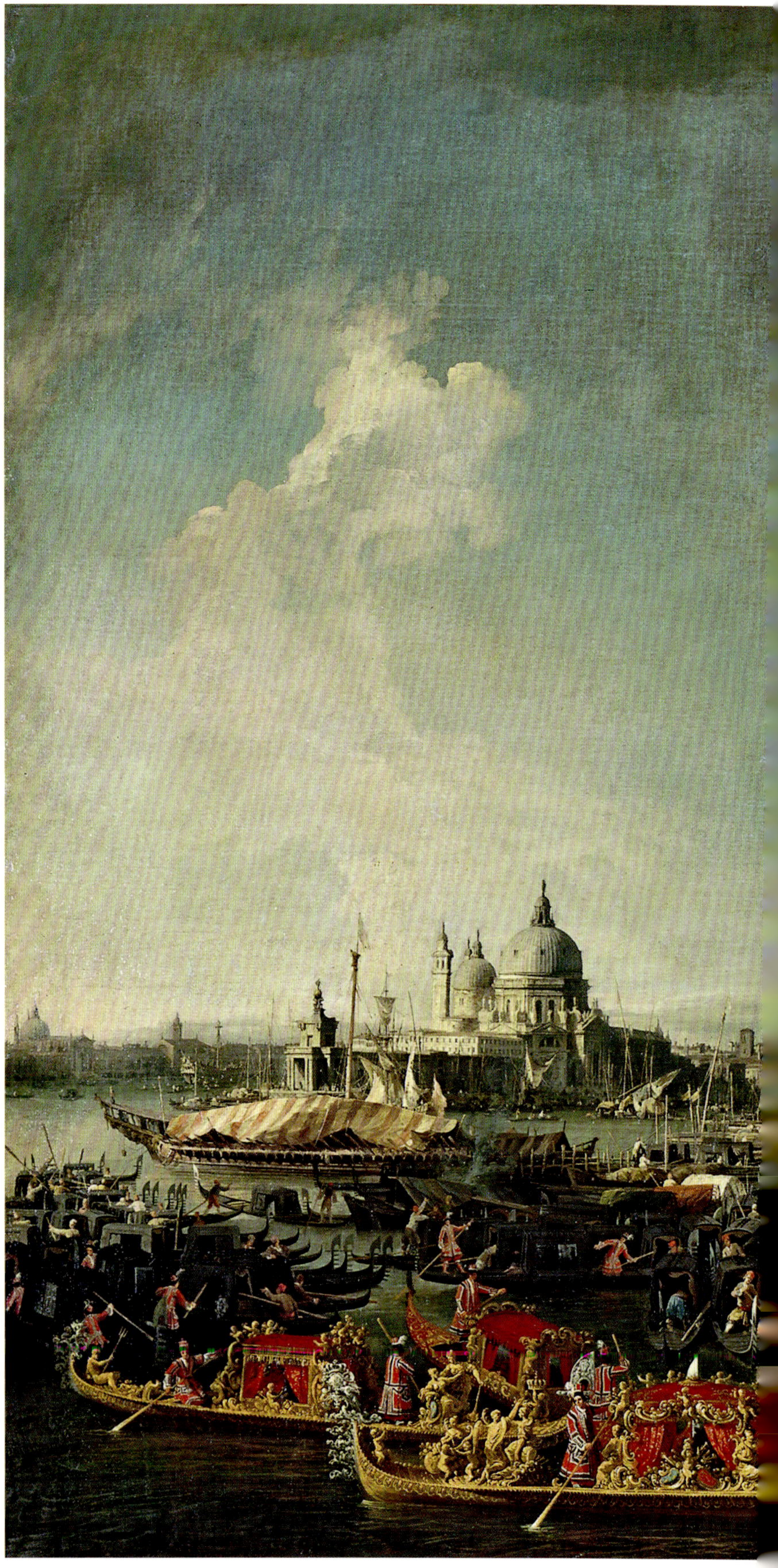

ANTONIO CANAL, CALLED CANALETTO. *The Reception of the French Ambassador in Venice.* 1726–27. OIL ON CANVAS. $71\frac{1}{4} \times 102\frac{1}{8}$ IN. (181 × 259.5 CM).

Canaletto belonged to the school of Venetian artists who painted *vedute*, or urban landscapes. This canvas gives a panoramic view of the most celebrated part of Venice: the Palace of the Doges, the Biblioteca Marciana, and the church of Santa Maria della Salute. Smartly dressed Venetians are crowding on the embankment to greet the delegation of the French ambassador, Jacques Vincent Languet, Count of Gergy. The urban landscape produced by Canaletto is marked by topographical precision and a distinctive romantic interpretation.

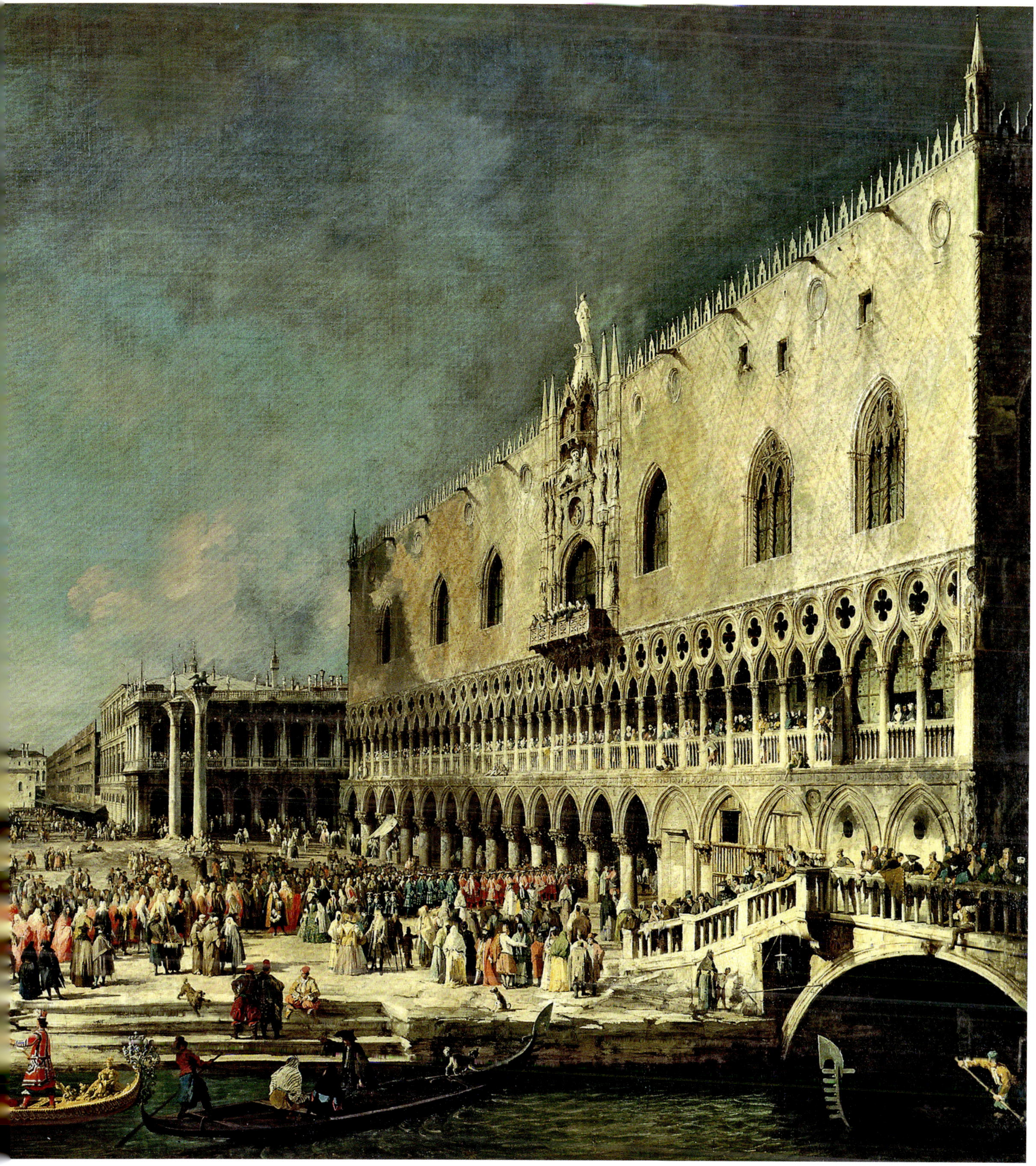

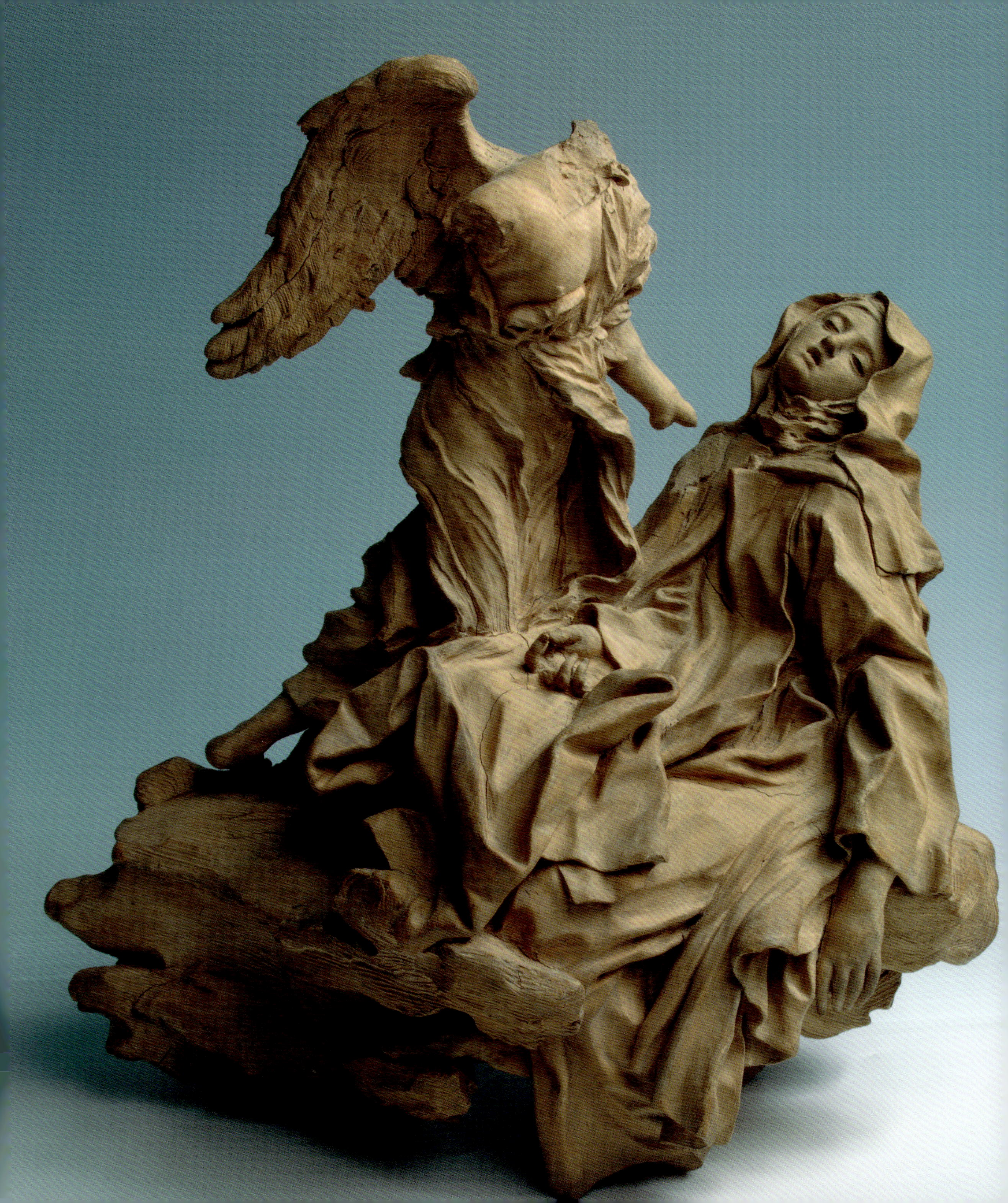

Western European Sculpture, 15th–Early 18th Century

GIAN LORENZO BERNINI. *The Ecstasy of St. Theresa.* 1640S. TERRACOTTA. 18 1/2 IN. (47 CM) HIGH.

The marble sculptural group that Bernini produced on this subject for the Cornaro chapel in Rome's Church of Santa Maria della Vittoria is the apogee of Baroque sculpture. The "sweet torment" that Theresa of Avila experienced through a vision of an angel piercing her body with a spear found almost literal expression in the combination of the soft treatment of the face and hands and the sharp folds of the clothing that seems to be fluttering in a gust of wind.

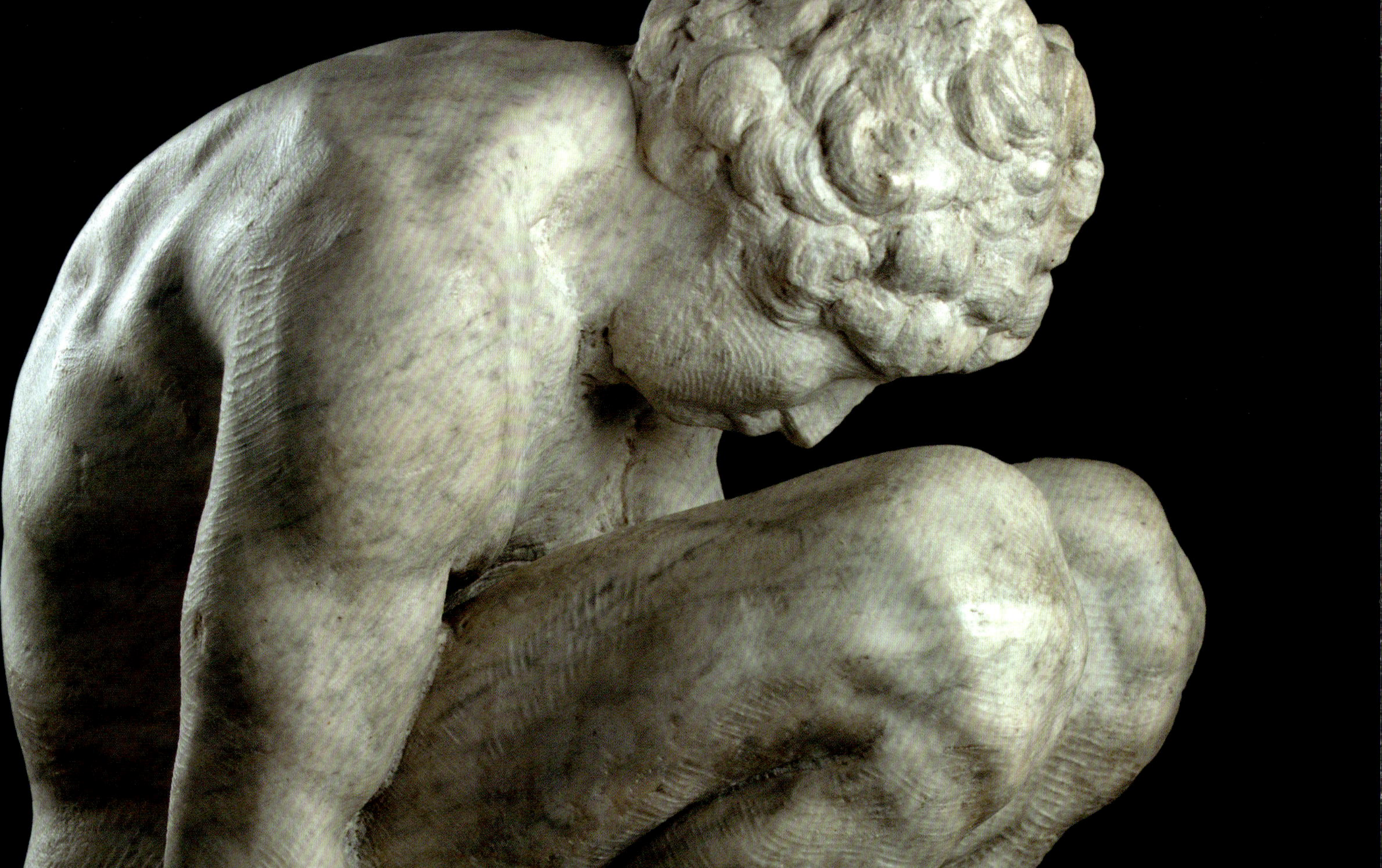

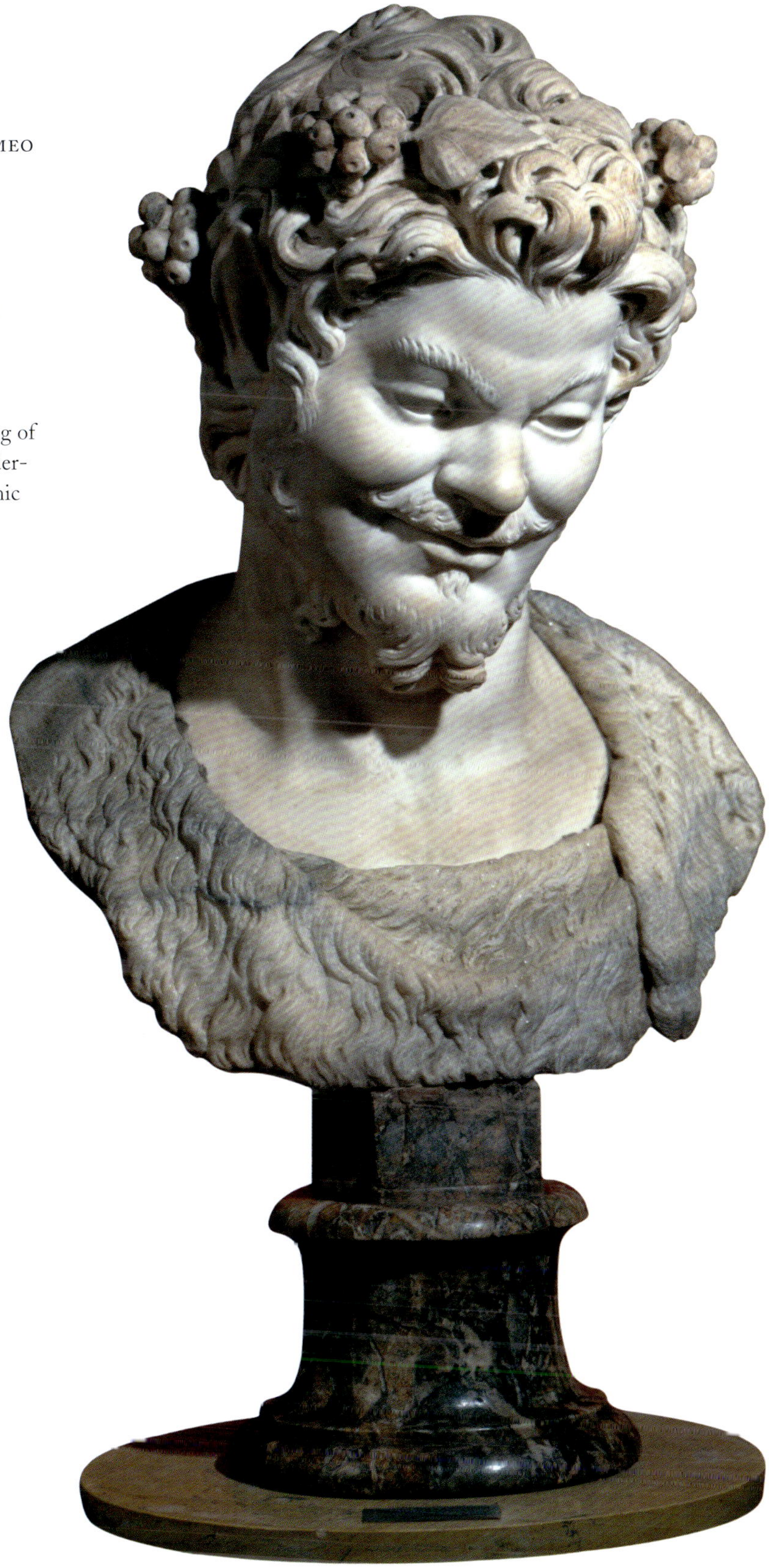

right: BACCIO BANDINELLI (BORN BARTOLOMMEO BRANDINI). *Faun.* 1540S. MARBLE. 22 7/8 IN. (58 CM) HIGH.

The talents of Baccio Bandinelli—an ambitious imitator and rival of Michelangelo, who found success at the court of Cosimo I Medici—revealed themselves particularly in drawing and small-scale plastic art. His monumental sculptural groups are full of contradictions and compositional discord, but his smaller works demonstrate the clear molding of volumes, smooth treatment of the marble, and moderate use of detail that laid the foundation for academic Classicism.

opposite: MICHELANGELO BUONARROTI. *Crouching Boy.* BETWEEN 1530 AND 1534. MARBLE. 21 1/4 IN. (54 CM) HIGH.

Judging by a surviving drawing, Michelangelo intended this figure for the Medici tombs in Florence's Basilica of San Lorenzo, one of his greatest achievements. The memorial ensemble, conceived as an allegory of the inexorable march of time, was not completed in accordance with the original project. The statue of a boy may have been made for one of the niches in a tomb and may symbolize the awakening soul or, on the contrary, death—all proposed interpretations are disputed.

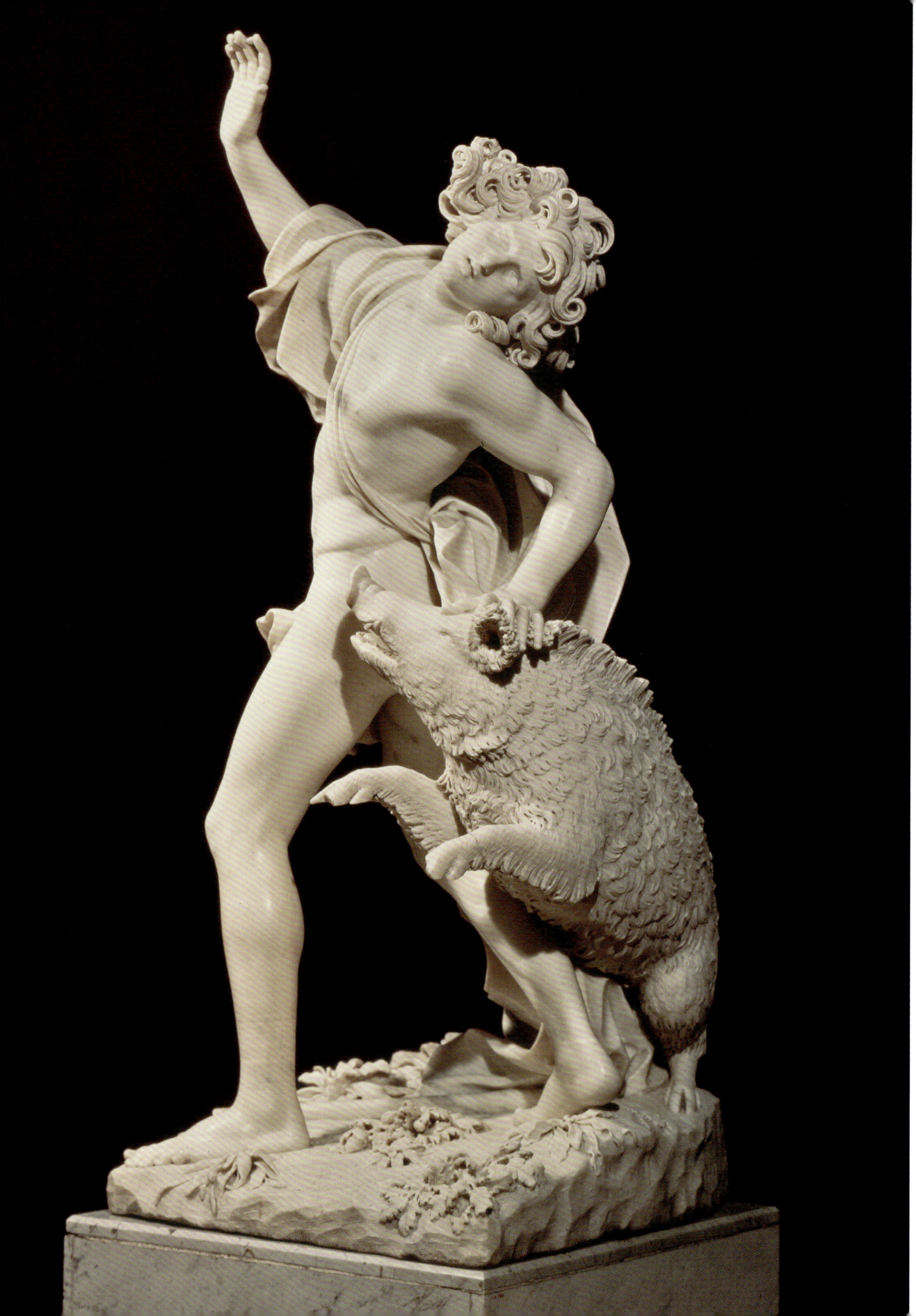

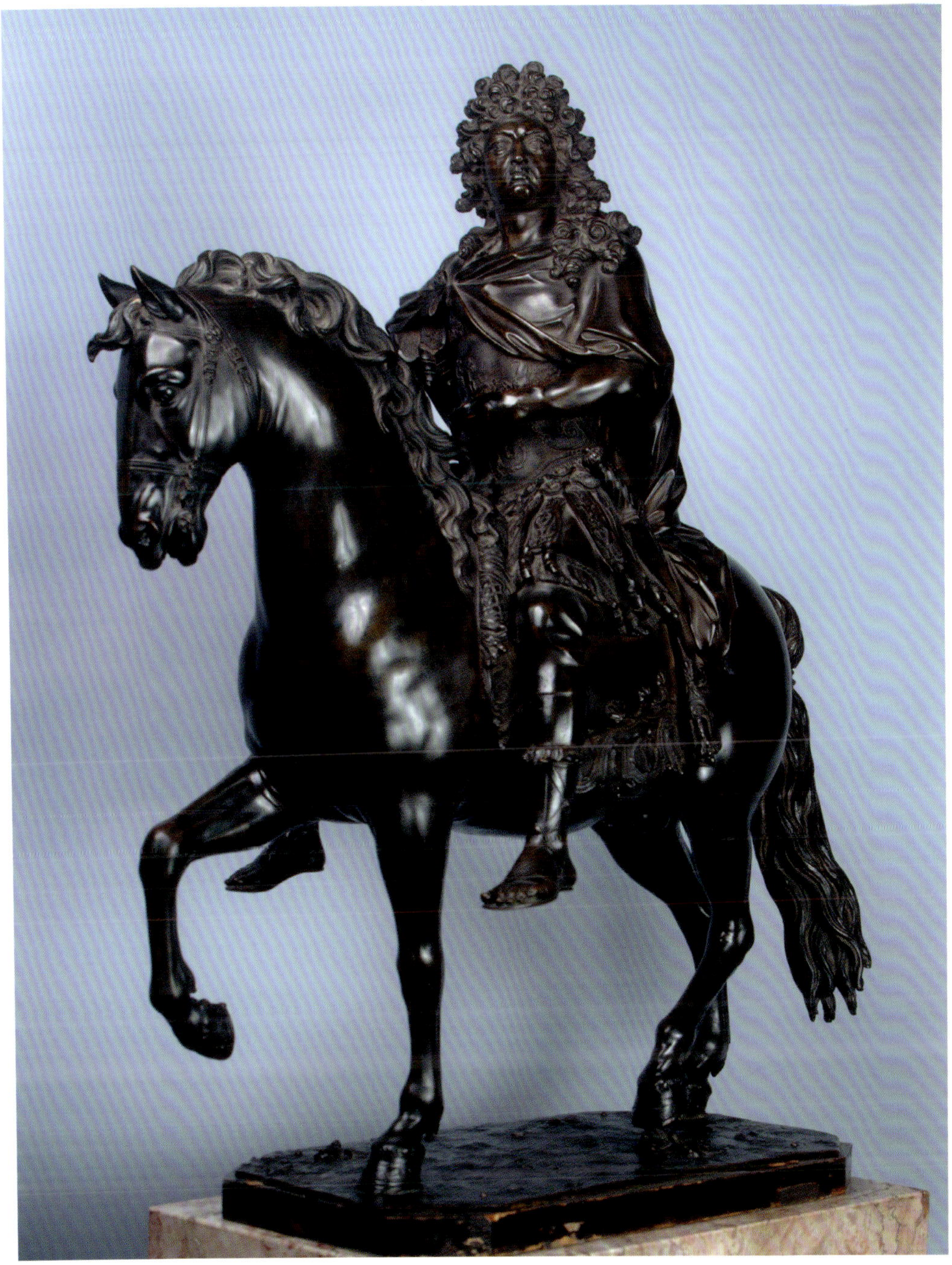

left: FRANÇOIS GIRARDON. *Model for an Equestrian Statue of Louis XIV.* 1680S–90S. BRONZE. 40½ IN. (103 CM) HIGH.

This sculpture was commissioned in 1685 to adorn the Place Vendôme in Paris. Taking as his prototype the monument to Marcus Aurelius in Rome, Girardon depicted the king as a triumphant general astride a horse without a saddle or stirrups, in ancient dress but with the wig characteristic of his own time. The monument, fifty-six feet high with the pedestal, was destroyed during the French Revolution and is known today only by a few scale models.

opposite: GIUSEPPE MAZZUOLA. *The Death of Adonis.* 1709. MARBLE. 76 IN. (193 CM) HIGH.

The exceptional beauty of this child, the fruit of an incestuous union engineered by the insulted Aphrodite, caused an argument among the gods that could only end in his death: he was killed by a boar while hunting. In devoting one of his chief works to that fatal incident, Mazzuola expressed—in a typically Baroque depiction of a dramatic moment—the idea of the transience of beauty.

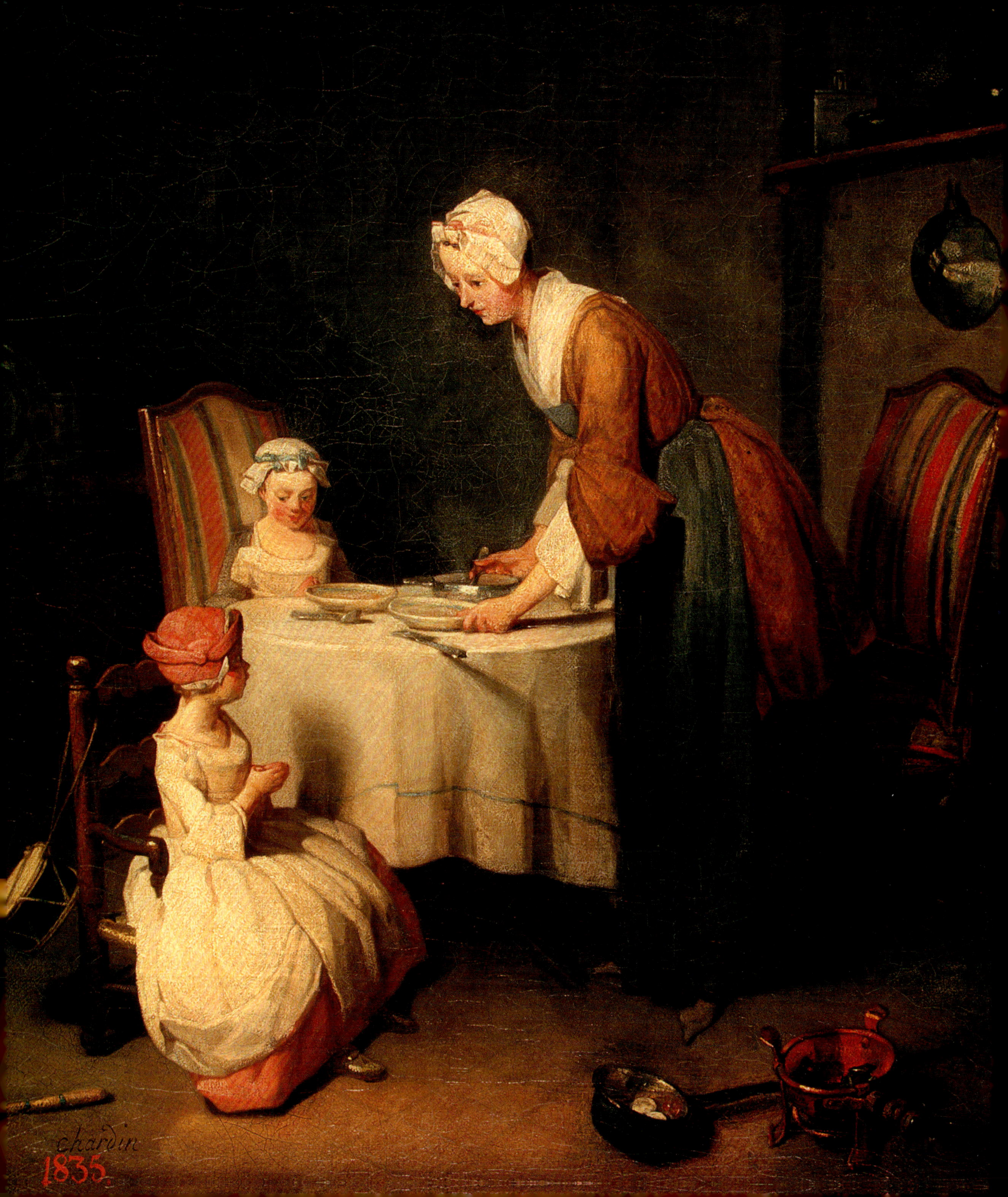
chardin
1835

Western European Painting, Mid-18th–19th Century

JEAN-BAPTISTE SIMÉON CHARDIN. *Saying Grace.* 1744.
OIL ON CANVAS. 19 1/2 × 15 1/8 IN. (49.5 × 38.4 CM).

In this understated scene, the younger girl is instructed to say grace while the older girl looks on. The didactic meaning of this common 18th-century subject—prayer before a meal—is clear. Chardin's meticulously painted dramatis personae paired with his refined execution create a quietly bewitching, intimate scene.

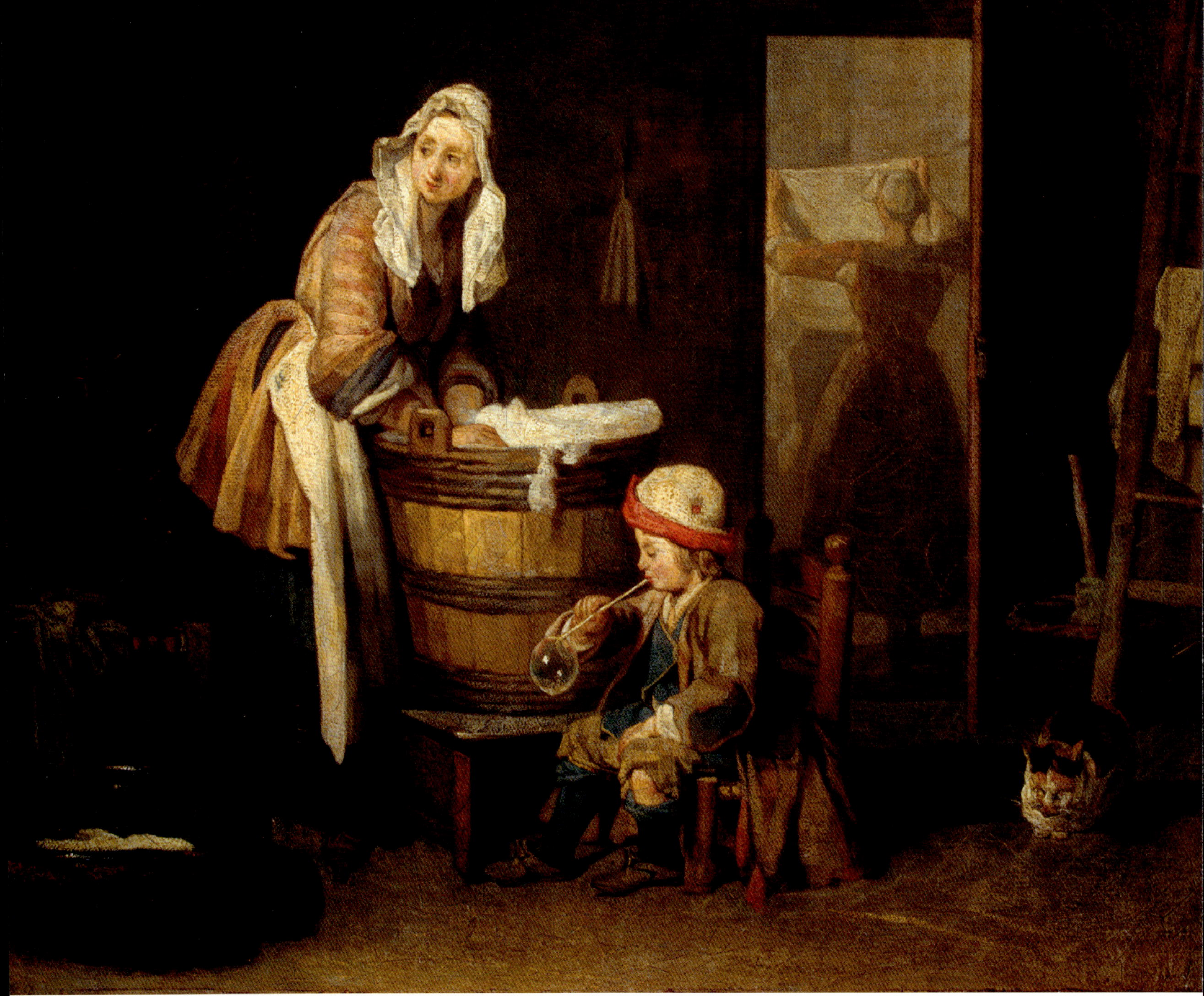

JEAN-BAPTISTE SIMÉON CHARDIN. *Laundress.* 1730S. OIL ON CANVAS. 14¾ × 16⅞ IN. (37.5 × 42.7 CM).

Praised highly by the critics and accepted into the Royal Academy of Painting and Sculpture at age twenty-nine as "a painter of animals and fruit," Chardin stands apart as a figure in French 18th-century painting. Neither the theatrics of Classicism nor the didacticism and frivolity of the Rococo are found in his works. Even the Dutch influence, evident throughout his oeuvre, has an unusual nuance: Chardin's self-absorbed characters do not point toward any moral but rather invite thoughtful reflection.

JEAN-BAPTISTE SIMÉON CHARDIN. *Still Life with Attributes of the Arts.* 1766. OIL ON CANVAS. 44 × 55 3/8 IN. (112 × 140.5 CM).

This painting, commissioned by Catherine II, is an allegorical representation of the arts: the palette and paint box stand for painting; the technical drawings and drawing instruments, architecture; the morocco-leather case for papers, drawing; and, finally, a small statuette by Jean Baptiste Pigalle, sculpture. On the left is the cross of the Order of St. Michael, the highest decoration awarded to Chardin. The still life pleased Catherine so much she kept it in her private apartments.

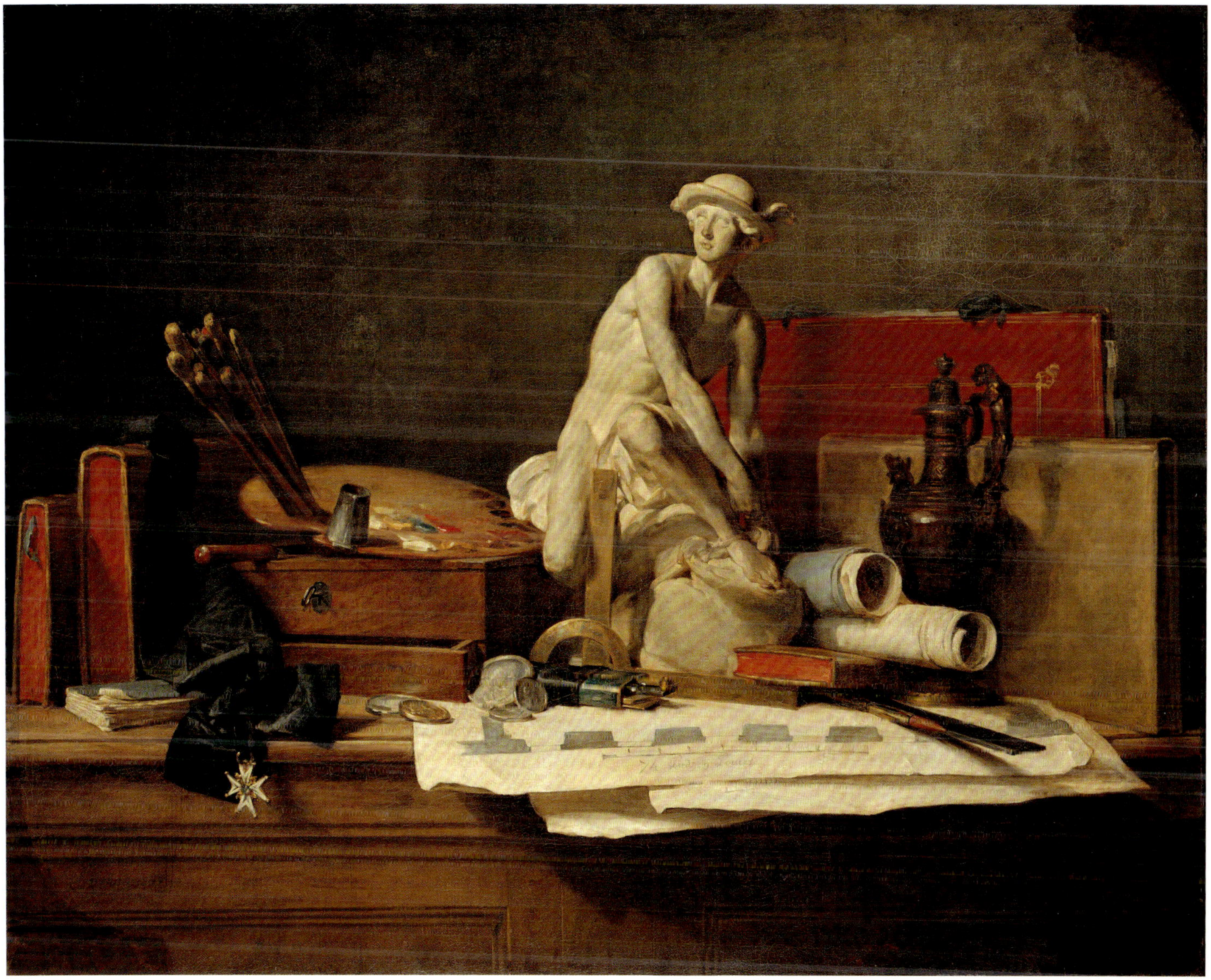

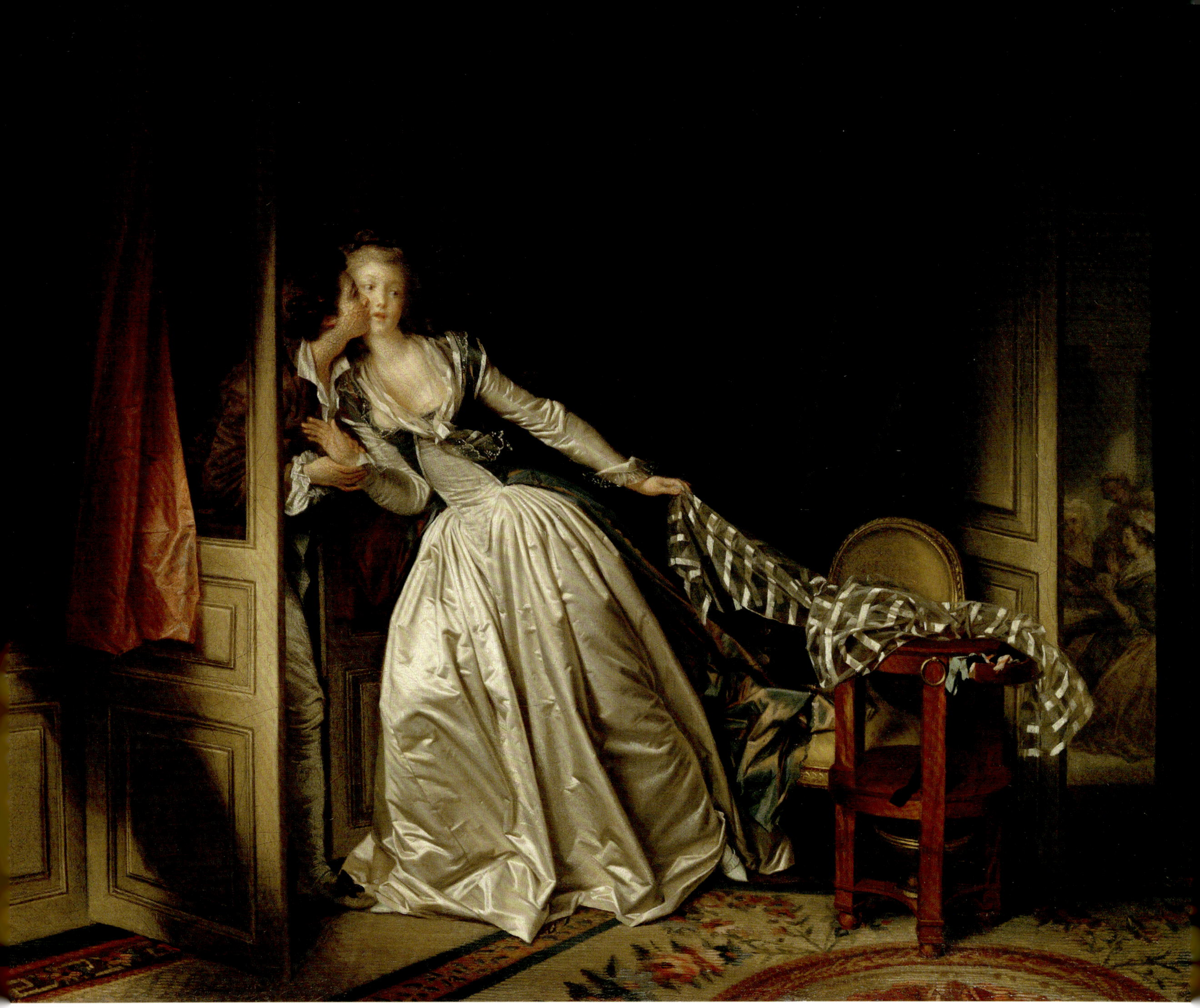

JEAN-HONORÉ FRAGONARD. *The Stolen Kiss.* CA. 1786–88. OIL ON CANVAS. 17 3/4 × 21 5/8 IN. (45 × 55 CM).

It is said that this painting reminded its first owner, the Polish king Stanislaw Poniatowski, of his affair with the future empress Catherine II. This piquant, intimate scene accords with the spirit of the late Rococo. The light, flowing outlines of the shapes and dashing smoothness of the brushstrokes combine with a particular attention to texture: the artist conveyed with especial care the furnishings, clothing, light wrap, patterned lace, and ribbons. This canvas belonged to Fragonard's "Kiss Series."

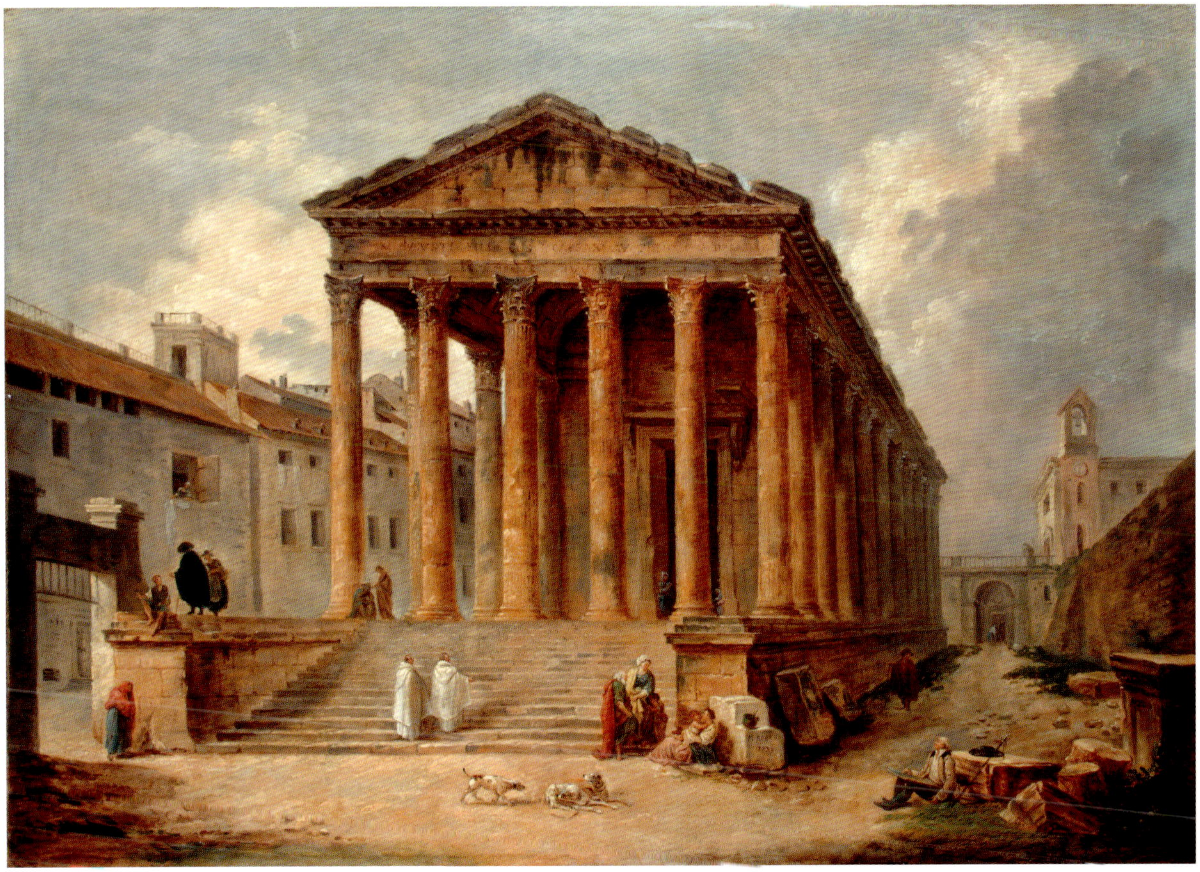

above: HUBERT ROBERT. *The Ancient Temple, Known as the Maison Carrée, in Nîmes.* 1783. 40 1/8 × 56 3/8 IN. (102 × 143 CM).

Both Vernet and Robert were among the artists most popular with the Russian aristocracy. The latter, a specialist in depicting romantic ruins, played a significant role in the spread to Russia of a fashion for landscape parks containing replicas of ancient edifices. The Maison Carrée in Nîmes is a 1st-century Roman temple that has survived virtually intact, and it served as one of the main models for Neoclassical architecture.

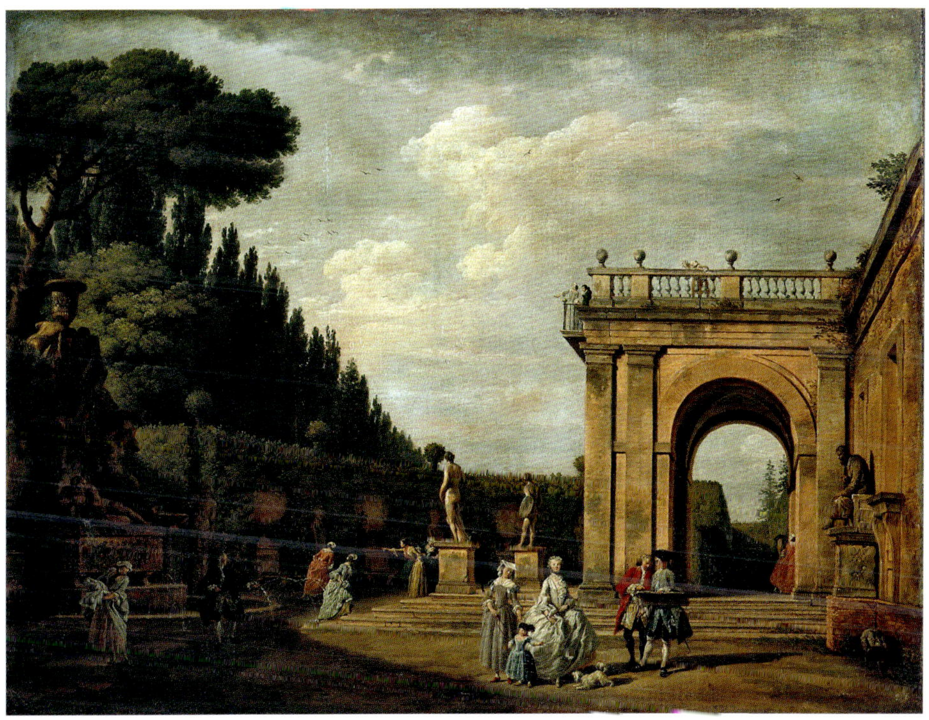

right: (CLAUDE-)JOSEPH VERNET. *View in the Park of the Villa Ludovisi in Rome.* 1749. OIL ON CANVAS. 29 3/8 × 39 1/8 IN. (74.5 × 99.5 CM).

The antiquities uncovered at the villa that Cardinal Ludovisi created in the 17th century on the site of ancient Rome's celebrated Sallustian Gardens made it a place of pilgrimage for artists, writers, and travelers. Vernet, who worked in Rome for twenty years, depicted himself in the right foreground with his wife and young son. The artist and a friend are discussing a sketch, perhaps one of the lost studies in oils made on location that endow Vernet's finest landscapes with the precision of immediate observation.

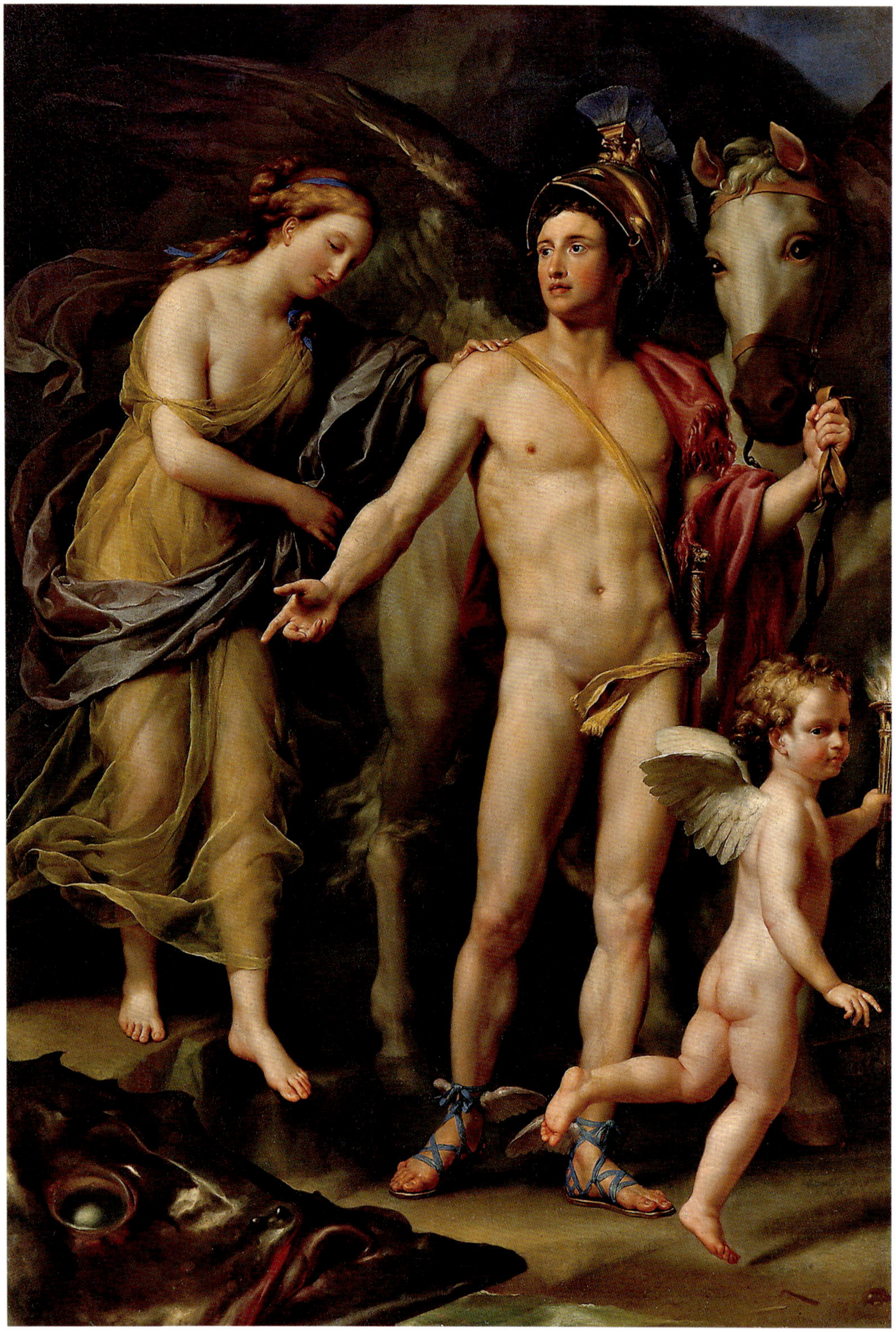

ANTON RAPHAEL MENGS. *Perseus and Andromeda.* 1777. OIL ON CANVAS. 89 3/8 × 60 1/2 IN. (227 × 153.5 CM).

Catherine II was among those collectors who held Mengs in high regard. Viewers were delighted with his mastery of antiquity's artistic vocabulary. Here, the composition and figures are borrowed directly from ancient Greek works. The scene of a maiden saved at the last moment from being devoured by a monster is devoid of drama and reflects the breadth of the artist's knowledge more than his interest in the myth's content.

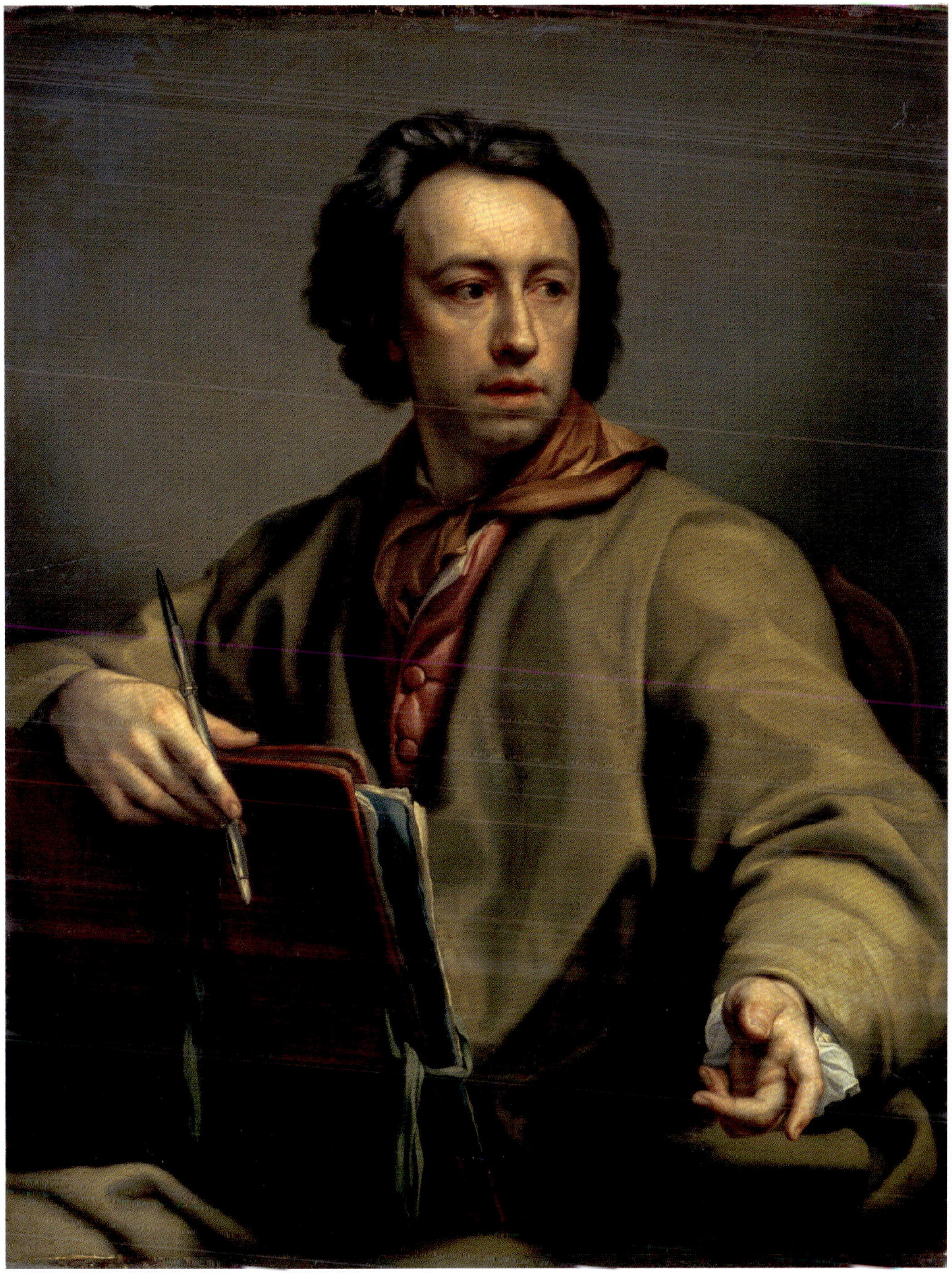

ANTON RAPHAEL MENGS. *Self-Portrait.* CA. 1775. OIL ON PANEL. 40 1/8 × 30 3/8 IN. (102 × 77 CM).

Mengs's father gave his son the first names of Correggio (byname of Antonio Allegri) and Raphael and instilled in him an admiration for the art of the Italian masters. The style of this founder of Neoclassicism became an embodiment of the ideas promulgated by the aesthetician J. J. Winckelmann, intended to summarize the best achievements of ancient Greece and the Renaissance. The artist's choice proved correct: in his own lifetime he was deemed "the greatest of the great" and worked on commissions for all the royal houses of Europe.

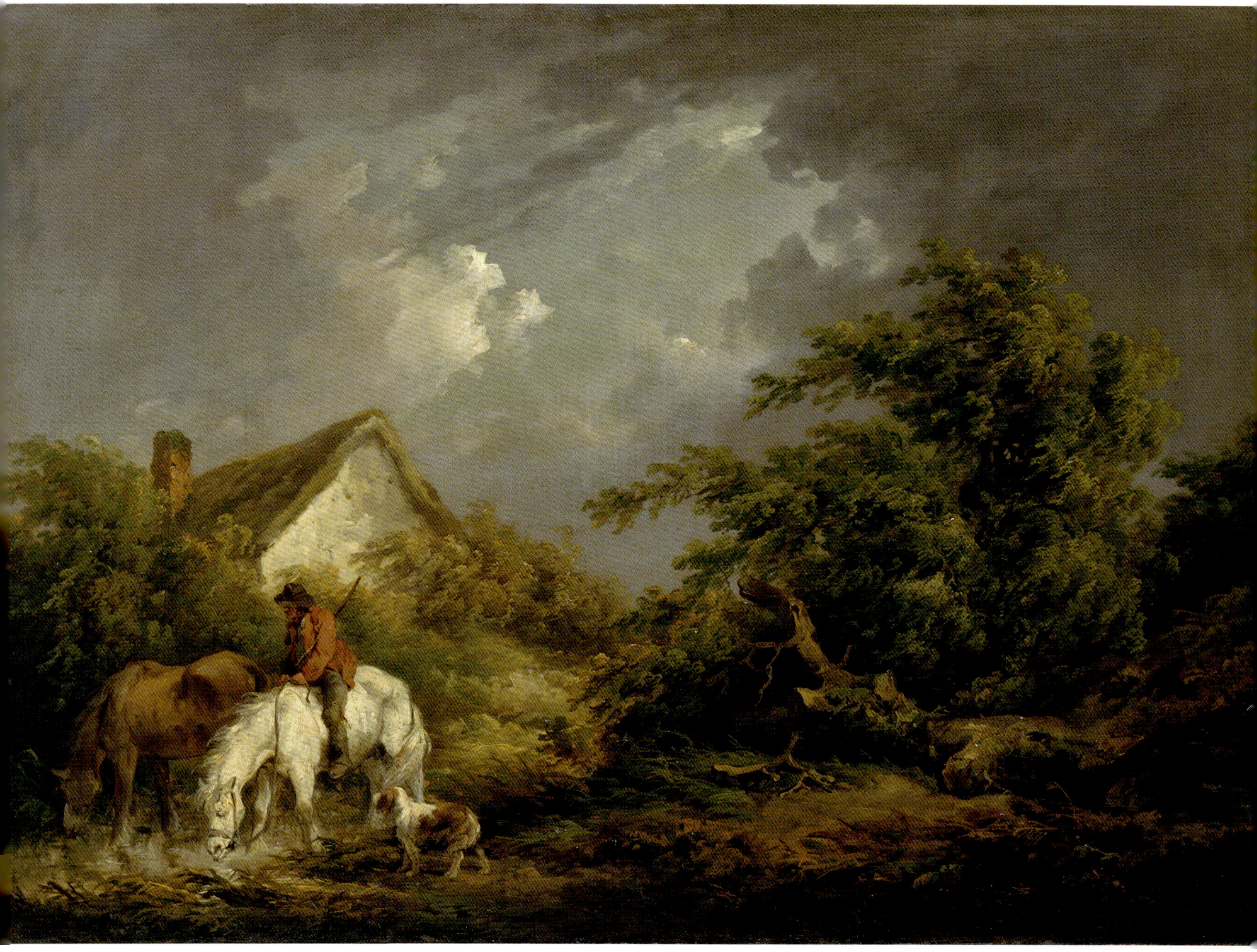

GEORGE MORLAND. *Approaching Thunderstorm.* 1791. OIL ON CANVAS.
33½ × 46 IN. (85 × 117 CM).

Morland, an older contemporary of Turner and Constable, represents the previous stage in the development of English landscape art, for which the main reference point in the 18th century was the Dutch tradition associated with names such as Jacob van Ruisdael and Meindert Hobbema. On British soil their landscapes lost only dramatic effect, becoming brighter and more sentimental in mood.

JOSEPH WRIGHT, CALLED WRIGHT OF DERBY. *An Iron Forge Viewed from Without*. 1773. OIL ON CANVAS. 41 3/8 × 55 1/8 IN. (105 × 140 CM).

Wright was friendly with many notable English scientists, naturalists, and businessmen and became a sort of chronicler of the first stages of the industrial revolution that began in England during the Age of Enlightenment. The era's materialistic creed—of science bearing the light of civilization—found near-literal expression in this painting through the sharp contrast of light and shade.

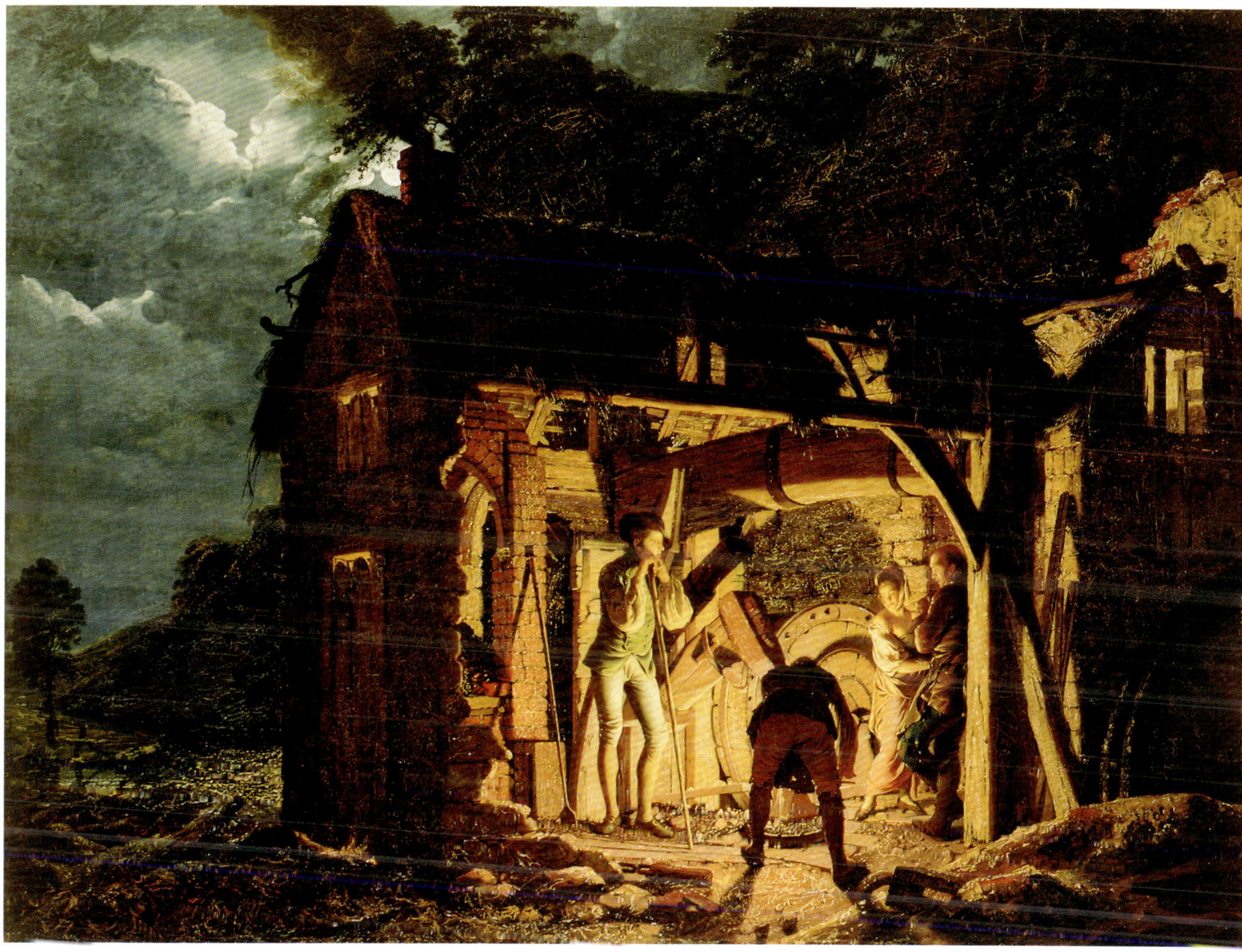

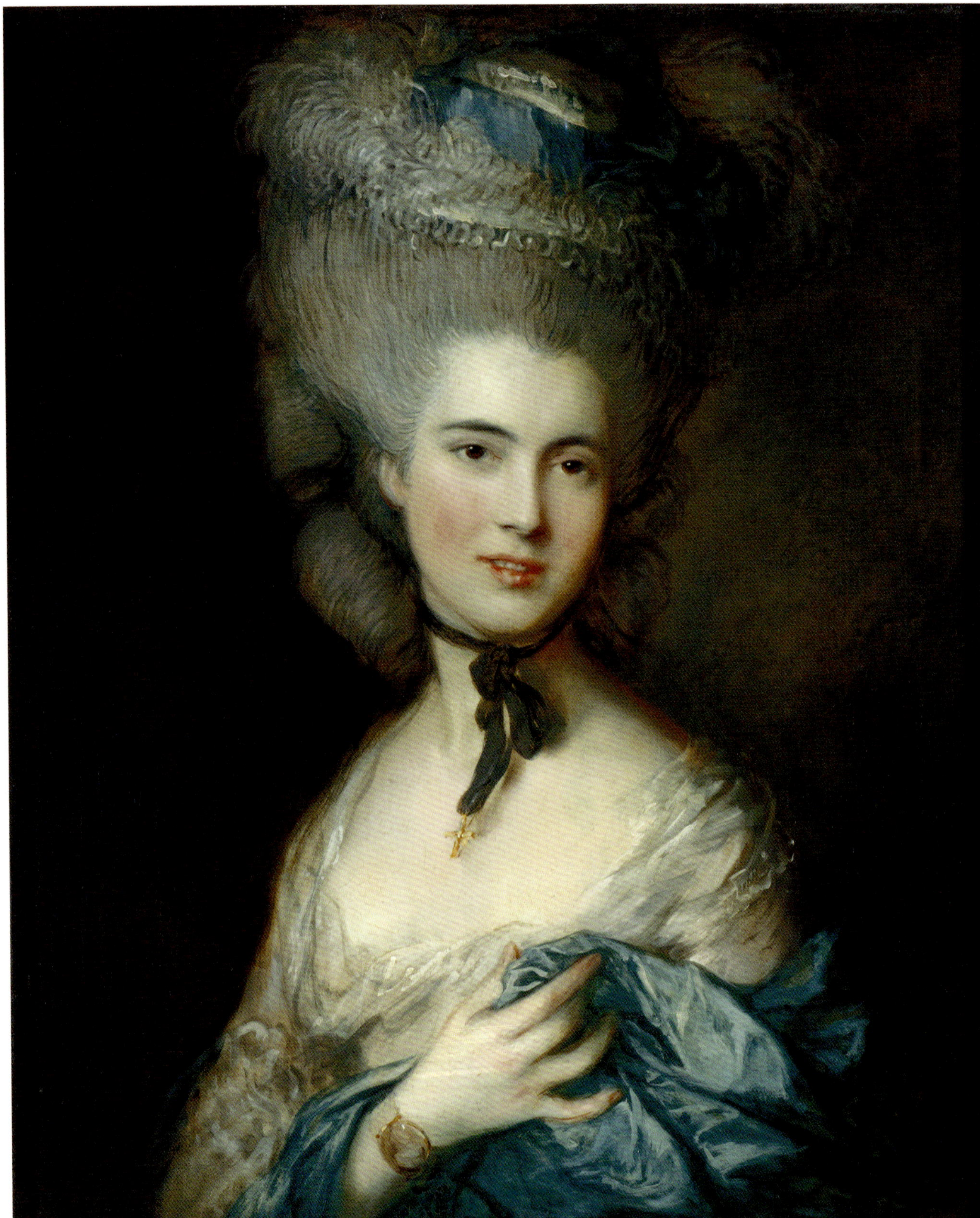

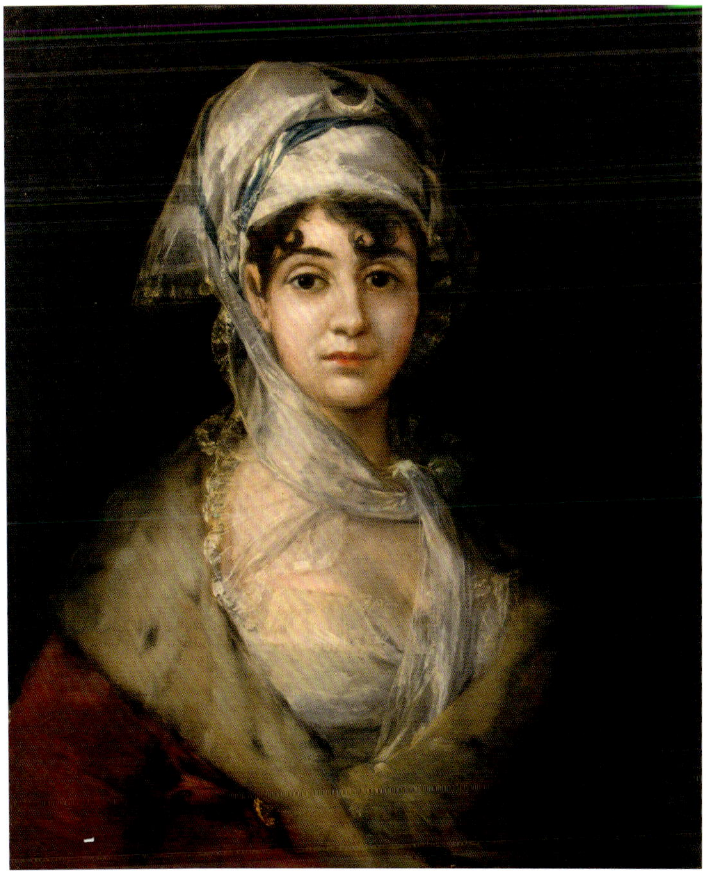

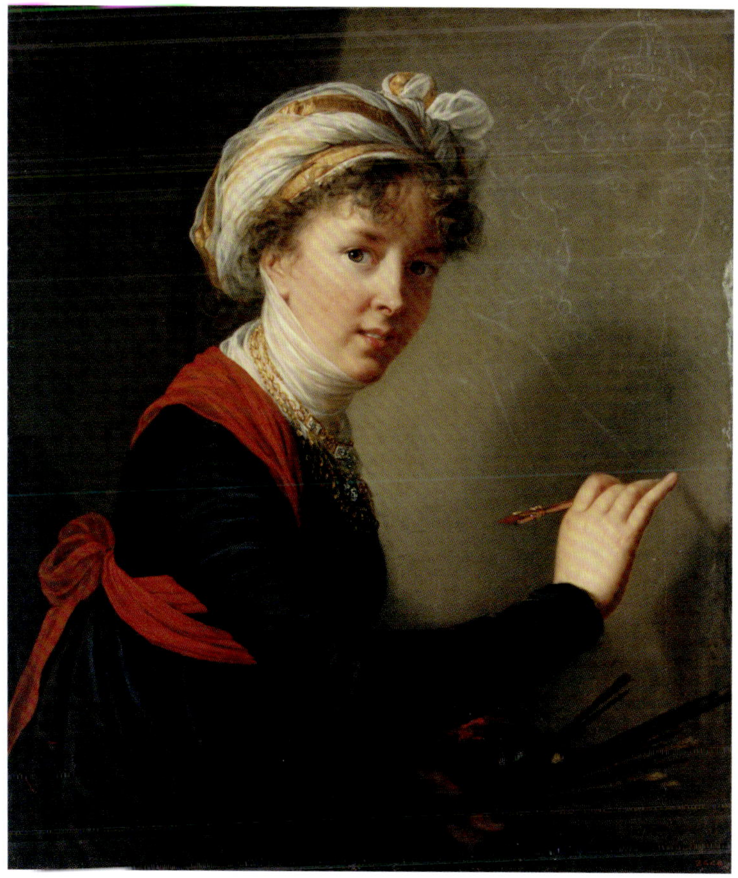

opposite: THOMAS GAINSBOROUGH. *Lady in Blue.* LATE 1770S. OIL ON CANVAS. $30 \times 25\frac{1}{8}$ IN. (76×64 CM).

Gainsborough was a master of the formal portrait and a favorite among society ladies. Avoiding the conventionalities of formal portraiture, Gainsborough invested this image with vitality. The relaxed pose, unforced gesture of the hand, slightly open lips, and dreamy gaze convey a real impression of the sitter. The refined harmony of cold hues—light and dark blues as well as silvers—the light, rapid translucent strokes applied with virtuoso skill and the abundance of half-tones invest this image with poetry and refinement.

above, left: FRANCISCO GOYA. *Portrait of Antonia Sarate.* 1810–11. OIL ON CANVAS. $28 \times 22\frac{7}{8}$ IN. (71×58 CM).

The transition from Thomas Gainsborough to Francisco Goya, whose portraits were considerably influenced by the English artist, provides a vivid impression of the beginning of the modern era in painting. In Goya's work, the combinations of color, already almost independent in Gainsborough but still intended to delight the eye, become an expression of the artist's mood. To Lionello Venturi's statement that this work is "far more a portrait of the soul than the face" could be added, "and of Goya's soul no less than of the model's."

above, right: ELISABETH-LOUISE VIGÉE-LEBRUN. *Self-Portrait.* 1800. OIL ON CANVAS. $31 \times 26\frac{3}{4}$ IN. (78.5×68 CM).

Thanks to talent and connections, Vigée-Lebrun was accepted into the Royal Academy of Painting and Sculpture at age twenty-eight and became a favorite of Queen Marie-Antoinette. When the French Revolution broke out, she fled with her daughter, and for the next thirteen years, lived and worked at the courts of Rome, Vienna, London, and St. Petersburg. Her manner of painting captures the reign of Louis XVI, when, in her words, "women ruled who were then stripped of power by the revolution."

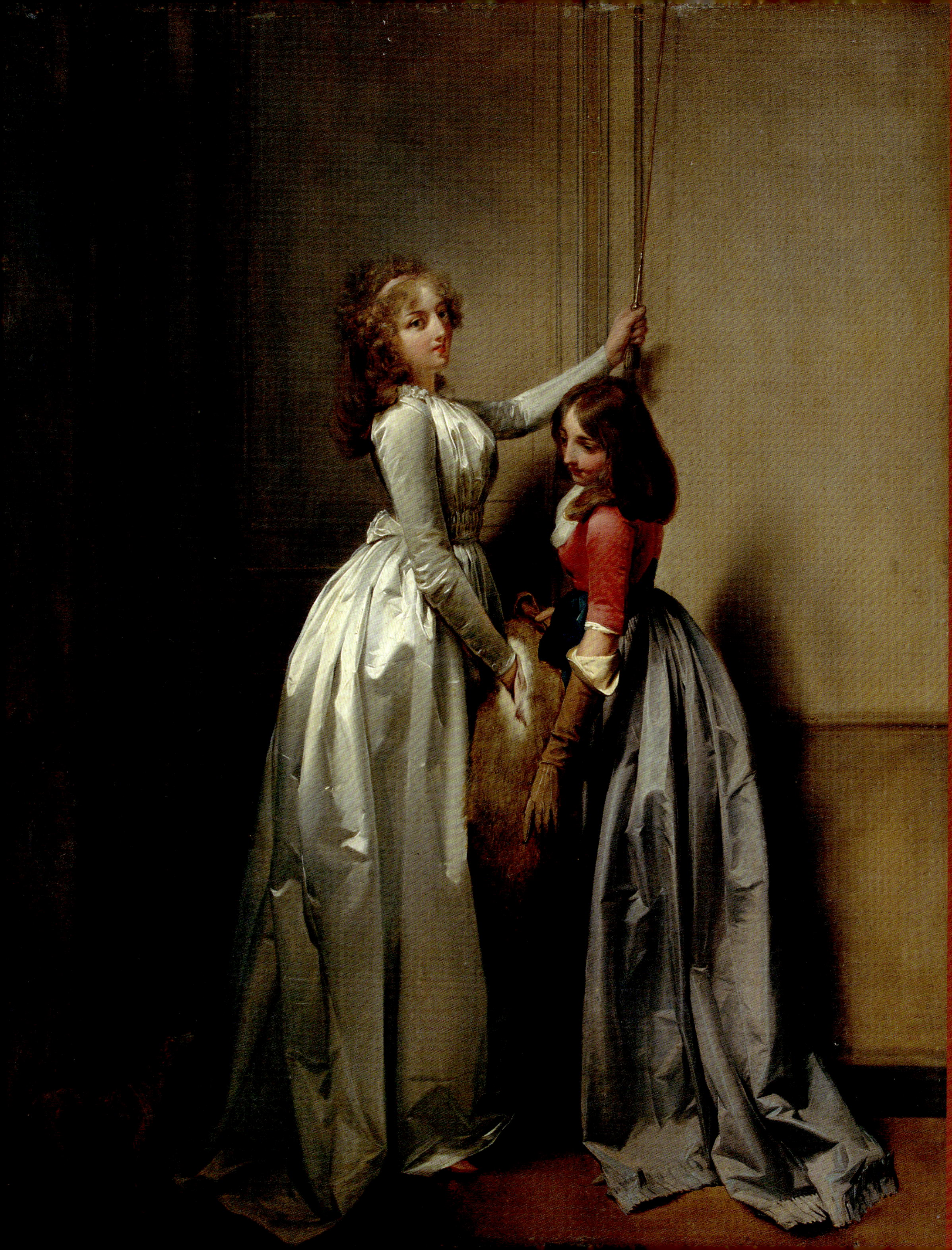

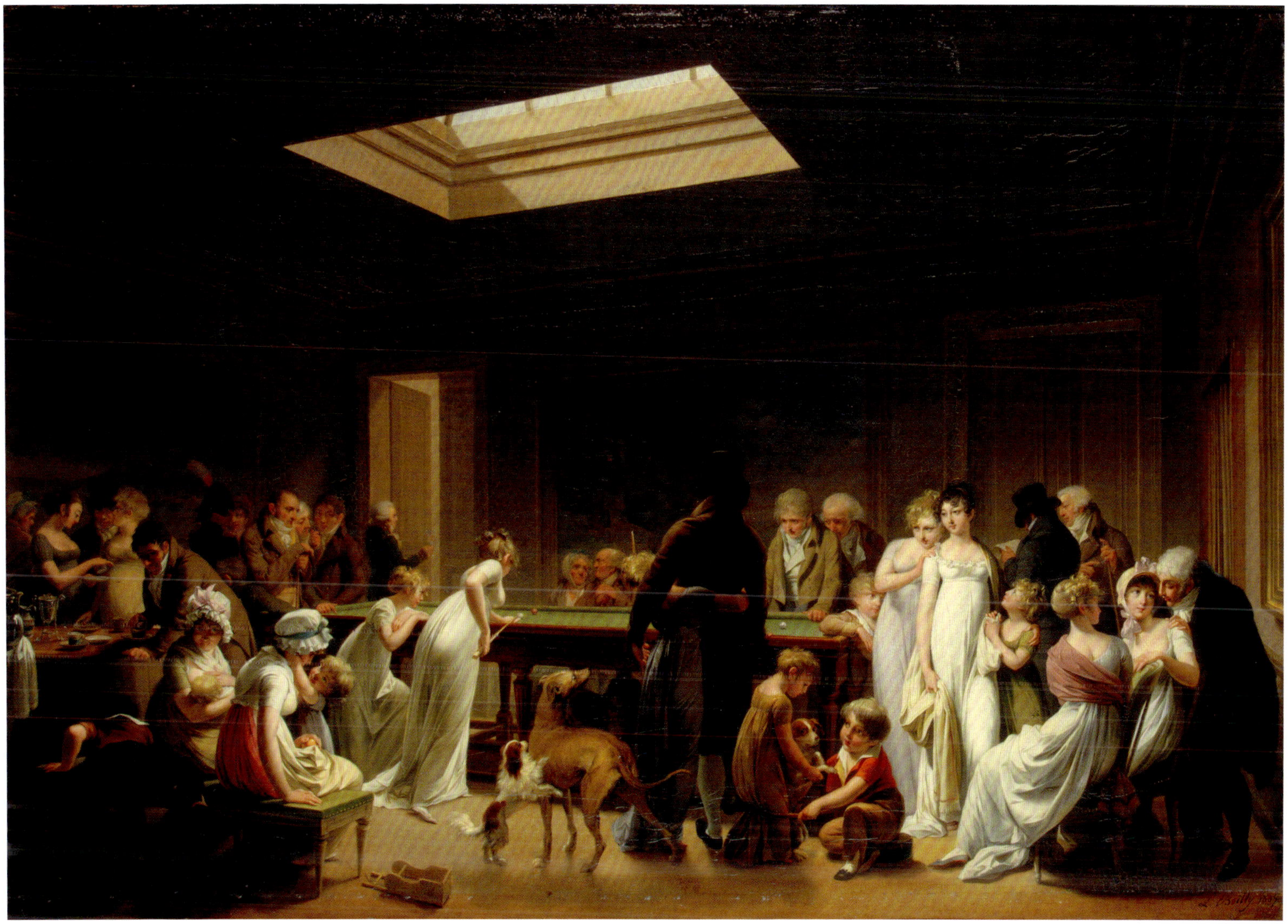

opposite: LOUIS-LÉOPOLD BOILLY. *At the Entrance.* 1796–98. OIL ON PANEL. 15¾ × 12¼ IN. (40 × 31 CM).

Boilly made his name in the early 1790s thanks to frivolous scenes capturing the spirit of the late Rococo. After being censured for such subjects during the first years of the French Revolution, he produced a series of patriotic works. He soon returned to genre painting, however, and gained a reputation as a chronicler of early 19th-century daily life in Paris. In this painting, created "at the entrance" to the 19th century, he recorded the fashion of France's Directory era.

above: LOUIS-LÉOPOLD BOILLY. *Billiards.* 1807. OIL ON CANVAS. 22 × 32 IN. (56 × 81 CM).

A master of genre painting based on the Dutch patterns and an artist sensitive to the individual features of his characters, Boilly created captivating scenes of contemporary Paris life. A good example is *Billiards*, which communicates the antique-style fashions of the First Empire; the free morals of this period, when women in light, transparent dresses were allowed to play billiards with men; and the game itself—in this case, carambole, which is played with three balls on a pocketless table.

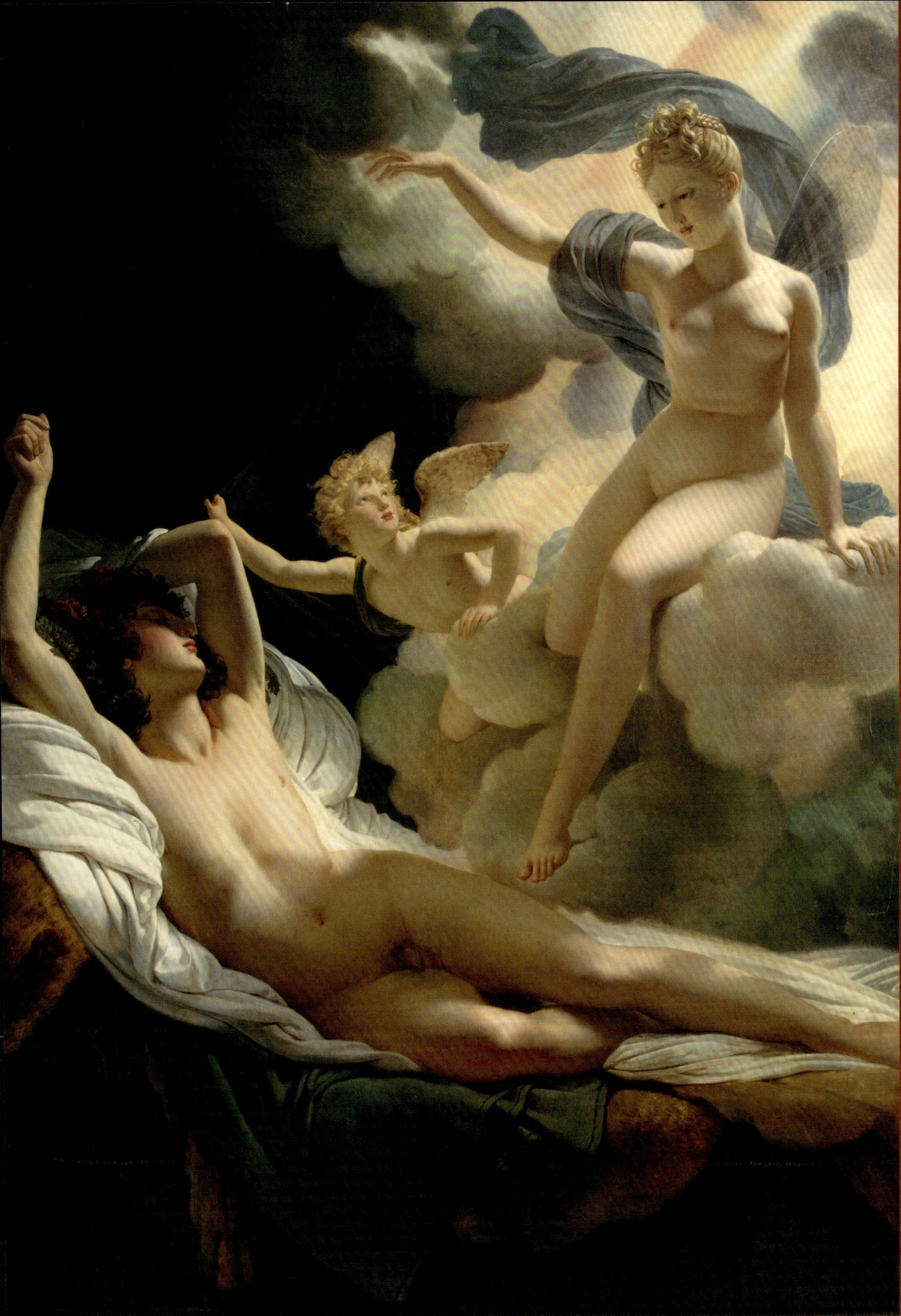

opposite: PIERRE-NARCISSE GUÉRIN. *Morpheus and Iris.* 1811. OIL ON CANVAS. 98 7/8 × 70 IN. (251 × 178 CM).

Guérin, a superb draftsman, is best known in art history as the teacher of Théodore Géricault and Eugène Delacroix. His works are dominated by the mood of quiet contentment typical of the official art of the Napoleonic empire. Paintings such as this one adorned the imperial residences, and the subject is indeed ideally suited to luxurious private apartments: Iris, the goddess of the rainbow, descends to her lover, Morpheus, the god of sleep.

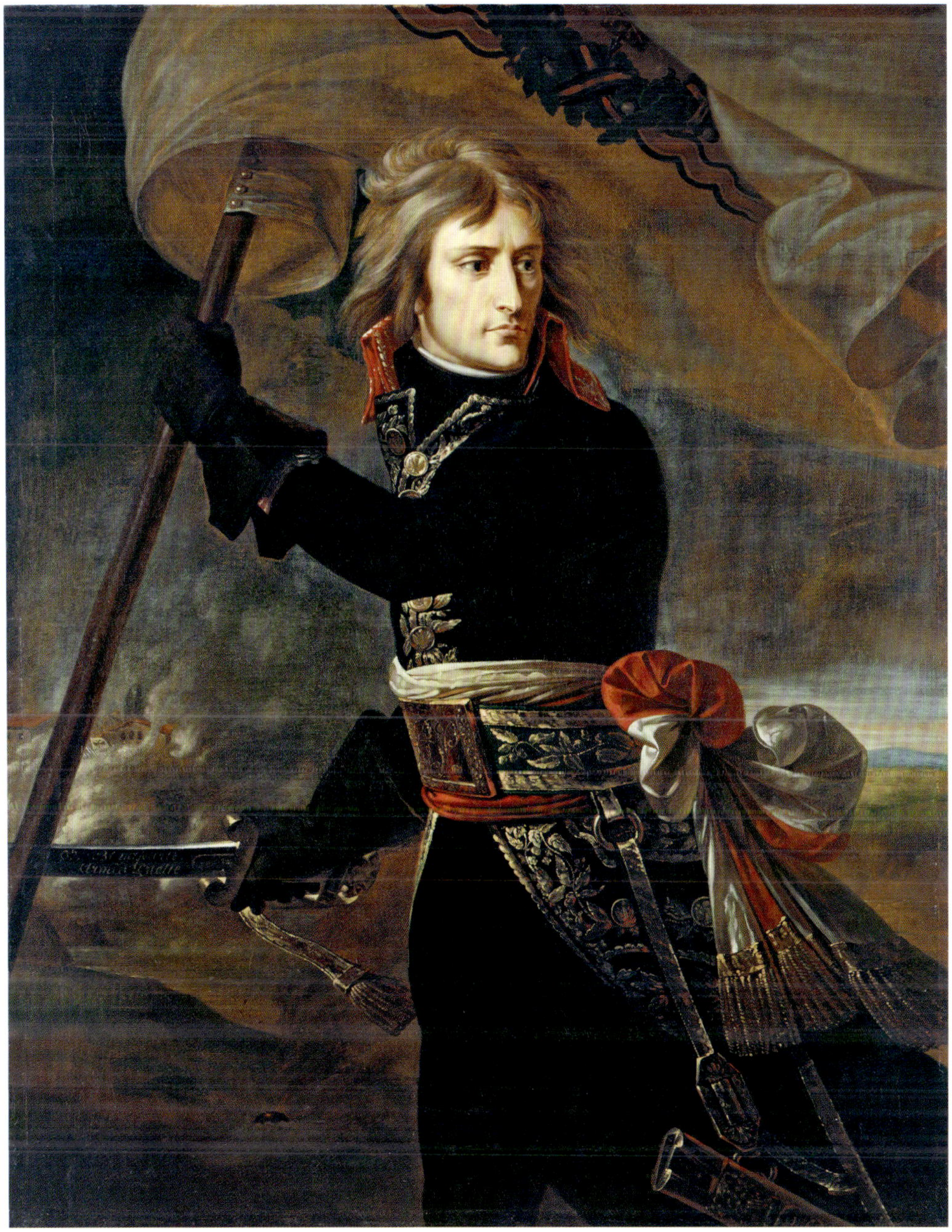

above: ANTOINE-JEAN GROS. *Napoleon on the Bridge at Arcola.* 1796–97. OIL ON CANVAS. 52 3/4 × 41 IN. (134 × 104 CM).

Among the major names in French painting in the late 18th and early 19th centuries, Gros was probably the only one who remained loyal to the national school's traditional values, seen in this work's dense textures and elaborate color scheme. Thanks to these qualities, the conventional heroic portrait acquires an emotional charge that foreshadows Romanticism. The persuasiveness is heightened because Gros witnessed the event while accompanying Napoleon on his Italian campaign in 1796.

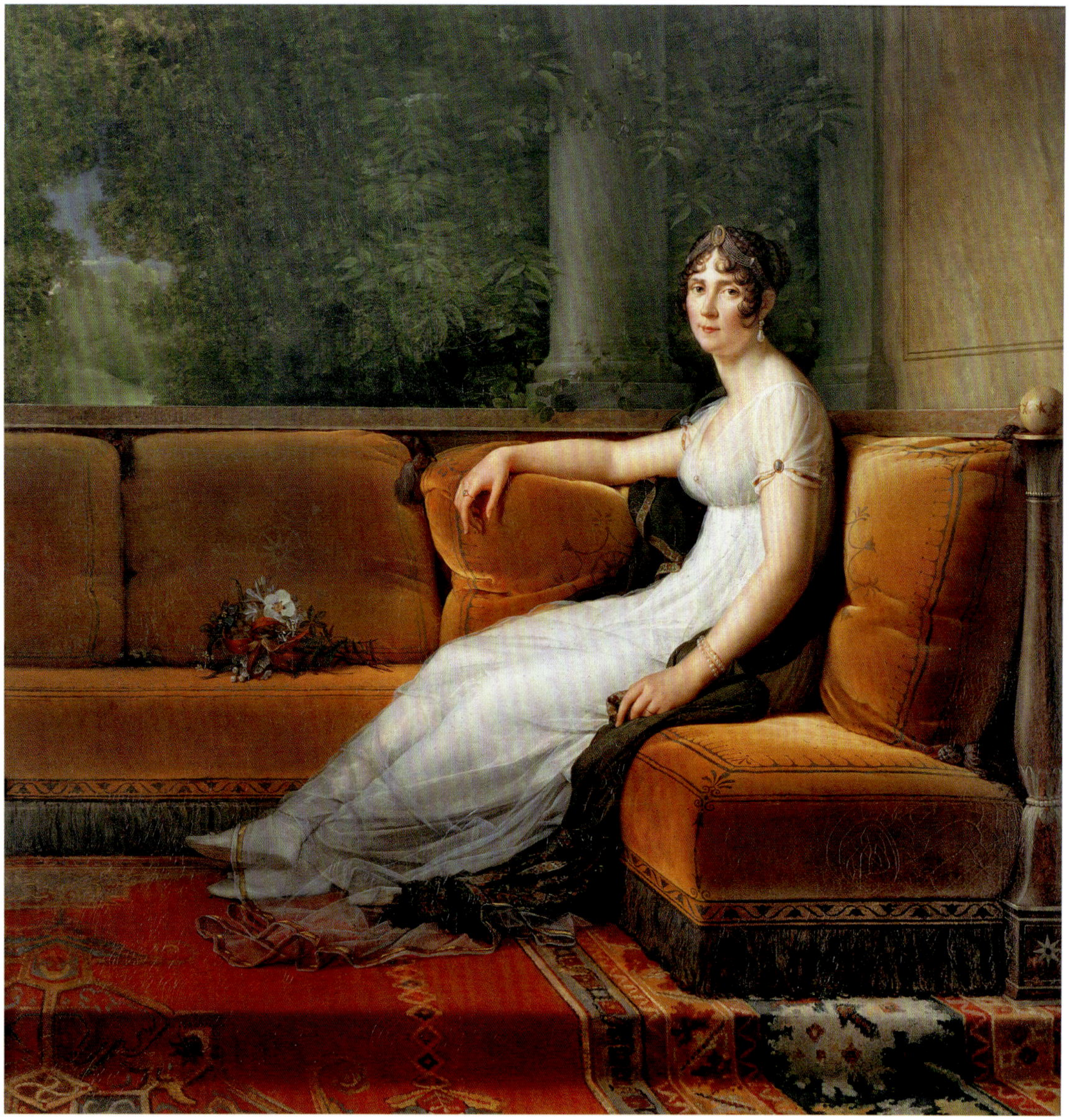

above: FRANÇOIS GÉRARD. *Portrait of Joséphine de Beauharnais.* 1801. OIL ON CANVAS. 70 × 68 1/2 IN. (178 × 174 CM).

One of the most fashionable portraitists of the Napoleonic era, Gérard had a fine feeling for artistic trends. Here, he successfully combines a refined classical composition, the imperial taste, and a light palette. Gérard worked as a decorator at Malmaison, among other places, and this painting depicts Joséphine de Beauharnais, the château's mistress and the wife of the future French emperor, Napoleon Bonaparte.

opposite: PIERRE-PAUL PRUD'HON, WITH MARIE-FRANÇOISE-CONSTANCE MAYER-LAMARTINIÈRE. *Innocence Preferring Love to Wealth.* 1804. OIL ON CANVAS. 95 5/8 × 76 3/8 IN. (243 × 194 CM).

This composition, executed with a young female pupil, was acquired by Prince Nikolai Yusupov, a Russian statesman and diplomat who lived in Paris from 1803 to 1810. A connoisseur of the arts, Yusupov acquired paintings for the Hermitage during Catherine II's reign and managed the museum's affairs under Paul I, later assembling his own remarkable collection of French painting.

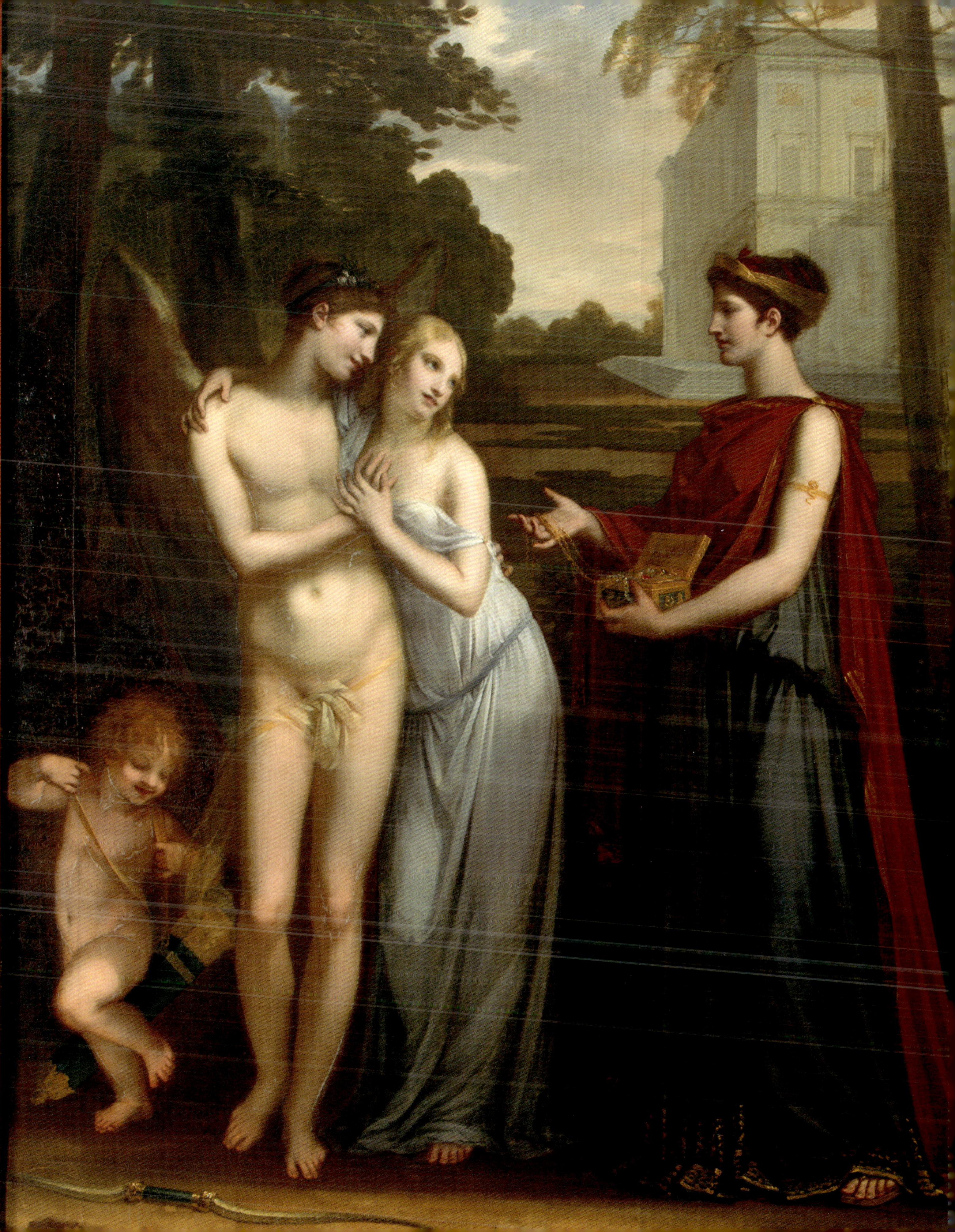

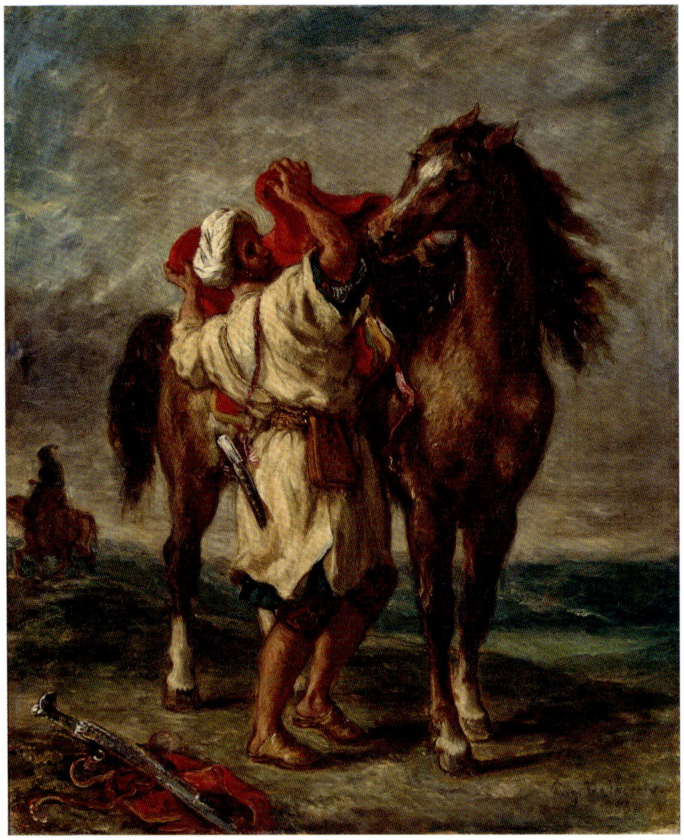

right: EUGÈNE DELACROIX. *A Moroccan Saddling a Horse.* 1855. OIL ON CANVAS. 22 × 18½ IN. (56 × 47 CM).

Delacroix's Romanticism is virtually the opposite of German artists' interpretation of the style, but his interest in depicting animals—the lions in the grip of death's fury, the spirited horses, alongside which the humans seem like frozen statues—connects him with the prose of German Romantic writers, in which the themes of the human in the beast and the bestial in the human play a substantial role.

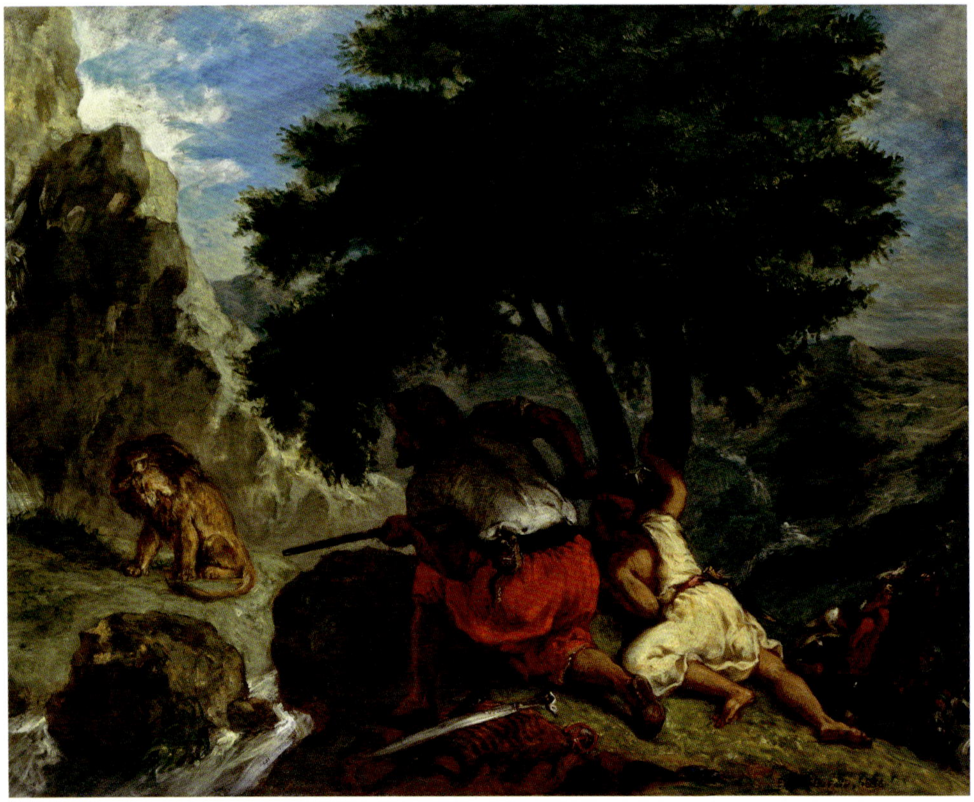

below: EUGÈNE DELACROIX. *Lion Hunt in Morocco.* 1854. OIL ON CANVAS. 29⅛ × 36¼ IN. (74 × 92 CM).

Delacroix visited Morocco in 1832 as part of a French delegation sent by King Louis-Philippe after the conquest of Algeria. His impressions of North Africa left their mark on all his subsequent work, and sketches he made during the journey formed the basis of many painted variations. Here, the subject is stripped of exotic details and subordinated to the unbridled energy of painting, founded on the contrast of complementary colors, which Delacroix was the first to employ consistently as a means of artistic expression.

opposite: CASPAR DAVID FRIEDRICH. *Dreamer (The Ruins of Oybin Monastery).* CA. 1835. OIL ON CANVAS. 10⅝ × 8¼ IN. (27 × 21 CM).

These ruins, geometrically regular to the point of strangeness, are a variation on Friedrich's beloved theme of the window—the boundary between worlds, the exit to eternity, and the eternity of the dream. In this work the dreamer, who has found a perch on the old stones, is the Romantic poet immersed in thought. He is poised on the threshold between reality and fantasy, the twilight of his native land and the bright abyss of the transcendental, and clarity and unpredictability.

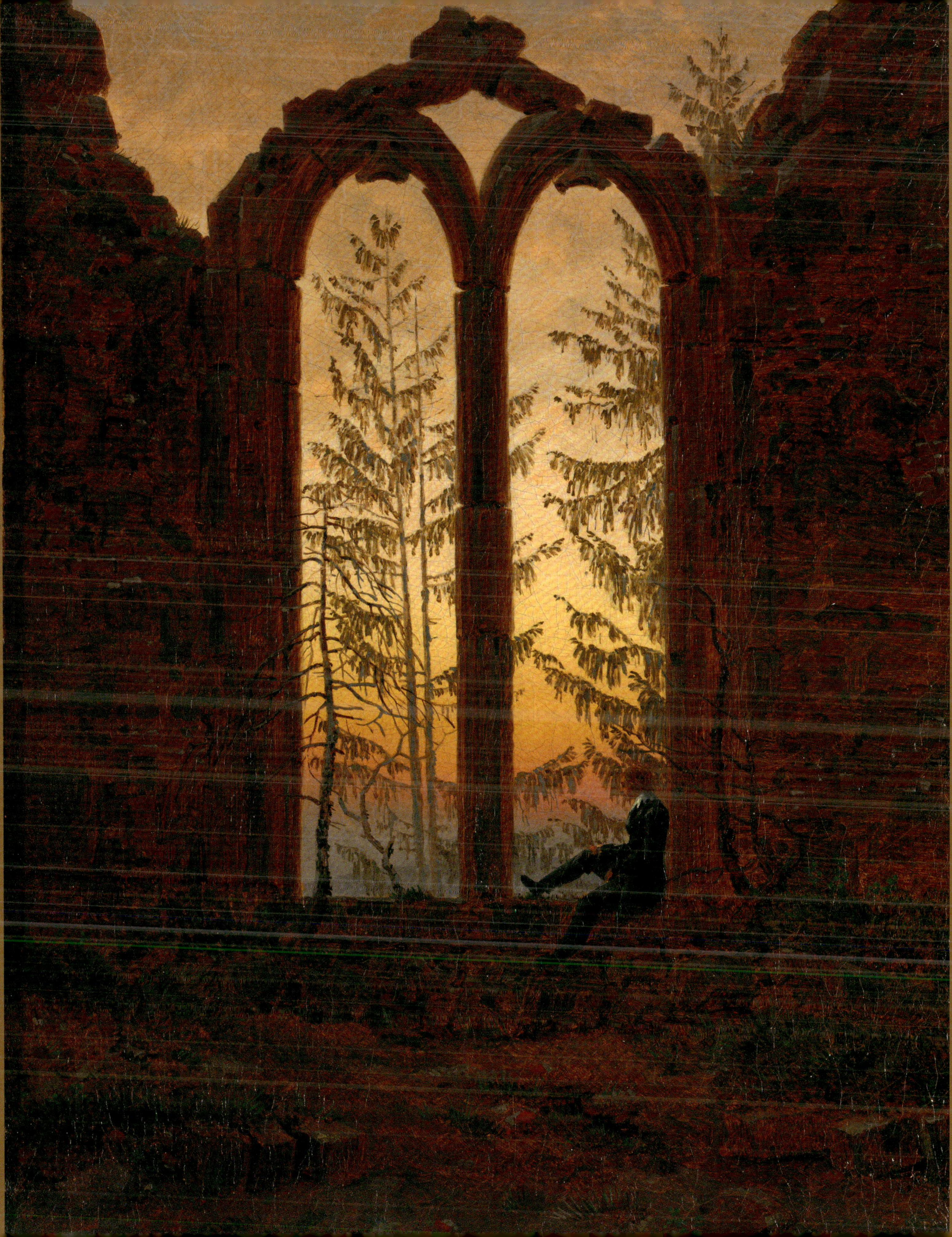

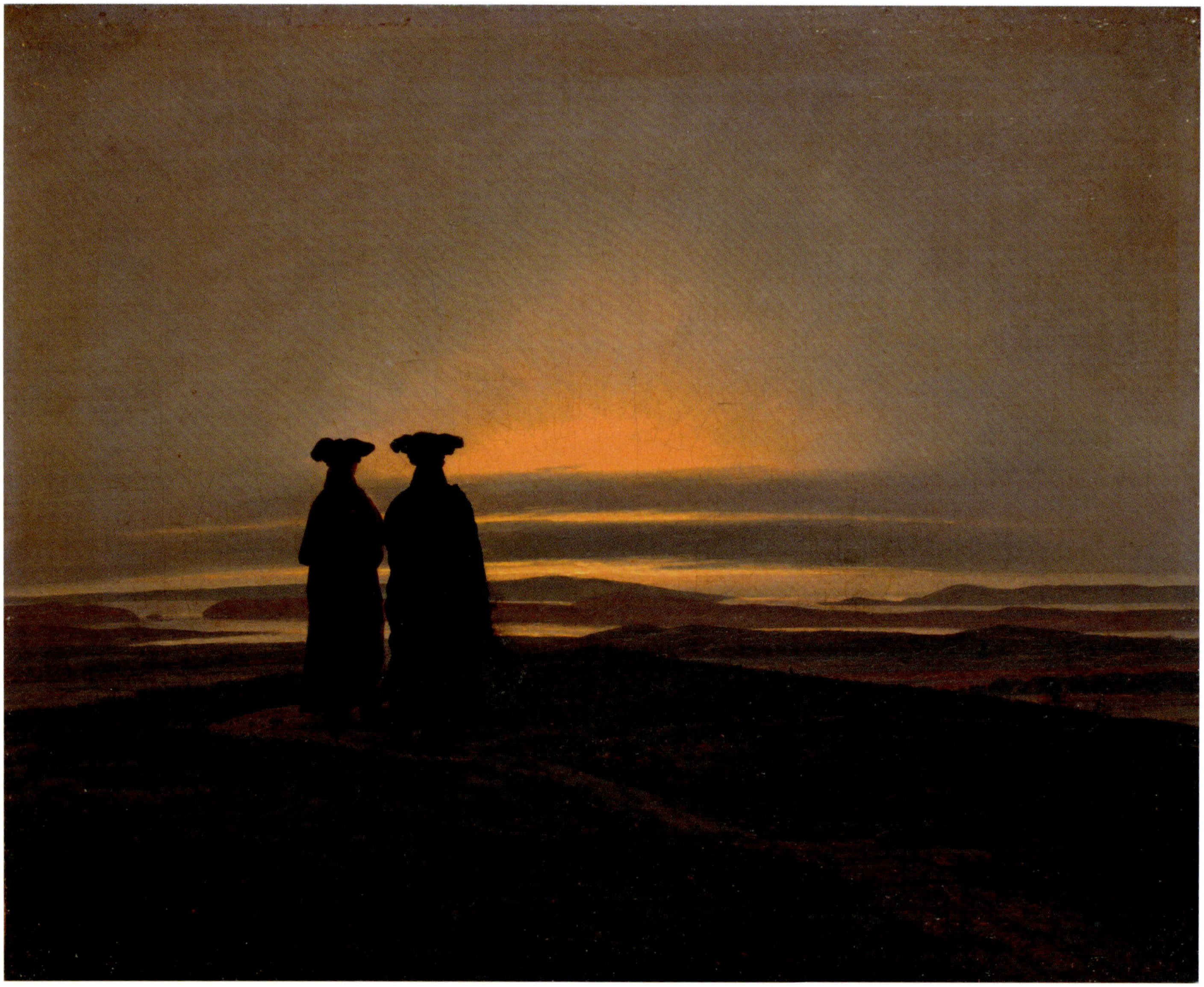

above: CASPAR DAVID FRIEDRICH. *Sunset (Brothers).* BETWEEN 1830 AND 1835. OIL ON CANVAS. 9 7/8 × 12 1/4 IN. (25 × 31 CM).

In Friedrich's work, the frequent motif of two male or female figures contemplating an empty expanse is usually associated with the cult of Romantic friendship that was adopted in the German Romantic milieu. This pairing prompts the viewer to perceive the landscape as not only a view but also a conversation between kindred souls, thus underlining the importance of its conceptual content.

opposite: CASPAR DAVID FRIEDRICH. *On a Sailing-Ship.* BETWEEN 1818 AND 1820. OIL ON CANVAS. 28 × 22 IN. (71 × 56 CM).

This work's unexpected composition might seem akin to the cropping practiced later in the century by the Impressionists, yet it is not evidence of a tendency on Friedrich's part to experiment with form. Its significance is metaphorical. As in many of his paintings, the ship denotes fate or destiny, in this case his own: the work was painted to mark his marriage. The couple has just embarked on a voyage from which, as with any Romantic journey, there is no turning back.

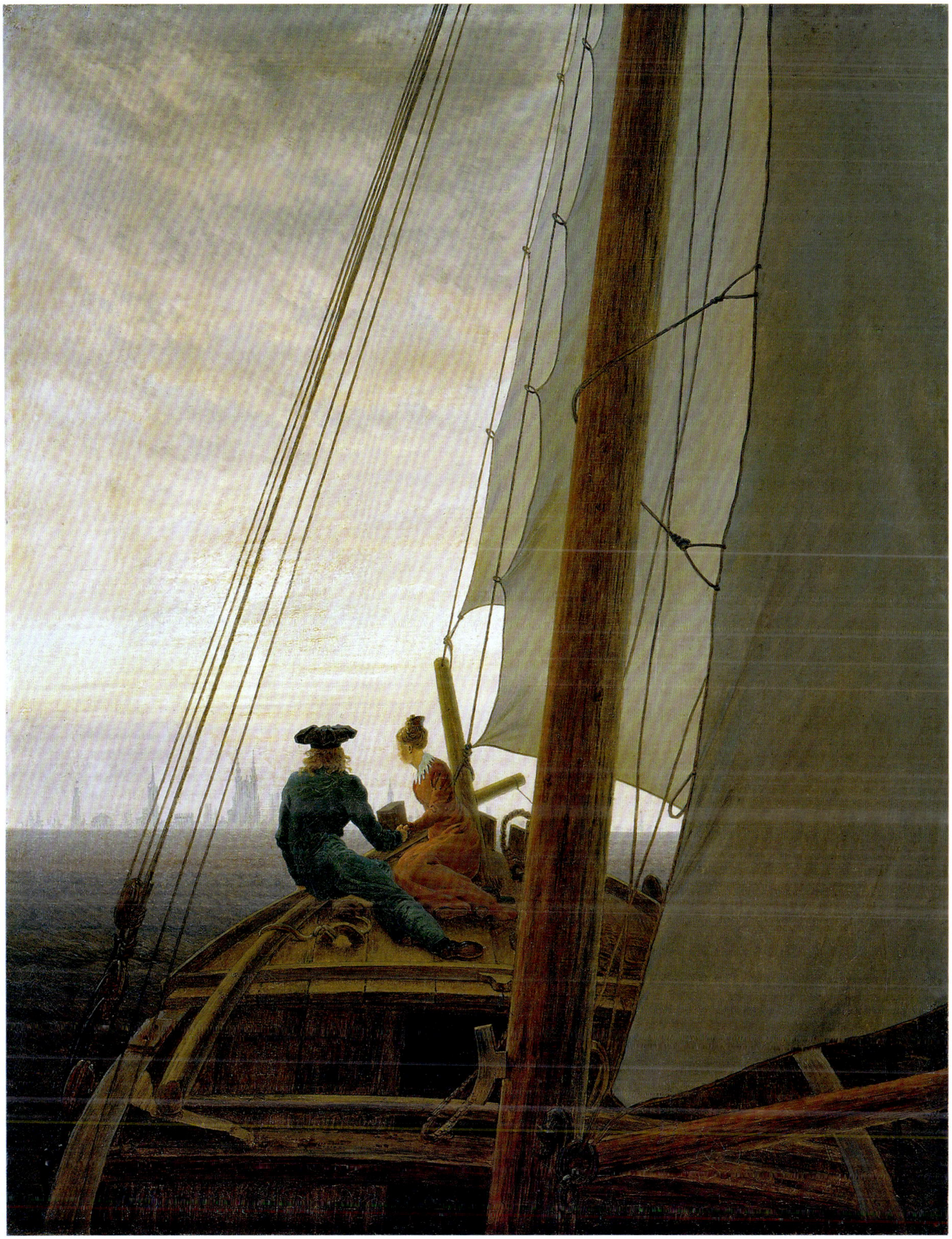

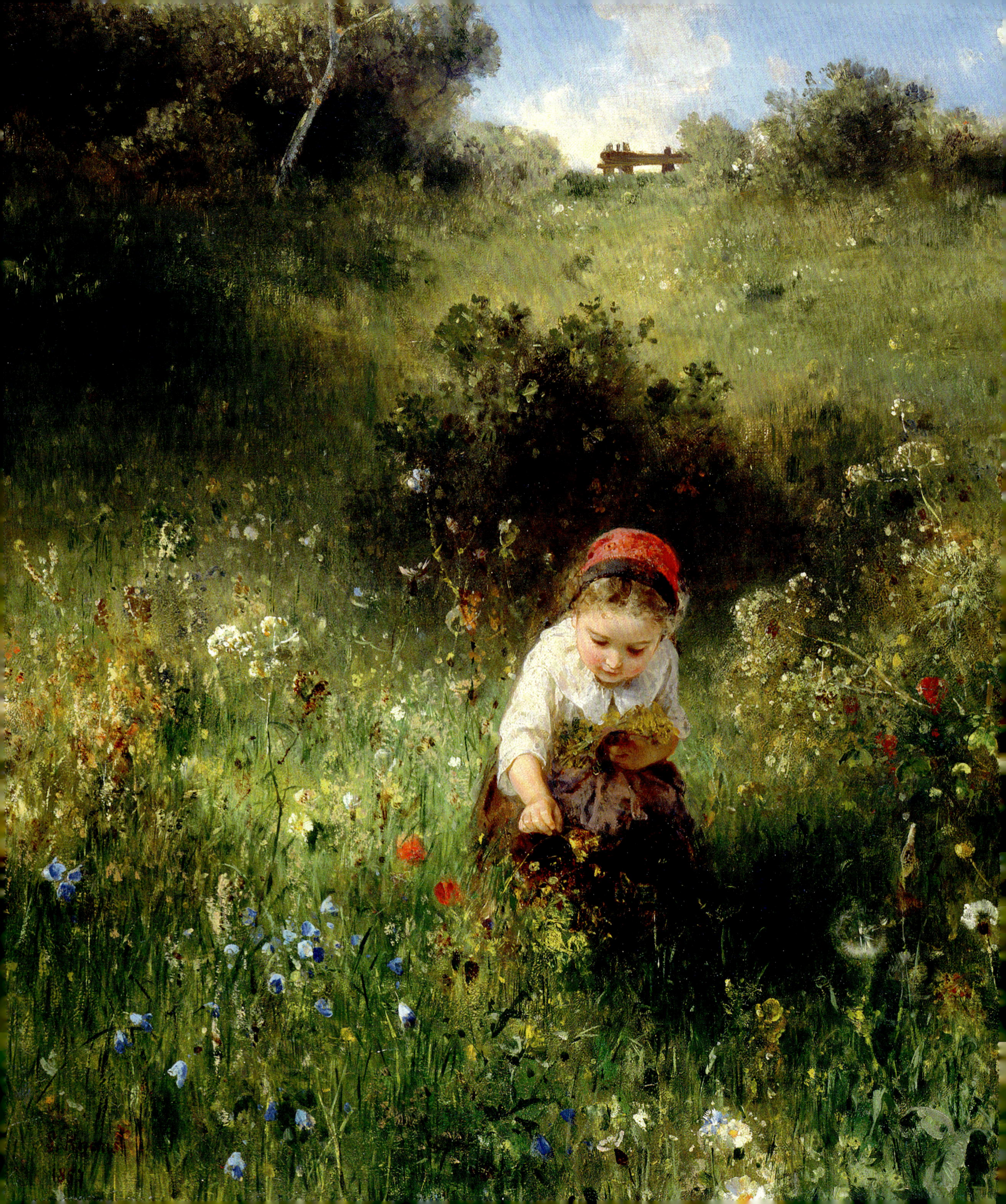

LUDWIG KNAUS. *Girl in a Field.* 1857. OIL ON CANVAS. 19 5/8 × 24 IN. (50 × 61 CM).

A considerable part of the late output of the Düsseldorf school is made up of sentimental genre paintings such as this one. Considered the leading figure of this style, Knaus enjoyed an excellent reputation in the second half of the 19th century. His works were appreciated by European aristocracy, including members of the Russian imperial court.

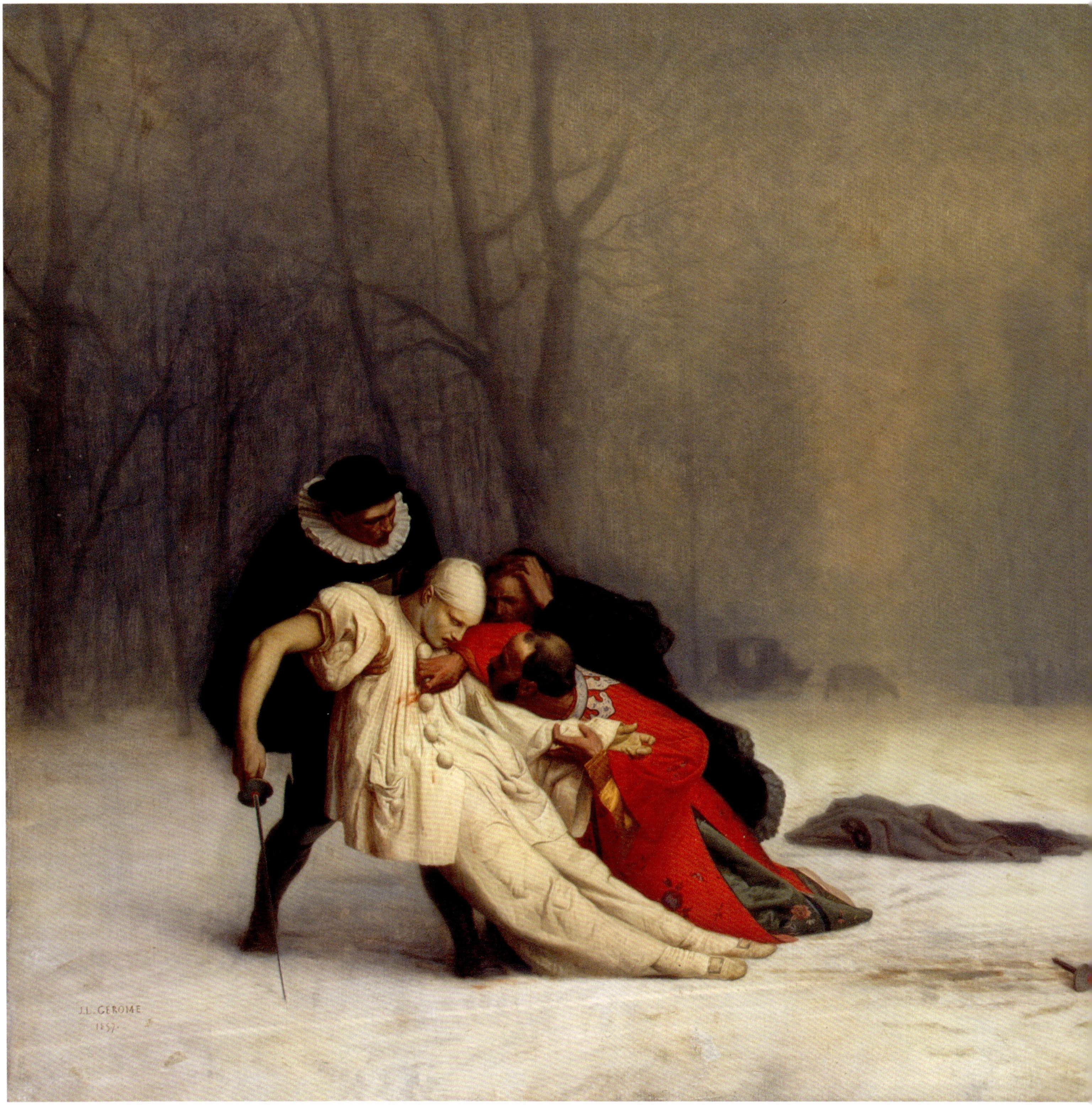

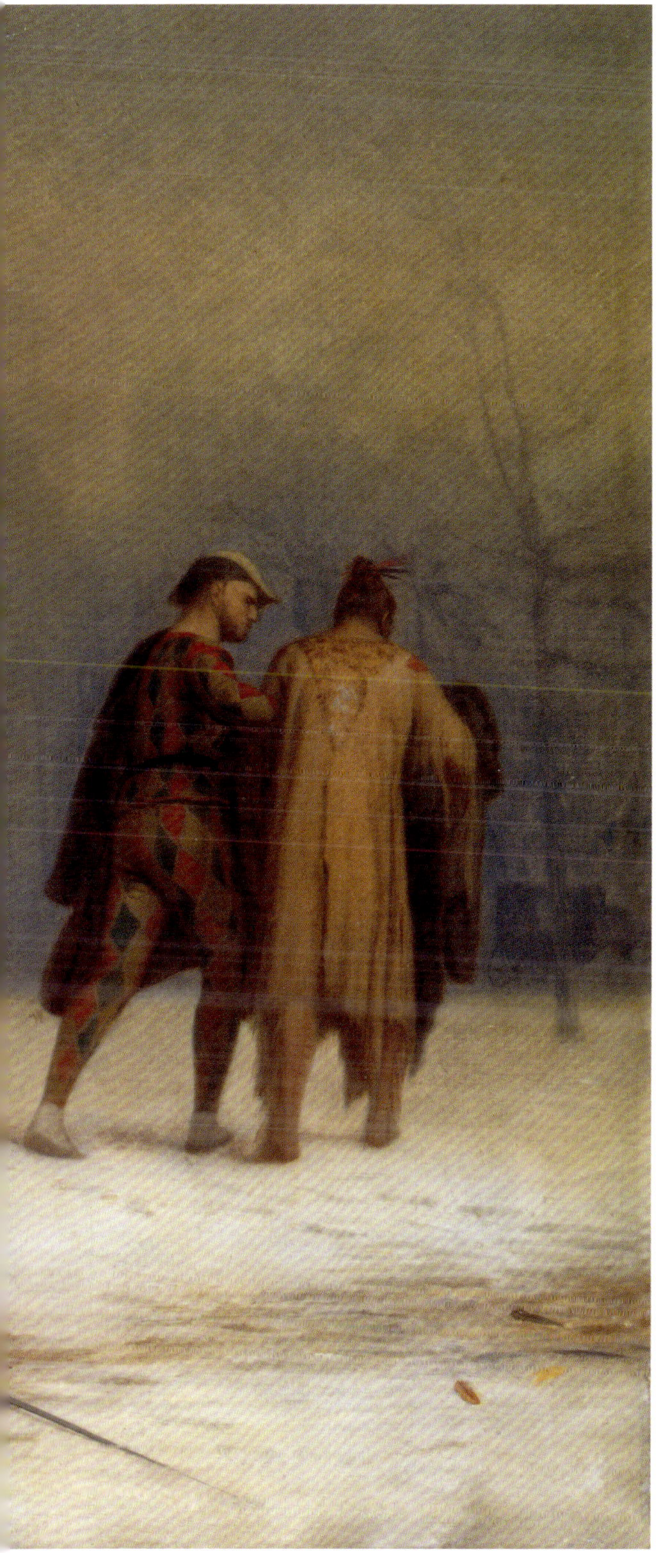

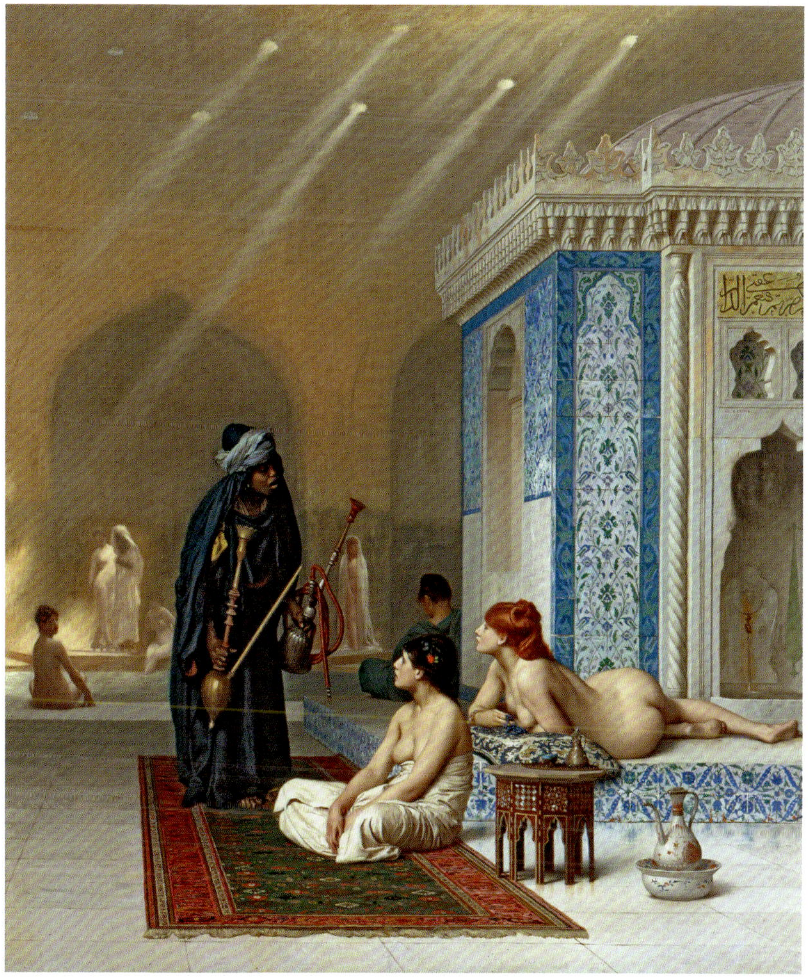

above: JEAN-LÉON GÉRÔME. *Pool in a Harem.* CA. 1876. OIL ON CANVAS. 29 × $24\frac{1}{2}$ IN. (73.5 × 62 CM).

This eye-catching canvas by Jean-Léon Gérôme, one of the most influential academic painters in Paris of his time, was purchased for the Imperial collection after it had been shown at the Salon of 1876. A fine example of a "costume" painting suitable for a study of an aristocrat (in fact, it adorned one of the royal studies of the Winter Palace), *Pool in a Harem* may also be reckoned among the artist's Orientalist works, marked by an ethnographic accuracy in its rendered details of architecture and household items.

left: JEAN-LÉON GÉRÔME. *Duel after a Masquerade.* 1857. OIL ON CANVAS. $26\frac{3}{4}$ × 39 IN. (68 × 99 CM).

Gérôme, a pupil and loyal follower of Paul Delaroche, became a vehement defender of academic tenets, which in the 1860s were shaken under the impact of Realism and Impressionism. After a few journeys to the East, Gérôme devoted himself entirely to sentimental, erotic exotica, working in a smooth, almost oleographic manner. This painting, executed in a fairly free manner, was a resounding success at the 1857 Salon, after which Gérôme repeated it several times.

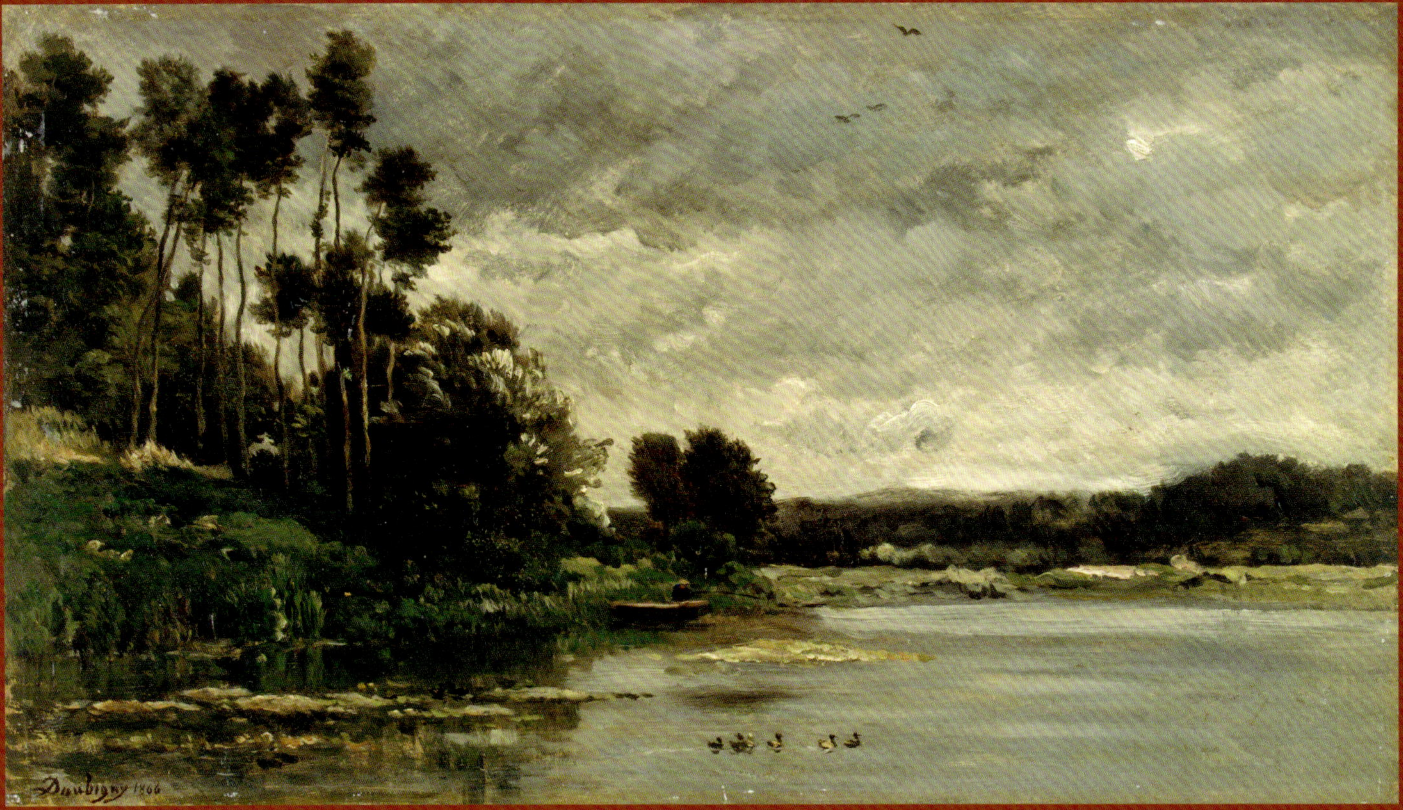

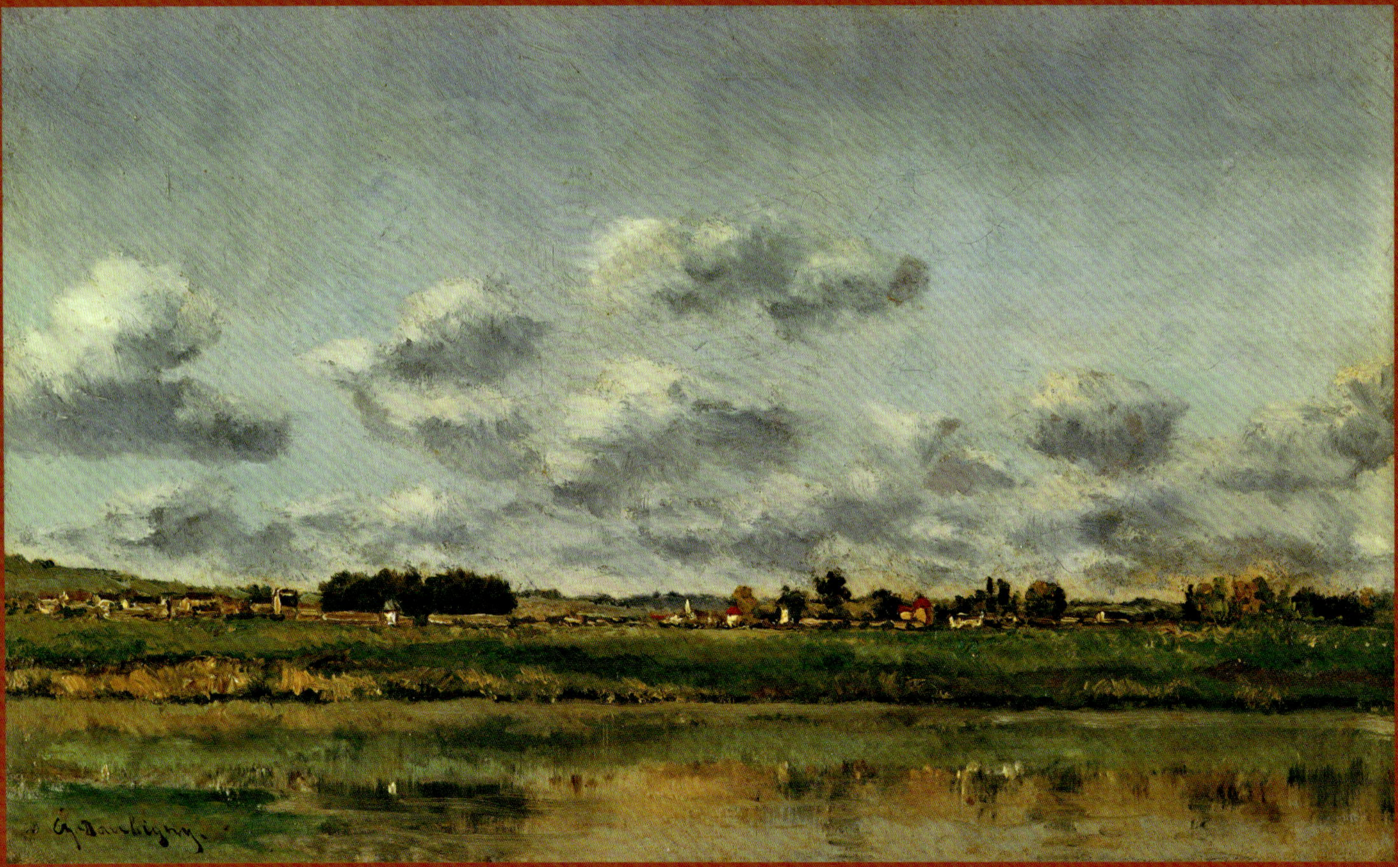

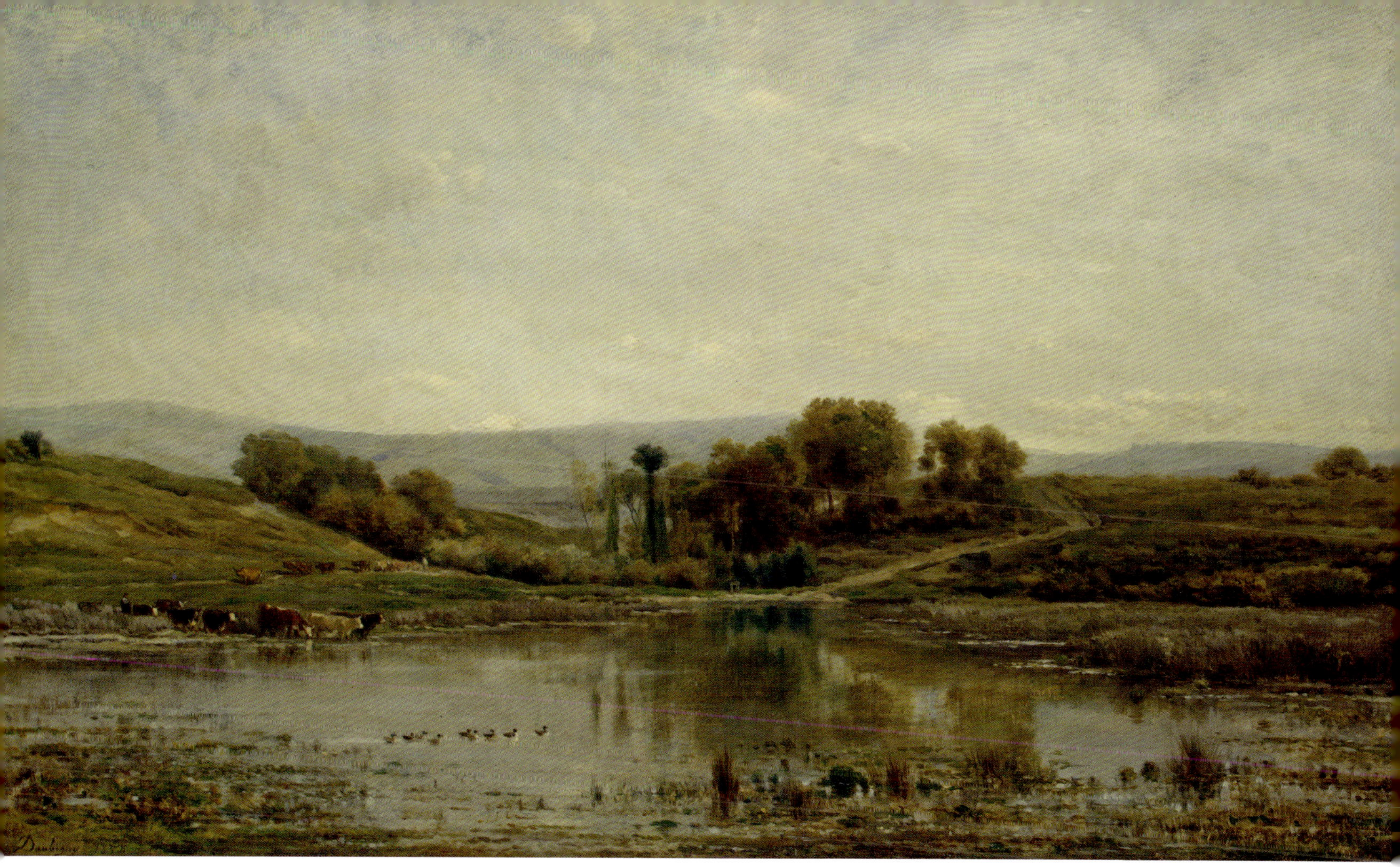

opposite, top: CHARLES-FRANÇOIS DAUBIGNY. *River Bank.* 1866. OIL ON PANEL. 10½ × 18⅛ IN. (26.5 × 46 CM).

Daubigny concentrated on simple provincial motifs, working increasingly en plein air as time went on. His paintings fully accord with the term "landscape of mood," which stresses his fundamental difference from the Impressionists about to burst onto the scene. An arbitrary viewpoint, interest in the optical construction of the image, and a sense of the decorative surface of the painting were alien to Daubigny, for whom emotional content was of primary importance.

opposite, bottom: CHARLES-FRANÇOIS DAUBIGNY. *Banks of the Loing.* LATE 1860S. OIL ON CANVAS. 10 × 16⅛ IN. (25.5 × 41 CM).

Increasingly uninhibited brushwork and an ever-freer use of color made Daubigny's work of the 1860s a direct forerunner of Impressionism. In this period he traveled along the rivers of northern France aboard a specially fitted studio-boat, producing landscapes that were variations on the Dutch theme of sky and water separated by a thin strip of land.

above: CHARLES-FRANÇOIS DAUBIGNY. *Pond.* 1858. OIL ON CANVAS. 22⅝ × 36⅞ IN. (57.5 × 93.5 CM).

Daubigny was one of the first artists to begin painting outdoors. He made the palette of the landscape substantially brighter, using a panoramic view of a flat piece of countryside—his favorite motif—in order to exclude dark areas as much as possible and to fill the painting with air.

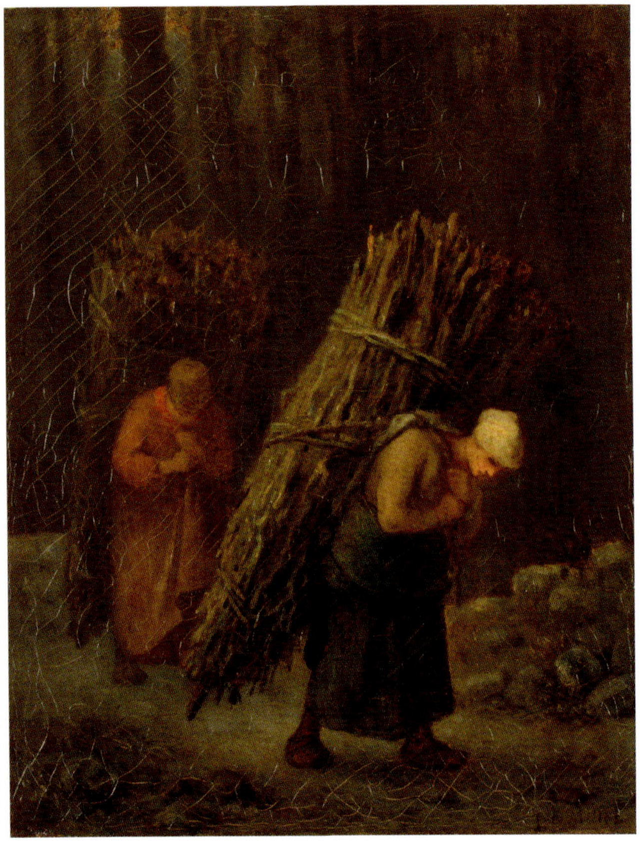

above: JEAN-FRANÇOIS MILLET. *Peasant Girls with Brushwood.* CA. 1858. OIL ON CANVAS. 14 3/4 × 11 5/8 IN. (37.5 × 29.5 CM).

"It seems to have been painted with the same soil that he is sowing," so Théophile Gautier wrote of *Sower*, another of Millet's works. In the artist's hands, the coarse materiality of painting (which had been rediscovered by the Barbizon school) serves to express the symbolic. In this work, the physical sensation of weight implied by the huge brushwood bundles expresses the abstract idea of humility.

below: JEAN-BAPTISTE CAMILLE COROT. *Peasant Woman Pasturing a Cow by the Edge of a Forest.* 1865–70. OIL ON CANVAS. 18 3/4 × 13 3/4 IN. (47.5 × 35 CM).

The austere yet inexhaustible range of silvery gray hues, together with the combination of a single mass of forest and a lightly drawn tree, make this painting characteristic of Corot's oeuvre. The figures in his late works appear to dissolve into nature. Here, the turn of the woman's body is presented so precisely that the entire landscape seems to be contained within her backward glance.

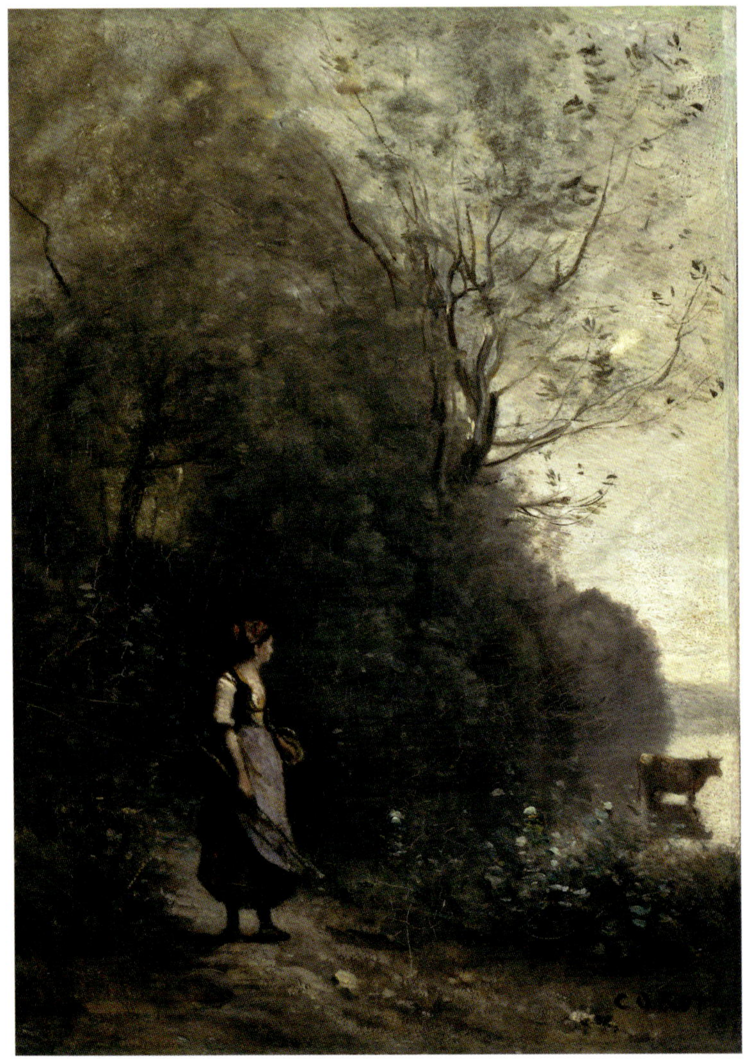

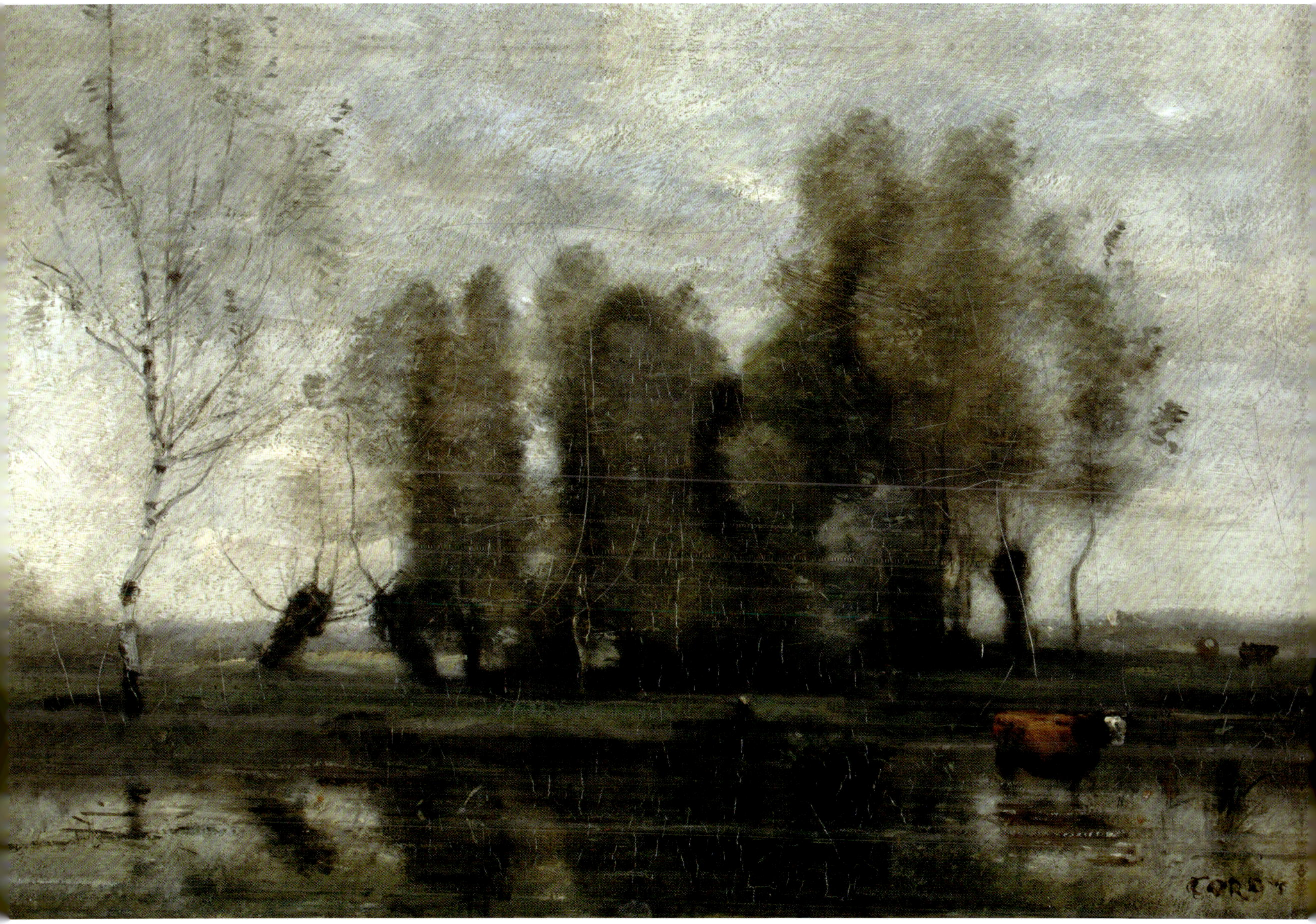

JEAN-BAPTISTE CAMILLE COROT. *Trees in a Marsh.* BETWEEN 1855 AND 1860. OIL ON CANVAS. 10 × 15 IN. (25.5 × 38 CM).

"Next to Corot, we are worth nothing," Claude Monet told a visitor admiring his paintings at an 1897 exhibition. It is true that working en plein air and the methodical use of different tonal values enabled Corot to fill his paintings with light and air, whose changing states the Impressionists would seek to capture. Those artists would reject classically elegant compositions, although in this landscape, that is precisely what makes the light and air particularly tangible.

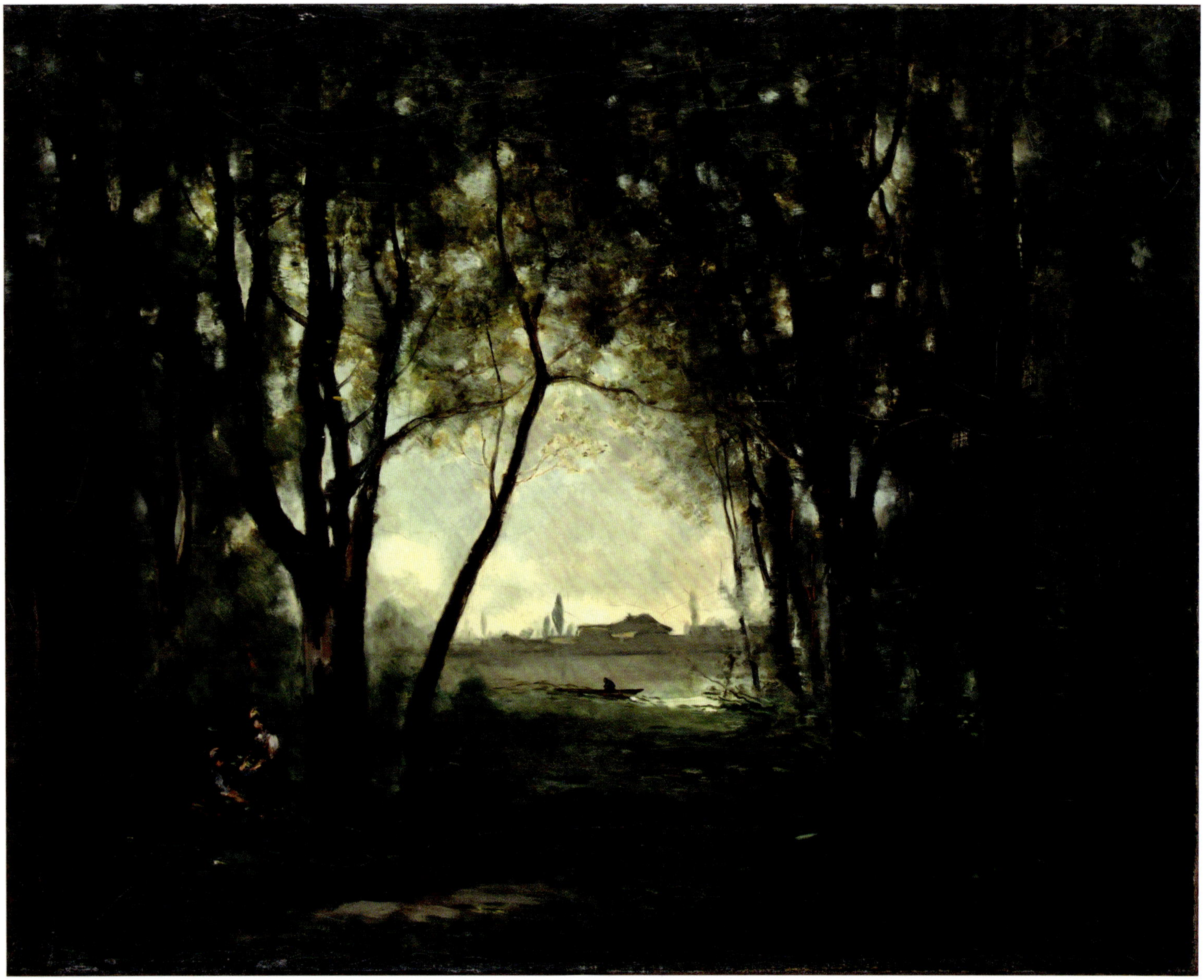

JEAN-BAPTISTE CAMILLE COROT. *Landscape with a Lake.* LATE 1860S–EARLY 1870S. OIL ON CANVAS. $20\frac{7}{8} \times 25\frac{3}{4}$ IN. (53×65.5 CM).

Corot clearly did not intend to make a powerful statement in this painting depicting a gap in a tangle of trees, with the resulting contrast of light and shade. The fuzzy shapes of the houses and boat do not draw the eye into the distance; rather, they present an invitation to thoughtful concentration.

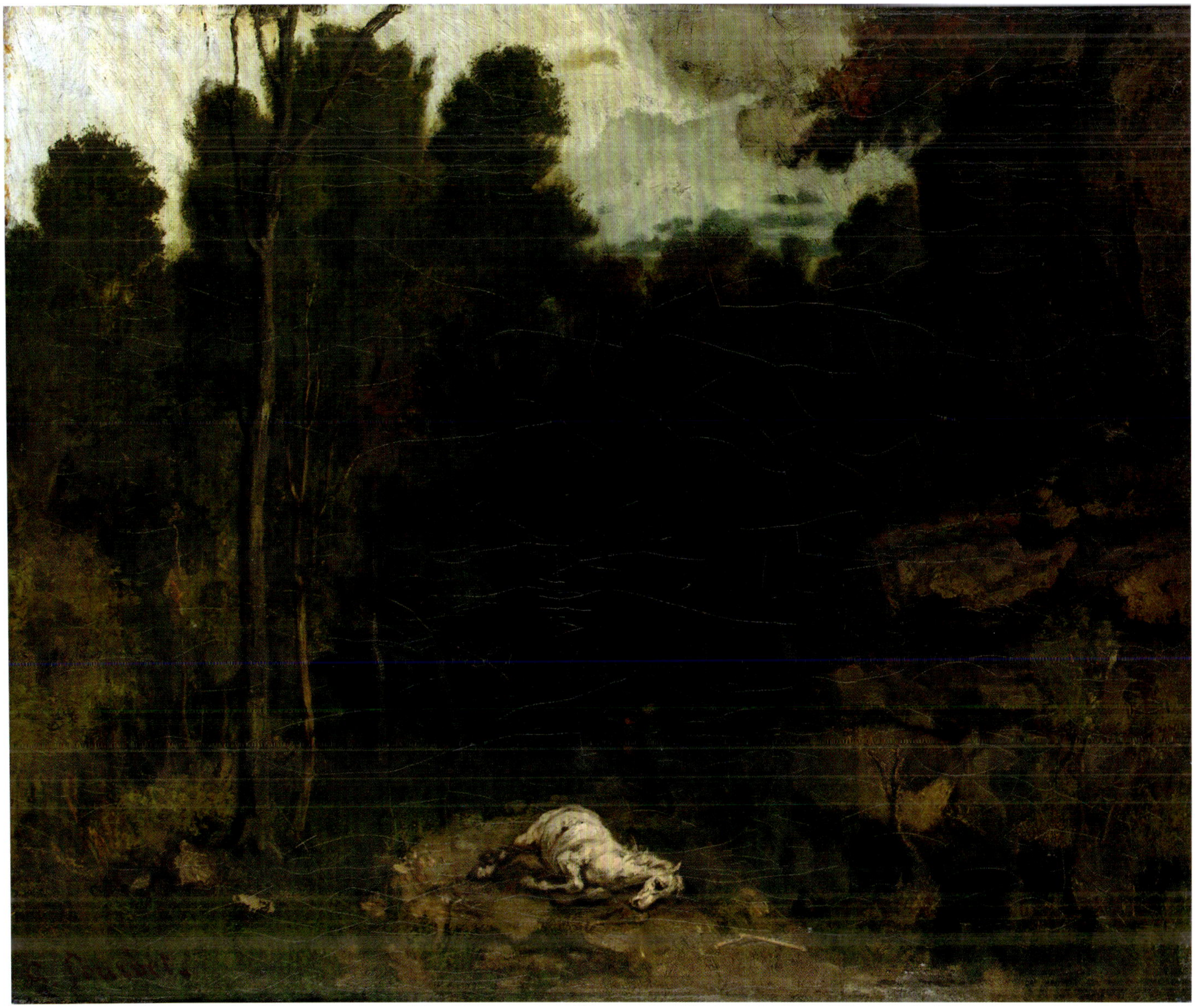

GUSTAVE COURBET. *Landscape with a Dead Horse.* SECOND HALF OF THE 1850S. OIL ON CANVAS. $17^{3}/_{4} \times 22$ IN. (45×56 CM).

The penetrating whiteness of the horse's corpse in the central foreground, contrasted with the sullen green of the forest, gives this provocative subject an elevated, almost religious inflection. The painting neatly illustrates the "inspired cynicism" that Charles Baudelaire detected in Courbet. Here, it may be interpreted in both a positive and a negative sense—as a true artist's ability to use any source of inspiration as well as a readiness to subordinate an eye sensitive to color to flamboyant naturalism.

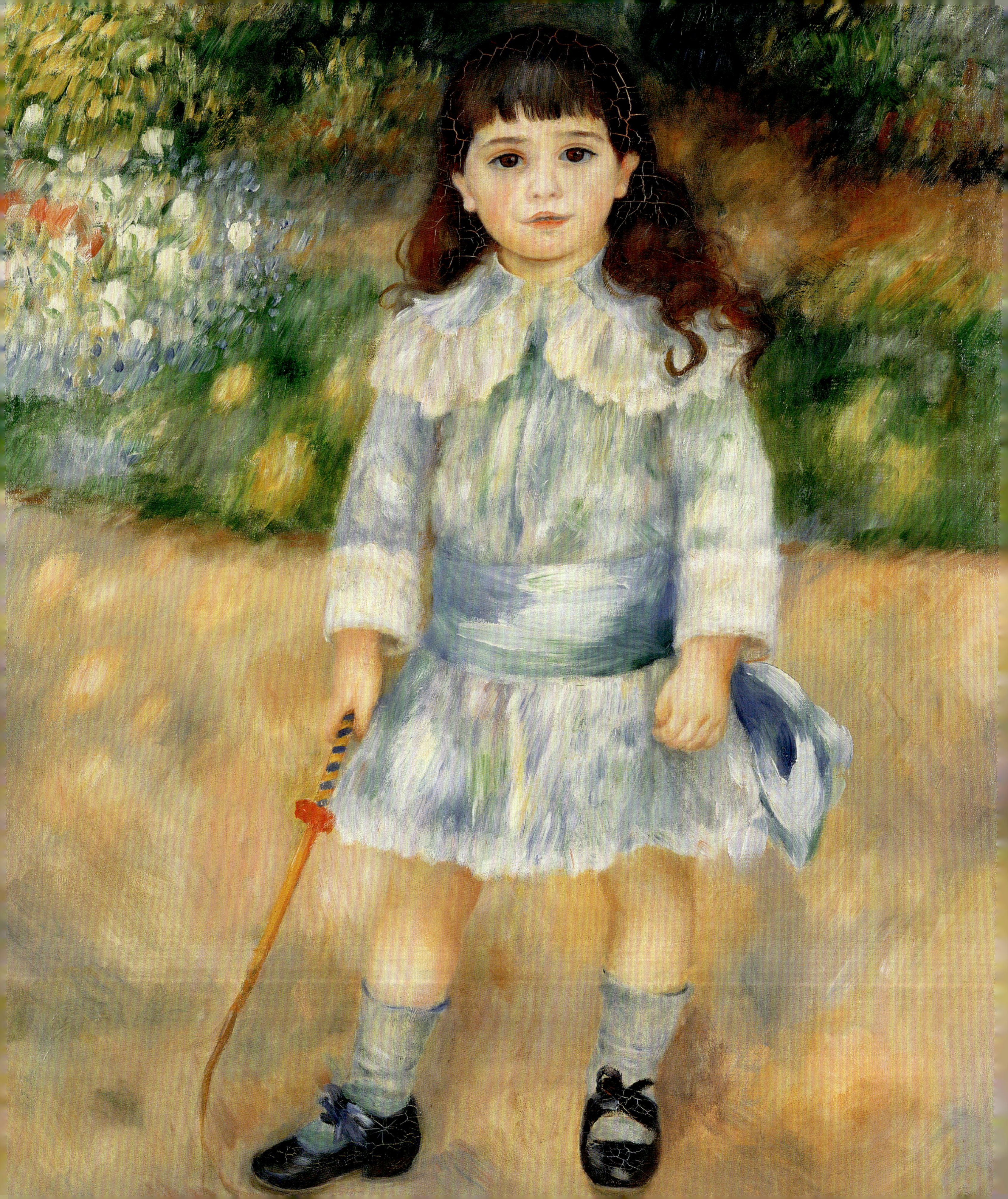

Impressionism and Post-Impressionism

PIERRE-AUGUSTE RENOIR. *Child with a Whip.* 1885. OIL ON CANVAS. 41 3/8 × 29 1/2 IN. (105 × 75 CM).

In the 1870s Impressionism was considered a rebellion against academic conventions, but by 1885 the two existed on equal ground. Sensitive to the decorative characteristics of the Impressionist style based on the rendering of fluid atmosphere and clear natural colors, Renoir used it as a background for a traditional, distinctly outlined portrait of Etienne Goujon, a five-year-old boy who is dressed according to Paris fashion of the 1880s.

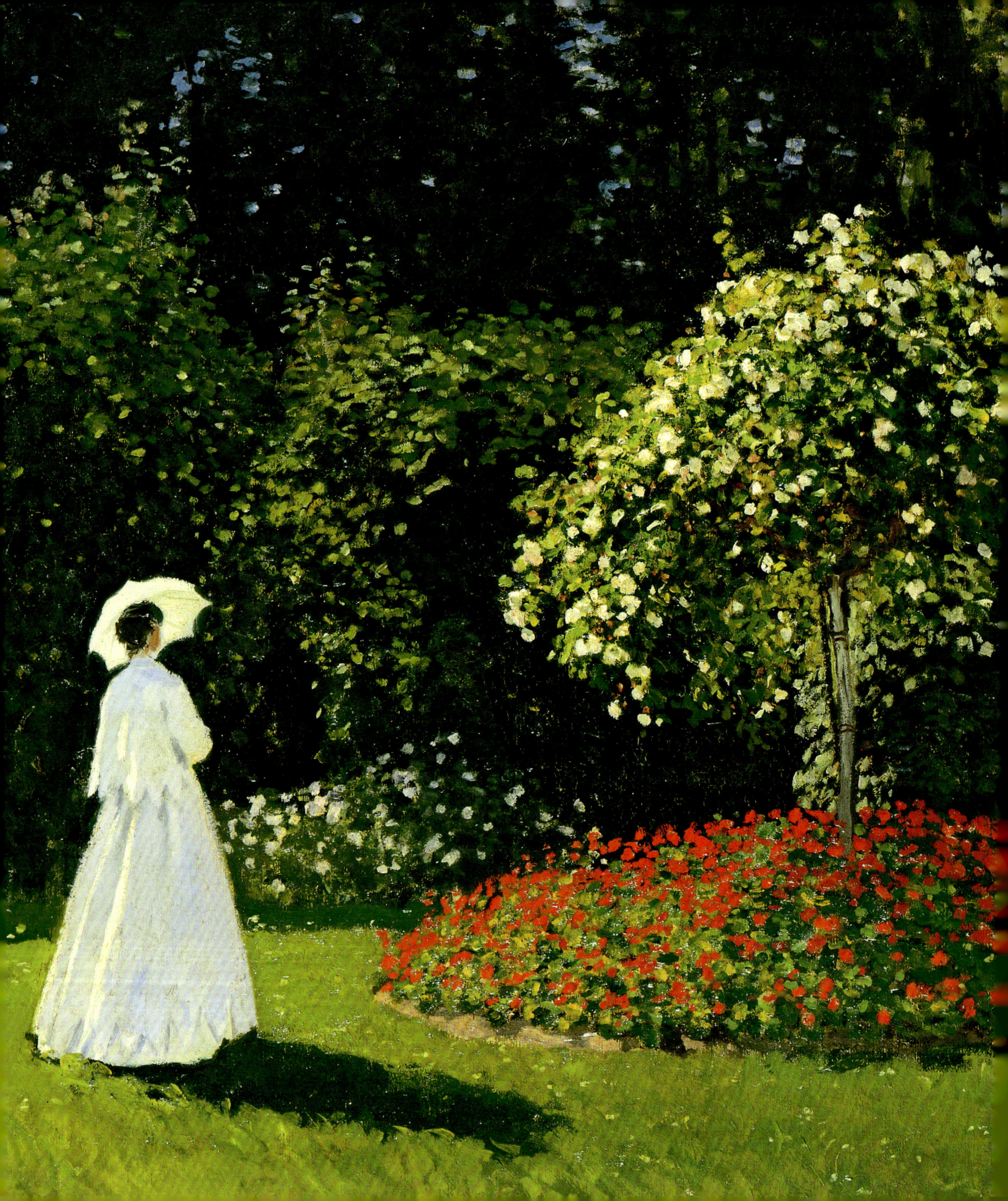

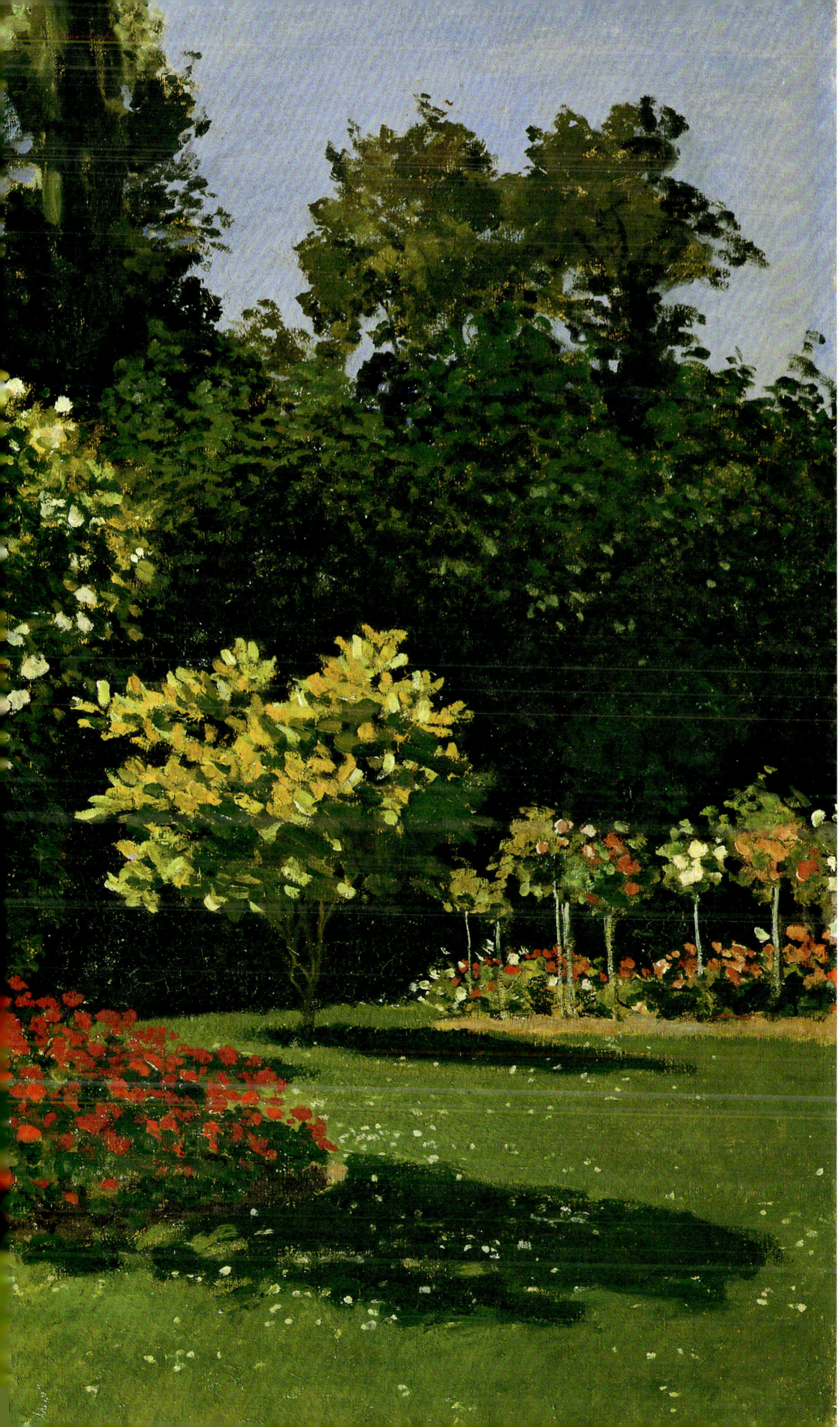

CLAUDE MONET. *Lady in a Garden.* 1867. OIL ON CANVAS. $32\frac{3}{8}$ × 40 IN. (82.3 × 101.5 CM).

The earliest of the Hermitage's eight works by Monet, *Lady in a Garden* is almost devoid of the signs of Impressionism. The white silhouette of the woman, whose dress and parasol precisely accord with the fashion of 1867, gleams in the sun and contrasts with the shady background in a visually effective way characteristic of Salon art.

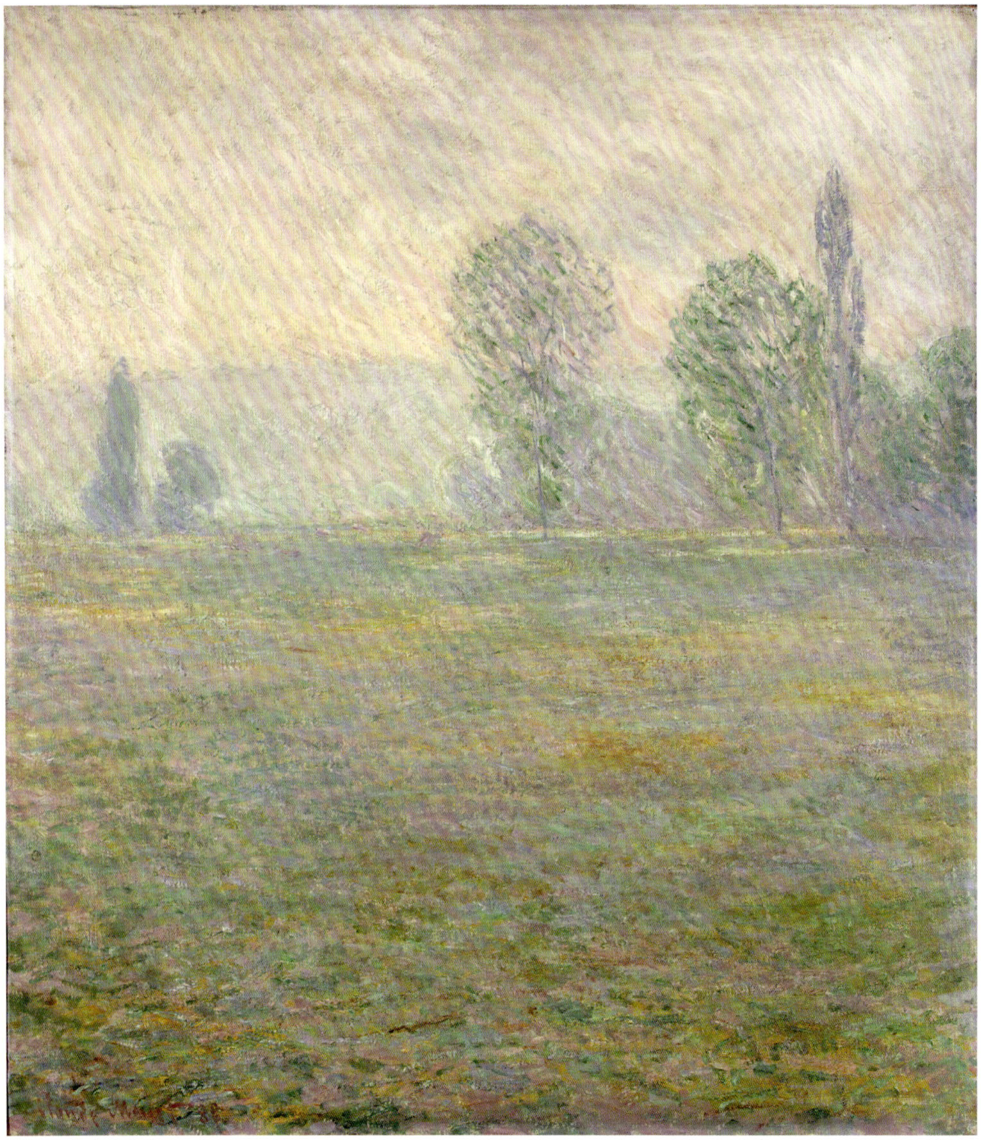

left: CLAUDE MONET. *Meadow at Giverny.* 1888. OIL ON CANVAS. $36\frac{3}{8}$ × 32 IN. (92.5 × 81.5 CM).

It was after moving to Giverny, eighty kilometers northwest of Paris, in 1883 that Monet first took a keen interest in rural landscape. While there he became fascinated with the effect of fog obscuring the boundaries of objects and softening colors. It was also in Giverny that he would later paint his celebrated series of water lilies.

opposite, top: CLAUDE MONET. *Poppy Field.* 1890–91. OIL ON CANVAS. 24 × $36\frac{1}{4}$ IN. (61 × 92 CM).

Painted in Giverny, this canvas belongs to the "poppy fields" series, which the artist created en plein air and that includes views depicted in different light and weather conditions. Such series were first introduced by Eugène Boudin, with whom Monet worked in the late 1850s. The simple composition—the landscape is represented by three contrasting stripes as if captured in their movement—is reminiscent of the works of another one of Monet's predecessors and teachers, Charles-François Daubigny.

opposite, bottom: CLAUDE MONET. *Waterloo Bridge: Effect of Fog.* 1903. OIL ON CANVAS. $25\frac{3}{4}$ × $39\frac{3}{4}$ IN. (65.3 × 101 CM).

The series of London landscapes, begun during Monet's visit to the British capital in 1899–1901 and later finished in Giverny, includes more than one hundred canvases, most of them misty views of the Thames with the Houses of Parliament, Charing Cross Bridge, or Waterloo Bridge. The diversity in the choice of colors was prompted by the artist's own observations made from the balcony of his room on the fifth floor of the Savoy.

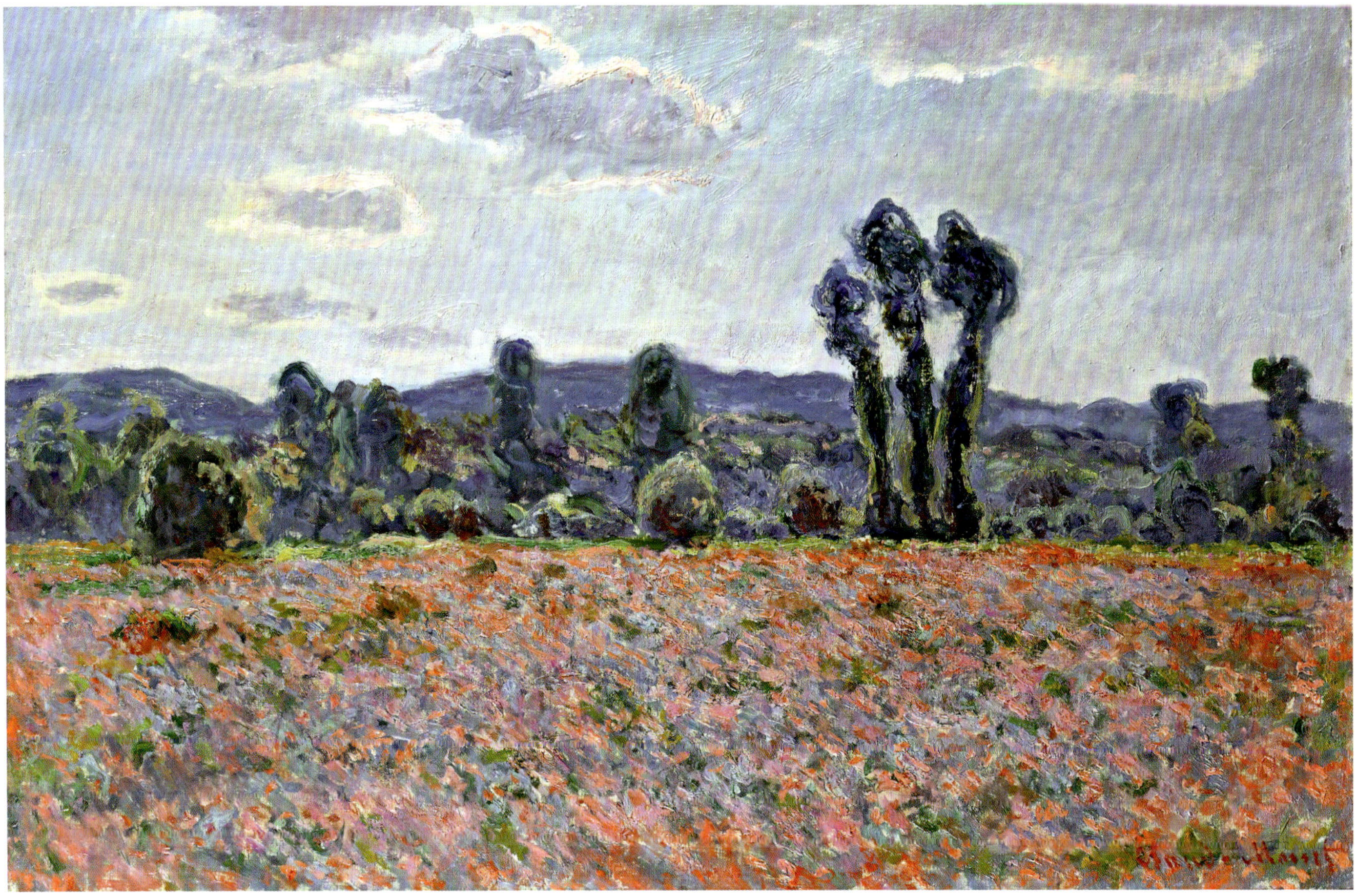

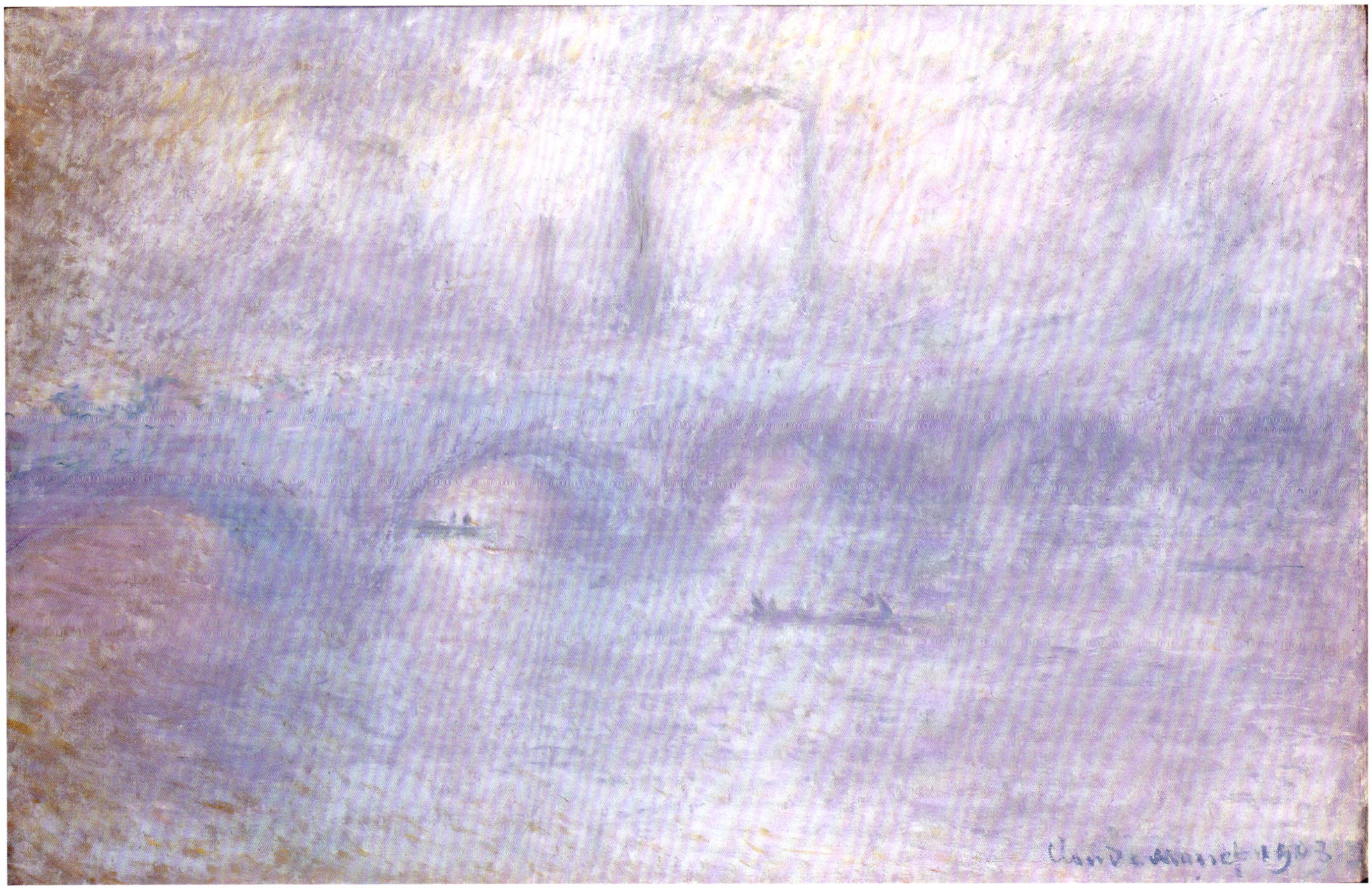

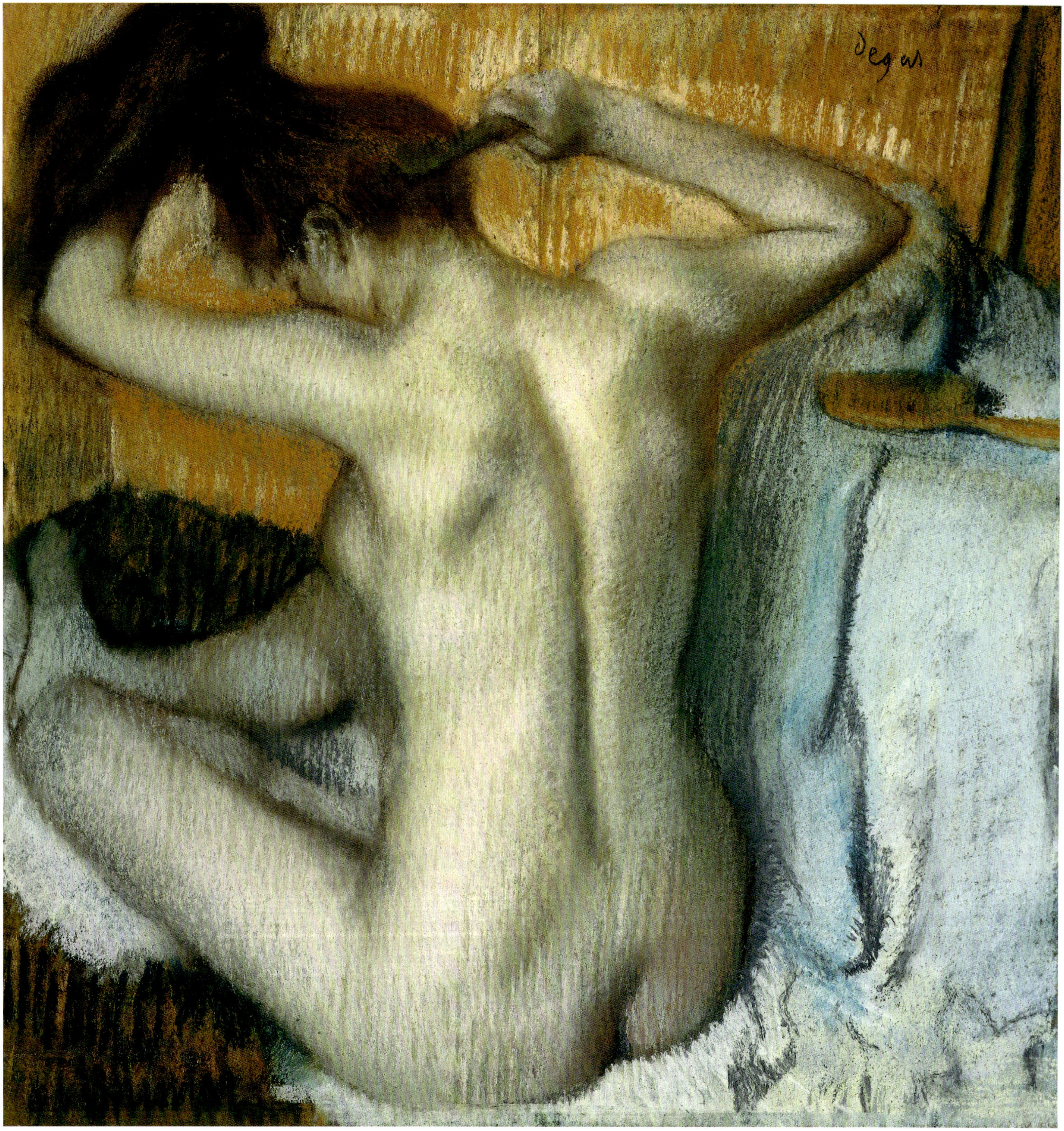
Degas

opposite: EDGAR DEGAS. *Woman Combing Her Hair.* CA. 1885. PASTEL ON GRAY-BROWN PAPER PASTED ONTO CARD. 20½ × 20½ IN. (52 × 52 CM).

Dynamic compositional shifts, bold cropping, tightly framed boundaries—these features make Degas's work akin to photography, a medium that would become his passion in the 1890s. In this and similar works, he precisely fixes the moment of movement while concentrating on the essential.

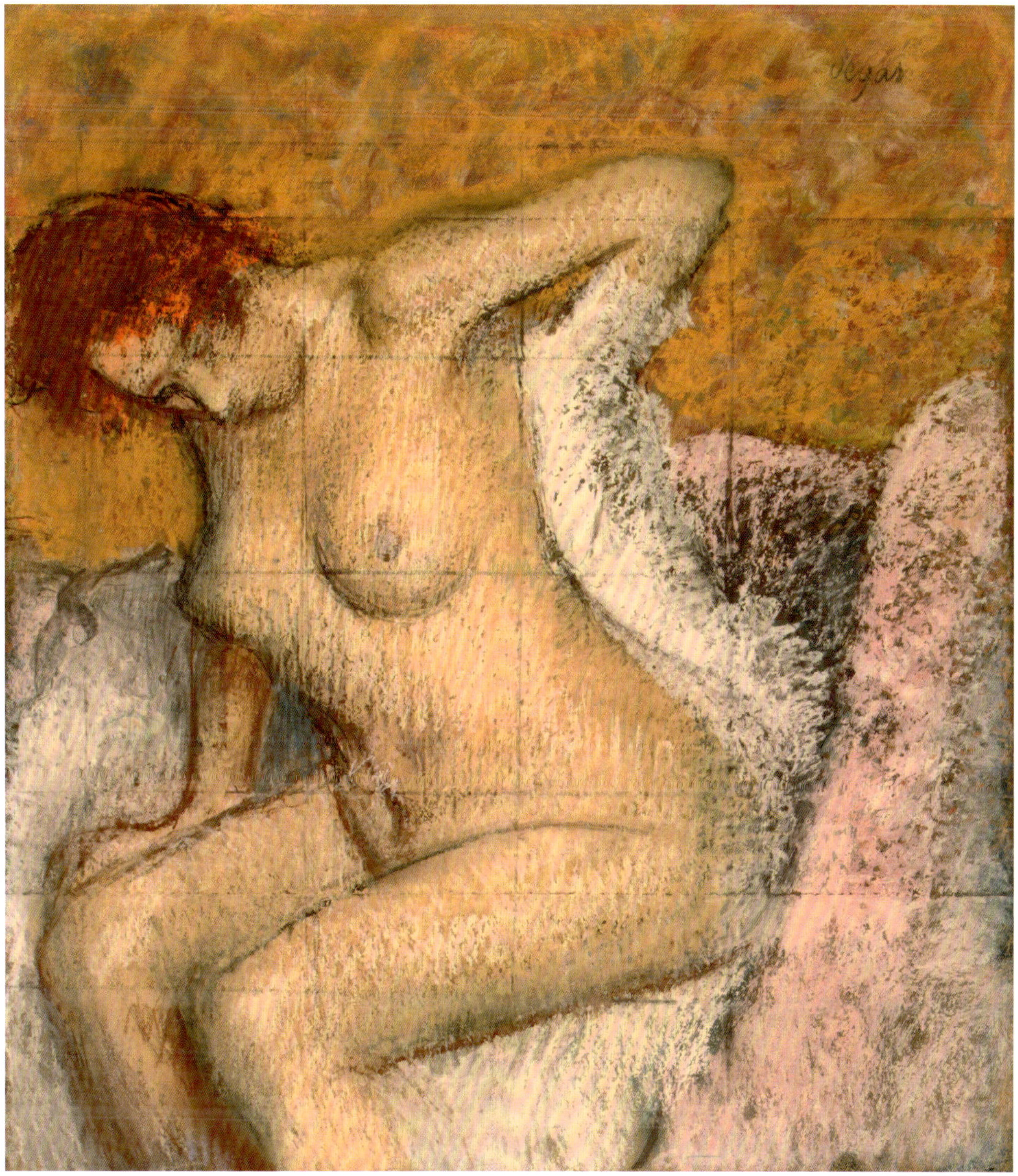

above: EDGAR DEGAS. *After the Bath.* CA. 1895. PASTEL, GOUACHE, TEMPERA, AND CHARCOAL ON BROWN PAPER PASTED ON CARDBOARD. 32⅕ × 28⅕ IN. (81.9 × 71.6 CM).

Pastel studies of female nudes were among Degas's main themes beginning in the 1880s. As time passed, such works, which technically are categorized as graphic art, acquired more complex pictorial features: the painter layered the pastel to attain more solid texture and deeper colors; he used not only pencils but also his brush and fingers to turn the surface of the paper into a vibrating mass; and he incorporated other mediums—in this case tempera and gouache.

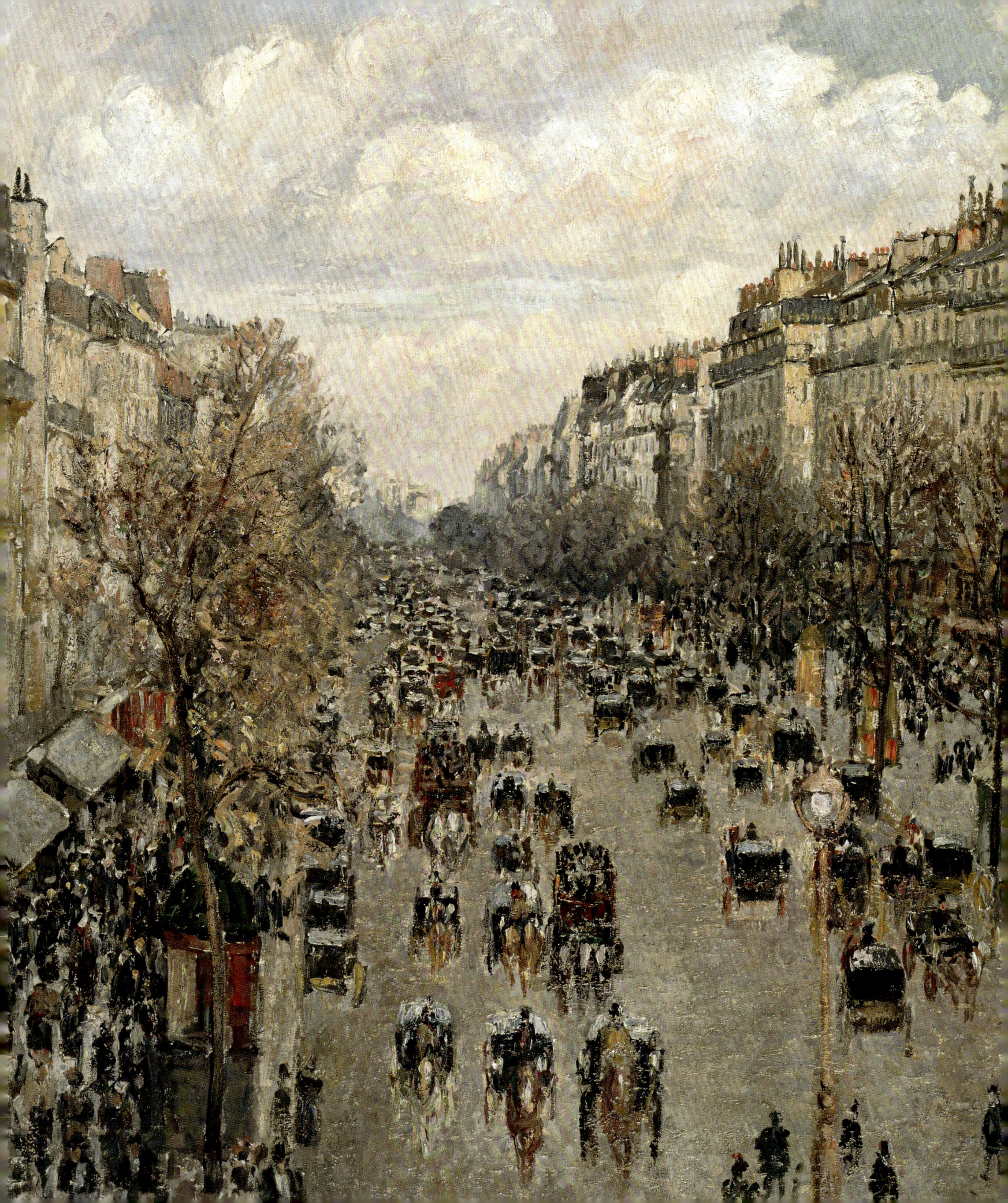

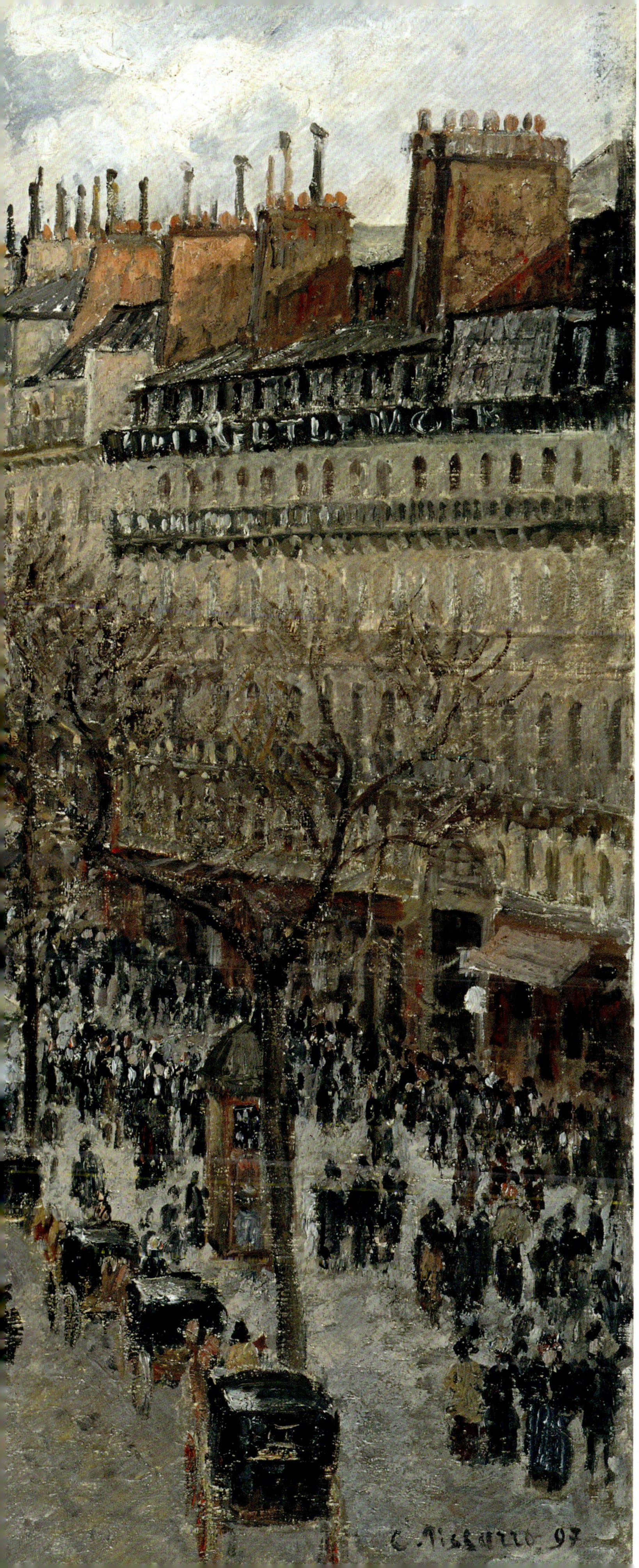

CAMILLE PISSARRO. *The Boulevard Montmartre in Paris (The Boulevard Montmartre in the Afternoon, Sunny Weather)*. 1897. OIL ON CANVAS. $29^{1}/_{8} \times 36^{1}/_{2}$ IN. (74×92.8 CM).

This painting's subtitle is a strong hint that Pissarro painted an entire series of Montmartre in different states from one viewpoint, chasing after (as was the Impressionists' habit) subtle atmospheric changes. His restrained color is woven from tiny brushstrokes and subtly conveys the charm of the everyday bustle on Parisian boulevards.

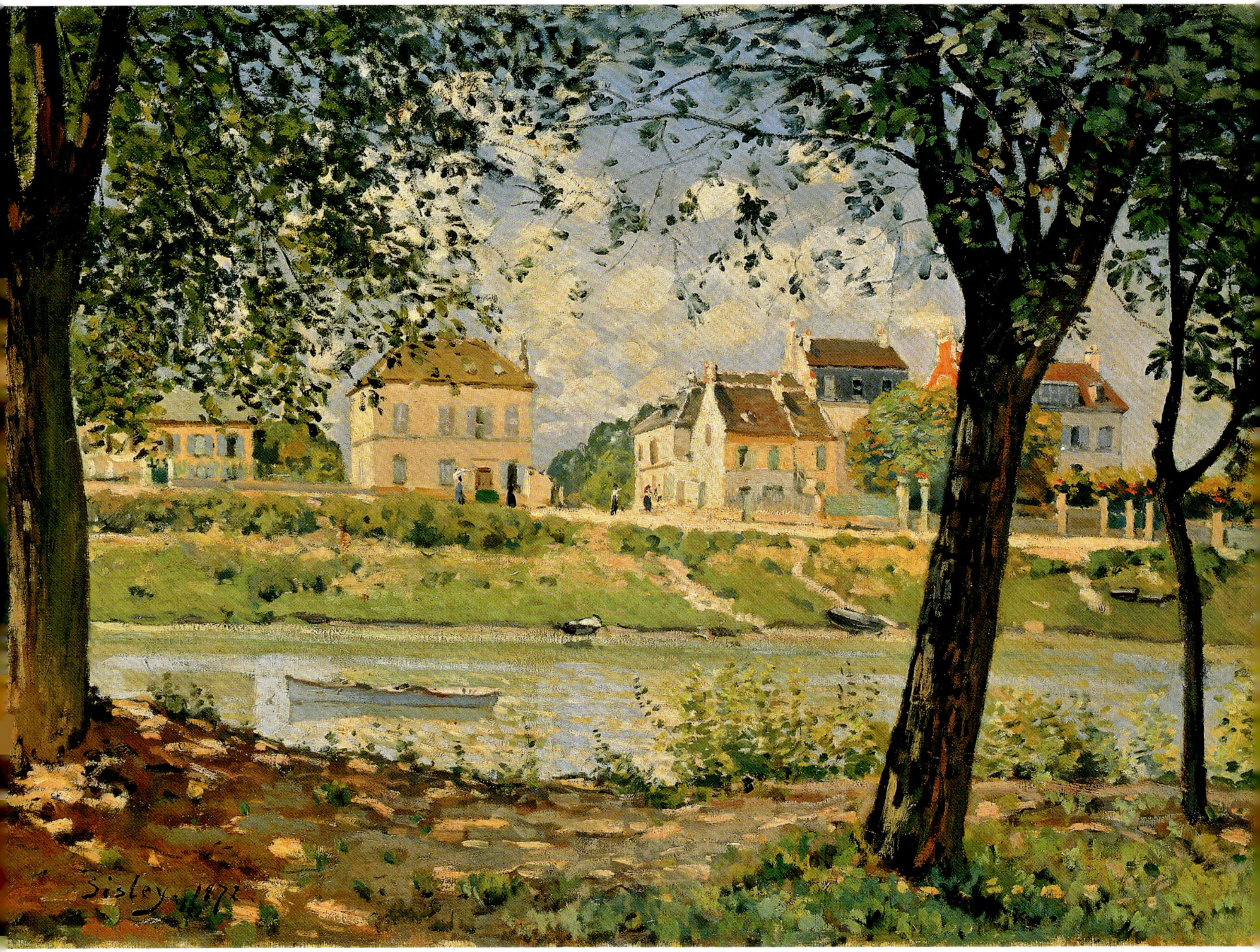

ALFRED SISLEY. *The Town of Villeneuve-la-Garenne on the Seine.* 1872. OIL ON CANVAS. 23 1/4 × 31 1/5 IN. (59 × 80 CM).

In this painting, created two years before the first Impressionist exhibition, light already reigns supreme. It floods the background in defiance of the traditions of aerial perspective, while the bank closer to the viewer is shrouded in shadow. Speaking of similar works by Sisley, Pierre-Auguste Renoir said, "They evoke . . . a desire to stroll into the depths."

EUGÈNE BOUDIN. *Beach at Trouville.* 1893. 22 × 35 7/8 IN. (56 × 91 CM).

In the 1890s Boudin, who had once been a mentor to Claude Monet, came in turn under Monet's influence and often worked en plein air on the Normandy coast. But, true to tradition, he subordinated color to the molding of form, thus giving his barely delineated groups on the seashore the persuasiveness of scenes from life.

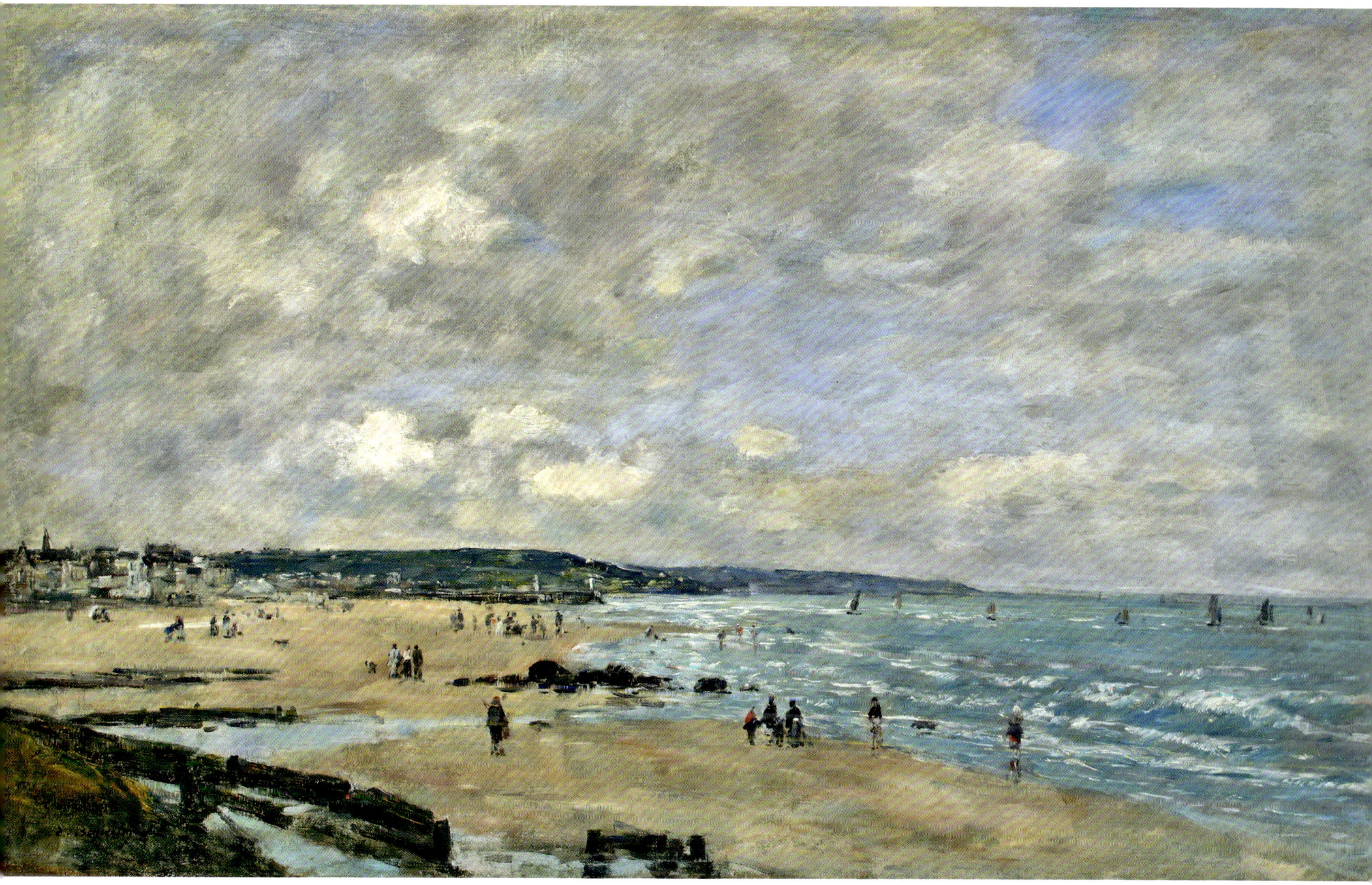

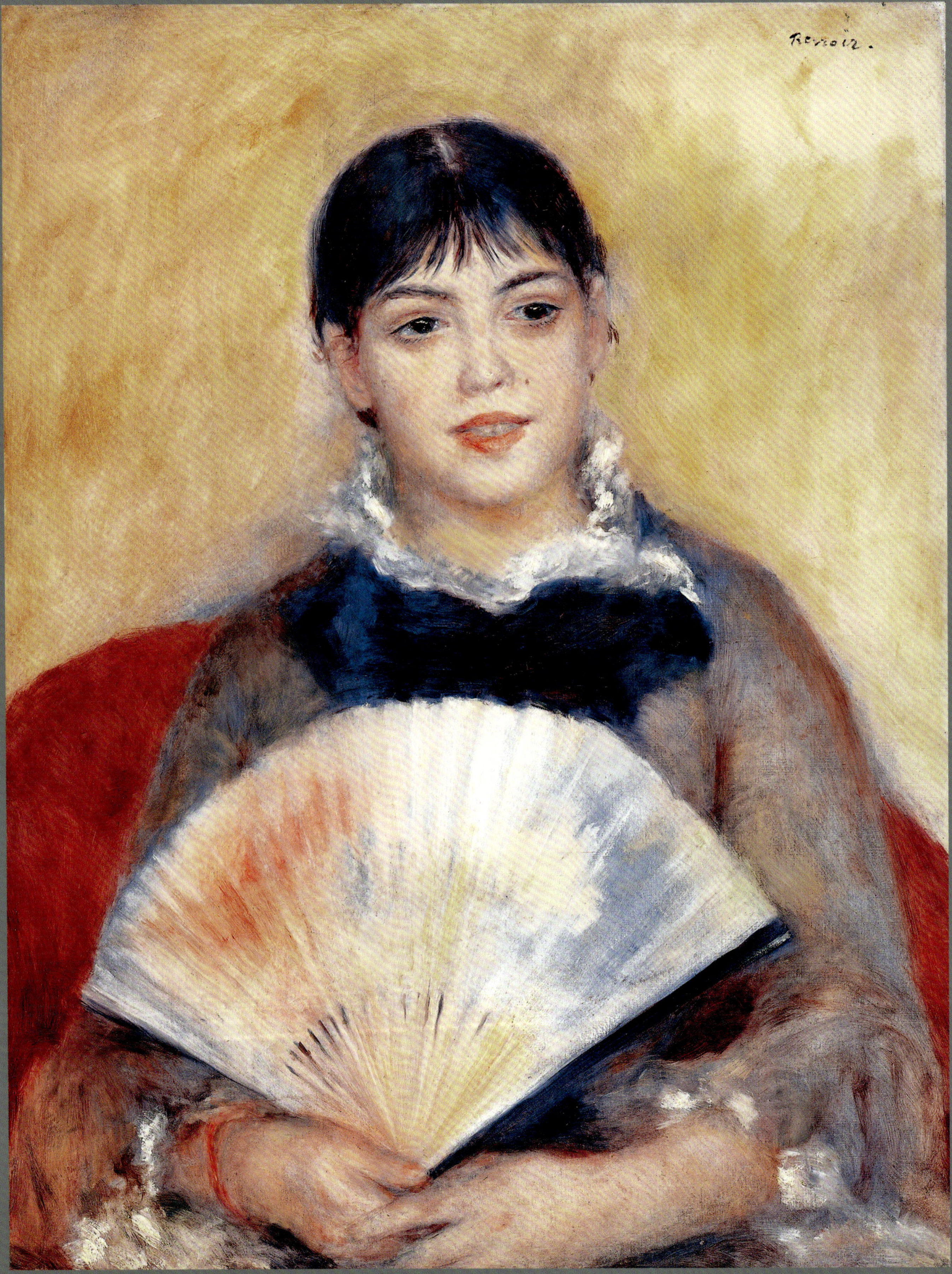
Renoir.

opposite: PIERRE-AUGUSTE RENOIR. *Girl with a Fan.* 1880. OIL ON CANVAS. 25½ × 19⅝ IN. (65 × 50 CM).

Renoir was exceptionally sensitive to details: earrings, a flower in the hair, and a neck scarf play no less a role in his heroines' outfits and his paintings' color schemes than does a dress or coiffure. This portrait is dominated by the fan, whose whiteness stresses the sheen of the model's dark hair and eyes while picking up, with a softening effect, the main colors of yellow, red, and blue. This painting was a great success at the seventh Impressionist exhibition, in 1882.

right: PIERRE-AUGUSTE RENOIR. *Portrait of the Actress Jeanne Samary.* 1878. OIL ON CANVAS. 68½ × 40 IN. (174 × 101.5 CM).

Renoir became acquainted with the twenty-year-old actress Jeanne Samary, who had already made her mark on the Parisian stage, at the home of his patron, Madame Charpentier. This large portrait of Jeanne in a ball gown—one of many Renoir painted—was intended for the 1879 Salon and reflected his pursuit of official recognition.

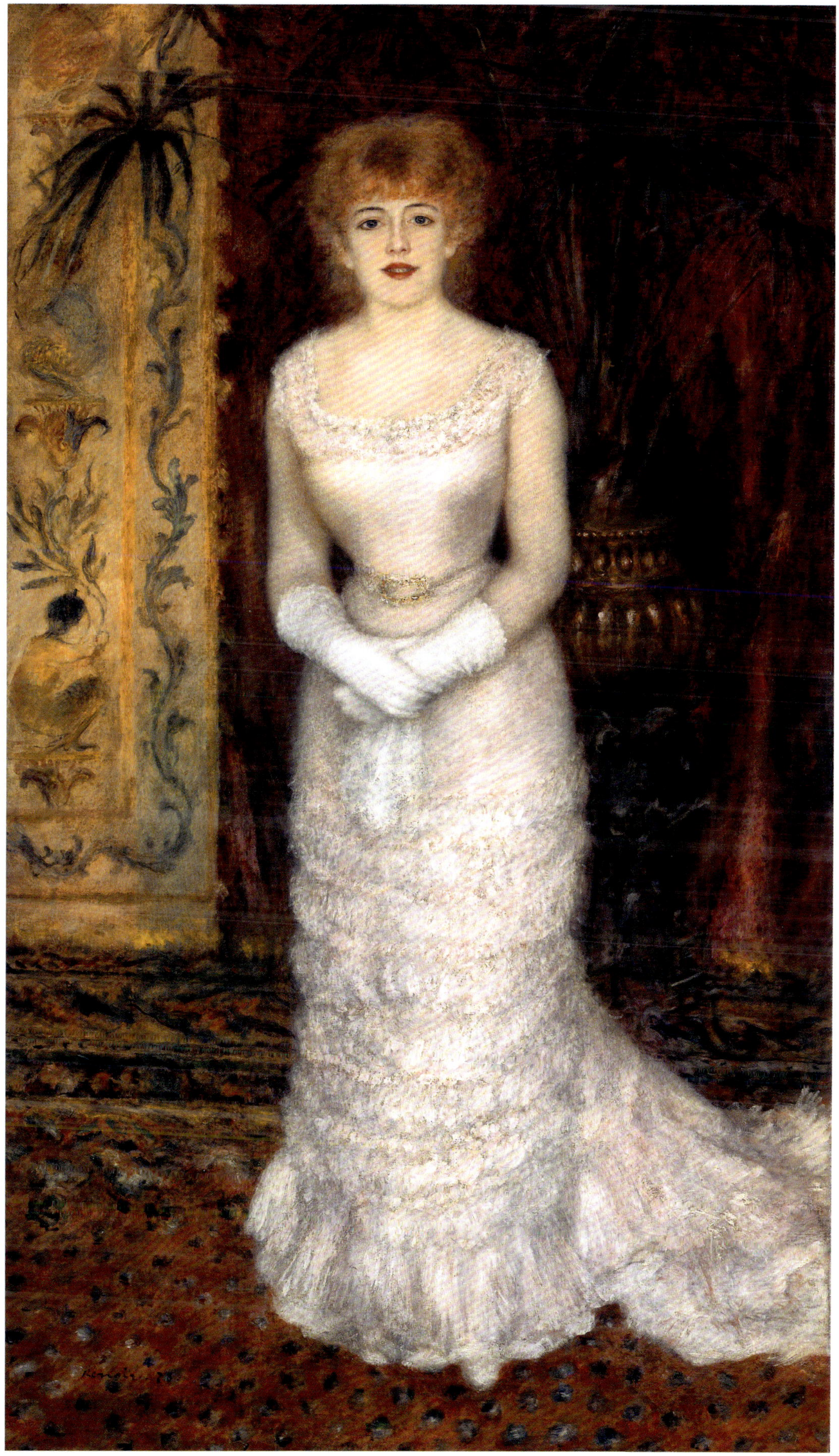

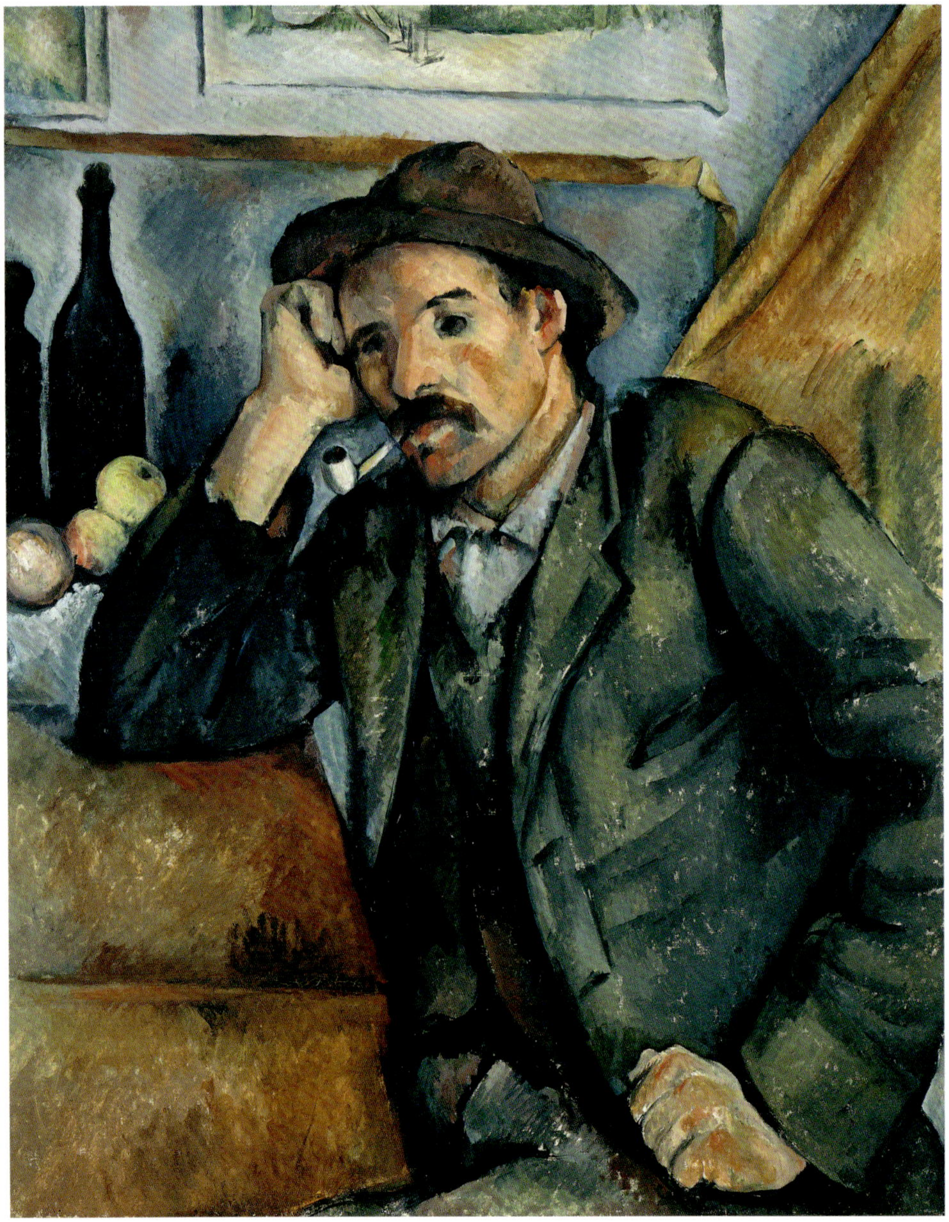

left: PAUL CÉZANNE. *The Smoker.* CA. 1890–92. OIL ON CANVAS. $36^{3}/_{8}$ × 29 IN. (92.5 × 73.5 CM).

While creating a balanced composition founded on a Renaissance painting attributed to Raphael, Cézanne painted the human being as an object, refusing to soften his manner or to be diverted by psychological details. (The model is believed to have been the peasant or gardener Alexander Polin.) For him, nature, objects, and people compose a single material world, reproducible through paint. This unity is underlined by one of his own still lifes, which serves as the portrait's background.

opposite: PAUL CÉZANNE. *Lady in Blue.* CA. 1900. OIL ON CANVAS. $35^{3}/_{8}$ × 29 IN. (90 × 73.5 CM).

We do not know exactly who posed as a model for this portrait. Maybe it was Madame Brémond, the artist's faithful housekeeper. Among Cezanne's later works, this painting is one of the most lyrical and touching. Besides, it gives us some idea of the individual character of the sitter. As the art historian Charles Sterling wrote, she is "unmistakably the provincial middle-class lady wearing her Sunday best for Mass, caparisoned in her haughty decency, yet with lips embittered."

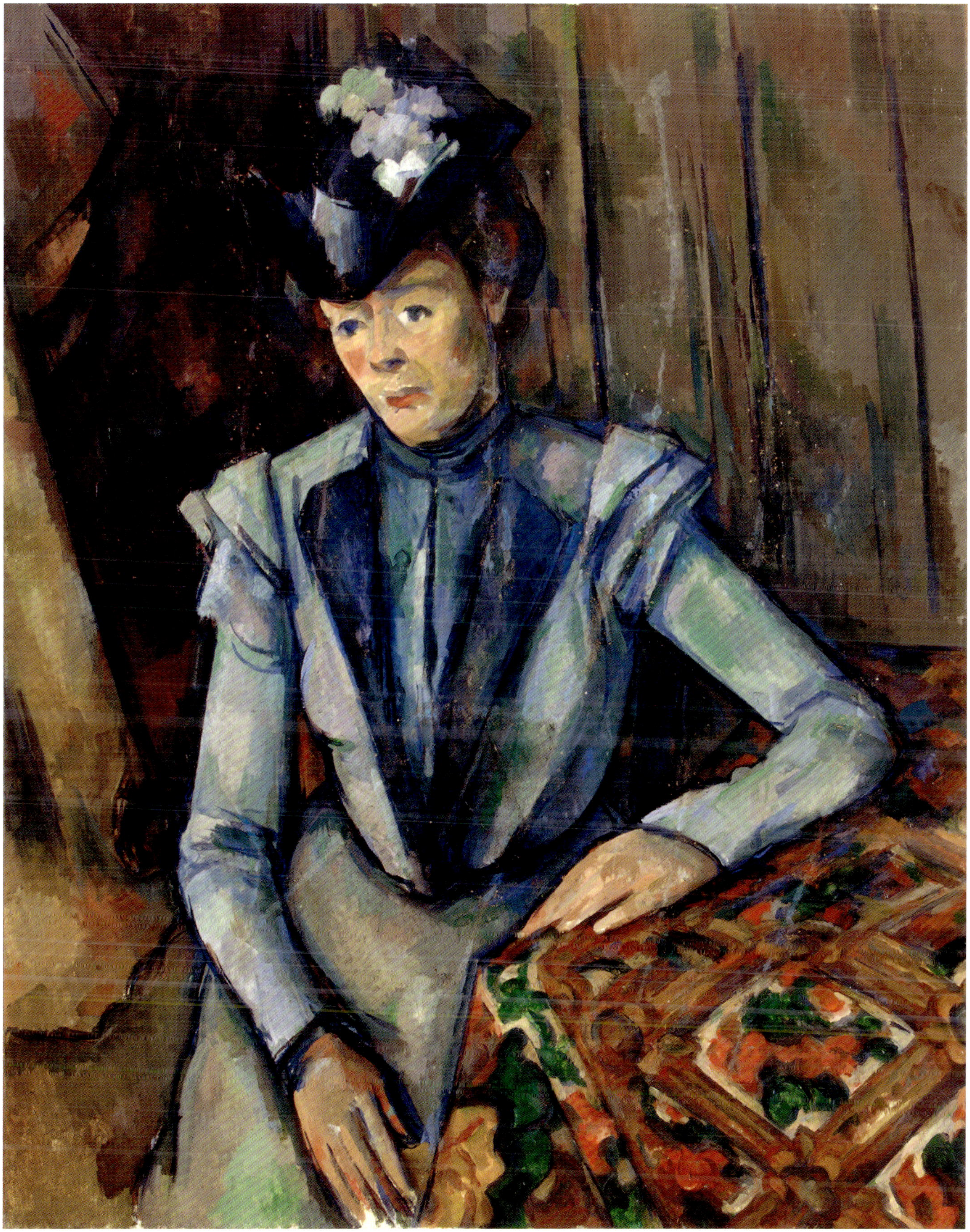

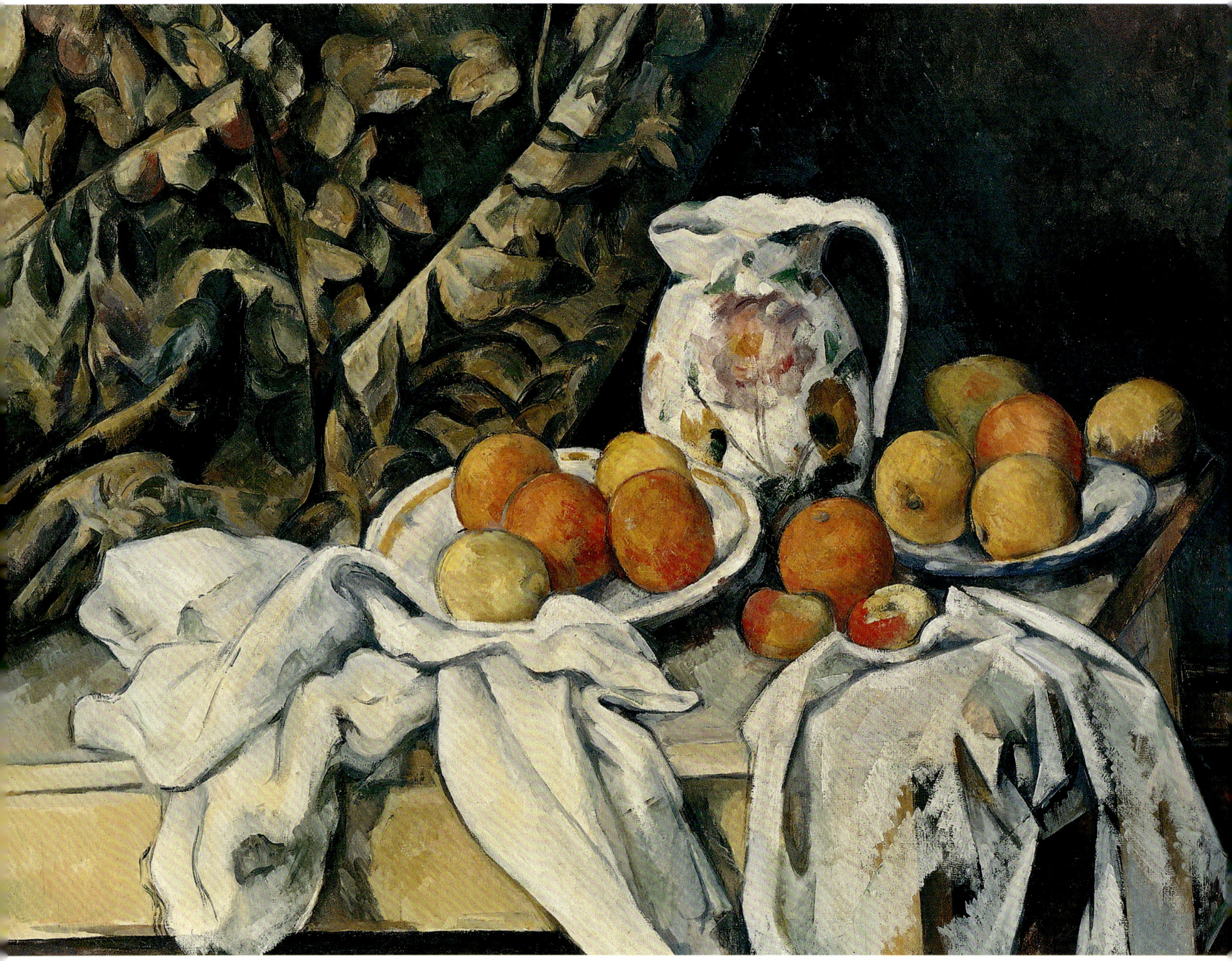

PAUL CÉZANNE. *Still Life with Drapery.* CA. 1894–95. OIL ON CANVAS. $20\frac{7}{8} \times 28\frac{3}{8}$ IN. (53 × 72 CM).

After visiting Cézanne's studio in the early 1900s, the writer Léo Larguier noted: "The apple was not very tasty; at the time two or three of that sort cost one sou. But those in the study, shiny and unwizened, will probably cost 1,500 francs later." He was not wrong. But in the last fifteen or so years of his life, Cézanne was concerned only with painting. Its power grew, together with his predilection for a transient motif.

PAUL CÉZANNE. *Mont Sainte-Victoire.* BETWEEN 1896 AND 1898. OIL ON CANVAS. 30 5/8 × 39 IN. (78 × 99 CM).

Mont Sainte-Victoire became a fetish for Cézanne, a sort of alter ego and, in fact, he often spoke of the mountain as a person. His alter ego in the history of painting was Poussin, whose *Arcadian Shepherds* featuring the same peak hung (in reproduction) at the head of his deathbed. It may indeed have been Poussin who prompted Cézanne to bring the mountain close to the foreground, concentrating the action and landscape elements in a single "mountain-forming" process.

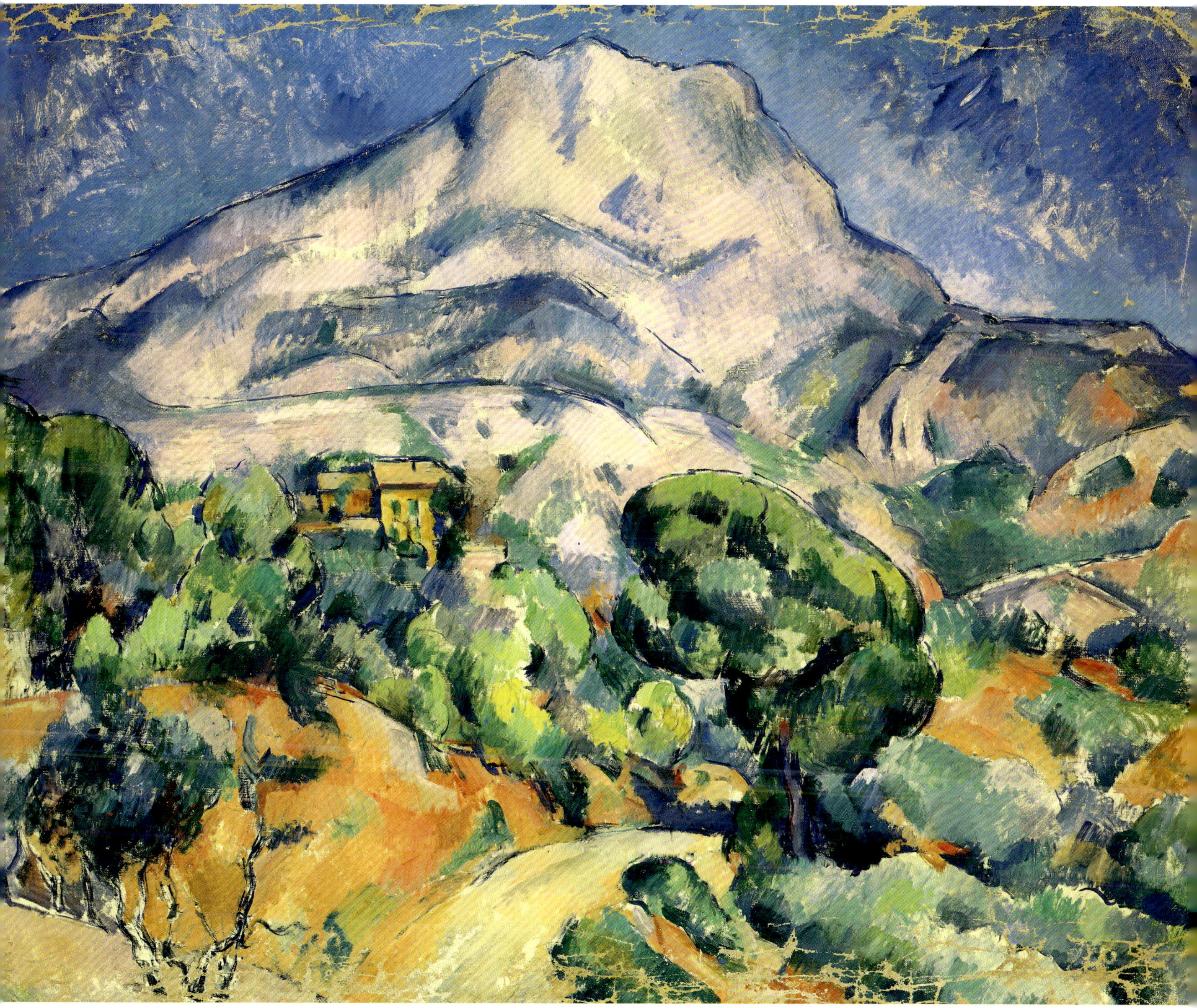

VINCENT VAN GOGH. *Cottages.* 1890. OIL ON CANVAS. $23^{3}/_{8} \times 28^{1}/_{2}$ IN. (59.5 × 72.5 CM).

In letters to family and friends, van Gogh most often described the subjects of his paintings in an idyllic manner, and the bright palette in this scene of peasant dwellings does indeed evoke a joyful springtime mood. But the artist's hand caused the locality to tumble in nervous waves, recording on canvas the abrupt swings of his psyche.

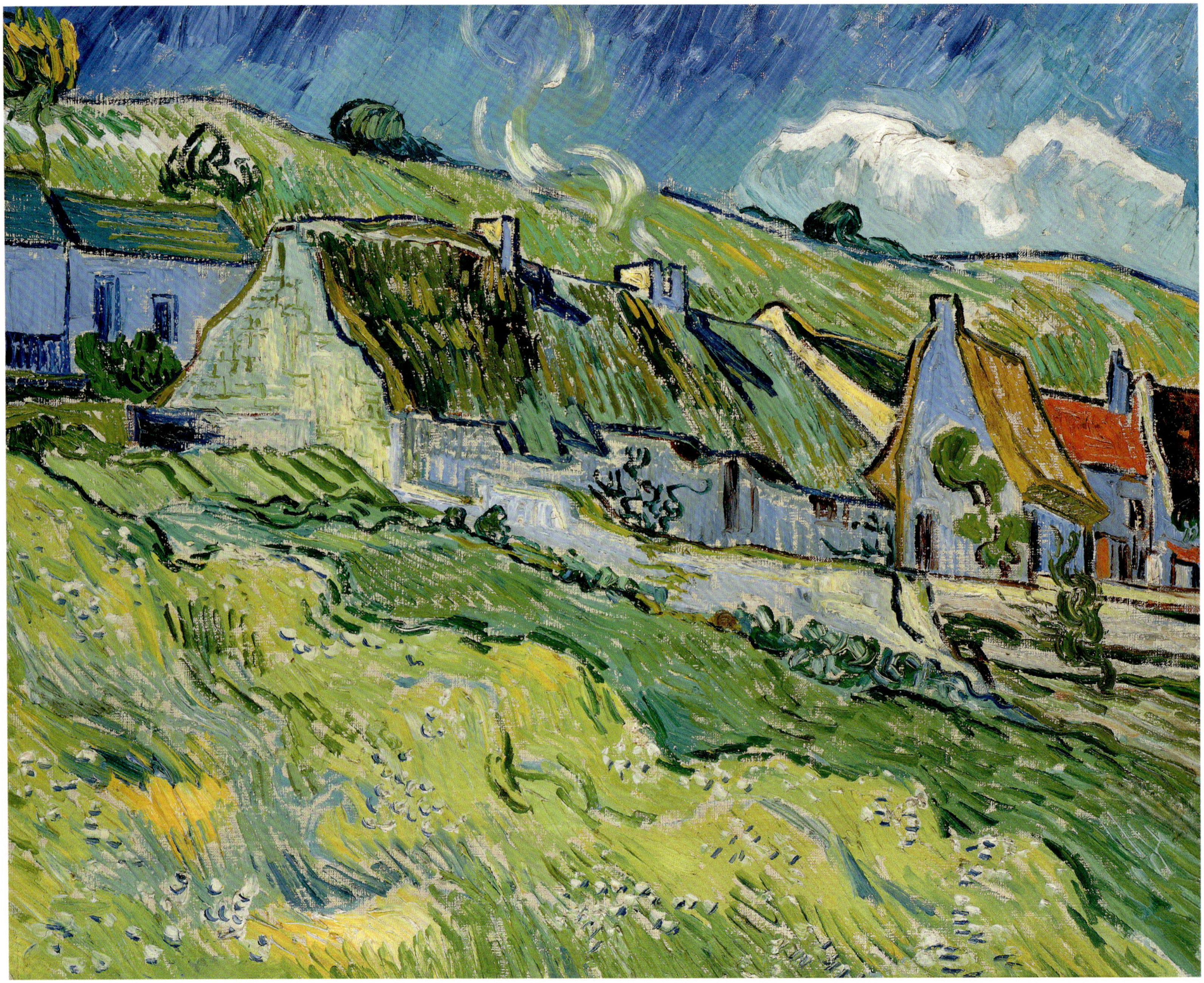

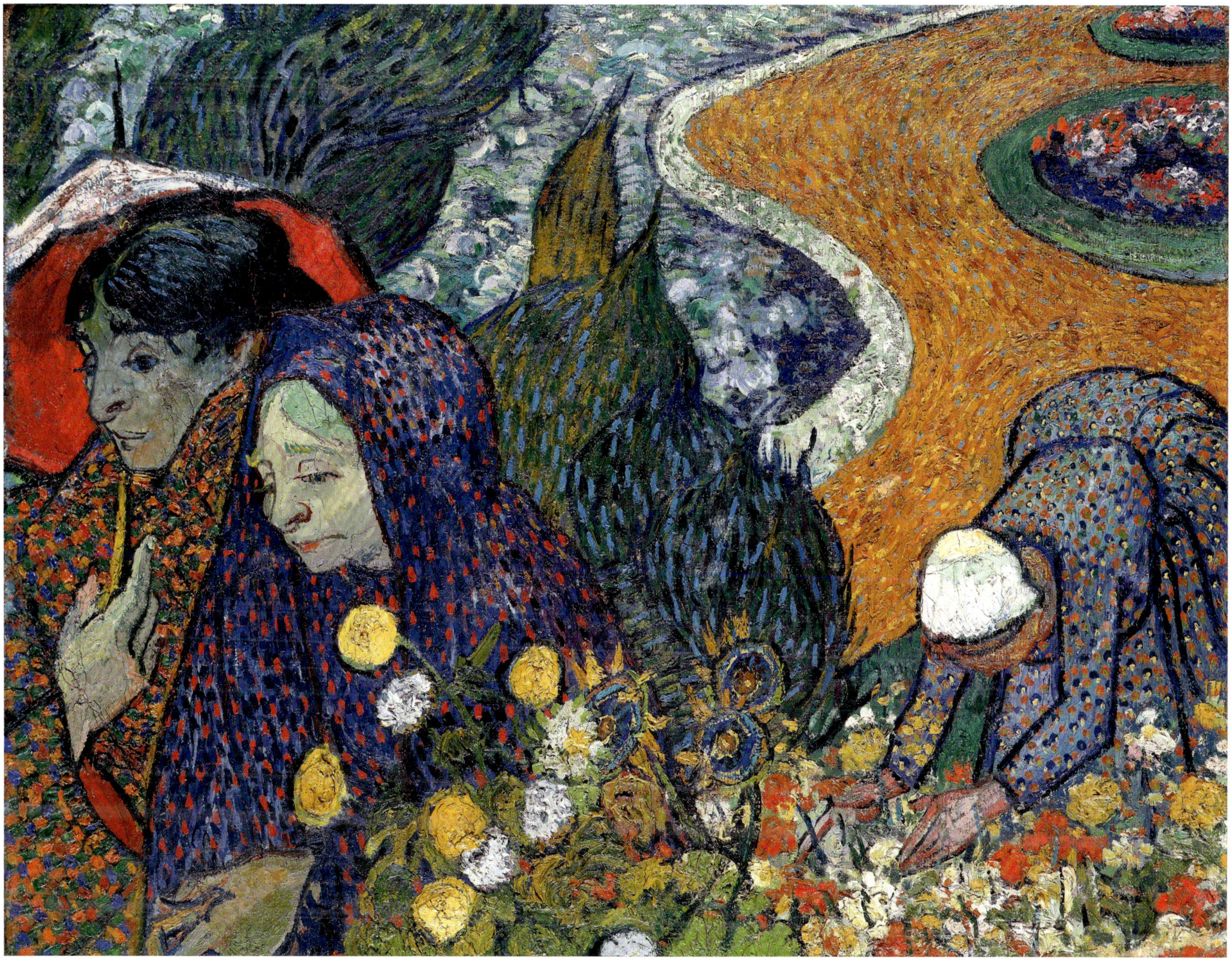

VINCENT VAN GOGH. *Memories of the Garden at Etten (Ladies of Arles)*. 1888. OIL ON CANVAS. 28 3/4 × 36 1/4 IN. (73 × 92 CM).

Etten is the Dutch town where an eighteen-year-old van Gogh lived with his parents in 1881. The women in the left-hand corner resemble his mother and sister. The landscape is utterly fantastic, painted from imagination at the advice of Paul Gauguin, with whom van Gogh was keeping company. But the painting displays far less Gauguin-esque symbolism than it does van Gogh's explosive temperament: the trees, like tongues of fire, are a reminder of the vividness of youthful experiences

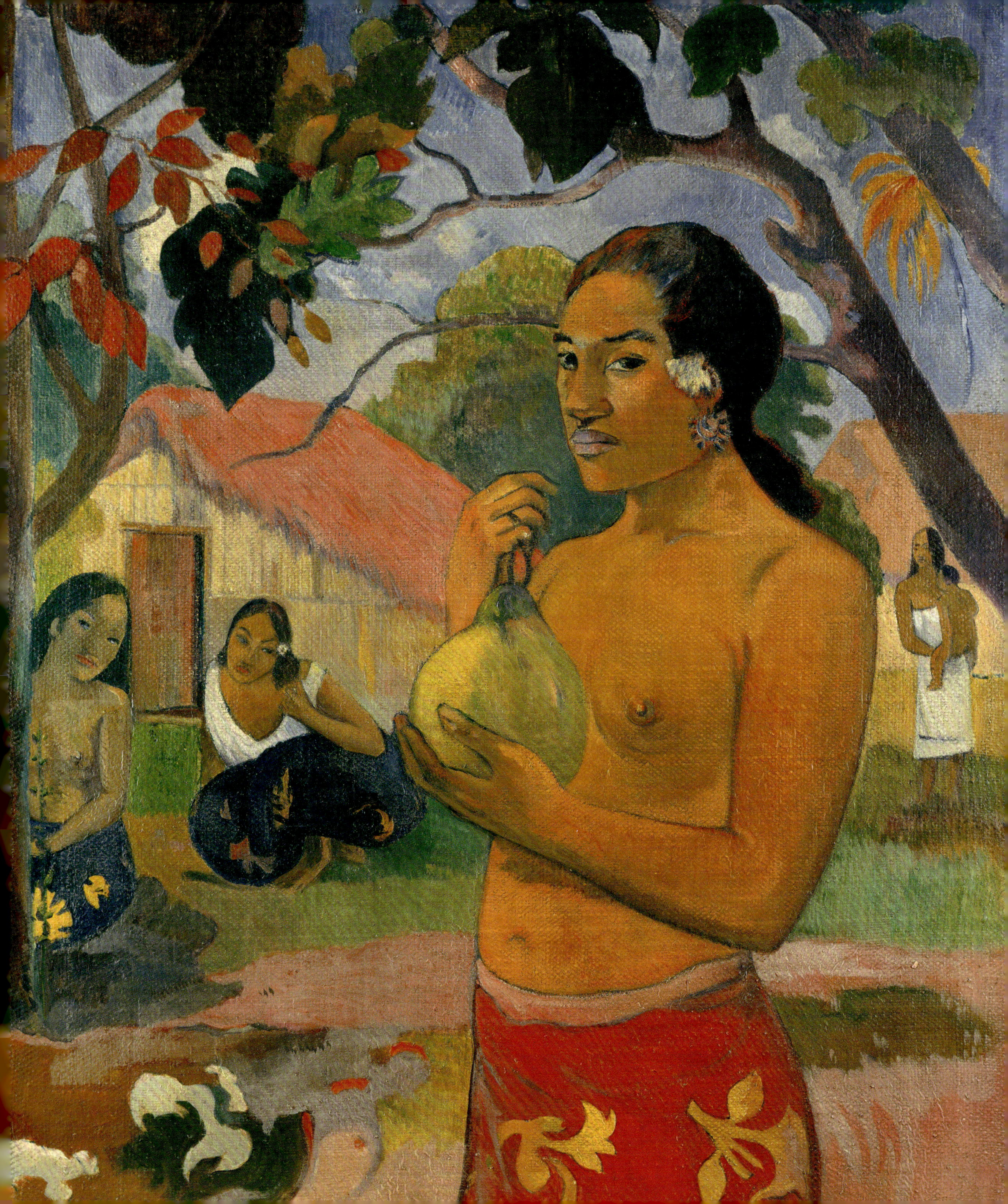

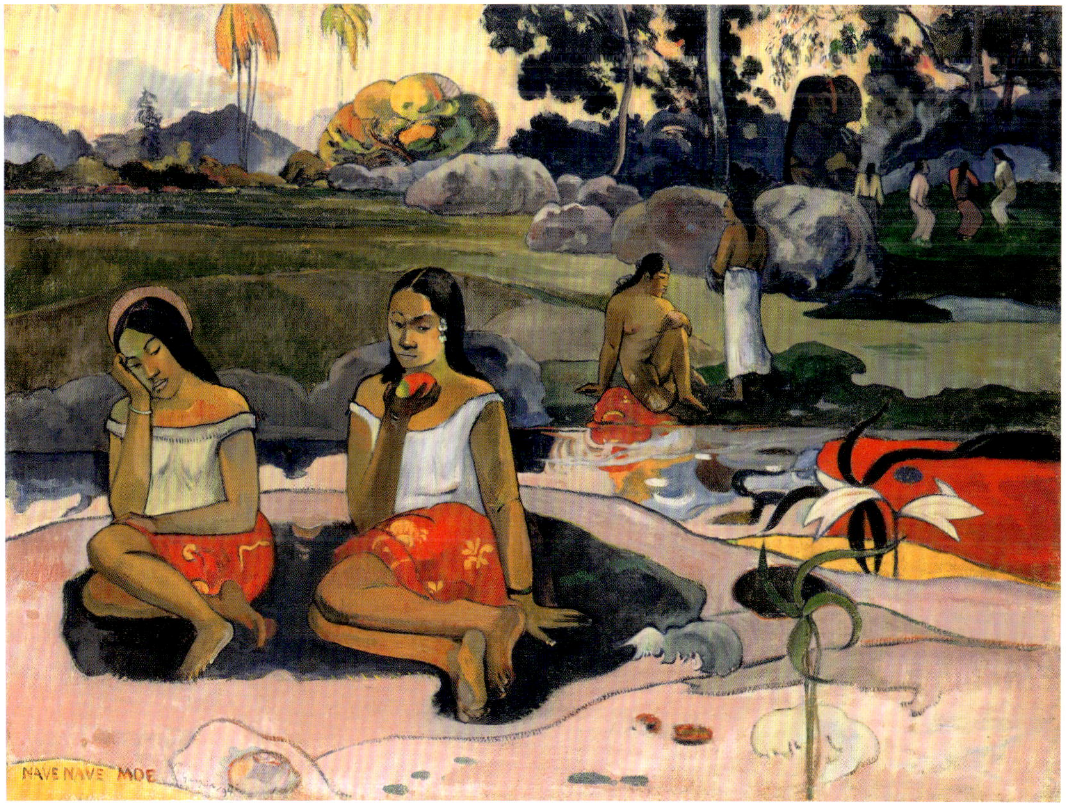

left: PAUL GAUGUIN. *Nave nave moe. Sweet Daydreams (Sacred Spring).* 1894. OIL ON CANVAS. 29 1/8 × 39 3/8 IN. (74 × 100 CM).

Gauguin said more than once that he was looking for an Eden where time did not exist. In this painting everything speaks of eternity, his own "sweet daydream": the majestic static poses of the heroines, the ancient idols, Eve and the apple, the Virgin Mary, and the simple Tahitian women all come together in a single space. Although produced after Gauguin's return to Paris, the painting differs in no way from his Tahitian cycle.

opposite: PAUL GAUGUIN. *Eü haere ia oe. Woman Holding a Fruit.* 1893. OIL ON CANVAS. 36 3/8 × 29 IN. (92.5 × 73.5 CM).

This painting's title, given by collector Ivan Morozov, stresses its connection with the primordial Eve, a theme that Gauguin touched upon repeatedly. The original Tahitian title translates as "Where are you going?" and adds another shade of meaning to the biblical subtext: the woman's look seems to be an answer to the words that echo Peter's question when Christ told the disciples about his departure to heaven (John 13:33–36).

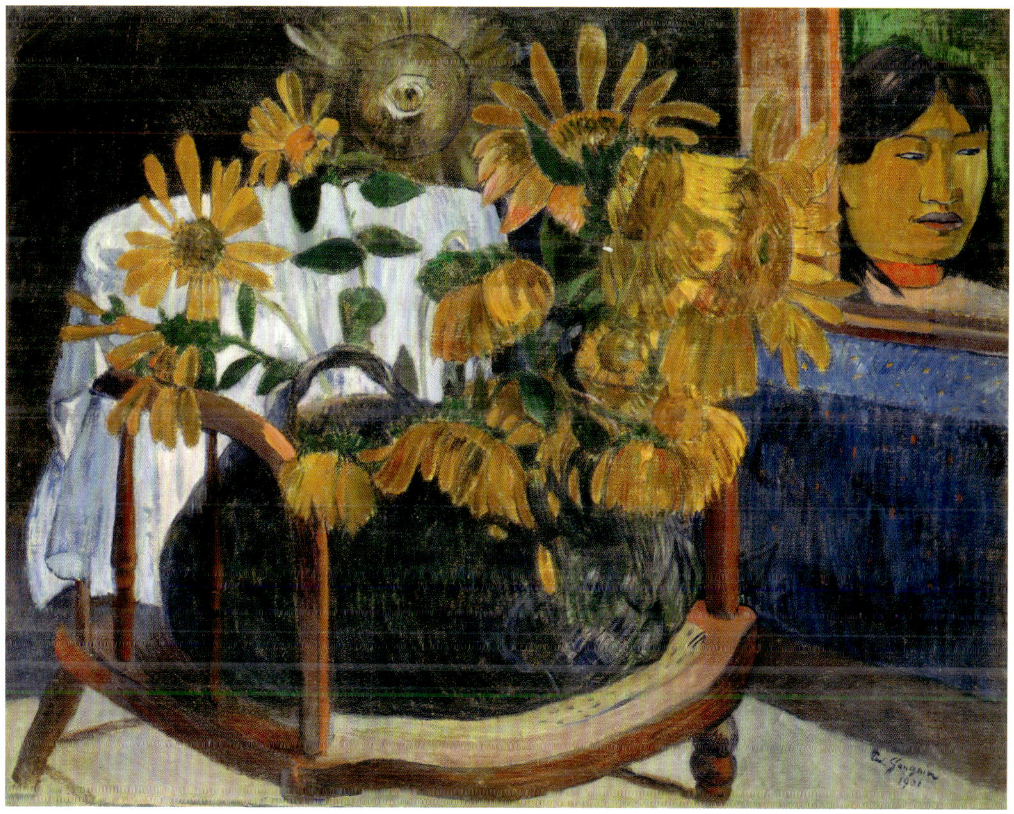

right: PAUL GAUGUIN. *Sunflowers.* 1901. OIL ON CANVAS. 28 3/4 × 36 3/8 IN. (73 × 92.3 CM).

It is likely that this still life painted by Gauguin toward the end of his life was prompted by memories of his work with Van Gogh in Arles in 1888. The motif of sunflowers borrowed from the dead friend is supplied here by symbolic elements: a Buddha-like head in the window and an eye in the middle of a sunflower that, looking straight at the viewer, evoke eternal time in which the past and the present endlessly watch each other.

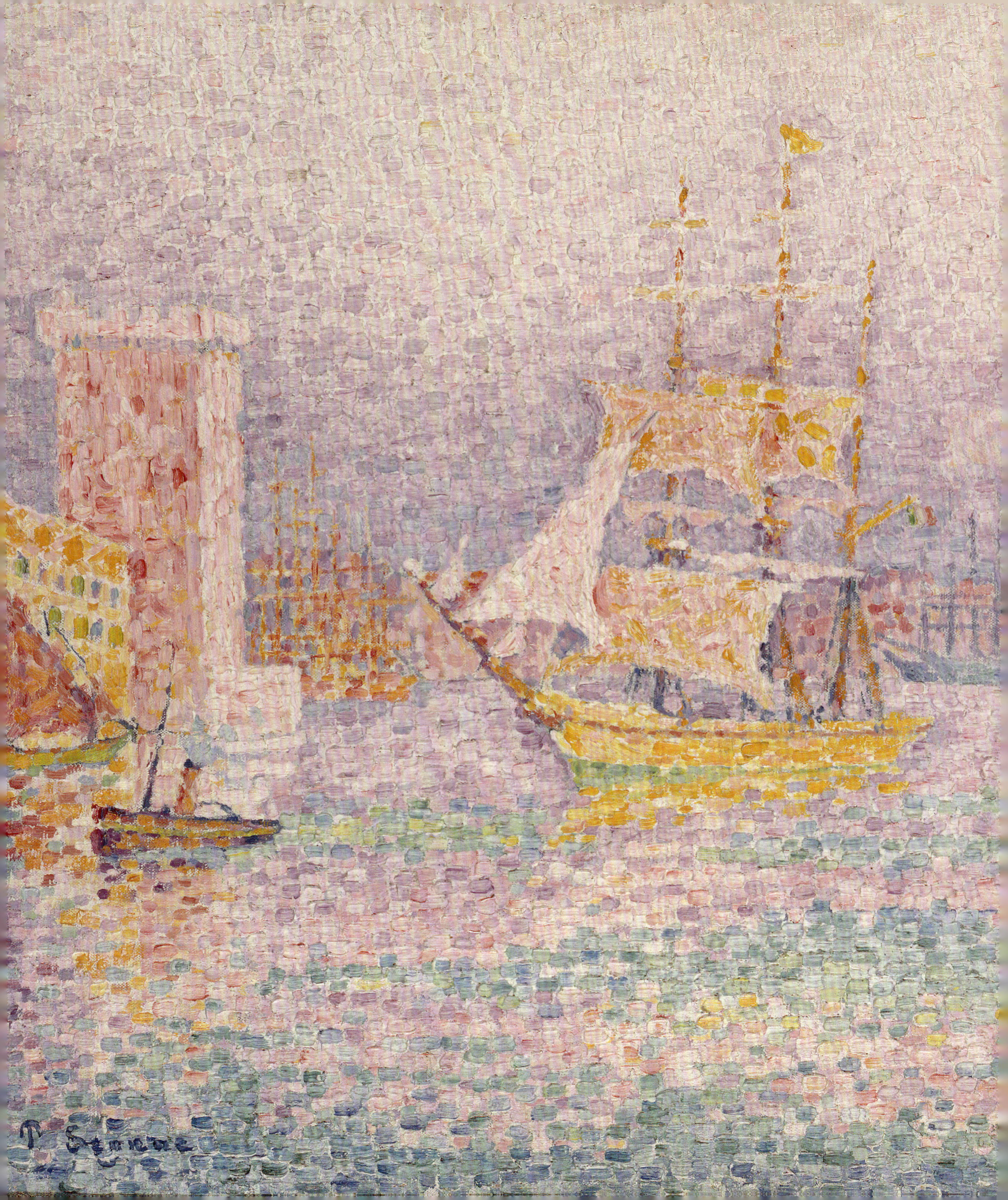

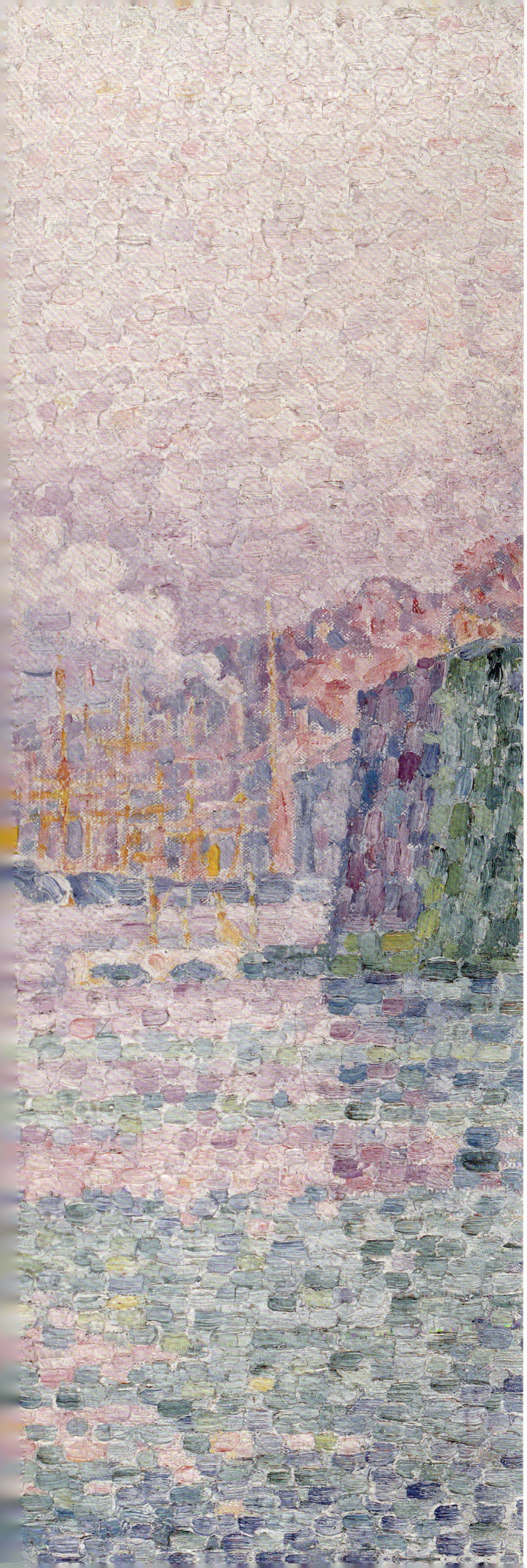

PAUL SIGNAC. *The Harbor at Marseilles.* 1907. OIL ON CANVAS. 18 1/8 × 21 5/8 IN. (46 × 55 CM).

Signac, for many years chairman of the Society of Independent Artists and a jury member of its salon, acted as a link between two generations of artists—the Post-Impressionists and the early 20th-century Modernists, many of whom worked with him in the south of France. Indeed, the paintings that Henri Matisse, André Derain, and Maurice de Vlaminck produced under his influence were a dress rehearsal for Fauvism.

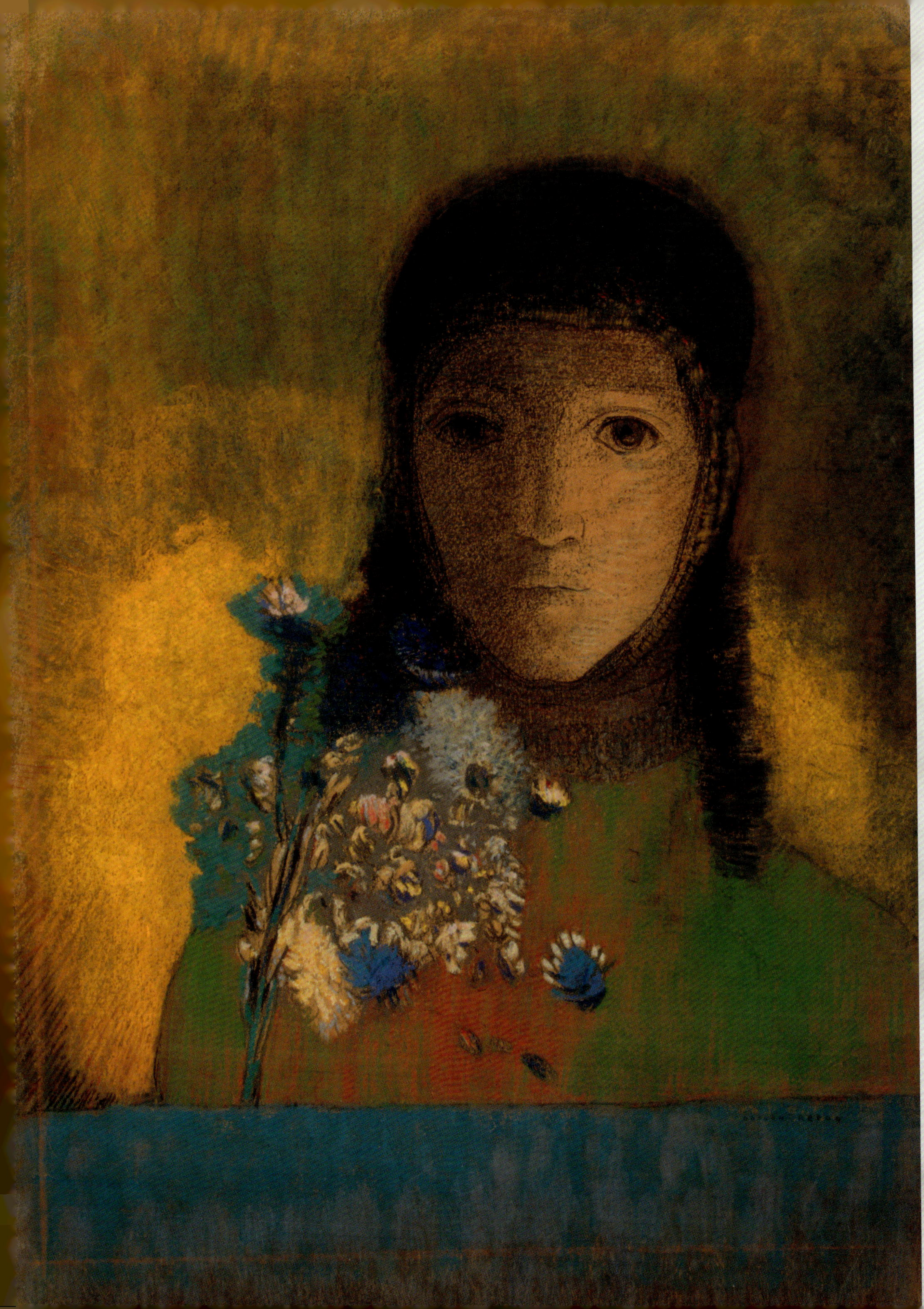

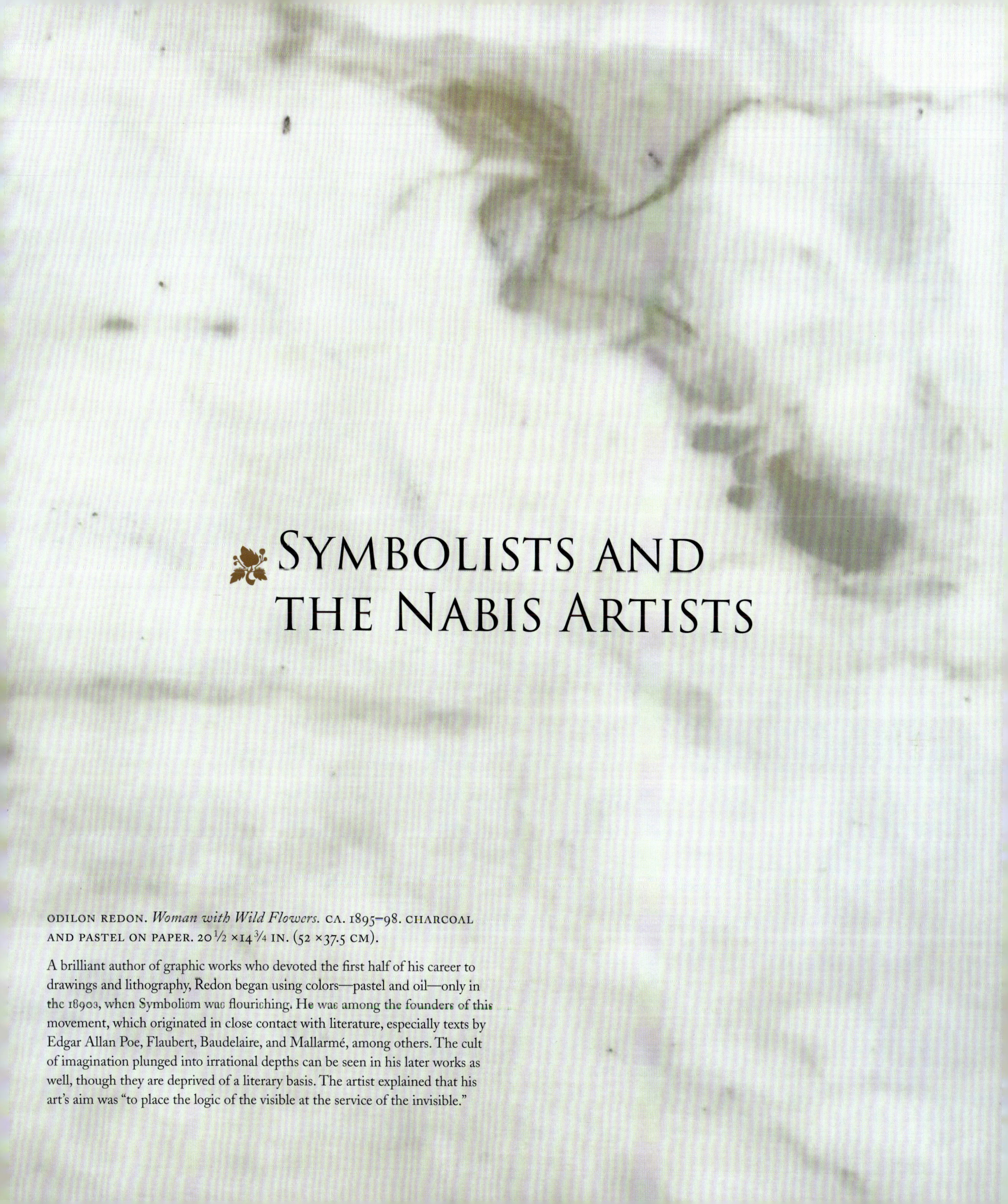

Symbolists and the Nabis Artists

ODILON REDON. *Woman with Wild Flowers*. CA. 1895–98. CHARCOAL AND PASTEL ON PAPER. 20½ × 14¾ IN. (52 × 37.5 CM).

A brilliant author of graphic works who devoted the first half of his career to drawings and lithography, Redon began using colors—pastel and oil—only in the 1890s, when Symbolism was flourishing. He was among the founders of this movement, which originated in close contact with literature, especially texts by Edgar Allan Poe, Flaubert, Baudelaire, and Mallarmé, among others. The cult of imagination plunged into irrational depths can be seen in his later works as well, though they are deprived of a literary basis. The artist explained that his art's aim was "to place the logic of the visible at the service of the invisible."

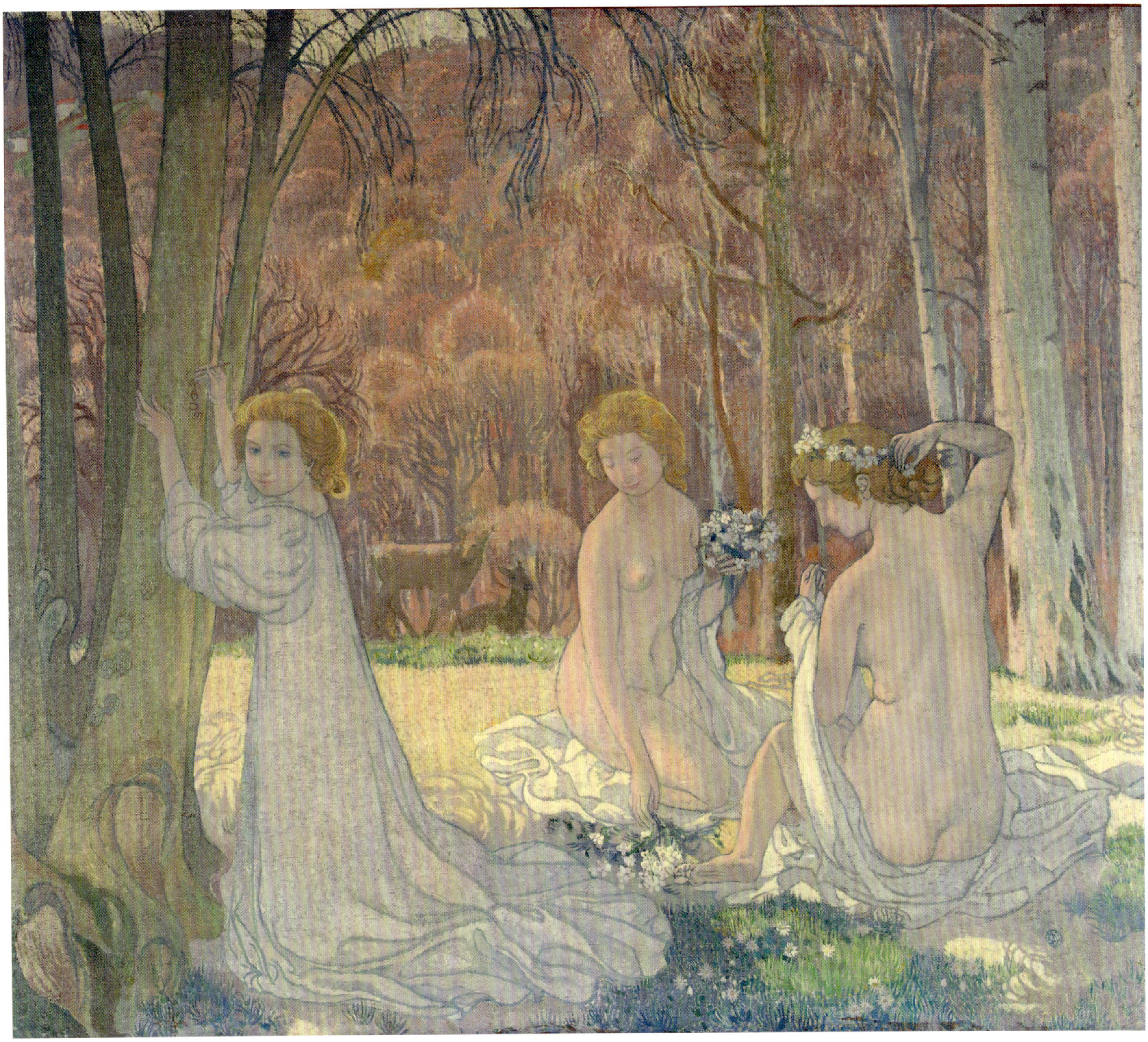

MAURICE DENIS. *Figures in a Spring Landscape (The Sacred Grove).* 1897.
OIL ON CANVAS. 61 7/8 × 70 1/2 IN. (157 × 179 CM).

The alternate title of this mature Symbolist work, apparently given by dealer Ambroise Vollard, alludes to a painting of the same name by Puvis de Chavannes. It contains a host of subtexts, including the three Graces meeting Spring in Botticelli's painting, and pagan beliefs, such as the May Rose. Based on an episode in Ariosto's *Orlando Furioso*, the motif of a girl writing her beloved's name on a tree trunk was used extensively in Italian baroque painting. Here, Denis's heroine inscribes the artist's initials.

MAURICE DENIS. *The Visitation.* CA. 1892. OIL ON CANVAS. 40½ × 36⅞ IN. (103 × 93 CM).

In this work, Denis projects onto the Christian subject of the imminent birth of a child circumstances from his own life. His son Jean-Paul was born in October 1894 (but lived only four months), and so the event that the Church commemorates in July is shown as occurring in autumn. The artist depicts with solemn simplicity the meeting between the women chosen by God to be the mothers of Christ and John the Baptist (Luke 1:39–56). The decorative background is full of symbols of the Virgin Mary: roses, the trellis of an enclosed garden, and the cloud all serve as a reminder of one of her epithets, the Gate of Heaven.

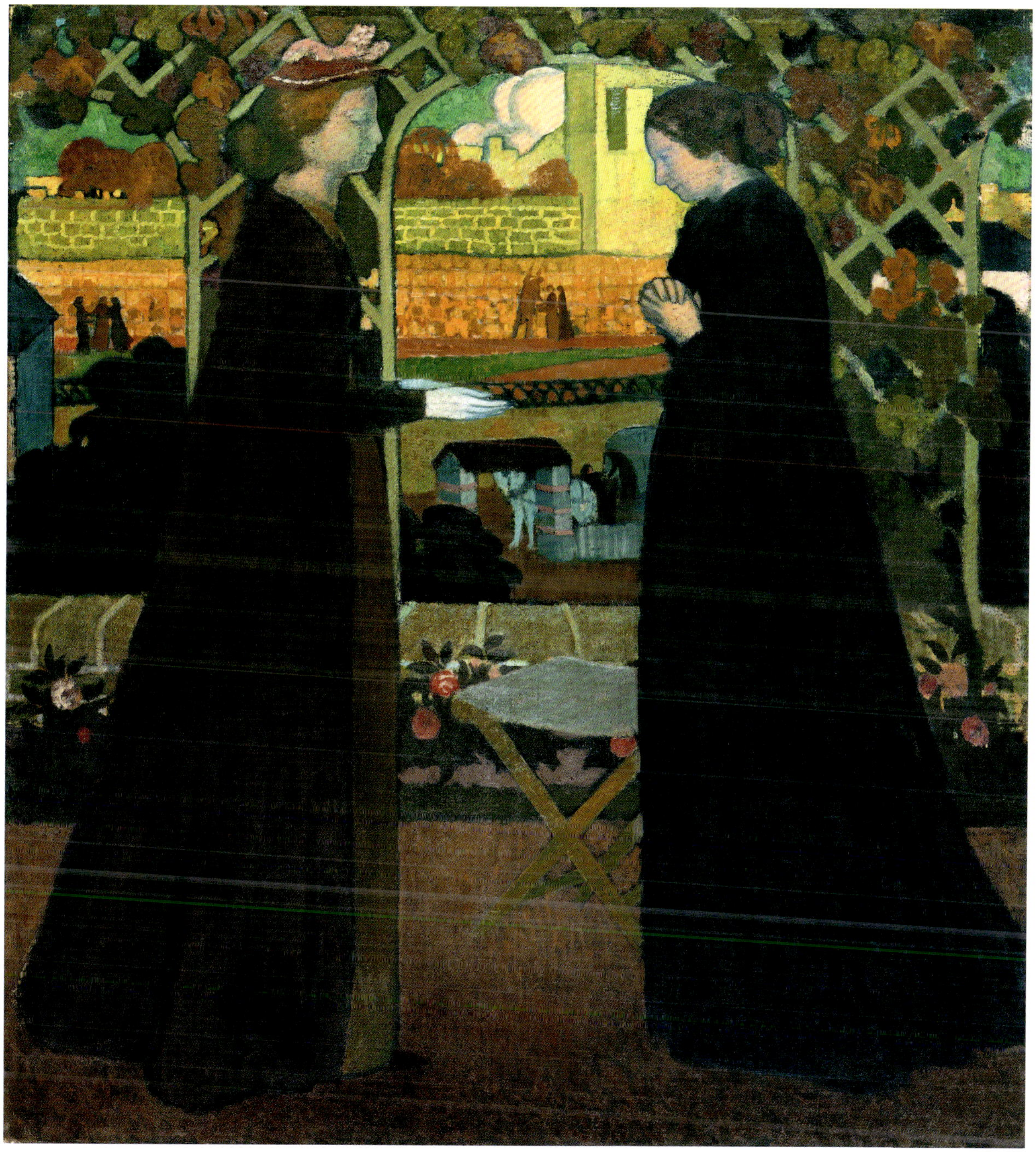

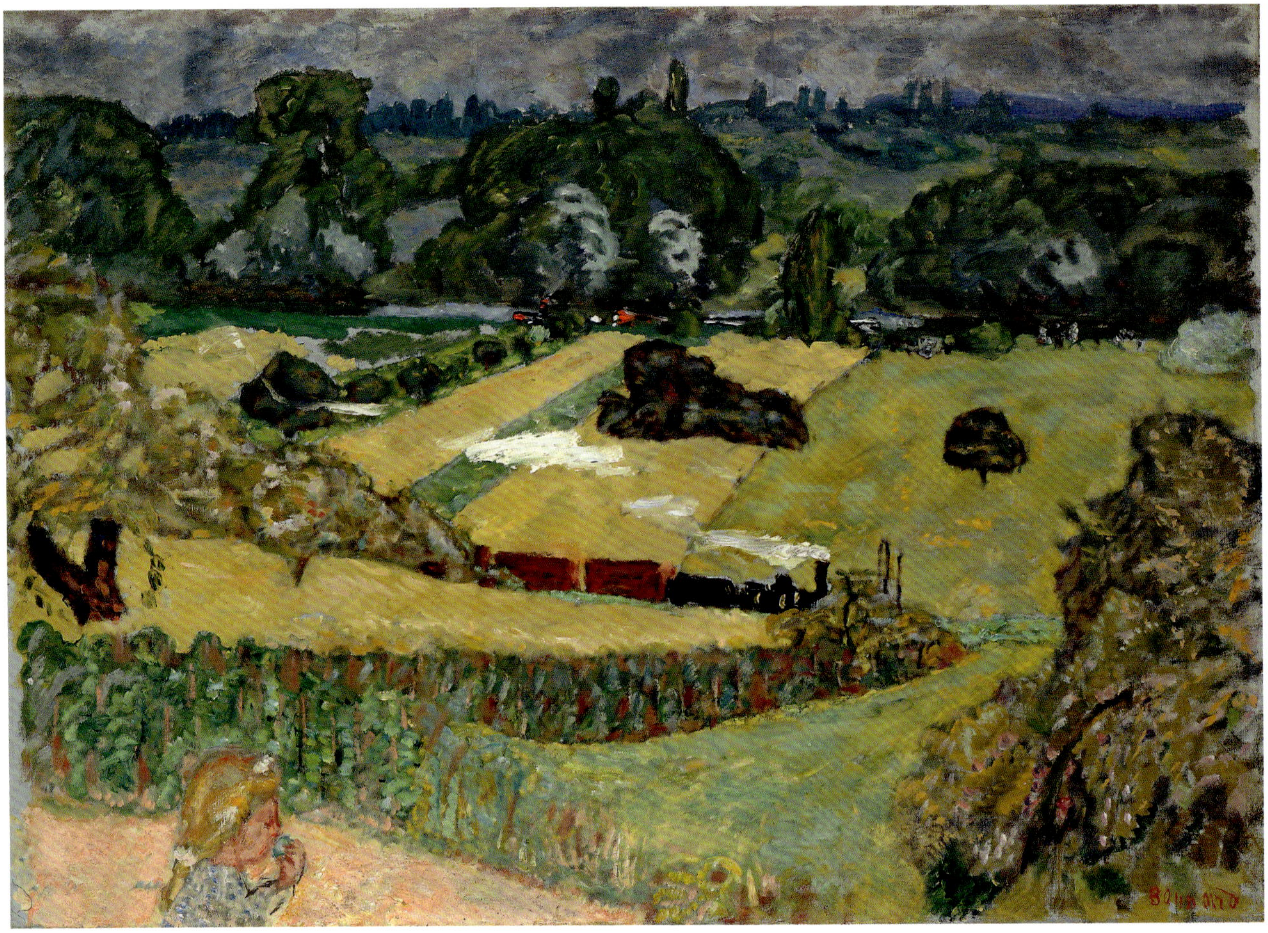

above: PIERRE BONNARD. *Train and Scows (Landscape with a Goods Train).* 1909. OIL ON CANVAS. 30⅜ × 42½ IN. (77 × 108 CM).

Reminiscent of an improvisation in verse, the lines of this landscape—boundaries of fields, stands of trees, the arrow of the train, the puffs of smoke—intersect at sharp angles to create a slightly irregular rhythm. Bonnard pursues the sense of immediacy with which the scene might be viewed by the young girl, who seems to have entered the picture by accident.

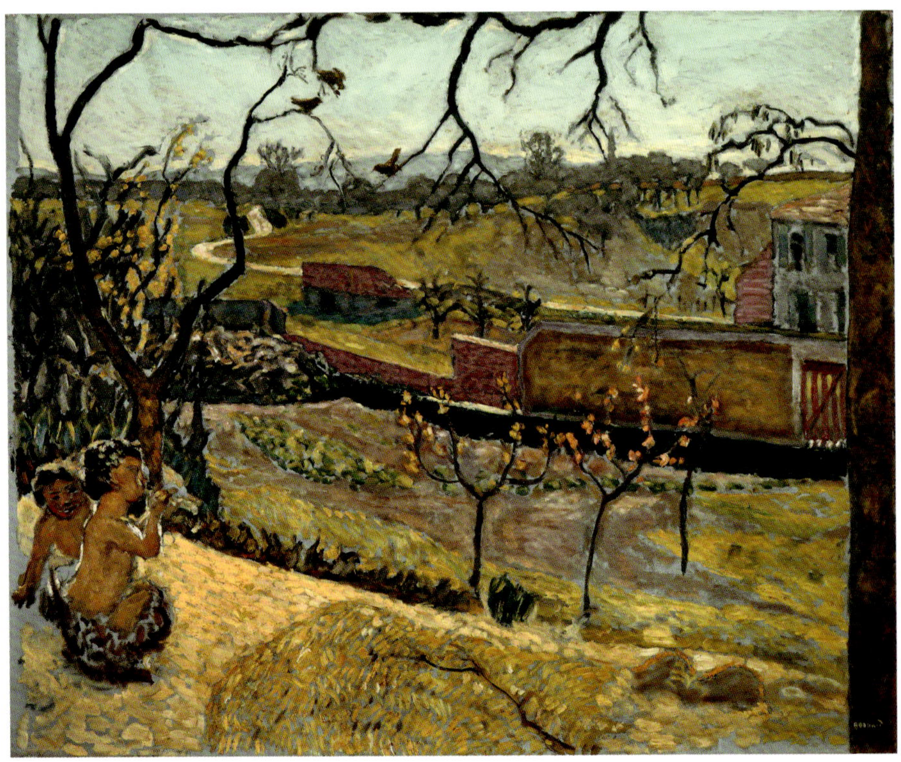

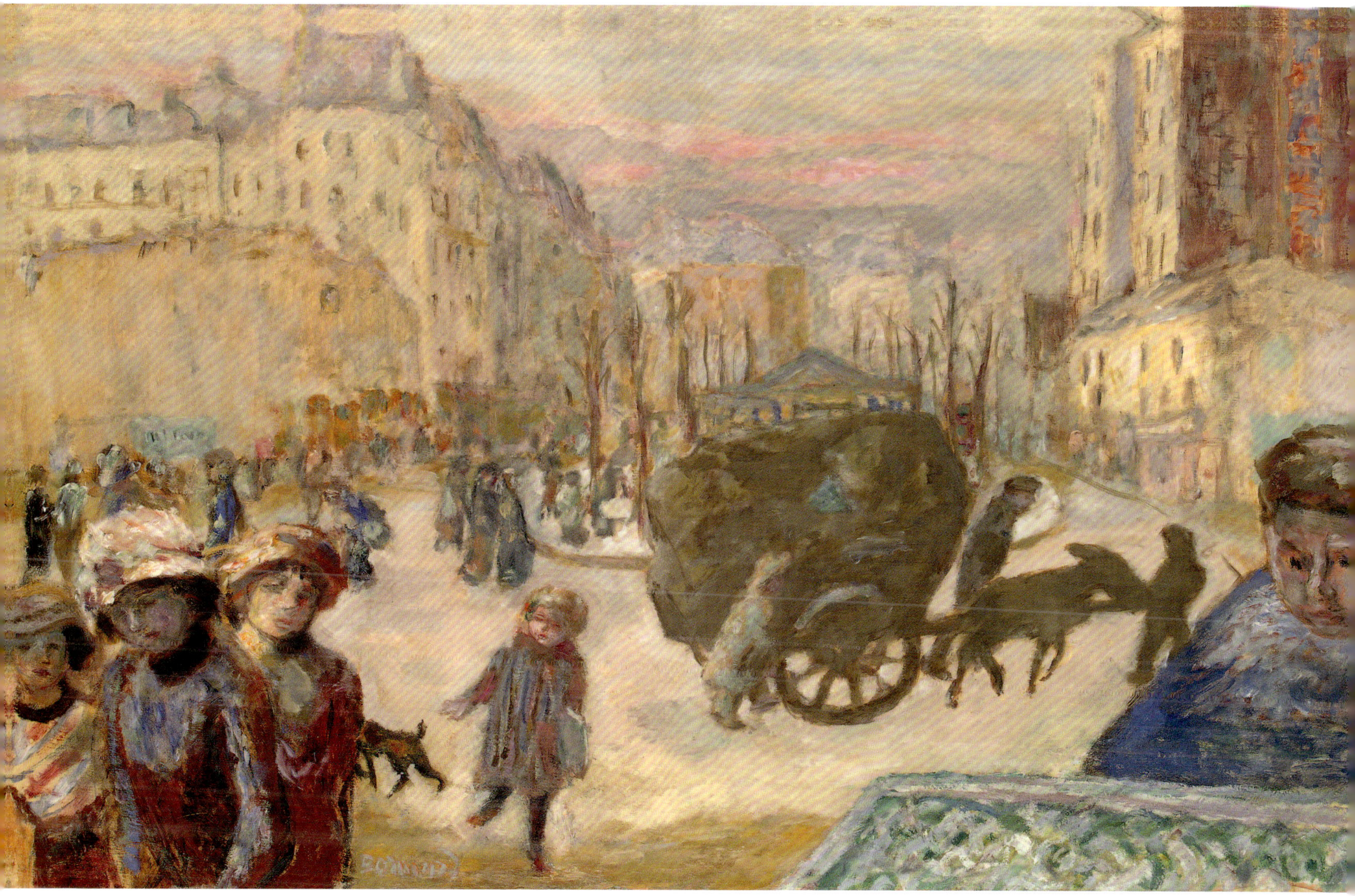

opposite, below: PIERRE BONNARD. *The Start of Spring (Little Fauns).* 1909. OIL ON CANVAS. 40 3/8 × 49 1/4 IN. (102.5 × 125 CM).

One of the best paintings by Bonnard in the Hermitage, *The Start of Spring* contains echoes of two key works for fin-de-siecle artistic culture: Stéphane Mallarmé's dramatic poem "L'après-midi d'un faune" and Claude Débussy's prelude of the same name. The Symbolist image that awakens to the sound of nature's pipes gives this canvas a dreamy remoteness uncharacteristic of the artist's earlier works.

above: PIERRE BONNARD. *Morning in Paris.* 1911. OIL ON CANVAS. 30 1/8 × 48 IN. (76.5 × 122 CM).

Bonnard painted two views of the French capital, *Morning* and *Evening*, for a commission from the Russian collector Ivan Morozov, who left the choice of subject to the artist. Through their disorderly movements, the personages of *Morning*, shrouded in the haze of dawn, convincingly convey a feeling of the start of the day. Their eyes are still, it seems, only half-open, and they bump into one another as they mix in the cheerful morning crowd.

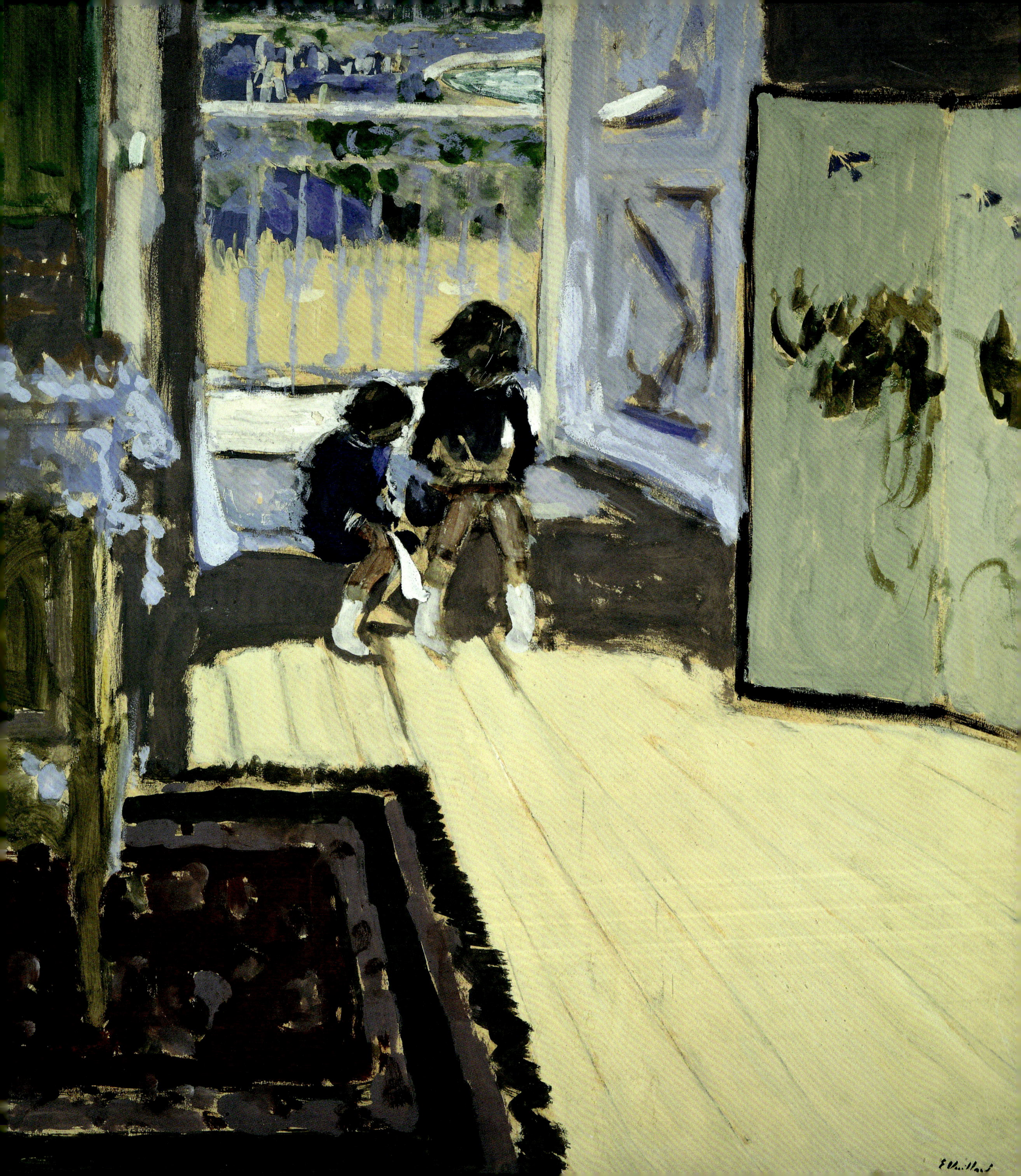
E Vuillard

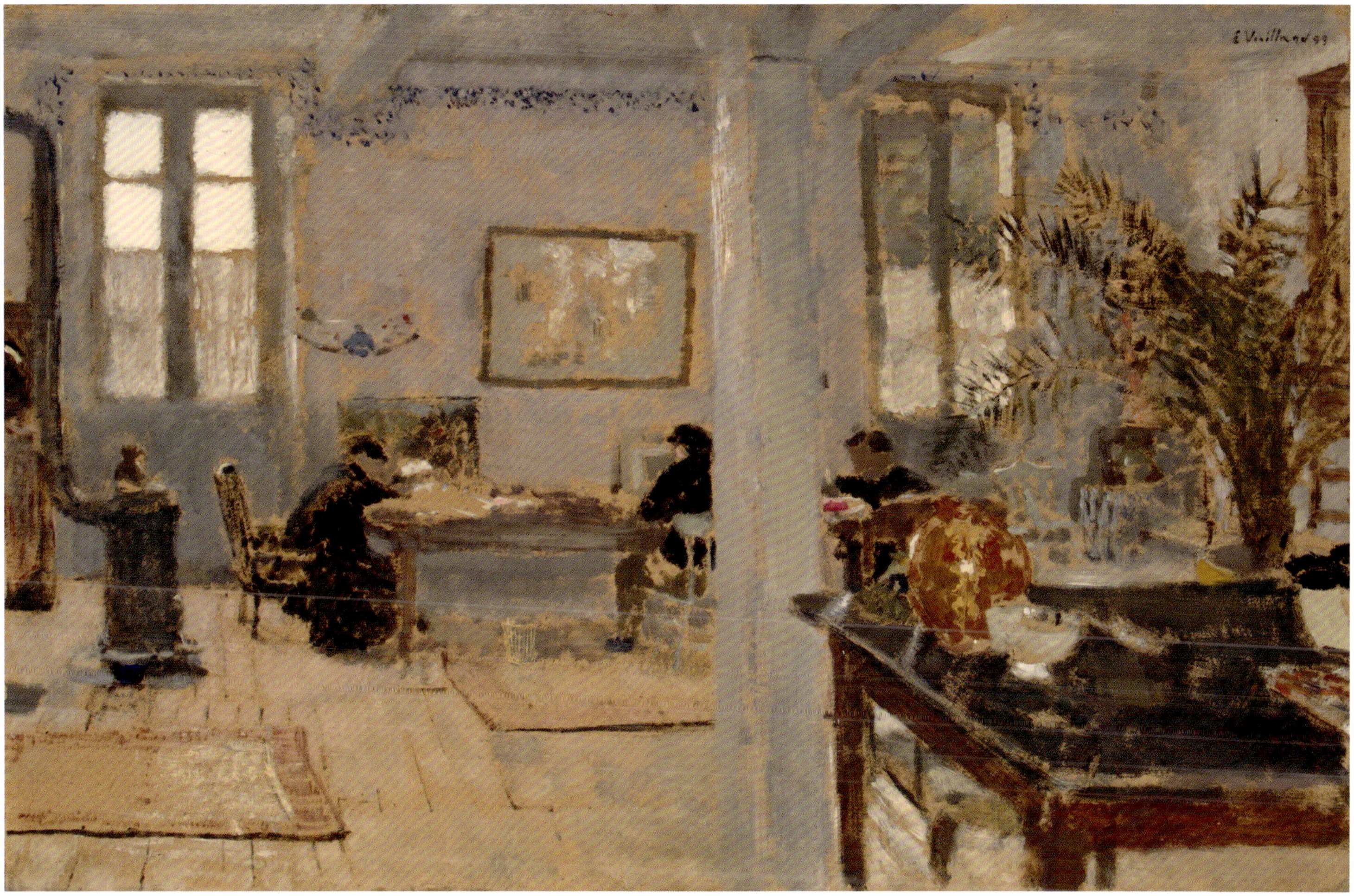

opposite: EDOUARD VUILLARD. *Children*. 1909. GOUACHE ON PAPER PASTED ONTO CANVAS. $33\frac{1}{4} \times 30\frac{1}{2}$ IN. (84.5×77.7 CM).

In this painting created in the house of the Nathanson brothers, who were the publishers of *La Revue blanche*, the French art and literary magazine, and who loved and valued Vuillard's works, we distinguish the painter's typical attributes—a carpet and a Japanese screen—which usually support his inclination toward a decorative two-dimensional approach. But here, they are much less significant than elsewhere, and with their subdued colors, give way to the energy of the pouring light.

above: EDOUARD VUILLARD. *In the Room*. 1899. OIL ON CARDBOARD. $20\frac{1}{2} \times 31\frac{1}{8}$ IN. (52×79 CM).

The palette of this early interior by Vuillard is constructed around a few closely related tones. Although they may seem excessively impoverished, these hues—gray-green, yellow ochre, and brownish black—make up the painting's protagonist: a tantalizing half-shadow that reigns in this room illuminated only slightly by light from the windows. The unexpected bouquet in the foreground is far more essential to the work's characteristics of color, scent, and feelings than the barely indicated, insignificant figures sitting at the table.

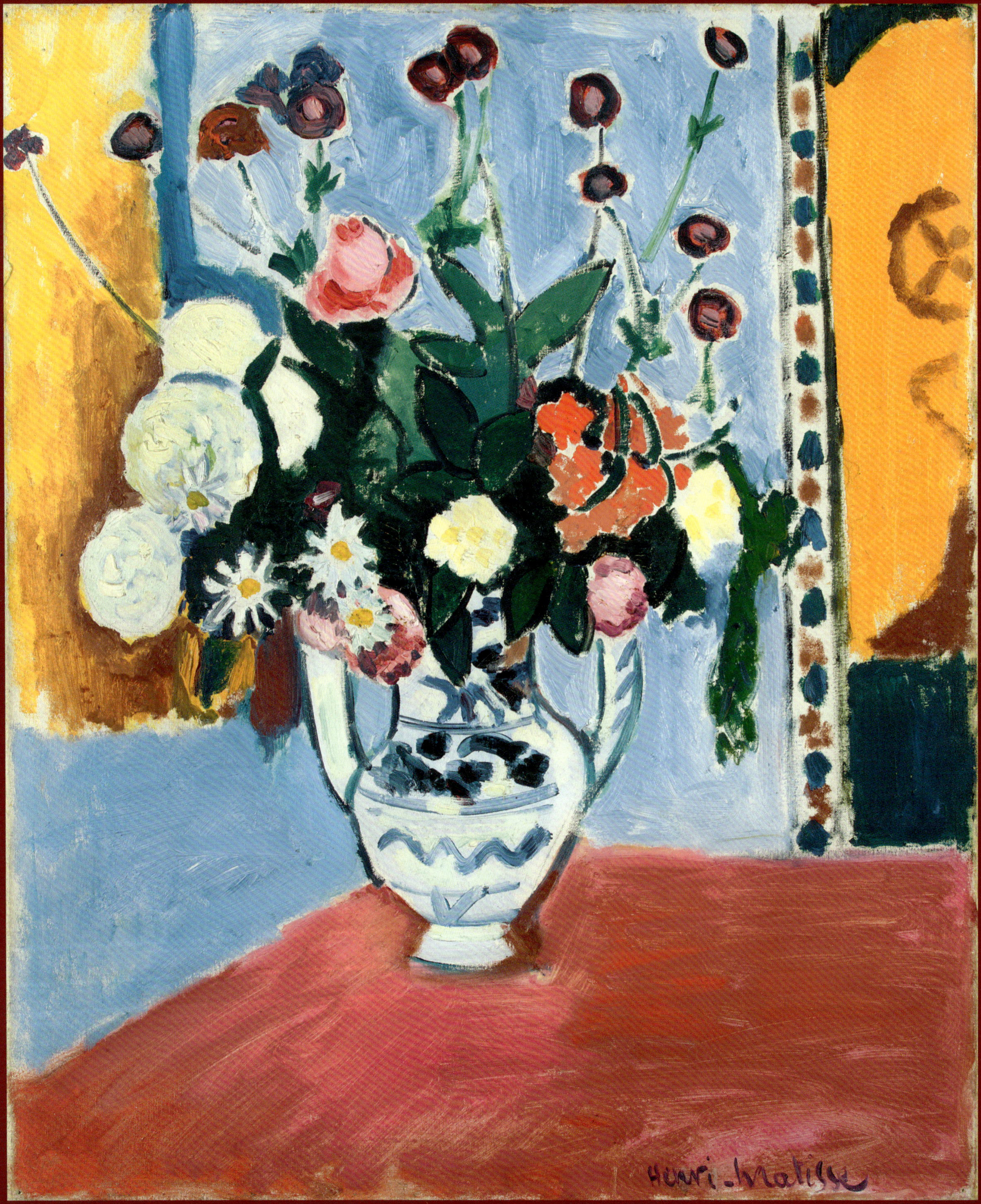

MATISSE AND THE FAUVES

HENRI MATISSE. *Bouquet (Two-Handled Vase).* 1907. OIL ON CANVAS. 29 × 24 IN. (74 × 61 CM)

In 17th-century Holland, a bouquet of flowers supplied an artist with unlimited possibilities to demonstrate his or her skills and inventiveness in various combinations of symbolic meanings. In the early 20th century, the bouquet again became a favorite subject of innovative painters, but this time as the main element around which to organize the space. Indeed, the object is not represented within a space but instead creates it: the vase gives its color to the sky-blue—and totally abstract—background; the yellow of the eyes of the daisies is echoed in the intense yellow of the "drop cloths"; and several pink brushstrokes accentuating a rosebud are repeated in the tablecloth.

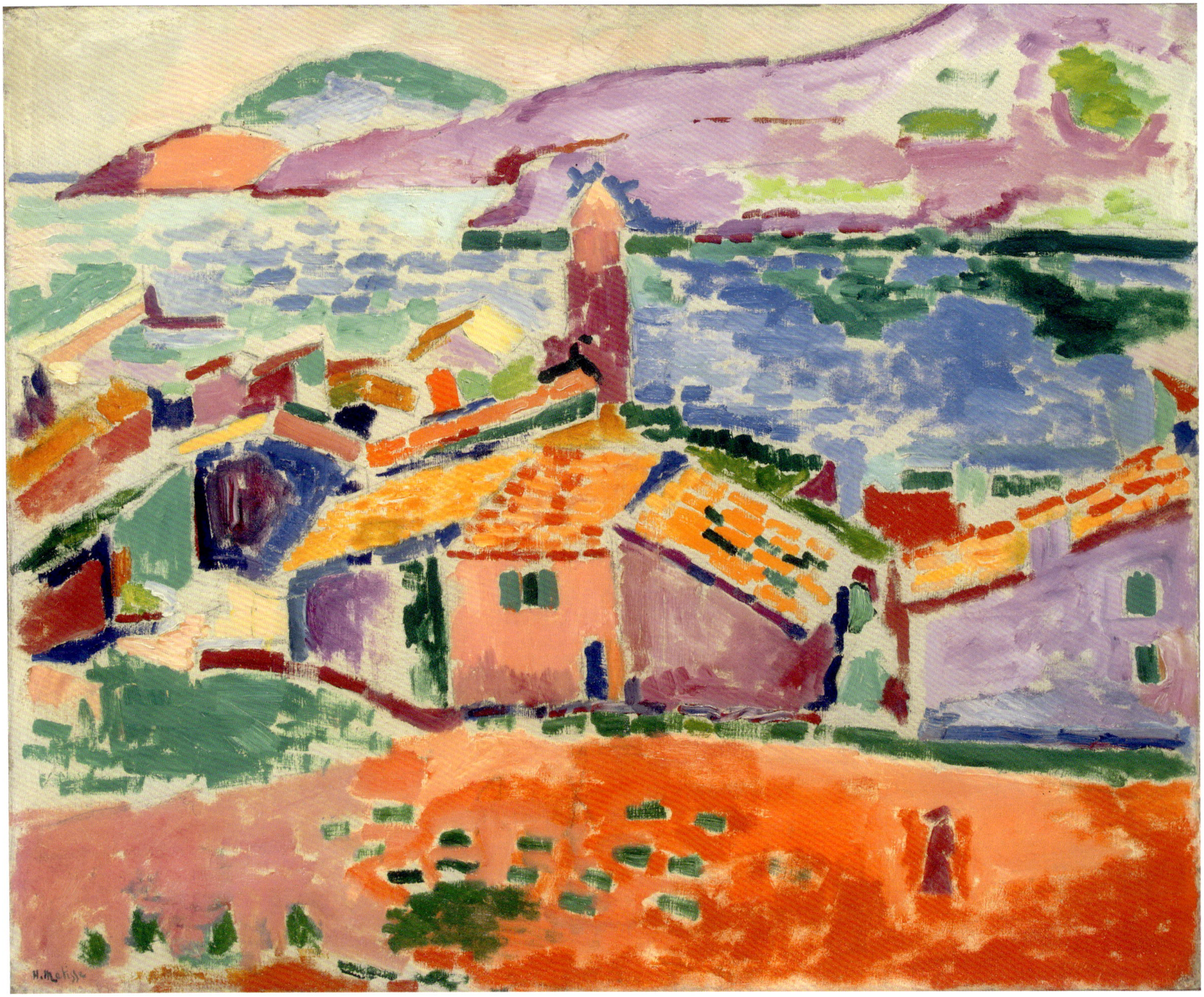

HENRI MATISSE. *View of Collioure.* 1905. OIL ON CANVAS. $23\frac{1}{2} \times 28\frac{3}{4}$ IN. (59.5×73 CM).

Bright, intensive, contrasting colors that seem to abandon their objects in the blinding Mediterranean light gave critics the reason to call Matisse and his friends who participated in the Salon d'Automne in 1905 "les fauves" (wild beasts). Matisse worked on the southern coast of France, in Collioure, together with Vlaminck. Their paintings of this period show the development of a new technique called divisionism, borrowed from Paul Signac, who made both artists adore the Mediterranean seaside.

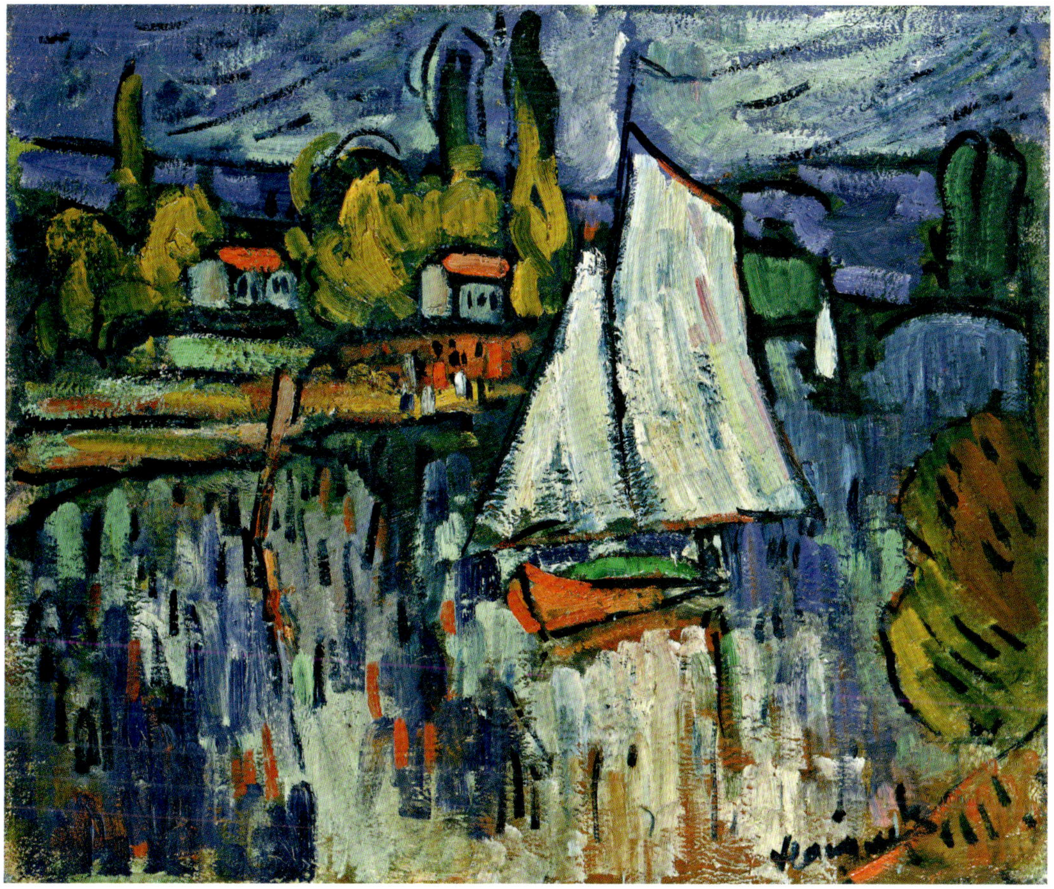

left: MAURICE DE VLAMINCK. *Town on the Bank of the Seine.* CA. 1909. OIL ON CANVAS. 32 × 39½ IN. (81.3 × 100.3 CM).

Vlaminck was a self-taught artist who began painting in 1899, at age twenty-three. On entering the refined artistic milieu of Paris, he set about mastering its traditions and styles, including Cézannism, and from then on, his painting became more restrained and subtle. But behind the constructive form and nuanced color there would always remain a sense of the explosive temperament of an anarchist.

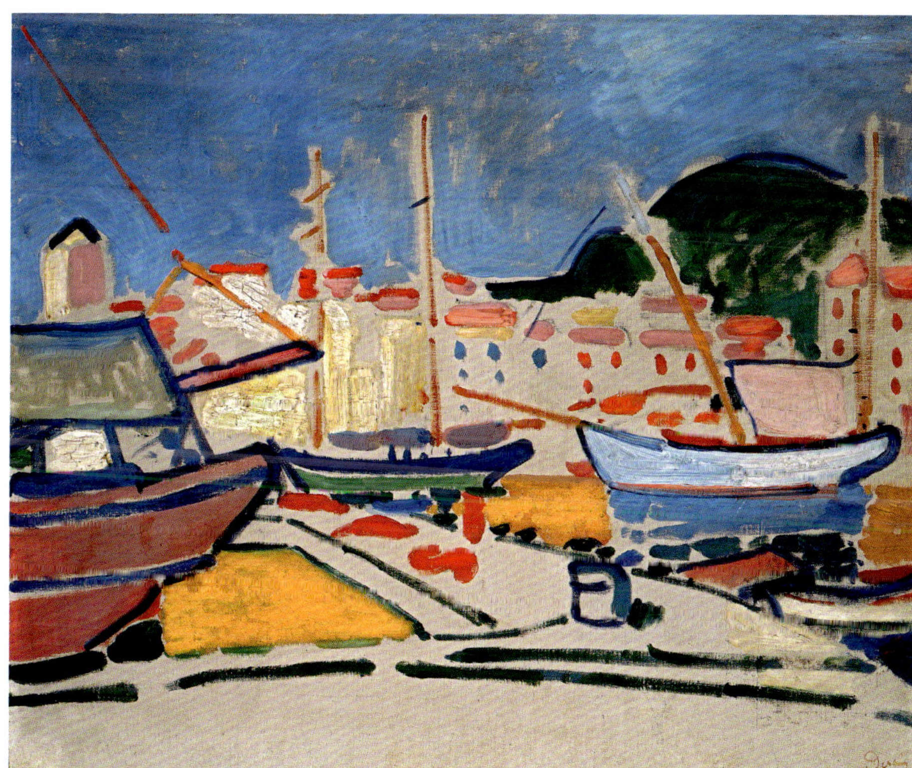

right: ANDRÉ DERAIN. *Port (Port-Vendres).* 1905–6. OIL ON CANVAS. 24½ × 28¾ IN. (62 × 73 CM).

Derain was one of the most noticeable figures among the Fauves, but he did not remain true for long to the ideas that united them. As early as 1908, under the influence of Picasso's *Demoiselles d'Avignon,* he destroyed the majority of his Fauvist works. But even in those that have survived, such as this one, there is an evident striving to bring the bright patches of color to a harmony, to gather them into a neat, balanced composition.

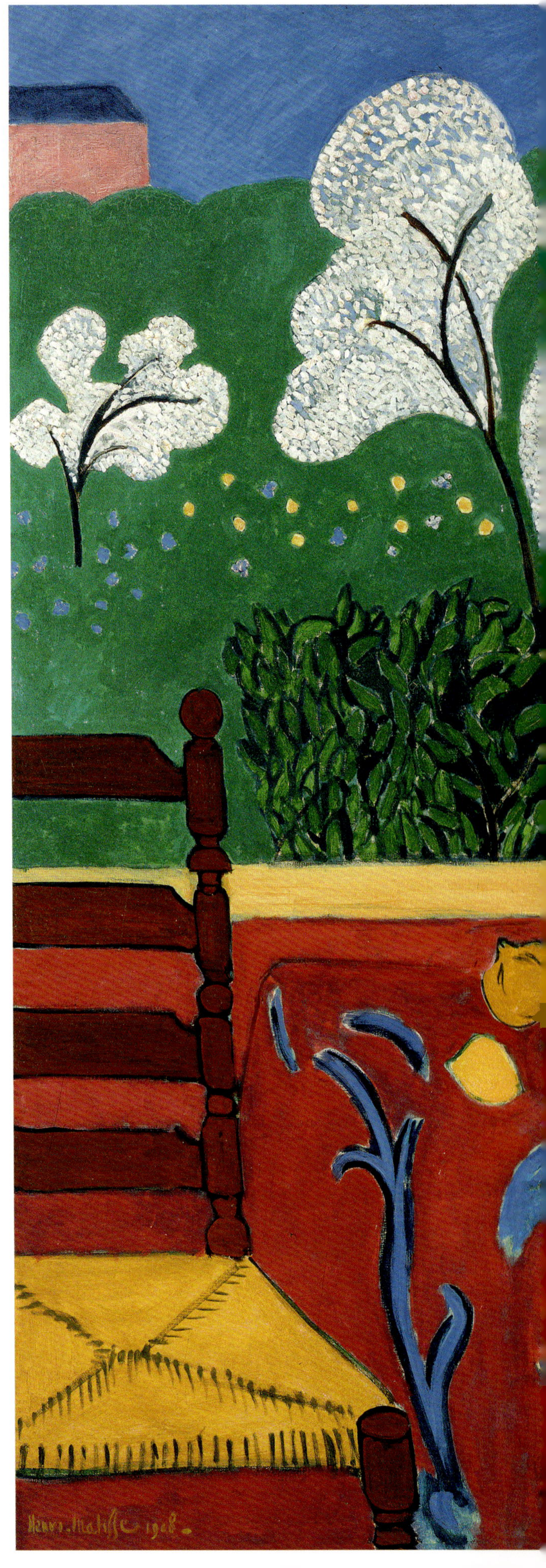

HENRI MATISSE. *The Red Room (Dessert. Harmony in Red).* 1908. OIL ON CANVAS. 71 × 86½ IN. (180 × 220 CM).

An important factor in the development of avant-garde painting in the late 19th and early 20th centuries was the heritage of primitive and traditional cultures. For Gauguin, these were Polynesian idols; for Picasso, Iberian sculpture; and for Matisse, ornament. *The Red Room* is a manifesto of sorts, stating the ornamental, rhythmical structure of the universe: the pattern of the cloth taken from real life (although the original piece was not red but blue) governs everything around it—the still life objects, the lines of the trees and horizon, and even a woman's figure.

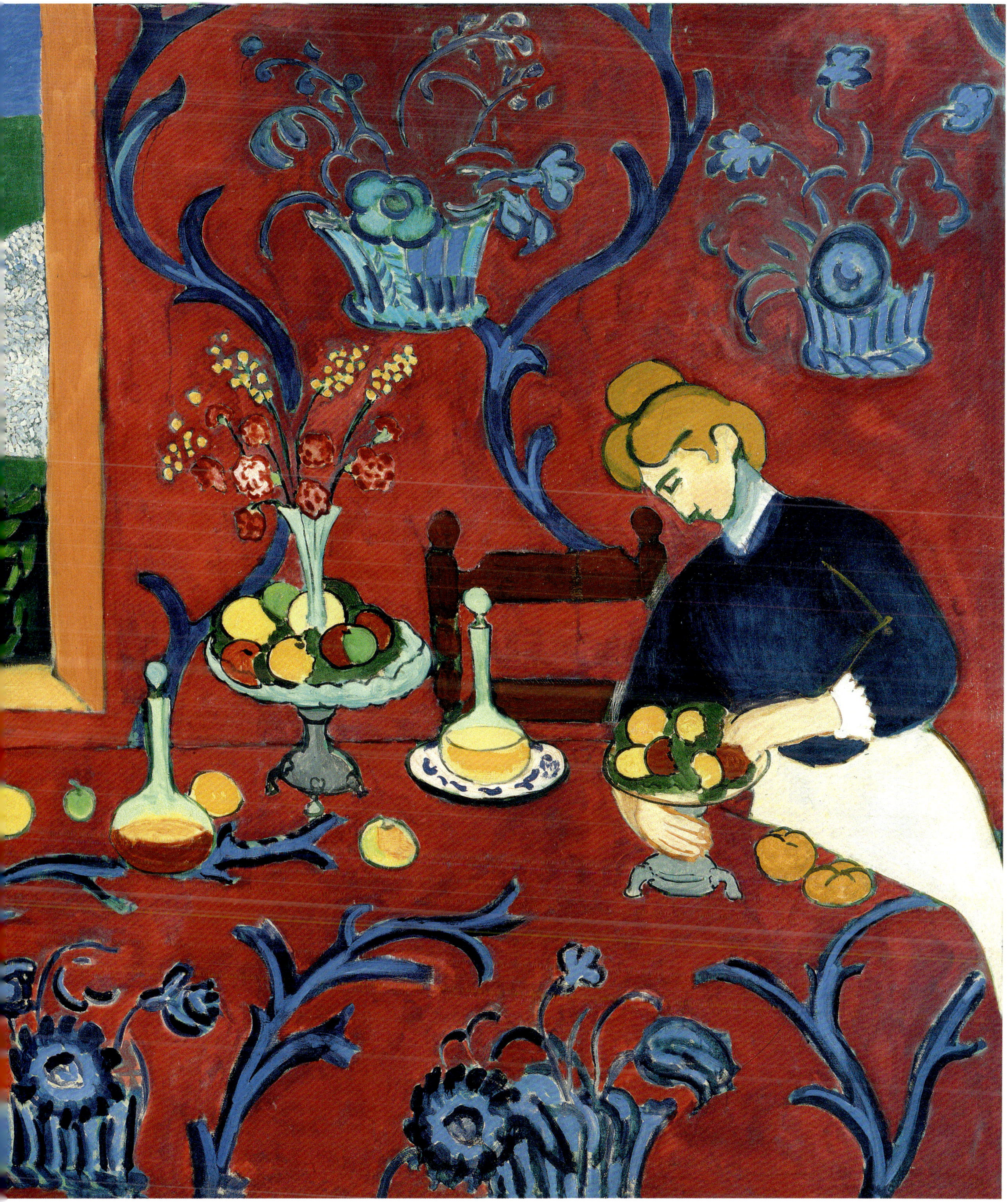

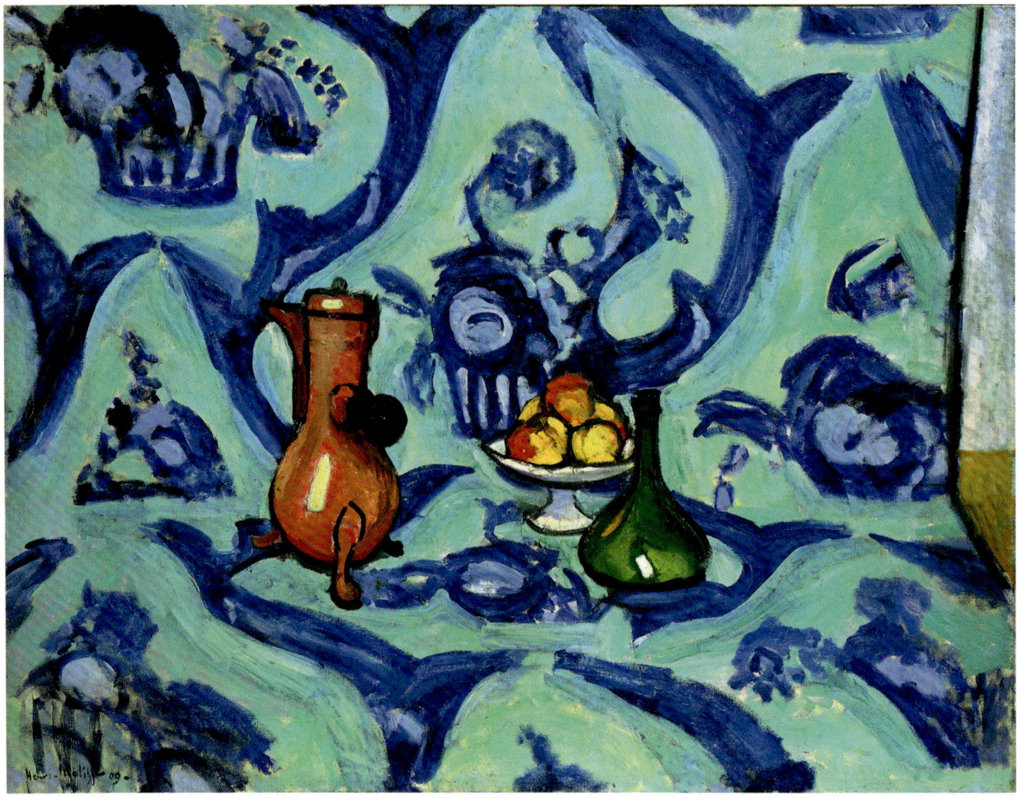

opposite: HENRI MATISSE. *Girl with Tulips (Portrait of Jeanne Vaderin).* 1910. OIL ON CANVAS. 36¼ ×29 IN. (92 × 73.5 CM).

Having created a background clash of complementary colors—blue and yellow that evoke the dramatic tension of van Gogh's palette—Matisse seems to set himself the task of calming their commotion. The tumult dies down behind the vernal chords of blue and pink that form the model's figure and the bunches of tulips in the foreground. Depicted is Jeanne Vaderin, a neighbor of the Matisses in the Paris suburb of Issy-les-Moulineaux, where the artist then worked.

above: HENRI MATISSE. *Still Life with a Blue Tablecloth.* 1909. OIL ON CANVAS. 34¾ ×45⅔ IN. (88.5 × 116 CM).

The fabric celebrated the previous year in *The Red Room* is, in this work, depicted in blue. Descending over the entire canvas, it masterfully takes charge of the image, drawing everything into its own movement and countering the "still life" of objects with the unstoppable flow of ornament.

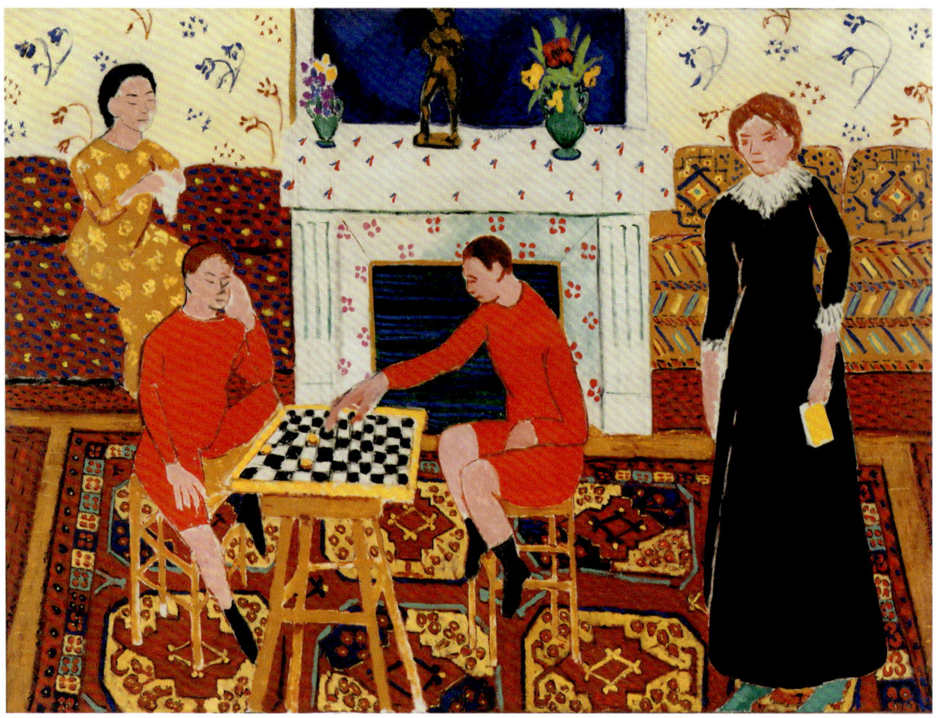

right: HENRI MATISSE. *Family Portrait.* 1911. OIL ON CANVAS. 17 × 76½ IN. (43 × 194 CM).

The nude figures in *Music* and *The Dance* caused concern for Matisse's patron, Sergei Shchukin, over how the panels would be received by the Moscovite public. Not wishing to upset the artist, the collector soon commissioned a new work, suggesting the subject of figures in an interior, "perhaps a portrait of your family." Shchukin's letter reached Matisse in Spain. In this family portrait, the artist expresses his admiration for Moorish art and Islamic art in general.

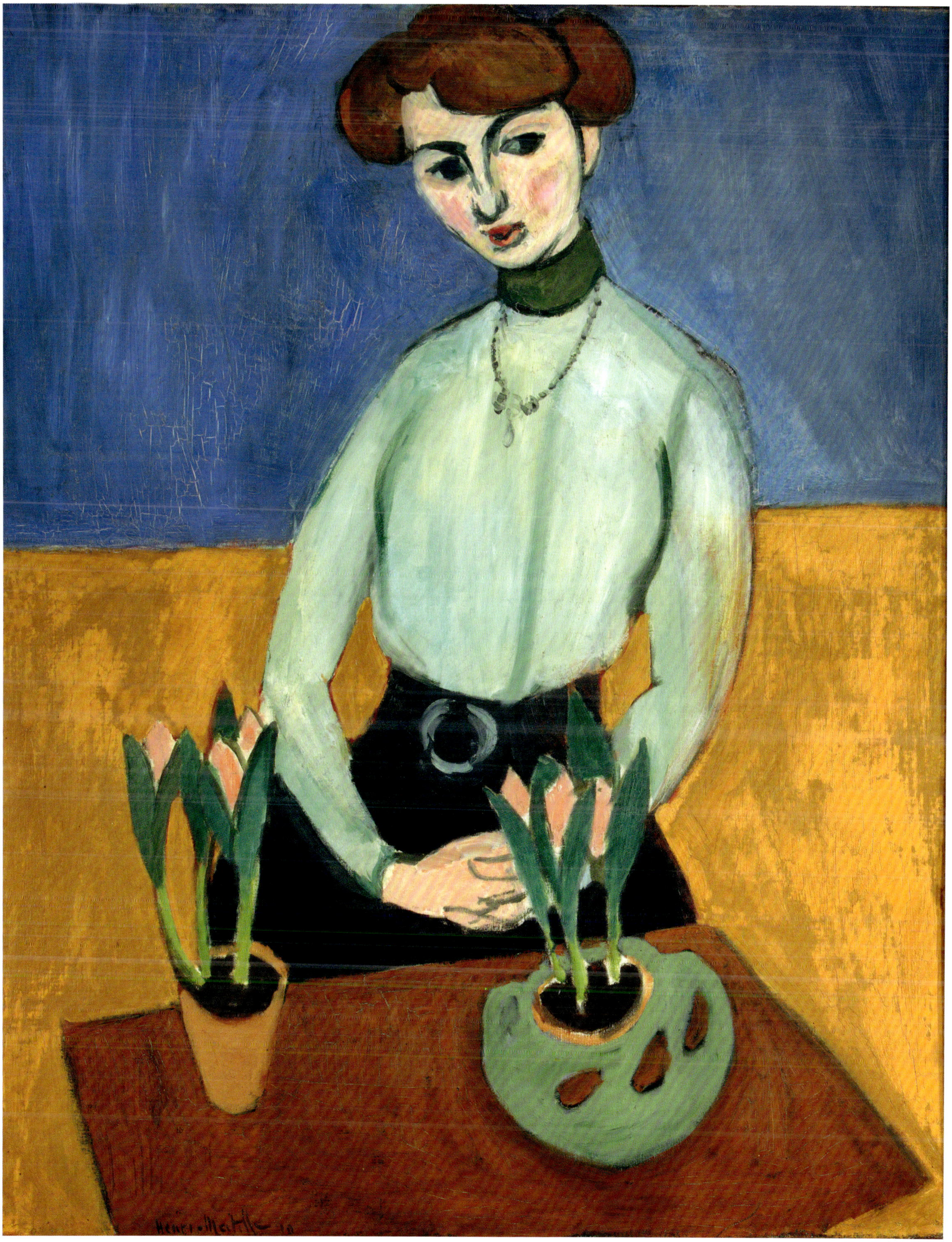

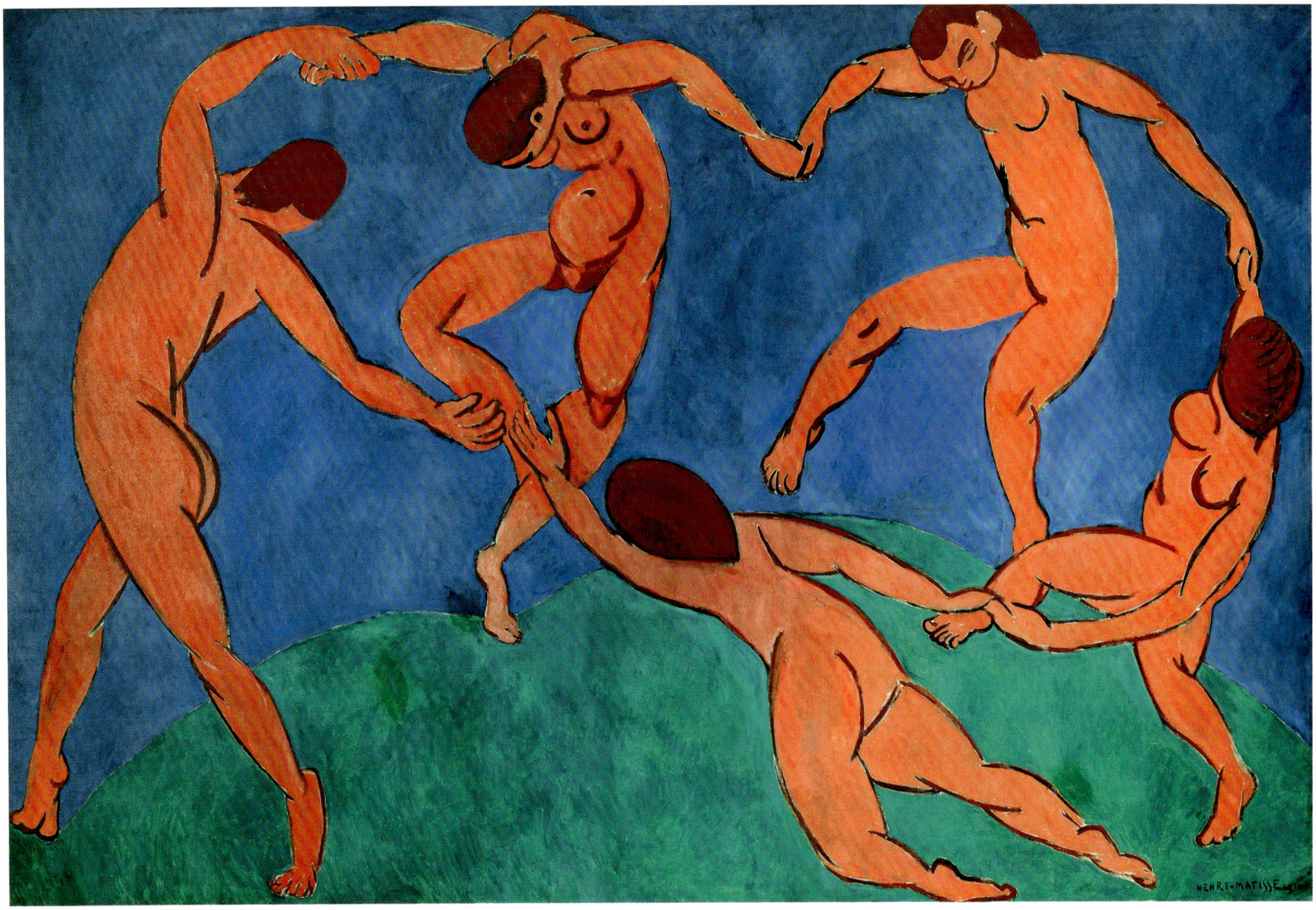

HENRI MATISSE. *The Dance.* 1910. OIL ON CANVAS. $102^{1}/_{3}$ × 154 IN. (260 × 391 CM).

In this panel created for the industrialist and collector Sergei Shchukin, the two main themes of Matisse's oeuvre in the early 1900s attain their fullest development: the energy of pure color (the space is formed by just red, blue, and green) and the power of the line, capable of depicting everything, from the human beings to movement itself. The artist achieves precision through simplification, depicting the moment when bodies caught up in a dance are transformed into an abstract pattern.

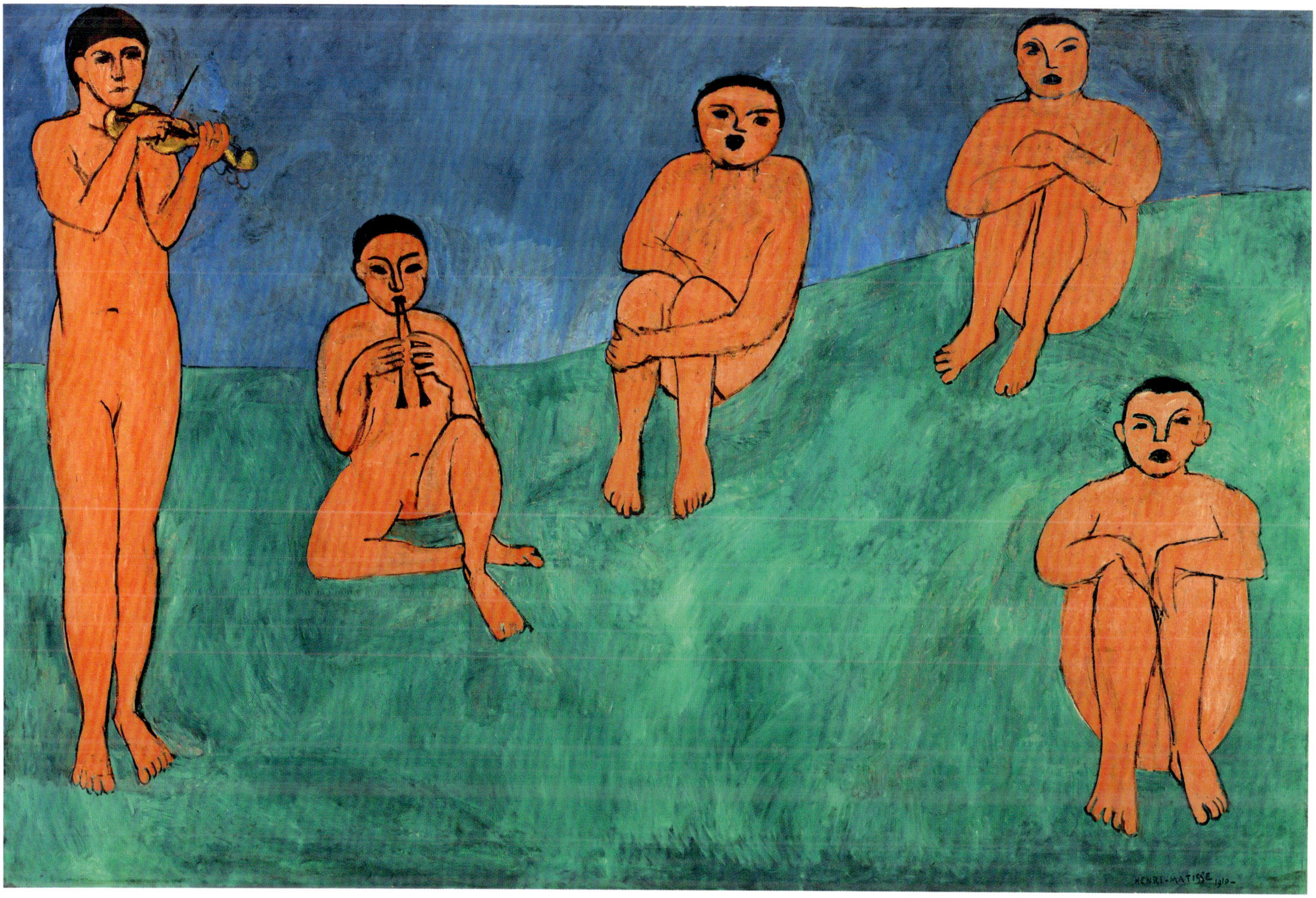

HENRI MATISSE. *Music.* 1910. OIL ON CANVAS. 102 1/3 × 153 IN. (260 × 389 CM).

Music decoratively complements and logically completes *The Dance*: the rhythm of the first panel acquires indisputable harmony. The laconic persuasiveness of its vertical figures, with circles for mouths, obliges us to include them among the "new signs," the quantity of which is, in Matisse's own words, "a measure of the significance of an artist."

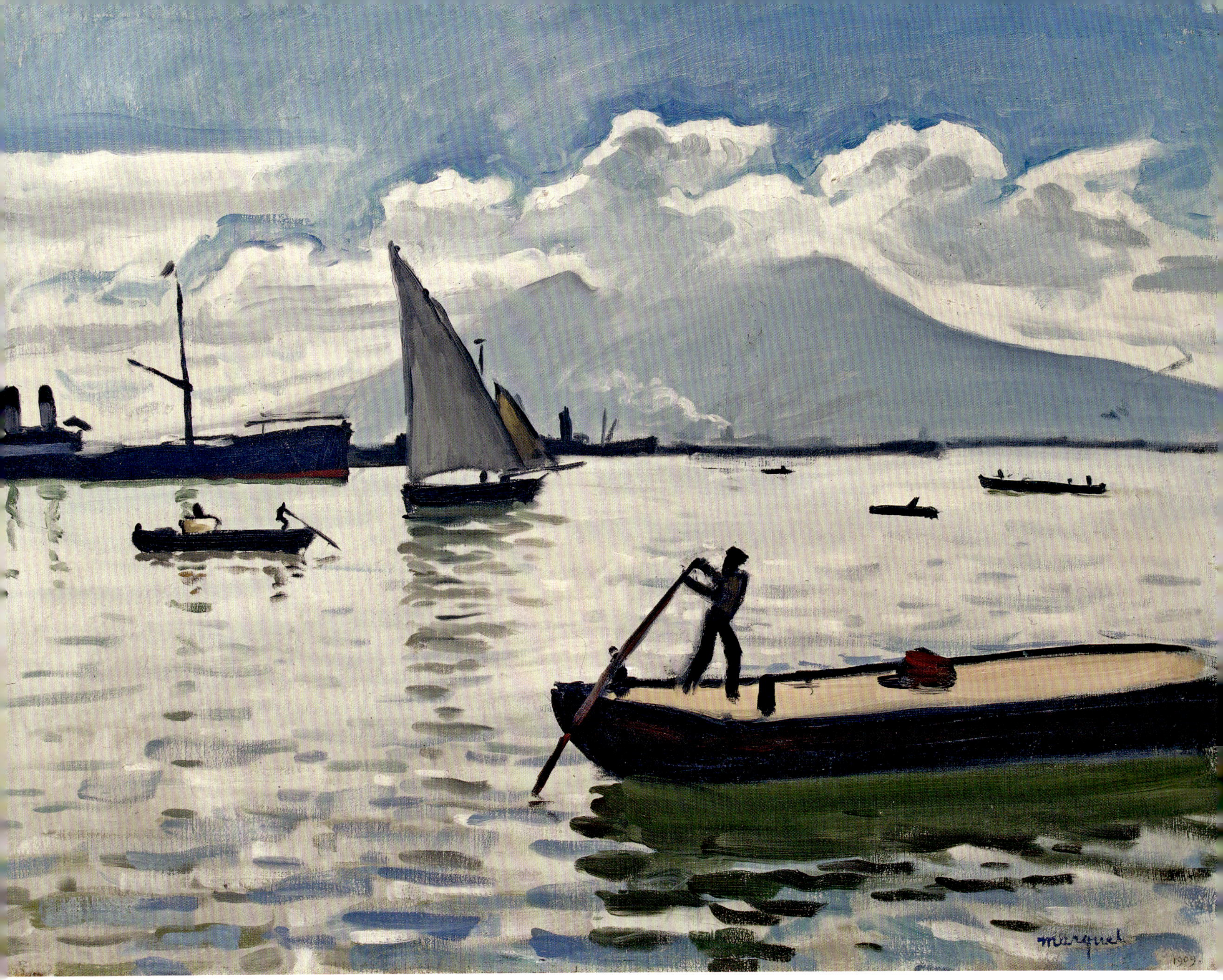

above: ALBERT MARQUET. *The Bay of Naples.* 1909. OIL ON CANVAS. $24\frac{3}{8} \times 31\frac{5}{8}$ IN. (62 × 80.3 CM).

Marquet traveled widely and was able to see many European cities through French eyes. A translucent light blue fills his vision of Naples with coolness and freshness; only the surface of the sea, whitened by the light and the sharp silhouettes of boats, reminds us of the bright, southern Italian sun.

opposite: ALBERT MARQUET. *The Place de la Trinité in Paris.* CA. 1911. OIL ON CANVAS. $31\frac{7}{8} \times 25\frac{3}{4}$ IN. (81 × 65.5 CM).

Marquet tames the throng of people—rare for him, but not at all for Paris—with orderly motion along the strictly drawn lines of the streets. The city is clearly more important for him than the human beings, and in the city the eternal is more important than the temporary. That is why everything, including the new buildings and the few indicators of modernity, fit into its smoothed, unshakeable silhouette.

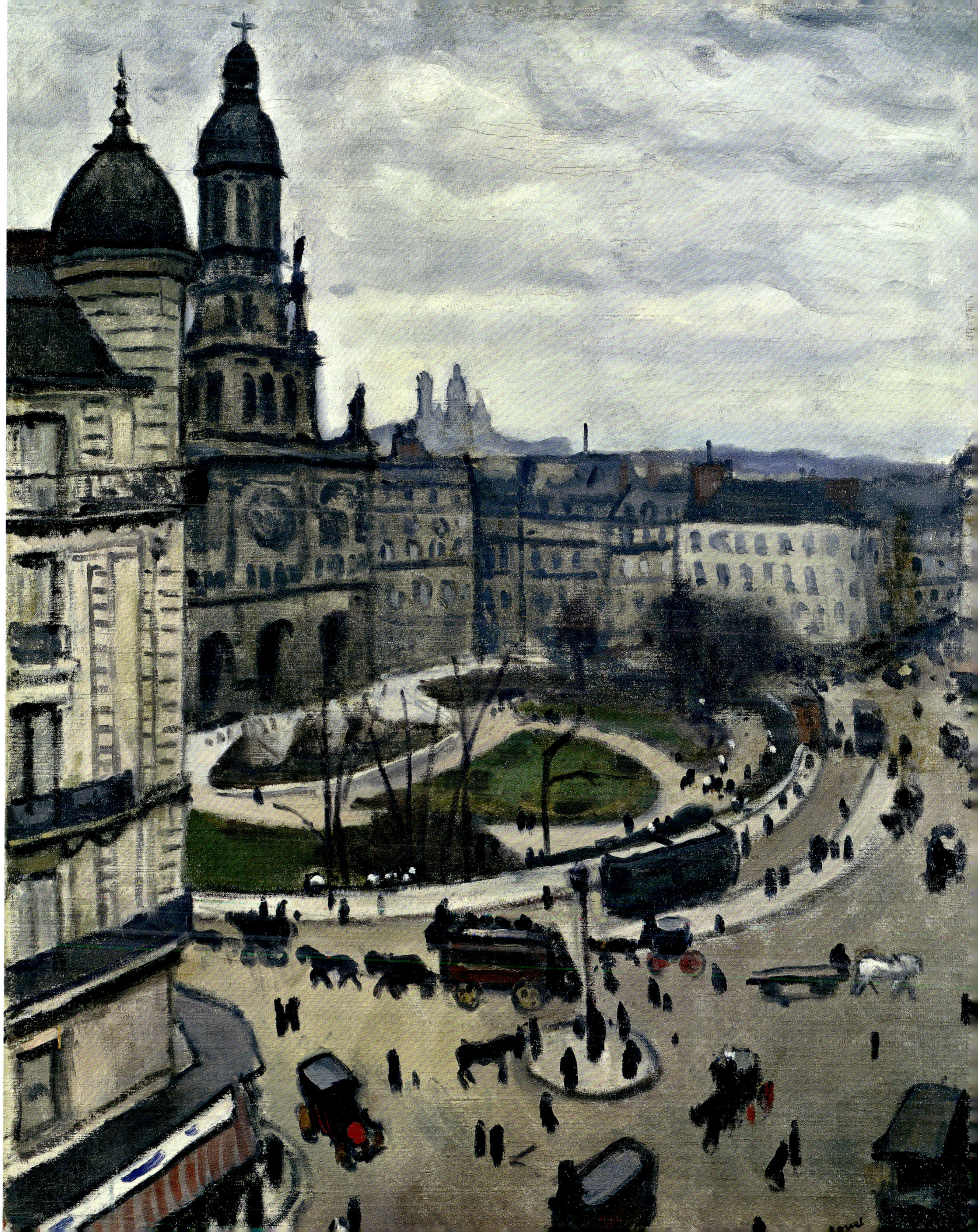

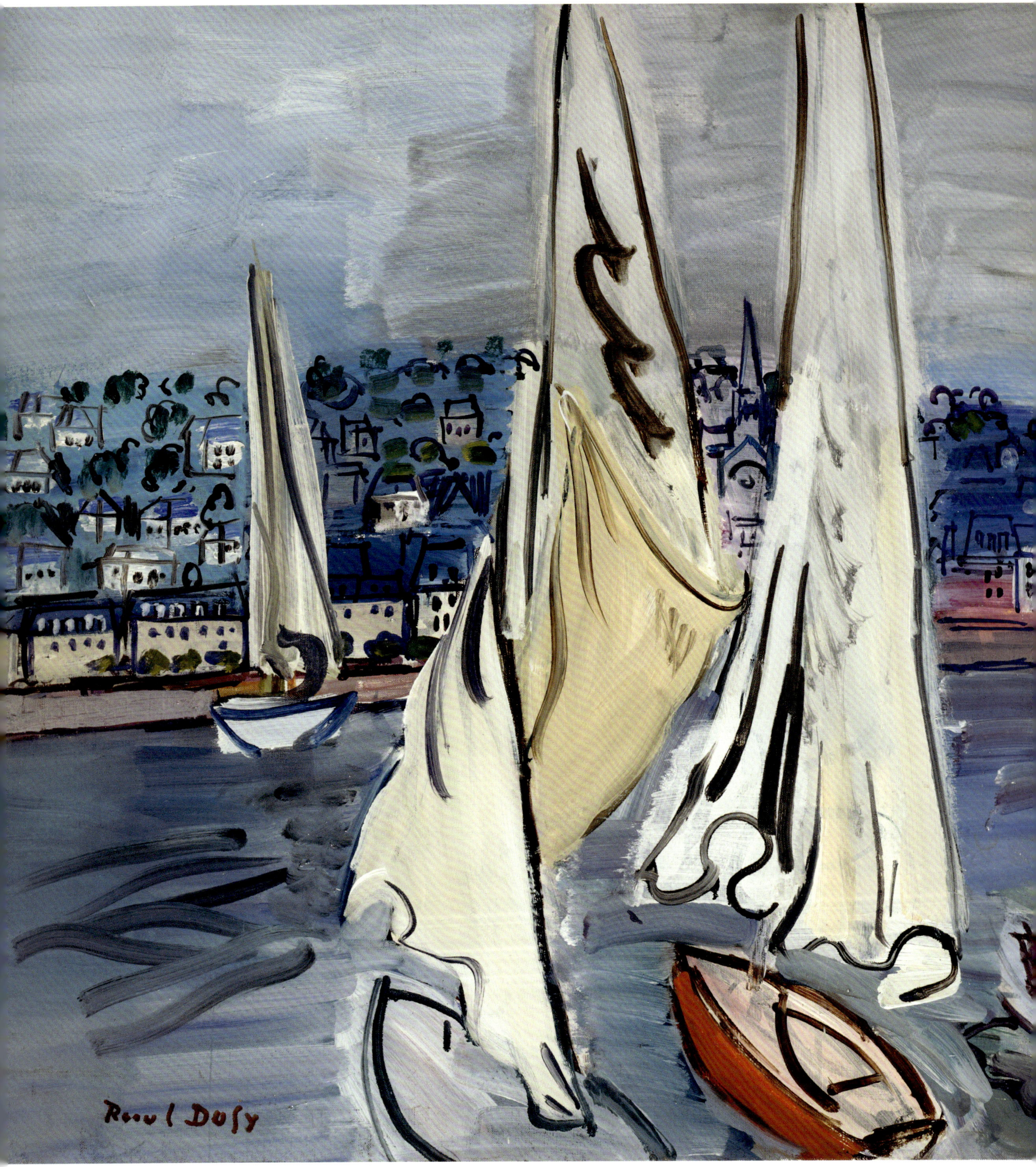
Raoul Dufy

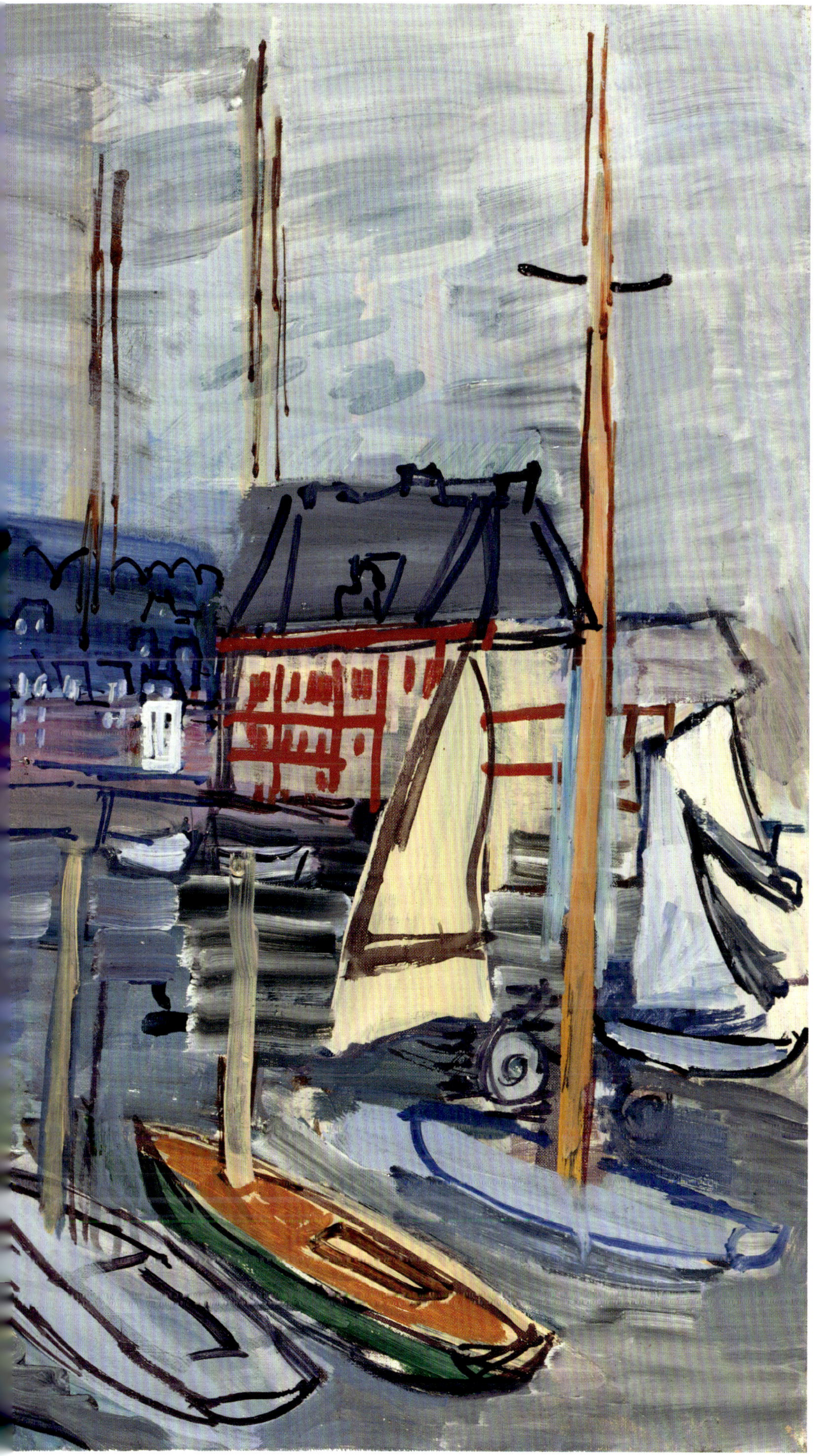

RAOUL DUFY. *Sailing Ships in Deauville Harbor.* CA. 1936. OIL ON CANVAS. $21^{1/4} \times 31^{7/8}$ IN. (54×80.8 CM).

In contrast to many of his contemporaries, Dufy never strove after thoroughness or expressive construction in a painting. With time his painting became less heavy. This exceptionally consistent evolution can easily be traced in the views of coastal towns in Normandy that this native of Le Havre painted in his youth.

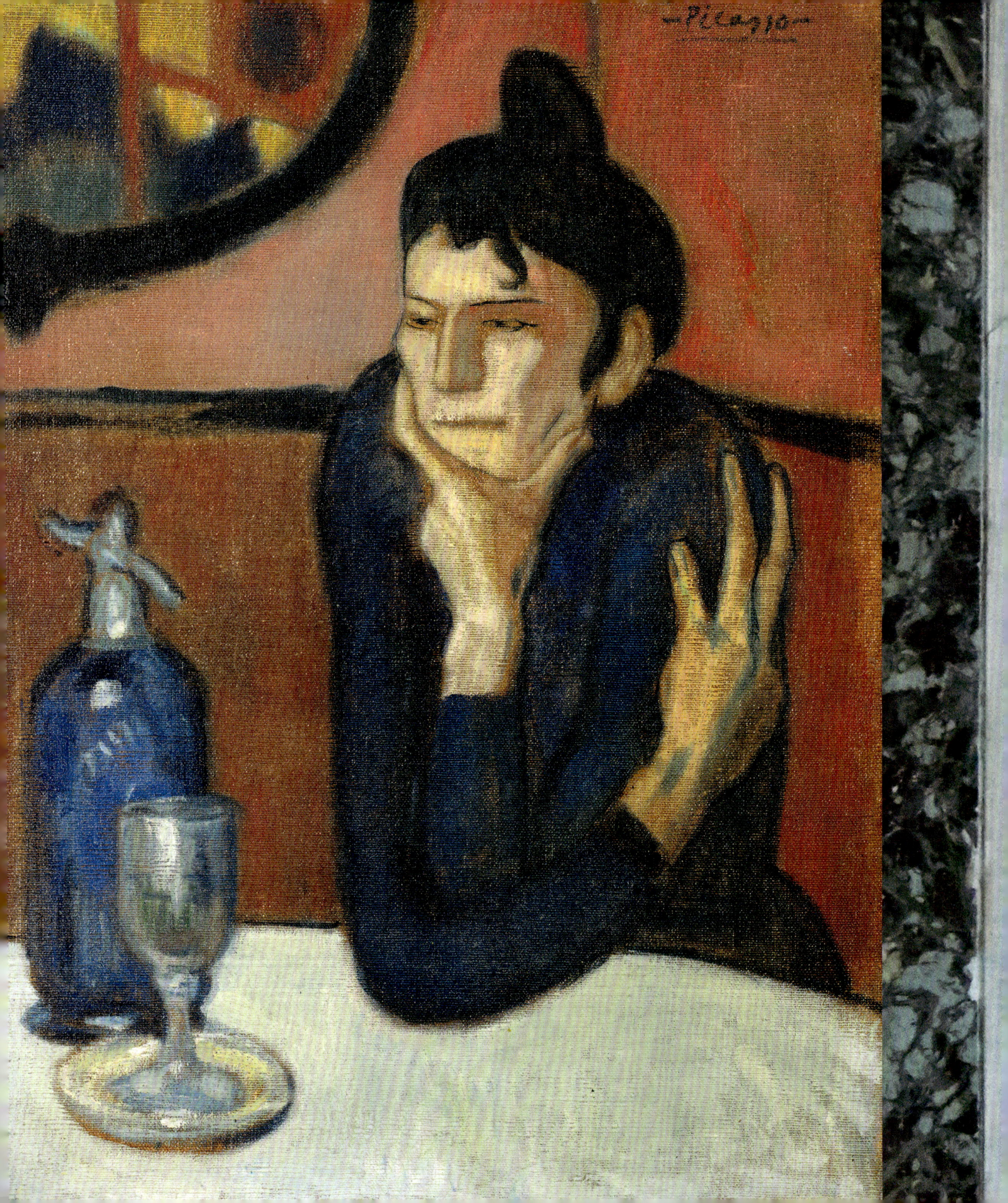
Picasso

THE EUROPEAN AVANT-GARDE

PABLO PICASSO. *The Absinthe Drinker.* 1901. OIL ON CANVAS. $28\frac{3}{4} \times 21\frac{1}{4}$ IN. (73×54 CM).

In May 1901 Picasso arrived in Paris for the second time, and until January of the following year, he worked in the studio of his friend Carlos Casagemas. He attracted the attention of critics after Ambroise Vollard organized an exhibition of his work in June. A variety of influences come together in Picasso's painting from this period, notably the expressive Symbolism of Edvard Munch and the social grotesques of Théophile Steinlen and Henri de Toulouse-Lautrec.

opposite: PABLO PICASSO. *Portrait of Benet Soler.* 1903. OIL ON CANVAS. $39\frac{3}{8} \times 28$ IN. (100×71 CM).

This portrait imbued with melancholia so typical of the painter's Blue Period is a reminder of his early work in Barcelona, of poverty and the longing for recognition that accompany a young artist. Benet Soler, Picasso's friend in those days, was a fashionable tailor who gave painters his attention and supported them with commissions. No wonder that in this canvas, the Spanish traits of Picasso's earlier manner are present: the pale face of a martyr; the tense, curving contours of the nose and fingers; and a sparkling glass of wine are reminiscent of the mystically distorted images in the paintings by Morales and El Greco.

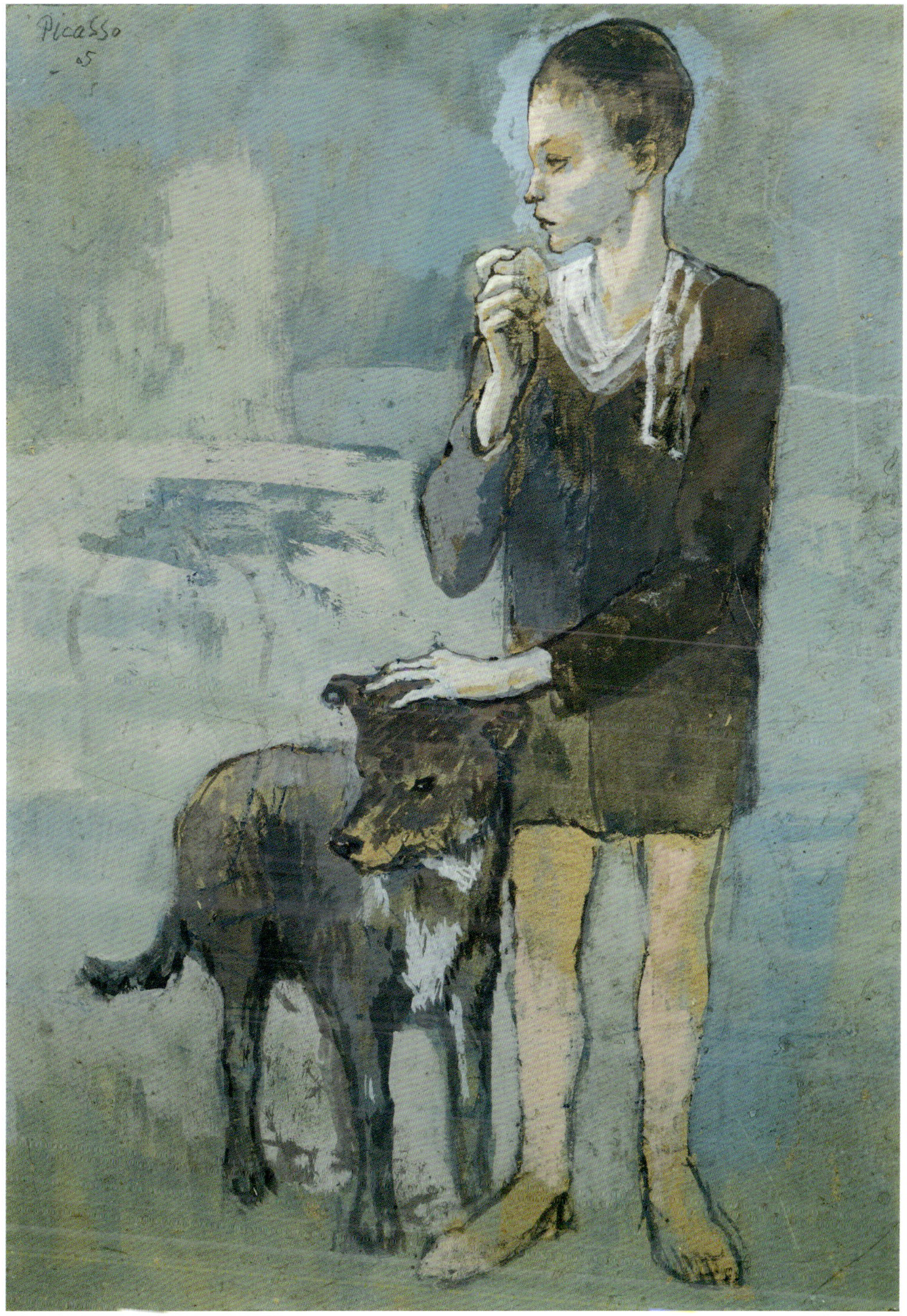

right: PABLO PICASSO. *Boy with a Dog.* 1905. PASTEL AND GOUACHE ON CARDBOARD. $22\frac{1}{2} \times 16\frac{1}{4}$ IN. (57.2×41.2 CM).

After moving to Paris in 1904, Picasso plunged into the French capital's tempestuous artistic life, living with his dog among the artistic community on Montmartre. The artist and his friends frequently amused themselves by visiting the nearby Circus Médrano, which undoubtedly influenced the subjects of his Rose period paintings. This pastel is a study for one of those, *The Family of Saltimbanques* (1905).

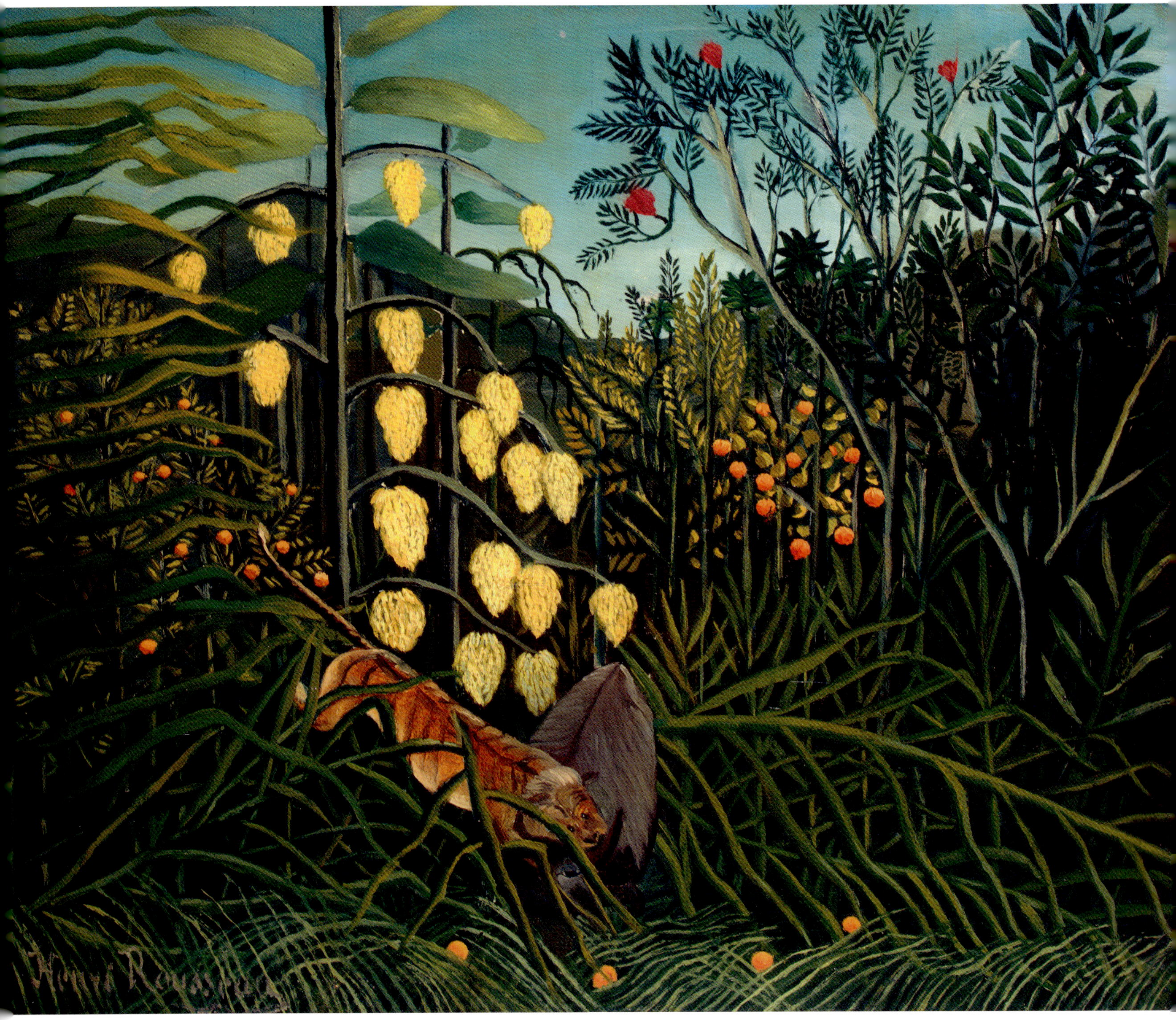

HENRI ROUSSEAU. *In a Tropical Forest. Struggle between a Tiger and a Buffalo.* 1908. OIL ON CANVAS. 18 1/8 × 21 5/8 IN. (46 × 55 CM).

It was Sergei Shchukin, a famous Russian art collector, who first noticed the works of "Le Douanier" (the customs inspector) Rousseau. Several years before, Rousseau's paintings had been extracted from obscurity and transported to the forefront of the avant-garde by Paris adepts of the new movement headed by Picasso and Apollinaire. In 1910–13, Shchukin bought seven paintings from the elderly artist, including this fantastic variation on the ancient theme of animal lacerations, the result of Rousseau's studies of illustrated magazines and his visits to the Paris Zoo.

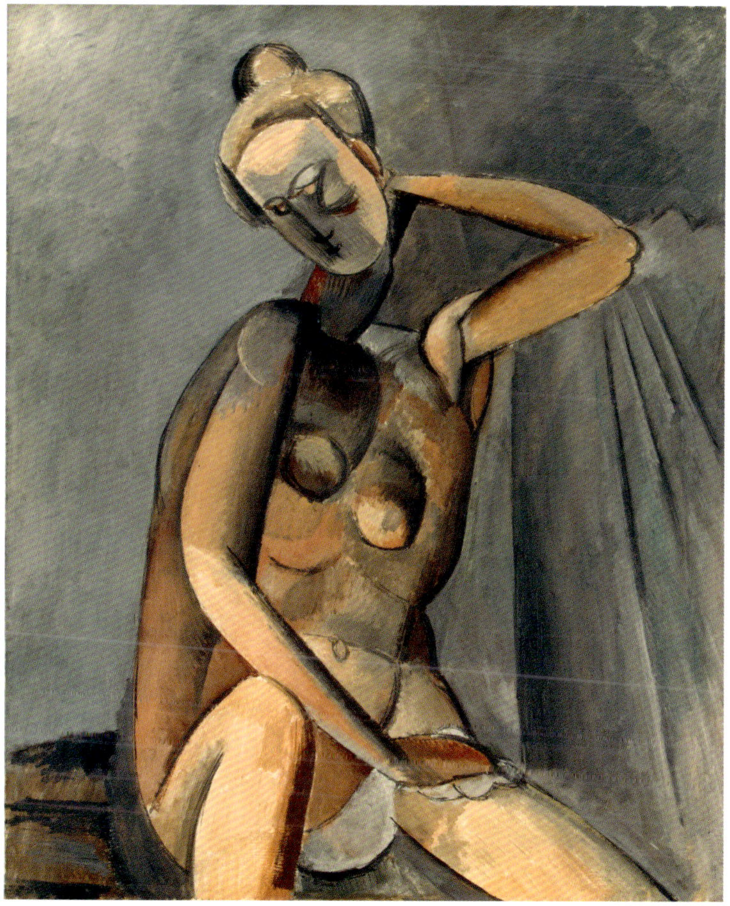

left: PABLO PICASSO. *Nude.* 1909. OIL ON CANVAS. 39 3/8 × 31 7/8 IN. (100 × 81 CM).

The device of combining two viewpoints, methodically implemented in this life study, is one that Picasso returned to often in his later career. With time this tour de force acquired more formal and decorative features. Yet here, in conjunction with the thorough molding of volumes, it seems to be a continuation of Ingres's anatomical experiments. Revealing the "interrupted motion" in the model's standard pose, it endows her body with a special materiality.

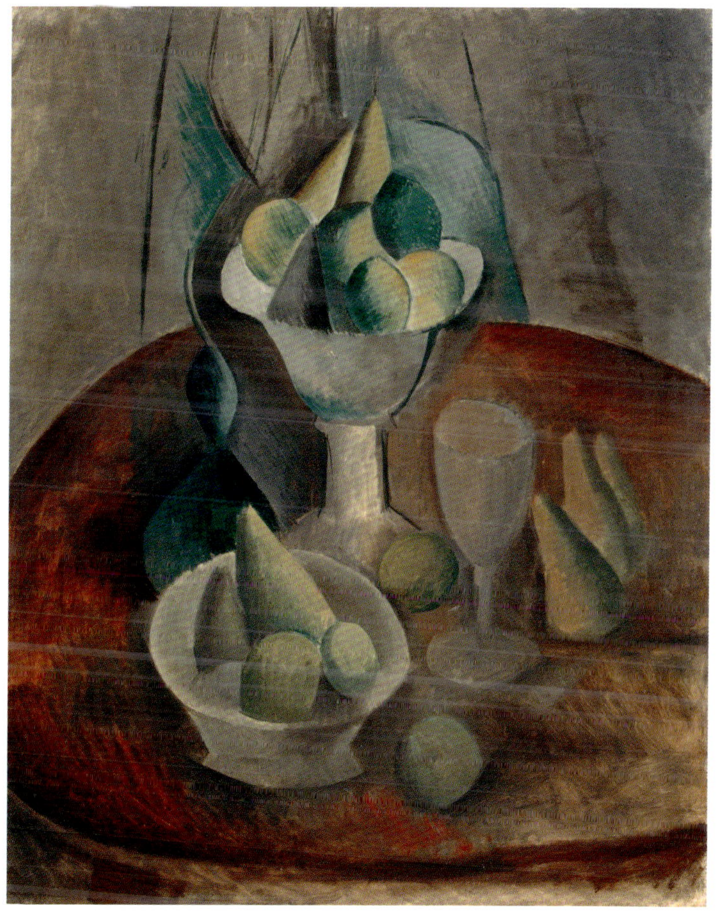

right: PABLO PICASSO. *Bowl of Fruit.* 1909. OIL ON CANVAS. 35 7/8 × 28 1/2 IN. (91 × 72.5 CM).

A few still lifes that Picasso painted in early 1909 make it possible to speak of him as a direct successor to Cézanne. "Everything comes from the sphere and cylinder," Cézanne told visitors to his studio in 1905. Precisely following this precept, Picasso "wraps" surfaces around the fruit and stresses the spherical basis of his space through the fanciful spiral of the bottle, which unites the elements and dissolves in space.

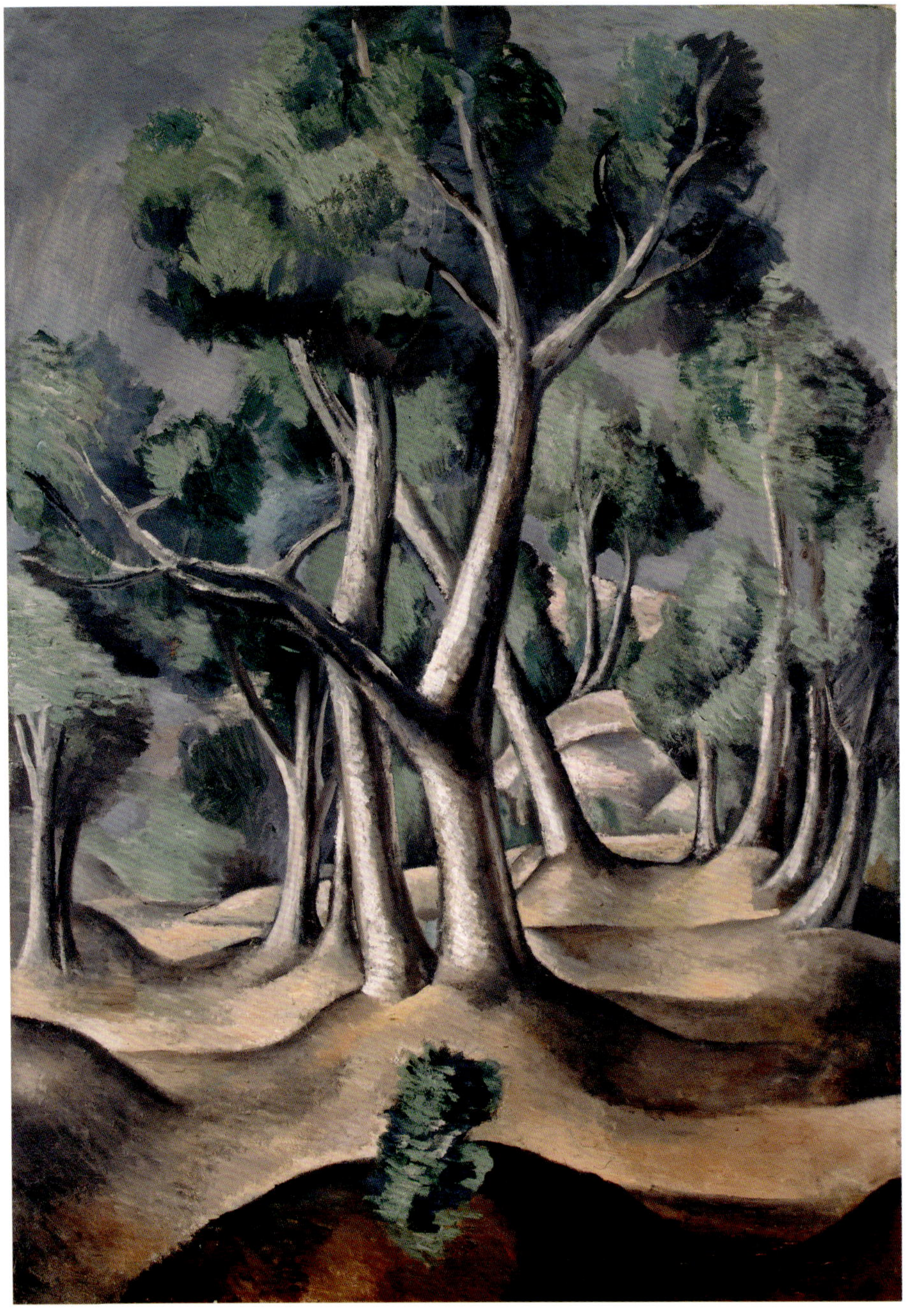

left: ANDRÉ DERAIN. *Grove.* 1912. OIL ON CANVAS. 45 7/8 × 32 IN. (116.5 × 81.3 CM).

Derain was one of the first to appreciate the originality of Rousseau's painting style and adopted some of his techniques, subordinating them to his pursuit of compositional clarity and constructional thoroughness. The smooth, rounded tree trunks, which Rousseau treated in a similar way to human figures, grow heavier in Derain's work and become threateningly alive, as does the earth mounded up by mysterious thrusts.

opposite: ANDRÉ DERAIN. *Harbor in Provence (Martigues).* 1913. OIL ON CANVAS. 55 1/8 × 35 IN. (140 × 89 CM).

In 1904–5, André Derain was among the founders of Fauvism. However, an early Neoclassical turn can be traced in his paintings, a shift that, in the second half of the 1910s, would not only become intrinsic for the majority of avant-garde painters but would also determine their quest during the next ten years. For Derain, its nature was of existential choice expressed in emotionally contrasting works—ominous claustrophobic portraits and landscapes like this one, but with a promise of peace and harmony.

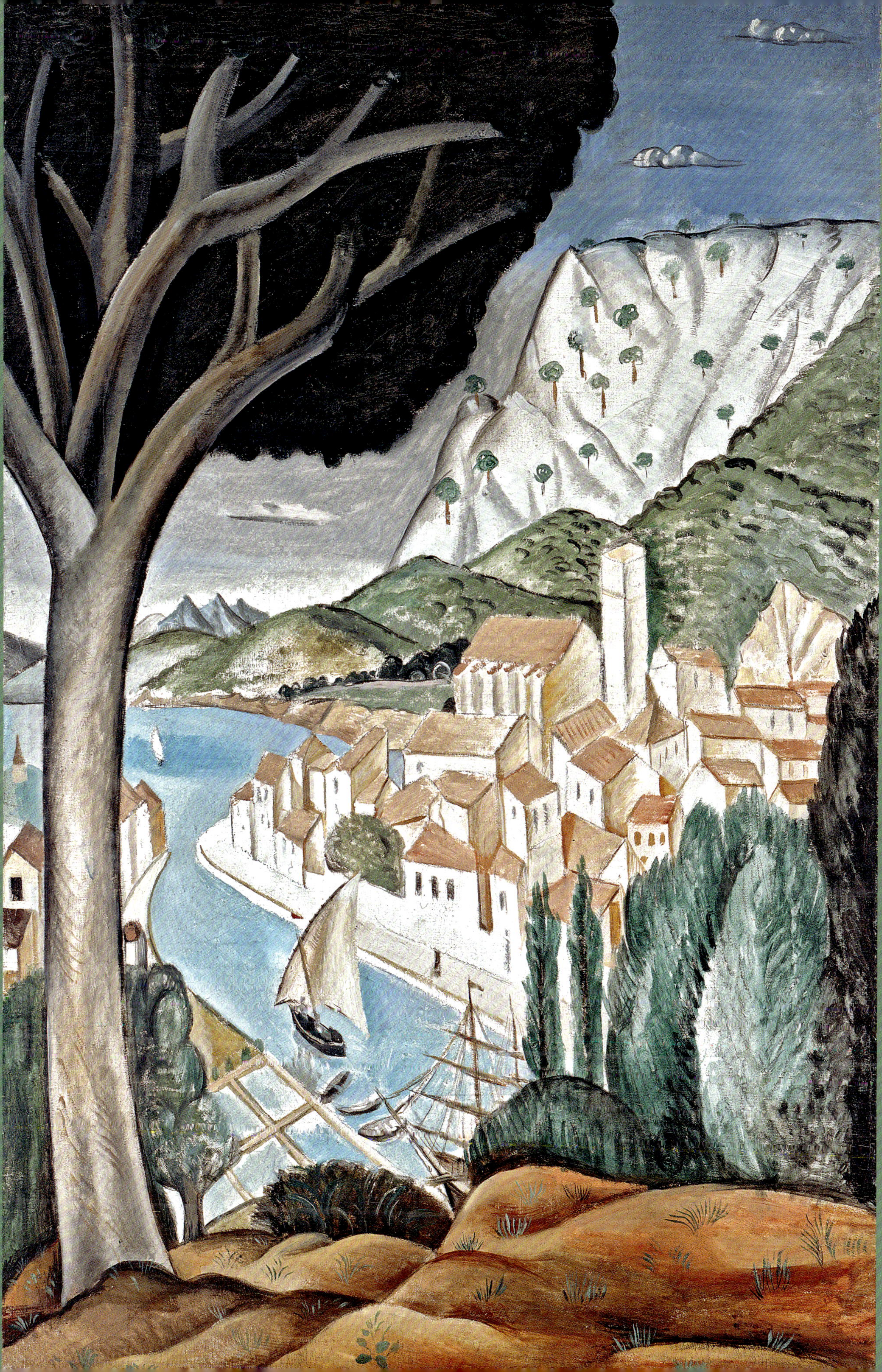

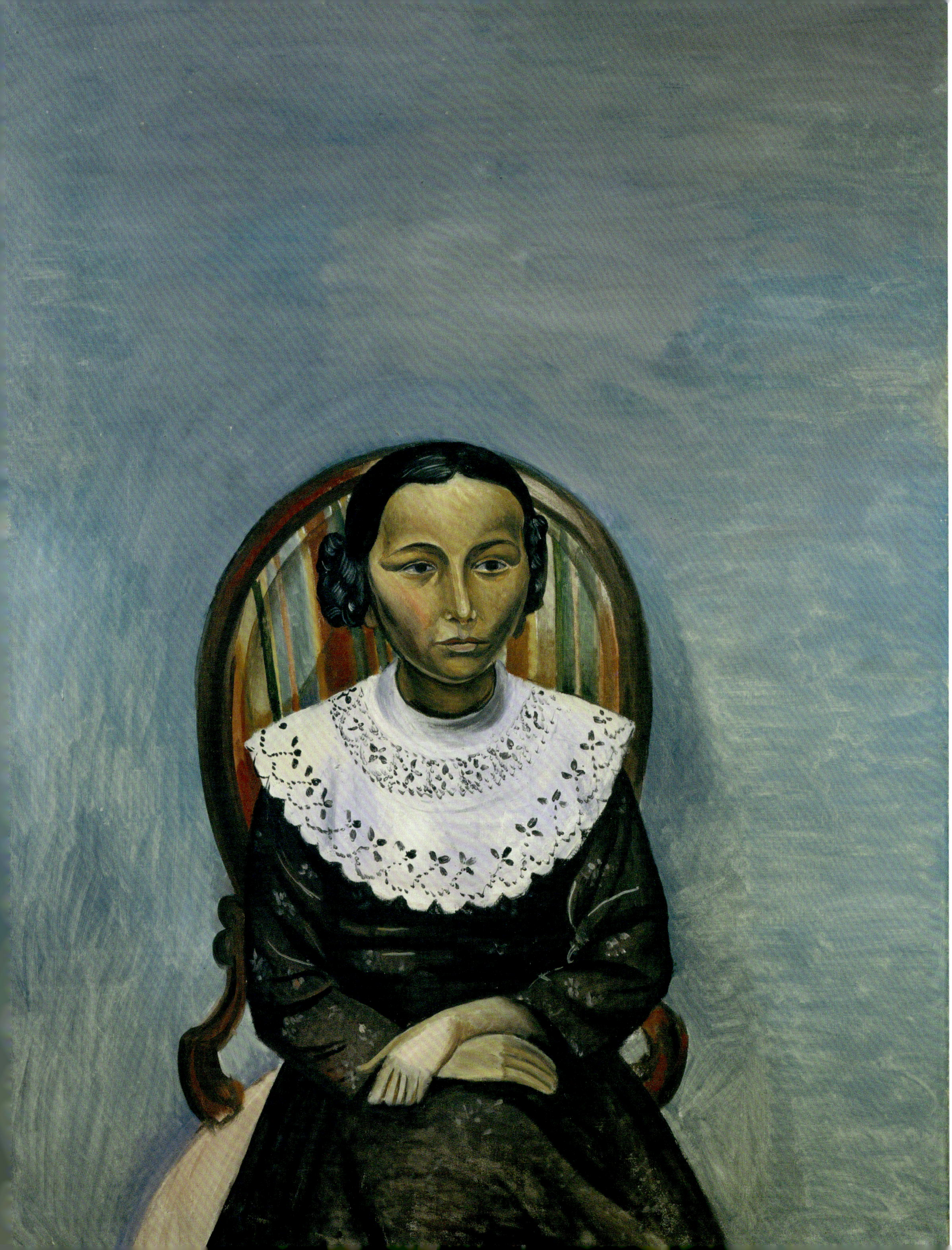

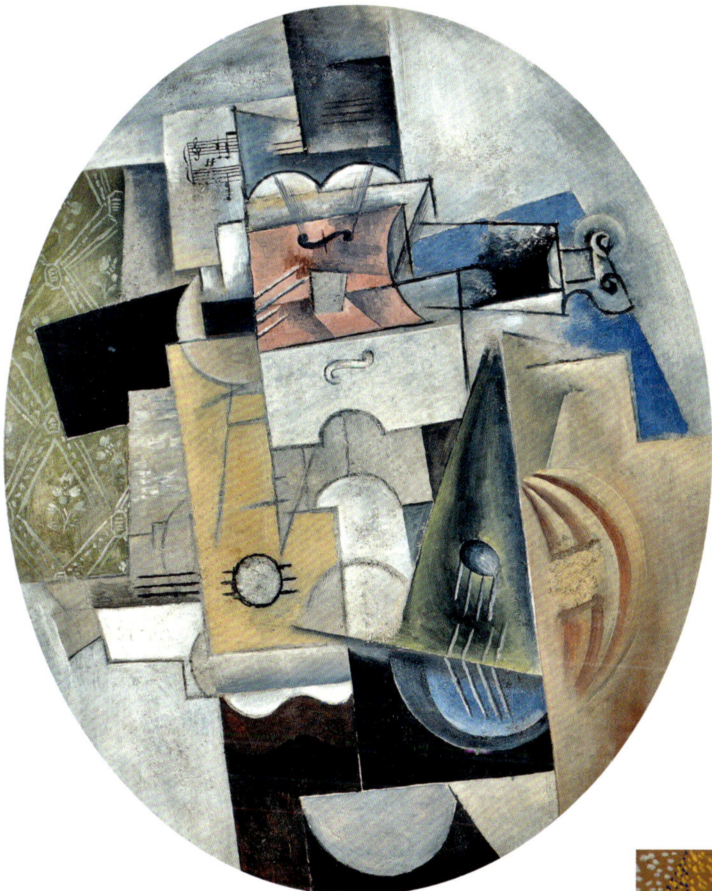

left: PABLO PICASSO. *Musical Instruments.* 1912. OIL, PLASTER, AND SAWDUST ON OILCLOTH. 38 1/2 × 35 3/8 IN. (98 × 90 CM).

The oval format, often found in Picasso's still lifes of 1912–14, may be a development of a theme he had already tried repeatedly—that of a table turned at right angles to the viewer. Now it is an operating table for the disassembly of the depiction into shape, color, texture, shadow, foreshortening, and other elements taken separately.

below: PABLO PICASSO. *Composition with a Cut Pear and a Bunch of Grapes.* 1914. CARDBOARD, COLLAGE ON BROWN PAPER, GOUACHE, DISTEMPER, GRAPHITE PENCIL, AND FIR SAWDUST. 26 5/8 × 20 1/2 IN. (67.6 × 52.2 CM).

Georges Seurat, who separated an image into spots, shows the viewer how he saw color. Picasso's fragmented shapes demonstrate how the same surface can appear to recede at one moment and protrude the next. In this collage, the only pasted-on paper element is the bunch of grapes. The different types of paper are drawn, everything is back to front, and the many shadows—effects of depth—reveal the multilayered surface. The artist's visiting card is stuck in among the layers.

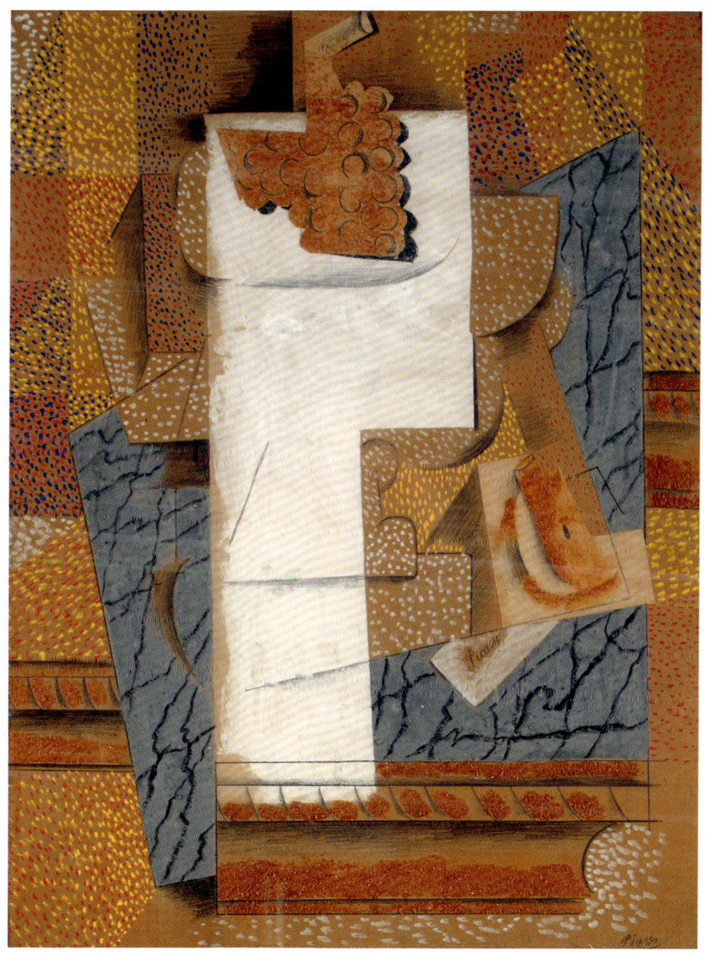

opposite: ANDRÉ DERAIN. *Portrait of a Girl in Black.* 1913–14. OIL ON CANVAS 45 × 34 5/8 IN. (114.5 × 88 CM).

Derain produced two known portraits of this model. This version's chief distinction is the even gray-blue background, which wraps tightly around the woman seated in an arm chair, an effect emphasized by the brushstrokes that outline her. An important role is played by the chair as well; precisely painted, it is large but clearly uncomfortable. The chair's austere refinement and the lace pattern of the subject's collar enhance a rather eerie impression of cold loneliness bordering on stupefaction.

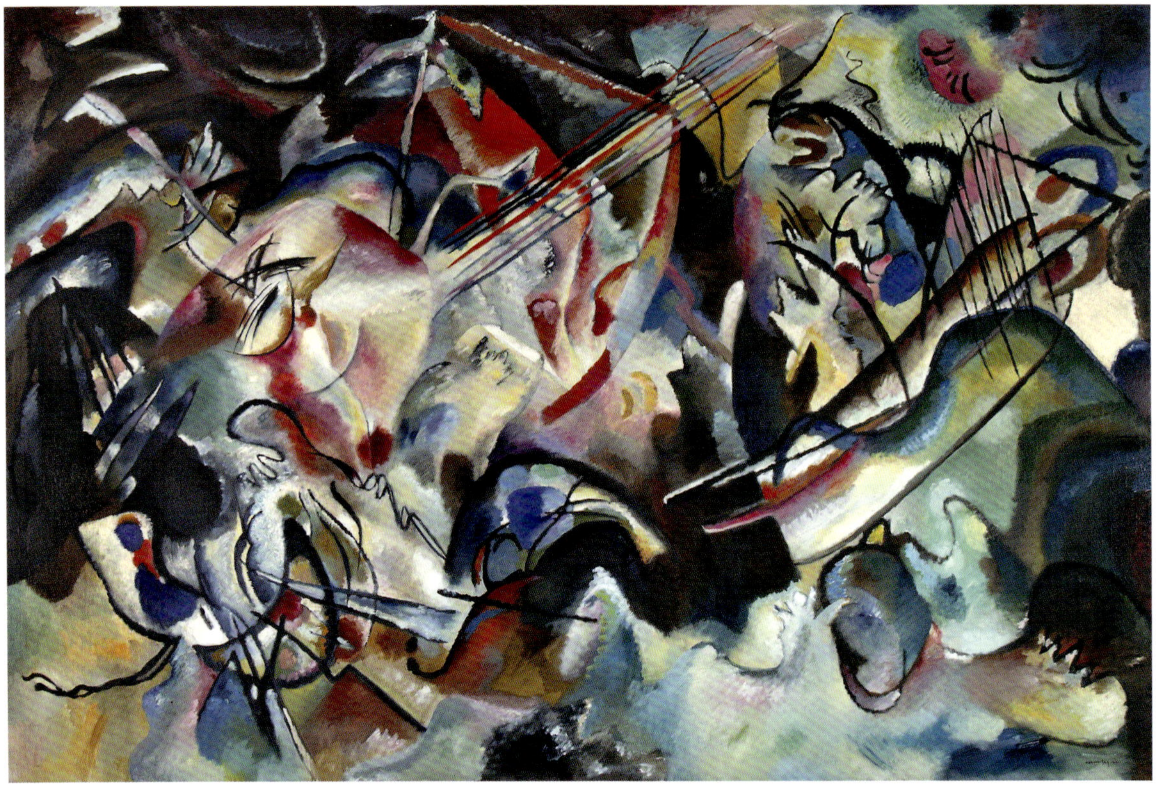

above: WASSILY KANDINSKY. *Composition VI.* 1913. OIL ON CANVAS. $76^{3}/_{8} \times 115^{3}/_{4}$ IN. (194 × 294 CM).

"A tremendous objectively occurring catastrophe is at the same time an absolute, independently sounding ardent song of praise, like a hymn to the new creation that follows the catastrophe." Thus, like the gradual unfolding of a piece of music, Kandinsky described this painting's content in a text specially devoted to it.

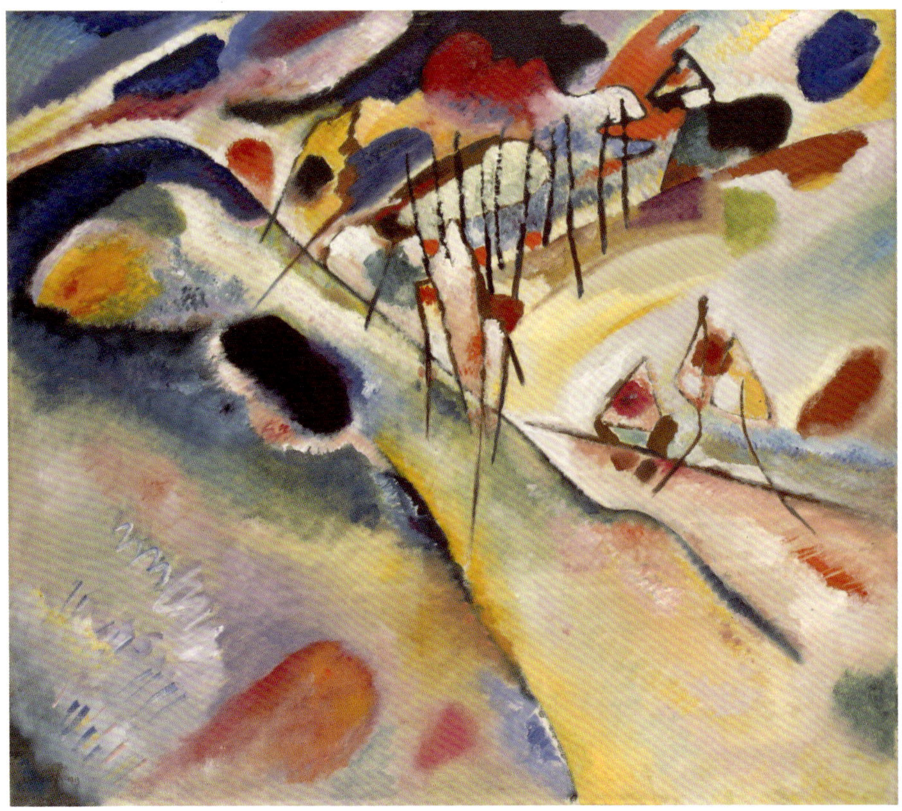

right: WASSILY KANDINSKY. *Landscape (Dünaberg near Murnau).* 1913. OIL ON CANVAS. $34^{5}/_{8} \times 39^{3}/_{8}$ IN. (88 × 100 CM).

In Kandinsky's mature work, the practical and the theoretical are inseparable. In practice, he proceeds from a physical (most often landscape) motif to the refinement of a sensual response to it. In theory, he seeks the exact meaning of every color and line with a particular direction and shape, creating a sort of musical notation for his painted composition.

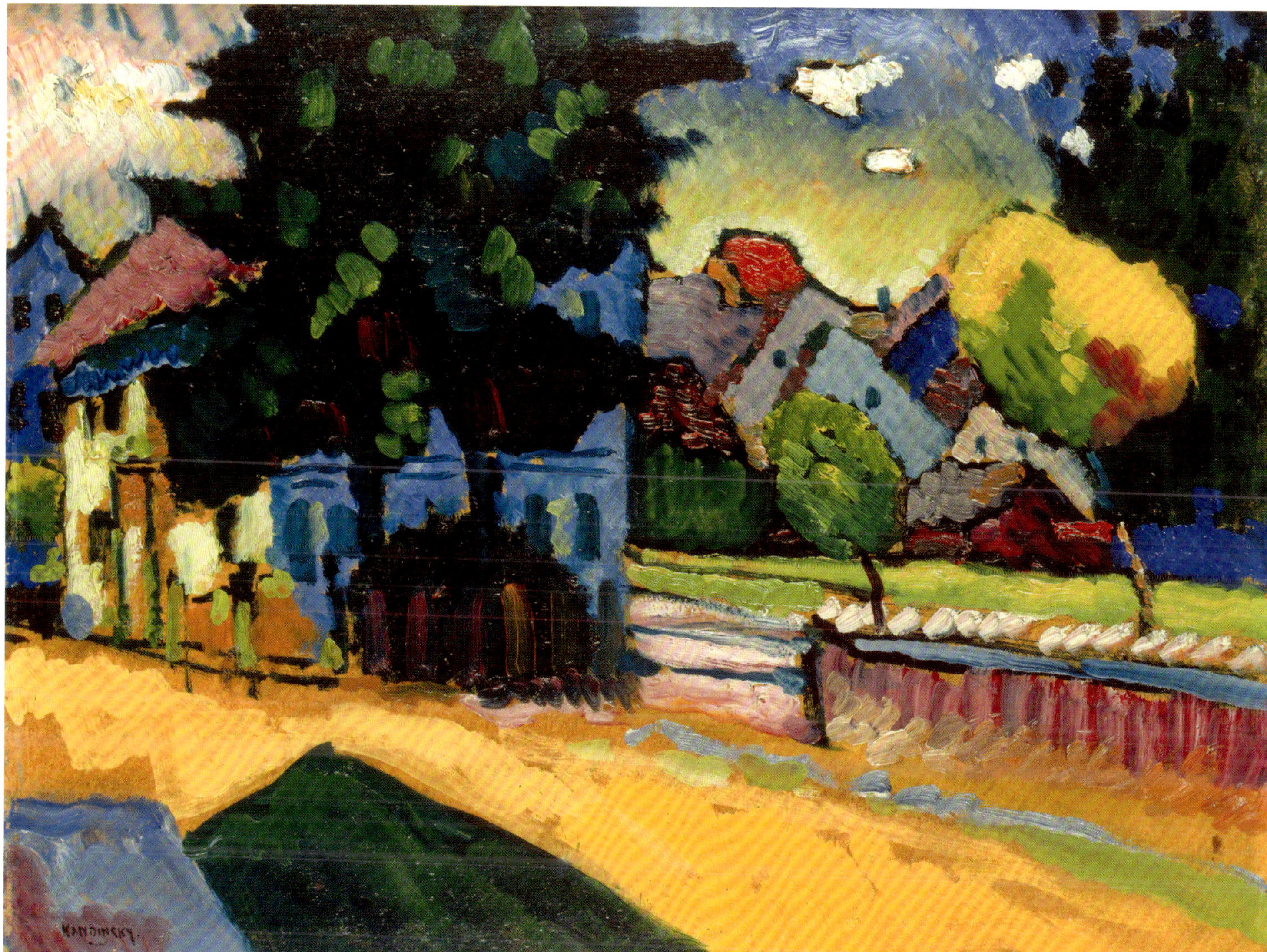

WASSILY KANDINSKY. *Murnau—Study for Landscape with Green House.* 1908. OIL ON CANVAS. 13 × 17 3/8 IN. (33 × 44 CM).

It was the youthful shock of the "inner life" of colors that led Kandinsky, at age thirty, to decide that painting was his true vocation. In less than two years in Murnau, the Bavarian Alpine village where he rented a house, he traveled the road that brought him to abstraction. A fascination with painting on glass, inspired by local folk tradition, helped him to realize the ornamental power of line while, in his landscapes, color was gradually liberated from objective restrictions.

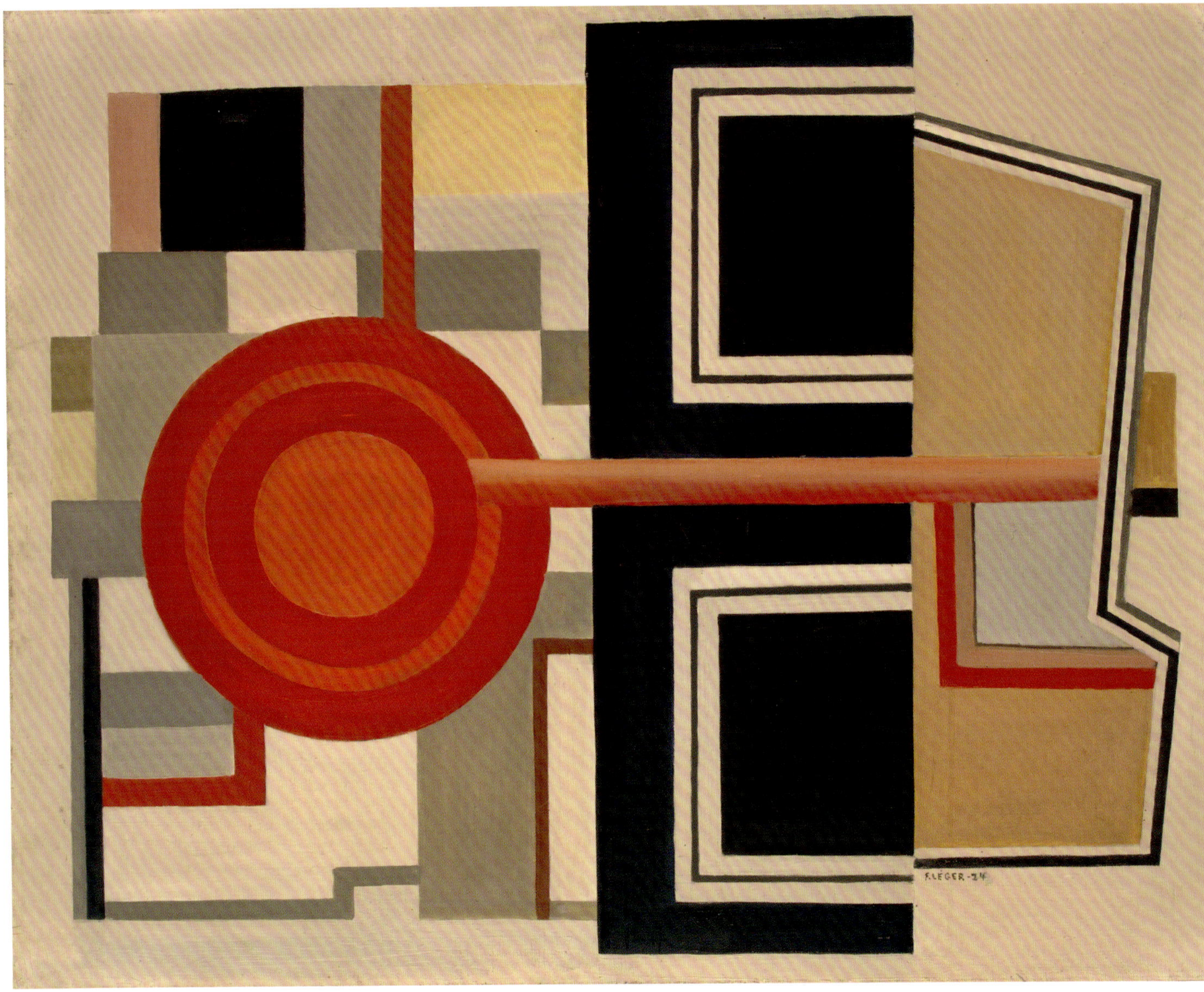

above: FERNAND LÉGER. *Composition.* 1924. OIL ON CANVAS. 28 3/4 × 36 1/4 IN. (73 × 92 CM).

An admirable image of the world of machines—and not its direct imitation, as with the Futurists—was the goal of Léger, who was fascinated by both industrial aesthetics and the pure colors of Jacques-Louis David's compositions. His "techno-classicism" is one of the most striking phenomena in French art of the 1920s, which was marked by a shift away from radical experimentation toward balanced clarity.

opposite: FERNAND LÉGER. *Postcard.* BETWEEN 1932 AND 1948. OIL ON CANVAS. 36 1/4 × 25 1/2 IN. (92 × 65 CM).

For the avant-garde artists of the late 19th and early 20th centuries, articles of mass culture became inspirational objects worthy of depiction. Léger went further, and for him the creation of such a seemingly insignificant thing became a respectable goal for art. The proximity of the women "assembled" from simple standard details and a stamp bearing a classic portrait of a woman's head seem to express the continuity of the tradition of artistically enhancing the world: the artist's credo.

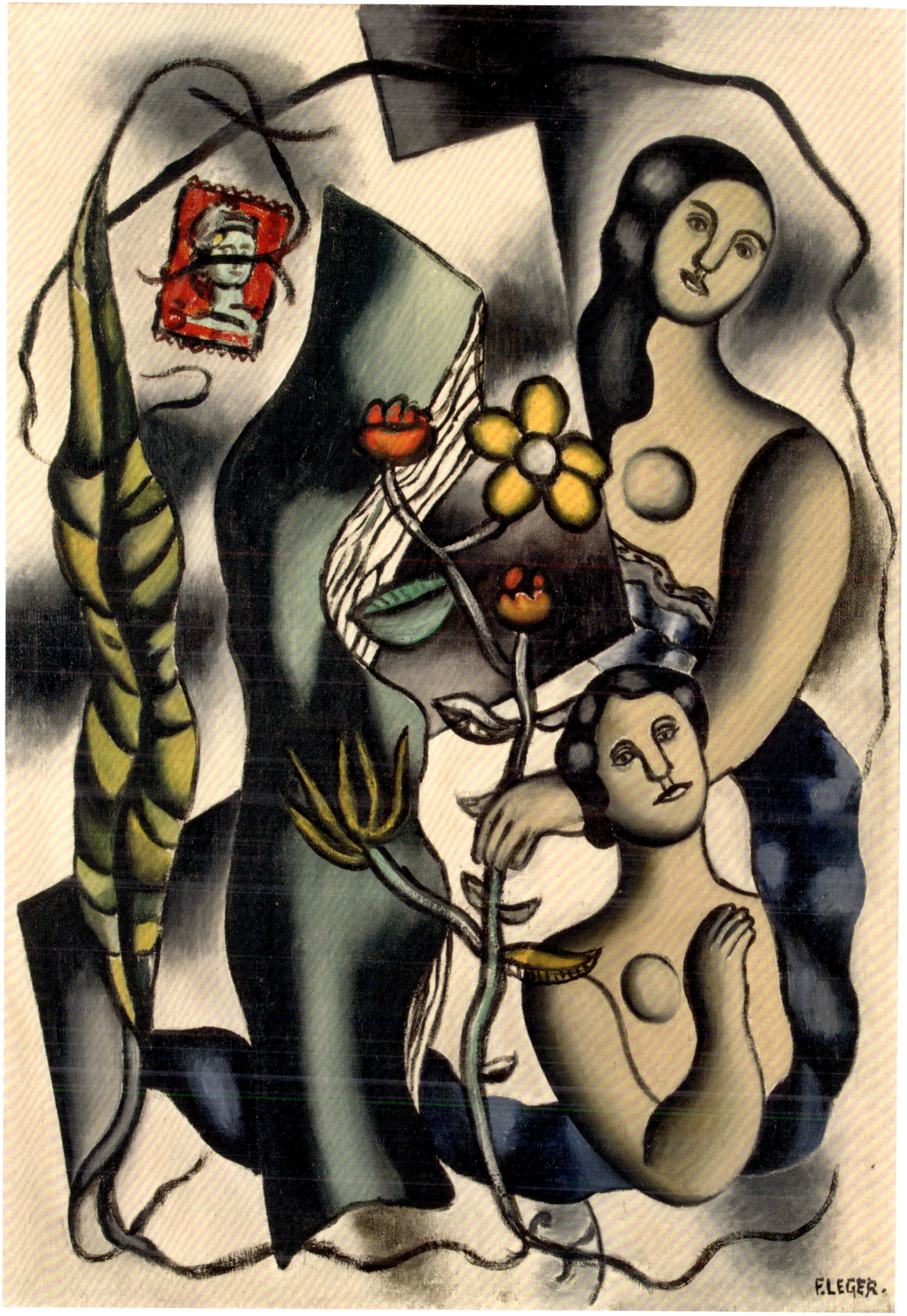
F.LEGER.

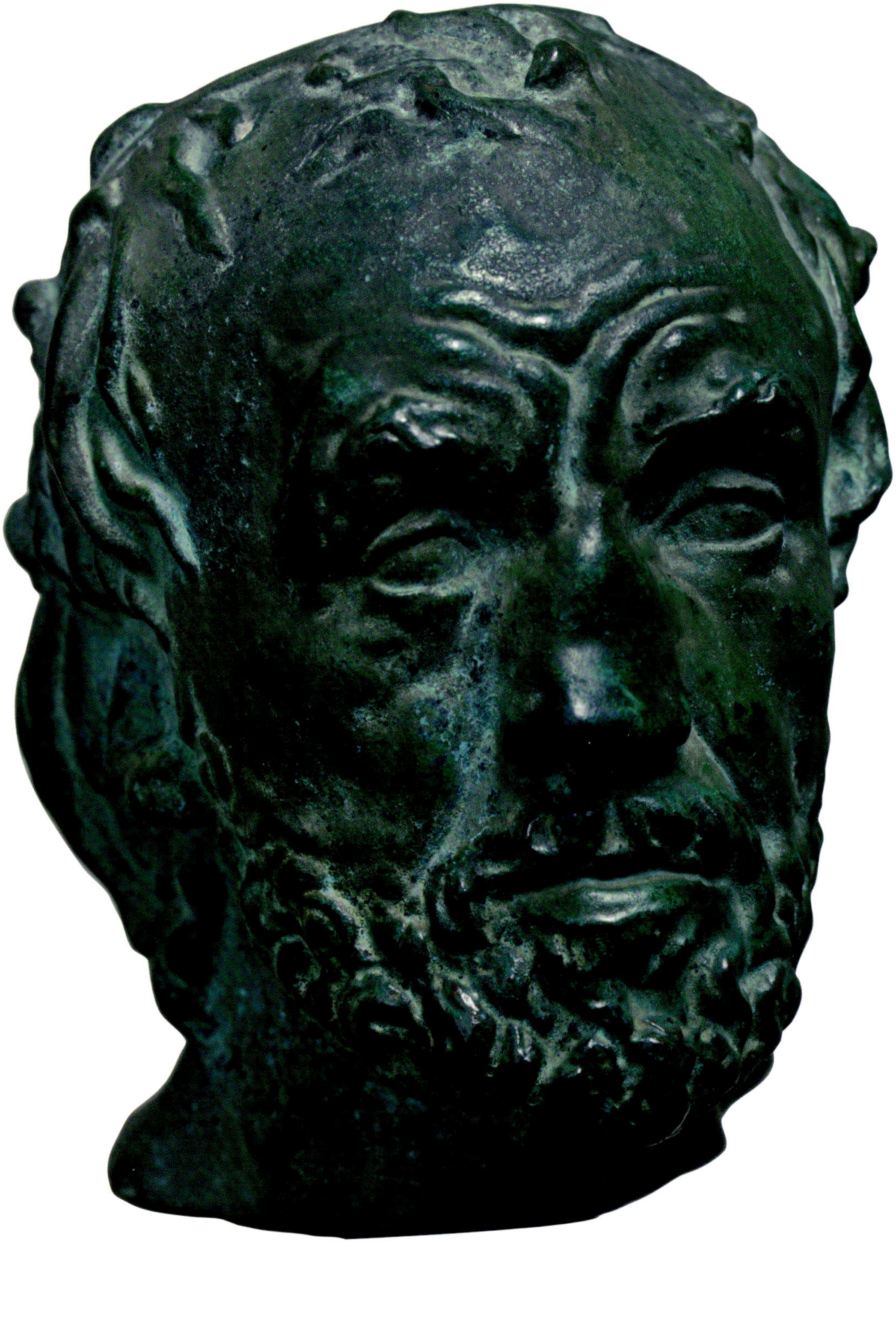

Western European Sculpture, 19th–Early 20th Century

AUGUSTE RODIN. *Man with a Broken Nose.* 1863–64. BRONZE. 23 5/8 IN. (60 CM) HIGH

Far from hindering Rodin from creating a striking artistic image, imperfection and asymmetry here make up its very foundation, conjuring the words of Renoir, who in one of his few theoretical declarations called on artists to follow the law of asymmetry as "the basic law of nature." Rodin discovered it for himself almost by accident—in the face of a tramp known as Bibi. The sculptor was struck by his appearance and invited him to work as a model.

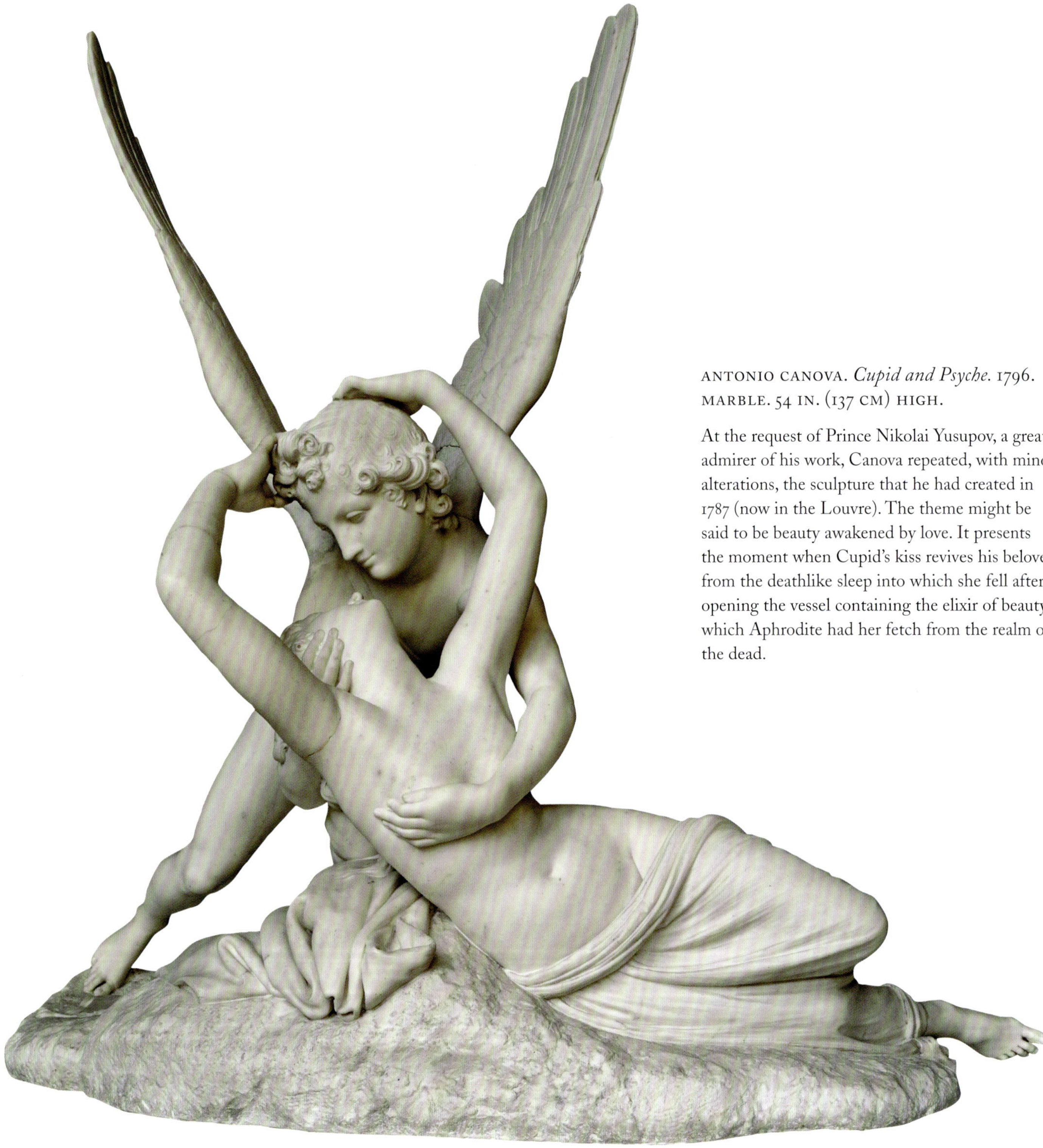

ANTONIO CANOVA. *Cupid and Psyche.* 1796. MARBLE. 54 IN. (137 CM) HIGH.

At the request of Prince Nikolai Yusupov, a great admirer of his work, Canova repeated, with minor alterations, the sculpture that he had created in 1787 (now in the Louvre). The theme might be said to be beauty awakened by love. It presents the moment when Cupid's kiss revives his beloved from the deathlike sleep into which she fell after opening the vessel containing the elixir of beauty, which Aphrodite had her fetch from the realm of the dead.

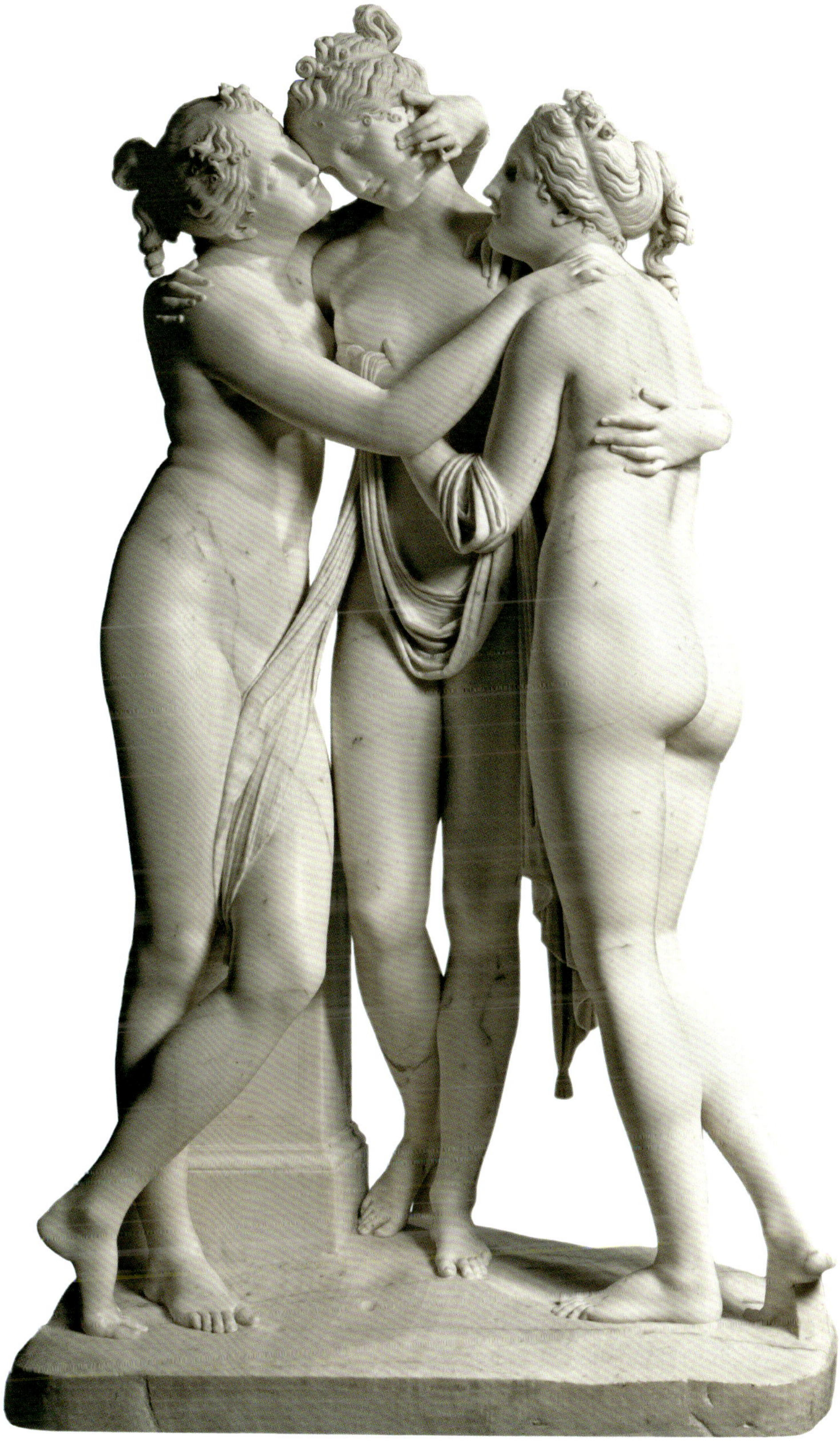

ANTONIO CANOVA. *Three Graces.* BETWEEN 1813 AND 1816. MARBLE. $71^{5}/_{8}$ IN. (182 CM) HIGH.

Canova's Neoclassicism is unusual in that it is free of both the quotation from ancient sources at the expense of plastic expressiveness (seen in Mengs and Thorvaldsen) and the loading of classical subjects and forms with contemporary ideas (found in David). The departure from the Greek schema, with two graces facing the viewer and the third looking away, seems dictated by the sculptor's striving to increase the complexity of the linear harmony and to fill the sculpture with a play of light.

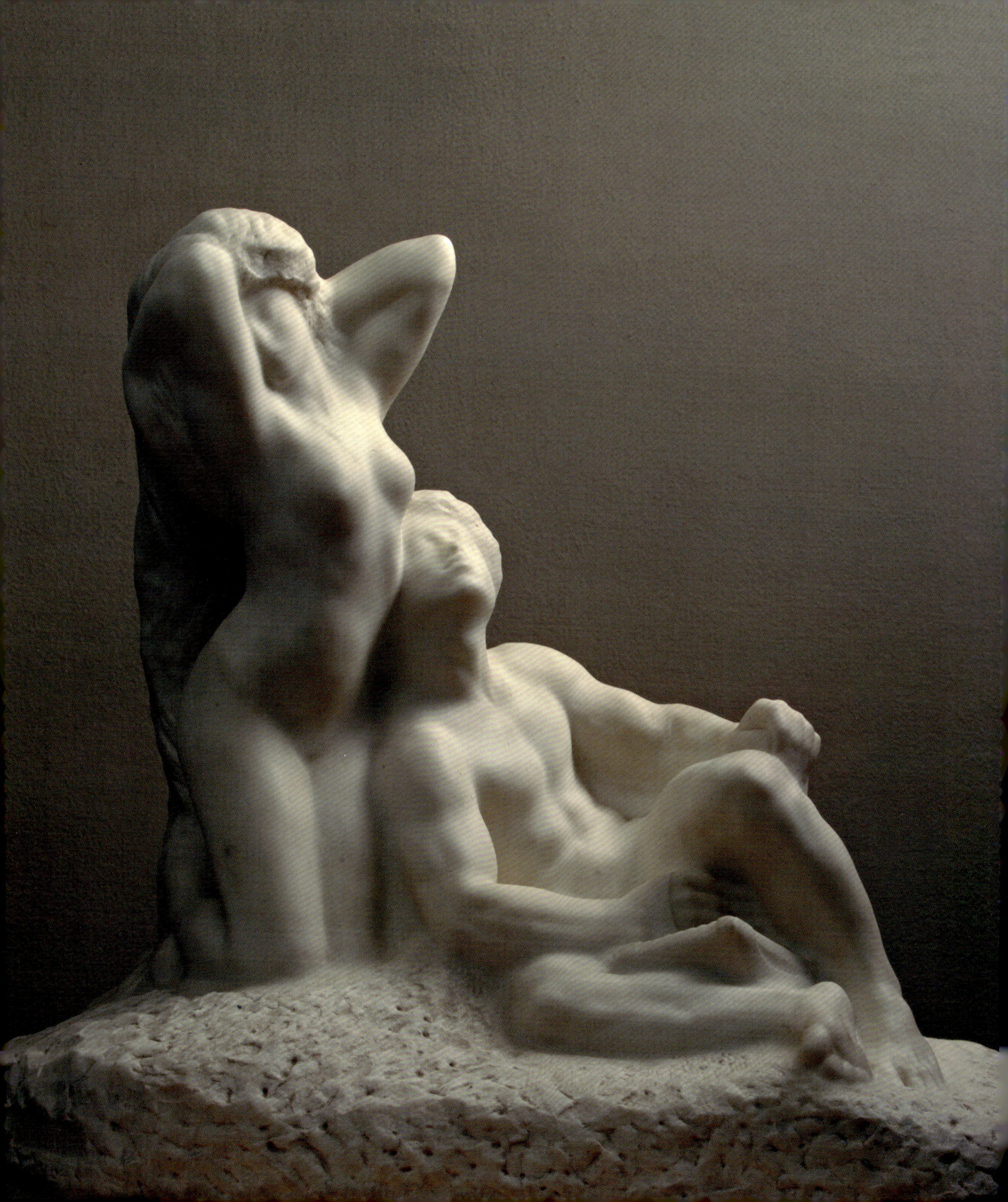

opposite: AUGUSTE RODIN. *Reveries (The Poet and the Muse).* CA. 1905. MARBLE. 24 7/8 IN. (63 CM) HIGH.

The male-female couple is among the central themes in Rodin's work. The German poet Rainer Maria Rilke, an admirer of the sculptor and his personal secretary in 1905–6, astutely observed that "the places of strongest contact are the beginning and culmination of his works; where something new arises, he sets to work and devotes all his skill to the mysterious phenomena that accompany the making of a new thing." In this case, poetic inspiration is such a thing.

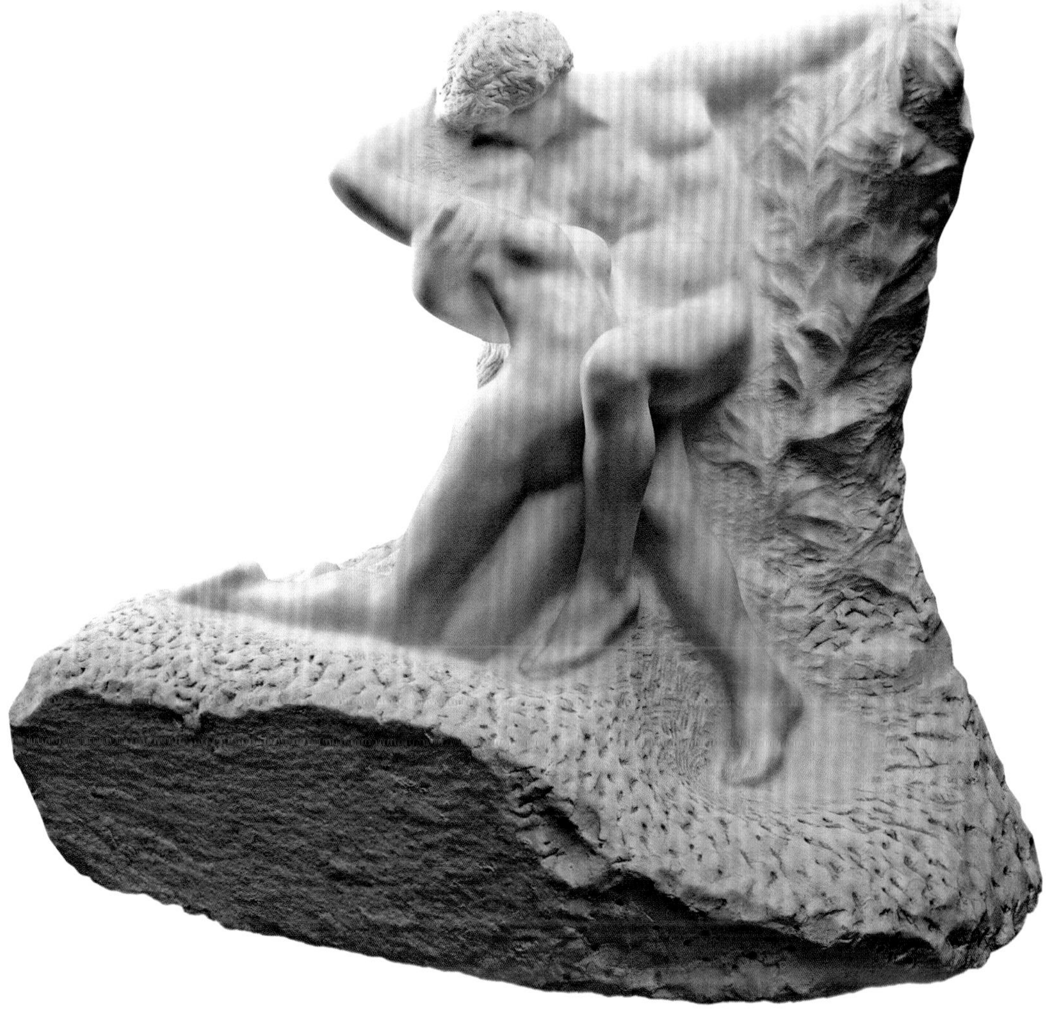

above: AUGUSTE RODIN. *Eternal Spring.* SECOND STATE; AFTER 1897. MARBLE. 30 3/8 IN. (77 CM) HIGH.

As part of *The Gates of Hell*, Rodin also intended to include a depiction of lovers condemned to eternal torments. This idea became the basis for many of his sculptures devoted to passion. The combination it proposed—of pleasure and torment, instantaneous ecstasy and eternity—proved exceptionally in tune with his striving to show a moment of swift movement and a paroxysm of emotion.

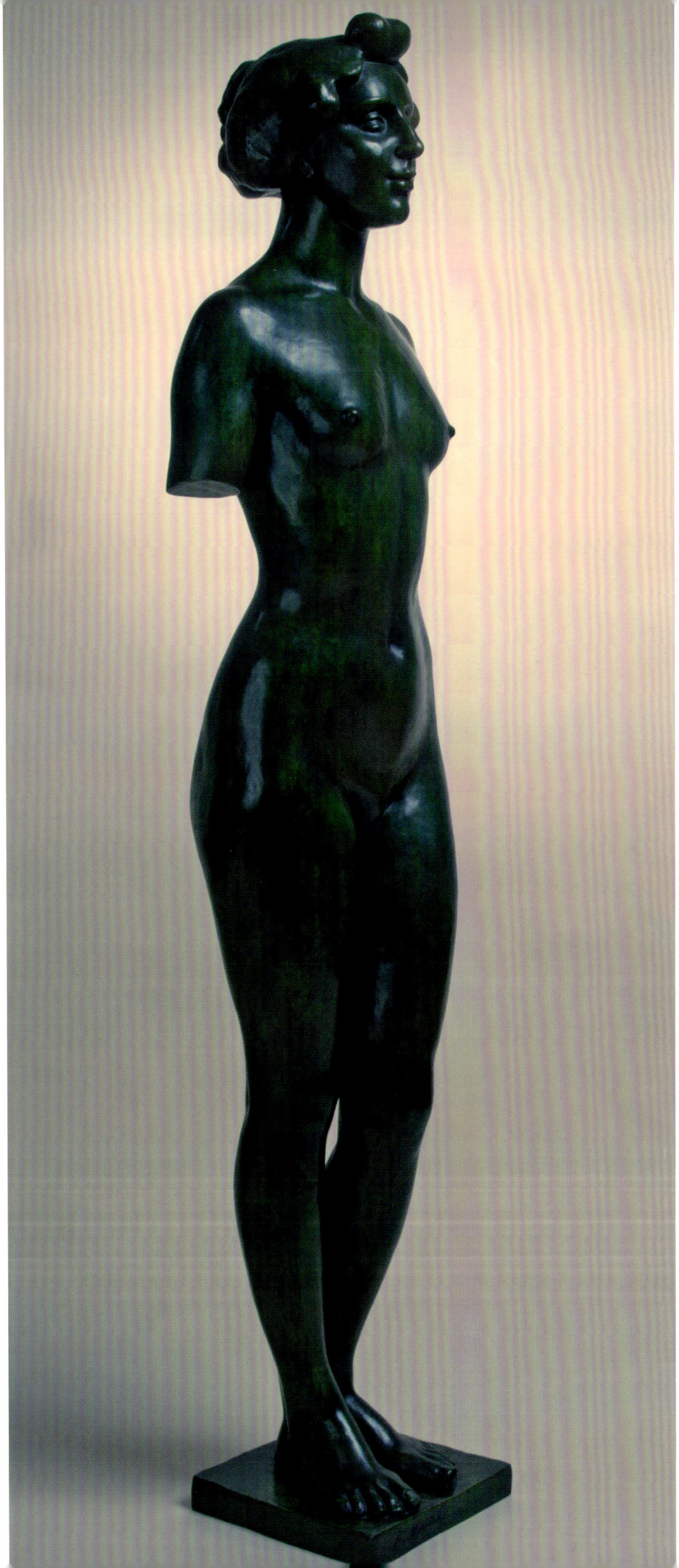

ARISTIDE MAILLOL. *Spring*. 1911.
BRONZE. $66\frac{1}{2}$ IN. (169 CM) HIGH.

This statue was intended for the music room in Ivan Morozov's Moscow mansion, where it would complement the decorative panels of *The Story of Psyche* painted by Maurice Denis. Where the latter reproduced an ancient subject in detail, modernizing it with a playful decorativeness, Maillol rejected any indications of a subject and, with an eye to ancient prototypes (the head was clearly inspired by Livia in the Louvre), produced an image of beautiful eternity.

Credits

INDEX

Note: Illustrations are indicated by page numbers in italic type.

PAGE 1: *The Raphael Loggias in the New Hermitage.*

PAGES 2–3: *The Gallery of the History of Ancient Painting in the New Hermitage.*

PAGE 4: REMBRANDT HARMENSZ. VAN RIJN. *Flora.* 1634. OIL ON CANVAS. 49¼ × 39¾ IN. (125 ×101 CM).

The twenty-eight-year-old-year-old Rembrandt depicted his bride, Saskia van Uylenburgh, in the guise of Flora. The flowers that adorn the classical goddess's hair and twine around her staff are almost the only ones in the artist's oeuvre, and although they are painted in a masterly manner, their role remains secondary. Along with the elegantly gleaming fabrics of Saskia's dress, they are details of a spiritual portrait of a young woman.

PAGES 6–7: *The Tent-Roofed Room in the New Hermitage.*

PAGE 8: PIETRO PERUGINO (PIETRO VANUCCI). *St. Sebastian.* BETWEEN 1493 AND 1494. TEMPERA AND OIL ON PANEL. 21⅛ ×15½ IN. (53.8 ×39.5 CM).

According to legend, Sebastian, a captain of the Praetorian Guard under Emperor Diocletian, was sentenced to death for his Christian faith. The Emperor's soldiers tied him to a post and shot arrows at him. Traditionally Italian artists depicted the full figure of Sebastian, but Perugino's painting shows only the upper part of the young man's figure and his face lit up by prayer. The artist wrote his own name in gold on the arrow that runs through the saint's neck.

PAGE 9: ANTHONY VAN DYCK. *Self-Portrait.* CA. 1622–23. OIL ON CANVAS. 45⅞ ×36⅞ IN. (116.5 ×93.5 CM).

After honing his natural talent in Rubens's studio, in the early 1620s van Dyck began his career as a society portraitist in Genoa, taking commissions from the local aristocracy while studying the legacy of the Renaissance masters. The young artist's haughty pose shows unshakable self-confidence, which had a good foundation: his style was already brilliant, both figuratively and literally. His virtuoso brush invests everything—from the material of the cloak to the glowing youthful skin—with the luster of solid prosperity.

PAGES 10–11: *The Large Skylight Hall in the New Hermitage.*

PAGE 12: JAMES COX. *The Peacock Clock.* BRITAIN. 1779–81. BRONZE, SILVER, STRASSES; GILDED.

The famous *Peacock Clock* was made by the most celebrated creator of mechanisms, the London jeweler and goldsmith James Cox. When it strikes the hour, the figures go into motion: the peacock spreads its tail, the owl turns its head, and the cockerel crows. The time is shown by figures in the cap of a large mushroom. This fantastic timepiece was bought by Prince Potemkin in 1780.

First published in the United States of America in 2014 by
Rizzoli Electa, a division of Rizzoli International Publications, Inc.
300 Park Avenue South
New York, NY 10010
www.rizzoliusa.com

Published in coordination with
ARCA Publishers
43 Moika Emb.
St. Petersburg, 191065, Russia

For ARCA Publishers:
Project Coordinator: Olga Borodyanskaya, Polina Yermakova
Editor of Russian text: Alexey Shestakov
Translation from Russian: Paul Williams
Translation Editor: Nina Zhutovsky
Photographers of The State Hermitage Museum:
Leonard Heifetz, Yury Molodkovets, Vladimir Terebenin, Valery Zubarov
Photographer of museum interiors: Max Gaskelberg (pages 1, 2–3, 6–7, 10–11, 14–15, 18–19)

For Rizzoli Electa:
Associate Publisher: Margaret Rennolds Chace
Project Manager: Giulia Di Filippo
Project Editor: Susan Homer
Book design by David Skolkin

2021 2022 2023 2024 / 10 9 8 7 6 5 4

Printed in China

ISBN-13: 978-0-8478-4209-4

Library of Congress Catalog Control Number: 2013957336

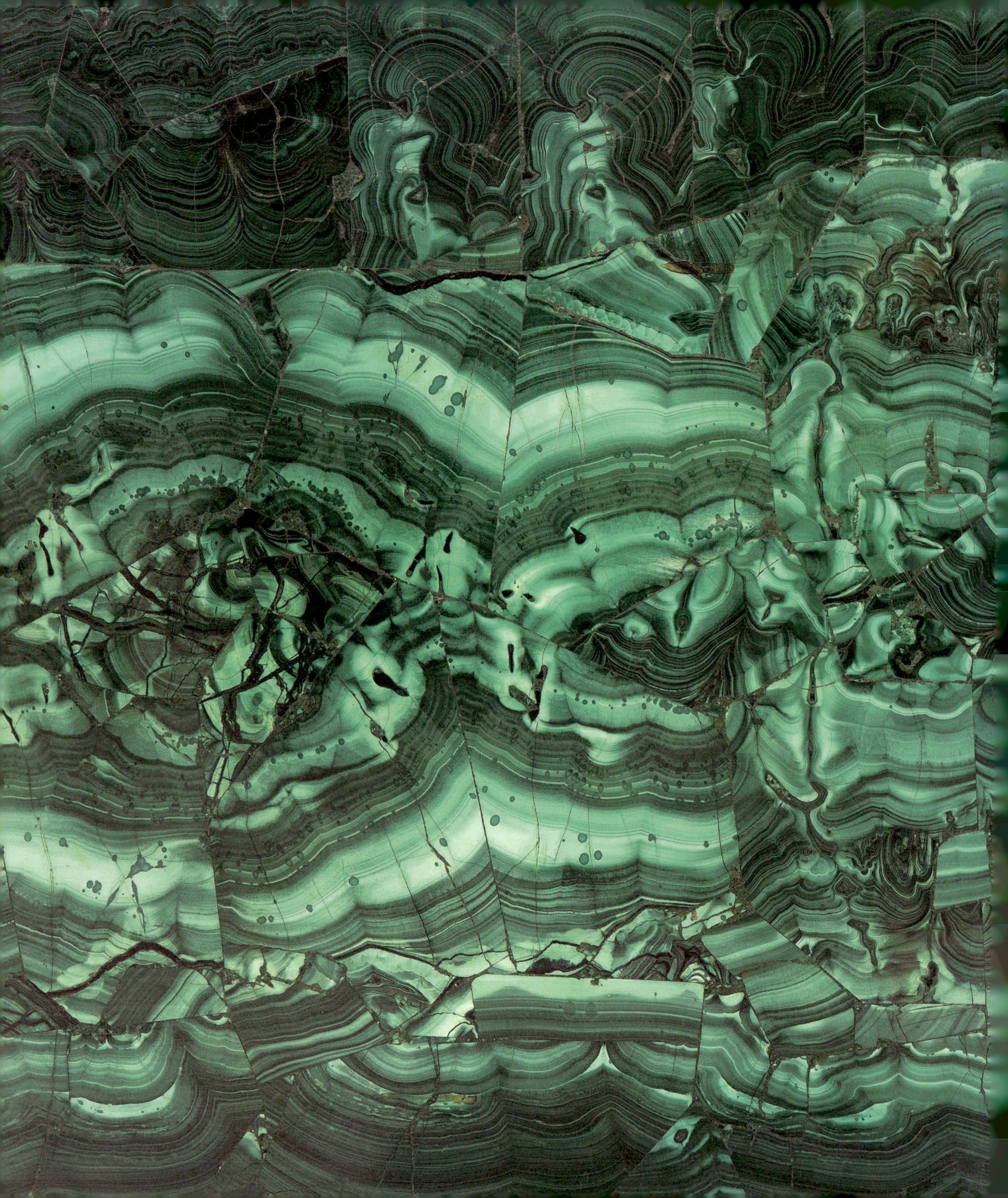